Pk

88 — option — r — rc

Macworld®
Mac® OS 8.5
Bible

*Freeze
813 815*

Macworld® Mac® OS 8.5 Bible

Lon Poole

IDG Books Worldwide, Inc.
An International Data Group Company

Foster City, CA ✦ Chicago, IL ✦ Indianapolis, IN ✦ New York, NY

Macworld® Mac® OS 8.5 Bible

Published by
IDG Books Worldwide, Inc.
An International Data Group Company
919 E. Hillsdale Blvd., Suite 400
Foster City, CA 94404
www.idgbooks.com (IDG Books Worldwide Web site)

Library of Congress Catalog Card Number: 98-75372

ISBN: 0-7645-4042-4

Printed in the United States of America

10 9 8 7 6 5 4 3 2 1

1B/QR/RS/ZY/FC

Distributed in the United States by IDG Books Worldwide, Inc.

Distributed by Macmillan Canada for Canada; by Transworld Publishers Limited in the United Kingdom; by IDG Norge Books for Norway; by IDG Sweden Books for Sweden; by Woodslane Pty. Ltd. for Australia; by Woodslane (NZ) Ltd. for New Zealand; by Addison Wesley Longman Singapore Pte Ltd. for Singapore, Malaysia, Thailand, and Indonesia; by Norma Comunicaciones S.A. for Colombia; by Intersoft for South Africa; by International Thomson Publishing for Germany, Austria and Switzerland; by Distribuidora Cuspide for Argentina; by Livraria Cultura for Brazil; by Ediciencia S.A. for Ecuador; by Ediciones ZETA S.C.R. Ltda. for Peru; by WS Computer Publishing Corporation, Inc., for the Philippines; by Contemporanea de Ediciones for Venezuela; by Express Computer Distributors for the Caribbean and West Indies; by Micronesia Media Distributor, Inc. for Micronesia; by Grupo Editorial Norma S.A. for Guatemala; by Chips Computadoras S.A. de C.V. for Mexico; by Editorial Norma de Panama S.A. for Panama; by Wouters Import for Belgium; by American Bookshops for Finland. Authorized Sales Agent: Anthony Rudkin Associates for the Middle East and North Africa.

For general information on IDG Books Worldwide's books in the U.S., please call our Consumer Customer Service department at 800-762-2974. For reseller information, including discounts and premium sales, please call our Reseller Customer Service department at 800-434-3422.

For information on where to purchase IDG Books Worldwide's books outside the U.S., please contact our International Sales department at 317-596-5530 or fax 317-596-5692.

For consumer information on foreign language translations, please contact our Customer Service department at 800-434-3422, fax 317-596-5692, or e-mail rights@idgbooks.com.

For information on licensing foreign or domestic rights, please phone +1-650-655-3109.

For sales inquiries and special prices for bulk quantities, please contact our Sales department at 650-655-3200 or write to the address above.

For information on using IDG Books Worldwide's books in the classroom or for ordering examination copies, please contact our Educational Sales department at 800-434-2086 or fax 317-596-5499.

For press review copies, author interviews, or other publicity information, please contact our Public Relations department at 650-655-3000 or fax 650-655-3299.

For authorization to photocopy items for corporate, personal, or educational use, please contact Copyright Clearance Center, 222 Rosewood Drive, Danvers, MA 01923, or fax 978-750-4470.

 is a trademark under exclusive license to IDG Books Worldwide, Inc., from International Data Group, Inc.

ABOUT IDG BOOKS WORLDWIDE

Welcome to the world of IDG Books Worldwide.

IDG Books Worldwide, Inc., is a subsidiary of International Data Group, the world's largest publisher of computer-related information and the leading global provider of information services on information technology. IDG was founded more than 30 years ago by Patrick J. McGovern and now employs more than 9,000 people worldwide. IDG publishes more than 290 computer publications in over 75 countries. More than 90 million people read one or more IDG publications each month.

Launched in 1990, IDG Books Worldwide is today the #1 publisher of best-selling computer books in the United States. We are proud to have received eight awards from the Computer Press Association in recognition of editorial excellence and three from Computer Currents' First Annual Readers' Choice Awards. Our best-selling ...For Dummies® series has more than 50 million copies in print with translations in 31 languages. IDG Books Worldwide, through a joint venture with IDG's Hi-Tech Beijing, became the first U.S. publisher to publish a computer book in the People's Republic of China. In record time, IDG Books Worldwide has become the first choice for millions of readers around the world who want to learn how to better manage their businesses.

Our mission is simple: Every one of our books is designed to bring extra value and skill-building instructions to the reader. Our books are written by experts who understand and care about our readers. The knowledge base of our editorial staff comes from years of experience in publishing, education, and journalism — experience we use to produce books to carry us into the new millennium. In short, we care about books, so we attract the best people. We devote special attention to details such as audience, interior design, use of icons, and illustrations. And because we use an efficient process of authoring, editing, and desktop publishing our books electronically, we can spend more time ensuring superior content and less time on the technicalities of making books.

You can count on our commitment to deliver high-quality books at competitive prices on topics you want to read about. At IDG Books Worldwide, we continue in the IDG tradition of delivering quality for more than 30 years. You'll find no better book on a subject than one from IDG Books Worldwide.

John Kilcullen
Chairman and CEO
IDG Books Worldwide, Inc.

Steven Berkowitz
President and Publisher
IDG Books Worldwide, Inc.

Eighth Annual Computer Press Awards ≥1992

Ninth Annual Computer Press Awards ≥1993

Tenth Annual Computer Press Awards ≥1994

Eleventh Annual Computer Press Awards ≥1995

Credits

Acquisitions Editor
Michael Roney

Development Editors
Kathryn Duggan
Katharine Dvorak

Technical Editor
Dennis R. Cohen

Copy Editors
Richard H. Adin
Ami Knox

Project Coordinator
Tom Debolski

**Graphics and
Production Specialists**
Linda Marousek
Hector Mendoza
Christopher Pimentel
Mark Yim

Quality Control Specialists
Mick Arellano
Mark Schumann

Proofreading and Indexing
York Production Services

Cover Design
Murder By Design

About the Author

Lon Poole, based in Kensington, California, is a *Macworld* magazine contributing editor who answers readers' questions every month in his "Quick Tips" column. Lon helped create *Macworld* in 1983 and has written 65 feature articles for the publication. His 1988 article entitled "Installing Memory" won a Maggie award for Best How-To Article in a Consumer Publication. His feature article, "Here Comes System 7," was a finalist in the 1990 Excellence in Technology Communications competition. His three-part series about Macs, "How It Works," won First Place for Best In-Depth Technical Feature Article from the American Society of Business Press Editors.

Lon has been writing books about personal computers and their practical applications since 1976. He has authored five Macintosh books, including the best-selling *Macworld Guide to System 7,* as well as the now-classic *Apple II User's Guide,* which sold over 600,000 copies worldwide. Lon has a BA in computer science from the University of California, Berkeley.

Foreword

If you are like a great many Mac users, you understand the critical importance of your system software. After all, it's the first thing that's loaded or preloaded in your Mac. Plus, you're constantly being told to place new items in the system folders or find things within those folders. And when you find yourself troubleshooting, you're often digging around in the system software.

Alas, many people who use a Macintosh aren't sure why the system software works the way it does. Yet having an understanding of the system software and how to work with it efficiently is one of the greatest boons to anyone's computing productivity. Because the system software underlies every application program you use, mastery of it can augment nearly every aspect of your work.

Now, thanks to the expertise of Lon Poole and his *Macworld Mac OS 8.5 Bible,* our path to a productive Mac life is made easier. Lon has created the most thorough, accurate, and useful guide to the many recent incarnations of the Mac OS. I can personally and professionally attest to the Mac wizardry of Lon Poole. Lon writes the popular "Quick Tips" column for *Macworld.* As an editor, I appreciate Lon's attention to detail, devotion to technical accuracy, and focus on providing Mac users with the most helpful tips and guidance. He accomplishes all of this in an entertaining and readable manner, belying the wealth of technical information contained within the text.

Lon is well equipped to provide comprehensive coverage of Mac OS 8.5 (and more). He has been a devotee of Apple and contributor to *Macworld* from the very beginning. He helped found the magazine back in 1983 and continues to be one of the key reasons *Macworld* is recognized as the Macintosh authority. Lon's own authority is well established in volumes of issues and books in which he provides highly specific and truly useful guidance that addresses a wide range of Macintosh computing solutions — making Lon one of the most knowledgeable Mac experts around.

Enjoy this excursion through the system software tour. Lon will tell you which system version is best for your needs, and he will tell you how to use your system software in order to work faster, smarter, and more efficiently.

— Adrian Mello
former Editor-in-Chief
Macworld

Preface

According to popular legend, a Mac is so easy to use that you don't need to read books about it. Alas, if only that were true. In fact, discovering all the power that the Mac OS gives your computer would take months of exploring and experimenting. Yes, exploring and experimenting can be fun. But do you really have months to devote to your computer's operating system? Save your time for having fun with games and multimedia, exploring the Internet, or maybe getting some work done. Benefit from the experience of others (in this case, the author and his collaborators). Read this book so you can put the full power of the Mac OS to work for you without a lot of poking around the Mac desktop.

Maybe you think you don't need this book because you have Apple's manuals and onscreen help. It's true these are good sources of information. But the *Macworld Mac OS 8.5 Bible* contains a great deal of information you won't find in the manuals or help screens. This book also provides a different perspective on subjects you may not quite understand after reading the manuals. And because this book describes the Mac OS completely, you can use it instead of Apple's manuals if you don't happen to have them.

Who Should Read This Book

This book is aimed at people who already know Mac OS fundamentals such as choosing commands from menus, moving icons on the desktop, and selecting and editing text. If you have spent more than a few days with any Mac OS computer, you know how to do these things and are ready for what's inside this book.

Read this book to learn all about Mac OS 8.5 — how to use it if you have it, and why to get it if you don't. Actually, this book tells you how to use all the recent versions of the Mac OS from 7.6 on. (If you have System 7.5.5 or earlier, read this book to find out what you're missing and why you should upgrade.)

You can stick to the basics if you're new to the Mac OS. When you're ready to go beyond the basics, you can learn how to take advantage of the power in your version of the Mac OS.

What's Inside

Macworld Mac OS 8.5 Bible covers Mac OS 8.5 and Mac OS 7.6–8.1 progressively in six parts. Following is an overview of each part.

✦ Part I takes a quick look at the features of the Mac OS. Use it to get started right away or to see the big picture. You get an overview of what's special about Mac OS 8.5, as well as what's hot and what's cool in all recent versions of the Mac OS.

✦ Part II describes in depth what you'll encounter when you first start using the Mac OS. Windows, icons, and menus appear from the moment you start up a Mac, but look closely and you may find some new and useful aspects of these elements. When you get beyond looking around the desktop, you can organize your disks, folders, and files with the Finder. You get to work by opening programs and documents (including documents from Windows and DOS computers), moving document contents around, and saving documents. You can modify the Mac OS appearance and behavior, and you can get help onscreen when you need it.

✦ Part III tells you how to use some important Mac OS capabilities. You learn how to fine-tune the system by making changes in the special System Folder and adjusting a multitude of settings in software control panels. You discover how handy aliases can be. You learn to deal with fonts and typography, and also learn to control printing. You find out why the Mac OS deserves its reputation as the multimedia leader among personal computer operating systems. You also learn how the Mac OS makes it easy to explore the Internet, including the Web and e-mail.

✦ Part IV takes you beyond the Mac OS basics — way beyond. You learn to be comfortable with managing your Mac's memory. You learn how to set up a simple network of computers, share your files with others on the network, and use their shared files. You get to know how any Mac can speak and how some can listen. This part of the book also introduces AppleScript, and teaches you how to use it to automate repetitive tasks. In addition, you learn to create compound documents with OpenDoc plug-in software or with the Mac OS publish and subscribe technology.

✦ Part V presents many ways to make the most of the Mac OS. You'll find that the accessory programs included with the Mac OS come in handy on occasion. If they're not enough, included is a chapter devoted to describing over 125 low-cost software utilities you can use to enhance the Mac OS. Two more chapters reveal over 100 Mac OS tips and secrets. Another chapter guides you through troubleshooting procedures.

✦ Part VI details how to upgrade or install the Mac OS, including how to install a clean copy. You see how the various recent Mac OS versions compare and what their requirements are, so you can decide whether to stick with the version you have or upgrade it. You find out how to get ready to install, and you can follow step-by-step instructions for installing Mac OS 8–8.5, Mac OS 7.6–7.6.1, and Mac OS enhancements.

In addition to these six parts, this book includes a glossary and coverage of QuickDraw GX printing, which works with Mac OS 7.6–7.6.1 but not with Mac OS 8–8.5.

If you read this book from front to back, you will find that some information appears in more than one place. In particular, everything that Part I covers in summary appears elsewhere in the book, in more detail. Also, some of the tips and secrets in Chapters 27 and 28 appear first amidst relevant subject matter throughout earlier chapters. This duplication is intentional and is meant for your benefit.

Conventions Used in This Book

This book makes use of established conventions in an effort to help guide you through the material.

Mac OS Version References

As you may have realized from reading this preface, this book uses the term *Mac OS* to include all versions of the Macintosh operating system, also known as the system software, unless a specific version number is stated (such as Mac OS 8.5). References to specific versions apply only to the version number cited. When you see a range of version numbers, such as Mac OS 8–8.5, the topic under discussion applies to all versions in the stated range.

Apple named earlier versions of the operating system *System* instead of *Mac OS*. You may notice occasional references in this book to System 7.5.5 and earlier. Just remember that *Mac OS* and *System* are two terms for the Mac operating system.

Sidebars

Certain discussions in this book are expanded with sidebars. These are shaded boxes that contain background information, expert tips and advice, areas where caution is needed, and other helpful information.

All sidebars have a title that categorizes the information contained in the sidebar. These titles are designed to alert you to the type of information presented. Here's what to look for:

- ✦ A *Backgrounder* sidebar provides background detail about an issue under discussion.

- ✦ A *Quick Tips* sidebar points out a useful tip (or tips) that can save you a great deal of time and trouble.

- ✦ A *Caution* sidebar alerts you to potential problems with an issue under discussion. Solutions and ways to avoid such scary situations are also included.

- ✦ A *Secrets* sidebar includes concepts and ideas missing from or not easily found in Apple's documentation of the Mac OS. The information is the result of countless hours of tinkering, troubleshooting, and asking questions of expert sources.

✦ A *Step-by-Step* sidebar provides detailed instructions that show how to perform tasks with the Mac OS. Many issues in the Mac OS can be complex, but these sidebars help break the desired goal into manageable components.

Feedback, Please

The author and publisher appreciate your feedback on this book. Please feel free to contact us, care of IDG Books Worldwide, with questions or comments.

Acknowledgments

When you're going to write a book of this size about a subject as deep and wide as the Mac OS, you can't be shy about asking for help. I have many people to thank for their contributions to this book. First, I would like to thank the people whose contributions to earlier editions of the book live on in the *Macworld Mac OS 8.5 Bible*. David Angell and Brent Heslop researched and wrote first drafts of material that appears in Chapters 12, 20, 21, and 24 in this book. Nancy Dunn and Rita Lewis helped reorganize and update an earlier edition of the book, and much of their work survives in Chapters 13, 14, 15, 22, and Appendix A. Tom Negrino compressed the entire Internet into Chapter 17. Derrick Schneider applied his AppleScript expertise to Chapter 23. Roxanne Gentile, former curator of the Macworld Online software library, put together the collection of utility software in Chapter 26 for the previous edition of this book. Rob Terrell wrote drafts of material that now appears in Chapters 30 and 31. I most gratefully acknowledge all their contributions.

For the *Macworld Mac OS 8.5 Bible*, I wish to thank Seth Novogrodsky for the dynamite troubleshooting information in Chapter 29, the overview of Mac OS 8.5 in Chapter 1, and the careful revision of Chapters 2 and 3. He also updated Chapter 23 for Mac OS 8.5. Many thanks to Katherine Ulrich for bringing Chapters 11, 25, and 26 up-to-date for Mac OS 8.5. I also wish to acknowledge Suzanne Courteau, the former editor of my "Quick Tips" column in *Macworld* magazine, for updating the tips in Chapters 27 and 28.

I also want to express my appreciation to the editorial and production teams at IDG Books Worldwide, whose diligence made all the difference. In particular, Dennis Cohen as technical reviewer did a great job of filtering out technical impurities. I also want to thank Mike Roney for tirelessly urging me onward. (It's done, Mike, but my fingers still type in my sleep.) In addition, I want to thank Kathi Duggan, who once again has done splendid job as development editor. (Believe me, you are glad she went over this book before you did.)

I reserve my deepest gratitude for my wife, Karin, and sons, Adam and Ethan, without whose love and support this work would have been impossible and pointless. Thank you from the bottom of my heart.

Contents at a Glance

Contents

Part II: Getting Started with the Mac OS   57

Chapter 8: Modify Appearance and Behavior 195

Part IV: Beyond the Basics of the Mac OS   487

Chapter 18: Manage Your Memory 489

Chapter 26: Enhance with Utility Software 707

Part VI: Installing the Mac OS   829

Introduction

When it comes to working on a personal computer, nothing quite equals working on an Apple Macintosh or Mac-compatible computer. What creates this unique working environment is the Mac operating system, known as the Mac OS.

The Mac OS displays the windows, icons, menus, pointer, and other elements of the graphical user interface (GUI, pronounced "gooey"), and the Mac OS responds to your input through the keyboard and mouse. And that's just the beginning. The Mac OS provides a raft of other services; the following is a partial list:

✦ Filing electronic documents and software items

✦ Opening application programs and documents and saving document changes

✦ Implementing basic text editing (inserting, deleting, replacing, and so on)

✦ Drawing two- and three-dimensional graphics on screen

✦ Composing text in a variety of typefaces, styles, and sizes

✦ Printing graphics and typeset text

✦ Displaying movies and 360-degree panoramas

✦ Playing sounds and music

✦ Accessing the Internet — e-mail, the Web, and more

✦ Managing the computer's memory

✦ Participating in a network of computers

✦ Working with documents from the MS DOS and Windows operating systems

✦ Synthesizing and recognizing speech

✦ Handling text in dozens of languages and writing systems

✦ Facilitating data exchange and communication among application programs

✦ Automating tasks with scripts

The Mac OS is not nearly as simple today as it was when Apple released the first Mac operating system in 1984. Over the years, Apple has added many improvements: a better filing system in 1985, color in 1987, and multitasking in 1988, to name a few. The system software entered a new realm of complexity in 1990 with the release of System 7.0. In 1994, System 7.5 integrated more than 50 additional features. Some were simple improvements, such as a digital clock in the menu bar, and some were more sophisticated, such as the ability to automate tasks with AppleScript.

Apple continues to revise the system software, adding more features and capabilities with each new version. Mac OS 7.6, released in January 1997 and the earliest version covered in this book, integrated some software updates with many Mac OS enhancements that were first distributed separately as add-ons. The major enhancements included Desktop Printing, Open Transport networking, QuickDraw 3D graphics, and the OpenDoc plug-in software infrastructure. Six months later, Apple delivered Mac OS 8, the biggest upgrade to the Mac system software since System 7.0. Its improvements included a sleek, three-dimensional appearance; new ways of working with windows, files, folders, and disks; integrated Internet access; better performance; and more stability. Another six months later, Mac OS 8.1 introduced the Mac OS Extended format and some minor improvements.

Mac OS 8.5 came along in October 1998, again spreading change across the Mac landscape. This version gives you much more control over your Mac's appearance. In addition, Mac OS 8.5 features further integrated Internet access, including the ability to conduct multiple, simultaneous searches of the Internet with ranked results and summaries of found items. You can also perform lightning-fast searches of the text in all the files on your disk, again with results ranked by relevance and the option of summarizing any found document. Mac OS 8.5 makes working with your computer faster and easier in lots of other ways, as you'll discover when you read the overview of it in the first chapter.

No matter how much or how little experience you have with the Mac OS, this book can show you something useful about it that you don't already know. The book describes both basic and advanced Mac OS features, and explains how you can use them to make working with your computer more productive and fun. Sure, you can discover a lot about the Mac OS by exploring it on your own, but your exploration will go faster and you'll find out more with this book as your guide.

Overview of
the Mac OS

What's Special About Mac OS 8.5

Although Mac OS 8.5 is not as great a leap in new features and capabilities as was the jump from Mac OS 7.6.1 to Mac OS 8, this release brings many changes that make the Macintosh OS more powerful and easier to use. Some of the changes are cosmetic, giving you the ability to customize the look and feel of the Mac OS to a greater extent than was ever possible before. Others are brand-new features and "under-the-hood" changes that make the Macintosh faster and more reliable.

New features include themes to easily alter the look of the Mac, a new way of getting help information, a complete makeover of the methods to open and save files (for applications that have been updated to take advantage of this new feature), enhancements for windows in the Finder and Mac applications, and new ways of accessing network resources. What's more, Mac OS 8.5 is better integrated with the Internet and Internet software.

This chapter gives an overview of the improvements that Mac OS 8.5 brings to the Mac system software. After reading this chapter, be sure to read the next two chapters for overviews of features and capabilities that this release shares with earlier Mac OS versions.

Reliability and Performance

Each new major release of the Mac OS offers better performance and greater stability than previous versions. Mac OS 8.5 is no exception.

Improved reliability

In addition to correcting bugs from previous releases, Mac OS 8.5 automatically performs a diagnostic check on the startup disk in the event of an improper shutdown, such as a forced restart after a crash. This automatic check performs the same function as running Apple's Disk First Aid utility, which detects and corrects problems with the directory structure of a Macintosh disk. This automatic check can correct errors before they turn into major problems.

Performance enhancements

Ever since the first Macintosh with a PowerPC chip appeared in 1994, each successive release of the Mac OS has contained more "native" code written specifically for the PowerPC architecture rather than the 680X0 architecture used in earlier Macintosh models. Mac OS 8.5 is the first version of the Mac OS to require a PowerPC chip.

With Mac OS 8.5, improvements in QuickDraw speed the display of screen images and make scrolling faster. QuickDraw is the part of the Mac OS that draws everything that you see — text, graphics, menus, and so on. In addition AppleScript — a language that you can use to automate tasks in the Finder and in some applications — has also gone native, and scripts now run as much as five times faster.

Mac OS 8.5 also brings with it the capability to copy files faster than ever before. The improvement is noticeable when copying files over a network and when copying to hard drives and removable disks such as Zip disks, Jaz disks, SyQuest cartridges, and magneto-optical disks.

Appearance

At first glance, Mac OS 8.5, with its "platinum" styling, looks very much like its direct predecessors, Mac OS 8 and 8.1. The differences, however, are far greater than it would appear; with Mac OS 8.5, you can change many aspects of your Mac's appearance all at once. Never before have users had this much direct control over how the Macintosh looks and feels.

Themes

Themes are a new concept introduced with Mac OS 8.5. Themes build on an overall look for menus, windows, and icons such as Mac OS 8–8.1's "platinum" look, which replaced the largely white, two-dimensional look that was used in previous releases with a metallic gray, three-dimensional look. Platinum is still around in Mac OS 8.5, but you will be able to replace it with other looks if they become available.

Themes are much more than a look. A theme is a collection of settings that control system fonts, the text highlight color, the color of window accents, the desktop background, and other features that you can set using the revamped Appearance control panel. You can pick from themes built into the Mac OS or create your own.

What follows are brief descriptions of some of the elements that can comprise a theme and a quick look at the Appearance control panel, which allows you to control themes and other aspects of your Mac's appearance. (To learn more, see Chapter 8.)

Appearance control panel

The Mac OS 8.5 Appearance control panel does a whole lot more than the Appearance control panel in Mac OS 8–8.1. The newer version allows you to change more aspects of the Macintosh's appearance. In addition, you can save all the appearance settings as a single theme, and switch to a different saved theme with a single mouse click. Different people who share one computer can select different themes, or you can select a theme to suit your mood. Figure 1-1 shows the section of the Appearance control panel in which you select a theme.

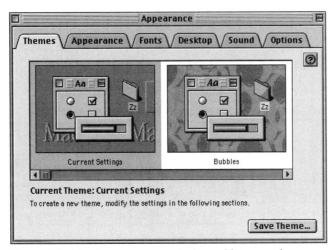

Figure 1-1: The Appearance control panel lets you change many aspects of how the Mac looks and operates.

System fonts

You have more choices than ever for the system font in Mac OS 8.5. This is the font that the Mac OS uses for menus, button names, window titles, and so forth. One choice is the classic Chicago font, which was the only choice until Mac OS 8. With Mac OS 8–8.5, the standard system font is Charcoal, but you can choose Chicago if you prefer it.

With Mac OS 8.5, you can choose from additional fonts such as Capitals, Gadget, Sand, Techno, and Textile. In addition, Mac OS 8.5 lets you separately choose the small system font. This font is used to display explanatory text in dialog boxes and labels. As in other Mac OS versions, you can also specify the Views font that the Finder uses for the text that identifies icons. In Mac OS 8.5, you choose the Views font in the Appearance control panel.

Sound tracks

The Macintosh OS has always provided audible feedback in some circumstances: for certain error conditions, when using the screen capture function, and, optionally, when collapsing windows. In Mac OS 8.5, you can choose to have the sound track provide sound effects for more operations, including opening menus and choosing menu items; dragging and resizing windows; activating controls such as buttons, checkboxes, arrows, and scrolling controls; and the Finder operations such as clicking and dragging and dropping. Each of these categories has a different sound effect, and you hear many of the sound effects in stereo if your computer has stereo speakers. You can select the categories for which you want to hear audible feedback, and you can choose an overall sound style for the entire set of sound effects. While shareware and freeware have enabled add-on sound tracks since 1987, Mac OS 8.5 has the first official sound tracks. Figure 1-2 shows the section of the Appearance control panel where you set sound track options.

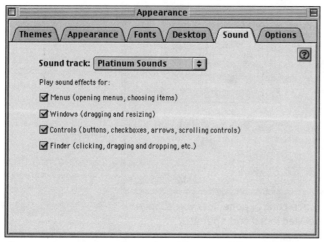

Figure 1-2: Sound tracks can provide you with audible feedback when you perform certain actions.

Desktop picture or pattern

Nothing affects the look of the screen like the desktop's background. Mac OS 8.5 gives you a wide choice of background patterns, and you can cover the pattern with a picture. Desktop pictures first appeared in Mac OS 8, but in Mac OS 8.5 you can select a pattern or a picture with the Appearance control panel and the pattern or picture becomes part of the theme, along with other aspects of the appearance.

Figure 1-3 shows the section of the Appearance control panel in which you select a desktop picture or pattern.

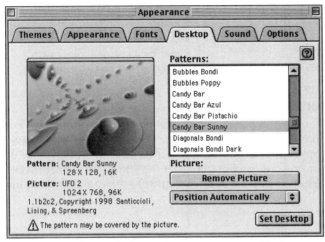

Figure 1-3: Select a desktop picture or pattern with the Appearance control panel.

Text smoothing

Mac OS 8.5 can smooth the appearance of text using a technique called antialiasing. In large font sizes, text characters may appear jagged because individual dots that make up the characters become visible around the edges. Antialiasing blends the edges of the text with its background to make text on the screen appear less jagged.

In the Appearance control panel, you can turn on text smoothing for the display of fonts larger than a font size you specify. It is best to pick a value of 12 points or larger; at smaller font sizes, text smoothing can make characters harder to read. The settings for text smoothing can be part of a theme.

New icons and icon features

The Platinum appearance introduced with Mac OS 8 features three-dimensional icons for disks, applications, desk accessories, documents, and folders. In addition, Mac OS 8.5 now allows larger icons that can contain millions of colors instead of just the maximum of 256 colors in Mac OS 8.1 and earlier. Applications need to be updated to make use of the more elaborate icons. (For more information about icons, see Chapter 4.)

Icon badges

Mac OS 8.5 now displays badges on icons that are aliases of other items, or folders with scripted actions, or folders that are shared on a network, or a locked item.

(Mac OS 8.1 and earlier also alter icons of shared folders.) Figure 1-4 shows examples of icons with badges.

Figure 1-4: You can easily tell whether an icon represents a locked item, an alias, a shared folder, or a scripted folder with Mac OS 8.5's badged icons.

Creating custom icons

Tired of the same old icons? You can replace individual full-size icons with your own designs. (This capability is not unique to Mac OS 8.5; it has been around since System 7.) First you copy a picture you want to use as an icon. Then you select the icon you want to customize, choose Get Info from the File menu, select the icon in the Info window, and paste. Figure 1-5 is an example of a custom icon in an Info window.

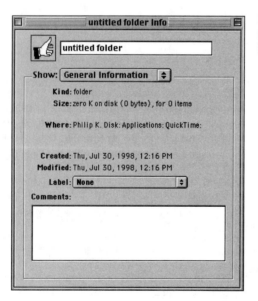

Figure 1-5: Customize an icon by pasting a picture into its Info window.

Ease of Use

There's more to Mac OS 8.5 than the improvements in speed, reliability, and customization of its appearance that we have discussed. It's also loaded with improved features and capabilities that make it easier to use than earlier Mac OS versions.

Application menu

Because the universal menu bar at the top of the Mac OS screen looks so much alike in many application programs, you can easily get confused about which application is currently active. Often the only surefire sign is the tiny icon that heads the Application menu in the right corner of the menu bar. Mac OS 8.5 eliminates all doubt by displaying the name of the active application next to its icon in the menu bar. You can eliminate the name altogether if you prefer.

A bigger change, however, is that in Mac OS 8.5 you can tear off the Application menu as a window called the Application Switcher. You tear off the Application menu by dragging the mouse pointer beyond its last menu item. The Application Switcher floats above ordinary application windows. It displays buttons labeled with miniature application icons and the corresponding application names. You can shrink the window to show just the small icons. To switch to a different application, click the button corresponding to the application you want to use. Figure 1-6 is an example of the Application Switcher.

Figure 1-6: You can tear off the Application Switcher from the Application menu for convenient switching between applications.

You'll find more information about the Application Switcher and the Application menu in "Managing Multiple Open Programs" in Chapter 7.

Help Viewer

Getting assistance onscreen has never been easier than with the Help Viewer. Help Viewer displays short how-to articles that you can search or browse via a table of contents. In addition, the articles contain links that you can click to see related articles, open the programs under discussion, or summon interactive step-by-step help. The interactive help is provided by Apple Guide, which was first introduced with System 7.5. Help Viewer articles provide detailed information about the Mac OS. Shortcuts and tips, troubleshooting information, and detailed descriptions of Mac OS features and capabilities are all available. (For more details, check out Chapter 9.) Figure 1-7 is an example of the Help Viewer.

Window enhancements

Mac OS 8.5 makes working with windows easier and more productive than ever. Described in the following paragraphs are the enhancements that you will see.

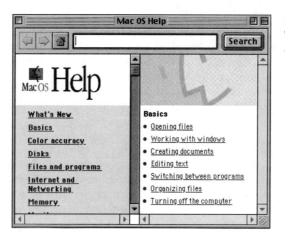

Figure 1-7: Help Viewer gives you easy access to information about your Mac.

Icons in title bars

Like Mac OS 8–8.1, Mac OS 8.5 windows have a collapse box to hide all but the title bar. In addition, the title bar now displays the icon of a folder or disk when you view its window in the Finder. You can drag this icon to move or copy the folder or disk to another location. Figure 1-8 shows an icon in a disk window's title bar.

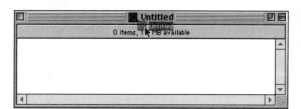

Figure 1-8: You can drag the icon in the title bar of a disk or folder window.

Standard view options

Being able to set view options separately for each window is a blessing in Mac OS 8–8.5. This blessing is a curse in Mac OS 8–8.1 if you want to apply the same change to many windows. Mac OS 8.5 addresses this predicament with standard view options. You can set any folder or disk window to use standard view options by choosing View Options from the View menu and clicking a button in the View Options dialog box. You can change standard view options for list views, icon views, and button views by choosing Preferences from the Finder's Edit menu. When you change the standard view options, all windows that adhere to them change at once. (You'll find more information in "Fine-tuning Views" in Chapter 6.) Figure 1-9 shows the Set to Standard Views button in a View Options dialog box alongside the corresponding standard view options as set in the Preferences dialog box.

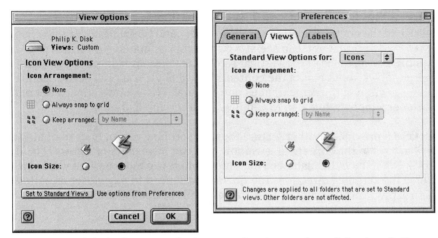

Figure 1-9: Click the button at the bottom of a View Options dialog box (left) to apply the standard view options defined by the Preferences command (right).

Resizing and rearranging columns in list views

Mac OS 8.5 gives you control over the width and arrangement of columns such as Name, Date Modified, Size, or Kind. Columns can be made narrower so that you can see more of them without enlarging the window. You can make columns wider to reveal truncated information. All columns except the Name column can be moved to the left or right so that they appear in a different order. To make a column wider or narrower, drag the borderline at the right edge of the column's heading. To move a column, drag its heading past another column on the left or right. These changes affect only the window you make them in. Figure 1-10 shows a column being moved to the left.

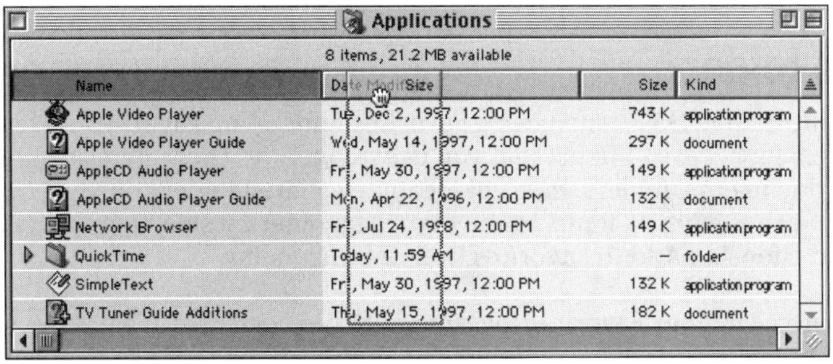

Figure 1-10: You can change column widths and positions in folder and disk windows.

Proportional scroll boxes and double scroll arrows

The size of the controls used to scroll vertically and horizontally can be changed in Mac OS 8.5 so that you can see at a glance approximately how much of a window is visible. For instance, if the vertical scroll box takes up half of the scroll bar, the window shows about half of the contents (vertically). You can set this feature in the Options section of the Appearance control panel. This feature applies not only to the Finder windows, but also to windows in other applications.

Mac OS 8.5 provides another feature to make scrolling easier. Instead of individual scroll arrows in the corners of a window, you can have pairs of arrows. The double-arrows can reduce the distance you have to move the mouse when you want to reverse the scrolling direction. You do, however, need to pay closer attention to which arrow you click. Figure 1-11 is an example of double scroll arrows and proportional scroll boxes.

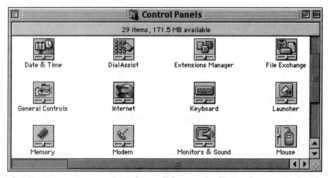

Figure 1-11: Proportional scroll boxes indicate how much of a window you can see, and double scroll arrows ease back-and-forth scrolling.

Favorites folder

The Apple menu in Mac OS 8.5 includes a Favorites folder. The Favorites folder can provide convenient access to items that you use frequently. These items can include applications, documents, folders, Internet locations, shared folders on your network, and so on. You can easily add items to the Favorites folder by selecting the item in the Finder and choosing Add to Favorites from the File menu.

What's more, items in your Favorites folder appear conveniently in a pop-up menu when you are opening and saving documents in applications that use Navigation Services (described next). You can also add favorites while using Navigation Services.

Navigation Services

For those applications that have been updated to take advantage of Navigation Services, which come with Mac OS 8.5, the standard dialog boxes for opening and saving files are a thing of the past. Although you can navigate through folders and disks as before, the Navigation Services dialog boxes provide three new buttons that make selecting the appropriate place to save or open a file much easier.

The Shortcuts button gives easy access to shared folders on file servers, which are computers on your network where you can save or open files. You can even use this button to connect to shared folders. The Favorites button gives you choices from the Favorites folder. Perhaps most convenient of all is the Recent button, which tracks those folders and documents that were used most recently. Figure 1-12 shows these three buttons in the upper-right corner of a Navigation Services dialog box.

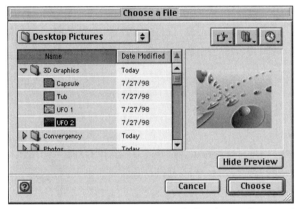

Figure 1-12: Navigation Services dialog boxes for opening and saving files have convenient buttons for shortcuts, favorites, and recent items.

You'll find complete coverage of Navigation Services in "Opening Programs, Documents, and More" in Chapter 7.

Improved Find

The Find File utility, first introduced in System 7.5, is greatly enhanced in Mac OS 8.5 to include flexible options for searching the contents of files and locating items on the Internet. Because of its expanded scope, the enhanced utility is named Sherlock in Mac OS 8.5. (In Mac OS 7.6–8.1, Find File is a utility program that can be opened with the Find command in the Finder's File menu.) Sherlock has three different tabs for specifying the type of search you wish to perform: Find File, Find by Content, and Search Internet.

Find File

The Find File section of the Sherlock program provides the same functionality as the old Find File program, but with the additional capability to save criteria to be used in future searches. The simplest form of the Find File window allows you to specify where to search and one attribute to match. For example, you can search all disks for items whose names contain the specified text. You can change where Find File looks for items and specify that it look at an attribute other than the item's name. You can also add more search criteria to the Find File window by clicking the More Choices button.

Find File displays the results of a search in an Items Found window. You can open a found item or the folder that encloses it. You can also drag found items to the desktop. In addition, you can change the file-sharing privileges, set the label, and open Info windows for found items. (A full description of Find File is found under "Finding Items" in Chapter 6.) Figure 1-13 shows the results of a Find File search.

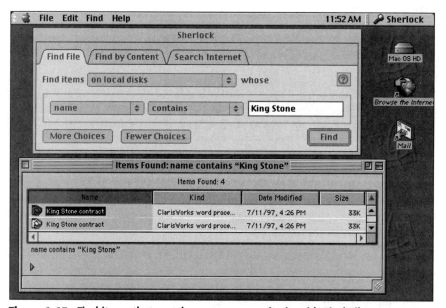

Figure 1-13: Find items that match one or more criteria with Find File.

Find by Content

Although the old Find File program can search the contents of text files, the Sherlock program searches by content a whole lot faster. You type a natural-sounding search request, such as "KEF board meeting minutes and agenda for January, February, and March" and within several seconds a list of files ranked by their relevance to your query appears. If you have file-translation software (not included with Mac OS 8.5), Find by Content uses it to search all kinds of documents that may contain text. Figure 1-14 is an example of the Find by Content section of the Sherlock program.

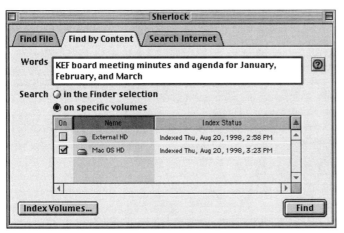

Figure 1-14: Find files that contain specific text.

The Find by Content section of the Sherlock program works by searching through indexes of file contents rather than files themselves. Before you can search the contents of files, you first must create an index by selecting the volumes that you want to search and clicking the Create Index button. You can schedule the indexes for automatic updating. (It can take hours to index a large hard drive for the first time.) You can't index floppy disks or locked disks such as CD-ROMs.

To learn more about Find by Content, see "Finding Documents by Content" in Chapter 7.

Search Internet

The Search Internet section of the Sherlock program gives you easy access to popular search engines on the Internet, including AltaVista, Excite, Infoseek, and the Apple Tech Info Library, Apple's technical support database. You can easily connect to the site where the item was found by double-clicking it or dragging it to an open window of your Web browser. (For details, see "Searching the Internet" in Chapter 17.) Figure 1-15 is an example of the Search Internet section of the Sherlock program.

File Exchange

The Mac OS helps you open documents created with programs you don't have. They may be documents created on a Windows, DOS, or Apple II (ProDOS) computer. When you insert a Windows, DOS, or Apple II (ProDOS) disk, the foreign disk's icon appears on your desktop and you can open it to see its contents. You can open PC-formatted floppy disks and other removable disks such as Zip, Jaz, SyQuest, and magneto-optical disks.

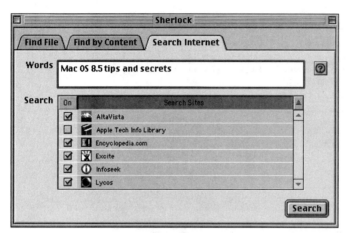

Figure 1-15: Search for items on the Internet using Sherlock.

Furthermore, you may be able to use an application on your Mac to open foreign files. If you don't have an application that can open foreign documents directly, you may need translation software to convert the foreign document to a format that your application can open. (For more detailed information, see "Translating Documents" in Chapter 7.)

In Mac OS 8.5, file translation and the mapping of PC files to Mac OS file types are set up using the File Exchange control panel. (In Mac OS 7.6–8.1, you use two different control panels, PC Exchange and Mac OS Easy Open.)

Using foreign files

If you have Mac programs that can open DOS or Windows files, you can use File Exchange to assign DOS filename extensions to specific Mac applications. Figure 1-16 is an example of the PC Exchange section of the File Exchange control panel.

Opening unidentified items

The File Exchange software relieves your frustration in trying to open a document when you don't have the application that created it. Instead of seeing a message that the document can't be opened a list of applications that can open that kind of document with or without file translation is shown. File Exchange knows which file translators are installed on your Mac and which kinds of documents your applications can open. File Exchange can work with translation software such as DataViz's MacLinkPlus. Figure 1-17 is an example of a File Exchange translator list.

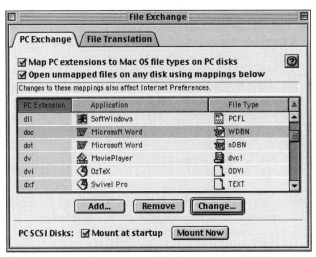

Figure 1-16: Assign Mac applications to open Windows and DOS files using File Exchange.

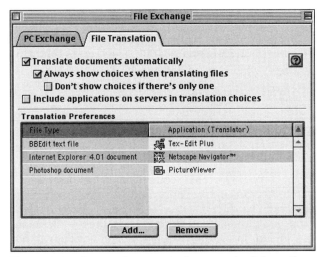

Figure 1-17: Open a document when you don't have the application that created it with the help of File Exchange.

AppleScript and folder actions

Mac OS 8.5 features several improvements to AppleScript—the system extension that enables you to automate multistep tasks with scripts (sets of instructions) that are either predefined or that you create. The most innovative improvement lets you specify automatic actions that happen whenever someone interacts with particular folders. For example, a folder action could automatically lock all items added to a folder. Attaching a script to a folder specifies an automated folder action. Folder actions can happen in response to opening a folder, closing it, adding items to it, removing items from it, or changing the size or position of its window.

Other AppleScript improvements in Mac OS 8.5 are more incremental in nature. First, programs written in AppleScript can run as much as five times faster than before. In addition, you can now script some tasks that cannot be automated in Mac OS 7.6–8.1. To learn more about AppleScript, see Chapter 23.

Internet and Networking

Mac OS 8.5 goes further than previous Mac OS versions in helping you connect to the Internet and access network services. This section gives a brief overview of new features that Mac OS 8.5 provides. Chapter 17 covers the Internet, and Chapters 19 to 21 cover networking in detail.

Network Browser

The Network Browser, which is found in the Apple menu, provides a convenient way to access shared folders and disks on your network. It has several advantages over the venerable Chooser (described in Chapter 20). A Shortcuts menu can be used in the Network Browser to connect to shared folders and disks that you use frequently. In addition, like the Recent Servers folder, the Network Browser tracks shared folders and disks that you recently connected. Finally, Network Browser provides direct access to shared items, the file servers they're on, and AppleTalk zones that you have added to your Favorites folder.

Connecting to the Internet

In Mac OS 8.5, the PPP (Point-to-Point Protocol) control panel has been incorporated into the Remote Access control panel. The Remote Access control strip module can be used to establish a connection to an Internet service provider using PPP, which is the most common method to connect to the Internet using a modem and telephone line. In addition, there is a DialAssist control panel that simplifies dialing PBX, long distance, international, credit card, and calling card numbers for remote access.

Internet control panel

The Internet control panel allows you to set options for many Internet services all in one place. You can specify your name, e-mail address, the location of your initial home page on the Web, your preferred Web browser, and the server that you use for accessing Internet newsgroups. Most current applications for accessing Internet services observe these settings. In addition, you can save groups of settings, which can be quite helpful if other people use your computer or if you have accounts with different Internet service providers. (The Internet control panel stores your preference settings in a file that's compatible with the Internet Config program, which is included with Mac OS 8–8.1 and works with other Mac OS versions as well.) Figure 1-18 shows the Internet control panel.

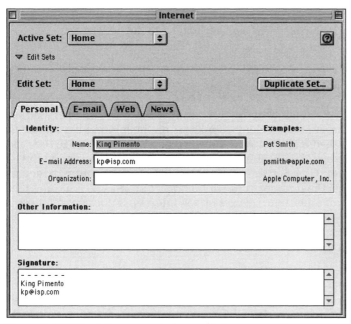

Figure 1-18: The Internet control panel lets you specify many different Internet preferences all in one place.

Internet and network location files

Because of the rapid expansion of the Internet and network services in general, it has become harder to keep track of where useful resources are located. Mac OS 8.5 provides a convenient way to save locations of items on the Internet such as Web pages, newsgroups, and e-mail addresses, as well as the locations of AppleShare file servers on your network. You can create a location file by selecting any text containing an Internet address, such as http://website.com/, and dragging it to the desktop. You can also create a location file by dragging items found by the Search Internet section of the Sherlock program. Similarly, you can create a location file by dragging a file server icon from the Network Browser to the desktop, a folder, or a disk. When you double-click a location file, the appropriate application opens and connects you to the location. Figure 1-19 has some examples of location files.

Figure 1-19: Create location files to help keep track of useful Internet and network resources.

Accessing network time servers

If you connect to the Internet, you can now easily make sure that your Mac's clock has the correct time. For years, many computers on the Internet have been using an Internet protocol called NTP (Network Time Protocol) to synchronize their clocks. You can now have your Macintosh reset its clock using a time server on the Internet with the Use Network Time Server feature in the Date & Time control panel. Apple runs time servers on the Internet in North America, Europe, and Asia, and there are literally thousands of other time servers on the Internet. It does not matter whether the time server is in a different time zone; the Date & Time control panel will compensate. You can have your Mac's clock synchronized automatically, at intervals you specify, or manually when you so choose.

Multilingual browsing

Although the Mac OS has provided advanced multilingual capabilities since the introduction of WorldScript (around the time System 7.1 was released), Mac OS 8.5 allows you to easily view foreign language content using Netscape Navigator or Microsoft Internet Explorer Web browsers.

Summary

This chapter provided a brief overview of some of the most exciting and useful features and capabilities of Mac OS 8.5. We started by looking at the "under-the-hood" changes, such as the automatic diagnostics after a crash and the increased use of native PowerPC code, that make this version of the Mac OS more reliable and faster.

This chapter then described how Mac OS 8.5 gives you far greater control over the Macintosh look and feel. We saw how themes allow you to alter multiple appearance attributes all at once using the Appearance control panel. These include system fonts, sound track, desktop picture or pattern, and text smoothing. This chapter also introduced some new icon features that you will see in Mac OS 8.5.

Next, this chapter provided an overview of many of the new features and enhancements that make using the Macintosh easier and more productive than ever. The Application Switcher, which you can tear off from the Application menu, allows you to switch among different applications at the click of a mouse. You can resize and reorder columns in lists, and you can choose standard views for windows in icon, list, or button view. You can have proportional scroll boxes and double arrows for scrolling. The Favorites folder gives easy access to frequently used items. In applications that use Navigation Services, opening and saving files is now more convenient, with shortcuts, recent items, and favorites buttons. An enhanced Find command provides powerful features for searching through the contents of files and locating items on the Internet. File Exchanges lets you access DOS disks and coordinates translation among different file formats. In addition, folder actions help automate repetitive tasks, and AppleScript is faster and more flexible.

Finally, this chapter told you about Mac OS 8.5's improved Internet and networking capabilities. You can use the Internet control panel to specify whole suites of Internet settings. You can now save addresses for network resources such as Web pages and e-mail addresses in location files. The Date & Time control panel can be used to synchronize your Mac's clock with highly accurate time servers on the Internet, and you can view foreign language content with your Web browser. Finally, with the Network Browser, you can easily find and connect to shared folders and disks on your network.

✦　　✦　　✦

What's Hot in Mac OS 8–8.5

Despite all the innovation in Mac OS 8.5, it has plenty in common with earlier versions of the Mac operating system. This chapter gives you an overview of the notable features and the capabilities present in Mac OS 8, 8.1, and 8.5.

This chapter draws your attention to some of the more powerful capabilities that make the Mac easy to use. Many improved methods make it easier to work with disks and their contents — collapsible windows, pop-up windows, view options for each window, spring-loaded folders, contextual menus, and sticky menus to name a few.

What's more, versions 8–8.5 of the Mac OS come with more software for accessing the Internet than did previous versions. For starters, a setup assistant program leads you through the confusing process of getting the computer ready to use the Internet for the first time. You also get top-notch programs for sending and receiving e-mail, browsing the Web, and publishing a simple Web site from your own computer.

Those capabilities are basic when compared to what the Mac OS can do with multimedia. This chapter introduces the system software extensions you get for watching movies and manipulating three-dimensional graphics: QuickTime, QuickDraw 3D, QuickTime VR, and the QuickTime MPEG extension.

Most of the features described in this chapter are not included with Mac OS 7.6–7.6.1. Nevertheless, some Macs that came with Mac OS 7.6–7.6.1 include Internet features that are similar to those described here as part of the Apple Internet Connection Kit. In addition, you can add Internet features to Macs running earlier system software by installing e-mail, Web browser, and Web-sharing software from Apple, Netscape, and Microsoft. Finally, you can add all the multimedia features described here to Mac OS 7.6–7.6.1 by installing QuickTime 3.0.

Ease of use: improved Finder responsiveness, using the collapse box, the revamped Views menu, contextual menus, sticky menus, and more

Internet: getting a glimpse of Internet setup, e-mail, Web browsing, Web sharing, and Java

Multimedia: watching QuickTime movies, manipulating QuickDraw 3D graphics, and giving QuickTime VR, MPEG movies, and new features in QuickTime 3.0 the once-over

✦ ✦ ✦ ✦

After reading this chapter, be sure to look through the next chapter for an overview of additional essential Mac OS features.

Ease of Use

The latest releases of the Mac OS have many improved features and innovations that make using the Mac easier and more productive.

Simultaneous operations

The Finder version in Mac OS 8–8.5 is more responsive than earlier versions. After opening a folder or disk that contains a large number of files and folders, you no longer have to wait for every item to appear in the folder or disk window before you can do anything else. The Finder continues updating the window while you proceed with other work, such as launching a program. What's more, you can do other work in the Finder while it copies files or empties the Trash. Figure 2-1 shows two batches of files being copied at the same time.

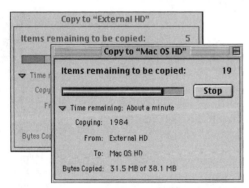

Figure 2-1: Keep working in the Finder while it copies files or empties the Trash.

Live scrolling

While you drag a scroll box in a folder or disk window in Mac OS 8–8.5, you see the items in the window scroll past continuously. In earlier versions of the Finder, you see only the scroll box move while you drag it; the items displayed in the window don't change until you release the mouse button after moving the scroll box to a new position.

Working with windows

Many windows in Mac OS 8–8.5 have controls not present in earlier system software. One of these is the collapse box, also known as the windowshade box, which you click to hide all of a window except its title bar and click again to expand the window. The collapse box sits at the far right end of a window title bar, bumping the zoom box to the left. You still have the option of collapsing and expanding a window by double-clicking its title (as described in "Collapsing Windows" in Chapter 8).

Another control not present in prior releases is the window frame, which you can drag with the mouse to move the window. It does the same job as the title bar, effectively giving you a bigger handle to grab and drag.

Viewing folder and disk contents

You change the view of a folder or disk window with a revamped View menu. You can choose to view files and folders as icons, buttons, or a list of names and other facts. If you're viewing icons or buttons, you can choose View menu commands that clean them up by aligning them to an invisible grid or that arrange them by name, date, kind, and so on. If you're viewing a list, you can sort it by those same criteria. (To learn more about the View menu, see "Fine-tuning Views" in Chapter 6.) Figure 2-2 shows the View menu for icons and buttons.

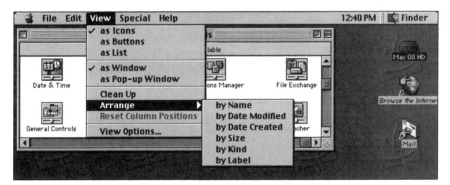

Figure 2-2: Choose the view for a folder or disk window from a revamped View menu.

Button views

If you choose "as Buttons" from the View menu, you see files and folders represented by square buttons. You open a button by clicking it once; you drag it by its name; and you select it by dragging across it. Figure 2-3 shows an example of a folder window viewed as buttons.

Figure 2-3: View files and folders as buttons, and open one by clicking it once.

Pop-up windows

You can make a pop-up window from a regular window by choosing "as Pop-up Window" from the View menu. This anchors the window to the bottom of the screen and changes its title bar into a tab. Clicking the tab at the top of a window closes it and leaves the tab at the bottom of the screen. Clicking a tab at the bottom of the screen makes the window pop up from there. (To find out more about pop-up windows, see "Using Pop-up Windows" in Chapter 6.) Figure 2-4 shows an open pop-up window and the tabs of closed pop-ups.

Figure 2-4: Click a pop-up window's tab to open and close it.

View options

By choosing View Options from the View menu, you can adjust several aspects of a window's appearance. Figure 2-5 shows the View Options dialog box for an icon view, a button view, and a list view.

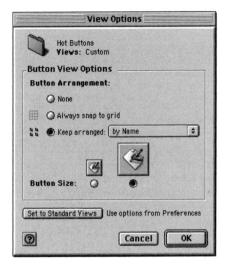

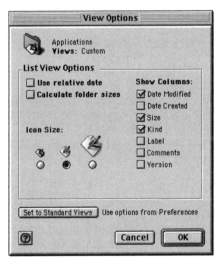

Figure 2-5: Adjust each window's appearance individually with the View Options command.

For a window viewed as icons or buttons, you can select an icon or button size and a forced arrangement. You can force icons or buttons always to snap to a grid when you move them, or you can keep them arranged by name, date, and so on. If you select any of the forced arrangement options, a small icon in the upper left corner of the window indicates which arrangement is in force. All these options are available not only for folder and disk windows, but for the desktop as well. Figure 2-6 shows the icons that indicate a forced arrangement.

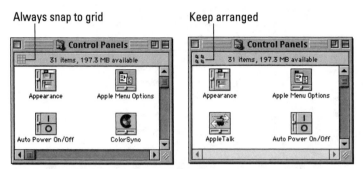

Figure 2-6: Small icons in a window's header indicate a forced arrangement of icons in Mac OS 8–8.5.

For a window viewed as a list, you can select an icon size, pick which columns to show, choose whether to take the time to calculate folder sizes, and specify whether to display relative dates such as "today" and "yesterday." You can also display a Date Created column in Mac OS 8–8.5 (which you can't do in Mac OS 7.6–7.6.1).

Note that the View Options command adjusts each window or the desktop individually. In Mac OS 8–8.1, normally you can't set view options for all windows or a batch of windows at once. (You can change view options en masse using utility software such as Neatnik by Karl Bunker, which is described in Chapter 26.) However, Mac OS 8.5 lets you change the view options of all windows that adhere to standard view options by changing the standard view options using the Finder's Preferences command (described next). You can make a window adhere to the standard view options by clicking the Set to Standard Views button in the window's View Options dialog box. (You'll find more information about view options in "Fine-tuning Views" in Chapter 6.)

Finder preferences

The Finder in Mac OS 8–8.5 has a Preferences command that you can use to set appearance and behavior options for all Finder icons and windows. You can simplify the menus to see just the essential commands. You can also configure spring-loaded opening of folders and disks (as described next). Other options replace similar options formerly found in the Views and Labels control panels. The Mac OS 8.5 Preferences dialog box has three tabs, one for general preferences, one for views, and one for labels. Figure 2-7 shows the Finder Preferences dialog box in Mac OS 8.5.

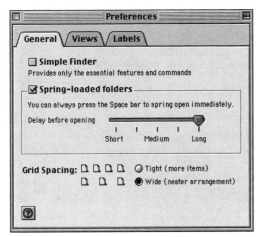

Figure 2-7: Set appearance and behavior options for all Finder icons and windows with the Preferences command.

For more information on Finder Preferences, see "Simple Finder" in Chapter 5, and "Fine-tuning Views," "Folder Ins and Outs," and "Labeling Items" in Chapter 6.

Spring-loaded opening

You no longer have to do a lot of double-clicking to travel through layers of folders in the Finder. Disks and folders spring open when you pause briefly over them with the mouse button held down. This behavior comes in handy when you're moving or copying items to a folder that's buried inside other folders. You can also make a disk or folder spring open by clicking it one-and-a-half times (like double-clicking, but hold down the mouse button on the second click). As long as you keep pressing the mouse button, you can open any folder or disk by pausing over its icon. You can adjust the delay factor or turn off the spring-loaded folders feature with the Finder Preferences command.

Contextual menus

Mac OS 8–8.5 brings menu commands closer to hand with contextual menus. You see a contextual menu of commands that can affect an icon, a window, or some text in the Finder when you press the Control key while clicking the object. What appears in the menu varies depending on the particular item you select. If you Control-click a group of selected items, the contextual menu lists commands that pertain to all of them. You can pop up contextual menus single-handedly with many alternative pointing devices such as two-button mice and trackballs made by companies other than Apple. Figure 2-8 shows an example of a contextual menu.

Figure 2-8: See a contextual menu by Control-clicking an icon, a window, or some text in Finder.

Sticky menus

When you open any menu on the Mac OS 8–8.5 menu bar, or any contextual or pop-up menu, it stays open even if you release the mouse button. You can then choose a menu item by clicking it, or you can open a different menu by moving the pointer to the menu title. The menu goes away if you click outside it or if you don't move the mouse for 15 seconds. You can also operate menus the old way, by holding down the mouse button.

File menu commands

The Finder's File menu has some additional commands in Mac OS 8–8.5, and several of which have useful keyboard shortcuts. The Move To Trash command disposes of items you have selected. The Show Original command locates an alias's original item and brings it into view in the window that contains it. You use the items in the Label submenu to apply a colored label to the items you have selected (like the Labels menu prior to Mac OS 8). In addition, the Sharing command's window is improved. Figure 2-9 shows the File menu.

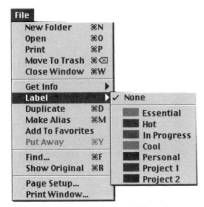

Figure 2-9: Use the additional commands in the Finder's File menu.

You'll find more information on labeling items in Chapter 6, on aliases in Chapter 12, and on sharing in Chapter 21.

The Internet

Mac OS 8–8.5 go a lot further than previous system software versions in helping you get connected to the Internet and get access to Internet services once you are connected. This section gives you an overview of what Mac OS 8–8.5 provide. (Some Internet features specific to Mac OS 8.5 were described in Chapter 1.) For the full story about the Internet and the Mac OS, see Chapter 17.

Setting up

Setting up an Internet connection can be an incredible nightmare, but not if you use the Internet Setup Assistant program. It interviews you to get the necessary information and then makes all the control panel settings behind the scenes. You don't have to open the control panels to get started, although you can always tweak them later. Figure 2-10 shows an example of the Internet Setup Assistant.

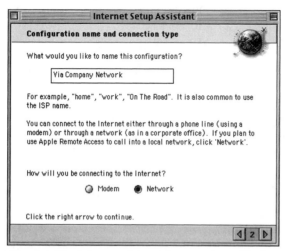

Figure 2-10: Set up an Internet connection with the Internet Setup Assistant program.

E-mail

Exchange electronic mail with people around the world or across the street by using the e-mail programs that now come with the Mac OS. More people use the Internet for sending and receiving e-mail than for any other purpose. Microsoft Outlook Express is the standard e-mail program in Mac OS 8.5, and Claris Emailer Lite is the standard in Mac OS 8–8.1.

Web browsing

It may not be as utilitarian as e-mail, but the World Wide Web is the flashiest part of the Internet. You can view text, pictures, and movies, and hear sounds from Web sites around the world with the Web browser programs you get with Mac OS. Microsoft Internet Explorer is the standard browser installed with Mac OS 8.1–8.5, although it does not replace any other browsers already installed on the computer. You can also install Netscape Navigator separately from the Mac OS 8.1–8.5 CD. Navigator is the standard browser installed with Mac OS 8, and you can install Internet Explorer from the Mac OS 8 CD. In addition, Apple's Cyberdog is included for optional installation with Mac OS 8 (and is available separately for installation with Mac OS 7.6–7.6.1 or 8.1–8.5).

Connect To

Mac OS 8–8.5 includes Connect To, which is a bare-bones program for quickly accessing any Internet site whose URL (Uniform Resource Locator) you know. You choose Connect To from the Internet Access submenu of the Apple menu (Mac OS

8.5) or directly from the Apple menu (Mac OS 8–8.1), type or paste the URL, and click the Connect button. Connect To accomplishes its magic by using systemwide Internet preferences set in the Internet control panel (Mac OS 8.5) or the Internet Config program (Mac OS 8–8.1). These preferences are preset during a standard installation of the Mac OS, but you can change them later. Figure 2-11 shows the Connect To program's dialog box.

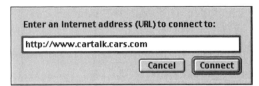

Figure 2-11: Access an Internet site quickly by typing its URL into the Connect To program's dialog box.

Personal Web Sharing

The Personal Web Sharing software included with Mac OS 8–8.5 makes it easy to host a Web site on your computer. You place your prepared Web pages in the Web Pages folder on your startup disk and click the Start button in the Web Sharing control panel. While you're connected to the Internet, anyone with an Internet connection and a Web browser can see your pages. The Web browser that views your site can be running on any kind of computer or even on an Internet connection device that hooks up to a TV. If you're connected to an intranet (a local TCP/IP network), anyone on the intranet can see your pages with a Web browser running on any kind of computer. Figure 2-12 shows the Web Sharing control panel.

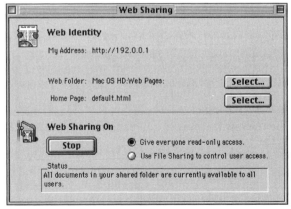

Figure 2-12: Share your Web pages on the Internet or an intranet with the Web Sharing control panel.

Mac OS Runtime for Java

Your computer can run programs written in the popular Java programming language with the Mac OS Runtime for Java software that's part of a standard installation of Mac OS 8–8.5. Small Java programs called *applets* are often embedded in Web pages to make the pages more interesting or useful. When you view a Web page with an embedded Java applet, the applet runs automatically. You can also run Java applets outside of Web browsers. The Apple Applet Runner is an application program that runs Java applets and is included with Mac OS Runtime for Java.

Multimedia

The Mac OS gives you many ways to enjoy audio and video on your computer. You can watch digital movies, interactively view "virtual reality" panoramas and objects, and manipulate three-dimensional objects displayed on the computer screen. You can play audio CDs in your computer's CD-ROM drive, and if your computer has video-input capability, it can display video from a camcorder or other video equipment. This section introduces you to movies, 3D graphics, QuickTime VR, the capability to play MPEG movies, and some new features introduced with QuickTime 3.0. Chapter 16 covers all the Mac OS multimedia capabilities in detail.

Watching QuickTime movies

With a standard installation of the Mac OS, your computer can play digital video and audio — movies — from its hard disk, a CD-ROM, or the Internet. The QuickTime system extension not only makes that possible, it makes movies ubiquitous. You don't need a special program to watch QuickTime movies. Most applications let you copy and paste movies as easily as you copy and paste graphics, and you can play a QuickTime movie wherever you encounter one.

What's more, the version of QuickTime included with Mac OS 7.6–8.5 enables the computer to play CD-quality digital sound and MIDI soundtracks. It can display closed-caption text along with the movie. It can also overlay the regular video track of a movie with independently animated sprites and three-dimensional graphics.

Applications use two methods for controlling movie playback. They can display a standard VCR-like controller just below the movie. You use this play bar to play, stop, browse, or step through the movie and adjust its sound level. Applications can also display movies without controllers. In this case, a badge in the lower left corner of the movie distinguishes it from a still graphic. To play a movie that has a badge and no controller, you double-click the movie. Clicking a playing movie stops it. Figure 2-13 shows one QuickTime movie with a playback controller and another movie with a QuickTime badge.

Figure 2-13: Play back a QuickTime movie by manipulating the controller along its bottom edge (left) or by double-clicking a movie with a badge in its lower left corner (right).

Because movies involve so much data, they are invariably compressed to save space on disk. QuickTime can display movies that have been saved using a variety of compression methods.

Manipulating QuickDraw 3D graphics

It takes a lot of work to draw and shade graphic objects to give them a three-dimensional appearance, but QuickDraw 3D enables the Mac OS to render 3D graphic objects that are in motion. In some cases, you watch 3D animation that someone else created. In other cases, you provide the motion by rotating, moving, and zooming a 3D graphic object with the mouse. QuickDraw 3D provides a standard viewer with controls for zooming, rotating, and moving a 3D object, and for viewing it from various preset angles. Because QuickDraw 3D renders at the Mac OS level, it's easy for any application to incorporate dynamic 3D graphics. The 3D graphics all have the same format so you can cut, copy, paste, drag, and drop them in any participating application. Figure 2-14 shows an example of the standard QuickDraw 3D viewer in the Scrapbook.

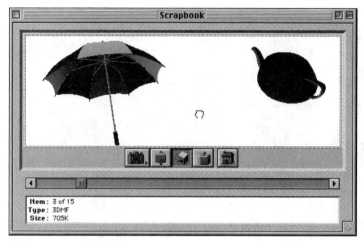

Figure 2-14: Change the view of a 3D graphic with the controls at the bottom of a standard QuickDraw 3D viewer.

Interacting with QuickTime VR scenes

Starting with Mac OS 8 you also get QuickTime VR, which lets you turn 360 degrees to view panoramas and turn objects to view them from different angles. You can view a QuickTime VR panorama or object anywhere you can view a linear QuickTime movie if you have QuickTime 2.5 or later installed.

When you view a QuickTime VR panorama, you can look up, look down, scan left, or scan right by dragging the pointer with the mouse. You can zoom in or out by pressing the Option or Control key. In addition, a VR controller appears across the bottom of the window if you have QuickTime VR 2.0 or later installed, as is standard with Mac OS 8–8.5. Figure 2-15 shows a QuickTime VR panorama being scanned to the right.

Pointer shows direction of movement

Figure 2-15: Drag the mouse to see another view of a QuickTime VR panorama.

When you view a QuickTime VR object, you can manipulate it to see a different view of it. You click the object and drag up, down, or sideways, and the object or some part of it moves. For example, it may turn around so that you can see all sides of it, or it may open and close. With QuickTime VR 2.0 and later, you can also zoom in and out on an object by pressing the Shift or Control key. Figure 2-16 shows a QuickTime VR object being turned to the left.

Figure 2-16: Drag the mouse to see a QuickTime VR object from other angles.

MPEG movies

The QuickTime MPEG Extension that comes with Mac OS 8–8.5 enables QuickTime to display MPEG movies on a PowerPC computer without any special equipment. MPEG (Motion Picture Experts Group) is a worldwide industry standard for compressing video.

QuickTime 3.0

QuickTime 3.0 is the version of QuickTime that comes with Mac OS 8.5, and it can be installed on Mac OS 7.6–8.1. New features of QuickTime 3.0 include:

✦ New compression methods that are optimized for streaming playback over the Internet, such as watching QuickTime movies in a Web browser.

✦ Increased flexibility in opening more types of multimedia files.

✦ Additional special visual effects and transition features for QuickTime movies.

✦ Roland's Sound Canvas instrument set to provide improved playback of MIDI music files.

✦ Support for DV/FireWire digital video streams.

Summary

This chapter introduced the features that make Mac OS 8–8.5 easier to use than earlier versions of the system software. The Finder is more responsive thanks to its live scrolling of windows and its capability to perform simultaneous operations. There are additional controls for moving and collapsing windows. The Finder's View menu is revamped, making it simpler to set the view of each folder and disk window and to keep it arranged. You can view files and folders as one-click buttons, and you can make any disk or folder window into a pop-up window. Many view options that previously applied to all folder and disk windows can now be set for each window separately. The Finder's Preferences command offers a Simple Finder option plus options that were formerly part of the Views and Labels control panels. You can make disks and folders spring open without lifting a finger. You can see a contextual menu of relevant commands by Control-clicking an icon, a window, or some text in the Finder. All menus stay open even if you release the mouse button, and several commands have been added to the Finder's File menu.

This chapter also gave you an overview of what Mac OS 8–8.5 provides for getting connected to the Internet and accessing Internet services. The Internet Setup Assistant simplifies setting up an Internet connection. You can use any of the supplied programs to exchange e-mail. You also have choices of Web browsers, and the Connect To program quickly connects you to any Internet location if you know its URL. The Personal Web Sharing software makes it easy to publish your own Web pages on the Internet or on an intranet. In addition, you can run Java applets that are embedded in Web pages and run Java programs outside Web pages with the Mac OS Runtime for Java software.

In addition to those basic capabilities, this chapter introduced the many ways that the Mac OS enables you to enjoy audio and video on your computer. These include watching QuickTime movies, manipulating QuickDraw 3D graphic objects displayed on the computer screen, interacting with QuickTime VR scenes, and MPEG movie playback.

✦   ✦   ✦

What's Cool in the Mac OS

The Mac OS has more features and capabilities worth noting besides the ones introduced in the previous chapters. This chapter draws your attention to some of the more powerful mousing techniques that are available with the Mac OS. You also learn about distinctive elements of the Mac OS menu bar, getting onscreen help, aliases, and desktop printing. Other basic features noted in this chapter include stationery pads, hierarchical outlines of disk contents, file searching, file sharing, custom icons, and item labels.

Moving beyond the basics, you also learn about the organization of the System Folder, different kinds of fonts, and what virtual memory does for you. These features are available in all system software versions. You also learn about the powerful Mac OS capabilities for managing system extensions, hearing the computer read text aloud, giving the computer spoken commands, and more.

Essential Maneuvers

The Mac OS has essential features and capabilities to help you with everyday tasks on your computer. This section takes a look at more than a dozen you're sure to find useful.

Editing by mouse alone

Instead of using the venerable Cut, Copy, and Paste commands to move text, graphics, or other material in document windows, you can simply drag it from one place to another. You can drag within a document, between documents, and between applications. You can drag material from a document to a Finder window or to the desktop, and the material becomes a clipping file. Conversely, you can drag a clipping file to a document window. This capability, called *drag-and-drop editing*, works only with applications designed to take advantage of it. (For more information, see "Moving Document Contents Around" in Chapter 7.) Figure 3-1 is an example of drag-and-drop editing.

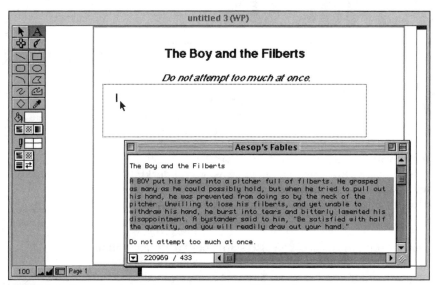

Figure 3-1: Dragging text from place to place within a document.

Translucent icon dragging

When you drag an icon on a PowerPC computer, the icon becomes translucent so you can still identify the icon while you look through it to see where you're dragging. If you drag a group of icons, only the icon under the pointer is translucent; the others in the group are outlines. Figure 3-2 illustrates translucent icon dragging.

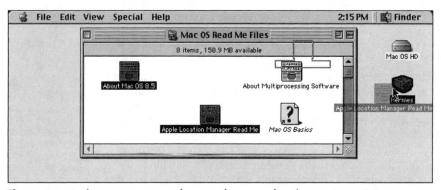

Figure 3-2: An icon appears translucent when you drag it on a PowerPC computer.

Dragging to open

You can open a document not only with the application that created it, but also with any compatible application you have. Drag the document icon to an application icon, and if they're compatible, the application icon becomes highlighted. Release the mouse button and the highlighted application opens the document. For example, you can drag a diverse collection of documents to an application that compresses them so that they consume less disk space. This drag-and-drop capability speeds your work and you can use it with aliases of documents and applications, as well as with the actual items. (For more information, check out "Opening Programs, Documents, and More" in Chapter 7.)

Tooling around with the Apple menu

The Apple menu is like the tool belt a carpenter wears. It doesn't hold all of the tools and equipment, but it holds the things the carpenter needs most often and the special things for the work the carpenter's currently doing. With the Mac OS, you can customize the Apple menu so that it gives you immediate access to programs, documents, folders, and anything else you use frequently or need for a current job. When you choose an item from the Apple menu, it opens right away. You don't have to root around a cluttered desktop or scrounge through folders with the Finder. The Apple menu is available in almost every program. It lists items alphabetically and shows their icons.

You put an item in the Apple menu by dragging its icon into the Apple Menu Items folder in the System Folder. The item becomes instantly available in the Apple menu — there is no need to restart your computer. To remove an item from the Apple menu, drag its icon out of the Apple Menu Items folder. (For more information on the Apple menu, see "Opening Programs, Documents, and More" in Chapter 7.) Figure 3-3 shows an example of the Apple menu and its special folder.

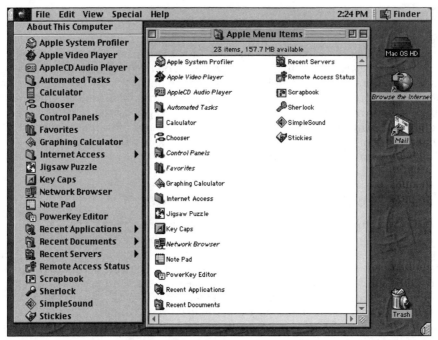

Figure 3-3: Open anything from the Apple menu, which lists whatever you put in the Apple Menu Items folder.

Multitasking

The Mac OS lets you keep more than one program open at a time and switch between the open programs. This capability is known as *multitasking*. You can have as many programs open simultaneously as fit in your computer's memory. You can switch to any open program, including the Finder, by clicking its window or by choosing it from the Application menu at the right end of the menu bar. (Chapter 1 described the Application menu briefly, along with its new tearoff counterpart, the Application Switcher, in Mac OS 8.5.) You can copy and paste among documents of open programs without closing documents and quitting programs. By switching to the Finder, you can open other programs, find documents, organize folders and disks, and so on. Figure 3-4 shows the Application menu and several programs open at once.

Having multiple programs open can lead to a confusion of windows. You can eliminate window clutter by using Application menu commands to hide windows temporarily.

Figure 3-4: Keep multiple programs open at the same time and switch between them with the Application menu.

Some programs can use the Mac OS multitasking capabilities to operate in the background while you work with another program. *Background programs* operate during the intervals — only split seconds long — when the active program isn't using the computer. Programs working in the background can print documents, send and receive e-mail, get files from the Internet, copy items in the Finder, back up disks to tape, and so on.

For more information about multitasking, background operations, and hiding windows, see "Managing Multiple Open Programs" in Chapter 7.

Checking the menu bar clock

You have the option of displaying a digital clock near the right end of the menu bar. Clicking the clock alternates between a display of the time and the date. You set the format of this clock with the Date & Time control panel and can set the clock to chime on the hour, at quarter past, at half past, and at quarter till. (For more information on the clock options, see "Date, Time, and Location Settings" in Chapter 11.) Figure 3-5 shows the clock settings in the Date & Time control panel.

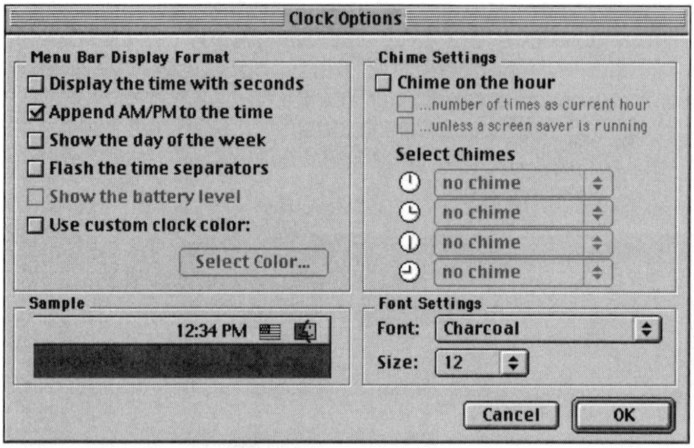

Clock Options

Menu Bar Display Format
☐ Display the time with seconds
☑ Append AM/PM to the time
☐ Show the day of the week
☐ Flash the time separators
☐ Show the battery level
☐ Use custom clock color:

Select Color...

Sample

12:34 PM

Chime Settings
☐ Chime on the hour
  ☐ ...number of times as current hour
  ☐ ...unless a screen saver is running

Select Chimes
🕐 no chime ⬍
🕐 no chime ⬍
🕐 no chime ⬍
🕐 no chime ⬍

Font Settings
Font: Charcoal ⬍
Size: 12 ⬍

Cancel   OK

Figure 3-5: Configure the optional menu bar clock to display the time and more.

Saving time with Stationery Pads

If you regularly create new documents with common formatting, contents, and so on, you can save time with stationery pad documents. Opening a stationery pad is like tearing off a page from a pad of preprinted forms — you get a new document with all common elements preset. Stationery pads have a distinctive icon that looks like a stack of document icons. You can make any document a stationery pad by setting the Stationery Pad option in its Info window. (For more details about making and using stationery pads, see "Creating Documents" in Chapter 7.) Figure 3-6 shows some sample stationery pad icons.

Stationery

4 items, 378.4 MB available

Document   Image   Press Release   Read Me

Figure 3-6: Open a stationery pad to get a new document with preset contents and formatting.

Printing with desktop printer icons

If you use more than one printer, you can choose one without using Chooser. The Mac OS desktop printing software creates desktop icons for each of your printers. Using the Finder's Printing menu you make one the default printer, which appears when you select a desktop printer icon. Desktop printers queue documents for printing and print them in the background while you do other work. You can open a desktop printer to see and manage the queue. It is also possible to switch between different printers using a Control Strip module or a printer menu in the menu bar. (For more information about desktop printing, see Chapter 14.) Figure 3-7 shows desktop printer icons and a desktop printer window.

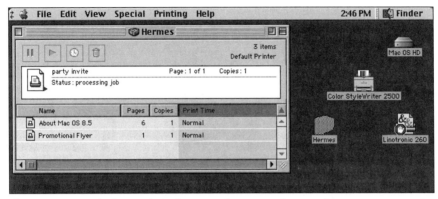

Figure 3-7: Use desktop printer icons to choose a printer and manage background printing.

Balloon help and Apple Guide

Although the Mac OS graphical interface is easier to learn and remember than a bunch of cryptic command words, it's hard to remember what every icon and graphical doodad means. Optional balloon help can assist your memory. Here's how it works: You choose Show Balloons from the Help menu (called the Guide menu in Mac OS 7.6–7.6.1). This action turns on balloon help, which works from any application, not just the Finder. Then you use the mouse to point to something — an icon, menu, part of a window, or some other object. A cartoon-style balloon pops up next to the object. Words inside the balloon describe the object to which the balloon points. The message usually tells you what the object is, what it does, or what happens when you click it. Figure 3-8 shows an example of a help balloon.

Figure 3-8: A help balloon describes an object and how it's used.

Balloon help is separate from Mac OS 8.5's Help Viewer, which was described in Chapter 1, and Apple Guide. Apple Guide is an interactive help system that shows and tells you how to get things done while you actually do them. Step-by-step instructions appear in a guide window, which floats above all other windows. As you move from step to step, the guide may coach you by marking an object onscreen with a circle, arrow, or underline. Figure 3-9 shows an example of Apple Guide.

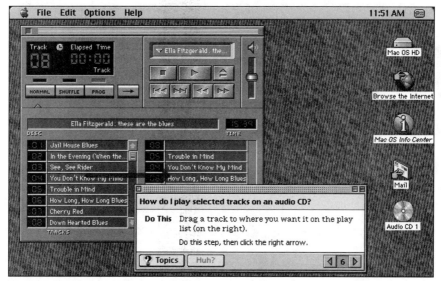

Figure 3-9: Apple Guide displays step-by-step instructions in a floating window and points out objects onscreen.

Apple Guide watches what you do and can adjust its steps if you work ahead or make a mistake. It can even perform a step for you, such as opening a control panel.

For more information on balloon help and Apple Guide, see Chapter 9.

Outlining in Finder windows

The Finder can display the contents of a folder or disk in a window as a list of item names and other information. Some of the items in a list may be folders, which may contain more folders. You can see the contents of all the enclosed folders as part of one list in an indented outline format. The levels of indentation in the outline clearly diagram the layers of folders listed in the window. You can expand or collapse any level in the outline to show or hide the corresponding folder's contents by clicking a small triangle next to the folder's icon. With folders expanded, you can select items from more than one folder at a time. (For more information, see "Viewing Folder and Disk Contents" in Chapter 5.) Figure 3-10 shows an example of the outline structure of a list view.

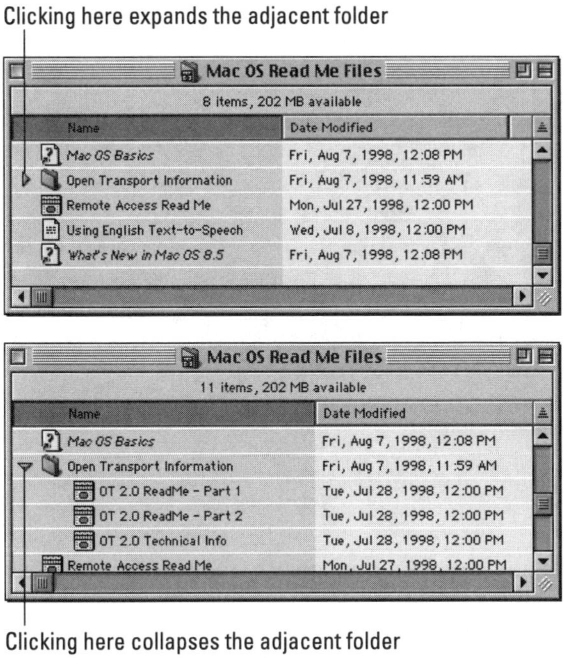

Clicking here expands the adjacent folder

Clicking here collapses the adjacent folder

Figure 3-10: Expanding and collapsing folder outlines in Finder windows.

Categorizing with item labels

Just as people use colored file folder labels to categorize folders of paper documents, the Mac OS can categorize folders or other items with color. Each color has an associated text label. You label an item with the Label submenu of the Finder's File menu (Mac OS 8–8.5) or the Label menu (Mac OS 7.6–7.6.1 and earlier). After labeling items, you can arrange a folder or disk window by label. You can also use Sherlock or Find File to search for items by label and apply labels to found items. Label colors and text are not fixed; you can change them by using the Labels control panel. (For a complete explanation of using and changing labels, see "Labeling Items" in Chapter 6.) Figure 3-11 shows some labeled items and a label being applied to another item.

Quick Tips

Folder Path Menus

The title of a Finder window appears to be static, but when you press ⌘ while clicking the window title, a menu pops up. This pop-up menu reveals the path through your folder structure from the active window to the disk containing it. You can open any folder along the path by choosing the folder from the pop-up menu. To close the active window while opening a folder along the path, press Option while choosing the folder from the pop-up menu.

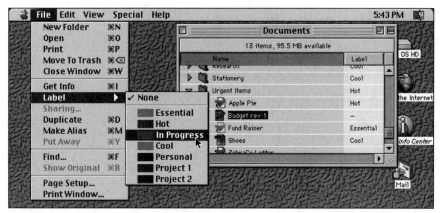

Figure 3-11: Setting an item's label.

Using aliases

You can't be in two places at once, but your documents, applications, and folders can be in many places at one time. Mac OS aliases make this virtual omnipresence possible. An *alias* is a small file that points to another file, folder, or disk. When you open an alias, the item it points to opens automatically. When you drag an item to the alias of a folder, the item you drag goes into the folder to which the alias points. You can put aliases anywhere — on the desktop, in the Apple menu, or in other accessible places — and leave the original items buried deep within nested folders. An alias looks like the original item except that its name is in italics, and its name may end with the word *alias*. To further differentiate an alias, Mac OS 8.5 displays a small badge that looks like a bent arrow on every alias icon. Figure 3-12 shows an alias and its original item.

Aliases have a variety of uses, including the following:

✦ Opening frequently used programs, documents, and folders from the desktop while the real items remain buried in nested folders.

✦ Adding items to the Apple menu without moving the original items from their folders.

✦ Organizing documents and folders according to multiple filing schemes without duplicating items. For example, you can file documents by project, addressee, date, and topic.

✦ Getting nearly automatic access to your computer's hard disks from another computer on the same network.

To learn how to make aliases and to discover more strategies for their use, see Chapter 12.

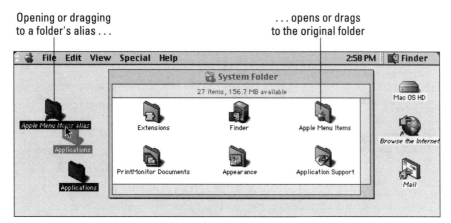

Opening or dragging to a folder's alias . . .

. . . opens or drags to the original folder

Figure 3-12: Things you do to an alias happen to its original item.

Sharing files

If your Mac is networked with other computers, the Mac OS makes it possible to share any of your folders, even whole disks, and their contents with other network users. Of course, you can access shared folders and disks on other networked computers as well. The remainder of this section briefly introduces Mac OS file sharing. Chapter 20 details how to access shared files, and Chapter 21 explains how to share your folders and disks.

Using someone else's folders

To use another computer's folder or disk, you can use the Network Browser (in Mac OS 8.5) or the Chooser (in all Mac OS versions). Both of these programs list the names of all computers that have shared folders or disks that you can connect to. After you choose one of the listed computers, the Network Browser or the Chooser asks you to connect as a guest or registered user and then presents a list of items you may share. Figure 3-13 shows how you connect to shared items using the Network Browser; the procedure is similar with the Chooser.

Sharing your folders with others

Before you can share your own folders or disks with other network users, you must start file sharing with the File Sharing control panel (Mac OS 8–8.5) or the Sharing Setup control panel (Mac OS 7.6–7.6.1). Your computer then shows up in the Network Browsers and Choosers of other network computers. Figure 3-14 shows the File Sharing control panel; the Sharing Setup control panel is similar.

To share one of your disks or folders, select it and then use the Finder's Sharing command to display the item's sharing information. This information appears in an item's Info window in Mac OS 8.5 or in an item's sharing window in Mac OS 7.6–8.1. There you specify who can see the item's folders, view its files, and make changes to these privileges. You can grant different access privileges to the owner of the item (usually you), to one other registered user or a group of registered users you designate, and to everyone else. Figure 3-15 shows an example of sharing information.

1. Open or expand a file server
in the Network Browser.

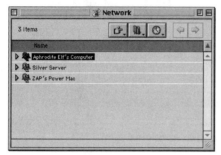

2. Connect as a guest or registered user.

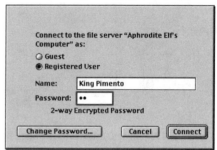

3. Open a shared item in the
Network Browser.

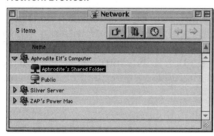

4. See the shared item's contents
in the Finder.

Figure 3-13: Connect to a shared folder or disk using the Network Browser.

Figure 3-14: Set up file sharing in the File Sharing control panel.

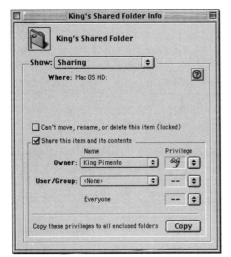

Figure 3-15: Use the Sharing command to share an item and set its access privileges in Mac OS 8.5 (left) or Mac OS 8–8.1 (right).

You identify registered users, set their passwords, and create groups of users with the Users & Groups control panel. You can see who is sharing what and how busy they're keeping your computer with the File Sharing control panel (Mac OS 8–8.5) or the File Sharing Activity Monitor control panel (Mac OS 7.6–7.6.1). You can also use either of these control panels to disconnect individual users who are sharing your folders and disks. Figure 3-16 shows an example of the Users & Groups and File Sharing control panels.

Important Mac OS Features

When you're ready to go beyond the basics, the Mac OS has many powerful features and capabilities to help you work more efficiently. This section takes a look at organizing the System Folder, fonts and typography, extending memory, managing startup items, and speech capabilities.

Organizing the System Folder

The system software consists of hundreds of files—system extensions, control panels, fonts, preference files, and many other kinds of files. The Mac OS organizes system software files in a number of special folders inside the System Folder. There's a Control Panels folder, a Preferences folder, an Extensions folder, a Fonts folder, and many more. Most of the special folders have distinctive icons. Moreover, the Finder knows which special folder to put many items in when you drag them to the System Folder icon. Figure 3-17 shows an example of the System Folder.

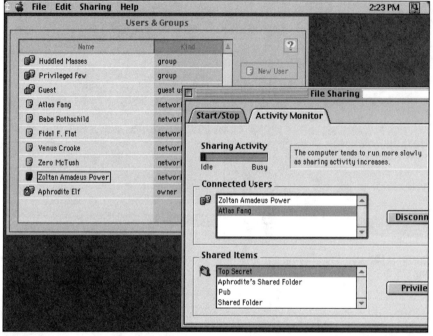

Figure 3-16: Identify who can use your shared items and see who's currently using them.

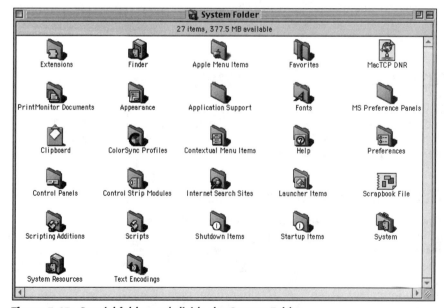

Figure 3-17: Special folders subdivide the System Folder.

In general, you should *not* move items from one special folder in the System Folder to another, because these files must be in specific locations to function. Likewise, you should not remove items from the System Folder unless you know for sure that an item is not needed. (To learn more about the System Folder's special folders, see Chapter 10.)

Tackling fonts and typography

The Mac OS works with three basic kinds of fonts: fixed size, TrueType variable size, and PostScript variable size. This section introduces some of the different kinds of fonts and typography. (Chapter 13 covers fonts in detail.)

Thanks to the TrueType font technology that is built into the Mac OS, text looks smooth at any size onscreen or on any printing device. TrueType fonts are variable-size outline fonts similar to the PostScript fonts that look so sharp on PostScript printers (and onscreen if you have installed Adobe Type Manager software). The Mac OS smoothly scales TrueType fonts to any size. Fixed-size fonts also look good on the screen at their prescribed sizes, but they appear lumpy when scaled to other sizes. Figure 3-18 shows how smoothly TrueType scales 36-point Times text compared with a scaled-up 18-point fixed-size font.

X ylophone　　Xylophone

Figure 3-18: The Mac OS scales TrueType fonts (left) more smoothly than fixed-size fonts (right).

Extending memory

Application programs are becoming more memory hungry all the time, and the Mac OS has a large memory appetite itself. Seems like a computer can never have too much memory. The Mac OS can increase the amount of memory available by using part of a hard disk transparently as additional memory. This extra memory, called *virtual memory,* lets you keep more programs open simultaneously and increase the amount of memory each program gets when you open it. Given more memory, programs may allow you to open additional or larger documents. Furthermore, on PowerPC computers, having virtual memory turned on substantially reduces the amount of memory that programs need. (For more information on memory management, see Chapter 18.)

Managing startup items

To help you manage the large number of items that load when you start up your computer, the Mac OS includes the Extensions Manager control panel. You can use it to disable and enable control panels, extensions, and other startup items either individually or in sets. The Extensions Manager that comes with Mac OS 7.6–8.5 provides many improvements over previous versions. For each item, it displays its status (enabled or disabled), name, size, and version, and in some cases the package it was installed with. You can view items grouped by the folders they're in, grouped by the package they were installed with, or ungrouped. You can enlarge the Extensions Manager window to display detailed information about a particular item. Figure 3-19 shows an example of the Extensions Manager.

Do not use the Extensions Manager to disable extensions unless you know for certain that a particular extension or groups of extensions are not needed; some extensions are essential to the proper functioning of your Macintosh.

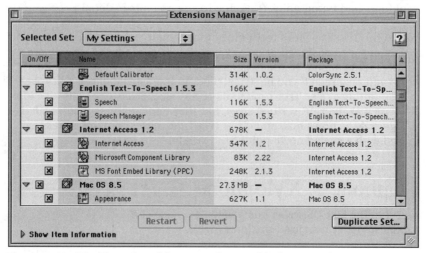

Figure 3-19: Disable and enable startup items with the Extensions Manager control panel.

To learn more about the Extensions Manager, see "Managing Startup Items" in Chapter 10.

Listening and speaking with PlainTalk

The very first Macintosh could speak — at its debut in 1984, it thanked Steve Jobs for being "like a father to me." Its voice, created by the MacinTalk system extension, had a heavy robot accent. Today, Apple's PlainTalk text-to-speech software can give your computer a clearer voice in English or Mexican Spanish. In addition, many computers can use PlainTalk speech recognition software to recognize spoken commands. You configure speech options with the Speech control panel, which is shown in Figure 3-20.

There are several ways to get your computer to speak. With English Text-to-Speech 1.5–1.5.3 (included with Mac OS 7.6–8.5), you can have the computer announce its alert messages. Some application programs use the text-to-speech software to read text aloud. And you can write AppleScript scripts that speak. The text-to-speech software synthesizes a variety of voices, male and female, with good inflection. It is quite accurate and can correctly pronounce most words and punctuation—even abbreviations. Almost any Mac OS computer can synthesize speech, although computers with a PowerPC or 68040 processor sound most natural.

English Speech Recognition (included with Mac OS 8.5 and available free for other Mac OS versions) enables the Mac OS to take spoken commands from anyone who speaks North American English. Applications can also take advantage of speech recognition software, but few do. When you speak commands, you just speak normally, without intense pauses, unnatural diction, or special intonation. You don't have to train the computer to recognize your voice. Speech recognition works on a computer with a PowerPC processor and 16-bit sound input (the Centris and Quadra AV models can also recognize spoken commands).

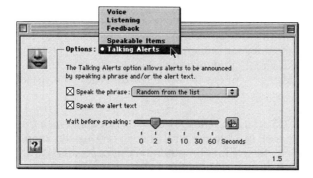

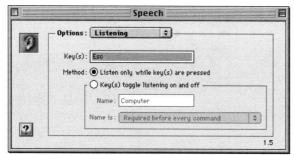

Figure 3-20: Set speech options with different sections of the Speech control panel.

For more information on speech, see Chapter 22.

Summary

This chapter introduced you to the special Mac OS features and capabilities that help you with everyday computer tasks. They include drag-and-drop editing, translucent icon dragging on a PowerPC computer, and dragging documents to open them with applications that didn't create them. The Mac OS also provides the Apple menu for opening your favorite items quickly and the Application menu for switching between open applications. You can check the time and date with the menu bar clock. Stationery pads save you time when you need to create duplicate documents with consistent formatting and content. Desktop printer icons make it easy to choose a printer and manage background printing. If you need help while using the Mac OS, you can use balloon help to get descriptions of items.

There are several ways the Mac OS makes it easier to work with your disks, files, and folders. You can see indented outlines of your layers of folders. You can categorize items with colored labels. For all practical purposes, you can keep items in more than one place at the same time by making aliases of them. And you can share files with other computer users on a network.

This chapter introduced you to more Mac OS features and capabilities that you're sure to find indispensable. They include special folders for organizing the contents of the System Folder, virtual memory for reducing program memory needs on PowerPC computers and making more memory available on all computers, and three kinds of fonts that the Mac OS works with — fixed size, TrueType variable size, and PostScript variable size.

To make the most of the Mac OS, you can manage your startup items with the Extensions Manager control panel. In addition, with English or Mexican Spanish text-to-speech software, you can hear your computer announce its alert messages and read other text aloud. With speech recognition software, you can speak commands.

✦   ✦   ✦

Getting Started with the Mac OS

Start on the Desktop

The desktop, with its menus, windows, and icons, serves as a home base for everything you do with your Macintosh. Because you use all these things so much, how they look and operate is important. You need to know what all this basic stuff is and how to use it: the menu bar, pop-up menus, contextual menus, regular windows, dialog boxes, alert boxes, window controls, other controls, and the active window. You also need to know how what different icon shapes mean, how to select one or more icons, and how to rename them. This chapter describes and illustrates all of these basic features of the Mac OS.

Menus

The Mac OS has always used menus to present commands and attributes from which you can choose. You see menu titles in the form of words and icons in a menu bar at the top of the screen. The menu bar contains some menus that are the same in all applications, as well as menus that are unique to the application program you're using at the time. Menus can also appear outside the menu bar. A menu that pops up from an icon or other object outside the menu bar has an arrow that indicates it is a menu. In addition, Mac OS 8–8.5 can display menus in some places based solely on the context of the mouse pointer. This section describes menus in the menu bar, pop-up menus, and contextual menus.

Menu bar

The menus in the menu bar at the top of the screen contain commands that are relevant to the application you are using at the time. The menus may also contain attributes that apply to objects you work with in the application. In addition, the menu bar has menus from which you can choose another application that you want to begin using. Menu titles appear in the menu bar, and you can use the mouse to display one menu at a time beneath its title. Figure 4-1 shows the menu bar as it initially appears in Mac OS 8–8.5, with one of its menus displayed.

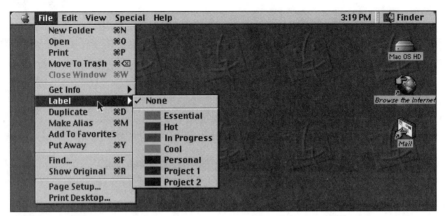

Figure 4-1: The menu bar is a permanent fixture at the top of the screen.

You can change some aspects of the menu bar appearance in Mac OS 8–8.5 as described in Chapter 8. In Mac OS 7.6–7.6.1, the menu bar and menus are white instead of gray.

Backgrounder

Why One Menu Bar

There are several reasons why the Mac OS has a permanent menu bar at the top of the screen. One reason is that a menu bar at the top of the screen is an easy target to hit with the mouse. You can quickly slide the mouse pointer to the top of the screen, where it automatically stops at the menu bar. If the menu bar were at the top of a window in the middle of the screen (like on a Windows computer), you would have to take more time to carefully position the pointer over it.

A second reason is that having a permanent menu bar at the top of the screen gives you a reliable place for every application's commands. If each window on the screen had its own menu bar, you'd have to think about which one you wanted to use.

How the menu bar works

To use the menu bar, you position the mouse pointer over a menu title and click or press the mouse button. The menu opens beneath the menu title so that you can see the items in it and choose one if you like. You must keep pressing the mouse button to make a menu stay open in Mac OS 7.6–7.6.1. You do not have to keep pressing the mouse button in Mac OS 8–8.5 (although you can if you want to).

In Mac OS 8–8.5, a menu stays open when you click it. You can leave your finger off the mouse button and move the pointer up and down the menu, highlighting each menu item as the pointer passes over it. The menu disappears if you move the pointer to the menu bar. You can display the same menu or another menu by moving the pointer over the menu title. You don't have to click again unless it's been more than 15 seconds since you last moved the mouse. To choose a menu item, you position the pointer over it and click. If you click outside a menu, or if you don't move the mouse for 15 seconds, the menu disappears and you have to click a menu title again to make menus stick open.

You can use menus the nonsticky traditional way with any version of the Mac OS. Position the pointer over a menu title and press the mouse button to display the menu. The menu disappears if you release the mouse button. To choose a menu item, hold down the mouse button as you drag the pointer to the menu item and then release the button to choose the item.

Standard menus

In most Mac OS applications, the menu bar includes these five standard menus:

✦ **Apple menu** is at the left end of the menu and has an Apple logo for its title. This menu usually includes an About item, which describes the application you're currently using, followed by an alphabetical list of programs, documents, and other items you can open. For information on using and customizing the Apple menu, see "Opening Programs and Documents, and More" in Chapter 7.

✦ **File menu** is next to the Apple menu and contains commands that affect a whole document, such as New, Open, Close, Save, and Print. The last item is usually Quit, which you use when you're done working with an application.

✦ **Edit menu** is to the right of the File menu and contains commands that you can use to change a document's contents, such as Undo, Cut, Copy, Paste, and Clear.

✦ **Help or Guide menu** gives you access to onscreen help. The menu title and its location are different in various Mac OS versions. In Mac OS 8–8.5, the help menu is labeled "Help," and the menu is immediately to the right of the last application menu in the menu bar. In Mac OS 7.6–7.6.1, the help menu is labeled with a question mark icon. It is near the right end of the menu bar, and is referred to as the Guide menu. For more information about onscreen help, see Chapter 9.

✦ **Application menu**, which is located at the right end of the menu bar, displays an alphabetical list of the applications that are currently running on the computer. Choosing a listed application makes it the active application so you can use it. You'll find more information about this menu in "Managing Multiple Open Programs" in Chapter 7.

Each application may add its own menus between the Edit menu and the Help menu. In addition, the menu bar normally includes a digital clock near the right end of the menu bar. The clock is not the title of a menu; clicking it does not display a menu.

Pop-up menus

Menus outside the menu bar must be marked so you can tell that clicking one will display a menu. By convention, an arrowhead next to some text or an icon indicates it is a menu title. The arrowhead may point down or to the right. It may also be double-headed and point up and down. This kind of menu is called a *pop-up menu*. Figure 4-2 shows some examples of pop-up menus.

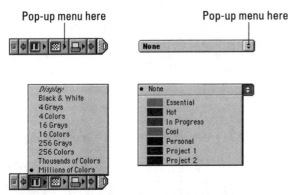

Figure 4-2: An arrowhead marks a pop-up menu.

Like menus in the menu bar, a pop-up menu stays open after you click it in Mac OS 8–8.5. You must keep pressing the mouse button to keep a pop-up menu open in Mac OS 7.6–7.6.1.

Contextual menus

If you're using Mac OS 8–8.5, you may not have to look through the menus on the menu bar to find a command or attribute. You can display a *contextual menu* by holding down the Control key while clicking an icon, a window, or some selected text for which you want to choose a command or attribute. The contextual menu lists commands that are relevant to the item that you Control-click. Figure 4-3 shows an example of a contextual menu for a window.

You can Control-click one icon or a selection of several icons. When several icons are selected, Control-clicking any one of them displays a contextual menu of commands that pertain to the whole group. For example, if you Control-click one folder icon in Mac OS 8.5, the contextual menu includes the command Attach a Folder Action. This command is not included in the contextual menu when you Control-click several folders because the command can only apply to one folder at a time. (For more information on selecting items, see "Icons" later in this chapter.)

Figure 4-3: Control-clicking an item displays a contextual menu in the Mac OS 8–8.5 Finder.

Contextual menus are not a universal feature of Mac OS 8–8.5. They are available when you're working with files, folders, and disks in the Finder (as described in Chapter 5), although they can be disabled in that context by selecting the Simple Finder option (also described in Chapter 5). Other applications can adopt contextual menus as well. In addition, you can extend contextual menus with shareware and freeware add-ons such as Apple Data Detectors and FinderPop (both of which are described in Chapter 26).

Although Mac OS 7.6–7.6.1 doesn't support contextual menus directly, some applications have contextual menus that work. Generally, you do something other than Control-clicking to display one of those contextual menus. For example, you display a contextual menu in Netscape Navigator by moving the pointer over an object in the browser window and pressing the mouse button for a few seconds.

If your Mac has a two- or four-button mouse or trackball, you may be able to display contextual menus by pressing the right button without holding down the Control key. If your multibutton mouse or trackball does not already work this way, you may be able to program it to simulate a Control-click whenever you press the button on the right. For instructions on programming a multibutton mouse or trackball, see the documentation that came with it. These alternative pointing devices are made by Kensington Technology (650-572-2700, http://www.kensington.com) and other companies, not by Apple.

Menu symbols

A menu item may be accompanied by a variety of symbols. A triangle pointing to the right indicates the menu item has a submenu. An ellipsis at the end of the item name indicates that choosing the item brings up a dialog box in which you must supply additional information before the command can be completed.

The following symbols indicate the status of a menu item:

- ✔ designates an attribute that applies to everything that is currently selected

- ● also designates an attribute that applies to everything that is currently selected

- – designates an attribute that applies only to some things that are currently selected

- ▶ designates a menu item with a submenu

- ◆ designates a program that's running in the background and that requires attention; to find out why, make it the active, foreground application

Other symbols are used to specify keyboard shortcuts for menu items. Pressing a specified combination of keys has the same effect as choosing the menu item. For example, pressing the ⌘ key and the X key is equivalent to choosing the Cut command from the Edit menu. The following symbols represent keys:

⌘ represents the Command key

⇧ represents the Shift key

⌥ represents the Option key

⌃ represents the Control (or Ctrl) key

⌦ represents the Delete key

When you use a keyboard shortcut for a command in a menu, the title of the menu flashes briefly to signal that the command has been issued. You can change how many times the title flashes or turn off the signal altogether in the Menu Blinking section of the General Controls control panel (as described in Chapter 11).

Windows

You view and interact with the files stored on your computer in rectangular windows. This section describes how different types of Mac OS windows look and work.

Window types

There are several types of Mac OS windows, each designed to display a specific kind of information. Some windows display the files and other items stored on disks. Other windows display the contents of files, which may be text, pictures, movies, or other kinds of information. Windows called *dialog boxes* display options that you can set. *Alert boxes* are dialog boxes in which the Mac OS or an application program notifies you of a hazardous situation, a limitation in your proposed course of action, or an error condition. *Palettes* contain controls or tools, or display auxiliary information for the application program that you're currently using.

Each type of window has a standard structure, and it's basically the same in all versions of the Mac OS. The frame that borders every window looks different for a regular window, a movable dialog box, an immovable dialog box, an alert box, and a palette. Figure 4-4 shows examples of the different types of windows as they initially appear in Mac OS 8–8.5.

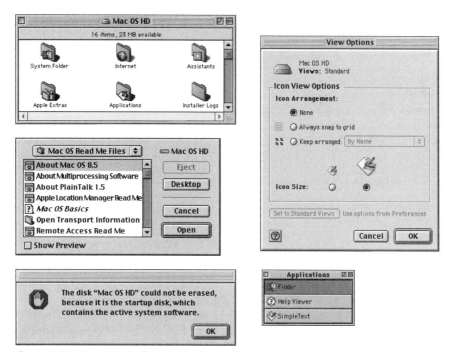

Figure 4-4: Mac OS windows include regular windows (top), immovable dialog boxes (middle left), movable dialog boxes (middle right), alert boxes (bottom left), and palettes (bottom right).

Although basic window structure is the same in all versions of the Mac OS, the overall look of windows is different in Mac OS 8–8.5 than earlier Mac OS versions.

Window controls

The design of a window has as much to do with function as with form. Many parts of a window's frame are actually control surfaces that you can use to move the window, size it, close it, or change the view of its contents. Figure 4-5 shows examples of window controls.

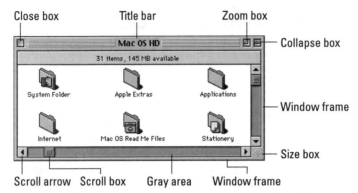

Figure 4-5: Manipulate windows with their many controls.

The window controls have these effects:

✦ **Title bar:** Drag to move the window. Double-clicking the title bar may collapse or expand the window and Option-double-clicking may collapse or expand all windows, like clicking and Option-clicking the collapse box. (To set up this option, see "Collapsing Windows" in Chapter 8.)

✦ **Close box:** Click to make the window go away. Press the Option key and click to close all windows.

✦ **Zoom box:** Click to make the window as large as it needs to be to show all its contents, up to the size of the screen. Click again to make the window resume its previous size and location. Press the Option key and click to force the window to fill the screen. (The zoom box usually leaves a margin on the right side of the screen.)

✦ **Collapse box:** Click to hide all but the window's title bar, or if the window is collapsed, click to show the entire window. Press the Option key and click to collapse (or expand) all windows. (This control is not included in Mac OS 7.6–7.6.1.)

✦ **Scroll bar arrow, box, gray area:** Click or press the arrow to scroll the window's contents smoothly; click or press the gray area to scroll in chunks; drag the box to quickly bring another part of the window's contents into view. The scroll bar controls do not appear if scrolling would not bring anything else into view. In Mac OS 8.5, you can make the scroll arrows bidirectional and the scroll box proportional to the window content. (To set up this option, see "Scroll Bar Controls" in Chapter 8.)

✦ **Size box:** Drag to adjust the size of the window.

✦ **Window frame:** Drag to move the window. (This function is not included in Mac OS versions prior to Mac OS 8.)

You won't find all the window controls on every kind of window. Document windows have all or most of the available controls, movable dialog boxes have fewer controls, and immovable dialog boxes and alert boxes have no controls built into their borders.

Other controls

Inside many windows are a variety of controls that you operate by clicking and dragging with the mouse. Examples include buttons with text or picture labels, checkboxes, radio buttons, sliders, little arrows for increasing or decreasing numeric values, disclosure triangles, scrolling lists, and tabs. Figure 4-6 shows examples of some controls in Mac OS 8–8.5.

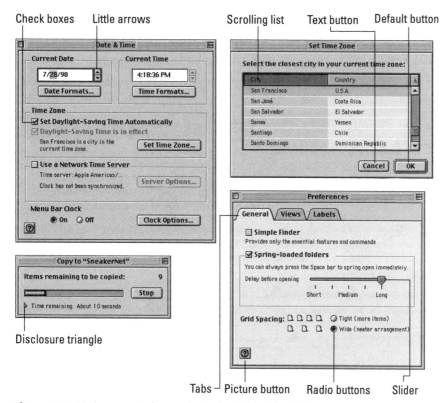

Figure 4-6: Various controls may be included inside windows.

Buttons, checkboxes, radio buttons, and other controls look somewhat different in Mac OS 7.6–7.6.1. They look flat instead of three-dimensional.

Controls have these effects:

✦ **Buttons** cause an action to take place when clicked. Many dialog boxes have OK and Cancel buttons. Clicking OK accepts all the settings and entries in the dialog box. Clicking Cancel rejects any changes you may have made in the dialog box and restores all settings and entries to their states when the dialog box appeared. One button in a dialog box or alert box may have a heavy border; this is the *default button*. It represents the action you'll most often want to take, except that if the most common action is dangerous, a button representing a safer action may be the default button. As a shortcut for clicking the default button, you can press the Return key or the Enter key.

✦ **Radio buttons** let you select one setting from a group. They're called radio buttons because they work like the station presets on a car radio. Just as you can select only one radio station at a time, you can select only one radio button from a group. To select a radio button, you click it. Although you can't select more than one radio button, several radio buttons in a group may be partly on and partly off because the group indicates the state of more than one thing, such as the right or left alignment of multiple paragraphs.

✦ **Checkboxes** let you turn options on or off. When an option is on, a check mark or a cross appears in the checkbox. When an option is off, the checkbox is empty. When an option is partly on and partly off because it indicates the state of more than one thing, such as the format of a range of text, a horizontal line appears in the checkbox. Checkboxes are not mutually exclusive like radio buttons. You can turn on checkboxes in any combination. Clicking a checkbox reverses its state.

✦ **Sliders** display a range of values or magnitudes. An indicator shows the current setting and you can drag the indicator to change the setting.

✦ **Little arrows**, which point in opposite directions, let you raise or lower a value incrementally. Clicking an arrow changes the value one increment at a time. Pressing an arrow continuously changes the value until it reaches the end of its range.

✦ **Disclosure triangles** control how much detail you see in the window. Clicking a right-pointing triangle reveals additional detail and may automatically enlarge the window to accommodate it. Clicking a down-pointing triangle hides detail and may automatically shrink the window to fit.

✦ **Scrolling lists** display a list of values in a box with an adjacent scroll bar. If there are more values than can be displayed at once, the scroll bar becomes active and you can use it to see other values in the list. Clicking a listed item selects it. You may be able to select multiple items by pressing the Shift key or the ⌘ key.

✦ **Tabs** look like the tabs on dividers used in card files and ring binders, and they have a similar function. They divide the content of a window into discrete pages, or sections, with each tab connected to one section of window content. You see one section at a time, and you switch to a different section by clicking its tab.

Active window

When more than one window is open, one is active and you can use its controls.
You can't use the controls in windows that are open but inactive. In fact, you can't
even see controls in the frames of inactive windows. You can tell the active window
not only by its visible controls but also by the fact that it overlaps inactive windows
that touch it. The active window is considered to be in front of inactive windows.
Figure 4-7 shows an active window and inactive windows in Mac OS 8–8.5.

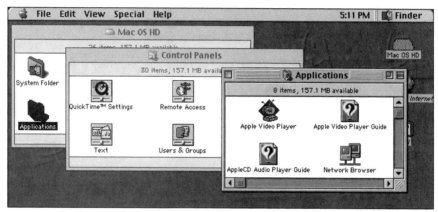

Figure 4-7: The active window has visible controls and overlaps inactive windows
that touch it.

To make an inactive window active, click any part of it that you can see. This brings
it to the front and moves the former active window behind. If a dialog box or alert
box is displayed, you must dismiss it before you can make another window active
in the same application program. Some dialog boxes allow you to make a window
from a different application that is currently open active, thereby switching
applications (see "Managing Multiple Open Programs" in Chapter 7).

There is an exception to the rule that only one window is active at a time. Palettes
are always active when they are open. They float in a layer above other types of
windows. If you are using an application with palettes, and switch to another
application with palettes, the palettes from the first application should close
automatically and any palettes that were previously open in the second application
should reopen automatically.

Secrets

Window Tricks

Although inactive windows don't have visible controls, you can move and collapse or expand them while they're in the background. If you have more than one program open at the same time, these tricks only work with windows of the program you're currently using.

To move an inactive window, press the ⌘ key while you drag the window's title bar or its frame (title bar only in Mac OS 7.6–7.6.1).

To collapse or expand an inactive window, press the ⌘ key while double-clicking the window's title bar. Pressing ⌘ keeps the window from becoming active.

To collapse or expand all windows, press the Option key while double-clicking any window's title bar. Option-clicking a collapse box does the same thing in Mac OS 8–8.5.

Icons

Many entities in the Mac OS are represented by small pictures called *icons*. In particular, you use the programs, documents, folders, and disks in your computer by manipulating icons on the computer screen. This section explains what the look of an icon tells you about it and how you use icons.

Icon appearance

An icon's basic appearance tells you what kind of item it represents. Icons that look like a sheet of paper with a dog-eared corner represent document files, which contain the text, pictures, sounds, and other kinds of data stored on your computer. Icons based on a diamond shape usually represent application programs that you use to work on documents. Many application icons have other shapes, but the diamond shape was the original standard for Mac programs. Icons that look like folders represent the folders in which programs, documents, and other items are organized on your disks. These are just a few of the icons you learn to recognize on a typical Mac; you'll find many other icons described in other chapters. Figure 4-8 shows examples of document, program, and folder icons in Mac OS 8.5.

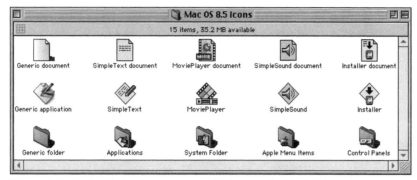

Figure 4-8: An icon's basic appearance indicates the kind of item it represents.

Selecting Icons

The look of an icon has no bearing on how you use it. Everyone who uses a Mac quickly learns how to select icons by clicking, but even some seasoned veterans don't know that in windows and on the desktop you can select more than one icon at a time. In addition, you can select icons individually by typing instead of clicking.

When you select an icon, the Mac OS highlights it by making it darker and displaying its name in white type on a black background. If the icon you select is on a monitor that's set to display black and white, the Mac OS highlights the icon by inverting its colors; white becomes black and black becomes white. Figure 4-9 shows examples of icons that are highlighted and icons that aren't.

Figure 4-9: Icon highlighting on a color or grayscale monitor (left) and a black-and-white monitor (right).

Multiple selection by Shift-clicking

Ordinarily, clicking an icon selects it (highlights it) and deselects the icon that was highlighted. You can select a group of icons in the same window or a group of icons on the desktop by pressing the Shift key while clicking each icon in turn. At any time, you can deselect a selected icon by pressing the Shift key and clicking it again.

Multiple selection by dragging

In addition to Shift-clicking to select multiple icons, you can select adjacent icons by dragging the mouse pointer across them. As you drag, the Mac OS displays a rectangle, called a *selection rectangle,* and every icon it touches or encloses is selected. Icons are highlighted one-by-one as you drag over them, not en masse after you stop dragging. All items must be on the desktop or in a single window. Figure 4-10 shows an example of selecting several icons with a selection rectangle.

Figure 4-10: Selecting adjacent items by dragging a selection rectangle.

You can combine dragging with the Shift key. Pressing Shift while dragging a selection rectangle across unselected icons adds the enclosed icons to the current selection. Conversely, pressing Shift while dragging a selection rectangle across selected icons deselects the enclosed group without deselecting other icons (if any).

Selection by typing

When you know the name of an icon you want to select but aren't sure where it is in a window, you can select it more quickly by typing than by clicking or dragging. Typing also may be faster than clicking if the icon you want to select requires lots of scrolling to bring into view.

To select an icon by typing, simply type the first part of its name. You need to type only enough of the name to uniquely identify the icon you want. In a window in which every icon has a completely different name, for example, you need to type only the first letter of a name to select an icon. By contrast, in a folder where every icon begins with *Power,* you have to type those five letters plus enough additional letters to single out the icon you want. When selecting by typing, uppercase and lowercase letters are interchangeable.

While typing, you can select the next item alphabetically by pressing Tab or the previous item alphabetically by pressing Shift-Tab. Pressing an arrow key selects the icon nearest the currently selected icon in the direction that the arrow key points. To select the icon of the startup disk, press ⌘-Shift-up arrow(↑). Table 4-1 summarizes keyboard selection techniques.

Table 4-1
Selecting Icons by Typing

To Select This	Do This
An icon	Type the icon's partial or full name
Next icon alphabetically	Press Tab
Previous icon alphabetically	Press Shift-Tab
Next icon up	Press up arrow (↑)
Next icon down	Press down arrow (↓)
Next icon left	Press left arrow (←)
Next icon right	Press right arrow (→)
Enclosing folder or disk	⌘-up arrow (↑)
Startup disk icon	Press ⌘-Shift-up arrow (↑)
Multiple icons	Press Shift while clicking each icon or while dragging to enclose them

Renaming Icons

Clicking an icon highlights the icon and its name but does not select the icon name for editing. This behavior protects your icons from being accidentally renamed by your cat walking across your keyboard (which has actually happened). If you select an icon and begin typing, expecting your typing to rename the selected icon, you may be surprised to discover that your typing selects another icon whose name most closely matches what you're typing (as described previously).

To rename a disk, folder, program, document, or other item, you must explicitly select its name. Either click the name directly, or click the item's icon and then press Return or Enter. An icon whose name is selected for editing has a distinctive look: the icon is highlighted as usual, and the name has a box around it. The box does not appear when you just click the icon. Figure 4-11 shows an icon with its name selected and another icon with its name not selected.

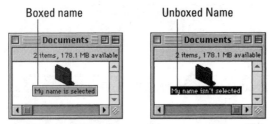

Figure 4-11: A boxed icon name is ready for editing.

For an additional visual cue that you have selected a name on a color or grayscale monitor, make sure the text highlight color is something other than black and white. Then you know that a name highlighted in color (or gray) is ready for editing, whereas a name highlighted in black and white is not. To set the text highlight color, use the Appearance control panel (in Mac OS 8–8.5) or the Colors control panel (in Mac OS 7.6–7.6.1) as described in "Accent and Highlight Colors" in Chapter 8.

Selecting all or part of an icon name

Right after you select an icon name, the whole name is selected. With the whole name selected, you can replace it completely by typing a new name. If you just want to change part of the name, you can select that part and replace or delete it. You can also select an insertion point and type additional text.

To select part of an icon name or an insertion point in one, you must first select the name for editing (as just described). Now position the mouse pointer (which should be shaped something like a capital I) where you want to place an insertion point or begin selecting in the name. Click to place an insertion point, or hold down the mouse button and drag the pointer to select part of the name. As you drag, the Mac OS highlights the text you are selecting. Release the mouse button to stop selecting. If you select an insertion point, you see a thin flashing line that marks its position. Figure 4-12 shows one icon name entirely selected, another name partially selected, and an insertion point in a third name.

Figure 4-12: Select all of an icon name (left), part of an icon name (middle), or an insertion point (right).

Quick Tips

Stop Waiting for the Editing Box

After clicking an icon name to edit it, you have to wait and wait for the editing box to appear around the name. To cut the wait short, just twitch the mouse and the name is highlighted for editing. You don't have to wait after clicking an icon's name if you immediately move the pointer.

Another way to avoid waiting after clicking an icon's name is to move the insertion point by pressing the arrow keys. Click the name and immediately press the up arrow (↑) or the left arrow (←) to move the insertion point to the beginning of the name, or immediately press the down arrow (↓) or the right arrow (→) to move the selection point to the end. Once the selection point is established, pressing the left arrow (←) moves it left and pressing the right arrow (→) moves it right.

The length of time you must wait for the editing box to appear around an icon name you clicked depends on the duration of a double-click interval—approximately 1.9 seconds, 1.3 seconds, or 0.9 second, as set in the Mouse control panel. If you have trouble editing icon names without opening the item, try setting a briefer double-click speed with the Mouse control panel (see "Keyboard and Mouse Adjustments" in Chapter 11).

If you want to select part of an icon name or an insertion point in the name, be sure you wait until the selection box appears around the name. The Finder may think you're double-clicking an icon and open it if you click the name and then immediately click, double-click, or drag in the name to select part of it. (You'll find more discussion of opening icons in "Opening and Closing Disks, Folders, and Files" in Chapter 5.)

Copy, Paste, and Undo

While editing a name, you can use the Undo, Cut, Copy, and Paste commands in the Edit menu. These commands are also available in a contextual menu while you are editing an icon name in Mac OS 8–8.5.

To copy all or part of an icon name, select the part you want to copy and choose Copy from the Edit menu. The Copy command places the selected text on the Clipboard, which is an internal holding area. Then you can paste what you copied by selecting all or part of another icon's name and choosing Paste from the Edit menu. At this point you can make changes to the name that you pasted; you must make changes if the icon whose name you're working on is the same as that of another icon in the same folder. Whatever you copied remains on the Clipboard until you use the Copy command or the Cut command. The Cut command works like the Copy command, but Cut also removes the selected text while placing it on the Clipboard.

While editing an icon name, you can undo your last change by choosing Undo from the Edit menu. The Undo command works only as long as the icon name remains selected for editing. You cannot undo your changes to a name after you finish editing it.

To finish editing an icon name, press Return or Enter, or click anywhere outside the icon name. You can cancel all the changes you made to an icon name since you began editing it by deleting the entire name (choose Select All from the Edit menu and press the Delete key) and then pressing Return or Enter. Because the icon now has no name when you press Return or Enter (ending the editing of the name), the Mac OS restores the name the icon had when you began editing it.

Besides selecting all or part of a name and copying it, you can copy the entire name of any item by selecting its icon and choosing Copy from the Edit menu. You do not have to select the name to copy it; you can just select the icon. Then you can choose the name of another icon (not just the icon this time) that's not in the same folder and choose Paste from the Edit menu to give it the copied name.

You can copy the names of multiple icons by selecting the icons and using the Copy command. This creates a list of icon names on the Clipboard. You can paste this list into a document such as a Stickies note, a SimpleText document, or the Note Pad, but you can't paste the copied icon names onto a group of selected icons. If the total length of all selected icon names exceeds 256 characters, Mac OS 7.6–8.1 copies only the first 256 characters. This limit does not apply in Mac OS 8.5.

Renaming locked items

You can't change the name of a locked item or an item that you are sharing on a network. However, you can copy its entire name as just described. (For information on locking and unlocking items, see "Protecting Files, Folders, and Disks" in Chapter 6. For information on sharing items on a network, see "Designating Your Shared Items" in Chapter 21.)

Taking a Screen Picture

You can take a picture of the whole screen — menu bar, windows, and icons — at any time by pressing ⌘-Shift-3. Each picture you take appears at the root level of your startup disk as a file named Picture 1, Picture 2, and so on. You can view the screen pictures with the SimpleText application, which is normally located in the Applications folder of the startup disk.

Rather than taking a picture of the whole screen, you can take a picture of a window or any rectangular portion of the screen. To do so, use these keystrokes:

✦ **Rectangular region:** Press ⌘-Shift-4 and then drag to select a rectangular region that you want to take a picture of (omits the pointer from the picture).

✦ **Window:** Press ⌘-Shift-4 and Caps Lock, and then click a window that you want to take a picture of (omits the pointer from the picture).

✦ **Cancel:** Press the Space bar (or any other key that normally types a character) to cancel a ⌘-Shift-4 combination.

✦ **Picture on Clipboard:** Add the Control key to any of the screen capture keystrokes to copy the picture to the Clipboard instead of saving it as a picture file on the startup disk. With the ⌘-Shift-4 combinations, you can alternatively press the Control key while selecting the region or window you want to take a picture of.

Summary

After reading this chapter, you know all about menus, windows, and icons. You know that the menu bar at the top of the screen normally contains five standard menus. You know how to use menus in the menu bar, as well as pop-up menus and contextual menus. You understand the meaning of check marks and other special symbols in menus.

You can tell the difference between a regular window, a dialog box, and an alert box. You know the function of scroll bars, zoom boxes, buttons, radio buttons, checkboxes, and other controls found on window frames and inside windows. You can tell which window is currently active.

When you see some icons, you can tell which represent documents, application programs, and folders. You know how to select one icon or a group of icons. You can rename an icon.

You even know how to take a picture of all or part of the screen by pressing a combination of keys.

✦　　✦　　✦

Get Organized with the Finder

◆ ◆ ◆ ◆

In This Chapter

Simplifying the Finder in Mac OS 8–8.5

Opening and closing disks, folders, and files

Viewing folder and disk contents in different formats and levels of detail

Working with files and folders

Working with disks

Doing background work

◆ ◆ ◆ ◆

Ask 100 Macintosh users to name the application program they use most often and only a few would come up with the correct answer: the Finder. People don't think of the Finder as a program they use or need to learn to use. In fact, it is a very rich application program that is included with the Mac OS for managing your disks and their contents.

This chapter describes the simple ways you can organize the stuff on your computer with the Finder. You can open and close disks, folders, and files. You can view the contents of each folder and disk as icons, as a list, and, in Mac OS 8–8.5, as buttons. You can create folders and you can copy, move, duplicate, and delete folders and files. You can also remove or erase disks, if you have more than one on your desktop. Some of these tasks are time-consuming, but in most cases the Finder can finish them in the background while you work.

Once you've mastered the skills presented in this chapter, you're ready to continue learning about the Finder in other chapters. The next chapter gets into the more elaborate ways you can organize your disks and their contents. Chapter 7 discusses opening and saving programs and documents using the Finder. And in Chapter 12, you learn how to create aliases in the Finder to expedite your work in almost all applications.

Simple Finder

A quick scan of the Finder's menus gives you an idea of its capabilities. Not all of them are essential. If you'd rather not bother with the Finder's more advanced capabilities, you can simplify its menus using the Finder's Preferences command. To do this, choose Preferences from the Edit menu to display the Finder's Preferences window. If you have Mac OS 8.5, you see tabs at the top of this window; in this case, click the General tab to see the general preferences. Then click the Simple Finder option to turn it on. (The option is turned on when you see a check mark in the option's checkbox.) Figure 5-1 shows the Simple Finder option turned off.

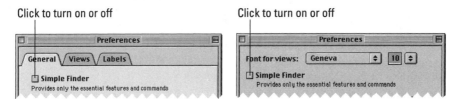

Figure 5-1: Set the Simple Finder option in the Finder's Preferences window in Mac OS 8.5 (left) or Mac OS 8–8.1 (right).

In the interest of simplicity, you can ignore the other options in the Preferences dialog box for now. For more information about them, see Chapter 6.

The Preferences command and the Simple Finder option are available only in Mac OS 8–8.5. If you're using Mac OS 7.6–7.6.1, you can't suppress the Finder's more advanced features and commands, you can only ignore them.

Opening and Closing Disks, Folders, and Files

When you want to see what's in a disk, folder, or file, you open it. Opening a disk, a folder, or a file that is a document displays its contents in a window. Opening a file that is a program displays the program's menus in the menu bar and may display a document window for that program (not all programs automatically display a document window). You open a program when you want to use it to view or edit the kinds of documents it can create.

When you don't want to see a window any more, you can close it. (In Mac OS 8–8.5, you can also make a window into a pop-up window in the title bar, as described in Chapter 6.)

There are two ways to open a disk, folder, or file. You can select its icon and choose Open from the File menu, or you can double-click the icon. Instead of double-clicking an icon, you click it once if it's part of a square button in a Mac OS 8–8.5 window (more about these buttons in the next section). Note that the File menu shows a keyboard shortcut for the Open command, ⌘-O, which means you can also open an icon by selecting it and pressing ⌘-O. Another keyboard shortcut for the Open command is more of a secret: ⌘-down arrow (↓).

There are also two ways to close a window. You can choose Close from the File menu (its keyboard shortcut is ⌘-W or ⌘-up arrow (↑)), or you can simply click the window's close box. To close all open windows at once, press the Option key while closing one of the windows you want to close. This shortcut works with the Close command and the close box.

The Open and Close commands also appear in the contextual menu that pops up when you hold down the Control key and click an icon in Mac OS 8–8.5, as described in the previous chapter. (To see contextual menus, the Simple Finder option must be turned off with the Preferences command in Mac OS 8–8.5's Finder.)

You can open a folder or file and close the window it's in at the same time. Just press the Option key while opening the item. This trick works whether you double-click or choose the Open command.

Viewing Folder and Disk Contents

After opening a folder or disk, you see in its window the files and folders it contains. You can choose to see the contents of a folder or disk window as icons that you can move around or as an ordered list of item names and other facts. If you're using Mac OS 8–8.5, you can also choose to see the contents of a folder or disk window as buttons that you open by clicking once (instead of double-clicking).

Regardless of a window's view format, you can scroll or size the window to see more of its contents.

Choosing a view

You choose a view format from the View menu. In Mac OS 8–8.5, you choose one of three basic formats: icons, buttons, or list. (The View menu has additional commands for choosing variations of the basic formats if the Simple Finder option is turned off in the Preferences dialog box, as described in the next chapter.) Figure 5-2 shows examples of the three basic view formats.

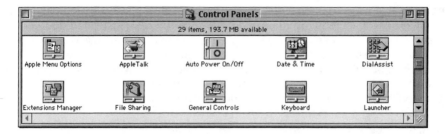

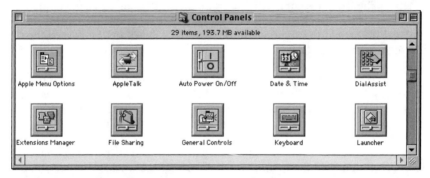

Figure 5-2: Window contents viewed as icons (top), as buttons (middle), or as a list (bottom).

In Mac OS 7.6–7.6.1, you choose one of seven specific formats from the View menu: icon, small icon, name, size, kind, label, or date. The icon view is the same as the icon view in Mac OS 8–8.5, and the small icon view is a variation of it. The other views are all variations of the list view in Mac OS 8–8.5. You can't view a folder or disk window as buttons in Mac OS 7.6–7.6.1. A window set to button view in Mac OS 8–8.5 appears in icon view if you display it in Mac OS 7.6–7.6.1.

Working with list views

List views can pack a lot of information into a window, and you can use that information to organize the list view. You can sort the list by any of the column headings at the top of the view. You can see the contents of enclosed folders in an indented outline format. Also, you can select items contained in more than one enclosed folder.

Changing the sort order

When you initially view a window as a list, the items are arranged alphabetically by name. You can sort the list in a different order by clicking one of the column headings near the top of the window. For example, to list the items in the order in which they were last modified, click the Date Modified heading.

A quick glance at the column headings tells you the sort order. The dark heading indicates the sort order in a Mac OS 8–8.5 window. In Mac OS 7.6–7.6.1, the heading that indicates sort order is underlined.

You can reverse the sort order in Mac OS 8.1–8.5. Simply click the triangular sort direction indicator at the right end of the column headings. This indicator is not present in Mac OS 7.6–8.

Rearranging and resizing columns

The columns of a list view are adjustable in Mac OS 8.5 (but not in Mac OS 7.6–8.1). You can change the size of a column by moving the mouse pointer to the right edge of the column heading, where the pointer shape looks like a sideways pointing arrow. Then press the mouse button and drag left or right. Figure 5-3 is an example of resizing a column in a Mac OS 8.5 list view.

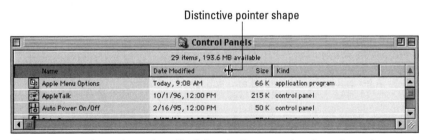

Figure 5-3: Drag a column-heading's borderline to resize the column in Mac OS 8.5.

You can also change the order of columns in a Mac OS 8.5 list view. Simply drag the column heading to the left or right. As you drag, the pointer looks like a hand and you see a pale image of the column you are moving. You can't move the Name column. Figure 5-4 is an example of rearranging columns.

To reset a window's column width and order to the standard configuration, choose Reset Column Positions from the View menu. The Finder asks if you're sure you want to reset the columns. This command affects only one window at a time.

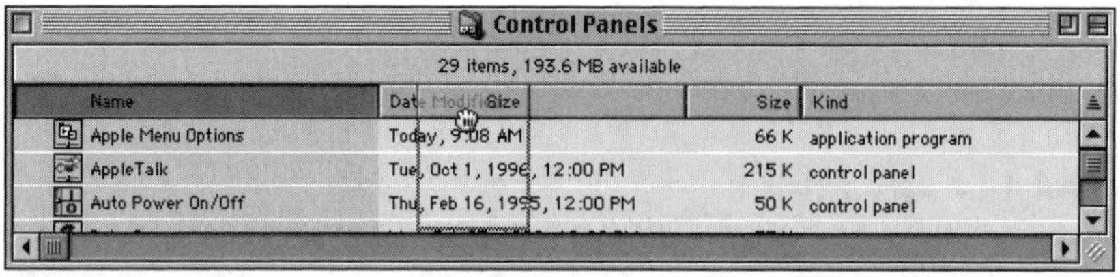

Figure 5-4: Drag a column heading to move the column in Mac OS 8.5.

Expanding and collapsing folders

You can open folders to see what's inside, but if you layer lots of folders within folders, windows clutter your screen by the time you reach the innermost folder. There is a faster and easier way. The Finder displays list views in an indented outline format. The levels of indentation in the outline show how folders are nested. The indented outline provides a graphical representation of a folder's organization. You can look through and reorganize folders without opening additional windows. Figure 5-5 is an example of a list view with both expanded and collapsed folders.

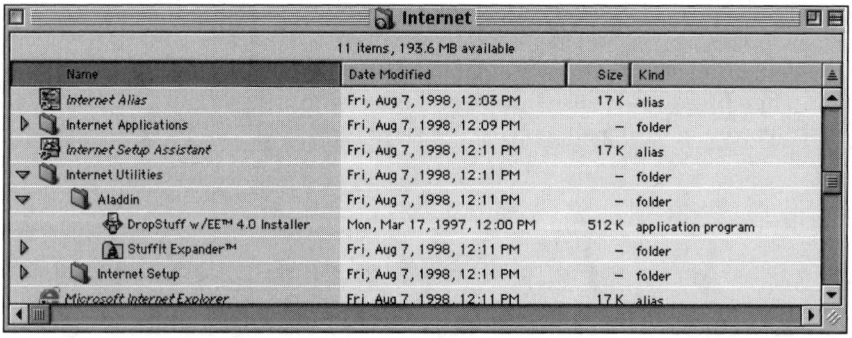

Figure 5-5: A list view with expanded and collapsed folders.

Disclosure triangles next to folder names tell you whether the folders are expanded or collapsed. If a triangle points to the right, the folder next to it is collapsed and you cannot see its contents. If the triangle points down, the folder is expanded and you can see a list of the items in the folder indented below the folder name.

To expand a folder, click the triangle to the left of the folder's icon. When you expand a folder, Finder remembers whether folders nested within it were previously expanded or collapsed, and restores each to its former state. Figure 5-6 shows a folder before and after expanding it.

Figure 5-6: Click a left-pointing triangle (Apple Extras on the left) to expand a folder and display its contents (right).

To collapse a folder, click the triangle to the left of the folder's icon. Figure 5-7 shows a folder before and after collapsing it.

Figure 5-7: Click a down-pointing triangle (QuickTime on the left) to collapse a folder (right).

To collapse a folder and all the folders nested within it, press Option while clicking the disclosure triangle of the outer folder. To expand a folder and all the folders nested within it, press Option while you click the disclosure triangle.

Selecting from multiple folders

After expanding several folders in a list view, you can select items from more than one of the expanded folders. To select an additional item, press Shift while clicking it. You can also select consecutive items by pressing Shift while dragging a selection rectangle across them. If you need to deselect a few items, Shift-click each item or Shift-drag across consecutive items. Figure 5-8 shows a window with items selected from two folders.

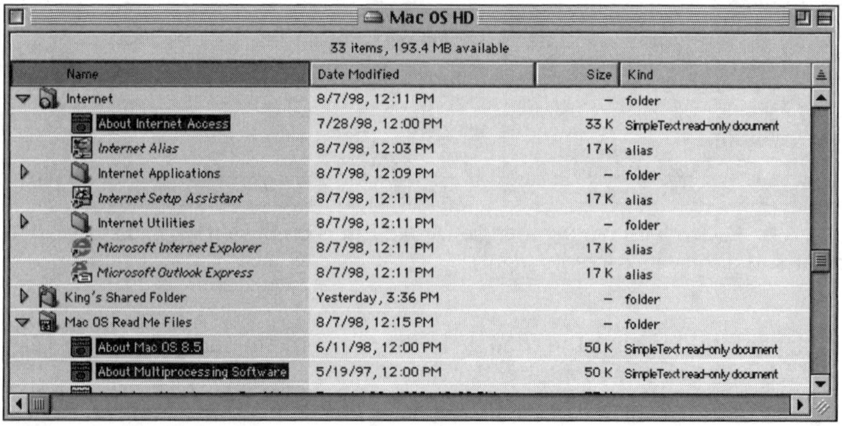

Figure 5-8: Items selected from multiple folders.

Selected items remain selected if you expand folders in the same window. Selected items also remain selected if you collapse folders in the same window, except that any selected items in a folder you collapse are no longer selected.

Seeing more contents

If you can't see everything in a window, you can scroll the window or change its size to see more. Each scroll bar becomes active only if using it would bring more into view.

You can scroll a folder or disk window in Mac OS 8.5 by holding down the ⌘ key and dragging inside the window. While you ⌘-drag, the pointer looks like a gloved hand.

Smart zooming

A window may not fit its content optimally after you expand or collapse folders in a list view, rearrange icons or buttons in an icon or button view, or simply change from one view to another. You can quickly size a window up or down to fit its contents and view format by clicking the zoom box. The Mac OS makes the window just as large as it needs to be to show as much of the window's contents as will fit on the screen. This smart zooming helps you make best use of your screen's real estate.

If you do want to zoom a window to fill the screen (instead of just large enough to show the window's contents), press Option while clicking the zoom box.

Finder Keyboard Shortcuts

Much of what you do with the mouse you can do with keyboard shortcuts instead. For instance, you can select an item in a folder or disk window (or the desktop, if no window is active) without using the mouse by typing the item's name or the first part of its name. Other keystrokes select an item near the currently selected item, open the item, and so on. Table 5-1 gives the details.

Table 5-1 Finder Keyboard Shortcuts	
Objective	*Action*
Icon Shortcuts	
Select an icon by name	Type the icon's full or partial name
Select the next icon alphabetically	Tab
Select the previous icon alphabetically	Shift-Tab
Select the next icon up, down, left, or right	Up arrow (↑), down arrow (↓), left arrow (←), or right arrow (→)
Select the startup disk	⌘-Shift-up arrow (↑)
Select multiple icons	Shift-click each icon or Shift-drag across the icons
Begin editing the selected icon's name	Return or Enter
Insert at the beginning of a selected icon name	Up arrow (↑)
Insert at the end of a selected icon name	Down arrow (↓)
Move the insertion point in a selected icon name	Left arrow (←) or right arrow (→)
Align (or don't align) icons or buttons (countermands View Options or Views control panel setting)	⌘-drag icon or button, Options, or Views
Copy an icon to the desktop or another folder	Option-drag on the same disk
Make an alias (Mac OS 8–8.5 only)	⌘-Option-drag
Move selected icons to the Trash (Mac OS 8–8.5 only)	⌘-Delete
Open the selected icon	⌘-O or ⌘-down arrow (↓)
Open the selected icon and close the active window	⌘-Option-O or ⌘-Option-down arrow (↓) or Option-double-click

(continued)

Table 5-1 *(continued)*

Objective	Action
Icon Shortcuts	
Open the selected icon's enclosing folder or disk	⌘-Up arrow (↑)
Open the selected icon's enclosing folder or disk	⌘-Option-up arrow (↑) and close the active window
Open an enclosing folder or disk of the active window	⌘-click the window title and then choose from the pop-up menu
Window Shortcuts	
Zoom a window to its full size	Option-click zoom box
Expand the selected folder in a list view	⌘-right arrow (→)
Expand the selected folder and its enclosed folders	⌘-Option-right arrow (→) or Option-click the triangle
Expand all folders in the active window	⌘-A and then ⌘-right arrow (→)
Expand all folders and their enclosed folders	⌘-A and then ⌘-Option-right arrow (→)
Collapse the selected folder in a list view	⌘-Left arrow (←)
Collapse the selected folder and its enclosed folders	⌘-Option-left arrow (←) or Option-click the triangle
Collapse all folders in the active window	⌘-A and then ⌘-left arrow (←)
Collapse all folders and their enclosed folders	⌘-A and then ⌘-Option-left arrow (←)
Close a window	⌘-W
Close all windows	⌘-Option-W or Option-click the close box
Close a pop-up window and remove its tab (Mac OS 8.1–8.5 only)	⌘-Shift-W
Close all windows and put away all pop-up window tabs (Mac OS 8.1–8.5 only)	⌘-Shift-Option-W
Close a window while opening the selected item	⌘-Option-O or ⌘-Option-down arrow (↓)
Close a window and make the desktop active	⌘-Option-up arrow (↑)
Collapse all windows	Option-click the collapse box

Objective	Action
Window Shortcuts	
Move a background window	⌘-Drag its title bar
Collapse a background window	Option-double-click its title bar
Hide the active program's windows	Option while making another program active
General Shortcuts	
Switch to the next open application (Mac OS 8.5 only)	⌘-Tab*
Switch to the previous application (Mac OS 8.5 only)	⌘-Shift-Tab*
Make the desktop active	⌘-Shift-up arrow (↑)
Skip Trash warnings	Option while choosing Empty Trash
Erase a floppy disk	⌘-Option-Tab as you insert the disk
Cancel the operation in progress	⌘-Period(.)
Start without extensions	Shift while starting up
Start with Extensions Manager open	Space bar while starting up
Start without internal hard disk	⌘-Option-Shift-Delete
Start from a CD-ROM (most Macs)	C while starting up
Sleep now (PowerBook only)	⌘-Shift-0 or Control-click menu bar clock
Sleep now (any capable Mac)	Power or ⌘-Option-Power
Restart safely	Power or ⌘-Shift-Power
Shut down safely	Power or ⌘-Option-Shift-Power
Force the active program to quit *and lose unsaved work!*	⌘-Option-Escape
Restart a crashed computer *and lose unsaved work!*	⌘-Control-Power
Rebuild the desktop	⌘-Option during startup or while inserting a disk
Reset Chooser and control panel settings stored in parameter RAM (PRAM)	⌘-Option-P-R while starting up

*Using ⌘-Tab as a shortcut for switching applications in Mac OS 8.5 conflicts with some application programs, including FileMaker Pro, ClarisWorks, and AppleWorks. See the discussion of the Application Switcher in "Managing Multiple Open Programs" in Chapter 7 for a way to eliminate this conflict.

Working with Files and Folders

There's a lot you can do with the Finder besides fiddling with the way you view the content of folders and disks. You can organize your files in folders, creating new folders as needed and putting files and folders in other folders. You can duplicate a file or folder in the same folder. You can also get rid of files and folders that you don't want to keep.

Creating a new folder

You create a new folder with the New Folder command in the File menu. The new folder is created in the active window or on the desktop if no window is active. This means that you must open a disk or folder before you can create a folder inside it. If the disk or folder is already open but its window is covered by another window, click the window in which you want to create the folder to bring that window to the front. To create a folder on the desktop, click the startup disk icon (or any other desktop icon) to make the desktop active.

If you create a folder in the wrong place, don't sweat it. You can move it as described next.

Moving items

To move an item to a different folder on the same disk, you just drag it to the window or icon of the destination folder. Similarly, you move an item to the *root level* (main level) of a disk by dragging it to the disk icon or window. To drag an item, you position the pointer over it, press the mouse button, and continue pressing while you move the mouse. The pointer moves across the screen and drags the item you pointed at along with it. You release the mouse button when you get the item positioned over the destination folder icon, disk icon, or window. You can tell when you have the item positioned over the destination because the Finder highlights it. The Finder highlights an icon by making it darker, and it highlights a window by drawing a gray or colored border inside the window frame.

You can move an item by dragging its icon or its name. In a list view, you can also drag an item by any text on the same line as the item's icon, such as its modification date or kind. In a Mac OS 8–8.5 window viewed as buttons, you can drag an item only by its name.

If a folder or disk is open in Mac OS 8.5, you can move it by dragging the small icon in the title bar of its window. To drag a title bar icon, you must place the pointer over it and hold down the mouse button a second before dragging the icon away. If you don't pause with the mouse button down, you end up dragging the window instead of the icon.

Quick Tips

Drag to the Main Folder

If you're working in a list view and want to move an item from an enclosed folder to the main level of the window, just drag the item to the window header as shown in the figure. A window header is the space just below the title bar where the number of items in the window is reported.

The file moves
to the main level of the window

Drag a file to the window header

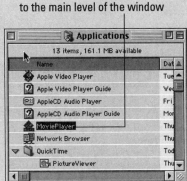

Quick Tips

Cancel a Drag

Oops! Accidentally dragged the wrong icon, or changed your mind while dragging and want to return the item you're dragging to its original location? Just drag it up to the menu bar and release the mouse button as shown in the figure. The Finder returns it to its original location.

1. Drag a file to the menu bar   2. The file returns to its original location

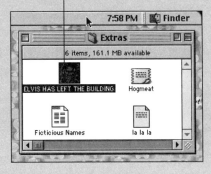

Copying items

To copy an item to another folder on the same disk, press Option while you drag the item to the destination folder. If you're using Mac OS 8–8.5, the pointer has a little plus sign when you Option-drag to remind you that you're making a copy.

The Finder always copies an item when you drag it to a folder that's on another disk (or to another disk itself). Again, the Mac OS 8–8.5 the Finder displays a little plus sign on the pointer when you drag an item over a folder (or a folder window) of a different disk. When you drag an item to another folder, the Finder figures out whether the destination folder is on the same disk as the source folder. If so, the Finder moves the items you're dragging to the destination folder. If the items you're dragging come from a different disk than the destination folder, the Finder copies the items you're dragging.

When you copy an item to a disk or folder that already contains an item by the same name, an alert box asks whether you want to replace the item at the destination. The alert tells you which of the like-named items is newer. If you copy a group of items and more than one of them has the same name as items at the destination, the alert doesn't name the duplicates. Figure 5-9 shows examples of the alerts that the Finder displays to verify replacement.

Figure 5-9: Confirm imminent replacement of an item (left) or items (right).

The Finder is also smart about copying an entire floppy disk to a hard disk. It puts the floppy disk's contents into a new folder on the hard disk and gives the folder the same name as the floppy. You can also copy a hard disk to a larger hard disk. You can even copy a disk to a folder on another disk.

Quick Tips

Autoscrolling While Moving

You can scroll a window in the Finder without using the scroll bars. Simply place the pointer in the window, press the mouse button, and drag toward the area you want to view, as shown in the figure. Drag the pointer up, down, left, or right past the window's active area to begin scrolling. Dragging past a window corner scrolls diagonally.

As you drag, you can vary the scrolling speed. To scroll slowly, drag just to the window's edge (and continue pressing the mouse button). Increase scrolling speed by dragging beyond the window's edge.

You can use this scrolling technique, known as *autoscrolling,* while performing these operations:

✦ Dragging an icon or group of icons to a new place in any visible window (Mac OS 7.6–7.6.1 autoscrolls only the active window)

✦ Dragging an item or group of items to any visible folder or disk icon

✦ Dragging a selection rectangle around adjacent items in the active window to select them all

Be careful when autoscrolling while dragging a selected item or items, especially when autoscrolling to the left. If you accidentally move the pointer completely out of the window and release the mouse button, the Finder places the selected items on the desktop. You can return items from the desktop to their original folder by selecting them and using the Finder's Put Away command.

Drag past any edge or corner of the window

Duplicating an item

You can duplicate an item in the same folder by selecting it and choosing Duplicate from the File menu. If the item is a folder, the duplicate contains duplicates of everything in the original folder. You can also duplicate an item by Option-dragging it to another place in the same window. One more way to duplicate an item: choose Duplicate from the contextual menu that pops up when you Control-click the item. (To see contextual menus, you must be using Mac OS 8–8.5 and the Simple Finder option must be off.)

The Finder constructs the name of a duplicate item you create with the Duplicate command by suffixing the name with the word *copy*. Additional copies of the same item also have a serial number suffix. Figure 5-10 shows an example of several duplicates of an item in the same folder.

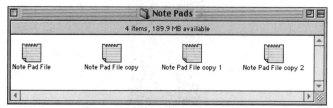

Figure 5-10: How the Finder names duplicated items.

If any suffix results in a name longer than 31 characters, the Finder removes characters from the end of the original item's name. For example, duplicating the item named "June Income and Expense Report" results in an item named "June Income and Expense Re copy."

Secrets

Colons are Special

Icon names can't include colons because the Mac OS uses colons internally to specify the path through your folder structure to a file. A path name consists of a disk name, a succession of folder names, and a file name, with a colon between each pair of names. For example, the path name "Mac OS HD:System Folder:Control Panels:Memory" specifies the location of the Memory control panel on a startup disk named Mac OS HD. Putting a colon in a file name would interfere with the scheme for specifying paths, so the Finder won't let you do it.

Deleting files and folders

You get rid of files and folders you no longer want by dragging them to the Trash icon. When you drag a folder to the Trash, everything inside that folder goes to the Trash as well. You can also move an item to the Trash by choosing Move To Trash from the contextual menu that pops up when you Control-click the item. (To see contextual menus, you must be using Mac OS 8–8.5 and the Simple Finder option must be off.)

You don't have to drag things to the Trash with the mouse. Pressing ⌘-Delete moves all selected items to the Trash. (This shortcut doesn't work if the Simple Finder option is turned on in Mac OS 8–8.5. It also doesn't work in Mac OS 7.6–7.6.1 unless you install the free control panel Finder Options or an equivalent, as described in Chapter 26.)

Emptying the Trash

Your junk accumulates in the Trash until you explicitly tell the Finder to delete it. You do that by choosing Empty Trash from the Special menu or from the contextual menu that pops up when you Control-click the Trash.

The Finder does not remove locked items. If it encounters one while emptying the Trash, it displays an alert advising you that the Trash contains locked items and asking whether you want to delete the other items or stop deleting. To get rid of locked items in the Trash, press Option while choosing the Empty Trash command.

Secrets

Back from the Trash

When you delete files by emptying the Trash, the disk space occupied by deleted files becomes immediately available for other files. The Empty Trash command removes a file's entry from the disk's file directory. It also changes the disk's sector-allocation table to indicate that the disk sectors the file occupied are available for use by another file.

To save time, the command does not erase file contents in the now-available sectors. Until the system writes a new file over the deleted file's data, the Norton Utilities program from Symantec (408-253-9600, http://www.symantec.com) can resurrect the deleted file. Any blackguard with disk-utility software can retrieve files you deleted—or view any fragment of deleted files' contents—unless you erase their contents with Norton Utilities, SuperTools (described in Chapter 26), or equivalent software. There are actually companies that specialize in sifting through e-mail and other documents that unwary computer users thought they had eliminated by emptying the Trash.

Trash warnings

When you choose the Empty Trash command, the Finder tells you how many items the Trash contains and how much disk space they occupy. You decide whether to discard them all or cancel. You can disable the Trash warning by pressing Option while choosing the Empty Trash command. Figure 5-11 is an example of the alert that appears when you empty the Trash.

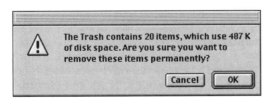

Figure 5-11: Confirm emptying the Trash.

Quick Tips

Disable Trash Warning

If you always suppress the Trash warning by pressing the Option key when you choose the Empty Trash command, you may prefer to disable the warnings more permanently. To do that, select the Trash icon and choose Get Info from the File menu. This brings up the Trash Info window. At the bottom of that window, turn off the "Warn before emptying" option by unchecking it and closing the Trash Info window. The figure shows the Trash Info window with the warning turned on.

Trash contents

If an item you move to the Trash has the same name as an item already there, the Finder renames the item that's already there. Suppose, for example, that the Trash contains an item named Untitled and you dragged another like-named item there. the Finder renames the item already there to Untitled copy. If you later add another item named Untitled, the Finder changes Untitled copy to Untitled copy 2, changes Untitled to Untitled copy, and leaves the name of the item you just added unchanged. In other words, the item most recently added has the plain name and the least recently added has the highest number suffix.

The Trash contains all the items that you have dragged to it from all the disks whose icons are on the desktop. The Empty Trash command deletes the items from all disks involved. If there's a disk whose trashed items you don't want deleted yet, remove the disk from the desktop as described in the next section. The Empty Trash command doesn't affect disks whose icons are not on the desktop. If you can't remove the disk, you have no choice but to open the Trash and drag the items you don't want deleted onto the desktop or into a folder. Then use the Empty Trash command.

If you eject a removable disk (and put away its icon in Mac OS 7.6–7.6.1) after dragging items from that disk to the Trash, those items disappear from the Trash, but the Finder does not delete them. They reappear in the Trash the next time you insert that disk. If you insert that removable disk in another Mac, they appear in its Trash.

Sometimes the Trash contains a folder named Rescued Items. This folder contains former temporary files that were found when you started up your Macintosh. The Rescued Items folder appears only after a system crash. Although it's unlikely, you may be able to recreate your work up to the time of the system crash by opening the contents of the Rescued Items folder.

Secrets

Shared Trash

If you're sharing someone else's disk or folder over a network and you drag an item from the shared disk to the Trash on your desktop, the item goes into your Trash, not into the Trash on the computer where the shared disk or folder resides. The item is removed from that computer if you use the Empty Trash command. From the opposite viewpoint, you do not know when someone sharing your folder drags items from it to his or her Trash. (The owner of a shared disk or folder can set access privileges to keep unauthorized people from dragging items from it to their Trash. Chapter 21 explains how.)

Working with Disks

There are two things you do with disks that you don't do with files or folders: remove them without deleting their contents and erase them so they can be reused.

Removing disks

There are two ways to remove a disk: one is to use the Eject or Put Away menu command and the other is to drag the disk to the Trash. With either method you can eject a removable disk and remove its icon from the desktop or you can eject and leave the icon behind.

Eject and Put Away commands

The official way to remove a floppy disk, CD-ROM disc, or other removable disk from your desktop in Mac OS 8–8.5 is to select its icon and choose Eject from the Special menu. You can also Control-click the disk icon to pop-up its contextual menu and choose Eject from it. (To see contextual menus, you must be using Mac OS 8–8.5 and the Simple Finder option must be off.) With Mac OS 7.6–7.6.1, you use the Put Away command in the File menu to remove a disk from the desktop. You can also use the Put Away command to remove a disk in Mac OS 8–8.5.

The Eject and Put Away commands remove the disk's icon from the desktop and make its contents unavailable. If the disk is a floppy disk, CD-ROM, or Zip disk, dragging its icon to the Trash ejects the disk from the disk drive. With other types of removable disks, you may have to push a button or flip a lever on the disk drive to remove the disk.

If folders on a removable disk are open when you eject the disk, then, as you might expect, the folders' windows disappear. The same windows appear again the next time you insert the disk (the folders remain open), even if you insert the disk in a different Mac. There is an exception to this behavior: If you eject a disk from a computer that has Mac OS 8–8.5 and later insert the disk into a computer that has an earlier Mac OS version, the windows are closed.

Dragging a disk to the Trash

The shortcut for removing a disk icon is to drag it to the Trash. Lots of people use this shortcut because it's so convenient, even though it doesn't exactly make sense. If you think about it, dragging a disk to the Trash could just as easily mean that you never want to use that disk again — that is, erase it. By convention, dragging a disk to the Trash means that you want to get rid of its icon, not its contents.

If you have more than one hard disk icon, you may be able to remove one that's not your startup disk by dragging the icon to the Trash. The Eject command doesn't work with most hard disk icons, but the Put Away command does. Removing a hard disk from the desktop, which is called *unmounting* the disk, makes its contents unavailable. The reverse process, which is called *mounting* the disk, happens every time you start the computer. You can also mount disks using the Drive Setup utility program that comes with Mac OS 8–8.5, or with a disk utility such as Mt. Everything (described in Chapter 26).

Ejecting a disk and leaving behind the icon

It's also possible to eject a disk without removing its icon from the desktop. To do this with Mac OS 8–8.5, you select the icon and press the Option key while choosing the Eject command. With Mac OS 7.0–7.6.1, you don't have to press the Option key while choosing Eject. The Put Away command never leaves the disk icon on the desktop.

When you eject a disk and leave its icon on the desktop, the icon turns gray to signify that the disk itself isn't available. You can insert a different disk in the same disk drive and the second disk's icon also appears on the desktop. Because both icons are on the desktop, it's possible to copy items from the now-inserted disk to the ejected disk's gray icon. This involves a lot of disk swapping as the Finder reads a little bit from the source disk, ejects it, asks you to insert the destination disk, writes a little bit to the destination disk, ejects it, asks you to insert the source disk, and so on. It's a very tedious process that is a leftover from the days when everyone used a Mac with one floppy disk drive and no hard disk.

Erasing disks

Erasing a disk removes all of the files and folders it contains. When you open a disk after erasing it, you see no folders and no files in its window. Be sure this is what you want *before* you erase a disk.

To erase a disk, you select its icon and choose Erase Disk from the Special menu. The Finder displays a dialog box that asks you to confirm that you really want to erase the disk and that includes a space to edit the disk name. The capability to change the name is purely for your convenience. You can edit the disk icon's name later, as described in the previous chapter. (However, if file sharing is turned on as described in Chapter 21, you cannot change the name of any disk larger than a floppy disk.)

Erasing a disk creates a blank disk directory, a process called *initialization,* which wipes out the means of accessing the existing files on the disk without actually touching the files themselves. The contents of all your old files are still on a disk after you erase it, but there's no easy way to get at them. It's sort of like someone erased the book catalog of a library. The books are still on the shelves, but there is no way to look them up.

In fact, you can recover deleted files after erasing a disk by using the Norton Utilities program from Symantec (408-253-9600, http://www.symantec.com). The same program can erase a disk so that no one can recover files from it.

Mac OS Extended (HFS Plus)

Mac OS 8.1 and 8.5 give you the option of erasing (initializing) large disk volumes (32MB or larger) with the Mac OS Extended format, also known as HFS Plus. This format has these advantages over the older Mac OS Standard format, also known as HFS (Hierarchical File System):

✦ The Mac OS Extended format uses less space than the Standard Mac OS format to store small files on a large disk. For example, a file that contains 4K or less of data will occupy 64K on a 4GB Mac OS Standard volume, but only 4K on a 4GB Mac OS Extended volume. Table 5-2 enumerates the minimum file sizes for disks of various capacities.

✦ The Mac OS Extended format permits a disk to store a far greater number of files (250,000 or more on a 1GB disk).

✦ The Mac OS Extended format allows for extremely large file sizes (up to 2 terabytes, which is 2000 gigabytes).

✦ The Mac OS Extended format reports the creation time and modification time of each file accurately in any time zone. For example, a file last changed at 9 a.m. in San Francisco will have a modification time of 12 p.m. in New York and 6 a.m. in Honolulu. (With Mac OS Standard format, this file would have a modification time of 9 a.m. in all time zones.) Mac OS Extended saves a file's creation and modification times in Greenwich Mean Time but reports the adjusted times for the current time zone, while the Mac OS Standard format saves the times in local time and cannot adjust for time zone changes.

Offsetting these advantages are these disadvantages:

✦ Mac OS 7.6–8 and earlier can't access files or folders on a Mac OS Extended disk. People who use Mac OS 7.6–8 and earlier cannot share your removable disks that use the Mac OS Extended format. If you ever want to go back to an earlier Mac OS version, you will have to reformat your disks that use the Mac OS Extended format.

✦ Macs without a PowerPC processor cannot use a Mac OS Extended disk as a startup disk. They also cannot use a Mac OS Extended disk as storage for virtual memory (set in the Memory control panel, as described in Chapter 18).

✦ Older Macintosh disk utility programs, including old versions of Disk First Aid and Norton Utilities for Macintosh, are incompatible with the Mac OS Extended format and can destroy data stored on a Mac OS Extended disk.

✦ Saving the creation and modification times of files in Greenwich Mean Time (instead of local time) can confuse backup and file synchronization programs (see the sidebar "Mac OS Extended Format Can Change File Dates" later in this chapter).

Table 5-2
Smallest File Sizes with the Mac OS Extended Format

Disk Size	Smallest File Size*
32MB–256MB	0.5K
256MB–512MB	1K
512MB–1GB	2K
1GB and larger	4K

*It is possible to set the smallest file size as low as 0.5K for disks up to 2048GB by using a utility program such as PlusMaximizer by Alsoft (281-353-409, http://www.alsoft.com). You potentially save disk space, but your disk may become fragmented sooner, sapping performance.

Converting to Mac OS Extended format

You can convert a disk to the Mac OS Extended format by erasing it. Obviously, before you erase a disk you must have an up-to-date backup copy from which to restore the disk's contents after erasing. Instead of erasing, you can also convert a disk to Mac OS Extended format using a utility program such as PlusMaker from Alsoft (281-353-409, http://www.alsoft.com) or SpaceMaker 1.0 from Total Recall (719-380-1616, http://www.spacemaker.recallusa.com). Just to play it safe, you should make a backup copy of the disk before converting with a utility program.

To erase a disk using the Mac OS Extended format, select the disk and choose Erase from Finder's Special menu. Then in the dialog box that appears, choose Mac OS Extended from the Format pop-up menu, as shown in Figure 5-12.

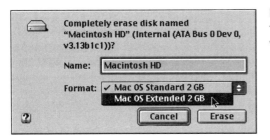

Figure 5-12: Store more small files on a large disk by erasing it with the Mac OS Extended format.

Do not erase your startup disk with the Mac OS Extended format unless you have a spare Mac OS 8.1 or 8.5 startup disk. In the event you have trouble starting from your regular Mac OS Extended startup disk, you will need the spare Mac OS 8.1 or 8.5 startup disk to access files on your Mac OS Extended disks. You can use a Mac OS 8.1 or 8.5 installation CD-ROM as a spare startup disk.

Determining a disk's format

To determine whether a disk has been formatted as Mac OS Standard or Mac OS Extended, look in its Info window. To display a disk's Info window, select the disk icon on the desktop. Then choose Get Info from the File menu. Figure 5-13 shows Info windows of disks that use the Mac OS Extended and the Mac OS Standard formats.

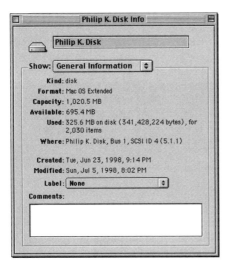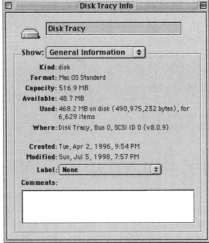

Figure 5-13: A disk's Info window tells you the disk's format: Mac OS Extended (left) or Mac OS Standard (right).

Caution

Mac OS Extended Format Can Change File Dates

When you change the time zone or the daylight-saving time setting, file modification times also change on disks that use the Mac OS Extended format in Mac OS 8.1. For example, if a file's modification time is 2:00 while the daylight-saving time setting is off, turning on the daylight-saving time setting in the Date & Time control panel (as described in "Date, Time, and Location Settings" in Chapter 11) immediately changes the file's modification time to 3:00. Besides being disorienting, this change makes an incremental backup application such as Dantz Retrospect think all files have changed and must be backed up. File synchronization applications such as PowerMerge from Leader Technologies are similarly affected. This problem can even break aliases.

This problem occurs because the Mac OS Extended format saves file modification dates (and creation dates) in Greenwich Mean Time (GMT). The Mac OS then calculates the local time by adding or subtracting an appropriate offset. For example, the offset for Pacific Standard Time is –8 hours. The offset is stored in the Mac's persistent memory and is updated when you change the time zone or the daylight-saving time setting. For example, turning on the daylight-saving time setting changes the Pacific Time offset from –8 hours to –7 hours. A file whose modification time is reported as 2:00 Pacific Standard Time (10:00 GMT –8 hours) would be reported as 3:00 Pacific Daylight Time (10:00 GMT –7 hours).

Basing modification dates on GMT instead of local time has a major benefit. It keeps the times accurate even if files are changed in more than one time zone. For example, suppose Ethan changes a file in New York at 4:00 Eastern, and then sends it to Adam in Oregon. Adam changes this file 20 minutes later, at 1:20 Pacific, and sends it back to Ethan. Without the Mac OS Extended format, Ethan would see a modification time of 1:20; this file incorrectly looks older to Ethan than the one he sent in the first place! With the Mac OS Extended format, Ethan sees a modification time of 4:20; now this file correctly looks 20 minutes newer than the file he sent.

You can eliminate the problem by upgrading to Mac OS 8.5. If you want to continue using Mac OS 8.1 when daylight-saving time goes into effect, you can make the occasion an opportunity to do a full backup of your Mac OS Extended disks. You can also dodge this problem with Mac OS 8.1 by changing the time directly in the Date & Time control panel instead of turning on the daylight-saving time setting.

Doing Background Work

The Mac OS 8–8.5 Finder can perform most of its time-consuming work in the background, while you continue doing other work in the Finder or other programs. For example, you can copy files or empty the Trash while opening folders, renaming icons, setting view options, or editing notes with Stickies. You can open control panels and applications (as described in Chapter 7) while the Finder works in the background. You can even start copying a batch of files before an ongoing copy operation finishes. Figure 5-14 shows two copy operations under way simultaneously while the Get Info command is about to be used.

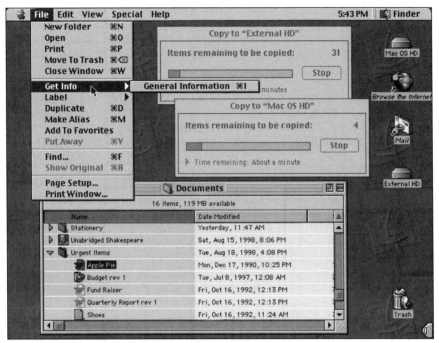

Figure 5-14: Use menus and do other work in the Finder while it copies items or empties the Trash.

The performance of your computer suffers while the Finder works on a task in the background. Furthermore, a background task proceeds more slowly than it does in the foreground. If the computer gets really busy with the background task, the mouse and keyboard may seem to stop working for a few seconds. If you type faster than the screen can display the characters, the system remembers the most recent 20 characters you type (about 5 seconds of typing at 40 words per minute). The system can also remember one click or double-click and can catch up with your dragging as long as you don't release the mouse button.

In Mac OS 7.6–7.6.1, the Finder's multitasking capabilities are limited to copying items, duplicating items, or emptying the Trash while you work in another application (not the Finder). During one of those operations, you can switch to another program by clicking in any of its windows or by choosing it from the Application menu or the Apple menu. You can't open a program or document by double-clicking its icon or using the Finder's Open command while the Finder copies, duplicates, empties Trash, or finds, but you can open programs and documents listed in the Apple menu. (Opening and switching applications is detailed in Chapter 7.) Also, you can't use most control panels while the Finder works in the background. None of these limitations applies to Mac OS 8–8.5.

Summary

After reading this chapter, you know how to boil down the Finder to its essential commands by turning on the Simple Finder option with the Preferences command in Mac OS 8–8.5. You know that double-clicking or using the Open command with a disk, folder, or file displays its contents in a window. Conversely, the Close command or close box puts a window away when you don't want to see it any more. While a folder or disk window is open, you can use the View menu to see the window's contents as icons, buttons, or a list. In a list view, you can change the sort order by clicking a column heading. You can rearrange columns by dragging their headings and you can resize columns by dragging the borderlines of their headings. Also, you can expand and collapse folders in a list view by clicking the disclosure triangles next to their names. With enclosed folders expanded, you can select items from multiple folders at the same time.

You also learned that you can do more with the Finder than just view the contents of your disks and folders. You can create a new folder with the New Folder command; drag items to copy or move them; duplicate items with the Duplicate command; drag items to the Trash to delete them; and to empty the Trash with the Empty Trash command. If there's more than one disk on your desktop, you can remove a disk by dragging it to the Trash or by using the Eject command (Mac OS 8–8.5) or the Put Away command (Mac OS 7.6–8.5). You can erase a disk with the Erase disk command. With Mac OS 8.1–8.5, you can erase using the Mac OS Extended format or the older Mac OS Standard format (the only format with Mac OS 7.6–8 and earlier). Aside from erasing disks, the Finder can do most of its time-consuming work in the background while you do other work with it or another program at the same time.

✦   ✦   ✦

Get More Organized with the Finder

Once you master the simple ways of organizing your disks, folders, and files with the Finder that were presented in the previous chapter, you're ready for the advanced techniques covered in this chapter. Here you learn how to make and use pop-up windows. You learn how to fine-tune the view in a folder or disk window by aligning icons, arranging items in a different order, setting a view font, and selecting an icon or button size for a view. You learn how to search for items by name and other criteria.

Using the techniques described in this chapter, you can make your way continuously into a folder's enclosed folders or out the other direction through enclosing folders toward the disk or desktop. You can return items from the desktop or the Trash to their previous locations. You can categorize items with text and color labels, and you can attach comments to an item. This chapter also tells you how to lock or otherwise protect files, folders, and disks. You learn how attach scripted actions to folders in Mac OS 8.5 so that the actions happen automatically whenever you interact with the folders. You find out why you might want to partition your hard disk and how to do it. Finally, you learn how to change the startup disk if you have more than one disk drive.

To use most of the techniques described in this chapter with Mac OS 8–8.5, the Simple Finder option must be turned off with the Finder's Preferences command. If the Finder's menus don't contain commands mentioned in this chapter, such as the Put Away command in the File menu, turn off the Simple Finder option as described in the previous chapter. (In Mac OS 7.6–7.6.1, there is no Simple Finder option to turn on or off.)

To learn even more ways to organize your disks and their contents, be sure to read the coverage of opening and saving programs and documents in the next chapter, the System Folder in Chapter 10, aliases in Chapter 12, and file sharing in Chapter 21.

Using Pop-up Windows

With Mac OS 8–8.5, you can change any folder or disk window to a pop-up window. A pop-up window is anchored to the bottom of the screen, and in place of a title bar it has a tab labeled with the window title. Clicking the tab at the top of a window closes the window and leaves the tab at the bottom of the screen. Clicking a tab at the bottom of the screen makes the window pop up from there. Figure 6-1 shows both states of a pop-up window.

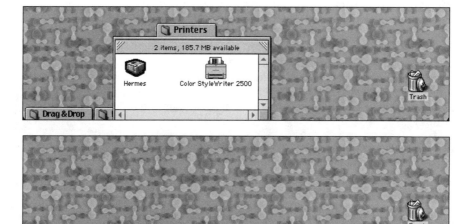

Figure 6-1: Clicking a tab at the bottom of the screen displays a pop-up window, and clicking the tab of an open window closes it and leaves its tab showing.

Pop-up windows are easy to find and open, so they're great places to keep stuff you use often. You can move or copy items into a pop-up window by dragging them to its tab. This works whether the pop-up window is open or closed. When you drag an item to the tab of a closed window, the window pops up. If the window is set for icon or button view, then you can continue dragging inside the window to place the icon or button where you want it.

When you drag something out of a pop-up window, the Finder automatically closes the window when the mouse button is released. If you need to drag several items from a pop-up window to a common destination, select them all and drag them as a group. If you drag them individually, you have to pop up the window for each one.

Pop-up windows are not available in Mac OS 7.6–7.6.1 and earlier.

Making a pop-up window

You can make a regular disk or folder window into a pop-up window by choosing "as Pop-up Window" from the View menu while the window is active (front-most). Another method is to drag the window's title bar to the bottom of the screen, where it changes into the tab of a collapsed pop-up window.

If you already have several pop-up windows and you try to make another one whose tab won't fit in the available space at the bottom of the screen, the Finder displays an alert explaining why you can't make another pop-up window. Remember that the length of a pop-up window's name directly affects the size of the window's tab. You can make room for more tabs by abbreviating the names of existing pop-up windows and by moving tabs as close together as possible at the bottom of the screen, as described under the next heading.

To make a pop-up window into a regular window, choose "as Window" from the View menu while the pop-up window is active; the pop-up window must be open to be active. You can also make a pop-up window into a regular window by dragging its tab up toward the top of the screen. As you drag, you see the outline of the window, and eventually the outline changes to the rectangular shape of a regular window. When you see the regular window shape, release the mouse button and you have a regular window.

Moving a pop-up window

You can move a pop-up window left and right by dragging its tab along the bottom of the screen. This allows you to arrange pop-up window tabs in any order you like. Be sure to drag a pop-up window's tab while the window is closed. If you drag the tab while the window is open, it becomes a regular window.

To move a tab as close to its neighbor as possible, drag the tab so that it partially overlaps its neighbor and release the mouse button. When you drag, don't let the pointer touch the neighbor or the tab you're dragging will snap back to its former location when you release the mouse button.

Sizing a pop-up window

While a pop-up window is open, you can change its size by dragging one of the two size boxes at its top corners. The size boxes can adjust the width and height of the window. You can also adjust the height alone by dragging the pop-up window's tab up or down. Remember that if you drag the tab high enough, you make the pop-up into a regular window.

Closing a pop-up window

As mentioned previously, clicking any pop-up window tab closes the pop-up window that's open. You can also close a pop-up window by pressing ⌘-W. In Mac

OS 8.1–8.5, you can close a pop-up window and convert it to a regular window (removing its tab from the bottom of the screen) by pressing ⌘-Shift-W. Pressing ⌘-Shift-Option-W converts all pop-up windows to regular windows and closes all Finder windows.

Fine-tuning Views

There are lots of ways to fine-tune the basic icon, button, and list views that were described in the previous chapter. You can cleanup icons or buttons by aligning them to an invisible grid whenever you want, or you can have the Finder keep them aligned automatically. You can arrange or sort items by name, kind, or another criterion. You can select an icon or button size for any view. In a list view, you can select which columns of information are displayed about items in the view, and in Mac OS 8.5 you can rearrange and resize the columns. An additional option in Mac OS 8–8.5 lets you force the contents of an icon or button view to stay arranged in a particular order, such as by name.

With Mac OS 8.5, you can fine-tune each window individually or you can make all the windows adhere to standard options. With Mac OS 8, you fine-tune each window individually. With Mac OS 7.6–7.6.1, some options apply to individual windows but others apply to all windows as explained later in this section.

Cleaning up icons or buttons

When icons or buttons are in disarray, you can have the Finder align them in neat rows and columns. You clean up the active window by choosing Clean Up from the View menu in Mac OS 8–8.5. In Mac OS 7.6–7.6.1, you choose Clean Up Window from the Special menu. If no window is open or active, the Finder cleans up the desktop icons. Figure 6-2 shows a window before and after being cleaned up.

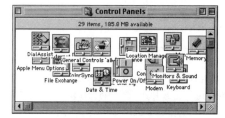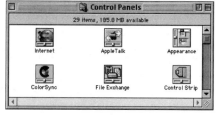

Figure 6-2: Cleaning up icons or buttons: before (left) and after (right) using the Clean Up command.

You can clean up individual icons by holding down the ⌘ key while dragging them singly or in groups—unless the Snap to Grid option is turned on (as described later in this section). If that option is turned on, the Finder aligns icons when you drag them normally—without pressing the ⌘ key.

In Mac OS 7.6–7.6.1, you can also use the Finder's Clean Up command to align only the icons you select in a window or on the desktop. Pressing Shift changes Clean Up to Clean Up Selection.

Arranging icons or buttons

While the Finder is cleaning up icons or buttons, you can have it arrange them in a particular order, such as by name or modification date. The Finder arranges icons first by the attribute you choose and second by name if necessary. For example, if you arrange by kind, then all application icons will come before all folder icons; the application icons will be arranged alphabetically by name before the alphabetically arranged folder icons. The first icon goes in the upper-left corner, and remaining icons fill the window from left to right and top to bottom.

The procedure for arranging icons is different in Mac OS 8–8.5 than in Mac OS 7.6–7.6.1.

Arrange in Mac OS 8–8.5

You arrange and clean up icons in Mac OS 8–8.5 by choosing the order you want from the Arrange submenu of the View menu. Note that you do not need to choose Clean Up as well. Figure 6-3 shows a window before and after being arranged (and simultaneously cleaned up) by icon name.

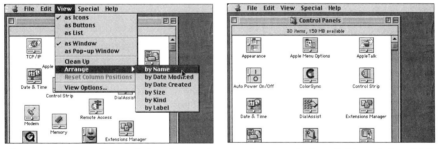

Figure 6-3: Arranging and cleaning up icons or buttons: before (left) and after (right).

You can cleanup the desktop by clicking any desktop icon to make the desktop active and then choosing the order you want from the Arrange submenu. In this case, the Finder puts the startup disk icon in the upper-right corner and fills the desktop from top to bottom and right to left. No matter which order you choose, the Finder always arranges desktop icons in groups in this order: hard disk volumes, desktop printers, floppy disks and other removable disks, shared disks and folders, and all other icons. The Trash icon always goes in the bottom-right corner of the desktop.

Arrange in Mac OS 7.6–7.6.1

You can use the Clean Up command in Mac OS 7.6–7.6.1 and earlier to arrange icons by any of the choices in the View menu. First, you must set the order you want by choosing it from the View menu. This has the side effect of temporarily changing to a list view. Change back to an icon view by choosing "by Icon" or "by Small Icon" from the View menu. Now press the Option key while choosing the Clean Up command and the Finder rearranges all icons in the window.

If you press Option while cleaning up the desktop (instead of a window), the Finder aligns all desktop icons in a standard configuration. It moves the startup disk's icon to the upper-right corner of the desktop, lines up other disk icons below it, puts the Trash in the lower-right corner, and arranges all other desktop icons in rows and columns next to the disk icons.

Sorting a list view

Much as you can have the Finder arrange icons in a window, you can have it sort a list view. The most direct method is to click the heading of the column by which you want to sort the list, as mentioned in the previous chapter. Alternatively, you can choose a sort order from the Sort submenu of the View menu in Mac OS 8–8.5. In Mac OS 7.6–7.6.1, you choose the sort order directly from the View menu. You may find the menu method more convenient if the window isn't wide enough to show the column by which you want to sort.

Setting view options in Mac OS 8–8.5

Additional view options let you change the format and contents of folder and disk windows. In Mac OS 8–8.5, you can set the icon size for each window, regardless of the type of view. You can have the Finder keep icons arranged automatically. You can set the spacing between icons and buttons. You can determine which columns appear in a list view. And you can choose a font for the text in all windows. You set these view options in Mac OS 8–8.5 with the Finder's View Options and Preferences commands; in Mac OS 8.5, you use the Appearances control panel in addition.

Text font and size in Mac OS 8–8.5

You can set the font and font-size that the Finder uses for text in all disk and folder windows. In Mac OS 8.5, you use the Appearances control panel. In Mac OS 8–8.1, you use the Finder's Preferences command. The Finder uses the font and font-size settings for icon names, the window information header (the number of items in the window and the space available on the disk), and all the text in list views. The settings for font and font-size affect all windows and the desktop — you can't set the font and font-size for windows individually. Figure 6-4 shows where you set the views font and font-size.

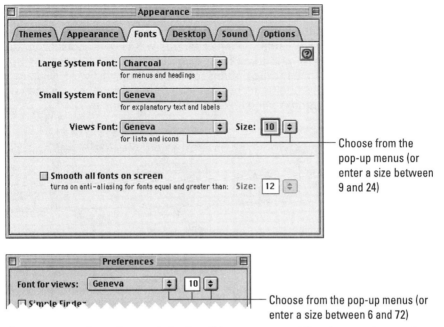

Choose from the pop-up menus (or enter a size between 9 and 24)

Choose from the pop-up menus (or enter a size between 6 and 72)

Figure 6-4: Setting a font and size for all icon names and list-view text in Mac OS 8.5 (top) and 8–8.1 (bottom).

To set the font and font-size used in all disk and folder windows in Mac OS 8.5, open the Appearances control panel (choose Control Panels from the Apple menu and then double-click the Appearances control panel in the Control Panels window). At the top of the Appearances control panel, click the Fonts tab. Then choose a font from the Views Font pop-up menu and choose a font size from the Size pop-up menu. If you want to use a size that isn't listed in the pop-up menu, you can enter any size between 9 and 24 in the space provided.

To set the font and font-size used for text in all disk and folder windows in Mac OS 8–8.1, choose Preferences from Finder's Edit menu. Choose a font and a size from the pop-up menus at the top of the Preferences window. If you want to use a size that isn't listed, you can enter any size between 6 and 72 in the space provided.

After changing the font or the font-size in Mac OS 8–8.5, you may want to use the Clean Up command to adjust the spacing of icons on the desktop and in windows. You must clean up each window individually.

In Mac OS 8–8.5, the standard font is Geneva and the standard font-size is 10, but you should try Geneva 9. The italic style used for alias names looks better and is easier to edit in Geneva 9 because there is a special italic Geneva 9 font installed in the system. (For more information on aliases, see Chapter 12, and for more information on fonts, see Chapter 13.)

Icon or button view options in Mac OS 8–8.5

You can set the size and automatic arrangement of icons or buttons on the desktop and in each Mac OS 8–8.5 window whose contents you view as icons or buttons. To set these view options for a window, bring it to the front and choose View Options from the View menu. To set these options for the desktop, click any desktop icon to make the desktop active and then choose View Options from the View menu. Figure 6-5 shows the View Options dialog box for icon and button views.

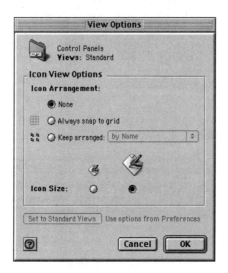
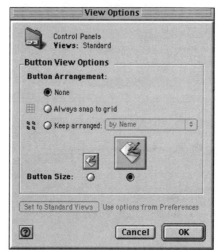
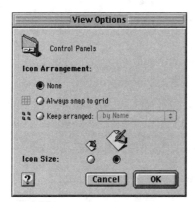

Figure 6-5: Setting view options for an icon view or button view in Mac OS 8.5 (top) or Mac OS 8–8.1 (bottom).

If you customize a window's view options in Mac OS 8.5, a button labeled "Set to Standard Views" becomes available in the View Options dialog box. Clicking this button makes all the settings in this particular View Options dialog box match the standard view settings from the Preference command. This button is disabled when the current settings match the standard settings. The button does not exist at all in Mac OS 8–8.1. (You'll find details on changing the standard view settings a little later in this section.)

Setting the Icon Arrangement or the Button Arrangement option to "Always snap to grid" or "Keep arranged" makes icons you drag in the window align to the same grid as the Clean Up command. When either of these settings is in effect for a window, you see an icon at the left end of the window's status bar, just below the close box. The icon in the window matches the current setting of the Icon Arrangement or the Button Arrangement option in the View Options dialog box.

You can temporarily reverse the state of an "Always snap to grid" or "Keep arranged" setting by pressing ⌘ while dragging icons. If either of those settings is selected, ⌘-dragging temporarily disables forced grid alignment. If neither of those settings is selected, then ⌘-dragging temporarily enables forced grid alignment.

The distance between aligned icons or buttons in Mac OS 8–8.5 is determined by the Grid Spacing option of the Preferences command. This option applies to all windows and the desktop, but affects each window only when you next make a change to it. Figure 6-6 shows the Grid Spacing option in the Preferences window.

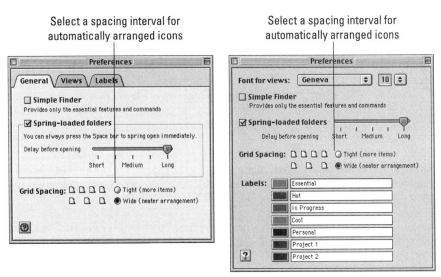

Figure 6-6: Setting the grid spacing for the Finder windows and the desktop in Mac OS 8.5 (left) and Mac OS 8–8.1 (right).

List view options in Mac OS 8–8.5

You can set the icon size and select what information you want shown in each Mac OS 8–8.5 window viewed as a list. To set these view options for a window, bring it to the front and choose View Options from the View menu. Figure 6-7 shows the View Options dialog box for list views.

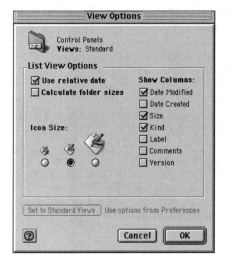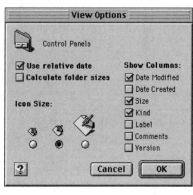

Figure 6-7: Setting view options for a list view in Mac OS 8.5 (left) or Mac OS 8–8.1 (right).

A list view includes an icon and a name for every item in the window. You can select which of seven other columns of information you want displayed. By selecting just the columns you need to see in a window, you can see most or all columns without scrolling the window. Click a window's zoom box to make it just wide enough to show all the columns you selected for display. If the window can't be made wide enough to show all the columns you selected for display, the window fills the screen and you have to scroll horizontally to see some columns. You may be able to reduce or eliminate horizontal scrolling in Mac OS 8.5 by making columns narrower. To resize columns, drag the lines that separate the column headings. (You cannot change the widths of columns in Mac OS 8–8.1.)

You can set the icon size in each window to standard (large), small, or tiny. Standard icons are the size you usually see on the desktop. Small icons are the size you see in the Apple and Application menus. Tiny icons are so small you don't see any unique detail, just a generic folder, application, or document icon.

The Comments column normally shows the first 25 characters of the comments entered in each item's Info window. In Mac OS 8.5, you can see more or less by dragging the right edge of the Comments header to change the column width. (For details on changing comments, see "Attaching Comments to Items" later in this chapter.)

The option "Use relative date" has the Finder display "today" instead of today's date or "yesterday" instead of yesterday's date in the Date Created and the Date Modified columns. For other dates, the Finder uses the date format set in the Date & Time control panel (as described in Chapter 11). If you resize a date column in

Mac OS 8.5, the Finder automatically changes the date format to fit. For example, a standard-width column that shows "Wed, Feb 25, 1998 12:00 PM" would show just "2/25/98 12:00 PM"; or "2/25/98" in a narrower column; or "Wednesday, February 25, 1998" in a wider column.

The option "Calculate folder sizes" has the Finder display the size of each folder in the window. It takes a while for the Finder to add up the sizes of items in a large folder. You can keep working on other tasks while the Finder calculates folder sizes, but calculating folder sizes reduces the system's performance for doing other work.

After you change view options in Mac OS 8.5, a button labeled "Set to Standard Views" becomes available in the View Options dialog box. Click this button to make all the settings in this particular View Options dialog box match the standard view settings from the Preference command. You can't use this button when the current settings match the standard settings. The button does not exist at all in Mac OS 8–8.1. (The details about changing the standard view settings are next.)

Quick Tips

Changing View Options Globally in Mac OS 8–8.1

There are no standard view settings for windows in Mac OS 8–8.1. You set view options for every folder window, disk window, and the desktop separately. It can be a lot of tedious work to make identical changes to a bunch of windows, let alone all windows. Fortunately, you can simplify this chore using shareware such as Finder View Settings by Alessandro Levi Montalcini (described in Chapter 26).

An alternative workaround takes advantage of the fact that copies of a folder — in this case copies of an empty folder — have the same view options as the original folder. You create a new folder, open it, and use the View menu to set its view as you wish. Then you duplicate the empty folder (⌘-D or Option-drag) on the same disk as an old folder whose view options you want to change, and drag the old folder's entire contents (⌘-A to select all) to the duplicate empty folder. If you drag from an old folder that contains icons you have hand-placed in a particular order, you should open the destination folder and drag all the icons as a group to the destination folder's window rather than to the folder's icon. This preserves the icon ordering as much as possible (the view options set for the destination folder may forcibly reorder the icons). Finally, copy the name from the old, now empty folder, trash the old folder, and paste the name on the replacement folder. Repeat with a new duplicate of the empty folder for each old folder that you want to have the same view options. This procedure is still a lot of work, but it is less work than applying multiple View commands to each old folder.

Standard view options in Mac OS 8.5

In Mac OS 8.5, windows that don't have custom view settings adhere to standard view settings from the Finder's Preferences command. You can change the standard settings by choosing Preferences from the Finder's Edit menu and clicking the Views tab at the top of the Preferences window. You change the standard settings for icon, button, and list views separately. Use the pop-up menu near the top of the Preferences window to choose the type of view whose settings you want to change. Changes you make to standard settings immediately affect all windows that don't have custom settings; windows with custom settings are not affected. Figure 6-8 shows the standard view settings in the Preferences window.

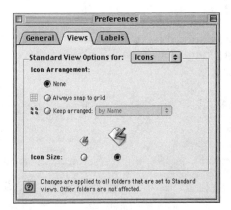

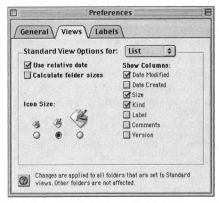

Figure 6-8: Changing standard view settings with the Preferences command in Mac OS 8.5.

You can make a window adhere to the standard view settings from the Preferences command by clicking the button labeled "Set to Standard Views" in its View Options dialog box (as explained previously in this section).

Setting view options in Mac OS 7.6–7.6.1

In Mac OS 7.6–7.6.1, you set view options with the Views control panel. You can choose a font and font-size for text, set icon alignment rules, and determine list view contents. All these options affect every disk and folder window as well as the desktop. You can't set any of these options separately for each window as you can with Mac OS 8–8.5. Figure 6-9 shows the Views control panel in Mac OS 7.6–7.6.1.

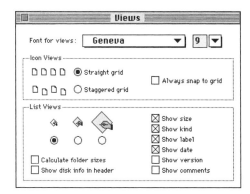

Figure 6-9: Setting view options with the Views control panel in Mac OS 7.6–7.6.1.

Text font and size in Mac OS 7.6–7.6.1

With Mac OS 7.6–7.6.1, you choose a text font and a font size for windows and the desktop from the pop-up menus at the top of the Views control panel. If the font size you want isn't listed, you can enter any size between 6 and 36. The Finder uses the font and font-size settings for icon names, the disk information header (number of items, disk space used, and disk space available), and all the text in list views. Your font and font-size settings affect all windows and icons.

Icon alignment in Mac OS 7.6–7.6.1

Other settings in the Views control panel determine how the Finder aligns icons in Mac OS 7.6–7.6.1. You can set the type of grid the Clean Up command uses and decide whether icons automatically align with that grid when you drag them. The settings affect icons on the desktop and in all windows with icon or small-icon views. You cannot set icon alignment options separately for each window as you can with Mac OS 8–8.5.

The "Staggered grid" option makes it possible to arrange icons close together without their names overlapping. Turning on the "Always snap to grid" option makes icons you have dragged align to the Clean Up command's grid. You can temporarily reverse the "Always snap to grid" setting by pressing ⌘ while dragging icons.

List view options in Mac OS 7.6–7.6.1

With Mac OS 7.6–7.6.1, you determine how much information the Finder shows in all windows with list views (name, size, kind, and so on) by setting numerous options at the bottom of the Views control panel. You cannot set list view options separately for each window as you can with Mac OS 8–8.5.

List views always include an icon and name for every item in the window. In addition, you select which of six other columns of information to include: size, kind, label, date, version, and comments. Your selections appear as choices in the Finder's Views menu. You cannot change the order of the columns or their widths, only whether each appears or not.

Judicious setting of list view options keeps your list view windows as small as possible. You can make a list view window narrower by reducing the number of items checked in the Views control panel and then clicking the window's zoom box.

You can set the icon size for all list views to standard, small, or tiny. Standard icons are like desktop icons. Small icons are like the icons in the Apple and Application menus. With tiny icons you see only generic folder, application, and document icons.

You can also set an option to have the Finder calculate and display folder sizes. Adding up the sizes of items in a large folder can take quite a while. Fortunately, the Finder only calculates sizes of folders you can see and does this work in the background so that you can get on with other tasks. But other tasks may slow if the Finder is concurrently calculating folder sizes.

Another list view option has the Finder show disk information in the header of all list view windows. The disk information includes the number of items in the window, the amount of disk space in use, and the amount of disk space available. This information is standard in icon and small-icon views.

Finding Items

No matter how carefully you organize your folders and disks, there comes a time when you can't find a file or folder without a lot of digging through layers of folders. The Finder's Find command fetches lost or buried items with less effort. When you choose Find from the Finder's File menu, you see a Find File window in which you can specify search parameters. You can set the parameters in this window to search for items that match a single attribute, such as the item's name, or many different attributes, such as the name, date modified, and kind of item.

The Find File window is not actually a part of the Finder — it's part of a separate utility program named Sherlock in Mac OS 8.5 and Find File in Mac OS 7.6–8.1. You open the utility program when you use the Finder's Find command. You can also open the Sherlock or Find File program by choosing it from the Apple menu.

Find File is one of three sections in Mac OS 8.5's Sherlock program. If you see one of the other sections after choosing Sherlock from the Apple menu, click the Find File tab at the top of the window. The other sections of the Sherlock program search for files by content and search for Web pages on the Internet. The "Finding Documents by Content" section in Chapter 7 describes how to search by content; Chapter 17 covers searching the Internet.

Making a simple search

The simplest form of the Find File window allows you to specify where you want to search and one attribute you want to match. Find File is preset to look on all disks for items whose names contain the text you specify. You can change where Find File looks for items and specify that it look at an attribute other than the item's name. Figure 6-10 shows the Find File window set up to search by name.

Figure 6-10: Setting up a simple search with Find File in Mac OS 8.5 (top) and Mac OS 7.6–8.1 (bottom).

You use the pop-up menus in the Find File window to specify which attribute you want Find File to look at and how you want Find File to compare that attribute with a value or a state you specify. Table 6-1 lists the possible combinations.

Table 6-1
Attributes that Find File Can Search For

Search By	Search How	Search For
Name	Contains/starts with/ends with/is/is not/doesn't contain	Text you enter
Size	Is less than/is greater than	Amount you enter, in kilobytes
Kind	Is/is not	Alias/application/clipping file/ control panel/desktop printer*/ document/extension/folder/font/ letter/sound/stationery
Label	Is/is not	Label you choose from pop-up menu
Date created	Is/is before/is after/is not; is within 1/2/3 days of; is within 1/2/3 weeks of; is within 1/2/3/6 months of	Date you specify
Date modified	Is/is before/is after/is not; is within 1/2/3 days of; is within 1/2/3 weeks of; is within 1/2/3/6 months of	Date you specify
Version	Is/is not	Text you enter
Comments	Contain/do not contain	Text you enter
Lock attribute	Is	Locked/unlocked
Folder attribute	Is/is not	Empty/shared/mounted
File type	Is/is not	4 characters you enter
Creator	Is/is not	4 characters you enter
Contents**	Contain/do not contain	Text you enter
Name/icon lock	Is	Locked/unlocked
Custom icon	Is	Present/not present
Visibility	Is	Invisible/visible

*Available only in Mac OS 8.5

**Superseded in Mac OS 8.5 by the Find by Content section of the Sherlock program

Secrets

Find and Find Again

Although the Finder's Find command ordinarily opens the Find File utility in Mac OS 7.6–8.1, you can have it bring up the old Find dialog box of System 7–7.1 by pressing Shift while choosing the Find command. The Find dialog box has a simple form and an expanded form. The simple form of the Find dialog box sets up a search by name of all disks. The Finder displays the first item it finds, opening the folder that contains the item and selecting the item. The figure below shows the simple form of the old Find dialog box.

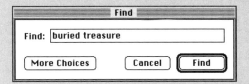

To find another match, use the Find Again command. If the active window contains another matching item, the Finder selects it and scrolls it into view. Otherwise, the Finder looks in other folders and disks.

Clicking the More Choices button in the Find dialog box extends your search options. You specify what you want to search for and where you want to search. The old Find and Find Again commands can find by two criteria not available in the Find File utility: a kind that contains or doesn't contain the text you enter, and a version number that is less than or greater than the text you enter. In addition, you can restrict Find and Find Again to searching just the active window. If you restrict the search to one disk, you can have the Finder select all the items it finds at once in a list view. The figure below is an example of the old expanded Find dialog box.

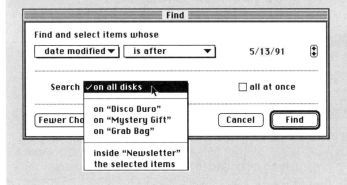

You can have Find File look in these places: on all disks, on all local disks (not including file servers), on mounted servers (whose icons appear on the desktop), on the desktop, in the Finder selection (the items currently selected), or on a specific disk by name. Find File does not look inside the System file or suitcase files for fonts, sounds, or desk accessories. It can, however, find those kinds of items in folders and on the desktop.

Find File can search for items based on any of 16 attributes, 4 of which are ordinarily hidden. The 12 attributes you can always see are name, size, kind, label, date created, date modified, version, comments, lock attribute, folder attribute, file type, and creator. The four hidden attributes are contents, name/icon lock, custom icon, and visibility. To see the extra four attributes, you press the Option key when you first click the left-most pop-up menu in the Find File window.

Making an expanded search

You can add more search criteria to the Find File window. Clicking the More Choices button adds a criterion at the bottom of the window. Clicking the Fewer Choices button removes a criterion. Alternatively, you can use the More Choices and Fewer Choices commands in Sherlock's Find menu (Mac OS 8.5) or Find File's File menu (Mac OS 7.6–8.1). If you have more than two criteria, you can remove them all by holding down the Option key (Mac OS 8.5) or the Shift key (Mac OS 7.6–8.1) and clicking the Fewer Choices button. Figure 6-11 shows a Find File window in Mac OS 8.5 with two criteria (Mac OS 7.6–8.1 windows look similar).

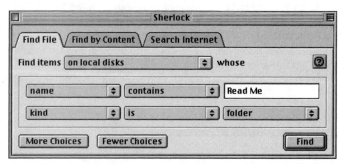

Figure 6-11: Setting up an expanded search with Find File in Mac OS 8.5.

Using search results

The search begins when you click the Find button in the Find File window. While the search progresses, a count of the number of items found appears in the window. You can also set Find File to display the name of the disk being searched and the name of the last item found, although this may slow the search somewhat. In Mac OS 8.5, choose Preferences from the Edit menu, select the option "Show current search status for Find File," and click OK. In Mac OS 7.6–8.1, press the ⌘ key while clicking the Find button in the Find File window.

While a search is underway in Mac OS 8.5, you can begin another search by choosing Find File from the Find menu. In Mac OS 7.6–8.1, Find File can only do one search at a time.

When a search ends, Find File displays all the found items in an Items Found window. There can be only one Items Found window in Mac OS 7.6–8.1 — the current search results replace any previous search results. There can be multiple Items Found windows in Mac OS 8.5. Figure 6-12 shows an example of an Items Found window in Mac OS 8.5 (Mac OS 7.6–8.1 windows look similar).

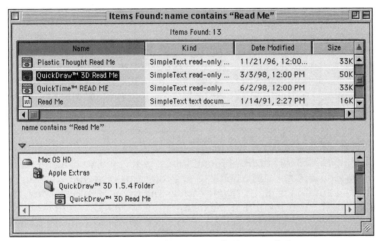

Figure 6-12: Viewing the results of a Find File search in Mac OS 8.5.

Adjusting the Items Found window

You can sort the list of found items, which appears at the top of the Items Found window, by name, size, kind, or modification date. To change the sort criterion, click the column heading in the Items Found window. In Mac OS 7.6–8.1, you can also choose a sort criterion from Find File's View menu.

You can also sort in reverse order. In Mac OS 8.5, click the triangular sort-direction control at the right end of the column headings in the Items Found window. In Mac OS 7.6–8.1, press Option and click a column heading or press Option while you choose from the Find File's View menu.

If you want to see more columns in the Items Found window, you can make the window larger by dragging its size box or clicking its zoom box. In Mac OS 8.5, you can resize the columns by dragging the lines that separate the column headings. You can't resize columns in Mac OS 7.6–8.1, and you can't rearrange columns in any Mac OS version.

Seeing a found item's folder location

While the top part of the Items Found window displays items that match your search parameters, the bottom part of this window displays a folder location for one found item. To see a found item's folder location, select the item (by clicking it) in the list of found items at the top of the Items Found window. If the selected item in the top part of the window is in a deeply nested folder, you may have to scroll the bottom part of the window to see the entire folder location. If you'd like to see more of a deeply nested folder location without scrolling, you can make the bottom part of the window taller (and the top part shorter) by dragging the line that separates the top and bottom parts of the window. In Mac OS 8.5, you can hide the bottom part of the Items Found window altogether by clicking the disclosure triangle next to the separator line.

You can select multiple items at the top of the Items Found window as you do in the Finder: by Shift-clicking or dragging a selection rectangle across them. To select all items, use the Select All command in Find File's Edit menu. When you select more than one item at the top of the Items Found window, no folder location is displayed at the bottom of the window.

Moving, copying, and deleting found items

In addition to seeing folder locations of found items, you can also drag items from the Items Found window to the desktop or to any folder or disk that you can see in the Finder. If the destination is on the same disk as the found item you drag, the found item moves to the destination. If the destination is on a different disk, the found item is copied to it. In Mac OS 7.6–8.1, you can drag items only from the top of the Items Found window. In Mac OS 8.5, you can drag from the top or the bottom of the window.

The Trash is another place to which you can drag one or more found items. Although you can drag multiple items as a group from the Items Found window to the Trash successfully in Mac OS 8.5 and Mac OS 7.6–7.6.1, this procedure does not work in Mac OS 8–8.1. You can work around this limitation by dragging the selected items from the Items Found window to an alias of the Trash. (To make an alias of the Trash, select the Trash and choose Make Alias from the Finder's File menu. See Chapter 12 for details on aliases.)

Doing more with found items

In addition to dragging found items, you can use these File menu commands to manipulate the items you selected in the Items Found window:

> ✦ **Open Item** opens the selected item or items (see "Opening Programs, Documents, and More" in Chapter 7 for details). You can also open an item by double-clicking it in the top or bottom of the Items Found window. If more than one item is selected, double-clicking one of them opens all of them.

✦ **Open Enclosing Folder** opens the folder that contains the selected item. The Finder automatically becomes active, the folder opens, and the Finder scrolls to and selects the item in the folder window.

✦ **Print Item** prints selected documents just as the Finder's Print command does (see Chapter 15 for details). You can also print documents by dragging them to a desktop printer icon that you can see in the Finder.

✦ **Move To Trash** puts the selected items in the Trash. This command is available only in Mac OS 8.5. In any Mac OS version, you can drag items from the Items Found window to the Trash icon on the desktop.

✦ **Get Info** displays the Info windows of selected items (see "Attaching Comments to Items" and "Protecting Files, Folders, and Disks" later in this chapter for more about Info windows).

✦ **Label** classifies the selected items with a color and text label (as explained in "Labeling Items" later in this chapter). In Mac OS 7.6–8.1, there is a Label menu instead of a Label command in the File menu.

✦ **Show Original** displays the selected alias's original item in the Finder. This command is only available when an alias is selected in Mac OS 8.5; it is not available in Mac OS 7.6–8.1. (For more information on aliases, see Chapter 12.)

✦ **Sharing** allows you to share selected folders (as described in Chapter 21) and link selected programs (as described in Chapter 23).

These commands can act either on items selected at the top of the Items Found window or on an item selected at the bottom of the window. The affected item is the one in the part of the window highlighted with a heavy border. You can alternate the highlight between the top and bottom parts of the window by pressing Tab or by clicking in the part you want to highlight.

Secrets

Find File Shortcuts

You can quit the Find File program while opening a found item by holding down the Option key while choosing Open from the Find menu (or while double-clicking an item in the Items Found window). This trick saves you the trouble of reactivating Find File to quit it. The Option key shortcut also works with other commands in Find File's File menu, such as Get Info, Sharing, Open Enclosing Item, and Print. The Option key shortcuts don't work in Mac OS 8.5's Sherlock program, but you can learn about others by choosing Mac OS Help from the Help menu. In the Help window, click "Files and programs" on the left and then click "Finding files" on the right. When the "Finding files" article appears, scroll down until you see the underlined text "Shortcuts for finding files" and click this text. In Mac OS 7.6–8.1, you can read several pages of additional shortcuts by choosing Find File Shortcuts from the Help menu while Find File is active.

Reusing searches

If you're using Mac OS 8.5, you can save the Find File parameters and use them later to do a new search. To save the current Find File parameters as a file, choose Save Search Criteria from the File menu. This displays a dialog box in which you can type a name and select a folder for the saved Find File parameters. Click Save in this dialog box to save the Find File parameters.

To do a new search using saved Find File parameters, choose Open from the File menu. In the dialog box that appears, locate the saved Find File parameters file, select it, and click the Open button.

Folder Ins and Outs

Getting to a folder where you want to move or copy an item can take a lot of double-clicking of folder icons as you travel in and out of folders on the way. Mac OS 8–8.5 has a couple of features that make it possible to traverse a folder hierarchy without a lot of double-clicking. You can make folders spring open as you delve deeper through layers of folders, and you can zip through folder layers toward the enclosing disk. The capability to zip through folder layers is also available in Mac OS 7.6–7.6.1.

Spring-open folders

With Mac OS 8–8.5, you can make a folder or disk spring open when you pause briefly over it. This behavior is normally turned on, but you can use the Finder's Preferences command to adjust the amount of time you must pause until a folder or disk springs open or to turn off spring-loaded opening altogether. (Spring-loaded opening is not available in Mac OS 7.6–7.6.1 and earlier.)

Making folders and disks spring open

A disk or folder springs open automatically if you drag an item to its icon and pause briefly with the pointer positioned over the icon and the mouse button held down. The folder or disk icon flashes twice and opens. This will also occur if you pause while dragging a group of items.

You don't have to pause briefly for a disk or folder to spring open in Mac OS 8.5. To make a disk or folder spring open immediately, drag to its icon and press the spacebar.

If you continue holding down the mouse button, you can then drag to a folder icon in the window that just opened and continue deeper into the layers of folders. You may need to travel through a folder that's already open to get into a folder it encloses. Go ahead and drag to the folder's open icon; its open window springs to the front so you can make a folder in it spring open. If you make the wrong disk or folder spring open by accident, simply drag the pointer out of its window and the window closes automatically.

When you release the mouse button, the Finder moves or copies the item or items you were dragging into the active window. The active window does not close, but all other windows of folders that you made spring open do close automatically. If any of the folders you made spring open were already open, their windows do not close either.

If you change your mind about moving or copying the item you're dragging, just drag it to the menu bar and release the mouse button. The Finder returns the item to the place you got it from.

Actually, folders spring open even if you're not dragging anything but the pointer. To make this happen, begin to double-click the first disk or folder you want to spring open, but don't release the mouse button after pressing it the second time. This gesture is called a *click-and-a-half,* because you make one click and half of a second click. After a brief pause while you continue to hold down the mouse button, the pointer changes to a magnifying glass, the icon flashes twice, and opens. As long as you hold down the mouse button, the pointer remains a magnifying glass and you can continue opening interior folders by pausing over them. Again, in Mac OS 8.5 you don't have to pause over a folder or disk icon. To make a folder or disk spring open immediately without dragging anything to it in Mac OS 8.5, do a click-and-a-half over the folder or disk icon and press the spacebar; the pointer becomes a magnifying glass and the folder or disk opens right away.

Setting spring-open options

To adjust the amount of time you must pause until a folder or disk springs open or to turn off spring-loaded opening altogether, choose Preferences from the Finder's Edit menu. In Mac OS 8.5, you may need to click the General tab to see the setting for spring-loaded delay time. Figure 6-13 shows the "Spring-loaded folders" option in the Preferences window.

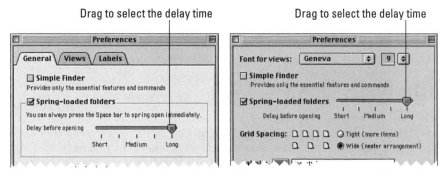

Figure 6-13: Setting options for spring-loaded opening in Mac OS 8.5 (left) and Mac OS 8–8.1 (right).

Finding enclosing folders

Rather than go deeper into your layers of folders, you can go the other direction and open a folder that encloses an open folder. If the open folder is nested inside several layers of folders, you can quickly open any of those enclosing folders or the disk that encloses them all.

To open any of the nested folders or the disk that encloses an open folder, make the open folder's window active (bring it to the front) and then press ⌘ while clicking the window title. A menu pops up showing the layers of nested folders and the disk that encloses the open folder. You open one of the folders or the disk by choosing it from the pop-up menu. If the outermost folder is on the desktop, the pop-up menu doesn't list an enclosing disk. Figure 6-14 is an example of a folder window's pop-up menu.

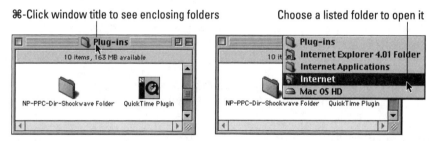

Figure 6-14: Opening an enclosing folder.

While opening one of the folders or the disk that encloses an open folder, you can simultaneously close the open folder's window. Simply hold down Option and ⌘, click the menu title, and choose a folder or the disk from the pop-up menu. You must start holding down Option and ⌘ before clicking the window title. If you ⌘-click the window title and then press Option while choosing from the pop-up menu, the window opens for the folder you chose but the previously active window doesn't close.

Putting Stuff Back

From time to time you may find that your desktop has become cluttered with files and folders you no longer need to have there. You could drag these items back to some folder, but if you just want to put them back where they came from, there's an easier way. Just select the items you want to put back and use the Put Away command. The Finder returns the selected items to their former locations without opening any folders.

The Put Away command also works with items in the Trash. You can open the Trash, select items you don't want to delete, and use the Put Away command to return them to their former locations.

The Put Away command returns items to the folders they were last in, but does not necessarily return items in their original order within the window.

Attaching Comments to Items

You can attach notes or comments to folders, files, and some disks in their Info windows. To display an item's Info window, select it and choose Get Info from the File menu. Alternatively in Mac OS 8–8.5, you can Control-click an item to display its contextual menu and then choose Get Info from it. At the bottom of the Info window, you can type anything you want (to a maximum of 199 characters) in the space provided for comments. Although the window has no scroll bar to see lengthy comments, you can scroll by pressing the arrow keys or by dragging the pointer past the borders of the entry box. Figure 6-15 shows comments in an Info window.

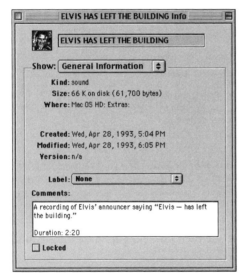
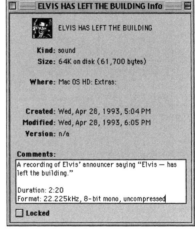

Figure 6-15: Viewing comments in an Info window in Mac OS 8.5 (left) and Mac OS 7.6–8.1 (right).

In Mac OS 8–8.5, you can't attach comments to floppy disks. The part of the floppy disk where comments are located in Mac OS 7.6–7.6.1 and earlier system software versions is used by Mac OS 8–8.5 to store view options for the disk and its folders.

Labeling Items

The Finder enables you to classify folders, programs, and documents by labeling them with a word or phrase. On monitors displaying at least 16 colors, labeling an item also colorizes it.

Applying labels

To label an item in Mac OS 8–8.5, select the item and choose a label from the Label submenu of the Finder's File menu. In Mac OS 7.6–7.6.1, use the Label menu. Figure 6-16 shows the Label submenu.

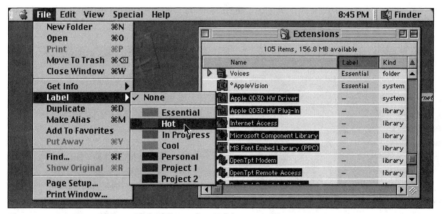

Figure 6-16: Specifying a label for selected icons with Mac OS 8–8.5.

In Mac OS 8.5, you can set an item's label in the item's Info window. Select the item, choose Get Info from the File menu, and use the Label pop-up menu in the Info window (previously shown in Figure 6-15).

You can also label items found by the Find File section of the Sherlock program (Mac OS 8.5) or the Find File program (Mac OS 7.6–8.1). Select items in the Items Found window that you want labeled alike, and choose a label from the Label submenu of Find File's File menu (Mac OS 8.5) or from Find File's Label menu (Mac OS 7.6–8.1).

When you label a color icon, the Finder blends the label color as if you covered the icon with a piece of acetate that is the same color as the label. To label an item without colorizing it, change the label color to solid black, as described later in this section.

Using labels

After labeling items, you can view a folder or disk window's contents arranged by label. You can also search for items by label with the Finder's Find command. Label colors also show up in the Apple menu and in the dialog boxes used by many programs' Open and Save commands. Figure 6-17 shows a folder window sorted by label, and Figure 6-18 shows how you find by label.

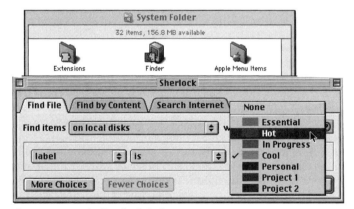

Figure 6-17: Sorting by label.

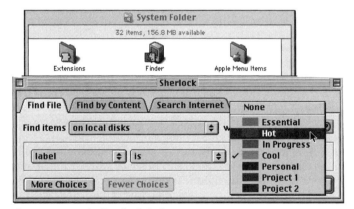

Figure 6-18: Finding by label.

Changing label names and colors

You change the standard label names and colors in Mac OS 8–8.5 with the Finder's Preferences command. In Mac OS 7.6–7.6.1, you use the Labels control panel. Figure 6-19 shows the Labels settings in the Preferences window of Mac OS 8.5 and 8–8.1, and the Labels control panel of Mac OS 7.6–7.6.1.

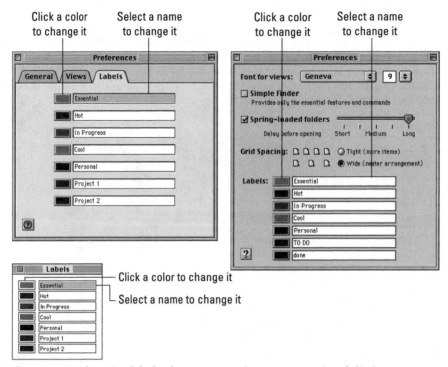

Figure 6-19: Changing label colors or names in Mac OS 8.5 (top left), in Mac OS 8–8.1 (top right), and in Mac OS 7.6–7.6.1 (bottom).

If you click a label color to change it, the Finder displays the standard Color Picker dialog box. You can select the type of color picker you want to use from the list on the left side of the dialog box. (In Mac OS 7.6–7.6.1, you have to click a More Choices button at the bottom of the dialog box to see this list.) You pick a new color by clicking a color wheel, adjusting sliders, typing numbers, or clicking a color swatch, depending on the type of color picker you selected. For example, the Crayon Picker has swatches that look like crayons. The HLS Picker has a color wheel, which you can use to specify hue (dominant color) and saturation (amount of color); a slider, which you can use to specify lightness (closeness to black or white); and spaces where you can enter hue, saturation, and lightness numerically. With Mac OS 8–8.5, you can also pick up any color displayed on the screen by holding down the Option key, which turns the pointer into an eyedropper, and clicking the color you want to pick up. Figure 6-20 shows the HLS picker in the Color Picker dialog box of Mac OS 8–8.5, and Table 6-2 lists the HLS settings for the standard label colors (in case you want to reset them after experimenting).

Select a type of picker   Cross marks current settings

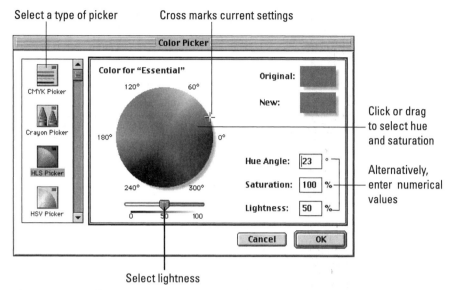

Click or drag to select hue and saturation

Alternatively, enter numerical values

Select lightness

Figure 6-20: Picking a custom label color.

Table 6-2
Values for Standard Label Colors

Label	Hue Angle	Saturation	Lightness
Essential	23°	100%	50%
Hot	1°	94%	45%
In Progress	328°	93%	49%
Cool	196°	98%	46%
Personal	240°	100%	41%
Project 1	131°	100%	20%
Project 2	29°	89%	18%

Secrets

An Apple-ish Red Label

Select the Crayon Picker while using the Color Picker in Mac OS 8–8.5 and you see a box of 60 crayons in various premixed colors with fanciful names such as Obsidian, Marigold, and Dirt. Instead of clicking each crayon to see a sample of its color and its name on the right side of the dialog box, you can drag across the crayons and watch the color sample and the name change. Hold down the Option key and click the edge of a crayon to pick up a lighter or darker shade of color, which is appropriately named with the suffix "-ish."

Secrets

Transparent Labels

If you've avoided icon labels because they discolor your beautiful color icons, you need shun them no longer. You can label a color icon without changing its color — provided the label color is black, white, or any shade of gray. (On a color monitor, icons with white labels are invisible unless they are selected.) You can still view the Finder windows by label, find items by label, and so on.

To make a label transparent, display the Finder's Preferences window (Mac OS 8–8.5) or open the Labels control panel (Mac OS 7.6–7.6.1) and click the color of a label you want to use. The standard Color Picker dialog box appears. On the left side of the dialog box, select the HLS Picker (Mac OS 8–8.5) or the Apple HSL Picker (Mac OS 7.6–7.6.1). Then set the Hue Angle to 0 degrees and Saturation to 0 percent, and set the Lightness to 100 percent for white, 0 percent for black, or a number between 0.01 percent and 99.99 percent for a shade of gray. You can type the three values in the spaces provided, or you can click the center of the color wheel and adjust the slider.

Protecting Files, Folders, and Disks

The Mac OS lets you protect files and folders individually so they can't be changed. You can lock a file with the Get Info command, lock folders with the Sharing command, and specially protect the System Folder and Applications folder with the General Controls control panel. In addition, you can lock a disk so it can't be erased and its contents can't be changed.

Locking a file

To lock a file, select its icon and use the Get Info command to display the file's Info window. At the bottom of the Info window is a Locked option. If you turn it on, you can open the file and copy its contents, but you can't change its contents or its name. In addition, the Finder does not delete locked files that are in the Trash unless you press Option while choosing the Empty Trash command (as discussed in the previous chapter). You can tell a file is locked in Mac OS 8.5 by the small lock-shaped badge on its icon. In Mac OS 7.6–8.1, a locked file has a small lock icon near its name in a list view. Figure 6-21 shows a locked file's Info window and several locked files.

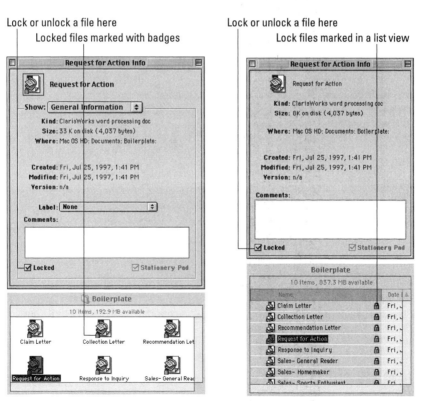

Figure 6-21: Locking a file with the Get Info command in Mac OS 8.5 (left) and Mac OS 7.6–8.1 (right).

Locking a folder

You can protect against moving, renaming, or deleting a folder by using the Finder's Sharing command. Normally, you use the Sharing command to control who can access your folder over a network (as described in Chapter 21), but you can also use the Sharing command for simple folder protection.

To lock a folder, select its icon and choose Sharing from the Get Info submenu of the Finder's File menu (Mac OS 8.5) or from the Finder's File menu (Mac OS 7.6–8.1) to display the folder's sharing information. Turn on the option labeled "Can't move, rename, or delete this item (locked)." You don't have to actually share the folder or change any other sharing settings for the folder. A locked folder has a small lock-shaped badge on its icon in Mac OS 8.5. In Mac OS 7.6–8.1, a locked folder has a small lock icon near its name in a list view. Figure 6-22 shows the sharing information of a locked folder and some locked folders.

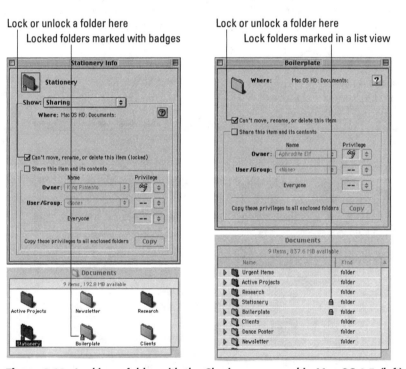

Figure 6-22: Locking a folder with the Sharing command in Mac OS 8.5 (left) and Mac OS 7.6–8.1 (right).

Protecting the System Folder and Applications folder

The Mac OS can protect the contents of two special folders in the startup disk, the System Folder and the Applications folder. You set this protection with the option

"Protect System Folder" and the option "Protect Applications folder" in the General Controls control panel. You can use these options only if file sharing is turned off (as detailed in Chapter 21). Figure 6-23 shows the General Controls control panel.

Turn folder protection on and off here

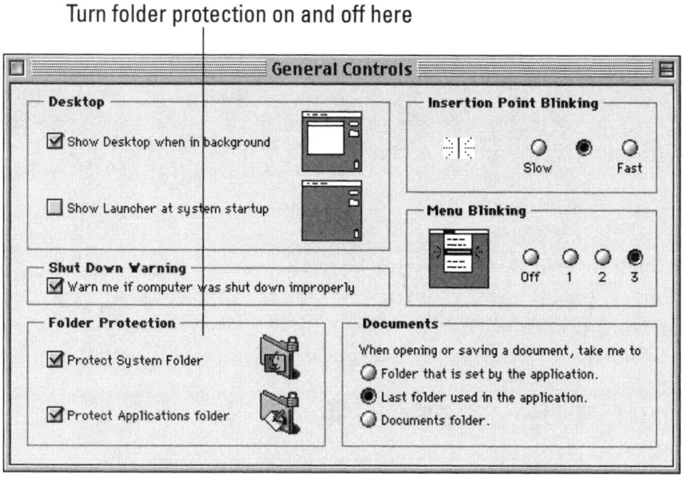

Figure 6-23: Setting folder protection with the General Controls control panel in Mac OS 7.5 and later.

Turning on folder protection prevents anyone from moving, renaming, or deleting items directly enclosed by the protected folder. The protection does not extend to items in folders enclosed by the protected folder. For example, with System Folder protection turned on, you cannot move, rename, or delete the Control Panels folder, but you can do all those things to individual control panels inside the Control Panels folder.

Locking a disk

You can lock floppy disks and some other disks. After locking a disk, you can't erase it, change its name, copy files onto it, duplicate files on it, or move files and folders it contains to the desktop or the Trash. A locked disk is said to be *write protected.*

To lock a floppy disk, you slide the tab in the corner of the disk so that the square hole is open. You unlock a floppy disk by sliding the tab so that the square hole is closed.

Some other removable disks have locking mechanisms on their cases. Check the instructions that came with your removable disks or disk drive for specific information about locking them.

Caution

You Can't Lock a Folder Without File Sharing

The Sharing command only locks folders while file sharing is turned on in the File Sharing control panel (Mac OS 8–8.5) or the Sharing Setup control panel (Mac OS 7.6– 7.6.1). In fact, you can't even bring up a Sharing window while file sharing is off. If you try, the Sharing command displays an alert saying you must turn on file sharing and offers to open the appropriate control panel so you can do so. If you lock some folders while file sharing is on and later turn file sharing off, the folders become unlocked until you turn file sharing on again.

You may be able to lock or write-protect your hard disk using the setup program that came with it. For example, you can write-protect an Apple hard disk with the Drive Setup program that comes with Mac OS 8–8.5.

Password-protecting a hard disk

If you have a PowerBook that you use in locations where you worry about people snooping through your files, you can block their access to the hard disk by protecting it with a password. With this protection in place, people must know the password to start up the PowerBook and optionally to wake it from sleep. You configure this protection in the Password Security control panel. Click the Setup button in this control panel to display a dialog box in which you can set or change the password, optionally specify a hint for remembering it, and specify whether you want sleep protected as well as startup. Before this dialog box appears, you must enter your password (if you have one). Figure 6-24 shows the Password Security control panel and its setup dialog box.

Turn on password protection

Specify the password here

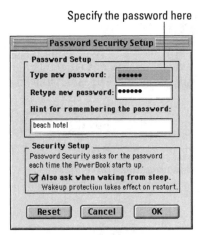

Figure 6-24: Protect a PowerBook by turning on password protection (left) and specifying the password (right).

If you have partitioned your PowerBook's hard disk into multiple volumes (as described at the end of this chapter), Password Security protects only one volume. If more than one volume has a System Folder, the computer may start up from a volume that is not protected.

Whatever you do, don't forget your password. You can't bypass the security dialog by starting up with the Shift key pressed, or by starting up from a Disk Tools floppy or Mac OS CD, because the password control is handled at the disk-driver level. You'll have to take your PowerBook with proof of purchase to an authorized service center, where a technician can bypass the security dialog.

Working with Folder Actions

Mac OS 8.5 introduces the capability to specify actions that you want to take place automatically whenever you interact with particular folders or disks. For example, you could specify that every time a file is added to a certain folder, a copy of the file is to be placed in another folder. Folder actions can take place in response to opening or closing a folder, adding items to or removing them from an open folder, or changing the size or location of a folder window. The Folder actions can also take place in response to the same kinds of interactions with disks and disk windows.

You determine the actions that apply to a folder or disk by attaching AppleScript scripts to it. Scripts are small programs written in the easy-to-understand AppleScript language. You can use scripts that come with Mac OS 8.5 as well as other scripts provided by Apple and other companies. You can also create your own scripts with the Script Editor program in the AppleScript folder inside the Apple Extras Folder on your startup disk. To learn how to create your own folder actions, see Chapter 23.

This section explains how to attach folder actions to a folder and describes the folder actions that come with Mac OS 8.5. This section also tells you how to remove folder actions. Before covering these topics, this section discusses some ways folder actions can compromise your computer's security.

Security with folder actions

You must be careful with folder actions because they can do almost anything you can do to your computer. They can automatically do all of the following and more:

✦ Create, move, duplicate, and delete files and folders

✦ Unmount disks (except the startup disk) and mount unmounted disks

✦ Set control panel options

✦ Connect to other computers on your local network or to the Internet

✦ Connect to Web sites on the Internet

✦ Transfer files to or from other computers on your local network or the Internet

✦ Send and receive e-mail

✦ Start other programs and use them to make changes to documents on your disk

To guard against your computer being controlled by another computer on your network, folder-action scripts must be located on a disk connected directly to your computer. The Folder Actions extension will not run a folder-action script unless it is located on your startup disk or a hard disk connected to your computer. Neither will it run scripts located on disks that can be removed (this excludes the startup disk, because it cannot be ejected until you shut down). Even folders on removable disks and network volumes must use folder actions from your startup disk or local hard disks. In other words, a folder on a removable disk can't use folder actions located on it.

Backgrounder

What Makes Folder Actions Happen

Folder actions can happen only under very particular circumstances. To trigger a folder action, a visible change must occur to a folder or disk's window or contents. For example, moving a file into a folder window would create a visible change, and could trigger a folder action. In contrast, moving a file into a closed folder would not create a visible change and would not trigger a folder action. Note that you may not be able to see a visible change happening in a folder window that is covered by an overlapping window. Likewise, you may not be able to see a visible change taking place in a part of a folder window that is currently scrolled out of view. (Philosophical question: If you can't see a change, is it truly visible? Answer: If a tree falls in the forest and no one is around. . . .)

It may seem at first glance that a folder must simply be open — its window must be displayed — to trigger a folder action. This is not true. A folder can trigger folder actions if its contents are visible in another folder window being viewed as a list. In other words, folders that are expanded in a list view — that have their disclosure triangles pointing down — can trigger folder actions. Folders that are collapsed in a list view — that have their disclosure triangles pointing to the right — can't trigger folder actions.

A special application named Folder Actions is responsible for running all folder-action scripts. If Folder Actions is not in the Extensions folder during startup, no folder actions will take place.

Caution

Use Scripts from Reliable Sources

To keep your computer secure and the information in it private, do not use any folder-action scripts from unfamiliar sources. The danger in folder-action scripts is that they are fairly easy to create, and an unscrupulous person could conceal side effects ranging from mischievous to destructive. This doesn't mean you should fear all folder actions or not use scripts from people you don't know personally. After all, you would probably consider using other kinds of software created by reputable strangers. You wouldn't use system extensions or utility applications from sources you weren't sure of, and you should treat folder-action scripts with the same caution.

Attaching folder actions

To attach a folder-action script to a folder or disk, choose Attach a Folder Action from its contextual menu (Control-click the folder or disk icon to display its contextual menu). A dialog box appears in which you select an AppleScript script file to use as a folder action. A folder with an attached folder action has a distinctive script badge on its icon. Figure 6-25 shows an example of attaching a folder-action script.

1. Choose Attach a Folder Action from the contextual menu

2. Select an AppleScript script file to use as a folder action

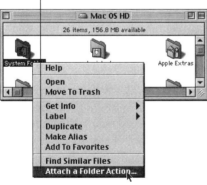

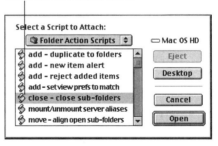

3. See a script badge

Figure 6-25: Attach an AppleScript script as a folder action in Mac OS 8.5.

Scripts for folder actions can be located anywhere on your startup disk or other hard disk connected to your computer. The standard location is the Folder Action Scripts folder inside the Scripts folder in the System Folder.

Sample folder actions

Ten folder-action scripts come with Mac OS 8.5:

✦ **add - duplicate to folders** tries to copy added items to other folders. The other folders must have aliases whose names begin "~!" in the attached folder (Chapter 12 explains aliases). The script labels items that were successfully copied by assigning them the penultimate label (initially named Project 1), and labels items that were not copied by assigning them the last label (initially named Project 2). Adding items to the attached folder triggers this script.

✦ **add - new item alert** advises that items have been added to the attached folder and offers to bring the folder window to the front so you can see what was added. Adding items to the attached folder triggers this script.

✦ **add - reject added items** places added items in a Rejected Items folder on the desktop, advises that this happened, and offers to bring the Rejected Items folder to the front. Adding items to the attached folder triggers this script.

✦ **add - set view prefs to match** changes the view options of added folders to match the attached folder. Adding items to the attached folder triggers this script.

✦ **close - close sub-folders** closes the windows of open folders contained in the attached folder. Closing the attached folder's window triggers this script.

✦ **mount/unmount server aliases** has two actions. On opening the attached folder, the script asks if you want to connect to each shared folder or disk that has an alias in the attached folder. On closing the attached folder, the script tries to unmount (put away) all shared folders and disks. Opening the attached folder or closing its window triggers this script.

✦ **move - align open sub-folders** staggers all open subfolder windows of the attached folder and resizes them to match it, so you can see all their title bars. Moving or resizing the attached folder triggers this script.

✦ **open - open items labeled 1** opens items in the attached folder that have the first label (initially named Essential). Opening the attached folder triggers this script.

✦ **open - show comments in dialog** displays a dialog box containing the comments for the attached folder and offers to clear the comments or open the folder's Info window. Opening the attached folder triggers this script.

✦ **remove - retrieve items** tries to return items that are moved out of the attached folder, and explains that items can't be removed from the folder. This script may fail to return items moved to closed folders. Removing items from the attached folder triggers this script.

There are additional sample scripts in the AppleScript folder on the Mac OS 8.5 CD.

You can use the scripts as-is or you can modify them to suit your needs. For example, most of the folder-action scripts that display advisory messages can be modified by changing one line of each script to not display messages. You modify the scripts using the Script Editor application (which is described in Chapter 23).

Removing folder actions

You can remove folder-action scripts from a folder or disk using the folder or disk's contextual menu. Control-click the folder or disk to display its contextual menu and choose the script you want to remove from the Remove a Folder Action submenu.

Partitioning Hard Disks

If you work with lots of small files, you may be able save a significant amount of disk space by dividing a large hard drive into several smaller disk volumes. This process is called *partitioning*. For example, a small preference file that takes 16.5K on a 1GB hard drive would take only 4K on a 250MB partition, saving 12.5K per small file. If you have lots of small files, the savings can literally add up to megabytes.

You don't need to partition a large hard disk to save space if you use Mac OS 8.1–8.5. Instead, you can convert the disk to the Mac OS Extended format, as explained in "Working with Disks" at the end of Chapter 5.

Each partitioned volume looks and acts exactly like a hard disk. Every volume has its own disk icon on the desktop, and all volumes appear at the desktop level of the dialog boxes you use for opening and saving files in an application (as described more fully in Chapter 7). Think of volumes as individual disks that happen to be stored on the same mechanism.

Partitioning has other advantages besides using disk space more efficiently. For one, items are easier to find on smaller volumes. You can secure an individual volume's contents with a password or lock it against overwriting. Accidental corruption of one volume is unlikely to affect other volumes.

On the downside, partitioning reduces storage flexibility. Each volume has a separate amount of available space. If you fill one volume, you can't store any more on it even though other volumes on the same drive have plenty of space available. Also, making multiple volumes increases the clutter of icons on the desktop. What's more, partitioning generally requires formatting a disk, which erases its contents. Backing up before and restoring after takes a lot of time and exposes your files to greater risk than doing nothing. For example, aliases may become unlinked from their original items when restored to a partitioned volume, which is essentially a new disk.

The disadvantages of partitioning are minor compared to the space savings you can obtain if you have a large hard disk. Unless you work mostly with files larger than 8K, you should consider partitioning a hard disk whose capacity is larger than 500MB. Either that, or convert the disk to the Mac OS Extended format in Mac OS 8.1–8.5.

Partitioning a hard disk

Before partitioning a hard disk you *must* back it up. You won't be able to access any of your existing files after partitioning until you have restored them from a backup. Make sure your backup program allows you to restore folders individually, because after partitioning you will have smaller disk volumes and all your folders may not fit on one volume. Restored aliases are more likely to work if you restore them to a volume whose name is identical to the disk they came from.

You partition a disk with a disk setup program. You can probably use the disk setup program that came with your computer, or with your hard disk if you have added another hard disk or replaced your original hard disk. For example, the Drive Setup program that comes with Mac OS 8–8.5 can partition an Apple hard disk but not other brands. You can also buy a disk setup utility, such as Hard Disk ToolKit from FWB (415-482-4800, http://www.fwb.com).

If you want to use a partitioned disk to start up your computer, you must install the Mac OS on one of the volumes. In some cases, your computer may not start up or may delay starting up unless you install the Mac OS on the preferred startup volume. The preferred startup volume is usually the first volume to appear on your desktop when you start up from another disk, such as a Mac OS installation CD or floppy disk. The preferred startup volume is also usually the first volume you create when you partition a disk. Some disk setup programs let you designate the preferred startup volume; Apple's Drive Setup does not.

You can install the Mac OS on more than one volume, but there is generally no reason to use up disk space this way. You may or may not be able to select which volume to start up from, as discussed in "Changing the Startup Disk" later in this chapter.

Optimum volume size

The most difficult decision to make when partitioning a hard disk is deciding how many volumes to create and what size to make each one. Generally, you want to make a volume large enough to hold all related items and leave room to add items in the future. For example, you can create one volume to hold all your software — application programs and system software — and another volume to hold all your documents. Unless you create very large documents (in which case you may be better off not partitioning), the volume for applications and the System Folder probably needs to be bigger than the volume for documents.

The size of a volume determines the minimum size of a file on that volume. The smallest amount of space that can be allocated to a file on a volume is called the *allocation block size*. Larger volumes have larger allocation block sizes. For example, a 100-word memo needs only about 600 bytes of storage space, but it uses up to 16.5K (16,896 bytes) on a 1GB volume or 8K (8,192 bytes) on a 500MB volume. Finder rounds file sizes up to the nearest whole number, so a list view would report the size of a 16.5K file as 17K.

Some documents and all programs get a minimum of two blocks. One block is for the file's data and the other block is for the file's resources. For example, a SimpleText document always occupies at least 33K on a 1GB hard disk.

Minimum allocation block size grows by 0.5K for every 32MB in volume capacity, as tabulated in Table 6-3.

Table 6-3
Smallest File Sizes for Various Volume Sizes Using Mac OS Standard Format

Volume Size	Smallest File	Volume Size	Smallest File	Volume Size	Smallest File
0 to 31MB	0.5K	832 to 863MB	13.5K	1664 to 1695MB	26.5K
32 to 63MB	1K	864 to 895MB	14K	1696 to 1727MB	27K
64 to 95MB	1.5K	896 to 927MB	14.5K	1728 to 1759MB	27.5K
96 to 127MB	2K	928 to 959MB	15K	1760 to 1791MB	28K
128 to 159MB	2.5K	960 to 991MB	15.5K	1792 to 1823MB	28.5K
160 to 191MB	3K	992 to 1023MB	16K	1824 to 1855MB	29K
192 to 223MB	3.5K	1024 to 1055MB	16.5K	1856 to 1887MB	29.5K
224 to 255MB	4K	1056 to 1087MB	17K	1888 to 1919MB	30K
256 to 287MB	4.5K	1088 to 1119MB	17.5K	1920 to 1951MB	30.5K
288 to 319MB	5K	1120 to 1151MB	18K	1952 to 1983MB	31K
320 to 351MB	5.5K	1152 to 1183MB	18.5K	1984 to 2015MB	31.5K
352 to 383MB	6K	1184 to 1215MB	19K	2016 to 2047MB	32K
384 to 415MB	6.5K	1216 to 1247MB	19.5K	2048 to 2079MB	32.5K
416 to 447MB	7K	1248 to 1279MB	20K	2080 to 2111MB	33K
448 to 479MB	7.5K	1280 to 1311MB	20.5K	2112 to 2143MB	33.5K
480 to 511MB	8K	1312 to 1343MB	21K	2144 to 2175MB	34K
512 to 543MB	8.5K	1344 to 1375MB	21.5K	2176 to 2207MB	34.5K

(continued)

Table 6-3 *(continued)*					
Volume Size	**Smallest File**	**Volume Size**	**Smallest File**	**Volume Size**	**Smallest File**
544 to 575MB	9K	1376 to 1407MB	22K	2208 to 2239MB	35K
576 to 607MB	9.5K	1408 to 1439MB	22.5K	2240 to 2271MB	35.5K
608 to 639MB	10K	1440 to 1471MB	23K	2272 to 2303MB	36K
640 to 671MB	10.5K	1472 to 1503MB	23.5K	2304 to 2335MB	36.5K
672 to 703MB	11K	1504 to 1535MB	24K	2336 to 2367MB	37K
704 to 735MB	11.5K	1536 to 1567MB	24.5K	2368 to 2399MB	37.5K
736 to 767MB	12K	1568 to 1599MB	25K	2400 to 2431MB	38K
768 to 799MB	12.5K	1600 to 1631MB	25.5K	2432 to 2463MB	38.5K
800 to 831MB	13K	1632 to 1663MB	26K	2464 to 2495MB	39K

Changing the Startup Disk

If your computer has more than one disk drive with a System Folder, the Startup Disk control panel determines which drive will be used when you start the computer. If you have partitioned a disk into multiple volumes, they all appear in the Startup Disk control panel. You may be able to specify which volume you want to be the startup volume by selecting it in the Startup Disk control panel, but your computer may ignore your selection and always start from the same volume. In this case, you can use the System Picker utility program (described in Chapter 26) to specify the startup volume. If you happen to select a disk that does not have a System Folder, the computer ignores your selection and starts up from the main hard disk. Figure 6-26 shows the Startup Disk control panel.

Figure 6-26: The Startup Disk control panel.

Summary

After reading this chapter, you know how to make a pop-up window with the View menu or by dragging any window to the bottom of the screen. You know how to move a pop-up window by dragging its tab, and how to change its size with its two size boxes.

You also know how to fine-tune folder and disk windows. You can choose a font and a font size for the text in all windows. You can clean up or arrange windows viewed as icons or buttons. You can sort a window viewed as a list and determine the columns it displays. In Mac OS 8.5, you can resize and rearrange the columns in a list view. In Mac OS 8–8.5, you know how to set the icon size for each window and have the Finder keep icons arranged automatically.

When you need to find items, you know how to use the Find File section of the Sherlock program in Mac OS 8.5 or the Find File program in Mac OS 7.6–8.1. In either case, you can specify a simple search with one criterion or an elaborate search with many criteria.

You know it's not necessary to do a lot of double-clicking to traverse layers of folders. You can zip through folder layers toward the enclosing disk, and in Mac OS 8–8.5, you can make folders spring open as you delve deeper through layers of folders.

If you find your desktop is cluttered with files and folders, you know that the Put Away command returns them to their former locations. It also works with items in the Trash.

You know how to classify folders, programs, and documents by applying labels. You can arrange a list view by label, and you can search for items by label with the Finder's Find command. You know how to change label names or colors.

In addition, you know how to attach comments to items and lock files with the Get Info command. You can lock folders with the Sharing command, protect the System Folder and the Applications folder with the General Controls control panel, and lock disks with locking mechanisms on their cases or with their disk setup programs.

Finally, you know that partitioning a hard disk or converting it to the Mac OS Extended format can save storage space if you have a lot of small files, and that you can change the startup disk with the Startup Disk control panel or the System Picker program.

✦   ✦   ✦

Work with Programs and Documents

It may seem reasonable that once you open a program or a document, you've left the Mac OS behind. True, the Mac OS does pretty much hand over control of the computer to a program when you open it, but many of the functions and capabilities of application programs are actually provided by the Mac OS. The Finder handles opening application programs, and the Mac OS manages to let you have more than one program open at the same time. You can also use the Finder to open documents, and you can open them from applications using standard dialog boxes provided by the Mac OS. Similar dialog boxes appear when you save a document from any application.

Many programs rely on the Mac OS for basic document editing, such as the Cut, Copy, and Paste commands. You don't need those editing commands as much in programs that adopt the Mac OS drag-and-drop editing technology, which lets you move material around in a document and between documents by dragging it with the mouse.

The Mac OS also makes it possible for you to open documents created by programs you don't have, including Mac programs and programs on Windows, DOS, and Apple II computers. You can even use removable disks from those foreign systems in your Mac.

Opening Programs, Documents, and More

You open a program when you want to work with it — this action is sometimes called *launching* a program. You open a document when you want to view or edit its contents. For example, you open SimpleText when you want to view, create, or edit a text document. (You can also work with text documents using other programs.) There are many ways to open programs, documents, other kinds of files, and folders. This section describes how to open items with the Finder, the Apple menu, the Launcher control panel, the Startup Items folder, the Shutdown Items folders, and any application.

Opening with the Finder

You already know the basic methods for opening a program or document with the Finder (assuming you read the previous chapter). To review: you either double-click the program or document icon or, in a Mac OS 8–8.5 button view, click the program or document button. If you prefer a more formal approach, you can select the icon by clicking it once and then use the Open command. The Open command is in the File menu; it also appears in the contextual menu that pops up when you Control-click a program in Mac OS 8–8.5.

When you open a document using one of these methods, you automatically open the application that created the document. The Finder figures out which application created it, opens that application, and tells the application to open the document. Quite a chain of events you start by double-clicking a document.

Suppose you want to open a bunch of documents. No problem, just select them all and then double-click one of the selected icons or use the Open command. If the documents were created by different applications, the Finder doesn't get ruffled. It opens each application and gives it a list of the documents you want opened.

Opening a document with any compatible application

Instead of opening a document with the application that created it, you can open it with any compatible application. For example, any word processing application can open plain text documents created by other applications.

To open a document with any compatible application, drag the document's icon to the icon of the application you want to use. If the application is compatible with the document, the application's icon becomes highlighted. Release the mouse button while the application icon is highlighted, and the application opens the document. If the application is not already open, the Finder opens it automatically. If an application can't open a document you drag to it, nothing happens — no highlighting, no opening. Figure 7-1 shows how an application icon looks if it can open a document that you drag to it.

Secrets

Multiple Drag

In Mac OS 7.6–7.6.1, you can drag multiple items at once to an overlapping window without moving or resizing the windows. Start by selecting the items in the source window. Next, activate the destination window by clicking along its right edge or its bottom edge (where its scroll bars would be if it were active). You can also click just below the title bar, where the column headings or disk information appears. But don't click anywhere inside the destination window or in its title bar, or you will deselect the items in the source window. Finally, drag the selected items from the now-inactive source window to the now-active destination window. You can drag the whole group of selected items by dragging any one of them, even if the target window covers some of them in the inactive source window. Unfortunately, this trick does not work in Mac OS 8–8.5.

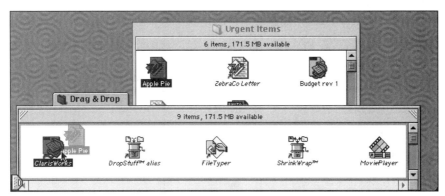

Figure 7-1: Opening a document by dragging it to a compatible application.

Opening the unknown

If you try to open a document by double-clicking its icon, clicking its button, or using the Finder's Open command, but you don't have the application that created it, you see an alert. Normally, this alert displays a list of alternate applications that can handle the kind of document you tried to open. You select the alternate application you want to have open the document and click the Open button in the dialog box. Then the alternate application you selected opens the document. The Mac OS remembers which alternate application you selected, and uses it to open the same document or any other like it (same type of document and same creator application) in the future. You don't see the alert box asking you to select an alternate application again for the same kind of document. Figure 7-2 shows the alert box in which you select an alternate application to open a document created by an application you don't have.

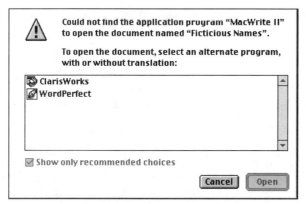

Figure 7-2: Select an alternate application to open a document created by an application you don't have.

Sometimes none of your applications can handle a document that you try to open. In this case, an alert tells you the document could not be opened because the application that created it could not be found. Usually the alert tells you the name of the creator application. Knowing the creator application, you may be able to obtain translator software that will enable you to open the document (see "Translating Documents" later in this chapter). Figure 7-3 shows an example of the alert you see when you don't have an alternate application to open a document.

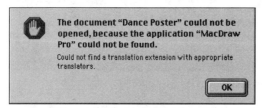

Figure 7-3: The application that created the document you want to open is not available and neither is an alternate.

If you'd rather not see alerts asking about alternate applications for opening documents, you can turn them off. Use the File Exchange control panel in Mac OS 8.5 or the Mac OS Easy Open control panel in Mac OS 7.6–8.1 to turn off automatic file translation, as explained in "Translating Documents" at the end of this chapter. Another way to stop these alerts is to disable or remove the File Exchange control panel or the Mac OS Easy Open control panel, as discussed in "Managing Startup Items" in Chapter 10.

After turning off automatic file translation, you see a different alert when you try to open a document created by an application you don't have. In this case, the alert tells you the document could not be opened because the application that created it could not be found, but the alert does not name the missing application. If the document is a type that SimpleText can open, the Finder asks whether you want to have SimpleText open it. SimpleText can open documents saved in plain text format by another program (but not word processing documents saved in a proprietary format). In addition, SimpleText can open pictures saved in the PICT format, movies saved in the QuickTime format, and 3D graphics saved in the QuickDraw 3D format (for details on viewing movies and 3D graphics, see Chapter 16). The PICT, QuickTime, and QuickDraw 3D formats are all standard Mac OS formats. Figure 7-4 shows examples of the alerts you see when automatic file translation is turned off and you try to open a document created by an application you don't have.

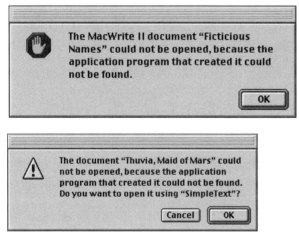

Figure 7-4: The application that created the document you want to open is not available and automatic file translation is turned off.

Opening with the Apple menu

The Apple menu expedites opening items you use frequently. Anything you can double-click in the Finder, including documents, application programs, desk accessories, folders, control panels, fonts, and sounds, you can also put in the Apple menu and open by choosing it there. Figure 7-5 shows an example of the Apple menu.

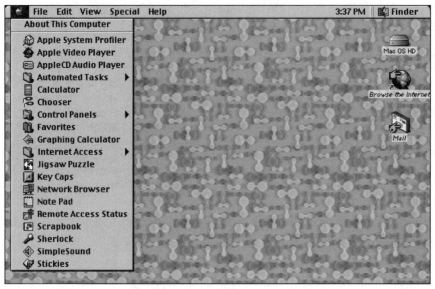

Figure 7-5: Opening an item by choosing it from the Apple menu.

Adding and removing Apple menu items

You put an item in the Apple menu by dragging it into the Apple Menu Items folder, which is inside the System Folder. The item becomes instantly available in the Apple menu (no need to restart your computer). Figure 7-6 shows how you add items to the Apple menu.

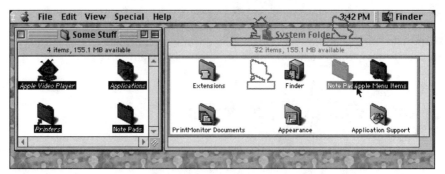

Figure 7-6: Adding items to the Apple menu by putting them in the Apple Menu Items folder.

To remove an item from the Apple menu, drag its icon out of the Apple Menu Items folder onto the desktop or into another folder.

Making submenus in the Apple menu

If your Apple menu has so many items that you must scroll to see them all, consider consolidating the less-used items in a folder or two within the Apple Menu Items folder. You can make the contents of folders within the Apple Menu Items folder appear as submenus of the Apple menu by using the Apple Menu Options control panel. You can also use this control panel to create submenus that list the items you have used recently. Figure 7-7 shows the Apple Menu Options control panel.

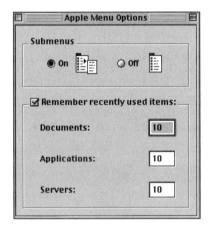

Figure 7-7: Adding submenus to the Apple menu and tracking recently used items.

Turning on the Submenus option creates a hierarchy of submenus in the Apple menu. After turning on the Submenus option, you see submenus whenever you highlight a folder listed in the Apple menu. A submenu lists the contents of the highlighted folder. Highlighting a folder listed in a submenu displays another submenu, up to five levels deep.

Turning on the option to remember recent items creates folders in the Apple menu for tracking the documents, applications, and servers that you most recently used. You can set the number of documents, applications, and servers that you want to track. The control panel tracks recent items by creating aliases of those items and placing the aliases in the Recent Applications folder, Recent Documents folder, or Recent Servers folder (where appropriate) in the Apple Menu Items folder (inside the System Folder). If you wish to suppress tracking of one type of item, set the number to be remembered to 0 (zero) and discard the appropriate recent items folder if it exists. (See Chapter 12 for more information on aliases.)

Organizing the Apple menu

The Apple menu always lists items alphabetically, regardless of their order in the Apple Menu Items folder. You don't affect the Apple menu when you rearrange the contents of the Apple Menu Items folder by dragging icons in its window or clicking column headings in a list view.

You can change the order of Apple menu items by beginning their names with certain characters. To make an item appear at the top of the Apple menu, begin its name with a blank space. You can group different types of items by prefixing different numbers of blank spaces to their names. The more blank spaces, the higher on the Apple menu the item appears. For example, you can prefix two blanks to the name of the most important item in your Apple menu, one blank to names of less important items, and none to other items.

To make items appear at the bottom of the Apple menu, begin their names with a hollow diamond (◊) or a bullet (•). Press Shift-Option-V for the hollow diamond or Option-8 for the bullet.

Rather than carefully prefixing icon names to arrange them in the Apple menu, you can install the shareware system extension AMICO, which stands for Apple Menu Items Custom Order, by Dennis Chronopoulos. With this extension installed, you determine the order of items in the Apple menu by arranging icons in the Apple Menu Items folder. In addition, you can add gray dividing lines like the ones you see in other menus. (See Chapter 26 for more information on shareware.)

Step-by-Step

Forcing Order Invisibly

Forcibly reordering items in the Apple menu by putting spaces or special symbols at the beginning of the items' names has side effects you may dislike. The spaces or symbols visibly alter the names and conspicuously shift the names to the right. Here's how to invisibly force the order you want:

1. Open the Note Pad or a new document in SimpleText.

2. Press Return to create a blank line, select the blank line, and copy it to the Clipboard.

3. Switch to the Finder. Open the Apple Menu Items folder, and click the name of an item that you want to appear at the top of the Apple menu to select the name for editing.

4. Press the up arrow (↑) key to move the insertion point to the beginning of the selected name and paste. The whole name goes blank, but don't fret.

5. Press Enter or click outside the name, and the name springs back into view. The renamed item jumps to the top of the window if you're viewing by name.

To increase an item's alphabetic buoyancy, paste the blank line two or more times at the beginning of the item's name.

Warning: Some applications don't work properly with files or folders whose names contain blank lines (blank spaces are okay). Specifically, some versions of QuarkXPress and PageMaker generate an undefined PostScript error if you try to print a document that's in a folder whose name begins with a blank line (not a blank space). If you encounter problems after pasting blank lines at the beginning of file or folder names, you'll have to use blank spaces instead.

Opening with the Launcher

Another way to open items is with the Launcher control panel. The Launcher displays a window of large buttons and clicking a button (once) opens the item it represents. The Launcher is similar to a folder window viewed as buttons in Mac OS 8–8.5, but the Launcher has features a folder window doesn't have, as described in the following paragraphs. Moreover, button views aren't available in Mac OS 7.6–7.6.1, but the Launcher is. Figure 7-8 shows an example of the Launcher window.

Figure 7-8: Opening an item by clicking its button in the Launcher control panel.

Items in the Launcher window are actually aliases in the Launcher Items folder inside the System Folder. (For detailed information on aliases, see Chapter 12.)

Launcher categories

You can categorize items in the Launcher by placing them in specially named folders within the Launcher Items folder. The name of a category folder must begin with a bullet (press Option-8 to type a bullet). The names of up to eight category folders appear as button names in a panel at the top of the Launcher window, and clicking a category button displays the items in the corresponding category folder.

There is a shortcut for opening a category folder: press Option and click the folder's button in the Launcher window. To open the Launcher Items folder itself, Option-click the Applications button in the Launcher window.

Adding, moving, and removing Launcher buttons

You can choose one of three sizes for icons in the Launcher window. You can also drag icons to, from, and within the Launcher window (without opening the Launcher Items folder or its subfolders) and open a document by dragging it to a compatible application in the Launcher. Specifically, you can do the following:

✦ Add an item by dragging its icon to the Launcher window, including to a category button in the Launcher window.

✦ Move an item in the Launcher by pressing the Option key and dragging the item.

✦ Open a document by dragging its icon to a compatible application's icon in the Launcher. (An application icon becomes highlighted when you drag a document icon over it in the Launcher if the application is able to open the document.)

✦ Move or copy an item to a folder in the Launcher — drag the item's icon to the folder's button in the Launcher.

✦ Remove an item from the Launcher by pressing the Option key and dragging the item to the Trash. (Do not Option-drag an item from the Launcher over a desktop printer icon or your computer may crash.)

✦ Change the icon size for the visible Launcher category by pressing the ⌘ key, clicking inside the Launcher window, and choosing from the menu that pops up.

Opening at startup and shutdown

If you want to have a program, document, or anything else open every time you start your computer, or every time you shut it down, the Finder can do that for you. Just put the items you want to open during startup into the Startup Items folder, which is inside the System Folder. Put the items you want to open during shutdown into the Shutdown Items folder, which is also inside the System Folder. Actually, to avoid disorganizing your disk you should generally put aliases (not original items) in the Startup Items and Shutdown Items folders. (For more information on these special folders, see "Exploring the System Folder" in Chapter 10. For information on creating aliases, see Chapter 12.)

Opening from applications

Yet another way to open items is with the Open command in most applications. Choosing the Open command from any application's File menu (except the Finder's) displays a dialog box that shows a view of your files, folders, and disks that's more or less like a list view in the Finder. Most applications display a standard Open dialog box, but some display the Navigation Services dialog box introduced with Mac OS 8.5. Figure 7-9 shows examples of Open and Navigation Services dialog boxes.

Open dialog box

An Open dialog box shows items from the desktop, the main level of one disk, or one folder at a time in a scrolling list. The Open dialog box also has buttons and a pop-up menu for opening disks, folders, and ultimately the document you want. In some applications, the Open dialog box includes a place to display a preview of the document that's currently selected in the dialog box. Each application can also add its own unique controls to assist in opening documents. You can't move an Open dialog box on the screen, you can't change its size, and you can't switch to another application (as described later in this chapter) while an Open dialog box is displayed.

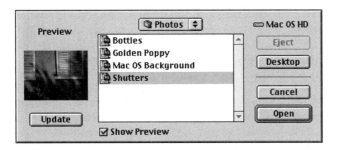

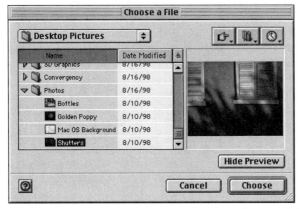

Figure 7-9: Opening an item using a standard Open dialog box (top) or a Navigation Services dialog box (bottom).

Navigation Services dialog box

The Navigation Services dialog box does the same job as the Open dialog box but eliminates many of its shortcomings. The scrolling list of files, called the *browser,* looks and operates a lot like the list view of the Finder. You see the icon, name, and modification date of every item in the folder or disk volume named at the top of the list. For each listed item, the modification date automatically expands from the longest date format (Friday, January 1, 1999) to the shortest format (1/1/99) depending on the space available. You can click the column headings to sort the list by name or date. You can also reverse the sort order by clicking the triangular sort direction indicator at the right end of the headings (above the scroll bar).

Next to each folder and disk volume icon you see a disclosure triangle. Clicking this triangle expands the folder or volume to display the items inside it.

As you can tell from the title bar, the Navigation Services dialog box is movable. You can drag it by its title bar or its frame. In addition, you can switch to another open application (including the Finder) while the Navigation Services dialog box is displayed.

Look closely at the bottom right corner of a Navigation Services dialog box. The textured area there is a size box that you can drag to resize the dialog box.

You may occasionally encounter a Navigation Services dialog box that you can't move or resize. If this happens, the application program you are using is restricting the Navigation Services dialog box because the application can't handle the screen updating that would be required if you were to move or resize the dialog box.

Opening a document

You open a document that's listed in an Open or Navigation Services dialog box by selecting it (click it once) and clicking the Open button. In some cases, especially in Navigation Services dialog boxes, the button may have a different name such as Choose or Select. You can also double-click a document to open it. Either way, the dialog box goes away and the document appears in a window.

You can select more than one document in a Navigation Services dialog box if the application program you're using allows this. To select additional documents, just press the Shift key while clicking them. You can even select multiple items from different folders. To select additional items in another folder, click the folder's disclosure triangle to expand the folder, and then Shift-click the items in it that you want to open.

If you realize while double-clicking an item in an Open or Navigation Services dialog box that you are pointing at the wrong item, you can cancel the operation as long as you have not released the mouse button. To cancel, hold down the mouse button on the second click and drag the pointer outside the dialog box before releasing the mouse button.

Instead of canceling a double-click in an Open dialog box, you can continue pressing the mouse button and drag the pointer to the item you want to open. When you release the mouse button, the currently selected item opens. This trick does not work in a Navigation Services dialog box, which lets you do other things by dragging items (more on this subject shortly).

Opening a folder

The only way to see documents in a folder that's listed in an Open dialog box, and one of the ways in a Navigation Services dialog box, is to open the folder. To open a folder, either select it and click the Open button or double-click it. When you open a folder, its contents take over the scrolling list and its name appears at the top of the list. The other way to see a folder's contents in a Navigation Services dialog box is to click the folder's disclosure triangle so that it points down. This method doesn't make the folder's contents take over the scrolling list or change the name above it.

The pop-up menu above the scrolling list in an Open or Navigation Services dialog box identifies the folder whose contents you see in the scrolling list. You can use the pop-up menu to go back through the folder layers toward the desktop. At the end of the pop-up menu is the desktop, and just ahead of it is the disk that contains the folder you currently see in the dialog box. Choosing an item from the pop-up menu takes you to that item and displays its contents in the dialog box. As a shortcut in the Open dialog box, you can move back one folder to the folder that contains the currently listed folder by clicking the name of the disk where it is displayed above the Eject button in the dialog box. This shortcut is not available in a Navigation Services dialog box.

You can quickly show a folder's contents in a Navigation Services dialog box if you can see the folder's icon outside the dialog box on the desktop or in a Finder window. All you do is drag the folder icon to the dialog box. This shortcut does not work in an Open dialog box.

Changing disks

If you use more than one disk, you may want to see folders and files from a different disk in an Open or Navigation Services dialog box. You can do this by showing the desktop in the dialog box and opening the disk there. One way to show the desktop in the dialog box is to choose it from the pop-up menu above the scrolling list in the dialog box. You can also show the desktop in an Open dialog box by clicking the Desktop button. A Navigation Services dialog box has no Desktop button; instead you use the Shortcuts button as described next.

You can eject a CD-ROM, floppy disk, or other removable disk in an Open or Navigation Services dialog box. When you insert a different disk, you see its contents in the dialog box. To eject a disk from an Open dialog box, click the Eject button. In a Navigation Services dialog box, use the Shortcuts menu (described next) to eject a disk. You don't have to go to the desktop before ejecting a disk in either kind of dialog box.

Shortcuts, Favorites, and Recent menus

At the top of a Navigation Services dialog box are three picture buttons that can speed your way through the dialog box. Each of these buttons displays a pop-up menu when you click the button. Figure 7-10 shows examples of these menus.

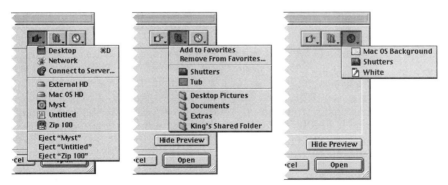

Figure 7-10: The Shortcuts (left), Favorites (middle), and Recent (right) pop-up menus speed your way through a Navigation Services dialog box.

The *Shortcuts* button looks like a pointing finger and displays a menu that lists every disk volume that has an icon on the desktop. Choosing a disk from this menu displays the disk's contents in the dialog box. The Shortcuts menu gives you easy access to the desktop, to your local network, and to file servers. In addition, the Shortcuts menu has an Eject command for every removable disk that you're currently using.

The *Favorites* button looks like a folder with a bookmark ribbon on it and displays a menu of your favorite files, folders, and volumes. (The application you're using can filter out all but the kind of items you're opening.) Choosing an item from the Favorites menu displays it in the dialog box. The Favorites menu also includes commands for adding and removing items on the menu. You can add an item by selecting it in the dialog box and choosing Add to Favorites from the Favorites menu. As a shortcut, you can simply drag the item from the scrolling list in the dialog box to the Favorites button. You can remove items by choosing Remove From Favorites from the Favorites menu. This displays a scrolling list of your favorites in a dialog box — select one or more on the list (Shift-click or ⌘-click to select multiple items) and click the Remove button. Your favorite items are also available in the Apple menu.

The *Recent* button looks like a clock face and displays a menu of documents that you recently opened. Choosing an item from this menu displays it in the dialog box. In some applications, the Recent menu also lists folders and volumes that you recently opened. Furthermore, the application you're using can restrict the Recent menu to showing only the kind of item you're opening. Navigation Services keeps track of recent items by storing aliases of them in a folder inside the Navigation Services folder in the Preferences folder, which is in the System Folder. (For details on aliases, see Chapter 12.)

The Shortcuts, Favorites, and Recent buttons are not available in Open dialog boxes, but you can endow Open dialog boxes with similar functionality by installing software such as Default Folder from St. Clair Software (http://www.stclairsoft.com), which is described in Chapter 26.

Navigating by keyboard

You can move through folders and open items by using the keyboard as well as the mouse. In an Open or Navigation Services dialog box, typing an item's full name or the first part of it selects the item. For example, pressing the M key selects the first item that begins with the letter *M* or *m*. Typing several letters quickly specifies a longer name to be selected, but pausing between keys starts the selection process all over again. The Key Repeat Rate setting in the Keyboard control panel determines how long you must pause to make a fresh start. After you have selected an item in an Open or Navigation Services dialog box (by any means), pressing Return or Enter opens the item. These dialog boxes recognize many other keyboard shortcuts. Table 7-1 has the details.

Table 7-1
**Keyboard Shortcuts for the Open and
Navigation Services Dialog Boxes**

Objective	*Keystroke*
Select a listed document, folder, or disk	Type the item's full or partial name
Scroll up in the list of items	Up arrow(↑)
Scroll down in the list of items	Down arrow(↓)
Open the selected item	Return, Enter, ⌘-down arrow(↓), or ⌘-O
Open the enclosing folder or disk	⌘-up arrow(↑)
Expand the selected folder	⌘-right arrow(→)*
Collapse the selected folder	⌘-left arrow(←)*
Go to the next disk	⌘-right arrow(→)**
Go to the previous disk	⌘-left arrow(←)**
Go to the desktop	⌘-Shift-up arrow(↑) or ⌘-D
Eject the current disk	⌘-E**
Eject the floppy disk in drive 1	⌘-Shift-1
Eject the floppy disk in drive 2	⌘-Shift-2
Click the Open button	Return or Enter
Click the Cancel button	Escape or ⌘-period(.)
Show the original of an alias (instead opening it)	Option-⌘-O, Option-double-click, or Option-of click Open

*Works in Navigation Services dialog box but not in Open dialog box.

**Works in Open dialog box but not in Navigation Services dialog box.

Managing Multiple Open Programs

With the Mac OS, you can have more than one program open at a time. When you open a program, the Finder remains open in the background. You can switch to the Finder without quitting the program you just opened. If your computer has enough memory, you can open additional programs without quitting. You can have as many programs open simultaneously as fit in your computer's memory. Figure 7-11 shows a desktop with windows from several programs open at the same time.

Figure 7-11: Keeping multiple programs open at the same time.

The capability to have multiple programs open simultaneously, which is called *multitasking,* can be very convenient. For example, you can copy and paste among documents of open programs without closing documents and quitting programs.

Multitasking's convenience has disorienting side effects. For example, a stray mouse click may make another open program active, bringing its windows to the front and covering the windows of the program you were using. If this happens unexpectedly, you may think that the program you're using has crashed when it is actually open and well in the background. You must get used to having multiple layers of open programs like piles of paper on a desk. Fortunately, you can hide program layers on the Mac—unlike layers of paper on your desk—as discussed later in this section under "Reducing window clutter."

No matter how many programs you have open, only one has control of the menu bar. The program currently in control is called the *active program.* Its icon appears at the right end of the menu bar, and normally its name also appears there in Mac OS 8.5. You can tell which open program is currently active by looking at that icon and icon name (if present), and at the titles of the other menus on the menu bar.

Switching programs

When you have more than one program open, there are several ways you can switch from one to the other. You can use the Application menu, the Application Switcher window (Mac OS 8.5 only), or the windows and icons you can see that belong to open programs.

Application menu

Not only do the program icon and name at the right end of the menu bar tell you which program is active, but it also marks the Application menu. The Application menu lists all open programs by name and small icon. You use the Application menu to switch from one open program to another. Figure 7-12 shows an example of the Application menu.

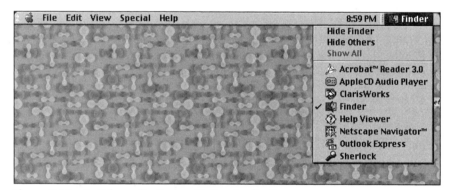

Figure 7-12: Switch applications with the Application menu.

To make a program in the Application menu the active program, choose it from the menu. When you do, that program takes over the menu bar and the program's windows come to the front. The program that was active becomes inactive. Its windows drop back but remain visible except for the parts covered by other open programs' windows.

Although the title of the Application menu in Mac OS 8.5 initially includes both the icon and the name of the active program, you can shorten the title to show only the icon. To resize the Application menu title, you drag the textured bar on the left side of the title. As you drag to the right, the Mac OS abbreviates the program name more and more in the menu bar. When you stop dragging, the name disappears and just the icon remains. If the Application menu title is only an icon, you can lengthen it to include the name by dragging the textured area to the left.

Program windows and icons

You can switch to a program by clicking any of its windows that you can see. All of the program's windows come to the front together, the program's menus take over the menu bar, and the program becomes the active program. Another way to accomplish this is by opening its icon or any of its document icons in the Finder.

Clicking the desktop or a Finder window makes the Finder active. On one hand, being able to bring the Finder to the front with a single mouse click can be very handy. On the other hand, it can be disorienting to have the application you're using suddenly disappear behind the Finder's windows due to a misplaced click on the desktop. If you find this behavior annoying, you can suppress the display of the desktop while you use other applications, as described under "Reducing window clutter" later in this section.

Application Switcher

You can switch among open programs in Mac OS 8.5 using a window that you get by tearing off the Application menu. This window, called the *Application Switcher,* has a button for each open program. Clicking a program's button in the Application Switcher makes it the active application. The Application Switcher initially displays the icons and names of all open programs, but you can change its size and orientation, as shown in Figure 7-13.

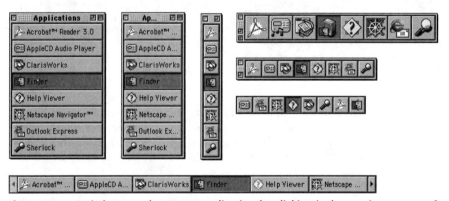

Figure 7-13: Switch to another open application by clicking its button in any one of the many forms of the Application Switcher in Mac OS 8.5.

Besides switching programs with the Application Switcher, you can open a document by dragging its icon to the button of a compatible application. You'll know an application is compatible with a document you're dragging because its button will become highlighted in the Application Switcher.

To tear off the Application Switcher, drag all the way to the bottom of the Application menu and then drag beyond it. When you see an outline of a window, release the mouse button.

The Application Switcher floats above other windows so it's always accessible. As a result, it can get in your way. You can move it like any other window, by dragging its title bar or window frame. In addition, you can move it by ⌘-dragging any part of it. To indicate this function, the mouse pointer looks like a gloved hand when it is over the Application Switcher and you are pressing the ⌘ key.

There are several ways you can make the Application Switcher's smaller or larger. You can alternate between the maximum button width (icon and full program name) and minimum button width (icon only) by clicking the zoom box. To adjust the widths of all buttons between these extremes, drag the right edge of any button. You can also alternate between large and small icons by Option-clicking the zoom box.

To alternate between vertical and horizontal orientation, Option-Shift-click the zoom box.

The Application Switcher normally has two keyboard shortcuts that you can use to switch programs. Press ⌘-Tab to switch to the next open program. Press ⌘-Shift-Tab to switch to the previous program. If necessary, you can disable or change these keyboard shortcuts. The simplest way to modify the Application Switcher's keyboard shortcuts is to use the onscreen help that comes with Mac OS 8.5. First, make sure the Finder is the active application, and choose Mac OS Help from the file menu. On the left side of the Mac OS Help window, click "Files and programs." Then on the right side of the window, click "Switching between open programs." Scroll down until you see the underlined text "Help me modify the keyboard shortcuts" next to a large diamond and click this text. A series of dialog boxes leads you through the process of modifying the shortcut keys. (For more information on using onscreen help, see Chapter 9.)

The Application Switcher has advanced features that you can control only through AppleScript. One feature is the capability to hide the title bar and window frame. You can also have programs listed in the order in which you opened them instead of alphabetical order. To give you an idea of the possibilities, Mac OS 8.5 comes with three AppleScript scripts for changing the Application Switcher. You can run these scripts by clicking underlined text at the very end of the "Switching between open programs" section of "Files and programs" in Mac OS Help. One of these scripts makes the Application Switcher a horizontal bar in the lower-left corner of the screen, without a title bar, window frame, or close box. Another makes the Application Switcher in an icon bar in the lower-right corner of the screen, with programs listed in the order in which they were opened. The third example resets the Application Switcher to its standard appearance. (For a detailed introduction to AppleScript, see Chapter 23.)

Reducing window clutter

With many programs open, the desktop quickly becomes a visual Tower of Babel. You can eliminate the clutter by choosing the Application menu's Hide Others command. It hides the windows of all programs except the currently active one. The icons of hidden programs are dimmed in the Application menu and the

Application Switcher, if you have it open in Mac OS 8.5. To make the windows of all programs visible, choose Show All from the Application menu.

You can hide the active program's windows and simultaneously switch to the most recently active program by choosing the first command from the Application menu. The command's name begins with the word Hide and ends with the name of the currently active program.

To hide the active program's windows as you switch to a particular program, press Option while choosing the other program from the Application menu. Or press Option while clicking the other program's window. You can hide the application you're using and switch to the Finder by pressing Option while clicking the desktop, a Finder icon, or a Finder window.

You can have the Mac OS hide the Finder's desktop automatically whenever you are working in another program. With the Finder's desktop hidden, you can't accidentally activate the Finder by clicking the desktop. To keep the Finder hidden, turn off the "Show Desktop when in background" option in the General Controls control panel, as shown in Figure 7-14.

Figure 7-14: Keep the Finder hidden with the General Controls control panel.

Memory partitions

Every application program and desk accessory you open has its own layer on the desktop and its own part of memory. You can see how your computer's memory is partitioned at any time. Just switch to the Finder and choose About This Computer from the Apple menu. (Chapter 18 explains how to manage your computer's memory.) Figure 7-15 shows an example of the About This Computer window.

Background operations

Some programs can operate in the background by using Mac OS multitasking capabilities. Background programs run during the intervals (typically less than $1/8$ of a second long) when the active program isn't using the computer. They usually work while the active program waits for you to do something. For example, the previous chapter explained that the Finder can copy files and empty the Trash in the background.

Secrets

Interacting with Background Programs

A background program can't use the menu bar and shouldn't interact directly with you in any way. It can, however, ask you to activate it by some or all of these means:

✦ Displaying a diamond symbol next to its name in the Application menu

✦ Flashing its icon on top of the Application menu's icon or the Apple menu's icon

✦ Playing the system alert sound (commonly a beep)

✦ Displaying a brief alert message which you must dismiss before continuing

In addition, a program in the background can interact with other open programs by sending them Apple Events messages (as described in Chapter 23).

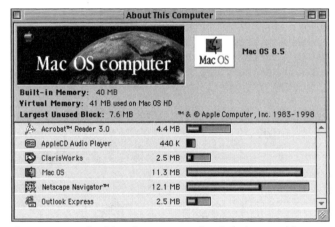

Figure 7-15: Checking the memory that is being used by open programs.

Moving Document Contents Around

While a document is open, you can generally move its contents to different places in the same document or other documents. The classic way to move contents is with the Edit menu's Cut, Copy, and Paste commands. Many programs also let you drag content from one place and drop it in another.

Cut, Copy, and Paste

Everyone quickly learns to use the Cut, Copy, and Paste commands to transfer material within a document and between documents. First you select the content you want to move—some text, a picture, a movie, or whatever kind of data the document contains. Then you choose Cut or Copy from the Edit menu to place the selected data on the Clipboard, which is a holding area for data in transit. The Cut command removes the selected data from its original location, but the Copy command doesn't. Next you select the location where you want to place the contents of the Clipboard and choose Paste from the Edit menu to put it there.

The Paste command does not empty the Clipboard. After pasting the contents once, you can paste the contents again. The Clipboard doesn't change until you copy or cut again (or until you shut down the computer).

You can copy-and-paste or cut-and-paste within the same document, between documents in the same application, or between documents in different applications. With a little practice, cut-and-paste and copy-and-paste become second nature, especially if you use the keyboard shortcuts (⌘-X for Cut, ⌘-C for Copy, and ⌘-V for Paste).

Drag-and-drop

The Mac OS provides a more direct way to copy text, graphics, and other material within a document, between documents, and between programs. This capability, called *drag-and-drop editing,* works only with programs that are designed to take advantage of it. Several programs that come with the Mac OS work with drag-and-drop editing, including SimpleText, Stickies, the Note Pad, and the Scrapbook.

To move material within a document, open the document and select the text, graphic, or other material that you want to move. Then position the mouse pointer over the selected material, press the mouse button, and drag to the place where you want to move it. As you drag, an outline of the selected material follows the pointer, and if you're dragging text, an insertion point shows where the material will appear when you stop dragging. If you want to copy rather than move selected material within a document, press the Option key before releasing the mouse button. Figure 7-16 shows some text being moved within a document.

To copy material between documents, first open both documents and position them so that you can see the source material and the place where you want to drop a copy of it. Select the text, graphic, or other source material and then drag the selected material to the place in the second document where you want the copy. As you drag, an outline of the selected material follows the mouse pointer. When the pointer enters the destination window, a border appears around the content area of the window, and if you're dragging text, an insertion point shows where the copy will appear when you stop dragging. Note that you do not have to press the Option key to make a copy when dragging between documents. You can use the same method to copy between two documents in the same application or between documents in different applications. Figure 7-17 shows some text being copied from one application to another.

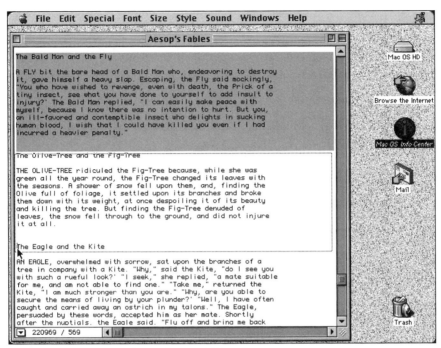

Figure 7-16: Drag-and-drop editing within a document.

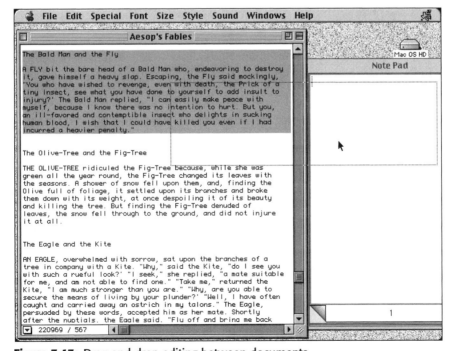

Figure 7-17: Drag-and-drop editing between documents.

Some people prefer drag-and-drop to cut-and-paste editing because they find it easier to use. Drag-and-drop has one clear advantage: It doesn't wipe out the contents of the Clipboard, so it's a good method to use when the Clipboard contains important material that you're not ready to replace.

Clipping files

You can also drag selected material from a document to the desktop or a folder window, where the Finder creates a clipping file that contains a copy of the dragged material. You can open a clipping file to see it in the Finder, but you can't select anything in a clipping file. You can copy the contents of a clipping file to a document by dragging the clipping-file icon to the open document's window. Clipping files can contain text, pictures, QuickTime movies, and sound.

You can use a clipping file over and over. For example, you can keep handy clippings that contain your letterhead, the company logo, a list of your e-mail addresses, and any other element that you use frequently.

Creating Documents

You can't always be opening documents that already exist. Sometimes you need to create new ones. Many application programs automatically create a brand-new, untitled document when you double-click the application icon. Most applications let you create a new document any time you want one by choosing New from the File menu.

You can also create a document by making a copy of an existing document. This method is especially useful if the existing document contains something you want to include in a new document, such as a letterhead or some boilerplate. To make a copy of a document, use the Finder's Duplicate command or one of the other methods described in "Working with Files and Folders" in Chapter 5.

Rather than duplicating a document every time you want a copy of it, you can make it a stationery pad. Opening a stationery pad — whether from the Finder directly, from the Apple menu, from the Launcher, or with the Open command in many applications — is like tearing a page from a pad of printed forms: you get a new document with a preset format and contents. Stationery pads generally have a distinctive icon that looks like a stack of document icons, although some types of stationery have generic (blank) stationery pad icons. Figure 7-18 shows some examples of stationery pad icons.

You can make any document a stationery pad by selecting the document in the Finder, choosing the Get Info command, and setting the Stationery Pad option in the Info window. Some applications enable you to directly save a document as a stationery pad (more about that in the next section, "Saving Documents"). Figure 7-19 shows the Stationery Pad option in an Info window.

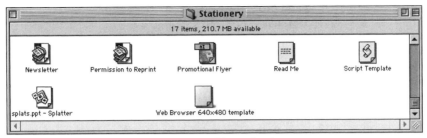

Figure 7-18: Stationery pad icons resemble pads of paper.

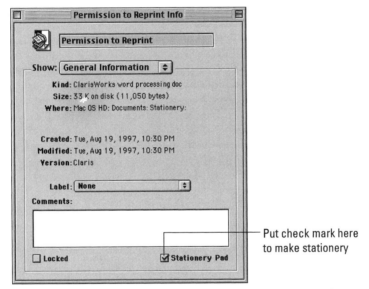

Figure 7-19: Making a stationery pad with the Finder's Get Info command.

What happens when you open a stationery pad depends on whether the application that opens it knows the difference between stationery pads and regular documents. What happens may also depend on how you open the application. If an application knows about stationery pads, it always creates a new untitled document with the format and content of the stationery pad. In this case, it doesn't matter how you open the stationery pad. If you use the Finder, the Apple menu, or the Launcher, the Mac OS figures out which application creates the type of stationery you're opening and tells that application to open the stationery. If you use the application's Open command, the application opens the stationery directly.

If you open a stationery pad for a type of document created by an application that doesn't know about stationery, the Mac OS creates a new document by making a copy from the stationery pad and has the application open the new document. With Mac OS 8–8.5, the Finder automatically names the new document. In Mac OS

7.6–7.6.1, you may get a dialog box asking you to enter a document name before opening the document. The dialog box appears only if you're using Mac OS 7.6–7.6.1 or earlier and the application that created the stationery document doesn't know how to open stationery properly itself.

If you open a stationery pad with the Open command of an application that doesn't know about stationery, the application opens the stationery pad itself, not a copy of it. A message warns you that you are opening a stationery pad. If you make changes, they will be saved into the stationery pad itself.

Quick Tips

When Locks are Better than Stationery

Opening a stationery pad creates a new document file. If you want to make a template that doesn't create a new file every time you open the template, don't make the template a stationery pad. Instead, make the template an ordinary document, but lock it by using the Finder's Get Info command. You may want to use this method with templates for single envelopes and mailing labels, for example. Then you can open the locked template, type or paste the recipient's address, print, and close without saving.

Saving Documents

After creating a new document or making changes to a document you opened, you need to save the document on disk so that the changes persist. Make sure the document's window is active (in front of other document windows) and choose Save or Save As from the File menu. For a new document, either of these commands brings up a dialog box in which you name the document and select the folder where you want it saved. For a previously saved document, the Save command does not bring up a dialog box; the application automatically saves the changed document in place of the previously saved document. The Save As command always brings up a dialog box so you can save a copy of a previously saved document.

In most applications, the Save and Save As commands display a standard Save dialog box, but in some applications, these commands display the Navigation Services dialog box introduced with Mac OS 8.5. These dialog boxes look and work much like the ones for opening documents (described earlier in this chapter). Figure 7-20 shows examples of Save and Navigation Services dialog boxes.

A Save dialog box shows the contents of the desktop, the main level of one disk, or one folder at a time, and has controls for opening a different disk or folder in the dialog box. In addition, the Save dialog box has a space where you enter a name for the document. The Save dialog box may have other controls for setting document format options.

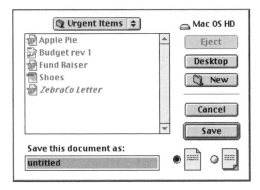

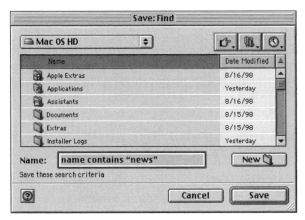

Figure 7-20: Saving a document using a standard Save
dialog box (top) or a Navigation Services dialog box (bottom).

Like a Save dialog box, a Navigation Services dialog box for saving a document
shows the contents of the desktop, the main level of one disk, or one folder at a
time. You cannot see the contents of multiple folders in the same list, because the
folders do not have disclosure triangles. In this regard, the Navigation Services
dialog box for saving is different than the one for opening files.

Although the Navigation Services dialog box for saving documents is similar to the
Save dialog box, it is improved nonetheless. The scrolling list of files and folders
shows item names and modification dates, like a list view of a folder window in the
Finder. You can sort the list by clicking a column heading in the dialog box, and you
can reverse the sort order by clicking the triangular sort direction indicator at the
right end of the column headings (above the scroll bar). Moreover, you can usually
move a Navigation Services dialog box, change its size, and switch to another
application while the dialog box is displayed. (Applications, however, can suppress
these last features.)

Specifying a name and location

The first time you save a document and every time you use the Save As command, you need to type a name for the document in the space provided in the dialog box. You also need to specify where you want the document saved. You do that by opening a folder, the main level of a disk, or the desktop in the dialog box. All the same methods described earlier in this chapter for opening folders, disks, and the desktop in dialog boxes for opening documents also work in dialog boxes for saving documents. You can open folders and disks by double-clicking them or by selecting one and clicking the Open button. You can use the pop-up menu (or click the disk name in a Save dialog box) to go back through the folder layers toward the desktop. You can eject a removable disk with the Eject button in a Save dialog box or the Shortcuts menu in a Navigation Services dialog box. You can also use the Favorites and Recent menus in a Navigation Services dialog box to open folders or disks quickly.

When you select a folder or disk in the Save or Navigation Services dialog box, there is an Open button but no Save button. To change the Open button to a Save button so you can save the document, select the document name in the dialog box by clicking it or pressing the Tab key.

Secrets

Copy and Paste in the Save Dialog Box

While you are entering a name for the document to save in a Save or Navigation Services dialog box, the Cut, Copy, and Paste commands may be available from the Edit menu. This means you can copy a name for a document from within the document before choosing the Save command, and then paste the copied name into the dialog box. When pasting a document name, only the first 31 characters are used; the rest are omitted. In some programs, you must use the keyboard equivalents: ⌘-X for Cut, ⌘-C for Copy, and ⌘-V for Paste.

Saving a stationery pad

In many applications you can designate in a Save or Navigation Services dialog box whether to save a document as a stationery pad or a regular document. Some applications offer this choice with two radio buttons, one labeled with a regular document icon and the other labeled with a stationery pad icon. Other documents offer more document format options in a pop-up menu in the dialog box.

Creating a new folder

A Save or Navigation Services dialog box usually includes a button that you can click to create a new folder. Clicking the New Folder button displays a small dialog box in which you type the name of the folder you want to create and click. The new folder is created in the folder, disk, or desktop whose contents are currently displayed in the Save dialog box. Figure 7-21 shows the dialog box in which you enter a new folder name.

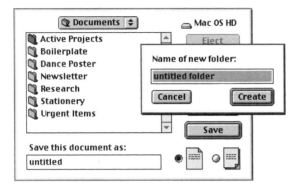

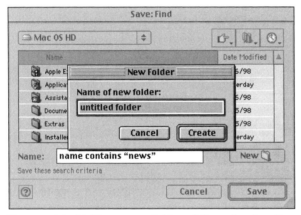

Figure 7-21: Making a new folder while saving in a Save dialog box (top) or in a Navigation Services dialog box (bottom).

Navigating with the keyboard

You can use the same keyboard shortcuts in dialog boxes for saving documents (previously listed in Table 7-1) as in dialog boxes for opening documents. You can also press ⌘-N to create a new folder. However, there is a trick to navigating with the keyboard in dialog boxes for saving. You must select the scrolling list in the dialog box so your keystrokes don't end up as part of the document name. You can alternate between the scrolling list and the name entry area by pressing the Tab key. Clicking in either area also makes it the keyboard target. The Mac OS indicates that your typing will affect the scrolling list by outlining it with a heavy black border. If, instead, you see a flashing insertion point or highlighted text in the document name, you know that your typing affects it. Figure 7-22 shows a Save dialog box where the contents list is the keyboard target and another where the document name is the target.

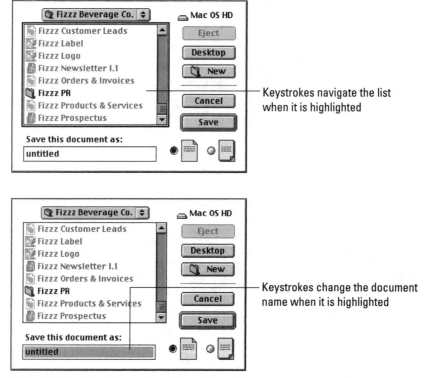

Figure 7-22: Using the keyboard in a Save dialog box to navigate the contents list (top) or edit the document name (bottom).

Finding Documents by Content

Finding a document is easy when you first start using your computer. As you acquire more and more documents, finding one you need gets harder. If you remember the file name, modification date, or some other attribute you can use the Find File section of the Sherlock program in Mac OS 8.5 or the Find File program in Mac OS 7.6–8.1 to find a document (as described in the previous chapter). After a while, you forget a document's file name and when you last changed the document. All you can remember is what the document is about. If you're looking for a text document and you have Mac OS 8.5, you're in luck. You can use the Find by Content section of the Sherlock program, shown in Figure 7-23.

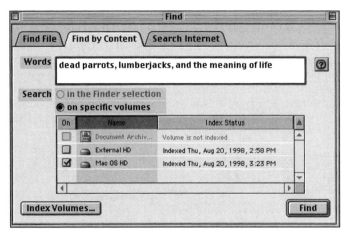

Figure 7-23: The Find by Content section of the Sherlock program quickly searches for documents whose content matches the query you type.

Find by Content quickly searches for documents that match a query that you specify. Then it displays a list of documents it found and ranks them by their relevance to your query. In some cases, you can have the Mac OS summarize a found item.

Find by Content can search your entire hard disk very quickly because it doesn't search through each document. It actually searches an index that you had it compile beforehand (as described after the next paragraph). The index contains significant words in the names and contents of your documents.

There's no comparison between Find by Content in Mac OS 8.5 and the capability of Find File in Mac OS 7.6–8.1 to search the content of text files. Find by Content is lightning fast and Find File is slug slow. Find by Content lets you type a natural-sounding query, but Find File limits you to typing one key word or key phrase. What's more, Find File searches only plain text documents, while Find by Content can also search formatted text documents such as the ones you create with Microsoft Word, ClarisWorks, and QuarkXPress. (You may need to obtain translation software to search your formatted documents.)

Creating an index

Before you can search by content, you must index the disks you want to search. Indexing takes a lot of time. Creating a new index can take an hour or more. Updating an index can easily take 15 minutes. The amount of time depends on the number of documents to index and their lengths. Because indexing is so time-consuming, you can schedule it to take place when you're not using your computer for anything else, such as at night.

To index a disk now or schedule indexing, open the Sherlock program (choose it from the Apple menu) and then choose Index Volumes from the Find menu. If the Sherlock program is already open, you can click the Search by Content tab in the Sherlock window and then click the Index Volumes button at the bottom of the window. Either action displays the Index Volumes window, which lists each disk that can be indexed and has buttons for creating indexes, deleting indexes, and setting up an indexing schedule. Figure 7-24 is an example of the Index Volumes window.

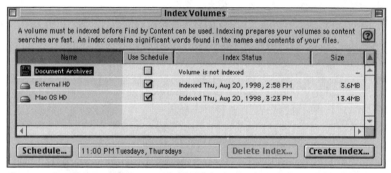

Figure 7-24: Create, delete, and schedule indexes for the Find by Content section of the Sherlock program.

To create or update an index for a disk right now, select it by clicking its name or icon in the Index Volumes window and click the button named Create Index or Update Index. You can index more than one disk at a time by selecting all their names (Shift-click each one you want to select) before clicking Create Index. When you click Create Index or Update Index, a dialog box advises you that creating or updating an index takes a long time. Buttons in the dialog box let you decide to schedule indexing, cancel indexing, or go ahead and create or update now. While indexing is underway, a dialog box indicates the status of the operation. If you decide it's taking too long to index a disk right now, you can click the Cancel button in this dialog box and then schedule the indexing to happen while you're away from the computer.

To put a disk on the indexing schedule, select its checkbox under Use Schedule in the Index Volumes window. To take a disk off the indexing schedule, clear its checkbox.

If you select disks to be indexed on a schedule, you must set up the schedule. Click the Schedule button in the Index Volumes window to display the Schedule dialog box. At the top of this dialog box you specify a time of day to begin indexing. Elsewhere in the dialog box you select the days of the week on which you want indexing to occur. If your computer has the Energy Saver control panel, you can make sure your computer is running at the time you have scheduled for indexing. Use Energy Saver to schedule a startup time a few minutes before the scheduled indexing time, as described in "Sleep, Startup, and Shutdown Settings" in Chapter 11.

You can't index floppy disks or locked disks such as CD-ROMs. (There's no way to save an index file on a locked disk.) Some CD-ROMs come preindexed, and there's no need to update their indexes because they can't be changed.

Searching indexed disks by content

To search the content of indexed disks, open the Sherlock program and click the Search by Content tab. In the space provided at the top of the window, type the words you would like to find and click the Find button. A short time later, an Items Found window lists the documents that matched your query, as shown in Figure 7-25.

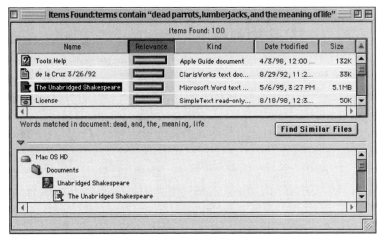

Figure 7-25: Viewing the results of a Find by Content search in Mac OS 8.5.

Initially, the found items are listed by their relevance to your search query. You can change the order by clicking a column heading in the Items Found window. To sort in reverse order, click the triangular sort direction indicator at the right end of the column headings (above the scroll bar). To resize columns, drag the lines that separate the column headings.

You can find out which words from your query are in a found document. Select the document in the list of found items and look just below the list to see the words that match enumerated.

The bottom part of the Items Found window shows the folder location of the document selected in the top part of the window. If you select more than one item in the top part of the window (by Shift-clicking or dragging across the names), the bottom part of the window doesn't show anything. You can adjust the relative size of the top and bottom parts by dragging the line that separates them. You can alternately hide and show the bottom part of the window by clicking the disclosure triangle next to the separator line.

You can find files that are similar to any of the found documents. Select a found document in the list and click the Find Similar Files button.

There are many other actions you can take with documents in the Items Found window. You can open them, open their enclosing folders, print them, move them to the Trash, display their Info windows, and set their labels. For details on these actions, refer to "Finding Items" in the previous chapter.

The results of searching by content may not be accurate if the content of a disk has changed since it was last indexed. If you have added, removed, or changed any files since the index was updated, you should update the index.

Summarizing a Document

You can have Mac OS 8.5 summarize the text content of documents that have been indexed for the Find by Content section of the Sherlock program. You do this in the Items Found window of the Sherlock program or in the Finder. In either place, you Control-click a document to display its contextual menu and choose Summarize File to Clipboard. If this command is not present in the contextual menu, then the item you're Control-clicking can't be summarized. The item may be a type that can't be summarized.

When the Mac OS finishes summarizing a document, the Finder displays its Clipboard window so you can see the summary. If the Finder is in the background, you may need to make it the active application to see this window.

The Mac OS summarizes a document by extracting the sentences that most typify the document. It takes a while to summarize large documents, and you can't use your computer for anything else while it's preparing a summary. To get a feel for how quickly the Mac OS can summarize documents on your computer, start with small ones and work up to larger ones.

Translating Documents

As the Mac OS has evolved, it has gradually simplified the process of opening documents created with programs you don't have. Someone else may have created the documents on another Mac OS computer or a PC, which uses the Windows or DOS operating system. You may have created the document with an application you don't have any more. In any case, you need to open the document with an application you do have. You may be able to use an application that can open foreign documents itself, or you may need translation software to convert the foreign document to a format your application can open.

PC disks

One of the ways you get PC files on your Mac in the first place is from PC disks. The File Exchange control panel enables Mac OS 8.5 to recognize PC floppy disks and SCSI disks, and the PC Exchange control panel enables Mac OS 7.6–8.1 to do the same. When you insert a PC floppy, a Zip disk formatted for PCs, or another removable PC disk, its icon appears on the desktop just like a Mac disk. If you attach a PC-format SCSI hard disk to your Mac and then start up the computer, an icon appears on the desktop for the PC hard disk.

You can open a PC disk and see its files and folders (which are also called *subdirectories* in DOS and Windows). You can open folders by double-clicking them, and you can open document files if you know which Mac applications can open them (more on this subject under the next heading).

If Mac OS 8.5 does not recognize a SCSI hard disk or removable disk, open the File Exchange control panel and click its Mount Now button. If you want PC SCSI disks to automatically appear on your desktop when you start up your Mac, select the "Mount and startup" option at the bottom of the control panel.

If Mac OS 7.6–8.1 does not recognize a SCSI hard disk or removable disk, open the PC Exchange control panel and click its Options button. After a few seconds, a dialog box appears with a list of SCSI devices attached to your computer. Select your PC SCSI device on the list. (You can't select devices that are listed in italics.) Click OK and restart your computer with the SCSI device on and removable disk ejected.

If you use PC floppy disks with Mac OS 7.6–8, you should install the DOS Format Fixer 1.0 utility, which is available from Apple's Software Updates library (http://www.apple.com/swupdates/). This utility corrects a problem with PC Exchange 2.1.1 that could corrupt floppy disks formatted with Windows 3.1 or DOS 5.0. You do not need this utility software with PC Exchange 2.2 or File Exchange.

You can't use PC disks larger than 1GB with the version of PC Exchange that comes with Mac OS 7.6–8. This limitation does not exist with PC Exchange 2.2, which comes with Mac OS 8.1, or File Exchange, which comes with Mac OS 8.5.

PC file mapping

If you have a file that came from a PC, the Mac OS can't use its standard method for determining which application should open it. Where a Mac file has internal codes that tell the Mac OS which applications can open it, a PC file has a code you can see in its name. This code, called a *file name extension* or *file name suffix,* comes at the end of the file name following a period. (File name extensions don't always show up on a computer that uses Windows 95–98 because it is possible and common to conceal them there. Windows 95–98 keeps track of file name extensions in a table called the Registry.)

Basically, the Mac OS (like Windows) uses a table to map file name extensions to applications. Mac OS 8.5 has a sizable table of file extension mappings built in. But in Mac OS 7.6–8.1, the table initially has only one entry, which maps the .txt extension to SimpleText. You can obtain free preconfigured file mapping tables from the Internet, such as the free PC Exchange Preferences from *Macworld* magazine's online software library (http://www.zdnet.com/cgi-bin/texis/swlib/mac/getit.bin?fcode= MC17162). You can also configure file name extension mappings yourself, as explained next. Table 7-2 lists some common file name extensions and the corresponding applications.

Table 7-2
PC File Name Extensions

Extension	Application and Document Type
.AI	Adobe Illustrator document
.BMP	Windows or OS/2 bitmap graphic
.CDR	CorelDraw document
.COM	A program
.DBF	Database file (various spreadsheet and database applications)
.DOC	Microsoft Word document
.DOT	Microsoft Word template
.EPS	Encapsulated PostScript file
.EXE	Self-extracting compressed file (PKzip format) or an application
.GIF	GIF graphic
.HTM	Web page (HTML file)
.IL5	Illustrator document (number is the application version)
.JPG	JPEG compressed graphic
.P65	Adobe PageMaker 6.5 publication file
.PCT	PICT graphic
.PCX	PC Paintbrush graphic
.PDF	Adobe Acrobat document
.PM6	PageMaker 6 document (number is the application version)
.PPT	Microsoft PowerPoint document
.PRN	Any print-to-disk file from many applications, including PostScript, PCL (HP LaserJet), or ASCII (for line printers)
.PS	PostScript file
.PSD	Adobe Photoshop document

Extension	Application and Document Type
.PT6	PageMaker 6 template (number is the application version)
.PUB	Microsoft Publisher document
.QXD	QuarkXPress document
.RTF	Rich Text Format word processing document (which can be opened in a word processor or placed in PageMaker)
.SAM	AmiPro document
.T65	Adobe PageMaker 6.5 template file
.TBL	Adobe table editor document
.TIF	TIFF graphic
.TXT	Plain text document
.WK1	Lotus 1-2-3 spreadsheet (the number is the application version)
.WKS	Microsoft Works document
.WMF	Windows Meta File graphic
.WP	WordPerfect document
.WPD	WordPerfect document (version 6.1 and higher)
.WPG	WordPerfect graphic
.WQ1	Quattro Pro spreadsheet (the number is the application version)
.WRI	Microsoft Write document
.WS2	WordStar document (the number is the application version)
.XLS	Microsoft Excel spreadsheet
.ZIP	Compressed file (PKzip format)

Configuring file mapping

To configure the mapping of file name extensions to applications in Mac OS 8.5, you use the PC Exchange section of the File Exchange control panel. In Mac OS 7.6–8.1, you use the PC Exchange control panel. Figure 7-26 shows examples of these control panels.

You can change the mapping of a PC file name extension by selecting one of the mappings listed in the File Exchange or PC Exchange control panel and clicking the Change button. You can also add a new mapping of a file name extension by clicking the Add button. These actions bring up a dialog box in which you type an extension, select a Mac application, and choose a document type, as shown in Figure 7-27.

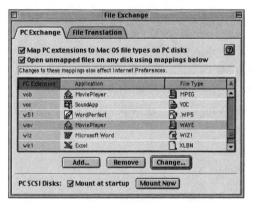

Figure 7-26: Mapping PC file name extensions to Mac applications in Mac OS 8.5 (left) and Mac OS 7.6–8.1 (right).

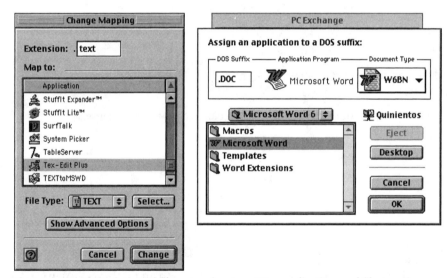

Figure 7-27: Assigning a PC file extension to a Mac application and file type in Mac OS 8.5 (left) and Mac OS 7.6–8.1 (right).

Clicking the Remove button in the control panel removes the currently selected extension mapping from the list. Before clicking Remove, you can select multiple items in the list by ⌘-clicking them (to select them individually) or Shift-clicking (to select a range).

Note that if the QuickTime Exchange option is turned on in the QuickTime Settings control panel, its mappings for graphics, sound, video, and other media files take precedence over the File Exchange mappings.

File mapping options

You can turn PC file mapping on or off in the File Exchange control panel or the PC Exchange control panel. In PC Exchange, select the On or Off setting in the lower-left corner of the control panel. In File Exchange, turn off PC file mapping by turning off the first option at the top of the control panel. If you turn off file mapping, then the files on PC disks are not mapped to Mac applications, and the PC files have generic PC icons. If you turn on file mapping, then PC files on PC disks are mapped; they take on Mac OS file types and have icons that look like Mac file icons.

File mapping happens only to PC files located on PC disks whose icons are on your desktop. The disks can be PC floppy disks, PC Zip disks, PC SCSI disks connected to your Mac's SCSI port (if it has one), and so forth. If you copy a PC file from a PC disk to a Mac disk, the copy on the Mac disk keeps the file mapping of the original on the PC disk.

If you have any unmapped PC files on a Mac disk, they will not be mapped to Mac applications; they must be on PC disks to be mapped. Unmapped files have generic PC icons, not the icons of Mac files. You can get unmapped PC files from many sources. They can come attached to e-mail. You can download them from the Web or FTP sites on the Internet. You can copy unmapped PC files from other computers on your local area network. You can also copy them from PC disks while file mapping is turned off.

In Mac OS 8.5, File Exchange can determine which Mac application should open any unmapped PC file according to its file name extension. The unmapped file still has a generic PC icon, but at least File Exchange helps you open it. The unmapped file can be on a PC disk or a Mac disk. To enable this feature, turn on the second option at the top of the control panel.

File translation

The Mac OS comes with a control panel that can help you open files created by applications you don't have. The File Translation section of the File Exchange control panel handles this in Mac OS 8.5, and the Mac OS Easy Open control panel handles this in Mac OS 7.6–8.1. These control panels step in when you try to open a file created by an application that you don't have. They suggest alternative applications of yours that may be able to translate and open the file, as explained in detail under the next two headings.

You may have files that none of your applications know how to open. In this case, software that comes with the Mac OS may be able to translate the files so that your applications can open them. Mac OS 8.5 comes with QuickTime 3.0, which can translate many types of graphics, sound, and video files. You can also get QuickTime 3.0 free from Apple's QuickTime Web site (http://www.apple.com/quicktime/) and install it on any Mac that has Mac OS 7.6–8.5. For more information on QuickTime, see Chapter 16.

Secrets

Long File Names

Mac and PC file names are not the same length. Mac file names can be as long as 31 characters. Windows 95–98 and NT 4.0 allow file names as long as 253 characters, but for compatibility with earlier Windows versions and DOS, these operating systems also store a truncated version of each file name. The truncated names can be as long as 12 characters and typically consist of up to eight characters that identify the file, followed by a period and a three-character file name extension. This short file name form is known as a DOS file name or an 8.3 file name.

File Exchange and PC Exchange take care of file name length differences. When you copy a Mac file to a PC disk or save a file directly onto a PC disk from a Mac, File Exchange or PC Exchange makes up an 8.3 version of the Mac file name. You still see the full Mac file name when you use the PC disk on a Mac. Someone using the same disk on a PC sees either the 8.3 name or the full name, depending on the Windows version installed on the PC.

When you look at PC files on a Mac, you may see 8.3 file names or long file names. File Exchange and PC Exchange 2.2, which come with Mac OS 8.5 and 8.1, can display the first 31 characters of a long PC file name. Of course, if the PC file was saved with an 8.3 name, that's what you see on a Mac. The older versions of PC Exchange that come with Mac OS 7.6–8 do not recognize long PC file names. With PC Exchange 2.1.1 and earlier, you always see 8.3 names for files saved on a PC.

Mac OS 7.6–8.1 comes with the MacLinkPlus translation software from DataViz, and you'll find it described in detail at the end of this section. However, some newer Mac models that have Mac OS 8.1 installed at the factory, such as the G3 desktop models, do not include MacLinkPlus. You can buy MacLinkPlus separately and install it on any Mac that has Mac OS 7.6–8.5.

Translation choices

File Exchange or Easy Open goes to work whenever you open a document that wasn't created by any of the applications you have. It doesn't matter how you open the document — by double-clicking its icon in the Finder, choosing it from the Apple menu, or using the Open command in an application.

When you try to open a document created by an application you don't have, File Exchange or Easy Open displays an alert box that lists your alternatives for opening the document. Each alternative identifies an application you have and may also specify an available translator that can translate the document you're opening for that application. A program may be listed more than once, each time with a different translator. For example, if you try to open an old PICT (picture) document created by MacDraw, which you no longer have, the alert might list ClarisWorks three times, once with no translator (ClarisWorks can open PICT documents directly), once with MacLinkPlus translation, and once with QuickTime translation. Figure 7-28 shows an example of the translation choices alert box.

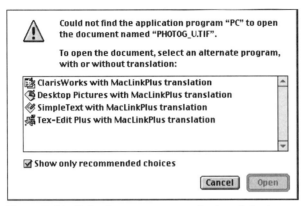

Figure 7-28: Selecting a program and a translator to open a document created by an application you don't have.

In the translation choices alert box, you select a translation alternative that looks promising (ideally a translation for a program closely related to the document) and click the Open button. You can alternatively just double-click a translation alternative. File Exchange or Easy Open applies the selected translator (if any) and has the selected application open the translated document.

You can see more choices in the translation choices alert box by turning off the "Show only recommended choices" option. With this option turned off, a list of all the applications that you have that can conceivably open the file is displayed. If you choose an alternative that's not on the short recommended list, the file probably won't translate well. For example, America Online can open a Word for Windows document, but the document comes across as unformatted text with a bunch of extraneous box characters. Some of the applications in the long list won't even open the file, so in general you save time when you stick with the recommended translations.

File Exchange or Easy Open keeps track of the application and translator that you choose to open each type of document. If you subsequently open another document of the same type, File Exchange or Easy Open automatically selects the same application and translator for you.

File Exchange and Easy Open setup

You can set several options in the File Exchange or Mac OS Easy Open control panel, as shown in Figure 7-29, that affect automatic file translation.

You can turn off automatic file translation altogether. In the File Translation section of the File Exchange control panel, turn off the option "Translate documents automatically." In the Easy Open control panel, set the "Automatic document translation" option to Off.

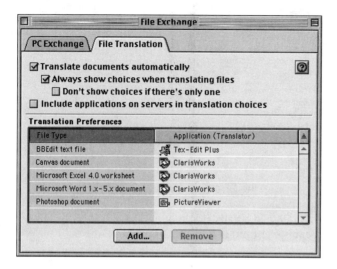

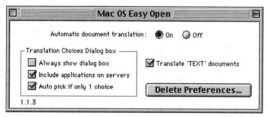

Figure 7-29: Setting automatic file translation options in Mac OS 8.5 (top) or Mac OS 7.6–8.1 (bottom).

You can set either control panel to display the translation choices alert box only the first time that you open a particular type of file. In the File Exchange control panel, turn off the option "Always show choices when translating files." In the Easy Open control panel, turn off the option "Always show dialog box." Turn on the option if you want the alert to appear every time you open a document that wasn't created by an application you have.

Another option lets you suppress the alert when there is only one translation choice. In the File Exchange control panel, turn on the option "Don't show choices if there's only one." In the Easy Access control panel, turn on the option "Auto pick if only 1 choice."

A fourth option controls whether the alert lists applications from file servers, which operate more slowly than applications on your local disks. In the File Exchange control panel, turn on the option "Include applications on servers in translation choices." In the Easy Open control panel, turn on the option "Include applications on servers."

In the Easy Open control panel, turn on the "Translate 'TEXT' documents" option if you want the control panel to look at the contents of the text files you open to see whether those contents can be translated to some type of formatted document. Turning off this option speeds the opening of plain text files, but also causes many PC files to be opened as unformatted text documents by SimpleText. (Many formatted PC files look like plain text files to the Mac OS.) If you want to translate any PC files, you should leave this option turned on.

Translating files with MacLinkPlus

If your computer has the MacLinkPlus software, it automatically expands the translation options you see in the alert box that File Exchange or Mac OS Easy Open displays when you try to open a document created by an application you don't have. Many of the translation options end "with MacLinkPlus translation." If you select one of these, a MacLinkPlus translator will translate the document you want to open. Each translator is a separate file located in the DataViz folder inside the System Folder. It's a good idea to disable MacLinkPlus translators you never use by dragging them to another folder. Disabling translators simplifies the translation choices alert box, decreases the startup time for your computer, and reduces the amount of memory used for the Mac OS.

With MacLinkPlus, you don't have to open a document to translate it. The Document Converter program can use the MacLinkPlus translators to translate a document without opening it. Look for Document Converter in the MacLinkPlus folder on the startup disk.

You use Document Converter to make a separate converter for each type of conversion you want to have on tap. Once you have the right converter, you can drag and drop files onto it to translate them in one step. When you drag a file to a converter, it automatically adds the word converted to the name of the translated file.

To make a converter, first locate the Document Converter and make a duplicate of it. Double-click the duplicate to see a long list of translation options. Scroll through the list to look for the combination of program and translator that you want to make a converter for. Select the program and translator combination you want and click the Set button. You can also just double-click the program and translator combination. Doing so creates a customized converter, renamed to indicate which file format it translates to. Figure 7-30 shows a few of the dozens of choices.

You can configure the MacLinkPlus software with the MacLinkPlus control panel. You choose an option from the Category pop-up menu at the top of the control panel, and then choose a setting for the option from the Preference pop-up menu lower in the control panel. A description of the current Category choice appears in the middle of the control panel. Figure 7-31 shows the MacLinkPlus Setup control panel.

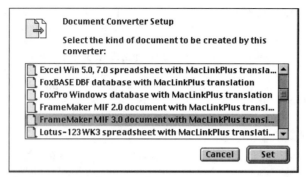

Figure 7-30: Setting up a document converter.

Figure 7-31: The MacLinkPlus Setup control panel.

These are the options you can set with the MacLinkPlus Setup control panel:

✦ **Languages** lets you specify the language used in the documents you are going to translate. This option determines the set of characters available in the document.

✦ **Graphic Clipboard** lets you have the translator automatically place a copy of a converted graphic file onto the Clipboard so that you can simply paste it into a document.

✦ **PCX Color Output** lets you pick the number of colors—256, 16, or monochrome—in documents you are going to translate to PCX format.

✦ **Drawing Size** lets you choose the size of PICT graphics translated from vector-based CGM, CDF, GEM, PIC, and WPG files.

✦ **Bitmap Compression** lets you decide if you want bitmaps to be compressed (using whatever compressor is normally used for the file format being used) or uncompressed.

✦ **Text Translations** lets you specify whether the PC text files you are going to translate use the DOS or Windows character set. If a text file contains extended-ASCII characters (for example, accent marks and symbols), the translator needs to know whether the file came from DOS or Windows, because they have different character sets.

✦ **AutoBullet, AutoNumber & Outlines** lets you indicate whether you want paragraphs that have been formatted for automatic renumbering, automatic bullets, or outlining to be converted to plain text with numbers or bullets, or to retain their original formatting attributes.

Summary

After reading this chapter, you know how to open documents in the Finder by dragging them to any compatible program. You know how to open anything from the Apple menu and the Launcher control panel, and how to have items opened during startup or shutdown. You are familiar with the dialog boxes used by all applications for opening documents and with the similar dialog boxes used by applications for saving new documents and document changes.

When you have more than one program open at the same time, you know how to make any of them active. You can deal with window clutter, and you understand how multiple programs share your computer's memory and work in the background.

You know several ways to create new documents. You can duplicate existing documents or create new ones from scratch with an application's New command. You can also make and use stationery pads for creating new documents.

When you need to find a document, you know that the Sherlock program in Mac OS 8.5 can quickly search the contents of your indexed disks. You know how to index your disks and how to keep the indexes up to date.

Finally, you know how the Mac OS helps you open documents created by applications that you don't have. The File Exchange control panel (Mac OS 8.5) or the PC Exchange control panel (Mac OS 7.6–8.1) enables your computer to use removable disks from Windows and DOS computers, and you can configure the control panel to have your applications automatically open compatible foreign documents according to their DOS file extensions. The File Exchange control panel (Mac OS 8.5) or the Mac OS Easy Open control panel (Mac OS 7.6–8.1) and the MacLinkPlus translation software enable you to open documents that aren't directly compatible with any of your applications.

✦　　　✦　　　✦

Modify Appearance and Behavior

If you don't like the way icons, windows, and menus look and act, there are several things that you can do about it. In the looks department, you can choose the accent and highlight colors that are used in menus, windows, and text. If alternate looks become available, you can change the overall look of menus, icons, windows, and controls in Mac OS 8.5. You can choose the system font that Mac OS 8–8.5 use in menus and titles, and choose a font for icon names and list views in the Finder. Mac OS 8.5 can smooth fonts on the screen. You can pick a desktop pattern or a desktop picture and you can replace individual icons with your own pictures.

In the behavior department, you can change what action makes the Mac OS collapse or expand a window. In Mac OS 8.5, you can also attach sound effects to system actions.

Overall Look

The overall look of windows, menus, and icons is different in various Mac OS versions. Mac OS 7.6–7.6.1 have black-and-white menus, predominantly white windows with some three-dimensional shading, and mostly two-dimensional icons. Mac OS 8–8.1 have what Apple calls the *platinum appearance*. This look is what you see in Mac OS 8.5 as well, but you will be able to choose a different look if alternate appearances become available. The platinum look features gray menus with color accents and three-dimensional shading. Many windows are also gray, and all have a lot of three-dimensional detail. In addition, the icons that represent folders, disks, and some files have the appearance of depth.

Choosing an appearance in Mac OS 8.5

Mac OS 8.5 can change its appearance much as you can change your outfit. These capabilities are useless without alternate appearances for Mac OS 8.5 or new outfits for you. Mac OS 8.5 does not come with alternate appearances, but it does provide the capability to change its appearance if Apple ever makes alternate appearances available. (An alternate appearance consists of a set of files that you put in the Appearance folder by dragging the files to the System Folder icon.) If you had a choice of appearances, you could pick one in the Appearance control panel. At the top of this control panel, you would click the Appearance tab and then choose the look you wanted from the Appearance pop-up menu. Figure 8-1 shows the location of this pop-up menu.

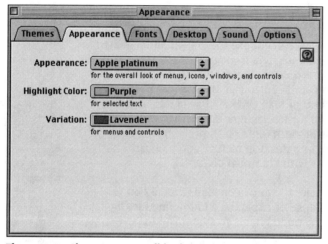

Figure 8-1: Choose an overall look for Mac OS 8.5 in the Appearance section of the Appearance control panel. (Mac OS 8.5 includes only the "Apple platinum" appearance.)

Systemwide platinum appearance in Mac OS 8–8.1

When Mac OS 8–8.1 apply the platinum appearance to all programs, you may notice some cosmetic flaws in older programs. These flaws are harmless, but if you don't want to see them, you can turn off systemwide platinum appearance with the Appearance control panel. (This function is not available in Mac OS 8.5.)

To turn the systemwide platinum appearance on or off, click the Options button on the left side of the Appearance control panel. Then on the right side of the control panel, turn the option "System-wide platinum appearance" on or off. You must restart your computer for a change to take effect. Figure 8-2 shows the Options section of the Appearance control panel.

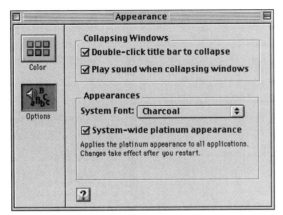

Figure 8-2: Set the systemwide platinum appearance
with the Appearance control panel in Mac OS 8–8.1.

If you make changes to the systemwide platinum appearance because it causes
problems with a program, contact the program's publisher to see if an updated
version is available.

Accent and Highlight Colors

The Mac OS uses color to accent menus and some window controls, and it uses
color to highlight text that you have selected. You can choose the color for text
highlighting. Depending on the Mac OS version you use and the current overall
appearance (in Mac OS 8.5 only), you may also be able to choose an accent color.

Variation and highlight color for Mac OS 8.5

In Mac OS 8.5, a highlight color for text is chosen by using the Appearance control
panel. If you are using the platinum appearance, you can choose a variation color in
this control panel, which highlights a menu item when you point at it and decorates
scroll boxes and other controls. You may not be able to choose a variation color
with other appearances, if any ever become available.

To set these colors, click the Appearance tab at the top of the Appearance control
panel. The Highlight Color pop-up menu lists nine colors and the option to mix your
own color. The Variation pop-up menu, if available, lists colors that are defined for
the overall look currently chosen in the Appearance pop-up menu. Figure 8-3 shows
the location of these pop-up menus.

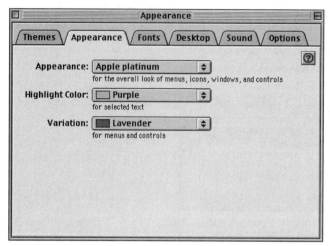

Figure 8-3: Set the Highlight Color or Variation in the Appearance section of the Appearance control panel in Mac OS 8.5.

Accent and highlight color for Mac OS 8–8.1

In Mac OS 8–8.1, you use the Appearance control panel to choose an accent color for controls or a highlight color for text. To set these colors, click the Color button at the top of the Appearance control panel. A sample of the current accent color is shown and you can scroll to see 17 alternatives; click one to make it the accent color. A pop-up menu lists possible highlight colors; choose the one you want to use. Figure 8-4 shows the Color section of the Appearance control panel.

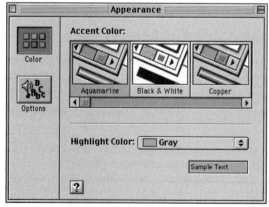

Figure 8-4: Set the accent color or highlight color with the Appearance control panel in Mac OS 8–8.1.

Setting the accent color to Black & White effectively disables the normal platinum appearance of Mac OS 8–8.1. The resulting high-contrast display is easier to see in poor light, such as when you use a PowerBook outdoors.

Window and highlight color for Mac OS 7.6–7.6.1

You can choose a window color or text highlight color with the Color control panel in Mac OS versions 7.6–7.6.1. For windows, a pop-up menu lists eight colors and black and white. Another pop-up menu lists eight colors, black and white, and the option to mix your own text highlight color. Figure 8-5 shows the choices in the Color control panel.

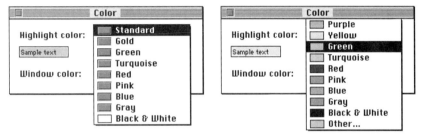

Figure 8-5: Set the window color (left) or highlight color (right) with the Color control panel in Mac OS 7.6–7.6.1.

The window color you choose does not apply to tool palettes and special-purpose windows created by some application programs. Although you can create your own text highlight color, you can't create your own window-shading color by using the Color control panel.

System Fonts

You have a choice of system fonts in Mac OS 8–8.5. You can choose the large system font that Mac OS 8–8.5 use for window titles, menus, buttons, and dialog boxes. Mac OS 8.5 also includes a pop-up menu for choosing the small system font, which is used for explanatory text and labels, but does not include alternative small system fonts.

CAUTION

Some Programs Require Chicago

There are some older programs that won't open when the system font set to anything other than Chicago. If this happens, change the system font to Chicago in the Appearance control panel. Contact the publisher of the program to see if an updated version is available that works with system fonts other than Chicago.

System fonts for Mac OS 8.5

To choose the system fonts for Mac OS 8.5, click the Fonts tab at the top of the Appearance control panel. The choices are listed in the Large System Font pop-up menu and the Small pop-up menu. Figure 8-6 shows the location of these pop-up menus.

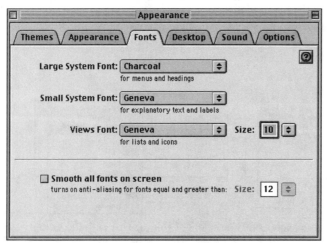

Figure 8-6: Set the Large System Font and the Small System Font in the Fonts section of the Appearance control panel in Mac OS 8.5.

System font for Mac OS 8–8.1

In Mac OS 8–8.1, you have two choices for the system font. You can choose the Charcoal font, which was introduced as part of the platinum appearance, or you can use the classic Chicago font. To set the system font, click the Options button on the left side of the Appearance control panel. Then on the right side of the control panel, choose a font from the System Font pop-up menu. A change takes effect after you restart your computer.

Font Smoothing

Mac OS 8.5 can improve the looks of text displayed on screen by smoothing the edges of fonts. Font smoothing works by blending the edges of text with the background, a technique known as *antialiasing*. To set font smoothing, click the Fonts tab of the Appearance control panel and turn on the option "Smooth all fonts on screen" (previously shown in Figure 8-6). The adjacent Size pop-up menu lets you choose a minimum font size for font smoothing. Font smoothing may make small font sizes blurry. In this case, increase the minimum font size for font smoothing.

Font smoothing can affect system performance. If you notice that it takes longer to display text on the screen and the slowdown bothers you, try increasing the minimum font size for smoothing, or turn off font smoothing altogether in the Appearance control panel.

Font smoothing may disfigure text in some applications. You may notice blemishes in highlighted text, especially when the text highlight color is set to black. You may see text alternate between smoothed and not. Or you may find text drawn incorrectly on a background that is not white. If you think font smoothing makes text unsightly or harder to read in one of your programs, turn off font smoothing and ask the publisher of the program if there is an update that fixes the problem.

Desktop Background

When it comes to the overall appearance of the screen, nothing has more impact than changing the desktop's background. In addition to changing the background pattern, with Mac OS 8–8.5 you have the option of covering the pattern with a picture. You set the desktop background with the Appearances control panel (Mac OS 8.5), the Desktop Picture control panel (Mac OS 8–8.1), or the Desktop Patterns control panel (Mac OS 7.6–7.6.1).

Desktop pattern in Mac OS 8.5

To change the desktop pattern in Mac OS 8.5, click the Desktop tab in the Appearance control panel. Select a pattern by name from the scrolling list on the right side of the control panel and look at the sample displayed on the left side of the control panel. If you can't see a pattern because a picture is covering it, there will be a Remove Picture button, which you can click to reveal the pattern sample. When you see a pattern you like, click the Set Desktop button to make that pattern the desktop pattern. Figure 8-7 shows a desktop pattern in the Mac OS 8.5 Appearance control panel.

You can remove the currently selected pattern from the control panel by choosing Cut or Clear from the Edit menu. After cutting a pattern, use the Paste command to store it in the Scrapbook.

To modify one of the patterns, first copy it by choosing Copy from the Edit menu. Then open a paint program and paste the copied image into it by choosing Paste from the Edit menu. Make changes to the pasted pattern with the program's painting tools and commands. Select the modified pattern in the paint program and use the Copy command to make a copy of it. Return to the Background section of the Appearance control panel and use the Paste command to add the copied pattern to the set of available desktop patterns.

You can create a new desktop pattern with a graphics program, a scanner, or other graphics source. Select the image you want to use as a desktop pattern, copy it, switch to the Background section of the Appearance control panel, and paste it.

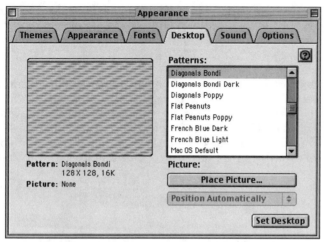

Figure 8-7: Set a desktop pattern in the Desktop section of the Appearance control panel in Mac OS 8.5.

After pasting a pattern into the Background section of the Appearance control panel, you can name it by choosing Pattern Name from the Edit menu. (You can't use this command to change the name of a preinstalled pattern.)

Desktop picture in Mac OS 8.5

To set or remove a picture as the desktop background in Mac OS 8.5, click the Desktop tab in the Appearance control panel. Then use the Place Picture or Remove Picture button and the pop-up menu near the bottom of the control panel. The control panel shows a reduced view of the current desktop picture or a sample of the current desktop pattern if there is currently no desktop picture. Figure 8-8 is a sample picture in the Mac OS 8.5 Appearance control panel.

If the control panel shows a desktop picture that you don't want to use, click the Remove Picture button. The Remove Picture button then changes to a Place Picture button, and the control panel displays a sample of the desktop pattern that's currently set.

When the control panel shows a sample of the current desktop pattern, you can select a picture to overlay it by clicking the Place Picture button. The control panel displays a Navigation Services dialog box in which you select a picture file that you want to use as a desktop picture. The button labeled Show Preview or Hide Preview controls the display of picture previews on the right side of the dialog box. (For more information on the Navigation Services dialog box, see "Opening Programs, Documents, and More" in Chapter 7.) Figure 8-9 is an example of the dialog box in which you select a desktop picture file.

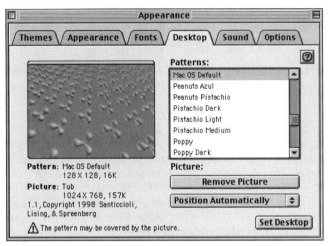

Figure 8-8: Set a desktop picture in the Desktop section of the Appearance control panel in Mac OS 8.5.

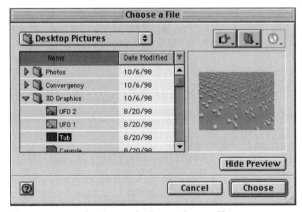

Figure 8-9: Selecting a desktop picture file.

The position of the currently selected picture on the screen can be adjusted by using the pop-up menu below the Remove Picture button in the control panel. This setting compensates for any difference between the size of the screen and the size of the selected picture. The Position Automatically setting uses optional alignment and positioning information stored in the picture file by the person who created the picture. If the picture doesn't have that information, the control panel scales the picture to fit the screen without changing the picture's aspect ratio. If you choose a different setting, you can see the effect by looking at the reduced view in the control panel.

Mac OS 8.5 comes with a collection of pictures for the desktop background. They're located in the Desktop Pictures folder that is inside the Appearance folder in your System Folder. You can also use picture files from other folders and disks.

To have Mac OS 8.5 randomly choose a different desktop picture each time you restart the computer, drag a folder of pictures to the sample desktop area of the control panel.

If the picture you select for a desktop picture is on a CD or other removable disk that is not available the next time you start or restart the computer, the desktop pattern is displayed instead. If you want your desktop picture to always be available, copy it to your hard disk and select that copy with the Appearance control panel.

If you have selected a desktop picture and your computer runs low on memory, you may notice the screen redrawing slowly after you close a window. If this happens, try using a desktop pattern instead of the desktop picture.

Desktop pattern in Mac OS 8–8.1

To set a desktop pattern in Mac OS 8–8.1, click the Pattern button in the Desktop Pictures control panel. The control panel shows one pattern from the set of available patterns; you can page through the available patterns by clicking the scroll arrows. When you see a pattern you like, click the Set Desktop button to make that pattern the desktop pattern. Figure 8-10 shows the desktop pattern controls in the Mac OS 8–8.1 Desktop Picture control panel.

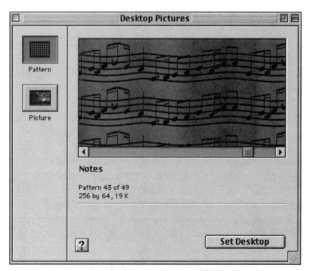

Figure 8-10: Set a desktop pattern with the Desktop Pictures control panel in Mac OS 8–8.1.

You can remove the pattern currently displayed in the control panel by choosing Cut or Clear from the Edit menu. After cutting a pattern, use the Paste command to store it in the Scrapbook.

To modify one of the patterns, first copy it by choosing Copy from the Edit menu. Then open a paint program and paste the copied image into it by choosing Paste from the Edit menu. Make changes to the pasted pattern with the program's painting tools and commands. Select the modified pattern in the paint program, and use the Copy command to make a copy of it. Return to the Pattern section of the Desktop Pictures control panel and use the Paste command to add the copied pattern to the set of available desktop patterns.

You can create a new desktop pattern with a graphics program, a scanner, or other graphics source. Select the image you want to use as a desktop pattern, copy it, switch to the Desktop Picture control panel, and paste.

After pasting a pattern into the Desktop Pictures control panel, you can name it with the Edit Pattern Name command in the Edit menu. (You can't use this command to change the name of a preinstalled pattern.)

Desktop picture in Mac OS 8–8.1

To set or remove a picture as the desktop background in Mac OS 8–8.1, click the Picture button in the Desktop Pictures control panel. The control panel shows a reduced view of the current desktop picture or a sample of the current desktop pattern if there is currently no desktop picture. You use the controls at the bottom of the control panel to set a picture as the desktop background. Figure 8-11 is a sample picture in the Desktop Picture control panel.

If the control panel shows a desktop picture that you don't want to use, click the Remove Picture button. The Remove Picture button then changes to a Select Picture button and the control panel displays a sample of the desktop pattern that's currently set.

When the control panel shows a sample of the current desktop pattern, you can select a picture to overlay it by clicking the Select Picture button. The control panel displays a standard Open dialog box in which you select a picture file that you want to use as a desktop picture. A checkbox at the bottom of the dialog box controls the display of picture previews on the left side of the dialog box. (For more information on the Open dialog box, see "Opening Programs, Documents, and More" in Chapter 7.) Figure 8-12 is an example of the dialog box in which you select a desktop picture file.

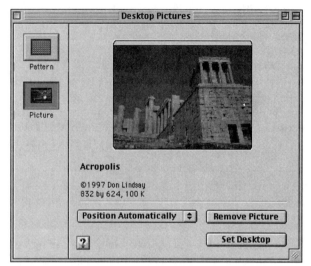

Figure 8-11: Set a desktop picture with the Desktop Pictures control panel in Mac OS 8–8.1.

Figure 8-12: Selecting a desktop picture file in Mac OS 8–8.1.

You can adjust the position of the currently selected picture on the screen by using the pop-up menu next to the Remove Picture button in the control panel. This setting compensates for any difference between the size of the screen and the size of the selected picture. The setting Position Automatically uses optional alignment and positioning information stored in the picture file by the person who created the picture. If the picture doesn't have that information, the control panel scales the picture to fit the screen without changing the picture's aspect ratio. If you choose a different setting, looking at the reduced view in the control panel shows its effect.

To have Mac OS 8–8.1 randomly choose a different desktop picture each time you restart the computer, drag a folder of pictures to the sample desktop area of the control panel.

If the picture you select for a desktop picture is on a CD or other removable disk that is not available the next time you start or restart the computer, the desktop pattern is displayed instead. If you want your desktop picture to always be available, copy it to your hard disk and select that copy with the Desktop Picture control panel.

If you have selected a desktop picture and your computer runs low on memory, you may notice the screen redrawing slowly after you close a window. If this happens, try using a desktop pattern instead of the desktop picture.

Desktop pattern in Mac OS 7.6–7.6.1

With Mac OS 7.6–7.6.1, you can select a desktop pattern from the Desktop Patterns control panel. It displays a sample of one desktop pattern from a set of available patterns, and you can scroll through the available patterns. Two numbers below the large sample of the pattern tell you which of the total number of available patterns you are seeing. When you see a pattern you want to use, click the Set Desktop Pattern button at the bottom of the window. Figure 8-13 shows the Desktop Pattern control panel.

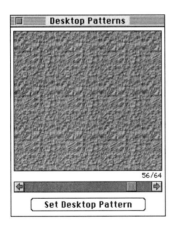

Figure 8-13: Set a desktop pattern with the Desktop Patterns control panel in Mac OS 7.6–7.6.1.

You can use the Cut, Copy, and Paste commands from the Edit menu to remove a pattern, copy it to a painting program for editing, or insert a new pattern copied from a graphics program.

With the Desktop Patterns control panel, you can also change the pattern that appears in the background of utility program windows such as Find File, Calculator, and Scrapbook. Here's how: Open the Desktop Patterns control panel and scroll to find a pattern that you like. Press Option to change the Set Desktop Pattern button to Set Utilities Pattern and click the button. Whatever pattern you set will be the same for all the utility windows; you can't set a different pattern for each utility.

Scroll Bar Controls

Scroll arrows and the scroll box are little things — too little and not as useful as they could be, some people say. If you agree and you use Mac OS 8.5, you can replace the single scroll arrows at both ends of every scroll bar with double scroll arrows at one end or both ends of every scroll bar. With double scroll arrows, you can scroll in either direction without moving the mouse pointer to the opposite end of the scroll bar.

You can also make the scroll box grow to indicate how much of a window's contents the window is displaying at its current size. A long scroll box means you can see most of the window's contents without scrolling, and a short scroll box means you need to scroll a lot to see all of the window's contents. A scroll bar with this type of scroll box is called a *proportional scroll bar*.

If you want double scroll arrows and a proportional scroll bar, click the Options tab of the Appearance control panel and turn on the Smart Scrolling option. Figure 8-14 shows this option in the Mac OS 8.5 Appearance control panel.

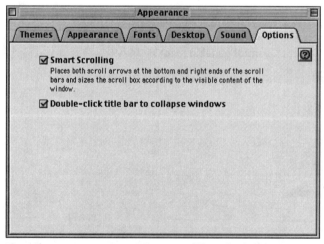

Figure 8-14: Set up Mac OS 8.5 scroll bars in the Options section of the Appearance control panel.

Sound Effects

Not only can you make Mac OS 8.5 look different, you can make it sound off when you do things with menus, windows, controls, and the icons of files, folders, and disks. Different sounds may accompany various actions in each of these categories. An entire set of related sounds is called a *sound track*. You can choose a sound track from among those installed on your computer, and you can turn sound effects on or off for the various action categories. (Mac OS 8.5 comes with only one sound track, Platinum Sounds. If Apple ever releases other sound track files, they go in the Sound Sets folder that is in the Appearance folder inside your System Folder.)

If your computer has stereo speakers, the sound effects are heard in stereo. The stereo sounds actually emanate from different locations as the mouse pointer moves from one side of the screen to the other while performing an action that has a sound effect.

To set sound effects, click the Sound tab in the Appearance control panel, choose a sound track from the pop-up menu, and use the checkboxes to turn sound effects on or off for each sound category. To turn off all sound effects, choose None from the pop-up menu. Figure 8-15 shows the Sound section of the Appearance control panel.

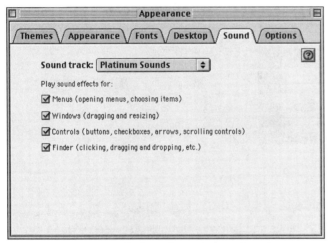

Figure 8-15: Set sound effects for various actions in Mac OS 8.5 in the Sound section of the Appearance control panel.

Collapsing Windows

It's up to you whether windows expand and collapse when you double-click their title bars. In Mac OS 7.6–8.1, you can also decide whether to hear special sound effects whenever you collapse or expand a window. In Mac OS 8.5, you can decide whether to hear all window sound effects or none; you don't have separate control over the sound effect for collapsing and expanding a window.

To control the collapsing window behavior in Mac OS 8.5, click the Options tab of the Appearance control panel and set the option "Double-click title bar to collapse windows" (previously shown in Figure 8-14). The option for hearing window sound effects, including the collapsing and expanding sound, is in the Sound section of the Appearance control panel (described in the previous section of this chapter).

You control the collapsing window behavior of Mac OS 8–8.1 with two clearly labeled checkboxes in the Options section of the Appearance control panel (previously shown in Figure 8-2).

In Mac OS 7.6–7.6.1, collapsing window behavior is controlled with the WindowShade control panel. In this control panel, you can set the number of times you must click a window's title bar to hide the window (or show the window if it's already hidden). You can designate one or more keys that you must press while clicking a window's title bar for WindowShade to do its work. You can also turn sound effects on or off. Figure 8-16 shows the WindowShade control panel in Mac OS 7.6–7.6.1.

Figure 8-16: Set up window collapsing with the WindowShade control panel in Mac OS 7.6–7.6.1.

Themes

Put together all the appearance and behavior options discussed so far and you have a group of settings that Mac OS 8.5 calls a *theme*. You can add your own themes to the preconfigured themes that come with Mac OS 8.5 and switch themes any time you like. When you switch to a different theme, you put in effect all its settings for overall look (appearance), variation color, text highlight color, system fonts, font smoothing, desktop background, scroll bars, sound effects, and collapsing windows.

To switch themes or to make your current settings a new theme, click the Themes tab in the Appearance control panel. Then you can scroll through previews of the available themes and click one that you want to put into effect. A theme goes into effect as soon as you click its preview in the control panel. Clicking the Save Theme button creates a new theme from the current settings in all the other sections of the Appearance control panel. Figure 8-17 shows the Theme section of the Appearance control panel.

If you click the Save Theme button, the Appearance control panel displays a dialog box in which you can type a name for the theme you're creating. You can change the name of any theme you have created by selecting its preview and choosing Theme Name from the Edit menu. You can't change the names of preconfigured themes.

To remove a theme, select its preview in the Appearance control panel and choose Clear from the Edit menu.

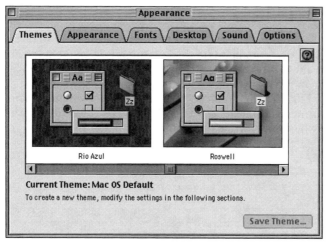

Figure 8-17: Select a theme or create a new one in the Theme section of the Appearance control panel in Mac OS 8.5.

Custom Icons

Would you like to see dinosaurs or hummingbirds on your desktop instead of ordinary icons? The Mac OS lets you replace the icons of individual documents, programs, folders, and disks with your own pictures. Figure 8-18 shows some examples of custom icons.

Figure 8-18: Icons your way.

There are free icon collections available on the Internet, from online information services such as America Online, and from user groups. You can also make icons from clip art that you get from those sources or on disk. You can even create your own icons with a graphics program.

Installing a custom icon

To replace an icon with a picture, first select the picture that you want to use for the icon and copy it with the Copy command (in the Edit menu). Then go to the Finder and find the icon you want to replace. Select the icon (click it once) and choose Get Info from the File menu. In the Info window, click the icon to select it and use the Paste command (in the Edit menu) to replace it with the picture you just copied. You can also copy an icon from an Info window and paste it into a different Info window. Figure 8-19 shows Info windows with custom icons.

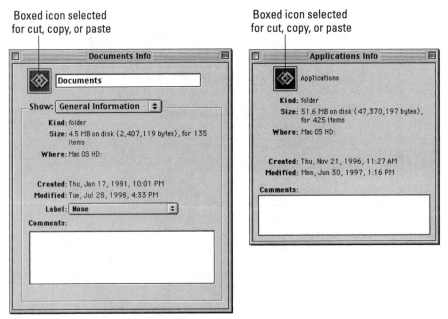

Figure 8-19: A custom icon pasted into an item's Info window in Mac OS 8.5 (left) and Mac OS 8–8.1 (right).

For best results, the picture you use for a custom icon should measure 32 x 32 pixels (dots). Multiples of this size, such as 64 x 64, 128 x 128, or 256 x 256, may also yield acceptable results. If your picture is larger than 32 x 32, the Finder reduces it proportionally to fit that amount of space when you replace an icon with it. Reducing a picture distorts it, especially if the original size is an odd or fractional multiple of the final size. If your picture is smaller than 32 x 32, the Finder centers it on a white 32 x 32 square.

If you duplicate or make an alias of an item with a custom icon, the duplicate or alias inherits the custom icon. (To learn about duplicating items, see Chapter 5. To learn about making an alias, see Chapter 12.)

You cannot replace the icon of a locked item, open document, or open program. Nor can you replace system software icons such as the System Folder, the Finder, Control Panels folder, and Trash. (You can replace individual control panel icons, however.)

Reverting to a standard icon

To revert to an item's standard icon, select the icon in the item's Info window and choose Clear or Cut from the Edit menu.

Summary

In this chapter, you learned how you can modify the appearance and behavior of the Mac OS. You can choose accent and text highlight colors. You can select a desktop pattern or, in Mac OS 8–8.5, a desktop picture. In Mac OS 8.5, you can also choose system fonts, set up font smoothing, configure scroll arrows and scroll boxes, and select sound effects. You can also select a group of settings all at once by choosing a theme in Mac OS 8.5. In addition, you can replace each icon with a custom picture.

✦　　✦　　✦

Get Help Onscreen

If you have a question about something displayed on your computer, or you aren't sure how to accomplish a task, the Mac OS provides three onscreen help systems. One help system briefly describes objects you point at on the screen. Another help system, available only in Mac OS 8.5, explains how to perform common tasks. You can search the text of this help and you can follow live cross-references in it by clicking them. A third help system interactively guides you step-by-step through tasks. In addition to the help you can get from the Mac OS, many application programs also provide onscreen help.

Help Menu and Help Buttons

The Mac OS provides onscreen help through the Help menu (referred to as the Guide menu in Mac OS 7.6–7.6.1). This menu lists the kinds of help that are available in the program you are currently using. The kind of help that you can get varies from program to program. You can always get balloon help (described in the next section), although it may be very limited. Additional commands in the Help menu may provide help through the Help Viewer program or through Apple Guide (each described in later sections of this chapter). Figure 9-1 shows examples of Help menus.

As a convenience, some control panels and other programs include a Help button that you can click to get help specifically about the part of the control panel or program that you are currently using. The Help button is a square button with a distinctive question mark on it. Clicking a Help button displays help that is relevant to the context in which the Help button appears. The help may be provided in the Help Viewer program (Mac OS 8.5 only) or by Apple Guide; both are described in later sections of this chapter. Figure 9-2 shows examples of the Help button.

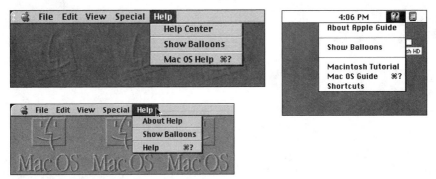

Figure 9-1: Get help onscreen with the Help menu in Mac OS 8.5 (top left) and Mac OS 8–8.1 (bottom left), or with the Guide menu in Mac OS 7.6–7.6.1 (right).

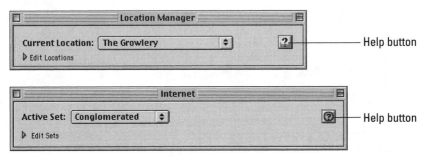

Figure 9-2: Get help by clicking a Help button.

Balloon Help

When you need immediate information about objects that you see onscreen, you can turn on Mac OS *balloon help*. With balloon help on, you position the pointer over an object and a concise description of it appears in a cartoon-style balloon. The balloon points to the object and tells you what the object is, what it does, what happens when you click it, or some portion of this information. You do not have to press any keys or click anything to make help balloons appear. Figure 9-3 shows an example of balloon help.

The Mac OS provides balloon help capability, but not all objects have help balloons. Many applications provide no balloon help at all (more on that shortly).

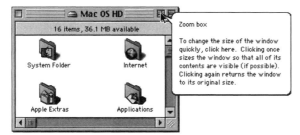

Figure 9-3: A help balloon describes the object under the pointer.

Turning balloon help on and off

You turn on balloon help by choosing Show Balloons from the Help menu. That command then changes to Hide Balloons, and choosing it again turns off balloon help. You can display balloon help by pressing keys if you install the shareware program Helium from Tiger Technologies (described in Chapter 26).

Working with balloon help on

Everything works normally when balloon help is on. Using balloon help does not put the Mac OS into help-only mode. It's similar to someone is standing over your shoulder and describing onscreen objects to you.

Help balloons appear whether or not you press the mouse button. You click, double-click, and otherwise use programs normally, except that you may perceive a slight delay as help balloons come and go when you move the pointer slowly across items that have balloon help descriptions.

The object that a help balloon describes may be large or small and individual or collective. For example, the Close box in the active window's title bar has its own help balloon. In contrast, an inactive window has one balloon for the whole window. Sometimes a help balloon describes a group of items. For example, one balloon tells you about all the scrolling controls in a scroll bar. Figure 9-4 shows the help balloons for a Close box and a scroll bar.

Figure 9-4: Help balloons vary in scope.

Moving the pointer slowly over several objects that have help balloons opens and closes balloons in sequence. To prevent excessive flashing of help balloons, they do not appear when you move the pointer quickly. For a help balloon to appear, the pointer must be in the same area for about one-tenth of a second or longer. You cannot change this timing.

What balloon help knows

Balloon help knows about all standard objects in the Mac OS. They include windows in general; system software icons; the Apple menu; the Help menu; the Application menu; standard parts of Open, Save, and Navigation Services dialog boxes (all of which described in Chapter 7); and the Page Setup and Print dialog boxes (described in Chapter 15). Balloon help cannot describe a specific program's menu commands, window contents, dialog boxes, and so on unless the program's developer or publisher has included the necessary information. For example, Apple has provided complete balloon help for the Finder, standard control panels, and many of the accessory and utility programs that come with the Mac OS.

Help Viewer

When you need more information in Mac OS 8.5 than balloon help provides, you can use the Help Viewer program to find and read short how-to articles. You can find help by browsing a table of contents or by searching for words that describe the help you need. Most of the articles you read have links that you can click to see related material. These links will be familiar to people who browse the Internet's World Wide Web, although you don't need to know how to use Web links to use the Help Viewer.

The Help Viewer is the main means of providing system-level how-to help in Mac OS 8.5. You can also get help on AppleScript via the Help Viewer in Mac OS 8.5. (For details on AppleScript, see Chapter 23.)

Displaying the Help Viewer

You can display the Help Viewer by choosing Help Center or Mac OS Help from the Help menu while you are using the Finder in Mac OS 8.5. If you choose Help Center, you see a list of all the help sections available in the Help Viewer. If you choose Mac OS Help, you see a list of system-level help categories. If these commands are not in the Help menu, choose Finder from the Application menu at the right end of the menu bar. Figure 9-5 shows what you see when you choose Help Center or Mac OS Help.

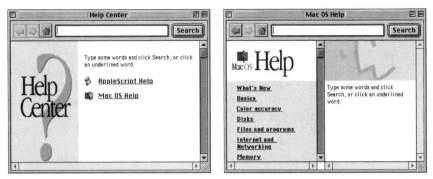

Figure 9-5: From the Help menu in Mac OS 8.5, choose Help Center to see a list of help sections (left) or choose Mac OS Help to see a list of system-level help categories (right).

Browsing Help Viewer links

All the underlined words you see in the Help Viewer are links that you can click to see related material. For example, if you choose Mac OS Help from the Help menu and then click one of the underlined help categories, you see a list of relevant topics. Clicking an underlined topic displays the article in the Help Viewer. Articles may also contain underlined links. Figure 9-6 is an example of browsing links in the Help Viewer.

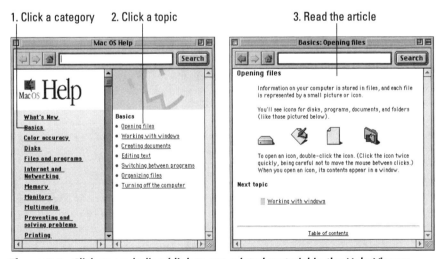

Figure 9-6: Click an underlined link to see related material in the Help Viewer.

Links in articles can take you to many places inside the Help Viewer and outside it. A link may show you another article in the Help Viewer window. A link that begins "Open..." probably opens the program that the article describes. A link that includes an Internet address probably connects to the Internet and shows you a page on the Web (after first asking whether you want to do this). A link may also display interactive, step-by-step help in an Apple Guide window (described later in this section). A link labeled "Table of contents" invariably shows you the list of help categories and topics that the article is part of. If the author of the help article writes clearly, you'll have a good idea about where the link will take you.

Besides clicking links, you can go places by clicking the picture buttons in the Help Viewer. Click the left-arrow (←) button to go back to the previous page in the Help Viewer. After going back, you can click the right-arrow (→) button to go forward. Click the Home button to go to the Help Center page.

If you go back to a page you have seen previously during your current session with the Help Viewer, note that the links you previously visited are green instead of blue.

Searching Help Viewer

If you're looking for help on a specific subject and don't want to browse through links until you find it, you can have the Help Viewer search all its articles for the help you need. To search, type some words that describe the subject and click the Search button. After a few seconds, the Help Viewer displays a list of topics that may help you. It ranks the topics according to their relevance, from five stars (most relevant) to one star (least relevant). Figure 9-7 shows an example of a search in the Help Viewer.

Figure 9-7: Search the Help Viewer for words that describe the help you need.

When typing words to search for, you can include special characters to more precisely describe the subject. Table 9-1 describes these special characters.

	Table 9-1 Special Characters for Help Viewer Searching		
Character	**Meaning**	**Search Example**	**Search Results**
+	and	picture + pattern	This example finds articles that include both "picture" and "pattern"
|	or	picture | pattern	This example finds articles that include either "picture" or "pattern"
!	not	picture ! pattern	This example finds articles that include "picture" but exclude "pattern"
( )	grouping	background + (picture | pattern)	This example finds articles that include "background" and either "picture" or "pattern"

Apple Guide

Apple Guide is another form of how-to help that is available in Mac OS 7.6–8.5 for some programs. Apple Guide shows and tells you how to get things done while you actually do them. Step-by-step instructions appear in a guide window, which floats above all other windows. As you move from step to step, Apple Guide may coach you by marking an object onscreen with a circle, arrow, or underline. Figure 9-8 is an example of an Apple Guide instruction and coaching mark.

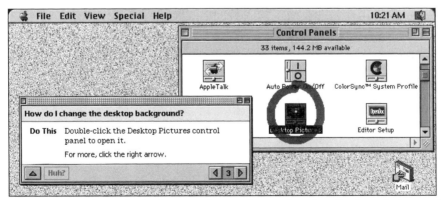

Figure 9-8: Apple Guide displays step-by-step instructions in a floating window and draws coaching marks to point out objects onscreen.

Apple Guide watches what you do and can adjust its steps if you work ahead or make a mistake. In some cases, Apple Guide will actually perform a simple operation for you, such as opening a control panel.

Notice that the Apple Guide window has a zoom box; in Mac OS 8–8.5, it also has a collapse box. You can use these controls to temporarily shrink the window so you can see what's underneath it, and then use them again to restore the window.

Apple Guide is the primary method for delivering how-to help on a broad range of system-related topics in Mac OS 7.6–8.1, but Mac OS 8.5 relies more heavily on the Help Viewer program (described previously). It's also available for SimpleText, AppleCD Audio Player, and some other programs that come with Mac OS 7.6–8.5. Some programs from companies other than Apple also use Apple Guide, but many do not. Program developers and system administrators can create additional help, which can cover tasks that involve multiple applications. Apple Guide's usefulness depends greatly on how well-crafted the help procedures for individual tasks are. Apple has set a good example with its system-level help procedures.

Displaying Apple Guide

While you are using a program that has Apple Guide help, you can generally display it by choosing a command from the Help menu (Mac OS 8–8.5) or the Guide menu (Mac OS 7.6–7.6.1). For example, while you're using Finder in Mac OS 8–8.1, choosing Help from the Help menu displays Apple Guide for system-related topics. While using Finder in Mac OS 7.6–7.6.1, you choose Mac OS Guide from the Guide menu. If you don't see these commands in the Help or Guide menu, choose Finder from the Applications menu at the right end of the menu bar and look again.

While using the Finder in Mac OS 8.5, the Help menu commands don't display Apple Guide help. Instead they display help in the Help Viewer program described in the previous section of this chapter. In the Help Viewer, a few underlined words are linked to specific Apple Guide help topics. Clicking one of these links brings up Apple Guide. These links typically begin with the phrase "Help me...," but there's no way to tell for sure which underlined words are linked to Apple Guide.

If you're using a program other than the Finder, look for a Help menu command that begins with the name of the program and ends with the word Guide, such as SimpleText Guide. If the Help menu lists only the About Help and Show Balloons commands, then the program you're using doesn't have Apple Guide help.

You can also display Apple Guide help from some control panels by clicking a button labeled with a question mark. However, the Help button often displays the Help Viewer program in Mac OS 8.5.

In many cases, the first thing Apple Guide displays is a topics window. A title at the top of the window tells you what software the help covers. For example, Mac OS Help covers a broad variety of system-related topics, but SimpleText Guide covers only topics related to SimpleText.

Secrets

Taking a Picture of Apple Guide

When using Apple Guide help, you can copy a picture of the Guide window to the Clipboard by pressing the Option key and clicking the panel. This function does not work in all Guide windows, and it does not apply to help windows that are not based on Apple Guide. Examples of help based on Apple Guide include Mac OS Help (Mac OS 8–8.1) and Mac OS Guide (Mac OS 7.6–7.6.1). Most application-specific online help is not based on Apple Guide.

The Apple Guide topics window generally includes three large buttons labeled Topics, Index, and Look For. You click one of those buttons to choose how you want to find help: by scanning a list of topics, by browsing an index, or by looking for words in the Guide. One of the three methods probably suits you better than the others, but try them all if you have trouble finding the help you need by using your favorite method.

The Apple Guide help that comes with some programs doesn't include the Topics, Index, and Look For buttons. An example is the AppleCD Audio Player program, which comes with Mac OS 7.6–8.5 and that offers only scanning by topic.

Browsing Apple Guide topics

To see a list of help topics, click the Topics button at the top of the Apple Guide topics window. Clicking a topic on the left side of the topics window displays a list of specific tasks and terms on the right side. If the list on the right includes headings in bold, you can show and hide a heading's subordinate phrases by clicking the disclosure triangle next to the heading. Figure 9-9 is an example of scanning Apple Guide topics with some headings expanded and others collapsed.

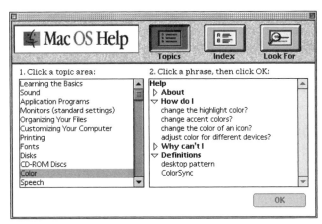

Figure 9-9: Scanning the list of topics in Apple Guide.

Browsing the Apple Guide index

To browse an Apple Guide index, click the Index button in the Apple Guide topics window. Apple Guide displays an alphabetical list of key terms used in the guide. You can scroll through the index with the scroll bar. You can type the first part of a term you want to look up in the index, and the index instantly scrolls to the index entry that most closely matches what you typed. You can also scroll the index to entries starting with a particular letter of the alphabet by dragging the pointer at the top of the index list to that letter or by simply clicking that letter. You can't see all 26 letters of the alphabet at the top of the index list, but you can see more by clicking and dragging the pointer slightly past the last letter you can see. Clicking an entry in the index displays a list of tasks in which that entry appears. Figure 9-10 is an example of browsing an Apple Guide index.

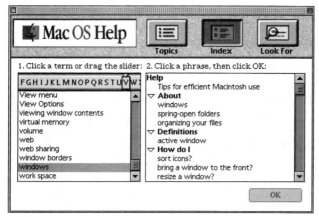

Figure 9-10: Browsing an index in Apple Guide.

Searching Apple Guide for key words

To have Apple Guide look for words you specify, click the Look For button in the Apple Guide topics window. Then on the left side of the window click the arrow button and type a key word or two that describe the step-by-step instructions you want to see. When you click the Search button (or press Return or Enter) a list of relevant tasks appears. Figure 9-11 is an example of searching Apple Guide for a key word.

Following step-by-step instructions

When you double-click an item on the right side of the Apple Guide topics window (or select the item and click OK), the topics window goes away. After a brief pause, another Guide window appears with an introduction to the task or a definition of the term you selected in the topics window. Figure 9-12 is an example of the step-by-step window.

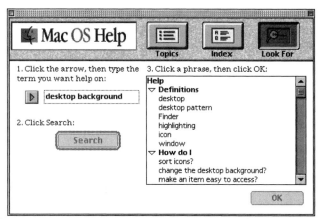

Figure 9-11: Searching for help in Apple Guide.

Figure 9-12: The first Apple Guide step describes the task or defines the term.

Read the information in the Guide window and follow any instructions it gives you. To go to the next step in a multiple-step task, click the right-pointing arrow at the bottom right of the Guide window. To back up one step, click the left-pointing arrow.

If you decide that you have selected the wrong task or term, you can return to the topics window by clicking the Topics button at the bottom of the Guide window. The Topics button may be labeled with an up-pointing arrow, a question mark, or the word Topics. You can also put away Apple Guide altogether by closing all guide windows.

At each new step, the guide may draw a circle, line, or arrow onscreen to point out a menu title or other object you must use to complete the step. These coaching marks appear in red or another color on a color monitor. If the step calls for you to choose from a menu, Apple Guide colors the menu item you should choose as well. On a black-and-white screen, it underlines the menu item.

If the Guide window mentions something you don't understand, try clicking the Huh? button at the bottom of the Guide window for clarification. (This button may be labeled I'm Stuck.) Clicking this button brings up another Guide window that may contain a definition of a term or begin step-by-step instructions for accomplishing a task related to the task you initially chose. For example, clicking Huh? in Step 2 of the task "How do I bring a window to the front?" brings up the task "How do I hide or show windows?" The Huh? button is dimmed when additional information is not available.

If you work ahead of the step currently displayed in the Guide window, Apple Guide can adjust itself to catch up. When you click the right-pointing arrow to go to the next step, Apple Guide skips ahead to the next step that matches your location in the task.

While you're following the steps in Apple Guide, you can still use your computer normally. If the Guide window is in your way, you can drag it somewhere else or click its zoom box to make it smaller; click again to make it larger. If you're using Mac OS 8–8.5, you can collapse a Guide window into its title bar by clicking its collapse box. If you're using Mac OS 7.6–7.6.1, you can collapse the Guide window according to the setup in the WindowShade control panel (described in "Collapsing Windows" in Chapter 8).

If you have not properly completed a step when you click the right-pointing arrow at the bottom of the Guide window, Apple Guide explains what you need to do to get back on track.

Other Help

Many programs add how-to help, onscreen reference material, or other items to the Help menu. For example, many applications published by Claris, FileMaker, and Microsoft list onscreen help commands in the Help menu. The help may appear in Apple Guide windows or the Help Viewer, but most applications use different help systems to display their onscreen help. For instructions on an application's own help system, check the documentation that came with the application.

Summary

After reading this chapter, you know about the different kinds of help the Mac OS makes available in the Help menu (the Guide menu in Mac OS 7.6–7.6.1). Balloon help briefly describes the object under the mouse pointer. In Mac OS 8.5, the Help Viewer program displays short how-to articles. You can search for articles, browse a table of contents, and click links in an article to go to a related article. In addition, Apple Guide shows and tells you how to complete a task as you do it.

✦   ✦   ✦

At Work with the Mac OS

Dig into the System Folder

Your computer has a special folder that contains all the essential software that gives the Mac OS its unique appearance and behavior. That folder is normally named System Folder, although the name is not mandatory. You can always spot the System Folder by its distinctive icon, which looks like a folder emblazoned with a miniature Finder icon.

The Mac OS uses additional special folders and files, several of them invisible, to keep track of items in the Trash, items on the desktop, and temporary files used by application programs. A desktop database matches documents with the applications that created them so that they all have the right icons and you can open documents from the Finder.

Exploring the System Folder

The System Folder contains several additional special folders, each with a distinctive icon, a unique name, and particular contents. The System Folder also contains a few files, such as the System file, which you can open like a folder, and the Finder. In addition, there may be some ordinary folders in the System Folder. Figure 10-1 shows an example of a System Folder.

Figure 10-1: A basic System Folder in Mac OS 8.5 contains essential files and folders.

Here's a brief rundown on some of the more common items that you may find in your Mac OS 7.6–8.5 System Folder:

✦ **Appearance** contains files that can change the look and sound of Mac OS 8.5: desktop pictures, themes, and sound sets (see Chapter 8).

✦ **Apple Menu Items** contains items listed in the Apple menu (see Chapter 7).

✦ **Application Support** contains items used by some application programs.

✦ **Clipboard** temporarily stores what you copy or cut (see Chapter 7).

✦ **ColorSync Profiles** contains color-matching profiles for specific scanners, monitors, and printers (see Chapters 11 and 15). With ColorSync 2.1, the version included with Mac OS 7.6–8.1, this folder is inside the Preferences folder.

✦ **Contextual Menu Items** contains plug-in software modules that add commands to contextual menus in Mac OS 8–8.5 (see Chapter 4). These modules require the SOMobjects for Mac OS file in the Extensions folder.

✦ **Control Panels** contains small programs for setting options and preferences (see Chapters 8, 11, and 17–22). This folder normally has an alias in the Apple Menu Items folder.

✦ **Control Strip Modules** contains the modules that appear in the Control Strip (see Chapter 11).

✦ **DataViz** contains the MacLinkPlus file translation software included with Mac OS 7.6–8.1 (see Chapter 7).

✦ **Editors** contains editors for the OpenDoc plug-in software included with Mac OS 7.6–8.1 (see Chapter 24).

✦ **Extensions** contains software that extends the capabilities of the Mac OS and application programs (see "Managing Startup Items" later in this chapter).

✦ **Favorites** contains aliases of items you want listed in the Favorites pop-up menu of the Navigation Services dialog boxes in Mac OS 8.5 (see Chapter 7). This folder normally has an alias in the Apple Menu Items folder.

✦ **Finder** is the application for organizing files, folders, and disks (see Chapters 5 and 6).

✦ **Fonts** contains fixed-size, TrueType, and PostScript fonts (see Chapter 13).

✦ **Help** contains the pages of the Mac OS Help and AppleScript Help that you see onscreen through the Apple Help Viewer in Mac OS 8.5 (see Chapter 9).

✦ **Internet Search Sites** specifies the means of searching you can use in the Search the Internet section of the Sherlock program in Mac OS 8.5 (see Chapter 17).

✦ **Launcher Items** contains items to be displayed in the Launcher window (see Chapter 7).

✦ **MacTCP DNR** is mostly obsolete in Mac OS 7.6–8.5, but some applications that use a TCP/IP network (as described in Chapter 19) may require it.

✦ **MS Preference Panels** contains preference settings for Microsoft Internet Explorer and other Microsoft applications (see Chapter 17).

✦ **Note Pad File** stores the text you write in the Note Pad (see Chapter 25).

✦ **Preferences** contains settings, status, and other information used by various programs (see "Investigating Preferences" later in this chapter).

✦ **PrintMonitor Documents** temporarily holds pending requests for background printing (see Chapter 14).

✦ **Scrapbook File** stores the text, pictures, and other items you add to and can copy from the Scrapbook (see Chapter 25).

✦ **Scripting Additions** contains files that extend the AppleScript language (see Chapter 23).

✦ **Scripts** contains AppleScript scripts, such as those used for folder actions (see Chapters 6 and 23).

✦ **Shutdown Items** contains items to be opened as the computer shuts down (see Chapter 7).

✦ **Startup Items** contains items to be opened as the computer starts up (see Chapter 7).

✦ **System** contains much of the Mac OS as well as sounds, keyboard layouts, and language script systems (as described in the next section, "Probing the System File").

✦ **System Enabler** has additional system software required by your Mac model. Most models with Mac OS 8.5 and many models with Mac OS 8–8.1 don't need a System Enabler.

✦ **System Resources** contains additional system software used by Mac OS 8.5.

✦ **Text Encodings** contains software that translates between different methods of encoding text, such as ASCII for Western European languages and Unicode for worldwide languages.

The names of most of these items can't be changed in Mac OS 8.5.

Your System Folder may contain items not listed here. For example, it may contain folders whose names end with "(Disabled)" but are otherwise the same as the names of folders listed here. Those folders contain items that you have deactivated using Extensions Manager, Conflict Catcher, or another program that manages startup files (see "Managing Startup Files" later in this chapter). Furthermore, additional items may appear in your System Folder after you install applications or other software.

Conversely, your System folder may not contain all of the items listed here. For example, if you have never used the Note Pad, you will not have a Note Pad file.

Probing the System File

One of the most important files in the System Folder, the System file, is unusual because you can open it like a folder. You can see some of the system resources it contains, and you can remove some or add more of the same.

Of all the items in the System Folder, there are two that must be present for the computer to start. One is the Finder and the other is the System file. The System file has long been terra incognita to all but the most intrepid resource-hacking Mac OS users. Although a large part of it remains an uncharted wilderness of basic system software, the Finder lets you see and work with some of the System file's contents.

Seeing System file contents

You can open the System file as if it were a folder and see which alert sounds, keyboard layouts, and script systems for foreign languages it contains. Several of these kinds of items do not appear when you open the System file because they are permanently installed in every computer that can use the Mac OS. These items include the simple beep sound, the U.S. keyboard layout, and the Roman script system for Western languages. Figure 10-2 shows examples of the items you can see by opening a System file.

SECRETS

False Alarm

If you use Mac OS 8.1 and an alert tells you the System file is damaged when you try to open it, the alert may be false. Check the version number of the Appearance Extension in the Extensions folder. If you have Appearance Extension 1.0.2, it is the Extension that is probably causing the spurious alert. To work around this problem, make a copy of the System file. You'll be able to open the System file copy. If you change the contents of this copy of the System and you want the changes to take effect, drag the System file from the System Folder to the Trash, rename the System file copy to System file, and drag it to the System Folder. Then restart your computer. If everything is working OK, you can empty the Trash to delete the old System file.

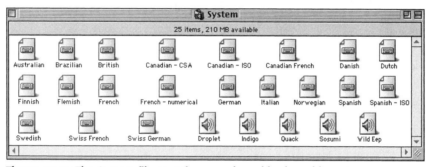

Figure 10-2: The System file contains sounds and keyboard layouts.

Working with System file contents

Not only can you see the contents of the System file, you can also drag items in and out of it as if it were a folder. Changes to sounds take effect as soon as you close the System file, but changes to other items require restarting your computer first. The Finder doesn't allow you to drag items in or out of the System file when other programs are open. You must quit all open programs except the Finder, make your changes to the System file contents, and then open the programs again.

Items you drag out of the System file become independent files. You can move them to any folder or the desktop and copy them to other disks. You can rename sounds but not other items in the System file. Opening a sound that's in or out of the System file makes the computer play it.

Installing sounds in the System file makes them candidates for the system alert sound, which you choose with the Monitors & Sound control panel or the Sound control panel (see "Sound Adjustments" in Chapter 11). There are many kinds of sound files that exist, but you can put only one kind into the System file. The kind of sound file that can go in the System file is sometimes called a *System 7 Sound* (it has an internal type code of sfil). Specifically, you can't put HyperCard sounds or AIFF sounds in the System file.

The keyboard layouts that you install appear as choices in the Keyboard control panel. Selecting a different keyboard layout there changes your Mac's arrangement of the keys on your keyboard. Selecting the Español (Spanish) layout, for example, makes the semicolon key on an U.S. keyboard produce an ñ (for details on foreign-language keyboard arrangements, see "Language Preferences" in Chapter 11).

Adding Items to the System Folder

Most of the items in the System Folder are placed there for you when you install the Mac OS, applications, and other software. Nevertheless, from time to time you may need to add items to the System Folder. Most items must go in a special folder or the System file inside the System Folder. The Finder can automatically route many kinds of items to the proper place, or you can drag items to specific folders yourself.

Automatic routing inside the System Folder

The Finder can automatically route many kinds of files to the proper place inside the System Folder. To take advantage of this service, you must drag the files to the System Folder icon, not to the System Folder window. The System Folder icon can be open (its window displayed), but you must drag files to the icon nonetheless. If you drag files to the System Folder window, they simply go into the main part of the System Folder, where some kinds of items will be effective but others will not.

When you drag the items to the System Folder icon (not the System Folder window), the Finder recognizes items that go in many of the special folders or the System file and asks whether you want the items put in their proper places. If you consent, the Finder automatically routes the items to special folders as enumerated in Table 10-1. Figure 10-3 is an example of the alert that appears if the Finder recognizes items you drag to the System Folder icon.

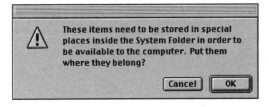

Figure 10-3: The Finder knows where to put some of the items that you drag to the System Folder.

Table 10-1
Automatic Routing to Special Folders in the System Folder

Kind of Item	Routed to
Theme file	Theme Files folder (inside Appearance)[1]
Sound Set file	Sound Sets folder (inside Appearance)[1]
JPEG picture	Desktop Pictures folder (inside Appearance)[1]
Internet Search Site	Internet Search Sites folder [1]
Contextual menu plug-in	Contextual Menu Items folder [1]
Control panel	Control Panels folder
Control Strip module	Control Strip Modules folder [3]
Apple Guide document	Extensions folder [4]
Chooser extension	Extensions folder
Communications tool	Extensions folder
Library	Extensions folder
System extension	Extensions folder
ColorSync Profile	ColorSync Profiles folder (inside Preferences folder in Mac OS 8.1)[2]
OpenDoc editor	Extensions folder (but belong in the Editors folder)
Desk accessory program	Apple Menu Items folder
Modem script	Modem Scripts folder (inside Extensions folder)
Scripting addition	Scripting Additions folder (inside Extensions folder in Mac OS 7.6–7.6.1)[3]
Location Manager module	Location Manager Modules folder (inside Extensions folder)[1]
Preference files of type "pref"	Preferences folder[1]
Text Encoding Converter document	Text Encodings folder [3]
Font or Font suitcase	Fonts folder
PostScript Font	Fonts folder
Sound (alert)	System file
Keyboard layout	System file
Script system	System file

1. Mac OS 8.5 only; goes to System Folder in Mac OS 7.6–8.1.

2. Mac OS 8.1–8.5 only; goes to System Folder in Mac OS 7.6–8.

3. Mac OS 8–8.5 only; goes to System Folder in Mac OS 7.6–7.6.1.

4. Some Apple Guide documents (those documents whose type code is "reno") in Mac OS 8–8.5 belong in the Global Guides folder inside the Extensions folder, but the Finder mistakenly puts them in the main System Folder.

Manual routing inside the System Folder

Some kinds of items can't be routed automatically to special folders because they are not a unique kind of item. For example, the Finder can't tell where to put a particular alias file — it may belong in the Apple Menu Items folder, Launcher Items folder, Favorites folder, Recent Applications folder (inside the Apple Menu Items folder), Recent Items folder (inside the Navigation Services folder), Startup Folder, or another special folder. Likewise, the Finder doesn't know it should put printer descriptions into the Printer Descriptions folder or PPP connection scripts inside the PPP Connect Script folder because both of these kinds of files are nothing more than plain text.

If you know where items belong inside the System Folder, you can drag them directly to the proper special folder or to the System file. Many items belong in folders you can see when you open the System Folder. Other items belong in folders located inside the folders at the main level of the System Folder. For example, most system extension files belong in the Extensions folder, but text-to-speech voices and printer descriptions belong in folders inside the Extensions folder. You need to be careful when putting items directly into folders inside the System Folder. You're not likely to damage anything by putting an item in the wrong place, but the item may not function if you put it in the wrong folder.

QUICK TIPS

How to Spot and Fix Routing Mistakes

The Finder sometimes makes mistakes when it puts items in special folders for you. It may put some items in the correct places and incorrectly leave others in the System Folder itself. For example, in Mac OS 8.5 the Finder correctly puts many preference files in the Preferences folder, but it incorrectly puts others in the System Folder.

You know that the Finder made a mistake if you don't see the expected alert when you drag items to the System Folder icon. If the Finder doesn't recognize items you drag to the System Folder icon, it doesn't put them in special folders. Of course, the System Folder is the right place for some items, such as a replacement Scrapbook File or Note Pad File.

You know that the Finder is about to make a mistake if you drag items to the System Folder icon and see an alert saying that some of the items need to be put in special folders. The key word here is *some*. In this case, you may want to cancel the alert and drag the items one at a time. This procedure takes a little longer than dragging a group of items, but you know more precisely which items do not go into special folders. The figure on the following page shows an example of the type of alert that you need to beware of.

When the Finder makes a mistake and puts an item in the System Folder itself rather than in the special folder where it belongs, you must open the System Folder and drag the misplaced item to the proper special folder yourself.

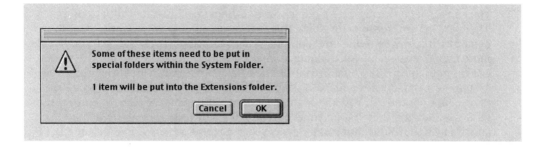

Removing Items from the System Folder

Before you can remove an item from the System Folder, you must know which inner folder contains it. If you're not sure where the item is, use the Finder's Find command to locate the item (see "Finding Items" in Chapter 6). Be sure to drag items from the special folders onto the desktop or into an ordinary folder. Some items you drag out of special folders remain effective if you merely drag them to the System Folder window.

Don't remove items from the System Folder unless you're sure your system doesn't need them. Sometimes a file name may sound like the item is used for one specific feature that you don't care about while it is actually required by the Mac OS or is used by other features that you don't want to deactivate. For instance, the Text Encoding Converter library in the Extensions folder may sound like you don't need it unless you want to read or write foreign languages. While you do need this library file to use foreign languages, you also need it to see the contents of a disk that uses the Mac OS Extended format in Mac OS 8.1–8.5.

If you happen to discard a special folder, you can make a replacement by using the Finder's New Folder command (in the File menu). After creating a new folder, change its name to that of the special folder you discarded. Wait a few seconds and you'll see its icon get the distinctive look of the special folder you discarded.

Managing Startup Items

Files from several places in the System Folder are loaded into the computer's memory when you start or restart the computer. Files from the Extensions folder, Control Panels folder, and the System Folder itself extend the capabilities of the Mac OS. Startup files are also known as *extensions* because many of them extend some part of the Mac OS. An extension used to be called an *INIT,* which is a common internal type code for a system extension, and you still hear this term applied to all startup files.

You can manage startup files so that some of them take effect but others don't. There are several reasons for doing this. For example, you may want to deactivate some startup files to reduce the amount of memory that the Mac OS uses and make more memory available for opening applications (see "Adjusting Mac OS Memory Usage" in Chapter 18). You may want to deactivate other startup files to improve system performance for special tasks such as digitizing movies (see "Apple Video Player" in Chapter 16). You may want to activate or deactivate startup files required for an application that you only use occasionally. You may want to deactivate startup files to troubleshoot a problem (see "Startup Problems" in Chapter 29).

BACKGROUNDER

Startup File Loading Sequence

Startup files may be in the Extensions folder, the Control Panels folder, or the System Folder itself. During startup, the Mac OS loads files from each of these folders in turn. First, it goes through the Extensions folder in alphabetical order. Then it loads startup files from the Control Panels folder, again alphabetically. Finally, the Mac OS checks the main level of the System Folder and alphabetically loads the startup files it finds there. This loading sequence can cause problems for a few combinations of startup files.

Some startup files in the Extensions folder, Control Panels folder, or System Folder need to be loaded before or after other files in the same folder. These files have peculiar names that put them first or last in the loading sequence. Names of files meant to come first usually begin with blank spaces or a character that has no visible symbol, so the Mac OS displays a hollow box (□). Names meant to come last often begin with a tilde (~) or a diamond (◊).

If a startup file from one of the special folders needs to load before or after startup files in another special folder, name prefixes alone won't suffice. You must also move the file into another folder. For example, to have a file from the Control Panels folder start before files in the Extensions folder, you must prefix its name with a blank space and put it in the Extensions folder. To have a file from the Control Panels folder load after startup files in the System Folder, you must prefix its name with a tilde or diamond and put it in the System Folder. For convenient access to control panels, you move out of the Control Panels folder, make aliases of the control panels, and put the aliases in the Control Panels folder. (See Chapter 12 for instructions on making aliases.)

You can also change the loading order of startup files without renaming them by using Conflict Catcher from Casady & Greene or another startup file manager program that offers this feature. The Extensions Manager control panel included with Mac OS 7.6–8.5 can't change the loading order of startup files.

The most direct way to manage startup files is to drag them in and out of folders. You can more easily activate and deactivate startup files with a startup management utility such as the Extensions Manager control panel or the Conflict Catcher program from Casady & Greene (831-484-9228, http://www.casadyg.com).

These programs can also manage items in the Startup Items and Shutdown Items control panels. In addition, Conflict Catcher can manage Control Strip modules, fonts, Internet plug-in software, and more.

Adding and removing startup files

Most startup files are placed in the proper folder as part of installing the Mac OS, an application, or utility software. As a result, you generally don't have to drag startup files into the Extensions folder or Control Panels folder. However, you can drag files out of these folders if you neither want nor need the capabilities they provide. For example, if you don't have an AudioVision 14 monitor, you don't need the PowerPC Monitors Extension file in your Extensions folder. After removing or adding startup files, you typically must restart your computer for the changes to take effect.

The best place to drag a startup file that you want to deactivate is to a specially named folder inside the System Folder. Drag files from the Extensions folder to the Extensions (Disabled) folder; from the Control Panels folder to Control Panels (Disabled) folder; and from the main level of the System Folder to the System Extensions (Disabled) folder. These folders may already exist in your System Folder, because Extensions Manager and Conflict Catcher create them automatically, or you may have to make new folders and name them yourself. If you use the specially named folders, you can switch back and forth between dragging startup files directly to them and using Extensions Manager or Conflict Catcher.

If you drag a startup file out of the Extensions folder or Control Panels folder, do not drag it to the main level of the System Folder. Startup files are still active there.

Using Extensions Manager

The Extensions Manager control panel can individually deactivate startup files in the Control Panels folder, the Extensions folder, and the main level of the System Folder, as well as items in the Startup Items and Shutdown Items folders. The Extensions Manager window has a scrolling list of these items. For each listed item, the Extensions Manager displays its status (on or off), name, size, version, and the package it was installed with. You can also display each item's type and creator codes by selecting options with the Preferences command (in the Edit menu). Figure 10-4 shows an example of the Extensions Manager.

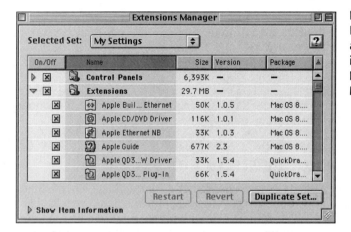

Figure 10-4:
Deactivate and
activate startup
items with
Extensions
Manager.

SECRETS

The Missing Extensions Alert

Sometimes when you open the Extensions Manager, it displays an alert asking if you'd like to save information about missing extensions. If you agree, Extensions Manager saves a text file with the name Missing Extensions (or another name you specify) in the folder you indicate. Do not be alarmed.

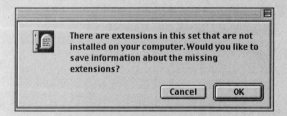

The Missing Extensions report itemizes startup files that the Extensions Manager expected to find in the folders it tracks — Control Panels, Extensions, Startup Items, Shutdown Items, and System Folder — but didn't. You probably dragged something from one of these folders since the last time you opened Extensions Manager. Another possibility is that you used a software installer to remove startup files or to install software that removed startup files.

Go ahead and save the missing extensions report. Switch to the Finder, open the report with SimpleText, and check it over just in case a startup file vanished mysteriously and you need to replace it by installing the software it came with.

Reorganizing the Extensions Manager list

You can reorganize the Extensions Manager list as follows:

✦ View items grouped by the folders they're in, grouped by the package they were installed with, or ungrouped by choosing from the View menu.

✦ Collapse and expand a group by clicking the disclosure triangle next to the group name or by double-clicking the name.

✦ Sort the list within each group by clicking any column heading to set the sort order.

✦ Adjust the widths of the Name and Package columns by dragging the right boundary line of the Name column heading or the left boundary line of the Package column heading. (You can't adjust the other column widths.)

Seeing detailed information about an item

To see more information about a particular item, you click its name to select it and then click the disclosure triangle labeled Show Item Information at the bottom-left corner of the Extensions Manager window. You can also select an item and choose Get Info from the Extensions Manager's File menu to open the item's Info window in Finder, or choose Find Item to open the folder that contains the item and select the item. If you want more information about any startup file in your System Folder, get the InformINIT shareware by Dan Frakes — the latest version is available on the Internet at http://cafe.AmbrosiaSW.com/DEF/InformINIT.html. Figure 10-5 shows the Extensions Manager expanded to show item information.

Activating and deactivating items

You deactivate or activate an extension or other item by clicking the checkbox next to the item's name. Activating or deactivating a group affects all the items in the group. You can save the current configuration of the Extensions Manager as a named set by choosing New Set from the File menu. Your named sets appear in the Selected Set pop-up in alphabetical order, and choosing a set from that pop-up changes Extensions Manager to the configuration saved for that set. To activate or deactivate all items, use the All On or All Off commands in the Edit menu.

Extensions Manager comes with two preconfigured sets: Mac OS All and Mac OS Base. Choosing the Mac OS All set turns on only the startup items that are installed by the Mac OS Installer. Choosing the Mac OS Base set turns on only the most essential startup items.

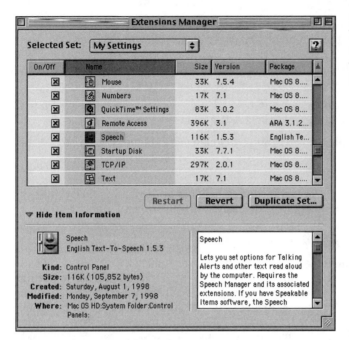

Figure 10-5:
The Extensions Manager expanded to show item information.

Changes you make to the status of any items take place when you restart. To restart immediately, click the Restart button. To restart later, quit Extensions Manager and press the Power key or use the Restart command in Finder's Special menu when you are ready to restart. To cancel the changes you've made, click the Revert button in the Extensions Manager window.

Extensions Manager puts deactivated items from the Extensions folder in a folder named Extensions (Disabled). Deactivated control panels are stored in a folder named Control Panels (Disabled). Deactivated items from the System Folder go into a folder named System Extensions (Disabled).

Using Extensions Manager during startup

You can activate or deactivate startup items while your computer is starting up. To bring up the Extensions Manager control panel at the beginning of the startup process, hold down the spacebar. Holding down the Shift key at the beginning of the startup process temporarily deactivates all extensions, without affecting settings in the Extensions Manager control panel.

Investigating Preferences

What you see in your Preferences folder depends on what you have installed on your hard disk. Many application programs save files of preference settings in the Preferences folder. Also, the Mac OS saves a plethora of preference files in the Preferences folder.

It's generally pretty easy to figure out which preferences file goes with what program by looking at the name of the preferences file. See if you can guess which control panels save settings in these preferences files: Date & Time Preferences, Keyboard Preferences, and Launcher Preferences. Here are descriptions of some of the items you'll find in the Preferences folder, excluding files that by their names obviously contain settings you make with like-named control panels:

✦ The **File Sharing** folder contains file-sharing access privileges for your disks and folders (as described in Chapter 21). You don't have this folder if File Sharing has never been turned on.

✦ **Finder Preferences** contains many of the settings you make with Finder's Preferences command in Mac OS 8–8.5 (as described in Chapters 5 and 6). In Mac OS 7.6–7.6.1, this file contains settings you make with various control panels.

✦ **Navigation Services** contains a folder of the items listed in the Recent pop-up menu in Navigation Services dialog boxes in Mac OS 8.5 (described in Chapter 7).

✦ **FBC Indexing Preferences** and **Find Preferences** contain settings for the Find program in Mac OS 8.5 (covered in Chapters 6, 7, and 17).

✦ **Internet Preferences** stores settings that you make with the Internet control panel in Mac OS 8.5 or the Internet Config program in Mac OS 7.6–8.1 (covered in Chapter 17).

✦ **AppSwitcher Prefs** specifies the current configuration of the Application Switcher (covered in Chapter 7). Remove this file to reset the Application Switcher to its standard configuration.

✦ **Users & Groups Data File** contains names and privileges for registered users and groups to whom you have given access to your computer (as described in Chapter 21).

✦ **ColorSync Profiles** stores color-matching information for specific scanners, monitors, and printers (as described in Chapters 11 and 15). This folder is in the main level of the System Folder in Mac OS 8.5.

✦ **AppleCD Audio Player Prefs** and **CD Remote Programs** contain album and song titles that you enter for individual audio CDs together with other settings for the AppleCD Audio Player program (as described in Chapter 16).

✦ **QuickDraw GX Helper Prefs** identifies the applications in which you have turned off GX desktop printing, if you have installed QuickDraw GX with Mac OS 7.6–7.6.1 (as described in Appendix A).

✦ **Jigsaw Picture** contains the picture that the Jigsaw Puzzle program uses to make its puzzles (as described in Chapter 25).

✦ **Stickies file** contains the text of notes that you post on your screen with the Stickies program (covered in Chapter 25).

Revealing More Special Folders

The Mac OS further organizes your disks with additional special folders outside the System Folder. The Finder creates these special folders as needed on each disk:

✦ The invisible **Temporary Items folder** contains temporary files created by the programs that you are using. A program normally deletes its temporary files automatically when you quit it.

✦ The **Trash folder** contains the items you drag from the disk to the Trash icon. Your disks' Trash folders are invisible, but you see their consolidated contents when you open the Trash icon. A visible Trash folder in a shared disk contains items from the disk that are located in the owner's Trash.

✦ The **Network Trash folder** contains items from your shared disk or folder that network users have dragged to the Trash — but have not yet permanently removed — on their computers. The discarded items appear in the network users' Trash, not yours.

✦ The **Rescued Items folder** contains items the Finder finds in the Temporary Items folder when you restart after a system crash (or after switching off the power without using the Shut Down command — tsk! tsk!). You may be able to reconstruct your work by opening them. If a Rescued Items folder exists, you can always see it by opening the Trash.

✦ **TheFindByContentFolder** stores files created by the Find by Content section of the Find program in Mac OS 8.5.

✦ The **Desktop folder** contains items located on the desktop. Although it is invisible on your disks, the Desktop folder of a shared disk is visible to others and contains items from the disk that are on the owner's desktop.

Checking the Desktop Database

Something you don't see in the System Folder is the invisible desktop database that Finder uses to keep track of:

✦ Which icons to use for documents created by all your applications (unless you have customized them, as described under "Custom Icons" in Chapter 8)

✦ What kind of file each icon refers to

✦ Where programs are located

✦ What comments you enter with the Finder's Get Info command

The Mac OS keeps this database hidden so users don't alter it inadvertently, but you can see some of the information the database contains by selecting a file in the Finder and choosing Get Info from the Finder's File menu.

The Finder creates and maintains a desktop database on every disk. On disks larger than 2MB, the desktop database consists of two invisible files named Desktop DB and Desktop DF. On smaller disks, the desktop database is kept in one file named Desktop. Finder creates these files automatically on new disks and updates them with new information whenever you install another application.

You can force the Finder to rebuild the desktop database by holding down the Option and ⌘ keys when starting the computer. After the Mac OS has loaded all startup files, the Finder displays an alert asking if you want to rebuild the desktop file on the startup disk. After rebuilding the startup disk, the Finder asks if you want to rebuild the next disk on the desktop, if you have more than one disk. The Finder asks about each disk on the desktop separately, even if you stop holding down the ⌘ and Option keys (so give your fingers a rest). See Chapter 29 for more information about rebuilding the desktop as a preventative measure and as a solution to some problems.

Summary

After reading this chapter, you know what's in the System Folder and why. You know that the Finder is there along with the System file, which contains much of the basic system software as well as sounds, keyboard layouts, and script systems for foreign languages. The Apple Menu Items folder contains items listed in the Apple menu, and the Favorites menu contains items listed in the Favorites pop-up menu in Navigation Services dialog boxes. The Startup Items folder contains items that are to be opened as the computer starts up, and the Shutdown Items folder contains items to be opened as the computer shuts down. The Extensions folder contains software that extends the capabilities of the Mac OS. Control Panels and Control Strip modules have their own folders. The Fonts folder contains fixed-size, TrueType, and PostScript fonts. The Preferences folder contains settings, status, and other information used by various programs. The System Folder contains many other items as well.

You read about adding items to the System Folder and removing items from it. You found out how to manage startup files in the Extensions, Control Panels, and main level of the System Folder.

This chapter also revealed other special folders that the Mac OS uses to keep track of items in the Trash, items on the desktop, and temporary files used by application programs. In addition, the Finder maintains a desktop database to match documents with the applications that created them so that they all have the right icons and you can open documents from the Finder.

✦   ✦   ✦

Adjust Controls and Preferences

Y our computer is highly configurable. You can set numerous options that affect various aspects of its operation, including the keyboard and mouse sensitivity, the screen resolution and color depth, the way the computer uses energy, and the alert sound you hear. All these options and many, many more are set with various control panels and the Control Strip.

In this chapter, you'll delve into ten types of customization that can adapt the Mac OS to fit your circumstances, making it easier to use and you more efficient.

General Preferences

The General Controls control panel sets a number of system options. Figure 11-1 shows the options you can set in the General Controls control panel.

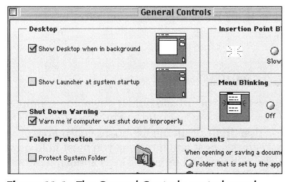

Figure 11-1: The General Controls control panel.

On the left side of the General Controls window, you can show or hide the Finder's desktop when the Finder is not the active application, and you can have the Launcher control panel open automatically during startup. You can have the Mac OS display a warning during startup if the computer crashed or was not shut down properly. In addition, you can individually protect the System Folder and the Applications folder on the startup disk, preventing items in them from being renamed or removed; to use these options, however, file sharing must be turned off in the File Sharing or Sharing Setup control panel, whichever your computer has.

On the right side of the General Controls window, you can set blinking rates for the text insertion point and menus. Another option determines which folder you see first in a dialog box for opening or saving a document. The first setting, "Folder that is set by the application," specifies the folder that contains the document you opened to launch the application, which is the application's folder if you opened the application directly instead of opening one of its documents. The second setting specifies the most recent folder used in the application. The third setting specifies the Documents folder on the startup disk.

Keyboard and Mouse Adjustments

Though you might think of the Mac OS as something you look at, there are also parts of it that you touch, namely, the keyboard and the mouse, trackpad, or trackball. Like many aspects of the Mac OS, the behavior of the keyboard and the mouse, trackpad, or trackball is adjustable to allow for differences among users. If you find yourself becoming frustrated or impatient as you use one of your input devices, you may be able to solve the problem by changing its sensitivity. Similarly, if you type a character repeatedly when you mean to type it only once, you can adjust the keyboard sensitivity. You make these adjustments using the Keyboard, Mouse, and Trackpad control panels.

If you have difficulty typing, moving the mouse, or clicking the mouse button, you can set up alternative methods of using them. These alternatives are especially helpful for people with disabilities. You configure these alternatives with the Easy Access control panel.

Setting keyboard sensitivity

When you press almost any key on the keyboard and hold it down, the computer types that character repeatedly as long as you keep the key pressed. (The ⌘, Option, Control, Caps Lock, and Esc keys don't repeat.) In the Keyboard control panel, you can change how quickly the characters repeat and how long you must hold down a key before the repeat feature kicks in. If you find repeating keys annoying rather than handy, you can disable the repeat by selecting Off in the Delay Until Repeat section of the keyboard control panel. Figure 11-2 shows the Keyboard control panel.

The Keyboard control panel also allows you to choose a keyboard layout. You use this option when you want to type in a different language. These adjustments are covered in "Language Preferences" later in this chapter.

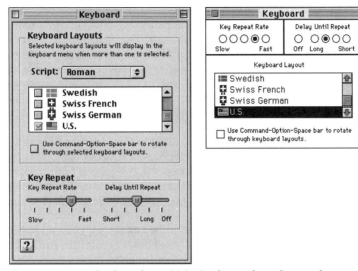

Figure 11-2: Set keyboard sensitivity in the Keyboard control panel of Mac OS 8–8.5 (left) and Mac OS 7.6–7.6.1 (right).

Setting mouse, trackpad, or trackball sensitivity

You can change the way the Mac OS responds to your manipulation of your computer's mouse or trackball by setting options in the Mouse control panel. On a PowerBook with a trackpad, you adjust its responsiveness with the Trackpad control panel. Figure 11-3 shows the Mouse and Trackpad control panels as they look in Mac OS 8.5.

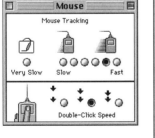 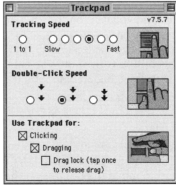

Figure 11-3: Set mouse or trackball sensitivity in the Mouse control panel and trackpad sensitivity in the Trackpad control panel.

The Mouse Tracking option (Mouse control panel) or Tracking Speed option (Trackpad control panel) determines the tracking speed — how fast the pointer moves as you glide the mouse, trackpad, or trackball. This setting is a matter of personal taste. If you feel that the pointer doesn't keep up, try a faster setting. If you often lose track of the pointer as you move it, try a slower one. Often, when you switch from a small monitor to a large one, you need to switch to a faster tracking speed because the pointer has a longer distance to travel from the menu bar to the Trash.

The Double-Click Speed option determines how quickly you must double-click for the Mac OS to perceive your two clicks as one double-click rather than two separate, unrelated clicks. When you select a double-click speed, the mouse button pictured in the Mouse control panel or the trackpad button pictured in the Trackpad control panel flashes to demonstrate the double-click interval you've selected.

In addition, the Double-Click Speed option determines how long you can hold down the mouse, trackpad, or trackball button when you click a menu title and still have Mac OS 8–8.5 interpret the gesture as a click so that the menu stays displayed after you release the mouse button. The shorter the double-click speed, the more quickly you must press and release. If you don't release within the allotted time, Mac OS 8–8.5 interprets the gesture as a press instead of a click and puts away the menu when you release.

Many PowerBook models that can use Mac OS 7.6–8.5 have three additional options under "Use Trackpad for" in the Trackpad control panel. These options let you configure the trackpad so that you can click and drag without using the trackpad button. If you turn on the Clicking option, you can click by tapping on the trackpad as well as by pressing the trackpad button. The Dragging option lets you drag without pressing the mouse button. To drag an object when this option is turned on, begin to double-tap the object, but don't lift your finger on the second tap. Now move your finger across the trackpad to drag the object across the screen. If your finger reaches the edge of the trackpad and you need to drag further, you can lift your finger briefly, put it down again on the opposite edge of the trackpad, and continue dragging. Dragging ends when you keep your finger off the trackpad for a few seconds, unless you have turned on the "Drag lock" option in the Trackpad control panel. With this option turned on, you can leave your finger off the trackpad indefinitely, and you stop dragging an object by tapping it again.

Easy Access

The Easy Access control panel sets up three alternative methods of using the keyboard and mouse. The first, called *Mouse Keys,* lets you use the numeric keypad portion of the keyboard to move the pointer on the screen and to click as if you were using the mouse button. The second, called *Slow Keys,* filters out accidental keystrokes. The third alternative keyboard behavior, called *Sticky Keys,* lets you type combination keystrokes such as ⌘-Z one key at a time.

Easy Access gives you an audible warning when you turn one of its features on or off. You hear an ascending scale when you turn a feature on, and you hear a descending scale when you turn one off. You can eliminate the warning by turning off the audio-feedback option at the top of the Easy Access control panel.

To work, Easy Access must be in the Control Panels folder at startup time. Easy Access is not installed automatically with the rest of the control panels. With some Mac OS installations, you will find Easy Access in the Universal Access folder inside the Apple Extras folder on your startup disk. You can drag the control panel from there to your Control Panels folder. If it's not on your hard disk anywhere, you can install it by doing a custom installation of the Mac OS module and selecting the Universal Access component group of this module (as described in Chapters 31 and 32). Figure 11-4 shows the Easy Access control panel.

Figure 11-4: The Easy Access control panel.

Mouse Keys

The Mouse Keys feature of the Easy Access control panel enables you to click, drag, and move the pointer with the numeric keypad instead of the mouse, trackpad, or trackball. Mouse Keys is very handy for moving graphic objects precisely. You can turn on Mouse Keys by pressing ⌘-Shift-Clear instead of using the Easy Access control panel. You can turn it off by pressing Clear. When Mouse Keys is on, the 5 key in the keypad acts like a mouse button. Press once to click; press twice to double-click; or hold it down. The eight keys around 5 move the pointer left, right, up, down, and diagonally. Pressing 0 locks the mouse button down until you press the period key in the keypad.

Be careful not to press ⌘-Option-Escape, which, instead of activating the Mouse Keys feature, brings up a dialog box that asks whether you want to force the active program to quit.

SECRETS

PowerBook Mouse Keys

You can't use the Mouse Keys feature of the Easy Access control panel to point and click on a PowerBook because PowerBooks have no numeric keypad. To use this feature on a PowerBook, install the system extension called Mouse Keys, which Apple distributes free via the Internet (ftp://ftp.info.apple.com/Apple.Support.Area/disability-solutions/Mouse_Keys_-_PowerBook_1.0-.sit.bin). This extension modifies the Easy Access control panel to recognize different keys instead of the numeric keypad. It substitutes the K key and the keys next to it for the 5 key and the keys next to it on the keypad. The Esc key substitutes for the Clear key. Thus, after installing the Mouse Keys extension, you turn on Mouse Keys by pressing ⌘-Shift-Esc, and you turn it off by pressing Esc.

When Mouse Keys is on, the K key acts like the button on a trackball or trackpad. Press once to click; press twice to double-click; or hold it down. The eight keys around K move the pointer left, right, up, down, and diagonally. Pressing the spacebar locks the mouse button down until you press Enter.

Slow Keys

The Slow Keys feature of the Easy Access control panel makes the Mac OS wait before it accepts a keystroke, thereby filtering out accidental keystrokes. You can turn Slow Keys on or off from the keyboard by holding down the Return key for about 10 seconds. No icon indicates whether Slow Keys is on or off, but about five seconds after you begin pressing the Return key, the computer makes three short, quiet beeps. About four seconds after that, the computer plays an ascending scale to confirm that Slow Keys is being turned on or a descending scale to confirm that it's been turned off. You don't hear these sounds if you use the Easy Access control panel, however, and some applications (such as Microsoft Word) may mute the sounds.

Sticky Keys

The Sticky Keys feature of the Easy Access control panel enables you to type combination keystrokes such as ⌘-Shift-3 (which puts a snapshot of your screen in a picture document that SimpleText and most graphics programs can open) one key at a time. Sticky Keys also enables you to lock down any modifier key by pressing it two times in a row. You can turn on Sticky Keys by pressing Shift five times in succession. You can turn Sticky Keys off by pressing Shift five times again or by pressing any two modifier keys simultaneously. When Sticky Keys is on, an icon at the right end of the menu bar shows its status. Figure 11-5 shows the four states of the Sticky Keys status icon.

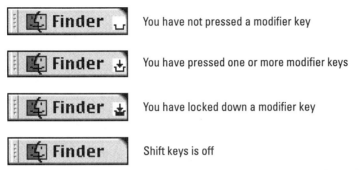

Figure 11-5: Checking the status of Sticky Keys (enlarged to show detail).

Sound Adjustments

There are many adjustments you can make to the sounds your computer generates itself or plays from external sources. You can set the sound level and a source for audio input. Depending on how your computer is equipped, you may also be able to set sound output options. In addition, you can select an alert sound and set its loudness.

You set sound options using the Monitors & Sound control panel or the Sound control panel, whichever is in your Control Panels folder. You can also use the Control Strip if it's available on your computer.

The Monitors & Sound control panel is installed in the Control Panels folder with Mac OS 8–8.5 and with Mac OS 7.6–7.6.1 on Macs with PCI slots. On other Macs with Mac OS 7.6–7.6.1, the Sound control panel is installed in the Control Panels folder.

If you have the Monitors & Sound control panel, you'll find the Sound control panel in the Apple Extras folder on your startup disk in case you need it. For example, you have to use the Sound control panel to adjust sound options while startup files are disabled (as described in "Managing Startup Items" in Chapter 10). Also, some older sound devices can't be controlled from the Monitors & Sound control panel. If you have difficulty controlling such a device from Monitors & Sound, try using the old Sound control panel instead.

Sound levels and sources

The available options for adjusting volume and choosing sound sources vary depending on the Mac OS version you are using as well as what type of hardware and sound-input and sound-output devices you have. In general, sliders let you adjust the relative volume of the computer's built-in speaker. (In Mac OS 8, but not Mac OS 8.1–8.5, you can also adjust the sound output level; for example, you can adjust the volume for your headphones separately from the computer's built-in speaker.) For computers that output stereo sound there are sliders that allow you to balance the right and left channels. Computers with other sound output capabilities, such as stereo surround sound, have options for controlling those capabilities. You may also be able to choose a sound output quality.

The options for sound input let you choose a source, such as the computer's microphone port, an internal CD-ROM drive, or the line input jacks if the computer has them. In addition, you can switch to other sound-input or sound-output hardware (NuBus or PCI card) if you have such a thing installed. You may not be able to change the sound input setting while an audio or video application such as Apple Video Player is open. If this happens, quit the video or audio application and try changing the sound input.

Sound levels and sources with Monitors & Sound

If your Mac has the Monitors & Sound control panel in the Control Panels folder, you generally use it to set sound level, input, and output options. You set these options in the Sound section of the control panel (click the Sound button at the top of the control panel to get there). Figure 11-6 shows typical sound input and output options from Monitors & Sound.

Sound levels and sources with Sound

If your Mac has the Sound control panel in the Control Panels folder, you use it to set sound options and volumes. If it's not in the Control Panels folder, you can use it from the Apple Extras folder. You choose a group of sound options from the pop-up menu at the top of the control panel. Figure 11-7 shows three groups of options available in the Sound control panel.

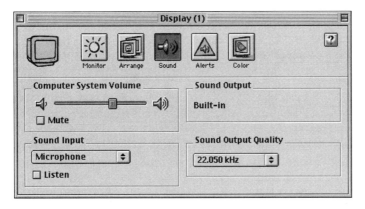

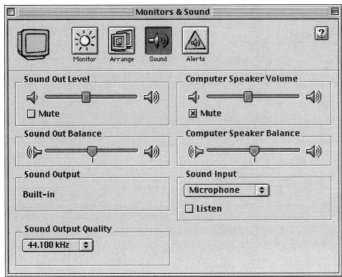

Figure 11-6: Sound input and output options in the Monitors & Sound control panel in Mac OS 8.1–8.5 (top)and Mac OS 8 (bottom). The specific options depend on the computer's sound capabilities.

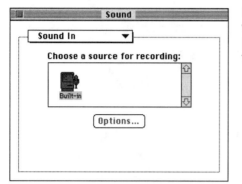

Figure 11-7: Sound input, output, and volume options in the Sound control panel. (The specific options depend on the computer's sound capabilities.)

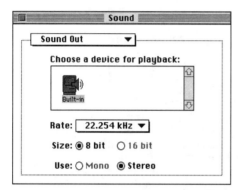

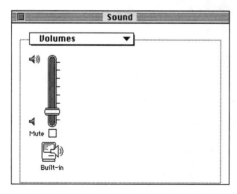

Sound levels and sources with the Control Strip

The Control Strip also offers modules for adjusting sound input and output. The Sound Volume module lets you change the volume of the computer's sound output. Clicking the speaker icon in the Control Strip pops up this module's volume slider. The Sound Strip module allows you to change the sound input source; for example, to switch to an audio CD or external microphone as your sound source. Clicking the microphone-plus-CD icon displays a menu of sound input sources. Figure 11-8 shows these two control panel modules.

Figure 11-8: Sound volume (left) and sound input options (right) in the Control Strip.

Alert sounds

You set the system alert sound and its volume separately from the other sounds played by your computer. To set these options, use the Monitors & Sound control panel or the Sound control panel, whichever is in your Control Panels folder.

Whether you use the Monitors & Sound control panel or the Sound control panel, you can always add and remove alert sounds by dragging them in and out of the System file (as described in "Probing the System File" in Chapter 10). If you get sound files in a format that can't be used as alert sounds, such as .wav format files from the Internet, you can convert them to the proper format for alert sounds using Norman Franke's free SoundApp program (described in Chapter 26). You can also record new alert sounds with the SimpleSound accessory program (described in Chapter 25).

Alert sounds with Monitors & Sounds

In the Monitors & Sound control panel, you set these options by clicking the Alerts button at the top of the control panel. Figure 11-9 shows the system alert options in Monitors & Sound.

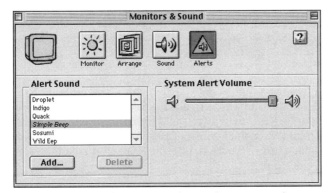

Figure 11-9: The Alerts options in Monitors & Sound.

If you don't like any of the sounds offered, you can record your own by clicking the Add button in the Alerts section of Monitors & Sound. This action brings up a dialog box that has buttons for controlling recording and playback, and a gauge that measures the duration of the recorded sound. Click the Record button to record or rerecord up to ten seconds of sound from the computer's microphone or another audio source. (You set the sound input source in the Sound section of this control panel.) Then click the Play button to hear your recording. When you're satisfied with your recording, click the Save button, and type a name for the new alert sound when you're asked. Figure 11-10 shows the dialog box in which you record an alert sound from the Monitors & Sound control panel.

Alert Sounds with Sounds

Alert Sounds is also one of the four options available from the pop-up menu at the top of the Sound control panel. Figure 11-11 shows the Alert Sounds options in the Sounds control panel.

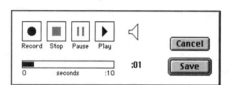

Figure 11-10: The dialog box for recording an alert sound.

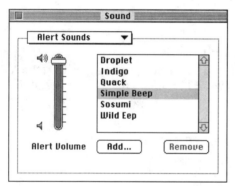

Figure 11-11: The Alert Sounds options in the Sound control panel.

In the Alert Sounds section of the Sounds control panel, there are two ways to add and remove system alert sounds. One way is to use the Edit menu's Cut, Copy, and Paste commands. For example, you can copy a sound from the Scrapbook (described in Chapter 25) and paste it into the Sound control panel. You can also record a new system alert sound by clicking the Add button, or remove an alert sound by selecting it and clicking the Remove button.

Monitor Adjustments

If you stare at your monitor for vast quantities of time, you want the view to be crisp and easy on the eyes. If you work with color, you want your monitor to display colors as accurately and consistently as possible. If you work with more than one monitor on your computer you need to have control over how the two work together.

In this section, you learn about changing the screen resolution, number of colors, and magnification; making multiple monitors work together; making onscreen color as accurate as possible by adjusting gamma and white points; matching onscreen color to the colors created by other input and output devices; calibrating your monitor to keep those colors consistent over time; and finding out the precise color of a pixel on your monitor, so that you can recreate it on the Web.

The way to adjust these settings differs according to which version of the Mac OS — and what kind of hardware — you use. With Mac OS 8–8.5, you adjust monitor settings using the Monitors & Sound control panel regardless of your Mac model. You also use this control panel to adjust monitor settings with Mac OS 7.6–7.6.1 on a Mac that has PCI expansion slots. You may occasionally need to use the Monitors control panel. For example, if you want to change the screen resolution or number of colors after disabling startup files (as described in "Managing Startup Items" in Chapter 10), you may need to use the Monitors control panel with Mac OS 7.6–8.5. If your Mac has Monitors & Sound in the Control Panels folder, look for the Monitors control panel in the Apple Extras folder on your startup disk.

If you use Mac OS 7.6–7.6.1 on a Mac that doesn't have PCI expansion slots, you adjust monitor settings with the Monitors control panel.

You can also change some monitor options via the Control Strip if your Mac has one.

Screen resolution and color depth

The two most basic monitor settings you can adjust are color depth and resolution. *Resolution* is the size of the rectangular screen image — the number of pixels (picture elements or dots) wide by the number of pixels high. *Color depth* is the number of colors available for each *pixel* of the screen image. Color depth is sometimes referred to as *bit depth,* which is a measure of the amount of memory it takes to store each pixel.

The higher the color depth, the more realistic the screen image can look. However, increasing the color depth doesn't necessarily make the screen display better, because the picture displayed onscreen may not make use of all of the available colors. For example, a black-and-white photograph will still be black, white, and shades of gray when displayed on a screen capable of displaying millions of colors.

The possible settings for color depth range from black and white to millions of colors, depending on the capabilities of your monitor and your computer's video-output circuitry. Typical settings include black-and-white, 16 grays or colors (4-bit grayscale or color), 256 grays or colors (8-bit grayscale or color), thousands of colors (16-bit color), and millions of colors (32-bit color). Some video circuitry cannot use color settings below 256 grays or colors.

The settings for resolution depend on the monitor and the computer's video-output circuitry, but in general range from 512 x 384 pixels (the nominal size of a 12-inch monitor) up to 1280 x 1024 pixels (the size of a 21-inch monitor). Some monitors can display only one resolution, while others can display multiple resolutions.

Resolution and color depth are related because increasing either requires more video memory. If you increase the resolution, the Mac OS may have to automatically reduce the color depth. Conversely, you may be able to set a higher color depth by decreasing the resolution. On some Mac models you can make higher resolutions and color depths available by installing more video RAM (VRAM). To learn how much VRAM is installed in your computer, use the free Newer Technology Gauge Series software (described in Chapter 26). Then you can use the free GURU program (also described in Chapter 26) to find out whether you can install more VRAM.

Resolution and color depth with Monitors & Sound

If your Mac has the Monitors & Sound control panel in the Control Panels folder, you use it to adjust resolution and color depth. Click the Monitor button at the top of the control panel to see the current settings. If your monitor can display more than one resolution, you can select one from the scrolling list on the right side of the control panel. On the left side of the control panel you can set the computer to display colors or grays. In addition, if your computer's video circuitry can display more than one color depth at the current resolution, you can select a color depth from the scrolling list on the left side of the control panel. Figure 11-12 shows the resolution and color depth options in the Monitors section of the Monitors & Sound control panel.

On a computer with more than one monitor, the Monitors & Sound control panel displays a separate window on each monitor. Each window has a Monitor button that you can click to adjust color depth and resolution for the monitor on which the window is displayed.

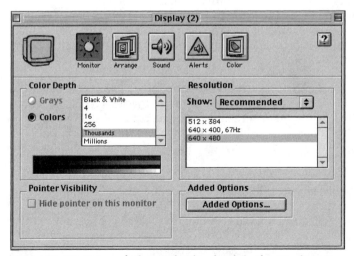

Figure 11-12: Set resolution and color depth in the Monitors & Sound control panel in Mac OS 8–8.5 and, if your computer has PCI expansion slots, in Mac OS 7.6–7.6.1.

Resolution and color with Monitors

If your Mac has the Monitors control panel, you can use it to adjust resolution and color depth. To set the color depth, choose the desired settings from the radio buttons and scrolling list at the top left of the control panel. Click the Options button to bring up a dialog box with additional monitor settings. Choose a resolution from the scrolling list under "Select a monitor setting." Figure 11-13 shows the color depth options in the Monitors control panel and the resolution options in the control panel's Options dialog box.

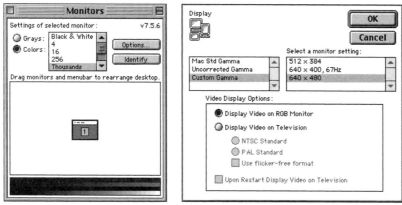

Figure 11-13: Set color depth and resolution in the Monitors control panel (left) and in its Options dialog box (right) in Mac OS 7.6–7.6.1.

On a computer with more than one monitor, you can use the Monitors control panel to adjust the resolution and color depth of each monitor separately. The control panel displays small images of each monitor, and you select the monitor you want to change by clicking its image. The currently selected monitor's image has a heavy black border.

Resolution and color in the Control Strip

Another place you can change your monitor's resolution and color depth is in the Control Strip. The Monitor Resolution module's icon looks like a monitor displaying a checkerboard pattern. Clicking this module displays a menu that lists the available resolutions of all monitors connected to the computer, and the current setting is marked with a bullet. The Monitor BitDepth module's icon looks like a monitor displaying a striped pattern. Clicking this module displays a menu that lists all the available color depths for each monitor connected to the computer. The bullet-marked menu item indicates the current color depth settings. Figure 11-14 shows the Control Strip modules and menus for setting the monitor's color depth and resolution.

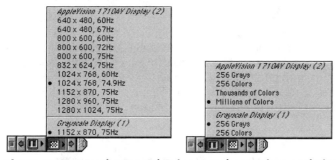

Figure 11-14: Use the Control Strip to set the monitor resolution (left) or color depth (right).

Multiple monitor setup

If your computer has two or more monitors, you can arrange them in an extended desktop, or you may be able to set them up to do video mirroring. In *video mirroring*, which is available on PowerBooks with external video ports and on some desktop Macs with two monitor ports, all monitors display exactly the same image—you get duplicate desktops. In the extended desktop mode, each monitor displays a different part of the desktop—as you move across the desktop, the pointer moves from one monitor to another. Some PowerBook models can use two monitors only for video mirroring, not for an extended desktop.

You can configure an extended desktop or set up video mirroring using the Monitors & Sound control panel or the Monitors control panel. You can also turn video mirroring on and off using the Control Strip.

Multiple monitor setup in Monitors & Sound

To configure an extended desktop or set up video mirroring using the Monitors & Sound control panel, click the Arrange button at the top of the control panel. Figure 11-15 shows the Arrange section of the Monitors & Sound control panel.

You can adjust the relative positions of the monitors by dragging the little images of them in the control panel. You can set which monitor has the menu bar by dragging the little menu bar to the appropriate little monitor in the control panel. You can also designate which monitor displays startup messages and icons. Turn on the option "Identify the startup screen" to display a tiny Macintosh icon that indicates the startup monitor. Then drag this icon to the little monitor image that you want to use during startup.

To turn on video mirroring, drag the little image of one monitor over the little image of the other monitor. To turn off video mirroring, drag the little monitor images apart.

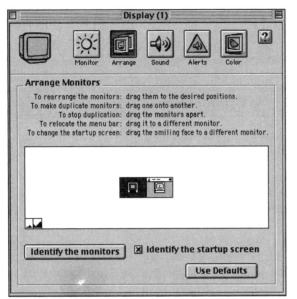

Figure 11-15: The Monitors & Sound control panel can configure an extended desktop or set up video mirroring.

Multiple monitor setup in Monitors

You can also configure an extended desktop using the Monitors control panel. To adjust the relative positions of the monitors, drag the little images of them that are found in the control panel. To set which monitor has the menu bar, drag the little menu bar to the appropriate little monitor in the control panel. To designate which monitor displays startup messages and icons, press the Option key and drag the miniature Macintosh icon that appears to the little monitor image that you want used during startup. Figure 11-16 shows multiple monitor setup in the Monitors control panel.

Figure 11-16: You can use the Monitors control panel to configure an extended desktop.

In the Monitors control panel, changes to the multiple-monitor arrangement normally take effect when you close the control panel. You can make them take effect immediately by pressing Option as you drag the monitors, menu bar, or startup icon. (These changes always take effect immediately in the Monitors & Sound control panel.)

Multiple monitor setup in the Control Strip

If your computer has two monitors and the Control Strip, you can use the Video Mirroring control strip module to set the second monitor to mirror the main monitor. Figure 11-17 shows this control strip module and its menu.

Figure 11-17: Use the Control Strip to make a second monitor mirror the main monitor.

Color accuracy

There's an inherent problem with the way we use digital equipment to produce color output: monitors, scanners, digital cameras, and so on create color with light, while any tangible output you create (from color laser printouts to four-color offset lithography) creates colors with pigment, and the two methods create slightly (or sometimes vastly) different sets of colors. In addition, each individual device has a specific range of colors that it can handle.

The ColorSync software built into the Mac OS can improve color accuracy by matching a color profile for your monitor to color profiles for printers, scanners, and other color equipment you use. Each profile specifies the range of colors that a particular type of monitor can display, printer can print, scanner can scan, and so on. The ColorSync software uses the profiles to shift colors so that they look as alike as possible on all compatible devices.

You specify the profile for your monitor with the Monitors & Display control panel, the ColorSync control panel, or the ColorSync System Profile control panel. You also need to specify ColorSync color matching when you print a color document, as described in "Setting LaserWriter 8 Options" and "Setting Color StyleWriter Options" in Chapter 15. In addition, you should take advantage of any ColorSync options that are available in application programs you use, for example, for scanning, image creation, image editing, page layout, and printing.

The ColorSync software, including the ColorSync control panel (Mac OS 8.5) or the ColorSync System Profile control panel (Mac OS 7.6–8.1) and profiles for several Apple monitors, is part of a standard installation of Mac OS 7.6–8.5. Profiles for other devices come with the devices themselves. You can create a custom ColorSync profile for your monitor using the Monitors & Sound control panel in Mac OS 8.5.

Choosing a monitor profile

In Mac OS 8.5, you can choose a ColorSync profile for your monitor using the Monitors & Sound control panel. Click the Color button at the top of the control panel to display a scrolling list of the available monitor profiles, as shown in Figure 11-18.

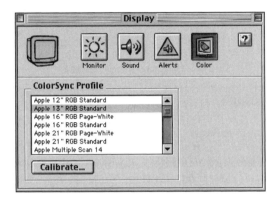

Figure 11-18: The Color section of the Monitors & Sound control panel.

The Calibrate button in the Color section of Monitors & Sound provides access to the Monitor Calibration Assistant. (You'll find detailed information about using the Monitor Calibration Assistant later in this section.)

Another place you can choose a profile in Mac OS 8.5 is the ColorSync control panel. In addition, you can use this control panel to choose profiles for RGB and CMYK colors, and to specify a color matching method. Figure 11-19 shows the Mac OS 8.5 ColorSync control panel.

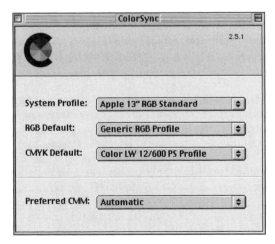

Figure 11-19: The ColorSync control panel in Mac OS 8.5.

With Mac OS 7.6–8.1 you must use the ColorSync System Profile control panel to specify a color profile for your display screen. Figure 11-20 shows the ColorSync System Profile control panel.

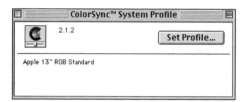

Figure 11-20: The ColorSync System Profile control panel.

Creating a custom monitor profile

All monitors change over time — the brightness of the CRT dims, the phosphors that make your monitor display color shift and fade. Mac OS 8.5's Monitor Calibration Assistant helps you account for these changes so that you will see consistent onscreen colors. It does this by creating a ColorSync profile tailored for your monitor. Before you use Calibration Assistant for the first time, you should adjust your monitor's brightness and contrast settings — either using the Monitors & Sound control panel (discussed in "Monitor Adjustments" earlier in this chapter) or using your monitor's own controls. You want the brightness to be at a level that is comfortable and clear for your viewing. Set the contrast to the highest setting. Also set the height, width, resolution, and position of the screen image as you want it.

To calibrate your monitor, click the Color button at the top of the Monitors & Sound control panel. At the bottom of the control panel, click the Calibrate button to display the Monitor Calibration Assistant. The assistant walks you through a six-step process for adjusting your monitor and creating and saving a ColorSync profile. Figure 11-21 shows the introductory screen of the Assistant.

In the Monitor Calibration Assistant's first step, you set your monitor to its highest contrast setting and then adjust the brightness. A test image helps you find the proper setting. If your monitor allows it, you should also set your preferred white-point at this stage.

In the second step, you give Assistant information about the monitor's current gamma. *Gamma* refers to the relationship between intensity of the computer's video signal and the resulting luminance of color on a display. You determine the current gamma by adjusting sliders until red, green, and blue test images look right.

The third step lets you specify a gamma setting that you want the monitor to use: 1.0 is linear gamma; 1.8 is the standard gamma setting for Mac OS computers; 2.2 is the standard gamma for television monitors and Windows computers. A low gamma setting makes colors appear more washed out. A high gamma setting makes colors appear more brilliant and with higher contrast.

BACKGROUNDER

Gamma Options

Gamma options in the Monitors & Sound and the Monitors control panels provide alternative color balancing for a video display. Color balancing is necessary because the intensity with which a monitor actually displays colors may not correspond uniformly to the intensity of the electronic signals that generate the colors. For example, on a monitor with a picture tube, a video electron beam traces the video picture on the phosphor coating inside the tube, but the phosphors are not equally luminous for all levels of light. The computer's video circuitry adjusts the strength of the electron beam to provide the most accurate color possible.

This compensation is commonly called *gamma correction.* Changing the gamma correction has no effect on video performance, only on color balance and luminance.

You set the gamma correction in Mac OS 8.5 by creating a custom ColorSync profile using the Calibrate button in the Color section of the Monitors & Sound control panel. In Mac OS 7.6–8.1, you set the gamma correction for most monitors in the Monitors section of Monitors & Sound control panel or the Options dialog box of the Monitors control panel. For some monitors, you set the gamma correction in the Colors section of the Monitors & Sound control panel.

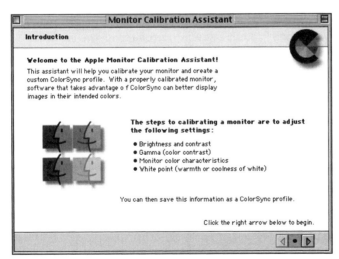

Figure 11-21: The Monitor Calibration Assistant's introductory screen.

In step four, you select your monitor type from a scrolling list. If your monitor's specific make and model is not listed, choose a generic description that fits your monitor, such as Generic LCD Color, Generic sRGB Monitor, or Generic Trinitron Monitor.

In step five, you select your target white-point: D50 is used mainly for graphic arts and attempts to match the white seen in printed matter; 6500 is a white that is the same as the sun at midday; 9300 is the white point used by most computer monitors and is the brightest white setting. You can also choose to make no white-point correction.

In step six, you create and name the custom profile for future use. You can create a number of profiles if you use your monitor at different resolutions or for different purposes.

For ColorSync Profiles to be most effective, you should repeat the calibration process monthly or when you change resolutions.

More monitor options

Some monitors have additional options that you can adjust via the Monitors & Sound control panel or the Monitors control panel. For example, the Geometry and Color buttons appear at the top of the Monitors & Sound control panel for an AppleVision 1710 or AppleVision 1710AV monitor. In the Monitors control panel, you can set the gamma correction for most monitors (see the sidebar "Gamma Options").

The Geometry section, if present in the Monitors & Sound control panel, includes options for changing how the monitor draws the screen picture. You can expand the display area, so that there is less of a black border around the visible area. You can also change the pincushion (how concave the sides of the picture are) and the rotation of the display. A Recall Factory Settings button resets the monitor to its presets.

The Color section of the Monitors & Sound control panel may include options for white-point, gamma curve, and ambient light. A monitor's *white-point* is, in essence, what color the monitor is displaying when it's displaying white. There are three standard settings for white point: D50 is used mainly for graphic arts and attempts to match the white seen in printed matter; 6500 is a white that is the same as the sun; and 9300 is the white-point used by most computer monitors and is the brightest white setting. The Gamma Curve setting controls how the computer adjusts the video signal for balanced contrast and intensity across the luminance range of the screen image. The Mac OS has traditionally used a gamma setting of 1.8. The Ambient Light option adjusts for the way surrounding room light affects how colors appear on the screen.

In the Color section of the Monitors & Sound control panel, you can save a collection of settings and switch back and forth between them using the buttons and the list on the right side of the control panel. Once you've changed some settings, you can save and name the settings by clicking the Save button. The Import and Export buttons are handy if you want to share your settings with others.

Screen magnification

You can use the CloseView control panel to magnify your screen 2 to 16 times and to invert the displayed colors. Several of the control panel options have keyboard shortcuts. The keystrokes are displayed in the control panel. Figure 11-22 shows the CloseView control panel.

Figure 11-22: The CloseView control panel.

CloseView is not installed automatically with the rest of the control panels. With some Mac OS installations, you will find CloseView in the Universal Access folder, which is in the Apple Extras folder on your startup disk. You can drag the control panel from there to your Control Panels folder. If it's not on your hard disk anywhere, you can install it by doing a custom installation of the Mac OS. In the last step of the Install Mac OS program, select the Mac OS module and click Start. When the Mac OS Installer window appears, choose Custom Install from the pop-up menu. Then select the Universal Access component group and click Install. (Chapters 31 and 32 have detailed instructions for doing a custom installation of Mac OS 7.6–8.)

Date, Time, and Location Settings

In addition to displaying a clock on your menu bar, your computer uses date and time information for a variety of operations. For example, your computer uses date and time information to provide files with creation and modification dates and to time-stamp e-mail. You use the Date & Time control panel to set the current date, time, time zone, and daylight-saving time status for your system. You can use the Map control panel to set the world location of your computer (latitude and longitude).

Setting the date and time

You set your computer's current date and time at the top of the Date & Time control panel. Through the Date Formats and Time Formats buttons, you can also choose how the date and time are displayed and the language of display. Figure 11-23 shows the Date & Time control panel.

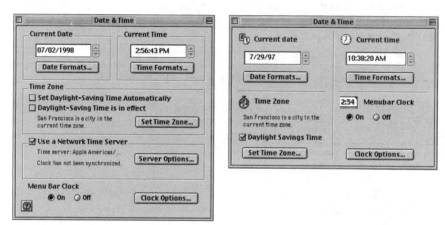

Figure 11-23: The Date & Time control panel for Mac OS 8.5 (left) and Mac OS 7.6–8.1 (right).

The Date & Time control panel offers a choice of preset formats for the language script system used by your version of the Mac OS, which for North American and Western European users is the Roman script system. Installing Apple language kit software so that you can write in additional languages does not add any preset formats to the Date & Time control panel, but you can set your own custom format. (For more information on using multiple languages, see "Language Preferences" later in this chapter.)

Setting the time zone

In the Time Zone area of the Date & Time control panel, you can see and set the time zone in which you are using your computer. Even if you never move your computer, you should set its location so that people receiving your e-mail in a different time zone can tell what time you sent the e-mail.

To set the time zone, click the Set Time Zone button. This displays a list of city names; select one in your time zone. (You can find out what time it is in a different zone by selecting a city in that time zone.)

Changing the current time zone in the Date & Time control panel also changes the computer's location as set in the Map control panel (described in "Setting World Location," later in this section). Likewise, setting a location in a new time zone in the Map control panel changes the time zone reported in the Date & Time control panel.

Time zone changes affect the file-modification dates and times on disks that use the Mac OS Extended format in Mac OS 8.1. For example, changing from Pacific time to Eastern time sets all file-modification dates three hours later. These changes can cause problems with file backup and synchronization, as discussed in "Working with Disks" in Chapter 5. This problem does not occur in Mac OS 8.5 or in Mac OS 7.6–8 and earlier.

Setting daylight-saving time

The Date & Time control panel lets you adjust the computer's clock for daylight-saving time. Turning on the Daylight-Saving Time Is in Effect option in Mac OS 8.5, or the Daylight Savings Time option in Mac OS 7.6–8.1, sets the Mac's clock ahead one hour; turning off this option sets the Mac's clock back one hour, returning it to standard time. The first time you set this option, you may have to adjust the hour displayed at the top of the control panel. In Mac OS 8.5, you can choose to have daylight-saving time applied automatically by turning on the Set Daylight-Saving Time Automatically option.

Changing the daylight-saving time affects the file-modification dates and times on disks that use the Mac OS Extended format in Mac OS 8.1. For example, turning on daylight-saving time sets all file modification dates one hour later. These changes can cause problems with file backup and synchronization, as discussed in "Working with Disks" in Chapter 5. This problem does not occur in Mac OS 8.5 or in Mac OS 7.6–8 and earlier.

Using the menu bar clock

In the Menu bar Clock area of the Date & Time control panel, you can turn on and off an optional digital clock near the right end of the menu bar. Clicking the Clock Options button in this section brings up a dialog box in which you can set the display format of the clock and set the clock to chime on the hour, half-hour, and quarter-hour. On a battery-powered Mac, you also can turn on or off a battery-level indicator, which appears next to the clock.

You can see the date instead of the time in the menu bar by clicking the clock in the menu bar. After a few seconds, the clock shows the time again.

You can hide the menu bar clock by Option-clicking it. To see the clock again, Option-click its usual location on the menu bar.

With Mac OS 7.6–7.6.1, you can even use the menu bar clock to put a computer to sleep (if it is capable of sleep). Control-click the battery indicator.

You can get ready for the millennium by having the clock display all four digits of the year. Click the Date Formats button in the Date & Time control panel and in the dialog box that appears, turn on the Show Century option.

Using a network time server

In Mac OS 8.5, you can set your computer to get the time from a time server on the Internet or your local network (if your local network has a time server). You set this up in the Date & Time control panel. First, turn on the option Use a Network Time Server. Then click the Server Options button. In the dialog box that appears, choose a time server from the pop-up menu and choose how to update the time. You can choose to synchronize your clock manually, have it updated whenever there is a discrepancy between it and the server's clock; or have it updated on a regular schedule. If you select either of the automated options, the Date & Time control panel automatically connects to the server when it's time to update your computer's clock. If the time server is on the Internet and you have a dial-up account, the Date & Time control panel automatically tries to establish a dial-up connection. Neither of the automated time update options can occur more than once every 12 hours.

Setting world location

You can set the world location (latitude and longitude) and the time zone of your computer using the Map control panel. The time zone setting in the Map control panel duplicates the time zone setting in the Date & Time control panel (described earlier in this section). The Map control panel can also compute the time difference and distance between any two places. Figure 11-24 shows the Map control panel.

You can enlarge the map by pressing Option while opening the Map control panel. To magnify more, press Shift-Option while opening the Map control panel.

In Mac OS 8.5, the Map control panel is installed in the Apple Extras folder, not in the Control Panels folder. You don't have to move the Map control panel to the Control Panels folder to use it. You can open it by double-clicking it in the Apple Extras folder.

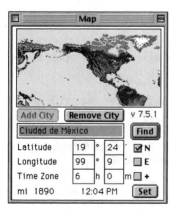

Figure 11-24: The Map control panel.

Finding and adding places on the map

Tiny flashing dots on the map mark known places; the preset locations include an idiosyncratic mix of major cities and obscure locations, among them the Middle of Nowhere. Click a dot or drag across one to see its name. You can type a place name in the space provided and click the Find button, or go through the list of known places alphabetically by pressing Option while clicking Find. The latitude, longitude, and time zone entries pertain to the most recently selected location, which Map marks with a flashing star. The map scrolls if you drag beyond its boundaries.

To add a new place, specify its latitude and longitude by clicking, by dragging, or by typing the coordinates in the spaces provided. Then type the place name and click the Add City button. After adding a new place, verify the estimated time zone and correct it, if necessary.

Setting your computer's location on the map

The Map control panel marks the location of your computer with a flashing dark cross. To change your current location, find or add it and then click the Set button. Alternatively, you can choose a new time zone location in the Date & Time control panel and then close and reopen the Map control panel. Map automatically adjusts the time and date of your system's clock according to the difference between the current and former locations. Your computer stores its location in its persistent memory, along with the time of day and other semipermanent settings.

CAUTION

The Map Control Panel versus Daylight-Saving Time

The Map control panel doesn't change the time zone correctly when the Date & Time control panel is set for daylight-saving time. This means that if you've turned on daylight-saving time in the Date & Time control panel (either automatically or manually) and you subsequently change your location in the Map control panel, your computer's clock will be set to the standard time for the new location. To keep daylight-saving time in effect, you must change time zones in the Date & Time control panel instead of the Map control panel. Do not use the Set button in the Map control panel if you want to retain the daylight-saving time setting in the Date & Time control panel.

If you want to set the time zone to a specific location that's not listed in the Date & Time control panel, you must use the Map control panel. Only the Map control panel lets you set the time zone by latitude and longitude. In addition, you can use the Map control panel to add cities (at latitudes and longitudes you specify) and subsequently use the added cities to change the time zone. Cities that you add to the Map control panel do not appear in the Date & Time control panel.

Before changing your computer's world location with the Map control panel, turn off daylight-saving time in the Date & Time control panel. (The clock should now show standard time, even if daylight-saving time is in effect.) Next, change the location in the Map control panel. Then you can turn daylight-saving time on again in the Date & Time control panel.

Getting distance, direction, or time to another place

The distance or compass direction from your Macintosh to the most recently selected location, which is marked with a flashing star, appears at the bottom of the control panel, along with the time at the distant place. Change from distance in miles to distance in kilometers or direction in degrees by clicking the unit of measurement in the lower-left corner of the control panel. To see the time difference between that place and your location, click the words Time Differ in the control panel. (If you don't see the words Time Differ, first click the words Time Zone.)

Control Strip Adjustments

The modular Control Strip control panel provides quick access to commonly adjusted features. Clicking a button in the Control Strip pops up a menu of related settings. Each button in the Control Strip corresponds to a module in the Control Strip Modules folder (inside the System Folder). Figure 11-25 shows the Control Strip on a PowerBook with Mac OS 8.5.

Figure 11-25: The Control Strip on a PowerBook with Mac OS 8.5.

This section explains how to resize and move the Control Strip, rearrange modules in it, remove modules from it, and install it if your computer doesn't have it.

Manipulating the Control Strip

The modules initially appear in the Control Strip in alphabetical order, from left to right. You can change a module's position by dragging it in the Control Strip while pressing the Option key.

The Control Strip floats above all application windows. You can collapse and expand the strip by clicking or dragging the tab at the end nearest the center of the screen. To collapse the strip to its smallest size, click the box at the opposite end. You can move the strip by pressing the Option key and dragging the tab, but the strip must touch the left or right edge of the screen.

Adding and removing modules

You add modules by dragging their files to the System Folder icon or to the Control Strip Modules folder. In Mac OS 8.5, you can also add modules by dragging Control Strip module files to the Control Strip itself. Option-dragging a module from the strip makes a copy of the module where you drag it on the desktop or in a folder. To remove modules in Mac OS 7.6–8.5, you must drag their files from the Control Strip Modules folder.

Installing the Control Strip

The Control Strip is part of a standard installation of Mac OS 8.5 on all computers. It's also standard on PowerBooks with all Mac OS versions.

You can install the Control Strip in Mac OS 7.6–8.1 by doing a custom installation of the Mac OS. In the last step of the Install Mac OS program, select the Mac OS module and click Start. When the Mac OS Installer window appears, choose Custom Install from the pop-up menu. Then select the Control Strip component, which is part of the Control Panels component group, and click Install. (Chapters 31 and 32 have detailed instructions for doing a custom installation of Mac OS 7.6–8.)

Groups of Settings

Originally designed for PowerBooks, the Location Manager provides an easy way to save a group of settings for your computer. As its name implies, the Location Manager is useful for computers that are often transported to different locations. If you have a PowerBook that you use at home and at the office, for instance, you'll often need to change the settings for your printer, network connection, or Internet connection each time you wake the computer from sleep. The Location Manager takes care of that by saving a group of settings for each location and letting you switch to any group of settings all at once.

You can also use the Location Manager to create groups of settings that you use for different work activities. For example, you might have one group of settings that opens your word processor and memo templates, and connects you to the printer that's stocked with your company's letterhead, while another group opens your graphics programs, switches your monitor's color depth to display more colors, and connects you to a color printer.

The settings you can save with Location Manager include sound volume, default printer, Extensions Manager configuration, file sharing on or off, AppleTalk and TCP/IP network configurations, time zone, and one or more items to be opened automatically. In addition, you can save settings for remote access and Internet connections in Mac OS 8.1–8.5. Figure 11-26 shows examples of the Location Manager control panel.

Location Manager 2.0 is part of a standard installation of Mac OS 8.1–8.5 on all computers. Location Manager 1.0 is part of a standard installation of Mac OS 7.6–8 on PowerBooks.

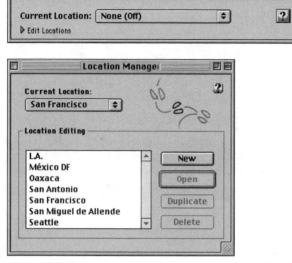

Figure 11-26: The Location Manager control panel in Mac OS 8.1–8.5 (top) and Mac OS 7.6–8 (bottom).

Changing to a different settings group

To switch to a different group of settings, simply choose the group's name from the Current Location pop-up menu at the top of the Location Manager control panel. If your computer has the Control Strip, you can also choose a group of settings from the Location control strip module. When you switch groups, a dialog box reports which settings were changed and tells you whether you need to restart to make any of the changes take effect. Figure 11-27 shows where you can change the settings group.

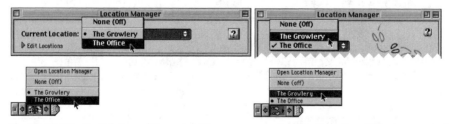

Figure 11-27: Switch to a different settings group using the Location Manager control panel or the Control Strip in Mac OS 8.1–8.5 (left) or Mac OS 7.6–8 (right).

Choosing a settings group during startup

If you want to choose a location when you start up the computer, you can set the Location Manager to display a pop-up menu of available locations in a dialog box during startup. You can have the Location Manager display this dialog box every time you start the computer, or only when you hold down a special hot key, or never. In Mac OS 7.6–8, the hot key is always the spacebar; in Mac OS 8.1–8.5, you can assign your own hot key. You select one of these options in the dialog box displayed by the Preferences command in the Location Manager's Edit menu. Figure 11-28 shows the Preferences dialog box for Location Manager.

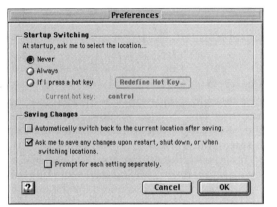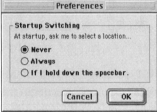

Figure 11-28: Startup preferences for the Location Manager control panel in Mac OS 8.1–8.5 (left) and Mac OS 7.6–7.6.1 (right).

Creating a new settings group

The way you create new groups of settings is somewhat different in Mac OS 7.6–8 and Mac OS 8.1–8.5.

New settings group in Mac OS 8.1–8.5

To create a new group of settings in Mac OS 8.1–8.5, you choose New Location from the Location Manager's File menu. Name the new group in the dialog box that appears and click Save. The control panel window expands to full size (if it was not already) and you can see a list of settings modules. You can include any settings module in your new group by selecting the module's checkbox. To remove a module from the group, deselect the checkbox. When you've selected all the modules you want remembered for the new group, choose Save Location from the File menu. Figure 11-29 is an example of a new settings group in Mac OS 8.1–8.5.

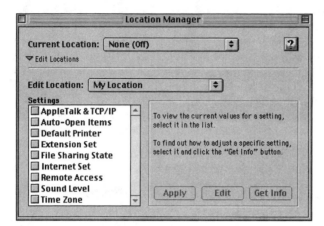

Figure 11-29: Select the settings that are part of a group in the Location Manager in Mac OS 8.1–8.5.

New settings group in Mac OS 7.6–8

In Mac OS 7.6–8 you begin creating a new group of settings by clicking the Location Manager's New button, which brings up a new location window. Enter a name for the new group in the space provided at the top of the window. Then one by one you add settings from a list on the left side of the window to a list on the right. To add a setting, select it in the list on the left and click the Add button. You can remove a setting from the list on the right by selecting it and clicking the Delete button. When the list on the right contains everything you want remembered for the new group of settings, save your changes and close the location window. Figure 11-30 is an example of a location window in Mac OS 7.6–8.

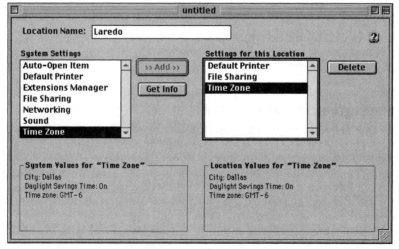

Figure 11-30: A location window specifies a group of settings in the Location Manager control panel in Mac OS 7.6–8.

What Location Manager remembers

When you add settings to a group, the Location Manager stores their current values as part of the group. This behavior is the same whether you use Location Manager 2.0 in Mac OS 8.1–8.5 or Location Manager 1.0 in Mac OS 7.6–8. For instance, if the computer's sound volume is set to 3 when you add Sound Level (Mac OS 8.1–8.5) or Sound (Mac OS 7.6–8) to a group, then the Location Manager stores a sound volume of 3 for that group, and whenever you switch to that group, your computer's sound volume will be set to 3.

If you add an Auto-Open Item to a group, the Location Manager displays a standard Open dialog box in which you select the program or document that you want automatically opened whenever you switch to the group. You can add more than one Auto-Open Item to a group.

Changing settings used for a group

You can change a group by adding, removing, or changing settings. The procedure is different in Mac OS 8.1–8.5 than the procedure in Mac OS 7.6–8.

Change settings in Mac OS 8.1–8.5

In Mac OS 8.1–8.5, you start by selecting the group you want to change from the Edit Location pop-up menu in the expanded Location Manager control panel. (To expand the control panel, click the disclosure triangle labeled Edit Locations.) To add a settings module, select its checkbox. To remove a settings module, deselect its checkbox.

To change the values stored in a settings module, select it in the Location Manager control panel and click the Edit button there. Because you must change the actual system settings, the Location Manager displays a dialog box that tells you which other control panels you must use to make the changes. You can open the necessary control panels by clicking buttons in this dialog box. (You can also open the necessary control panels by double-clicking them in the Finder, choosing them from the Control Panels submenu of the Apple menu, and so on). After making changes in a control panel, close the control panel or use the Application menu to switch back to the Location Manager. In the dialog box that's still open, click the Apply button to update the settings group with the change you just made. For example, if you select Time Zone and click Edit in the Location Manager dialog box, a dialog box that contains a button for opening the Date & Time control panel, where you actually change the time zone, opens. After changing the time zone, you close the Date & Time control panel (or switch to the Location Manager using the Application menu), and then click the Apply button in the dialog box that's still open.

If you need more help with changing a settings module in the Locations Manager, select it in the list on the left side of the Locations Manager window and click the Get Info button. You do not have to select a settings module's checkbox to use the Get Info button. You can simply select a settings module's name.

The Location Manger's Preferences dialog box (previously shown in Figure 11-28) includes several options that affect saving changes in Mac OS 8.1–8.5. One option determines whether Location Manager automatically switches or asks before switching back to the group that was active when you started editing a new or different group. Another option determines whether Location Manager offers to update the current settings group if you make changes to it outside the Location Manager. The Location Manager asks about updating the current settings group when you switch settings groups, restart, or shut down. For example, if the current settings group includes a setting for sound level and you change the system's sound level, then the Location Manager will ask if you want to update the current settings group when you shut down, restart, or change to another settings group that has a setting for the sound level. A related option determines whether your computer asks you to save each settings module individually or to save all changes at once.

Change settings in Mac OS 7.6–8

In Mac OS 7.6–8, you start by selecting a group to change in the Location Editing list on the left side of the Location Manager window and clicking the Open button (or double-clicking the location) to open the window for that group of settings. To add a setting, select it in the list of available system settings on the left side of the window and click the Add button. To remove a setting, select it in the list of location settings on the right side of the window and click the Delete button.

To change a setting, you must leave the Location Manager and make the change using the applicable control panel or other software. Next, you return to the window of the settings group you're editing in the Location Manager. Then in either list of settings in this window, you select the setting you just changed and click the Update button. (The Add button changes to an Update button when you select a setting that has a new system value.) For example, to change the sound volume stored for a group of settings called MyGroup, open MyGroup with the Location Manager's Open button, set the system volume with the Monitors & Sound control panel or the Sound control strip module, then select the Sound setting in the MyGroup window and click the Update button in that window.

If you're not sure how to change the value of a setting, select the setting in the window for the group and click the Get Info button there. This displays a dialog box that explains how to change the value of the selected setting.

Removing a settings group

To remove a settings group in Mac OS 8.1–8.5, choose Delete Location from the Location Manger's File menu. This command displays a list of groups. You delete a group by selecting it in the list and clicking the Delete button.

In Mac OS 7.6–8, you delete a group by selecting the group's name in the Location Editing list on the left side of the Location Manager control panel and clicking the Delete button.

Sharing settings groups

You can share groups of settings by importing and exporting them as location files. Choose Import Location or Export Location from the Location Manger's File menu. The Export Location command displays a standard Save dialog box in which you can name the exported location file and select a place to save it. The Import Location command displays a standard Open dialog box in which you can select a location file you want to import.

Sleep, Startup, and Shutdown Settings

All Macintosh PowerBooks and many Mac desktop models can go to sleep or automatically shut down to save energy while they are inactive. In the sleep state, the computer uses very little power. Shutting down the computer conserves even more energy, but there are advantages to making your computer sleep instead of shutting it down. The sleep state preserves your open programs, documents, and control panel settings so that when you "wake" the computer, you can start work from where you left off.

You can adjust how much energy your computer saves by setting how long it waits after becoming inactive before putting itself to sleep or shutting itself down. You may also be able to schedule times for a PowerBook to sleep and wake automatically or a desktop computer to shut down and start up automatically.

Over the years, Apple has produced a variety of software for setting these sleep, startup, and shutdown options. The control panels you use depend on what Mac model you have and which version of the Mac OS you use. This section covers the Energy Saver control panel version 2.0 and later, the PowerBook and PowerBook Setup pair of control panels, and an assortment of control strip modules. These are what all PowerBooks and many desktop models use with Mac OS 7.6–8.5.

If you use Mac OS 8.5 and your Mac is capable of sleep or scheduled shutdown and startup, you use the Energy Saver control panel version 2.1.1. This one control panel works on both desktop computers and PowerBooks that use Mac OS 8.5.

The situation with Mac OS 7.6–8.1 is not so simple. If you have a G3 Series PowerBook, you use Energy Saver 2.0.7 or later. Other PowerBook models use the PowerBook, PowerBook Setup, and AutoRemounter control panels with Mac OS 7.6–8.1. If you have a desktop computer with Mac OS 8.1, you use Energy Saver 2.0.7 or later. If your desktop Mac has Mac OS 7.6–8, you may use the CPU Energy Saver, Auto Power On/Off, or Energy Saver 1.0–1.1 control panels. These three control panels each do much less than Energy Saver 2.0 and later. Auto On/Auto Off can schedule times for startup and shutdown. CPU Energy Saver can schedule a shutdown time. Energy Saver 1.0–1.1 can only put external Energy Star monitors to sleep; this control panel can't make the computer sleep or schedule startup and shutdown times.

Setting sleep options

You can set sleep options that control how long your computer will remain idle before going to sleep. The sleep options are somewhat different for desktop computers and PowerBooks because the purpose of sleep is different on the two kinds of computers. A PowerBook sleeps to conserve battery power, and to achieve this goal it needs to go to sleep after a few minutes of inactivity. A desktop computer sleeps to save energy on a larger scale, and it can accomplish this without cycling in and out of sleep as frequently as a PowerBook.

Sleep or shutdown options on a desktop computer

If your desktop computer has the Energy Saver control panel, you can use it to set the amount of time before your computer goes to sleep or shuts down. To control these options, click the Sleep Setup button at the top of the control panel. You may see a single conservation-performance slider or you may see three sliders that enable you to set separate sleep timings for the whole system, the display, and the hard disk. You can alternate between these two views by clicking the Show Details button or the Hide Details button at the bottom of the control panel. In both views, you can select an option that makes your computer shut down rather than sleep. Figure 11-31 shows the two views of Energy Saver's sleep timings for desktop computers.

If you have configured sleep options on a PowerBook, you may wonder why desktop Macs have no provision for automatically reconnecting to network file servers and remounting shared folders and disks on wake-up. These actions are not necessary because shared disks and other network volumes remain mounted while a desktop computer sleeps.

BACKGROUNDER

Energy Star Savings

When you make an Energy Star computer and monitor sleep with the Energy Saver control panel, you reduce their power consumption to 60 watts or less (30 watts for the computer and 30 watts for the monitor). For example, a 150-watt Energy Star computer and monitor that sleeps half of each 10-hour weekday would cost $62 less per year to operate (at $0.10 per kWh) than a conventional system. Turning off an Energy Star computer nights and weekends would save another $42 per year. (*Energy Star* is a designation that the U.S. Environmental Protection Agency gives to computers, monitors, and other office equipment that meet its guidelines for energy conservation.)

Even more important than the cost savings is the reduction in air pollution that's a byproduct of generating electricity. According to the Rocky Mountain Institute (970-927-3851, http://www.rmi.org), "Computers and other electronic office equipment represent the fastest-growing electrical load in the United States, keeping at least a dozen 1000-megawatt power plants fully occupied." In an office, using the Energy Saver control panel and turning off your computer at night and over weekends also decreases the demand for air conditioning, which saves even more energy and reduces pollution.

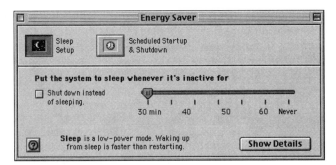

Figure 11-31: The Sleep Setup section of Energy Saver controls basic or detailed sleep timings for all desktop computers with Mac OS 8.5 and some with Mac OS 8–8.1.

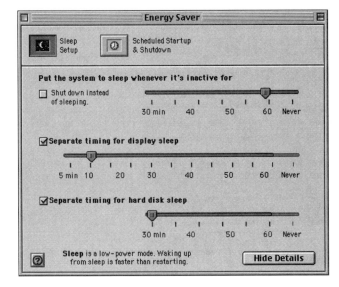

Sleep options on a PowerBook

If your PowerBook uses Mac OS 8.5, you use the Energy Saver control panel to set sleep options. Some G3 Series PowerBooks with Mac OS 8.1 also use the Energy Saver control panel to set sleep options. If your PowerBook uses Mac OS 7.6–8.1, you use the PowerBook control panel to set sleep preferences. These control panels look different but have similar options.

In the Energy Saver control panel, you set sleep options by clicking the Idle Sleep button at the top of the control panel. You may see a single conservation-performance slider or you may see three sliders that enable you to set separate sleep timings for the whole system, the display, and the hard disk. You can alternate between these two views by clicking the Show Details button or the Hide Details button at the bottom of the control panel. Figure 11-32 shows the two views of Energy Saver's sleep timings for PowerBooks.

In the PowerBook control panel, you always see a single conservation-performance slider. You may also see three additional sliders that let you set individual sleep timings for the system, screen, and hard disk. You can alternate between these two views by setting the Easy-Custom switch at the top of the control panel. Figure 11-33 shows the two views of the PowerBook control panel.

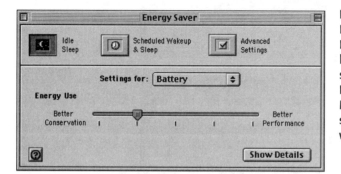

Figure 11-32: The Idle Sleep section of Energy Saver controls basic or detailed sleep timings for all PowerBooks with Mac OS 8.5 and for some PowerBooks with Mac OS 8.1.

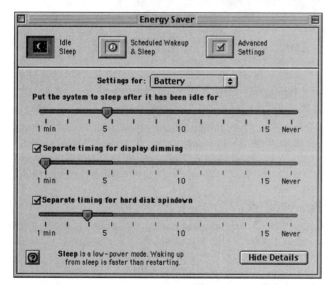

In both views of the Energy Saver control panel, and in the expanded view of the PowerBook control panel, you can set the timings differently for battery operation than for operation with the power adapter plugged into the computer. You choose the power mode from the pop-up menu in the control panel. With the PowerBook control panel, the computer determines whether to use the battery timings or the power-adapter timings as long as the Power Conservation option is set to Auto. When Power Conservation is set to Manual, the timings in the expanded section of the control panel stay in effect indefinitely.

Figure 11-33: The PowerBook control panel's easy and custom sleep options for PowerBooks with Mac OS 7.6–8.1.

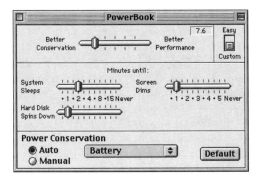

Instead of using control panels to set sleep options, you can set the basic power conservation level using the Control Strip. Figure 11-34 shows the control strip module you use.

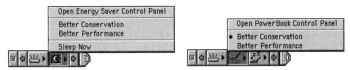

Figure 11-34: The Control Strip can set the basic power conservation level for PowerBooks with Mac OS 8.5 (left) or Mac OS 7.6–8.1 (right).

Advanced sleep options on a PowerBook

If your PowerBook has the Energy Saver control panel, you can click the Advanced Settings button to optimize energy use and control network connections on wake-up. The Power Cycling option lets the processor switch to a reduced-power mode when it is idle. The Reduced Processor Speed option makes the processor run at a slower speed, which may affect your PowerBook's performance. The option "Turn off the PowerBook Display instead of dimming it" conserves additional battery power by turning off the display back lighting altogether. The option "Turn off power to inactive PC Cards" forces all inactive PC cards to stop draining battery power, even those that normally require power when not in use. The Advanced section of the Energy Saver control panel also has options for reconnecting to file servers automatically on wake-up. Figure 11-35 shows the advanced options in the Energy Saver control panel.

If your PowerBook does not have the Energy Saver control panel, then you use the AutoRemounter control panel to configure network connections on wake-up. Select the After Sleep option to have the computer reconnect upon waking up. Select the Off option if you don't want the computer to reconnect automatically. If you want the computer to insist that each shared item's password (if any) be entered before reconnecting to the item, select the Always Entering Passwords option. If you want the computer to reconnect without asking for passwords, select the Automatically Remounting option. Figure 11-36 shows the AutoRemounter control panel.

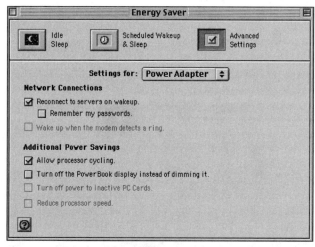

Figure 11-35: The Advanced Settings section of Energy Saver controls network connections and optimizes power use for PowerBooks with Mac OS 8.5.

Figure 11-36: AutoRemounter configures network connection options on wake-up for PowerBooks with Mac OS 7.6–8.1.

Triggering sleep manually

Although the Mac OS will put your computer to sleep after a user-specified period of inactivity, you gain additional energy savings by putting it to sleep manually if you know you won't use it for awhile. You can choose Sleep from the Special menu to make the computer sleep immediately. This command is available only while you're using the Finder.

You can make your computer sleep from any program by pressing the Power key on the keyboard. A dialog box appears asking if you want to restart, sleep, cancel, or shutdown. Click the Sleep button.

PowerBook users have other options for inducing sleep. Closing the lid puts many PowerBook models into the sleep state. Any PowerBook sleeps when you press ⌘-Shift-0. In Mac OS 7.6–7.6.1, you can make a PowerBook sleep by Control-clicking the battery monitor in the menu bar clock (if it is present). You can also make a PowerBook sleep or just spin down its hard disk using the Control Strip, as shown in Figure 11-37.

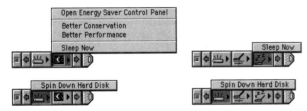

Figure 11-37: The Control Strip can make a PowerBook sleep or just spin down its hard disk in Mac OS 8.5 (left) or Mac OS 7.6–8.1 (right).

Waking up your computer

To make your Mac wake up, press the Power key or any other key on the keyboard. (On some models, the Caps Lock key and function keys may not work for this purpose.) You may hear a distinctive sound to let you know the computer is waking up, not restarting.

You can wake some desktop Macs by moving the mouse instead of pressing a key. (If you have a Macintosh Quadra model and Energy Saver 1.1, you should always use the mouse to wake the monitor; using the keyboard could freeze the computer.)

Scheduling wake up and sleep

You can schedule a PowerBook to wake itself up and, in some cases, to put itself to sleep. If your PowerBook has the Energy Saver control panel, you can set a recurring time or one time for wake-up and another recurring time or one time for sleep. You select these settings in the Scheduled Wakeup & Sleep section of the control panel. If your PowerBook has the PowerBook Settings control panel, you can use it to set a date and time for the PowerBook to wake itself. Figure 11-38 shows an example of the scheduled wake-up and sleep options.

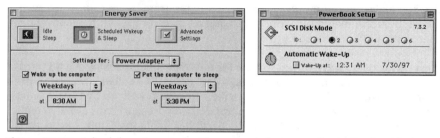

Figure 11-38: Schedule automated wake-up and sleep on a PowerBook with the Energy Saver control panel (left) or the PowerBook Setup control panel (right).

Scheduling startup and shutdown

If your desktop computer has the Energy Saver control panel, you can use it to schedule automated startup and shutdown times. This is a handy feature, especially if your computer takes a while to start. You could set your Mac to turn on automatically so it's ready when you get to work in the morning, or to shut down automatically to make sure it's off at night in case you forget. To see Energy Saver's scheduling options, click the Scheduled Startup & Shutdown button at the top of the Energy Saver control panel window, as shown in Figure 11-39.

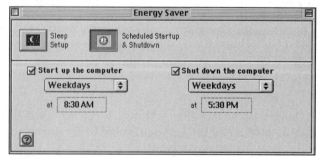

Figure 11-39: Schedule automated startup and shutdown on a desktop computer with the Energy Saver control panel.

To set a time for the computer to start up or shut down, turn on the "Start up the computer" option or the "Shut down the computer" option and enter a time in the space provided. Use the pop-up menu to choose the day or days you want the schedule to be effective: a specific day of the week, weekdays only, weekends only, or every day.

Language Preferences

The Mac OS puts all languages on an equal footing. It works with English, Spanish, French, German, and other languages that use the Roman alphabet and works equally well with Asian, Middle-Eastern, and other languages that use different alphabets. The Mac OS deals with the differences in language structure, writing direction, alphabetical sorting, calendar, date and time display, and currency. You're not limited to working in one language at a time. You can work in multiple languages and switch languages while you work. However, you may need to install additional software to use some languages, particularly languages that have a different alphabet than your system's primary language (the language used by the Finder).

To switch languages, you select a keyboard layout for a particular language and country, as described in this section. This section also explains how to change the text behavior and number format for a particular language and country. To change the date and time format, you use the Date & Time control panel (see "Date, Time, and Location Settings" earlier in this chapter). Finally, this section describes the software that you can install to add more languages to your Mac.

BACKGROUNDER

Language Script Systems and Keyboard Layouts

The world's languages have many different alphabets and methods of writing (vertical or horizontal, left-to-right, or right-to-left). The software that defines a method of writing is called a *language script system,* or simply a script. Do not confuse this kind of script with the kind of script you create with AppleScript (as described in Chapter 23).

A language script system tells the Mac OS which character in the specified language every keystroke produces, as well as how the characters should behave—for example, the direction in which text flows. The script also specifies sort order, number and currency formats, and date and time formats.

Multiple languages can use one language script system. For example, the Roman script is used in most Western languages, such as English, French, Italian, Spanish, and German.

Associated with each language script system are one or more keyboard layouts. A keyboard layout defines the relationship between keys you press and characters entered. For example, the keyboard layout for U.S. English produces a # symbol when you press Shift-3, but the same keystroke produces a £ symbol with the British English keyboard layout.

Selecting a keyboard layout

There are several ways to designate which keyboard layout you want to use of the ones installed on your computer. You can use the Keyboard control panel, a keyboard shortcut, or the Keyboard menu. With Mac OS 8.5, you can also synchronize the keyboard layout with the currently selected font. Remember, however, that only one keyboard layout matches the printed key caps on your keyboard. If you change to a different layout, some keys will no longer generate the characters printed on the keyboard.

Keyboard control panel

You can select a keyboard layout by opening the Keyboard control panel and clicking the name of the layout you want to use. With Mac OS 8–8.5, you can select more than one keyboard layout and you can choose a language script system in the Keyboard control panel. If you select more than one keyboard layout, the Keyboard menu appears near the right end of the menu bar (as described shortly). Figure 11-40 compares the Keyboard control panel from Mac OS 8–8.5 with the Keyboard control panel from Mac OS 7.6–7.6.1.

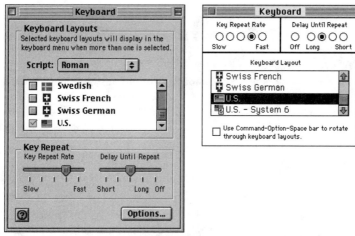

Figure 11-40: Select a keyboard layout in Mac OS 8–8.5 (left) and in Mac OS 7.6–7.6.1 (right).

Keyboard layout shortcut keys

The Keyboard control panel includes an option for enabling a keyboard shortcut. To set this option in Mac OS 8.5, click the Options button in the control panel. The option is in the control panel itself in Mac OS 7.6.1–8.1.

When you turn on this option, you can cycle through the available keyboard layouts by pressing ⌘-Option-spacebar while working in any application. Whether the keyboard shortcut option is selected or not, you can cycle through the installed script systems on your computer by pressing ⌘-spacebar.

Keyboard and font synchronization

If you use Mac OS 8.5, you can have the keyboard layout change automatically to match the font of text you select. This works because each font is implicitly associated with a particular language script system. To set this option, click the Options button in the Keyboard control panel. (This option is not available in Mac OS 7.6–8.1.)

Keyboard menu

If you regularly switch keyboard layouts with Mac OS 8–8.5, you can list the layouts you use in the Keyboard menu. You can then choose the layout from this menu while working in any application. To make the Keyboard menu appear, you select more than one keyboard layout in the Keyboard control panel that comes with Mac OS 8–8.5, and then close the control panel. The Keyboard menu is located near the right end of the menu bar next to the Application menu. The Keyboard menu's icon is a flag that indicates which keyboard layout is currently selected. Figure 11-41 shows an example of the Keyboard menu in Mac OS 8.5.

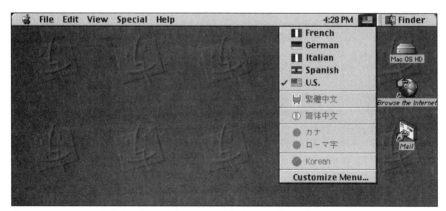

Figure 11-41: Switch keyboard layouts with the Keyboard menu.

If your computer has more than one language script system, switching keyboards may also change script systems. Each keyboard implicitly designates a script system because a keyboard layout can only be part of one script system. For example, if you switch from the U.S. keyboard layout to the Hebrew keyboard layout, you implicitly switch from the Roman script system to the Hebrew script system.

The Keyboard menu always appears if your computer has more than one language script system installed, because there must be at least one keyboard layout selected for each script system.

English and other Western languages typically provide only one way to enter text, and U.S. keyboards are based on that text input method. But in languages that are based on ideograms, such as Japanese and Chinese, text can be input in multiple ways. The Japanese language kit comes with an input method called Kotoeri that enables entering Kanji, Katakana, Hiragana, and Romaji. Other input methods are available. (Input methods are listed in the Keyboard menu.) The Chinese language kit comes equipped with Pinyin, Zhuyin, Cangjie, and Wubi input-method software, as well as two character sets: simplified and traditional.

Setting text behavior

Each language has its own rules of behavior, even though it may use the same script as another language. You teach the Mac OS the rules to use by setting the language behavior in the Text control panel. The options in this control panel tell the Mac OS how to produce text from characters. For languages that flow right-to-left, the control panel provides additional options. You can split the flashing vertical line that marks the insertion point so that you can see where your next typing will next appear for left-to-right writing as well as for right-to-left writing.

In the Text control panel, you also specify a set of rules for alphabetizing, capitalizing, and distinguishing words. First you choose among the installed language-script systems, such as Roman, Cyrillic, Arabic, Japanese, and Chinese. Then you choose among the regional rules for text behavior that the selected script system supports. For example, the Roman script system has text behavior rules for Brazilian, Danish, Dutch, English, Finnish, French, French Canadian, German, Italian, Norwegian, Spanish, and Swedish. Figure 11-42 shows the Text control panel options for the Roman and Hebrew scripts.

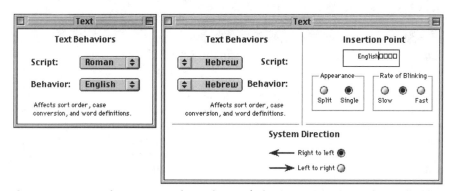

Figure 11-42: Use the Text control panel to set behavior options for each installed language.

Setting number formats

The Numbers control panel sets the number format — decimal separator, thousand separators, and currency symbol. You can choose a preconfigured number format for a region of the world that corresponds to one of the languages installed on your system. You can also specify a custom format by entering the punctuation marks to use as separators and the currency symbol. Figure 11-43 shows the Numbers control panel.

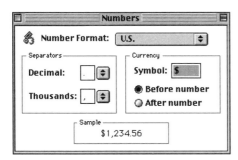

Figure 11-43: The Numbers control panel sets the format for numbers.

Installing multilingual software

To read or write in a language that uses a different alphabet than your system's primary language, you need to install additional software known as a *language kit*. A language kit includes a language script system, one or more keyboard layouts, and fonts.

Nine language kits are bundled with Mac OS 8.5, but installation is optional. The bundle includes Arabic, Devanagari, Gujurati, Gurmukhi, Hebrew, Japanese (display only), Korean (display only), Simplified Chinese (display only), and Traditional Chinese (display only). The ones designated as "display only" can be used only for reading text, not for writing it. To install these languages, do a custom installation of Mac OS 8.5 (as described in Chapter 31) and select the Multilingual Internet Access module.

Apple sells complete language kits for reading and writing in many languages. These language kits can upgrade the display-only language kits included with Mac OS 8.5, and they can add more languages to Mac OS 7.6–8.5. Apple's retail language kits require an updater with Mac OS 8.5. (The bundled language kits do not require updating.) If you upgrade an older system or install a language kit after installing Mac OS 8.5, be sure to run the Language Kit Updater program. It's included on the Mac OS 8.5 CD in the CD Extras folder. You can also get it free from Apple's Software Updates library (http://www.apple.com/swupdates/).

Besides language kits, you need applications that can use the languages installed on your computer. You get two such applications when you install the Multilingual Internet Access module with Mac OS 8.5: Microsoft Internet Explorer and Netscape

Navigator. You can use either one to browse foreign language Web pages on the Internet. (Web browsing is covered in Chapter 17.) In addition, you can buy applications that let you create multilingual documents as well as applications whose menus and dialog boxes are in a foreign language. For example, if you have English, Spanish, and Hebrew installed on your computer, you might use applications that are exclusively Spanish or Hebrew. You might also use a word processor that has English menus but lets you write documents in any combination of languages.

Compatibility Settings

The Cache Switch control panel on a Mac with a 68040 processor enables or disables the processor's internal caches. The setting of this control panel provides a trade-off between performance and compatibility. Figure 11-44 shows the Cache Switch control panel.

Figure 11-44: The Cache Switch control panel for computers with 68040 processors.

Selecting the Faster option improves performance by enabling the processor to store frequently used instructions and data in its internal caches. If you have programs that don't work correctly when the processor's caches are enabled, select the More Compatible option. It makes your computer run slower because the processor has to fetch all instructions and data from the computer's main memory.

The Serial Switch control panel provides compatibility for some applications that use the printer and modem ports. You can set the serial ports to Faster or More Compatible. This control panel works on Quadra 950 and IIfx computers. Figure 11-45 shows the Serial Switch control panel.

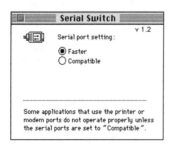

Figure 11-45: The Serial Switch control panel for Quadra 950 and IIfx computers.

Summary

In this chapter, you learned to use control panels to customize various aspects of your computer's operation to make your work more comfortable and productive. You learned how to set general preferences such as the preferred location for opening and saving documents, and the blinking rates for the insertion point and menus. You learned how to adjust the responsiveness of the keyboard and mouse. You learned how to change sound level and alert sounds; to adjust the way your monitor looks; and to set the current date, time, and location for your computer. You learned to install and modify the Control Strip. You learned how to use the Location Manager to create groups of settings and what control panels allow you to set sleep, startup, and shutdown times. Finally, you learned how to set foreign language preferences and adjust compatibility settings.

✦   ✦   ✦

Make Aliases Hop

Did you ever wish a file or folder could be in more than one place? You want to keep the contents of your disk organized by putting programs and documents in folders, and putting those folders in other folders. But when you want to open an item, you end up digging through folders to find what you want to open. *Aliases* cut through the organizational red tape. Think of an alias as a stand-in or an agent for a real program, document, folder, or disk. Aliases act like real items when you open them or drag items to them. You can place these agents at your beck and call in any handy location, such as on the desktop or in the Apple menu. Aliases even look a lot like the items they represent.

Understanding Aliases

Like the documents, programs, and other files on your disks, aliases are files that contain information. Aliases contain a different kind of information than other files. Where a document file contains text, pictures, or other data and a program file contains code, an alias file contains a pointer to a document, program, other file, folder, or disk. Figure 12-1 shows how aliases point to other items.

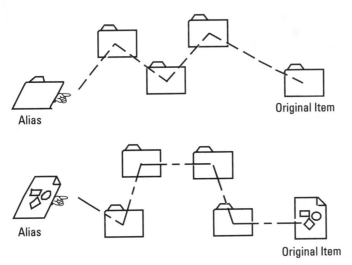

Figure 12-1: An alias points to its original item.

By analyzing the information in an alias, the Mac OS can locate the alias's *original item*. This process is called *resolving* an alias. The Mac OS can successfully resolve an alias to locate the alias's original item, even if you move or rename the original item or move the original item to a different folder. The only way you can break the connection between an alias and its original item is to drag the original item to the Trash and empty the Trash. The Mac OS cannot successfully resolve an alias whose original item no longer exists.

When you open an alias, the Mac OS uses the information in the alias to locate the original item and then opens the original. Dragging an item to the alias of a folder or disk in the Finder has the same effect as dragging it to the original folder or disk: the Finder uses the information in the alias to locate the original folder or disk and places the item you dragged there. Likewise, dragging a document to an alias of a compatible program opens the document. You can even drag an alias of a document to an alias of a compatible application; the Finder uses the information in both aliases to have the application open the document.

Making an Alias

You can make an alias for any item that you can open from the Finder. That means you can make aliases for documents, application programs, desk accessories, folders, disks, control panels, and even fonts and sounds. Making an alias is a simple procedure. In the Finder, select the item for which you want to create an alias and choose Make Alias from the File menu. A new item appears with the same icon as the original item, except that in Mac OS 8.5 the icon has a small curved arrow superimposed to indicate it is an alias. Every alias has an italicized name that matches that of the original item plus the suffix *alias*. Figure 12-2 illustrates the procedure.

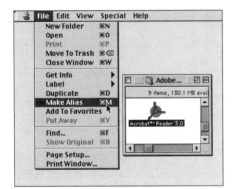

Figure 12-2: The Make Alias command (left) creates an alias that looks a lot like the original item (right).

Making an alias in Mac OS 8–8.5

In addition to the File menu, if your Mac has Mac OS 8–8.5 you can Control-click an item to pop-up its contextual menu and choose Make Alias from there. (For more information on using contextual menus, see "Menus" in Chapter 4.)

Mac OS 8–8.5 provides a convenient shortcut for making an alias. Just drag the original item to the place you want the alias, and then press ⌘-Option before releasing the mouse button. You can start pressing those keys any time while dragging, but you must hold them down while you release the mouse button if you want to make an alias. The pointer changes shape when you ⌘-Option-drag an item to a place where the Finder can make an alias, such as a folder, a disk, or the desktop. The pointer acquires a small right-pointing arrow in addition to its normal large left-pointing arrow. If you press ⌘-Option to make an alias at a location different from the original—for example, in another folder or on another disk— then the alias does not have the word "alias" at the end of its name. Figure 12-3 shows the pointer shape that means "make alias" in Mac OS 8–8.5.

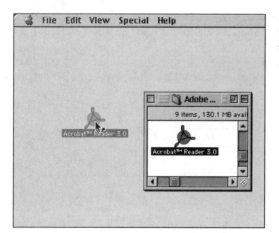

Figure 12-3: The pointer has a special shape when you ⌘-Option-drag to create an alias in Mac OS 8–8.5.

Making an alias in Mac OS 7.6–7.6.1

It normally takes two or three steps to make an alias at a location different from the original if you're using Mac OS 7.6–7.6.1. First you make an alias at the same location as the original item. Then you drag the alias to the place you want it. If that place is on a different disk than the original item, delete the alias you made that is next to the original.

If you want to make an alias anywhere in one step using Mac OS 7.6–7.6.1, you need to install the free utility software Finder Options (described in Chapter 26).

SECRETS

Same Alias, Different Size

Aliases vary in size from 1K to 17K or more, depending on the capacity and format of the disk they're on. For example, an alias takes up 1K of a floppy disk, a 20MB hard disk, or a 40MB hard disk. On a 100MB disk, an alias takes up 2K. On a 1GB disk in Mac OS Standard format, aliases occupy 17K each. The same aliases occupy 4K or less each on a 1GB disk in Mac OS Extended format. (Mac OS Extended format requires Mac OS 8.1–8.5.) If a hard disk is partitioned into multiple volumes (each having its own icon on the desktop), the volume capacity determines the size of the aliases on it. For details, see "Working with Disks" in Chapter 5 and "Partitioning Hard Disks" in Chapter 6.

Changing an Alias

After you make an alias, you can manipulate it as you would any other item. You can move it, copy it, and rename it. You can change its icon, comments, or locked status in its Info window.

Moving and copying an alias

If you move an alias to another folder on the same disk or to the desktop, the alias still knows where to find its original item.

You can copy an alias by using the Finder's Duplicate command or by dragging the alias to another disk or to a folder on another disk. To copy an alias or other item to another folder on the same disk, press Option while dragging. All copies of the alias point to the same original item.

Renaming an alias

You rename an alias as you would any other item on the desktop or in a Finder window. Immediately after you create an alias, its name is selected for editing. You can change the name by typing a replacement or by using other standard text-editing techniques (see "Icons" in Chapter 4). For example, you might want to shorten "Microsoft Word alias" to "Word" before adding the alias to the Apple menu or the Launcher. To keep the name as is, click anywhere outside the name or press Return or Enter.

If you want an alias to have exactly the same name as its original item, the two cannot be in the same folder. You must move one out. For example, if you make an alias with the idea of moving it to another folder and you don't want the alias to have the suffix "alias," you have to move the alias before editing its name. Of course, an alias and its original can be in the same folder if their names are very similar but not identical. For example, the alias name could have an extra blank space at the end.

Deleting an Alias

Like any item, you remove an alias by dragging it to the Trash. Remember that throwing away an alias doesn't affect the original item. You're only throwing away the alias, not the item to which it points.

QUICK TIPS

Removing the Suffix "Alias"

To remove the word *alias* quickly from the end of an alias's name, click the name once to select it for editing. Pause briefly (or avoid the pause by moving the mouse slightly to the right after you click the alias name). Double-click the last word of the name. Then press Delete twice (once to delete the selected word *alias* and a second time to delete the space before that word). If you double-click too soon after selecting the name, the Finder opens the item to which the alias points rather than selecting the last word of the name.

Alternatively, you can select the name for editing, press the down-arrow (↓) key or right-arrow (→) key to move the insertion point to the end of the name, and press Delete six times to erase the last word and the space preceding it. To conclude your name editing, click anywhere outside the name or press Return or Enter. If you want the Finder never to add the word *alias* as a suffix, you can modify the Finder with the free ResEdit utility program (see "Icons" in Chapter 27).

Changing an alias's icon

An alias inherits its icon from the original item. In Mac OS 8.5, an alias's icon normally looks like the icon of its original item with a small curved arrow superimposed. In Mac OS 7.6–8.1, an alias's icon normally looks exactly like the icon of its original item. If you subsequently change the original item's icon, the alias icon is updated automatically the next time you open it.

Like most other icons, you can customize an alias icon in its Info window. You bring up the Info window by using the Finder's Get Info command (see "Custom Icons" in Chapter 8). The alias's custom icon won't be affected by changes to the icon of the original item.

Locking an alias and entering its comments

Although an alias initially inherits the icon of its original item, the alias does not inherit the comments or the locked attribute of its original item. Every new alias is initially unlocked and has no comments. You can type comments about an alias and lock the alias in its Info window, which you display by using the Finder's Get Info command. The Info window has a space where you can enter comments (see "Attaching Comments to Items" in Chapter 6). The Info window also has a Locked option that you can turn on and off (see "Protecting Files, Folders, and Disks" in Chapter 6). Locking an alias prevents changing the name or icon of the alias — the same as locking any file. Locking an alias does not lock its original item.

Keeping Track of Original Items

Aliases are truly amazing at keeping track of their original items. Not only can you rename and move an alias's original item, but you also can replace it with another file that has the same name, all without breaking the link to the alias. You may wonder how the Mac OS can find an alias's original item after you rename or move the original item. If the Mac OS cannot find an item that has the same name and folder location as the original, it searches for the original item's unique *file ID number,* which the Mac OS internally assigns to each file. Once the Mac OS finds the item by using this ID number, it updates the alias with the original item's current name and folder location.

When you copy the original item referenced by an alias, the alias still points to the original item (not to the copy you just made). Sounds reasonable, but it doesn't feel reasonable when you want to move an alias's original item to a different disk. That's because moving and copying involve basically the same action — dragging an item. If you drag to a folder on the same disk, the Finder moves the item and the item's alias knows where to find the moved item. If you drag to a folder on another disk, the Finder copies the item. The alias knows where the original item is, but not the copy. If you then delete the original item (on the alias's disk), you break the alias's link to the item, even though a copy of the item exists on another disk.

Fixing Orphaned Aliases

If you use an alias whose original item has been deleted, the Mac OS tells you that it can't find the original item. Figure 12-4 shows the alert that you see in the Finder if the system can't resolve an alias.

You see a somewhat different alert when you try to open an orphaned alias in a standard Open or Save dialog box. This alert is smaller and does not name the alias. Moreover, in Mac OS 8.5 this alert has fewer buttons than the Finder's similar alert.

 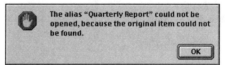

Figure 12-4: Finder displays an alert when it can't find an alias's original item in Mac OS 8.5 (left) and Mac OS 7.6–8.1 (right).

Quick fix in Mac OS 8.5

In Mac OS 8.5, the Finder offers a quick fix for an orphaned alias. When you try to open an orphaned alias, you see an alert that helps you delete an orphaned alias or select a new original for it. This alert has a Delete button and a Fix Alias button. Clicking the Delete button deletes the alias. Clicking the Fix Alias button brings up a Choose Object dialog box in which you can choose a new original for the alias. Figure 12-5 shows the Choose Object dialog box in which you choose a new alias.

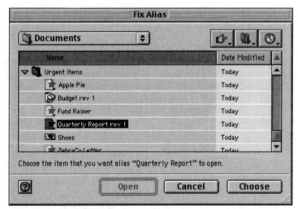

Figure 12-5: Choosing a new original for an orphaned alias in Mac OS 8.5.

Other fixes

In any Mac OS version, you can use utility software to connect an orphaned alias to its original file or to a copy of the original. For example, Spring Cleaning from Aladdin Systems (http://www.aladdinsys.com) can list the orphaned aliases on a disk and help you delete or fix them. The shareware programs Alias Crony by Rocco Moliterno and AliasZoo by Cliff McCollum have similar capabilities (see Chapter 26). But it's often easier just to create a new alias and throw out the broken one.

Finding an Original Item

You can find an alias's original item by choosing Show Original (in Mac OS 8–8.5) or Get Info (Mac OS 7.6–7.6.1) from the Finder's File menu. The Show Original command brings up the window that contains the original item, scrolls the original item into view, and selects it. The Get Info command displays the alias's Info window. In Mac OS 7.6–7.6.1, an alias's Info window includes a Find Original button, and clicking that button brings up the window that contains the original item, scrolls the original item into view, and selects it. In all Mac OS versions, an alias's Info window reports the disk and folder path to the original. Figure 12-6 shows examples of Info windows.

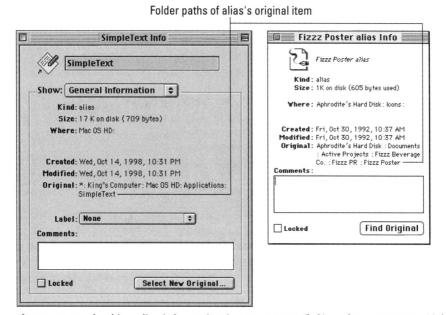

Folder paths of alias's original item

Figure 12-6: Checking alias information in Mac OS 8.5 (left) and Mac OS 7.6.1 (right).

If you try to find an original item on a removable disk that's not currently inserted, the Finder usually asks you to insert that disk. The Finder also ejects any currently inserted disk of the same type (floppy disk, Zip disk, and so forth). This can lead to a vicious bout of disk swapping, which you can cut short by pressing ⌘-period(.) repeatedly until the Finder stops asking you to insert disks. Then put away the currently inserted disk (by dragging it to the Trash or using Mac OS 8–8.5's Move To Trash command), insert the disk that contains the alias's original item, and try the Show Original command (Mac OS 8–8.5) or Find Original button (Mac OS 7.6–7.6.1) again.

Instead of asking you to insert a missing disk that contains an alias's original item, the Finder may display a message saying the original item couldn't be found. That happens with some types of removable hard disks unless another disk of the same type has been inserted since you started or restarted your computer.

Selecting a New Original Item

In Mac OS 8.5, you can change an alias so it opens a different item. Select the alias and use the Get Info command to display the alias's Info window. In the Info window, click the Select New Original button. This brings up a Choose Object dialog box (previously shown in Figure 12-5), in which you select the item that you want to become the alias's new original item.

To change an alias's original item in Mac OS 7.6–8.1, make a new alias and delete the old one. This method also works in Mac OS 8.5

Discovering the Many Uses of Aliases

There are many useful applications for aliases. The most common is quick access to programs and documents you work with frequently. For example, you can make an alias of a spreadsheet you use regularly to update sales figures and place the alias in a convenient location, such as the desktop. Some of the most important uses of aliases include adding items to the Apple menu or to the Startup Items folder; adding desktop convenience for accessing items; accessing archived information from removable disks; and streamlining access to shared items. The following sections provide a collection of scenarios to leverage the power of aliases, providing express service to a wide range of items.

Aliases in the Apple menu

The most convenient place from which to open application programs, desk accessories, control panels, documents, folders, and other items is the Apple menu. Because the Apple menu is always on the menu bar, items in the Apple menu are never more than a mouse click away. You can add to the Apple menu any item that you can open by using the Finder, including aliases.

Placing an alias in the Apple menu is as easy as dragging the alias icon to the Apple Menu Items folder, which is in the System Folder. The name of the alias appears instantly in the Apple menu in plain (not italic) text. Choosing the alias from the Apple menu opens the alias's original item. (You don't have to restart your computer for changes to the Apple Menu Items folder to take place.)

You can add as many aliases as you want to the Apple Menu Items folder. However, it's a good idea to keep the number within a reasonable range to avoid having to scroll through an extralong menu. To remove an alias from the Apple menu, drag its icon out of the Apple Menu Items folder.

One way to shorten the Apple menu is to put some related aliases in a submenu. You do this by putting the aliases in a folder inside the Apple Menu Items folder, or by putting the alias of a folder (or a disk) into the Apple Menu Items folder. For example, during installation of the Mac OS, an alias of the Control Panels folder is placed in the Apple Menu Items folder, making all the control panels appear in a Control Panels submenu of the Apple menu. Another example: the Finder places folders named Recent Applications, Recent Documents, and Recent Servers in the Apple Menu Items folder and puts aliases of recently used items in those folders. What's more, you can get universal access to your entire hard disk (up to the first five levels of nested folders) by putting an alias of your hard disk in the Apple Menu Items folder. However, don't be surprised if the overhead of keeping all the resulting submenus up-to-date slows your system somewhat.

To see submenus in the Apple menu and track recent items in submenus, you must have the options for submenus and recent items turned on in the Apple Menu Options control panel (as described in "Opening Programs, Documents, and More" in Chapter 7).

Adjusting an alias's position in the Apple menu

Items in the Apple menu appear alphabetically by name. You may want to change the name of your alias to adjust its position in the Apple menu. You can force an item to the top of the menu by putting a blank space at the beginning of its name or force it to the bottom of the list by beginning its name with a bullet (•). These and other techniques for organizing the Apple menu are described in more detail in "Opening Programs, Documents, and More" in Chapter 7.

Fast access to the Apple Menu Items folder

One useful alias that you can add to the Apple menu is an alias of the Apple Menu Items folder. Adding this alias allows you to quickly open the Apple Menu Items folder and to easily customize the Apple menu.

A frequent items menu

You can organize your frequently used items in the Apple menu by putting aliases of them in folders inside the Apple Menu Items folder. For example, you might have folders named Applications, Utilities, and Documents. (The folders create submenus in the Apple menu if you have the Submenus option turned on in the Apple Menu Options control panel.) The problem with this scheme is the time it takes to make aliases and place them in the appropriate folders.

One efficient way to manage favorite items the Apple menu is to place an alias of the Launcher Items folder in the Apple Menu Items folder. If you like, name this alias "Frequent Items" and put a space at the beginning of its name so it appears at the top of the Apple menu. Because Frequent Items is the alias of a folder, the items in the folder (in this case, the Launcher Items folder) appear in a Frequent Items submenu of the Apple menu. When you add items to the Launcher (by dragging them to its window), it places aliases of them in the Launcher Items folder. Then the Frequent Items alias makes the newly added items in the Launcher Items folder also appear in the Frequent Items submenu of the Apple menu. If you have created category buttons in the Launcher by creating inner folders whose names begin with a bullet (•), the categories appear as submenus of the Frequent Items submenu. (The Launcher is covered in "Opening Programs, Documents, and More" in Chapter 7.)

In Mac OS 8–8.5, you don't have to use the Launcher to manage frequently used items. Instead, you can create a folder named Frequent Items and leave it open as a pop-up window. Put an alias of the Frequent Items folder into the Apple Menu Items folder. Now the contents of the pop-up window appear as a submenu in the Apple menu. You can easily add and remove items from this submenu by dragging the corresponding items (preferably aliases) in and out of the pop-up window.

Universal Show Clipboard

Some application programs lack a Show Clipboard command and others that have one use a private clipboard whose contents may look different when pasted into another program. With an alias, you can put a Show Clipboard command in your Apple menu for reviewing the standard Clipboard contents from any application program. First, make an alias of the Clipboard file, which is in the System Folder. Then place the alias in the Apple Menu Items folder and rename the alias Show Clipboard. Now, choosing Show Clipboard from the Apple menu switches to the Finder and opens the Clipboard.

Aliases on the desktop

Other than the Apple menu, the desktop is the most accessible place for opening items and the most accessible place for folders to which you want to drag items. Rather than drag frequently used programs, control panels, documents, and folders themselves onto the desktop, make aliases of them and put the aliases on the desktop. Aliases on the desktop give you immediate access to items buried deep within nests of folders.

Putting aliases of programs on the desktop avoids the problems that can occur when you move the programs themselves onto the desktop. Such programs depend on support files being with them in the same folder (or on the desktop). For example, a word processor may also need a dictionary file on the desktop in order to check spelling. Aliases save you the hassle of guessing which support files a program needs to run correctly and avoid the mess that may result when you place those support files on the desktop. By creating an alias for an application, the alias accesses the original application in its folder, saving you from moving the application and its supporting files to get full access to the application.

By making aliases of documents and programs you use frequently and putting the aliases on the desktop, you don't have to always remember where you put the original items. Also, you can open several related items at the same time, even if the original items happen to be in different folders or on different disks, by opening aliases on the desktop.

Getting at buried desktop aliases

When windows of background applications cover desktop aliases, you can hide those windows by choosing Hide Others from the Application menu.

When windows of the foreground application cover desktop icons, you can collapse the windows. In Mac OS 8–8.5, click each window's collapse box, or Option-click any window's collapse box to collapse all the active application's windows. You can also collapse a window, or Option-double-click to collapse all windows, if the "Double-click title bar to collapse" option is turned on in the Appearance control panel. When this option is turned on, you can collapse a background window of the active application (but not a window of a background application) by ⌘-double-clicking its title bar. In Mac OS 7.5–7.6.1, you collapse windows of the active application according to the settings of the WindowShade control panel.

In all versions of the Mac OS, you can also close all the active application's windows at once by Option-clicking the close box of any window.

Clearing the desktop of alias clutter

If your desktop becomes too cluttered with aliases, you can put related aliases together in folders on the desktop. You can make these folders even more accessible by putting them (or aliases of them) in the Apple Menu Items folder. Choosing a folder from the Apple menu opens it and brings its window to the front even if the Finder was not the active application.

In Mac OS 8–8.5, you can put a folder full of aliases anywhere, open it, and drag its window to the bottom of the screen to make it a pop-up window. To see how this works, try opening the Favorites folder (choose it from the Apple menu) and make its window a pop-up window.

Multiple trash cans

If you have a big monitor, put aliases of the Trash in the upper-left and lower-left corners of the desktop. The extra Trash icons expedite discarding items when you're working on the left side of the desktop. Extending this idea, if you have two monitors, put a Trash alias on the desktop of the second monitor. That way, you never have to drag icons across two screens to throw them away.

"Remove disk" icon

In a few minutes you can solve a problem that has bothered Mac OS users since day one — the customary but dumb method of removing a disk from the Mac by dragging the disk icon to the Trash. You simply make an alias of the Trash, change the alias's name to Remove Disk, and paste a custom icon in the alias's Get Info window. Make the custom icon look like a hand removing a disk or a disk with an arrow pointing in the direction of ejection. Figure 12-7 shows an example of a "remove disk" icon.

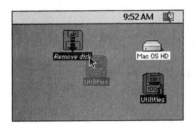

Figure 12-7: For removing disks, try an alias of the Trash with a custom icon.

Open, Save, and Navigation Services shortcuts

Alias names appear in italics in dialog boxes that list folder and disk contents. These dialog boxes include the Open and Save dialog boxes, and in Mac OS 8.5 the Navigation Services dialog box. Opening an alias in these dialog boxes (by double-clicking it, for instance) opens its original item. Instead of opening an alias's original item, you can quickly select the original item in an Open, Save, or Navigation Services dialog box by pressing Option while opening the alias. In this case, the system opens the folder containing the original item and selects the original item (but does not open the original item). Figure 12-8 shows an example of an alias in Open and Navigation Services dialog boxes.

To make an alias appear near the top of the list in Open, Save, and Navigation Services dialog boxes, put a blank space at the beginning of the alias's name. Items having initial blank spaces in their names float alphabetically to the top of the list in an Open, Save, or Navigation Services dialog box. (When you view the desktop level in an Open or Save dialog box, disks always appear at the top of the list above all other items. Navigation Services dialog boxes intermingle disks with other desktop items.)

If you don't like how initial spaces look, you can paste a blank line at the beginning of each name that you want to appear at the top of the list. Create the blank line by pressing Return in the Note Pad or any word processor. For step-by-step instructions and a caveat, see "Opening Programs, Documents, and More" in Chapter 7.

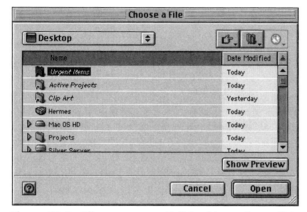

Figure 12-8: Alias names are italicized in an Open dialog box (top) and in Mac OS 8.5's Navigation Services dialog box (bottom).

Aliases as startup items

Every time you start (or restart) your computer, the Finder automatically opens everything in the Startup Items folder. For example, if you regularly use a particular program, you may want it ready to go immediately after you start your computer. But some programs must remain in a folder with other auxiliary files and won't work correctly if you move their icons to the Startup Items folder. Furthermore, returning items to their previous locations when you no longer want them opened at startup time can be a drag.

Moving an alias of a program, document, or other item to the Startup Items folder causes the original item to open during startup. To remove an alias from the startup sequence, drag the alias out of the folder.

Application programs in the Startup Items folder open in alphabetical order, so you can rename the alias of an application program to determine when it starts relative to other application programs in that folder. Aliases of desk accessories, control panels, and folders open alphabetically after all application programs have opened. (For more information about the Startup Items folder, see "Opening Programs, Documents, and More" in Chapter 7.)

QUICK TIPS

Quick Access to Favorite Folders

For quick access to a favorite folder in Open and Save dialog boxes, put an alias of the folder on the desktop. In an Open or Save dialog box, you can quickly get to aliases of favorite folders at the desktop level by clicking the Desktop button. Instead of working your way down through one branch of your folder structure and then working your way up another branch to the folder you want, you zip to the desktop level and there open the alias of the folder you want. It's as if you can jump from one branch of a tree to root level and then jump to a spot on another branch on another tree without having to crawl up the trunk and along the other branch.

Chances are you will only use aliases of favorite folders in Open and Save dialog boxes, never in the Finder. You also don't need to use desktop aliases of favorite folders in Navigation Services dialog boxes, where you can use the Favorites button instead (see "Opening Programs, Documents, and More" in Chapter 7.)

The specially named folder alias doesn't have to clutter your desktop to appear at the desktop level of Open and Save dialog boxes. Simply drag the alias to the bottom of the screen so that the alias name and most of its icon are out of view below the edge of the screen. Then cover up the remaining visible part of the icon by placing a pop-up window over it. (If you try to put an icon too low on the screen, the Finder automatically moves the alias to the left side of the desktop.) Try again, but don't drag the icon quite so low this time.

Startup messages

Do you like to have reminders at startup, but don't want to use the Stickies program? Create a clipping file of your notes, and place an alias of it in the Startup Items folder. Rename it to be alphabetically last (for example "zzNotes") so it opens after other startup items. At startup, the Finder does not have to launch an application to display the note, which you can easily dismiss by pressing ⌘-W. If you keep the clipping on your desktop, you will be able to view it anytime you want, within seconds. You can use a startup clipping in a lab setting to display general notes, update information, disclaimers, warnings, and so on. (For information on creating clipping files, see "Moving Document Contents Around" in Chapter 7.)

STEP-BY-STEP

Confirming Startup Items

Here's a trick if you use Mac OS 7.6–7.6.1 and want to open items in the Startup Items folder only some of the time:

1. Make a duplicate of an application (such as SimpleText).

2. Make an alias of the duplicate.

3. Drag the duplicate application to the Trash.

4. Empty the Trash.

5. Place the alias of the application you just deleted in the Startup Items folder.

6. Give the alias a name that alphabetically precedes all other items in that folder.

When the Finder encounters the alias, it displays an alert telling you that it cannot find the alias's original item, as shown in the figure below. Click Stop to cancel opening the startup items or click Continue to finish opening them.

This trick does not work with Mac OS 8–8.5.

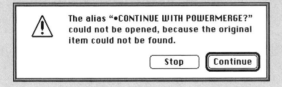

The alias "•CONTINUE WITH POWERMERGE?" could not be opened, because the original item could not be found.

[Stop] [Continue]

Audio CD autoplay

Would you like to have an audio CD play when you start your Mac? Putting an alias of any track from any audio CD into the Startup Items folder has the Finder automatically launch AppleCD Audio Player during startup and begin playing whatever CD is in the drive at that track. The track alias works with any audio CD, not just the one used to make the alias. If there's no CD in the drive, the Mac requests one. If you have QuickTime 2.5 or later, you can get a similar effect with the Enable Audio CD AutoPlay option in the QuickTime Settings control panel (see "Audio CDs" in Chapter 16). The control panel option always starts at track 1, but you can make an alias to start with any track.

Abridged System Folder

Aliases can help you quickly find folders in the System Folder whose contents you need to get at, such as the Startup Items folder and the Fonts folder. Here's how you do it: Make aliases for the System Folder items you access often—including the System Folder itself—and put all those aliases in a new folder. You can open and find an item in that new folder faster than in the System Folder. To make the new folder look like a System Folder, copy the icon from the System Folder's Info window and paste it into the new folder's Info window.

System Folder annex

If you need more space on your startup disk and you have another hard disk with space available, you can move large items such as the After Dark Files folder (which can easily be over 15MB) from the System Folder to a nonstartup disk. After copying an item from the System Folder to the nonstartup disk, make an alias of the copy (not of the original in the System Folder). Drag the original item from the System Folder to the Trash. Drag the alias from the nonstartup disk to the location that the original item formerly occupied in the System Folder. Then rename the alias so that it has exactly the same name as the original item. For example, an alias of the After Dark Files folder must be named After Dark Files and put in the Control Panels folder.

This technique doesn't work with all System Folder items. You'll have to experiment to see if it helps you.

Aliases of items on removable disks

You can use aliases to keep track of and quickly open items on removable disks— even the ones that aren't currently inserted. For example, you can keep the installation software for applications that you download from the Internet on removable hard disks and make an alias of each installation folder or installer program in a folder named Installers on your main hard drive. Then when you need to reinstall some software, you can quickly open the appropriate alias in your Installers folder. The system tells you the name of the disk to insert so that it can open the alias's original item.

QUICK TIPS

Personal Icon Library

A single floppy disk can use aliases to store hundreds of interesting icons for later use as custom icons for any file, folder, or disk. Just make aliases of files, folders, or disks having icons you want to save and copy the aliases to a floppy named Personal Icon Library. Whenever you want to use one of the custom icons from the floppy disk, copy the icon from the alias's Info window. Then paste it into the Info window of the file, folder, or disk whose icon you want to customize (as described in "Icons" in Chapter 4).

Be sure to make aliases of archived items *after* copying them to removable disks, not before. If you make aliases of the items while they are still on the hard disk, the aliases stop working when you delete the original items from the hard disk after copying them to a removable disk. (Remember, aliases point to the original items, not to copies of the originals on other disks.)

Aliases of shared items

The file-sharing capabilities of the Mac OS enable you to share items from someone else's computer if it is connected to the same network as yours. But getting access to shared items involves wading through a fair amount of bureaucracy in the Chooser.

Aliases cut through the red tape. Here's how: You access a shared disk or folder once by using the Chooser (see "Using Shared Folders and Disks" in Chapter 20). Next, select the shared item or any folder or file in it and make an alias of it on your hard disk. An alias keeps track of its original item even when the original item is on another networked Mac. Figure 12-9 shows some aliases of shared items.

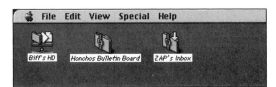

Figure 12-9: Aliases of a shared disk, a shared folder that you can't access, and a shared folder that you can put items into.

Once you make an alias of a shared item, you can get to the shared item by opening the alias. Dragging something to the alias of a shared disk or folder also automatically accesses that shared item. You still must enter a password unless you initially access the original item as a guest. If the shared item is not available — for example, because the Mac on which it resides is turned off — then the Finder tells you that it cannot find the item on the network.

Sometimes when you try to open an alias of a shared item, an alert tells you the alias's original item can't be found. An alias of a shared item may stop working for many reasons. Your Mac may be disconnected from the network, or the AppleTalk control panel may be set incorrectly (see "Configuring an AppleTalk Connection" in Chapter 19). The file server where the original shared item is located may be shut down or disconnected from the network. If the file server is someone's personal computer, that person may simply have turned off Mac OS file sharing (see "Turning File Sharing Off and On" in Chapter 21). If the computer is a PowerBook, it may be in sleep mode (sleep mode does not disable file sharing on a desktop Mac).

An alias of a shared item may not work correctly if the shared item is located on a file server that does not use the Mac OS. For instance, file servers in some organizations use the Windows NT operating system. Windows NT's Services for

Macintosh feature enables Macs to connect to and use files on a Windows NT computer, but some versions of Windows NT have trouble with aliases. Updating Windows NT to the latest version can usually clear up this trouble.

Server access from the Save dialog box

Don't you hate it when you get into a Save dialog box only to realize that you want to save on a server volume that you're not connected to? You don't have to cancel the Save dialog box, mount the server volume, and choose Save again if you take the time to make an alias of your Recent Servers folder and put it on your desktop. You can open that alias and get at recently used servers quite easily from within any Save dialog box. (Click the Desktop button in the Save dialog box for fast access to the Recent Servers alias.) If you find that the server you want to use is not included in the Recent Servers folder because you have not accessed it as recently as the servers that are included, you need to increase the number of servers that the Finder keeps track of in this folder. To do that, use the Apple Menu Options control panel (see "Opening Programs, Documents, and More" in Chapter 7).

Aliases of remote shared items

Not only do aliases work across a local network, they also work across a remote network connection made with Apple Remote Access (ARA, which is described in "Introducing Remote Network Connections" in Chapter 19). If you create an alias of a remote file, folder, or disk, disconnect the remote network, and then open the alias, the Mac OS tries to make the remote network connection again automatically.

Instead of locating the alias's original item on the remote network as it should, the Mac OS may locate another item that coincidentally has the same name on your local network. Sound far-fetched? Suppose the alias's original item is a shared disk with a common name such as "Mac OS HD" on a remote Mac with a common name such as "Power Mac 7600." Further suppose your Mac is connected to a local network on which someone is sharing a hard disk named "Mac OS HD" from a Mac named "Power Mac 7600." If you double-click the alias, your system will open the Mac OS HD on your local network, not the one on the remote network. A similar situation can occur if you sometimes connect to two remote Macs that are named alike and have shared hard disks with the same names.

Situations like these can develop unexpectedly when someone changes the name of a Mac or a shared disk; suddenly you discover that double-clicking an alias opens the wrong item. What's worse, the Mac OS updates the alias so that it now points to the wrong item. Even after you fix the conflicting aliases by changing one of the original item's names, the alias will continue representing the wrong item.

If an alias starts referring to an item on the wrong network or the wrong computer, delete the alias and make a new one. To prevent future problems, suggest to the owners of the computers with identical names that they give their computers and their hard disks unique names.

STEP-BY-STEP

Your Office on Disk

Aliases can give you nearly automatic access to your computer's hard disks by using a floppy disk in any other computer on the same network. To set up access to your office from a floppy disk, follow these steps:

1. Make sure that file sharing is turned on (see "Turning File Sharing Off and On" in Chapter 21).

2. Select all your hard disk icons. Then choose Sharing from the Get Info submenu of the File menu in Mac OS 8.5 or choose Sharing from the File menu in Mac OS 7.6–8.1. The Sharing command displays sharing privileges in a separate window for each selected disk.

3. In each sharing privileges window, set the options as shown in the figure. These settings restrict access to your disks so that only you can make changes or see files or folders.

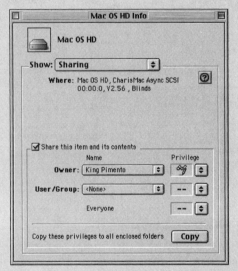
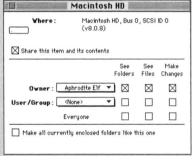

4. Make an alias of each hard disk and copy the aliases to a floppy disk.

Now you can use that floppy disk to access your hard disk from any Mac on your network, as long as file sharing is active on your Mac. You simply insert the disk, open the alias for the disk you want to use, and enter your password when asked. Correctly entering your password gives you access to all applications, folders, and documents on your disk from any remote computer. You don't have to bother opening the Chooser on a borrowed computer, selecting AppleShare, selecting your computer, and typing your name as the registered user.

STEP-BY-STEP

An Alias's Alias

When you move a drive from one AppleShare file server to another, network users have to tediously search all servers (by using the Chooser or the Network Browser in Mac OS 8.5) for the moved drive unless you inform them of its new location. That may happen if, for example, you have to move a shared drive from a busy server to an idle server or from a server needing repair to a temporary substitute.

You can solve this problem by creating an alias of an alias of every shared hard disk by following these steps:

1. Working from a shared hard disk that is always available to everyone, create an alias of every shared hard disk on the network.

2. Create aliases of those hard-drive aliases and copy the second set of aliases to each user's Mac.

With the double aliases in place, a shared hard disk named Crown Jewels, for example, can be accessed by double-clicking the alias named "Crown Jewels alias alias" on any user's Mac. That alias points to the alias "Crown Jewels alias" on the always-available shared drive, which in turn points to Crown Jewels itself.

Now, if you move Crown Jewels to a different file server, you merely make a new alias to replace the old Crown Jewels alias on the always-available shared drive. You do not have to update users' copies of "Crown Jewels alias alias," and users do not need to know that Crown Jewels has been moved.

This example uses the initial alias names that the Mac generates, but you can rename aliases freely. For example, both the alias and the alias's alias could be named Crown Jewels like the hard disk.

Aliases keep shared documents current

Besides providing easy access to shared items from other computers, aliases can help make sure that others who share your documents have the latest versions.

Suppose, for example, that you create a letter template that you want the rest of your group to use. By making an alias of the template and copying it to a shared folder, other users can copy the alias to their disks and use the alias to open the original template. If you later replace the original template with a version having the same name, the aliases that people already copied will open the new version. Users who share the alias always get the newest version of the original item it represents, even when the original frequently changes.

The only drawback to using an alias to share a template is that unless you're using a program that allows more than one person to open the same document, only one person can access the template document at a time. However, anyone who opens the template can quickly and easily save it with a different name and then close it to free it for someone else to open.

Summary

In this chapter, you learned that an alias is a file that represents another item such as a program, document, folder, or disk. Opening an alias or dragging something to an alias in the Finder has the same effect as opening or dragging to the alias's original item. But you can rename, move, or copy an alias or give it a custom icon without affecting its original item and without breaking the link between the alias and its original. An alias stays linked to its original item even if you move or rename the original. To see an alias's original item, you can use the Finder's Show Original command (Mac OS 8–8.5) or the Find Original button in the alias's Info window (Mac OS 7.6–7.6.1).

Aliases have a multitude of uses, some of which this chapter described. You can use aliases to add items to the Apple menu and Startup Items folder. You can use an alias to make a universal Show Clipboard command. An alias can be a "remove disk" icon on the desktop and can provide shortcuts in Open, Save, and Navigation Services dialog boxes. Aliases are also useful for archiving files on removable disks and easily accessing shared disks and folders. This chapter also described 16 other uses for aliases.

✦   ✦   ✦

Take Charge of Your Fonts

With the original Mac OS font technology, text looks great when displayed or printed as long as you stick to a half-dozen font sizes — usually 9, 10, 12, 14, 18, and 24 points. Apple's TrueType font technology, a standard part of Mac OS 7.6–8.5, makes odd sizes and big sizes like 11, 13, 36, 100, and 197 points look just as good. The optional QuickDraw GX software provides much more refined control of type, as long as the typefaces and programs that you're using take advantage of its advanced capabilities.

Introducing Fonts

Your computer can display and print text in three types of fonts: fixed-size, TrueType, and PostScript. Which looks best depends on the font size and the output device (display screen or type of printer).

Fixed-size fonts

Originally, all Macs used fixed-size fonts to display text onscreen and to print on many types of printers. A *fixed-size* font contains exact pictures of every letter, digit, and symbol for one size of a font. Fixed-size fonts often are called *bitmap fonts* because each picture precisely maps the dots, or *bits,* to be displayed or printed for one character. Figure 13-1 shows the dots in an enlarged view of a couple of fixed-size letters.

Each fixed-size font looks great in one size only, so fixed-size fonts usually are installed in sets. A typical set includes 9-, 10-, 12-, 14-, 18-, and 24-point sizes. If you need text in a size for which no fixed-size font is installed, the Mac OS must scale a fixed-size font's character bitmaps up or down to the size you want. The results are lumpy, misshapen, or blocky, as shown in Figure 13-2.

Figure 13-1: Times capital A and G bitmaps at fixed sizes 12, 14, and 18 points (enlarged to show detail).

Times 9. ABCDEFGHIJKLMNOPQRSTUVWXYZabcdefghijklmnopqrstuvwxyz123
Times 10. ABCDEFGHIJKLMNOPQRSTUVWXYZabcdefghijklmnopqrstu
Times 11. ABCDEFGHIJKLMNOPQRSTUVWXYZabcdefghijklmn
Times 12. ABCDEFGHIJKLMNOPQRSTUVWXYZabcdefghij
Times 13. ABCDEFGHIJKLMNOPQRSTUVWXYZabcde
Times 14. ABCDEFGHIJKLMNOPQRSTUVWXYZa
Times 16. ABCDEFGHIJKLMNOPQRSUVW
Times 18. ABCDEFGHIJKLMNOPQRST
Times 20. ABCDEFGHIJKLMNOPQ
Times 24. ABCDEFGHIJKLM
Times 30. ABCDEFGHIJ

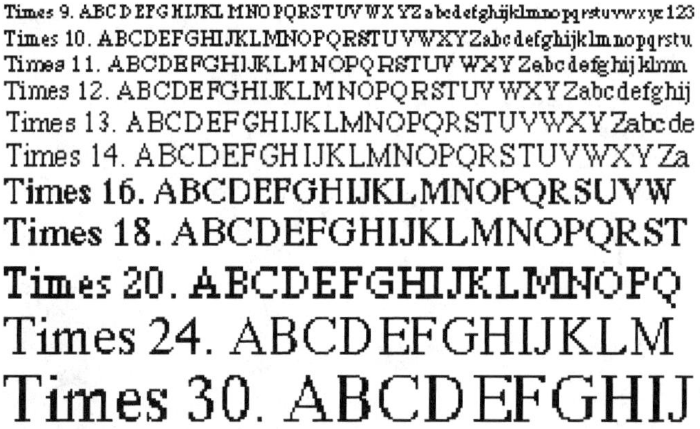

Figure 13-2: Fixed-size fonts look best at installed sizes — shown here for 9-, 10-, 12-, 18-, and 24-points at 72 dots-per-inch (enlarged to show detail).

TrueType fonts

TrueType is a variable-size font technology. Instead of fixed-size bitmaps, TrueType fonts use curves and straight lines to outline each character's shape. Because TrueType fonts are based on outlines, they sometimes are called *outline fonts*. Figure 13-3 shows the outline for an example TrueType letter.

TrueType fonts look good at all sizes. They work with all Mac OS applications and all types of printers, including PostScript printers. The Mac OS smoothly scales a TrueType font's character outlines to any size on a display screen and on printers of any resolution, all with equally good results. The Mac OS also lets you mix TrueType fonts with fixed-size and PostScript fonts. Figure 13-4 shows an example of TrueType font scaling.

Figure 13-3: Outline for TrueType Times capital G.

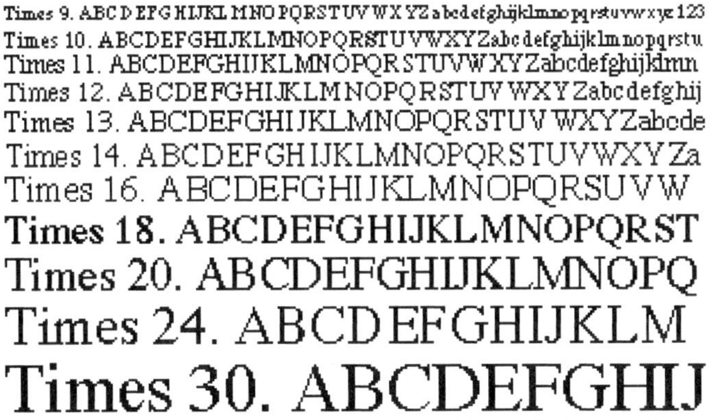

Times 9. ABCD EFG HIJKL MNO PQRSTUV WX YZ abcdefghijklmno pqrstuvw xyz 123
Times 10. ABCDEFGHIJKLMNOPQRSTUVWXYZabcdefghijklmnopqrstu
Times 11. ABCDEFGHIJKLMNOPQRSTUVWXYZabcdefghijklmn
Times 12. ABCDEFGHIJKLMNOPQRSTUVWXYZabcdefghij
Times 13. ABCDEFGHIJKLMNOPQRSTUVWXYZabcde
Times 14. ABCDEFGHIJKLMNOPQRSTUVWXYZa
Times 16. ABCDEFGHIJKLMNOPQRSUVW
Times 18. ABCDEFGHIJKLMNOPQRST
Times 20. ABCDEFGHIJKLMNOPQ
Times 24. ABCDEFGHIJKLM
Times 30. ABCDEFGHIJ

Figure 13-4: TrueType fonts scale smoothly to all sizes and resolutions (Times shown at 72 dots-per-inch and enlarged to show detail).

An enhanced form of TrueType fonts, known as TrueType GX fonts, accommodates much larger sets of characters and provides an advanced typographic control that otherwise requires special application programs. You'll find the details in "QuickDraw GX Typography" later in this chapter.

PostScript fonts

TrueType fonts look great in any size displayed onscreen or output on any printer, but they are not alone. *PostScript* fonts were the first to look great at any size and any resolution. They use an outline font technology invented by Adobe Systems. It's similar to TrueType but differs in how it mathematically specifies font outlines and how it adjusts the outlines for small font sizes and low resolutions.

There are actually two types of PostScript fonts, imaginatively called Type 1 and Type 3. Most of the PostScript fonts you see nowadays are Type 1 because it yields better results at small font sizes and low resolutions. Although Type 1 fonts generally look better, Type 3 fonts can be more elaborate. The characters in Type 3 fonts can have variable stroke weights, and they can be filled with something other than a solid color, such as shades of gray or blends that go from white to black.

Although PostScript fonts originally were designed for printing on LaserWriters and other PostScript output devices, Adobe Type Manager (ATM) software smoothly scales PostScript fonts to any size for non-PostScript printers and the display screen, just like TrueType. With ATM and PostScript fonts, you don't need a set of fixed-size or TrueType fonts for the screen display. Apple includes ATM with Mac OS 7.6–8.5, as described in "Setting Font Options," later in this chapter.

To make use of ATM, you must buy PostScript fonts for your System Folder — fonts built into your printer don't help. The Adobe Type Basics package includes the 11 standard LaserWriter font families — Avant Garde, Bookman, Courier, Helvetica, Helvetica Narrow, New Century Schoolbook, Palatino, Symbol, Times, Zapf Chancery, and Zapf Dingbats — along with 15 other font families. You'll find information on using ATM in the next section, "Managing Fonts." For more sources of fonts, see "Obtaining Fonts" at the end of this chapter.

TrueType fonts cannot replace PostScript for a number of reasons. For one, PostScript can set text at any angle or along a curve or other nonlinear path, which is possible with TrueType only with QuickDraw GX. In addition, PostScript offers more than outline fonts. It's a *page description language* that precisely specifies the location and other characteristics of every text and graphics item on the page.

PostScript or TrueType?

Which type of outline font should you use, TrueType or PostScript? Many longtime Mac OS users have invested thousands of dollars in PostScript fonts, and for them it makes sense to stick with PostScript and ATM. But PostScript fonts are messier than TrueType fonts. With PostScript fonts, each style of a font — bold, italic, bold italic, plain, and so on — is a different file on your hard disk. Moreover, PostScript font file names can be hard to figure out because they're a contraction of the full font name plus style name. For example, Helvetica Bold Italic has the file name HelveBolIta, and Garamond Demi Book comes out GaramDemBoo. So just to have the basic four font styles of a font you must have four PostScript font files. But that's not all. In addition, for each PostScript font family such as Times or Helvetica, you must also have at least one size of the same fixed-size font installed. ATM can't jigger the system without that fixed-size font. For example, to go with the four PostScript fonts AGarBol, AGarBolIta, AGarIta, and AGarReg you must also have at least one Adobe Garamond fixed-size font such as AGaramond 12.

In contrast, with most TrueType fonts you have just one item to deal with, a *font suitcase*. (Font suitcases are covered in the next section, "Managing Fonts.")

If you don't already have a collection of PostScript fonts, and especially if you don't print on PostScript printers, it is preferable to use TrueType fonts. More PostScript fonts are available than TrueType, but TrueType fonts sometimes cost less, and some are even free. For example, every version of the Mac OS from 7.0 onward includes TrueType versions of at least the Times, Helvetica, Courier, and Symbol fonts. Also, many applications from Apple (and its former subsidiary Claris) and Microsoft come with an assortment of TrueType fonts.

In fact, you will probably end up with a mixture of TrueType and PostScript fonts. This situation is perfectly acceptable. You can even use TrueType and PostScript fonts in the same document. However, it's best to avoid having TrueType and PostScript fonts with the same name on your computer. If you do, the Mac uses TrueType to display the document and PostScript to print it (on a PostScript printer), and you may notice differences in line lengths, line breaks, and page breaks between the displayed TrueType and the printed PostScript.

Backgrounder

Font Styles and Families

Text varies by style as well as size. The Mac OS can display and print four basic styles — plain, bold, italic, and bold italic — and many others (as listed in your friendly Style menu). The Mac OS can derive various styles by modifying the plain style, but you get better-looking results by installing separate styled versions of fonts, as shown in the following figure. Many fixed-size, TrueType, and PostScript fonts come in the four basic styles. Some PostScript font families include 20 or more styled versions. Collectively, the styled versions together with the plain version of a font are known as a *font family*. The figure illustrates the difference between installed styles and derived styles with enlarged type samples of text at display resolution (72 dots-per-inch).

Times, Times italic, Times bold italic, and Times bold	Only plain Times installed; other styles derived from it
Necessity never made a good bargain.	Necessity never made a good bargain.
Three may keep a secret, if two of them are dead.	*Three may keep a secret, if two of them are dead.*
Lost time is never found again.	**Lost time is never found again.**
He that lives upon hope will die fasting.	**He that lives upon hope will die fasting.**

How to recognize the best font sizes

You can usually tell which font sizes will look good onscreen by inspecting the Font menu of a program that you're using. The program highlights the best-looking sizes with outline-style numbers. All sizes of a TrueType font are highlighted (If you have PostScript fonts and ATM installed, all the sizes also look good.) Only the installed sizes of fixed-size fonts are highlighted, as shown in Figure 13-5.

A fixed-size font   A True Type font   **Figure 13-5:** Smooth sizes are outlined.

Managing Fonts

A basic set of fonts comes with the Mac OS. You can add more fonts whenever you need to use them and you can remove fonts that you no longer need to use. In addition, you can display samples of your fonts.

Fonts and font suitcases

The fonts you see in Font menus are represented in the Finder by icons. Each type of font has a distinctive icon. The icon of a fixed-size font bears a single capital A. A TrueType font's icon has three capital As, each a different size to suggest the variable sizing of the font. The icons of PostScript fonts may look like a generic laser printer, or they may have custom graphics designed by the companies that make the fonts. Figure 13-6 shows examples of different font icons.

For convenience, TrueType and fixed-size fonts are usually kept in *font suitcases*. You can think of font suitcases as special folders for holding fonts. Each font suitcase generally holds related fonts, such as the different sizes in a set of fixed-size fonts or the different styles of a TrueType font family. Font suitcases can't contain PostScript fonts. Figure 13-7 shows examples of font suitcases.

Figure 13-6: Each type of font has a different icon in Finder. From left: TrueType, fixed-size, Adobe PostScript, and two other PostScript fonts.

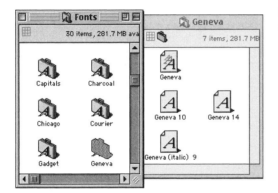

Figure 13-7: Font suitcases contain fixed-size and TrueType fonts.

You can create a new font suitcase by duplicating an existing font suitcase, opening the duplicate, and dragging the contents of the duplicate to the Trash. You can put any number of fonts in a suitcase as long as the total size doesn't exceed 16MB.

Adding fonts

To make a font available in your applications' Font menus, you add the font to the Fonts folder that is in your System Folder. The simplest way to add fonts is to drag their icons to the System Folder icon (not the System Folder window). You can drag font suitcases, folders containing fonts, or loose fonts to the System Folder icon. The Finder knows to put the fonts and font suitcases in the Fonts folder. However, the Finder does not distribute items for you if you drag them to the System Folder window instead of the System Folder icon. Figure 13-8 shows some fonts being dragged to the System Folder icon.

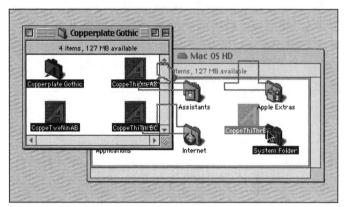

Figure 13-8: Install fonts by dragging them to the System Folder icon.

Before putting the fonts where they belong, the Finder displays an alert asking if that's what you want to do. This alert lets you know that the Finder has recognized the items you dragged to the System Folder icon, and it gets your OK before putting them in their places. Figure 13-9 shows an example of the alert in Mac OS 8.5.

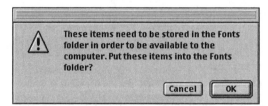

Figure 13-9: Finder knows where fonts go.

If you prefer, you can drag TrueType, PostScript, and fixed-size fonts directly to the Fonts folder icon. You also can open the Fonts folder and drag TrueType, PostScript, and fixed-size fonts to its window.

Newly added fonts become available in each application the next time you open it. If an application is open when you add fonts or font suitcases to your Fonts folder, you must quit the application and open it again to use the added fonts in it. The Finder displays an alert that notifies you when this condition exists.

Removing fonts

When you no longer want to use a font, you remove it or the suitcase that contains it from your Fonts folder. You can drag fonts and suitcases from the Fonts folder to another folder, the desktop, or the Trash. All applications except the Finder must be closed before you can remove any TrueType or fixed-size fonts from the Fonts folder. You can remove PostScript fonts any time. If you want to remove PostScript fonts but can't find them in the Fonts folder, look in the Extensions folder and the System folder. (PostScript fonts went in the Extensions folder or the System Folder prior to System 7.1.) Figure 13-10 shows some fonts being removed to a folder on the desktop.

By removing unneeded font suitcases and loose fonts from your Fonts folder, you make your system perform better. Many applications start faster with fewer fonts, because it takes less time to initialize their Font menus. You'll find a shorter Font menu easier to use as well.

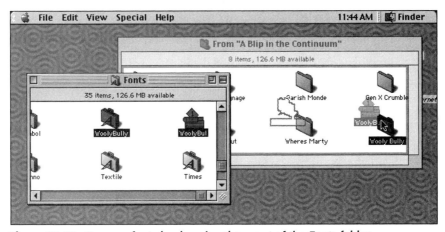

Figure 13-10: Remove fonts by dragging them out of the Fonts folder.

Viewing font samples

You can see a sample of any TrueType or fixed-size font by opening the font. Note that when you open a font suitcase you see not a font sample, but a window of fonts. Opening one of these fonts shows you a sample of it. Figure 13-11 shows examples of TrueType and fixed-size font samples.

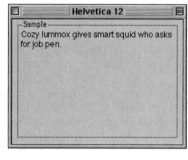

Figure 13-11: TrueType and fixed-size font samples.

The Mac OS doesn't display samples of PostScript fonts. If you open a PostScript font, the Finder displays a message that describes the font and tells you to put it in your Fonts folder. Remember that each PostScript font in your Fonts folder should contain a corresponding fixed-size or TrueType font. If you want to see a sample of a PostScript font, open the corresponding fixed-size or TrueType font instead.

Setting Font Options

Although the Mac OS handles font display and printing automatically, you can set a few options that affect how fonts look. If you use Mac OS 8.5, you can set a font-smoothing option. If you use ATM with any Mac OS version, you can adjust how it scales PostScript fonts.

Font smoothing

Mac OS 8.5 can smooth fonts on screen by blending their jagged edges with the background color. This process is called *antialiasing*. You turn font smoothing on or off in the Font section of the Appearance control panel. When font smoothing is turned on, you can also specify the smallest font size that you want smoothed. The Mac OS will antialias all TrueType fonts this size or larger on monitors set to display at least 256 colors or grays (see "Monitor Adjustments" in Chapter 11). The Mac OS will not antialias any fixed size (bitmap) fonts. ATM, as described next, handles antialiasing of PostScript fonts. Figure 13-12 shows the font smoothing options in the Appearance control panel of Mac OS 8.5.

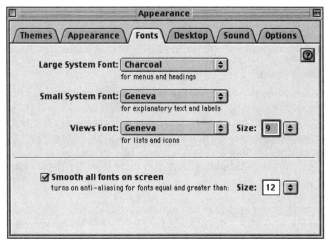

Figure 13-12: Setting font smoothing options in Mac OS 8.5.

Adobe Type Manager

You can set several options that affect how the optional Adobe Type Manager (ATM) software scales PostScript fonts onscreen and on printers that don't use PostScript. In addition, you can set options that affect ATM's performance. You make these settings in the ATM control panel. Figure 13-13 shows the ATM 3.8.3 control panel, which comes with Mac OS 7.6–7.6.1, and the ATM 4.0.2 control panel, which comes with Mac OS 8–8.5.

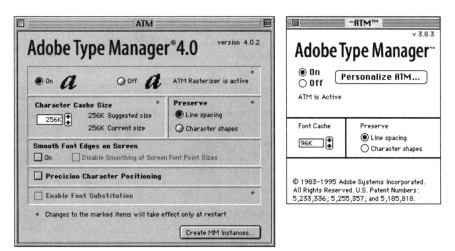

Figure 13-13: Setting ATM font options in Mac OS 8–8.5 (left) and Mac OS 7.6–7.6.1 (right).

ATM options

The Character Cache (ATM 4.0.2) or Font Cache (ATM 3.8.3) option affects performance. If applications seem to scroll more slowly with ATM turned on, try increasing this size.

The Preserve option determines whether ATM preserves line spacing or character shapes when it scales text. Preserving line spacing keeps line breaks and page breaks from changing with and without ATM, but this setting may clip the bottoms of some letters and vertically compress some accented capital letters. Preserving character shapes reduces the clipping but may change line breaks. The clipping occurs only onscreen and on output devices that don't use PostScript. No clipping occurs on a PostScript printer.

The Smooth Font Edges on Screen option (not available in ATM 3.8.3) smoothes font edges onscreen in the same way Mac OS 8.5 does, by blending their jagged edges with the background color. Whereas Mac OS 8.5 works with all TrueType fonts, ATM works in Mac OS 7.6–8.5 on Type 1 PostScript fonts. ATM can antialias color text only when the monitor is set to display thousands or millions of colors. If the monitor is set to display 256 colors, ATM can antialias only black-and-white text.

The Precision Character Positioning option (not available in ATM 3.8.3) displays more accurate spacing, especially at small font sizes. Turning on this option causes ATM to calculate character positions on a fractional pixel basis, which may slow text display of some documents on slower computers.

The versions of ATM included with Mac OS 7.6–8.5 does not have all the features of ATM Deluxe. ATM Deluxe can create substitute fonts dynamically when you open a document that contains fonts your system doesn't have. This font substitution feature preserves line breaks in documents but only approximates the look of missing fonts. Other ATM Deluxe features facilitate reviewing, organizing, adding, and removing large numbers of fonts. Adobe sells ATM Deluxe separately (408-536-6000, http://www.adobe.com).

ATM installation

ATM is not part of a standard installation of Mac OS; you install it separately. You may find separate installation software for ATM 4.02 on the CD that came with your Mac or on your Mac OS CD. If not, you can install ATM by doing a custom installation of the Mac OS. For Mac OS 8.5, do a custom installation of the Mac OS, select the QuickDraw GX module, and choose Customized Installation from its pop-up menu. In the dialog box that appears, select the ATM for QuickDraw GX component, click OK, and then click Start. For Mac OS 7.6–8.1, do a custom installation of the Mac OS and select the QuickDraw GX module. When the QuickDraw GX Installer window appears, choose Custom Install from the pop-up menu. Then select the ATM for QuickDraw GX and click Install. (See Chapters 31 and 32 for detailed Mac OS installation instructions.)

Determining Font Priorities

If your Fonts folder contains fixed-size, TrueType, and PostScript versions of the same font, you may wonder how you specify the one you want to use. In fact, you don't specify. The Mac OS picks one for you according to its own priorities. These priorities are different for the display screen, a PostScript printer, and a printer that doesn't use PostScript.

Displaying fonts on screen

For screen display, the Mac OS first tries to find a fixed-size font in the exact size needed. If it can't find that, it looks for a TrueType version of the font that it can scale to the needed size. Lacking that, it tries to have ATM, if installed, scale a PostScript font to the needed size. Some versions of ATM can even use Adobe Multiple Master fonts to display temporary substitutes that closely match PostScript fonts not installed on your computer. If no other font is available, the Mac OS scales the best-available fixed-size font.

Curiously, when both fixed-size and TrueType versions of the same font are present, the Mac OS always derives styled fonts from the fixed-size version, even if a styled TrueType version is installed. For example, if you have a fixed-size 12-point Times plain and a TrueType Times italic installed (but no fixed-size 12-point Times italic), the Mac OS derives a 12-point Times italic by slanting the fixed-size 12-point Times.

Individual programs can tell the Mac OS to ignore fixed-size fonts if a TrueType equivalent is available, and current versions of many popular programs now work this way. You may be able to turn this behavior on and off in some of your programs. Check each program's preference settings for one that tells the program that you prefer outline fonts. A decision to ignore fixed-size fonts in one program does not affect other programs — the Mac OS always prefers fixed-size fonts unless an application specifically overrides it.

Printing fonts on PostScript printers

When choosing among fixed-size, TrueType, or PostScript versions of the same font for printing on a PostScript printer, the Mac OS looks first for a PostScript font from the printer's ROM, RAM, or hard disk (if any). If the printer doesn't have the PostScript font, the Mac OS tries to download (copy) it from the computer's Fonts folder, Extensions folder, or System Folder. Failing that, the Mac OS tries to use a TrueType font; as a last resort, the Mac OS uses a fixed-size font.

If the Mac OS can find no PostScript equivalent for a TrueType font, it sends the TrueType font to the printer before sending the document to be printed. If the printer is one that can't handle TrueType fonts, the Mac OS converts the TrueType font to PostScript, with some loss of quality at small point sizes, and sends that. Either way, sending fonts causes a significant delay on many printers. If you use TrueType-only fonts with a PostScript printer that has its own hard disk or a large amount of memory, you may be able to reduce printing time by downloading (sending) the TrueType fonts to the printer in advance of printing documents. Fonts you download to a printer's hard disk remain there unless you remove them. Fonts you download to a printer's memory remain there until you turn off the printer, or (in some cases) until someone else prints on the printer with a different version of printer software than you use.

Printing fonts on a non-PostScript device

On a printer or other device that doesn't have PostScript, the Mac OS tries to use TrueType fonts. If your Mac doesn't have a needed TrueType font but does have ATM installed, the Mac OS looks for a PostScript version of the font. If neither type of outline font is available, the Mac OS uses a fixed-size font.

Secrets

Comparing Fixed-Size and TrueType Fonts

Look closely at some text in a TrueType font and at the same text in an equivalent fixed-size font. You'll see differences in letter shape, width, and height that may affect text spacing. The TrueType fonts match the PostScript fonts used in printers better than fixed-size fonts do. Fixed-size fonts display faster, however, and many of them look better onscreen in sizes smaller than 18 points. The following figure illustrates the problem with enlarged type samples of text at display resolution (72 dots-per-inch).

Today we are on the verge of creating new tools that will empower individuals, unlock worlds of knowledge, and forge a new community of ideas.	TrueType Times 12-point plain
Today we are on the verge of creating new tools that will empower individuals, unlock worlds of knowledge, and forge a new community of ideas.	Fixed-size Times
Today we are on the verge of creating new tools that will empower individuals, unlock worlds of knowledge, and forge a new community of ideas.	Fixed-size Times 12-point bold italic
Today we are on the verge of creating new tools that will empower individuals, unlock worlds of knowledge, and forge a new community of ideas.	TrueType Times 12-point bold italic

If you print on a non-PostScript printer such as an Apple StyleWriter, Hewlett-Packard DeskJet, or Epson Stylus, and have both fixed-size and TrueType fonts installed, text may not look quite the same onscreen as it does on paper. Character shapes may be different. More importantly, the spacing of words in the line may not match. When this happens, the Mac OS has used a fixed-size font for display (at 72 dots-per-inch) and a TrueType font for printing (at a higher resolution). You can fix the problem by removing the fixed-size font from your System file. In some programs, you may also be able to set an option that tells the Mac OS to ignore fixed-size fonts.

Understanding Outline Fonts

To understand why TrueType fonts look different from equivalent fixed-size fonts, you need to know how outline-font technology works. Like PostScript fonts and other outline fonts, a TrueType font defines each character mathematically as a set of points that, when connected, outline the character's shape. The Mac OS can vary the font size by moving the points closer together or farther apart and then drawing the character again.

After scaling the outline to the size you want, the Mac OS fills the outline with the dots that make up the text you see onscreen and on paper. The dot size, which is determined by the resolution of the screen or other output device, governs the smoothness of the result at a given size. Devices with more dots-per-inch produce smoother results, particularly in smaller point sizes. Figure 13-14 shows how dot size affects smoothness.

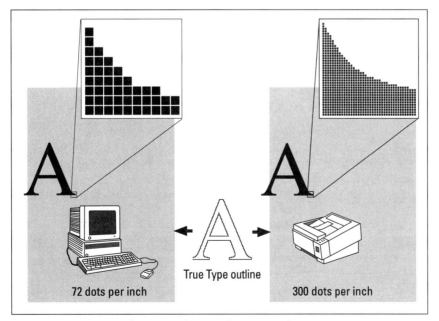

True Type outline

72 dots per inch   300 dots per inch

Figure 13-14: Output device resolution affects smoothness.

At small sizes, however, simply scaling the font outlines results in text that has unpleasant problems, such as gaps in diagonal lines or unwanted dots on the edges of curves. These imperfections occur because the outline does not precisely fit the grid in small point sizes, especially if the dots are relatively large, as they are on the computer's 72-dots-per-inch screen. On the display screen, the Mac OS must draw a typical 11-point letter in a space 8 dots square. At small sizes and relatively low resolutions, deciding which dots to darken is difficult. The Mac OS reduces the character outline, lays it over the grid, and darkens the dots whose center points fall inside the outline, as shown in Figure 13-15.

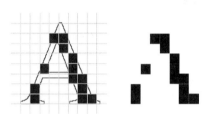

Figure 13-15: Scaling a font outline to a small size may leave gaps.

TrueType and PostScript fonts include a mechanism for adjusting the outline at small sizes on low-resolution devices. The font designer provides the font with instructions (also known as *hints*) that tell the Mac OS how to modify character outlines at small font sizes, as shown in Figure 13-16. This process is called *grid fitting*.

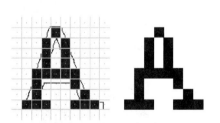

Figure 13-16: Hints modify outlines at small sizes.

High-resolution devices such as typesetters and film recorders usually don't need grid-fitting instructions — their grids are so fine that the character outlines don't need adjusting to get filled with dots. A 300-dots-per-inch grid is 4 times finer than a 72-dots-per-inch grid, and a 1,270-dots-per-inch grid is more than 16 times finer.

Scaling and grid fitting occur so quickly that you usually don't notice a delay. TrueType and PostScript fonts are not as fast as fixed-size fonts, however, and occasionally the lag is perceptible onscreen.

QuickDraw GX Typography

QuickDraw GX, which is included as an option with Mac OS 7.6–8.5, makes it possible for any application to use some precise typesetting techniques and achieve special effects that otherwise are available only in specialized publishing programs. The catch is that you need TrueType GX fonts together with programs designed to use QuickDraw GX typography. With TrueType GX fonts and a program that has adopted GX typography, you can have these special effects generated automatically:

✦ Fancy swashed initial or final characters in words or lines

✦ Lowercase (or old-style) numerals

✦ Ligatures (linked characters)

✦ Small caps instead of standard caps

You can also type diagonal fractions from the keyboard and format subscript or superscript in one step. In compatible programs, QuickDraw GX also makes it possible to customize certain fonts, making them bolder, lighter, skinnier, or wider. In any QuickDraw GX-compliant program — not just in high-end page-layout or illustration programs — you can easily control the letter spacing within words. Not every font will include all the possible GX options. Figure 13-17 shows the pop-up menu from a demonstration program that offers most of the type options.

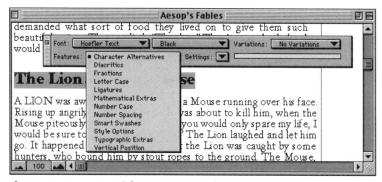

Figure 13-17: Any QuickDraw GX-compliant program can offer a multitude of typography options.

QuickDraw GX is not automatically installed when you install the Mac OS. With Mac OS 7.6–8.5, you must deliberately select QuickDraw GX in the Mac OS Install program (Mac OS 8–8.5) or the Install Mac OS program (Mac OS 7.6–7.6.1). The typography features described in the rest of this chapter work only if you've installed QuickDraw GX in addition to the basic Mac OS.

PostScript fonts with QuickDraw GX

You can use Type 1 PostScript fonts after installing QuickDraw GX, but you must have Adobe Type Manager (ATM). In addition, you must convert your Type 1 fonts to fonts that are compatible with QuickDraw GX.

ATM for QuickDraw GX

ATM smoothly scales PostScript fonts so that they look good onscreen—and printed on non-PostScript printers—at any size. A version of ATM comes with QuickDraw GX, although that version of ATM can't substitute multiple-master PostScript fonts for missing PostScript fonts as can some versions of ATM that are available from Adobe. (Adobe's ATM versions work fine with QuickDraw GX.)

ATM is installed automatically when you install QuickDraw GX with Mac OS 7.6–7.6.1. With Mac OS 8–8.5, you must do a custom installation of QuickDraw GX to get ATM. (You'll find information on installing and using ATM in "Managing Fonts" earlier in this chapter.)

Type 1 font conversion

You can make most PostScript fonts compatible with QuickDraw GX by using the Type 1 Enabler program. This program creates GX-compatible copies of Type 1 PostScript fonts, leaving the original fonts untouched. The program does not work with Type 3 PostScript fonts. Most PostScript fonts are Type 1, including all fonts from Adobe. However, if you have any Type 3 fonts, you will not be able to use them with QuickDraw GX.

If you use Mac OS 7.6–7.6.1, you may find that some of your Type 1 fonts have been converted for you. All Type 1 fonts in your Fonts folder are converted automatically when you install the version of QuickDraw GX that comes with Mac OS 7.6–7.6.1. Type 1 fonts in other folders are not converted during installation. You can convert these fonts yourself using the Type 1 Enabler.

To get the Type 1 Enabler program you must do a custom installation of QuickDraw GX. For Mac OS 8.5, do a custom installation of the Mac OS, select the QuickDraw GX module, and choose Customized Installation from its pop-up menu. In the dialog box that appears, select the ATM for QuickDraw GX component, click OK, and then click Start. For Mac OS 7.6–8.1, do a custom installation of the Mac OS and select the QuickDraw GX module. When the QuickDraw GX Installer window appears, choose Custom Install from the pop-up menu. Then select the ATM for QuickDraw GX component (Mac OS 8–8.1) or the QuickDraw GX Utilities component (Mac OS 7.6–7.6.1) and click Install. (See Chapters 31 and 32 for detailed Mac OS installation instructions.)

Before you can convert Type 1 fonts for QuickDraw GX, the fixed-size fonts for each PostScript font family to be converted must be in its own font suitcase. In addition, those font suitcases should not include TrueType fonts. The Type 1 Enabler program will not enable multiple PostScript font families whose fixed-size fonts are all in the same font suitcase. Related font families such as Helvetica and Helvetica Condensed are considered separate families and their fixed-size fonts must be in separate font suitcases.

After isolating each fixed-size font family in its own font suitcase, create a new folder named Old Fonts (or another name you like). Move the Type 1 PostScript fonts that you want to convert and the matching font suitcase into the Old Fonts folder.

Open the Type 1 Enabler program, and in the Open dialog box that appears, select the Old Fonts folder and click the button labeled Select "Old Fonts." The program inspects the fonts and displays a dialog box in which you select the destination for the converted fonts. Open your Fonts folder and then click the button labeled Select "New Fonts" to select it as the destination, unless you have a reason for selecting a different destination. (If the program finds a problem with the unconverted fonts, it displays a message in its log window.)

The Type 1 Enabler program converts the fonts to GX versions. Its log window reports the outcome of the conversion process. When it finishes, you may quit.

If you look in your Fonts folder for the converted fonts, you will see a suitcase with the same name as the one containing the original fixed-size fonts. Inside the new suitcase, you will find copies of the fixed-size fonts together with new icons for the converted Type 1 fonts. These new fonts look like TrueType fonts, but are actually Type 1 PostScript GX fonts.

TrueType GX

Part of QuickDraw GX is an improved kind of font called *TrueType GX fonts*. They work pretty much the way that conventional TrueType fonts work, but they include additional typographic information that gives QuickDraw GX-compatible programs more convenient access to the fonts' sophisticated features. TrueType GX fonts should work fine on Macs without QuickDraw GX. TrueType GX fonts do not completely replace regular TrueType fonts. You can use regular TrueType fonts with QuickDraw GX installed, although application programs will be unable to access the special features of the TrueType GX fonts.

Ligature substitution

Some GX fonts (Type 1 PostScript GX and TrueType GX) include *ligatures*. Each ligature is a group of linked letters that appear run together in a word. For example, diphthongs such as *ae* are ligatures, and so are *ff* or *fi* in words such as *afflicted* and *official*. When you use a GX-compliant application and a GX font that contains ligatures, QuickDraw GX handles the ligatures automatically. Figure 13-18 shows examples of QuickDraw GX ligatures.

Figure 13-18: With QuickDraw GX and a compliant application, ligatures automatically appear as you type.

Without QuickDraw GX and a compliant program, you'd have to type an awkward key combination to generate a character that looks like a ligature. When you use one of these two-letters-in-one characters, you can't select each letter of the ligature separately as you can with QuickDraw GX ligatures. Furthermore, spelling checkers do not recognize one-character ligatures, and hyphenation routines in programs do not properly divide words in the middle of ligatures. QuickDraw GX corrects these problems.

Automatic swashes

Some GX fonts include alternate *glyphs,* or characters, that have fancy tails called *swashes* on some of the strokes, usually on ascenders and descenders. The swashed alternatives are meant to be optional decorative characters, usually for letters that begin or end a line. Programs that take advantage of QuickDraw GX fonts allow you to decide just how swashbuckling you want your type to be (assuming that you have a font that includes alternate swashed glyphs), as shown in Figure 13-19.

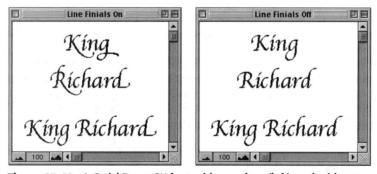

Figure 13-19: A QuickDraw GX font with swashes (left) and without swashes (right) at the ends of lines.

Numeral and fraction options

Some fonts offer more than one set of numerals, perhaps both proportional and monospaced numerals, or both uppercase numerals that stand as tall as capital letters and lowercase (or old-style) numerals that dip below the baseline of the type. Programs that take advantage of QuickDraw GX allow you to choose which of a font's number sets to use. Figure 13-20 shows examples of different QuickDraw GX numerals.

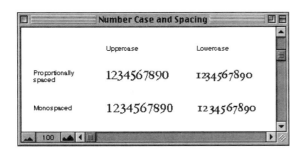

Figure 13-20: QuickDraw GX and compliant applications make it easy to choose among a font's numeral sets.

In addition, because QuickDraw GX provides more control of the vertical and diagonal spacing of characters, compatible programs can let you type professional-looking fractions with either diagonal or horizontal lines. You don't need a specialized fractions font. Furthermore, you don't need to remember arcane key combinations to type special fraction characters.

Font variations

If you're familiar with Adobe Systems' Multiple Masters line of fonts, you'll immediately understand the font-weight and width-variation controls that QuickDraw GX makes available in applications that take advantage of them. Here's how they work: A type designer can build into a font some leeway to allow you to change the font's weight (making the characters bolder or lighter) and width (extending or condensing the font characters). A program that includes QuickDraw GX font-variation controls offers a pop-up menu, sliders, or some other simple control that allows you to modify selected text instantly. Figure 13-21 shows some of the variations you can make to a GX font's weight and width with QuickDraw GX-compatible applications.

Figure 13-21: With an application that takes advantage of QuickDraw GX, you can control the weight and width of some QuickDraw GX fonts.

Letter-spacing controls

Without QuickDraw GX, only programs for publishing and design specialists include decent tools for moving characters closer together or farther apart. With QuickDraw GX, any compatible program can offer simple letter-spacing controls.

Tracking

The overall spacing between letters in an entire document or text selection is called *tracking*. Text with loose tracking has extra space between the characters in words. Text with tight tracking has characters squeezed close together. Figure 13-22 shows examples of tracking from a QuickDraw GX demonstration program.

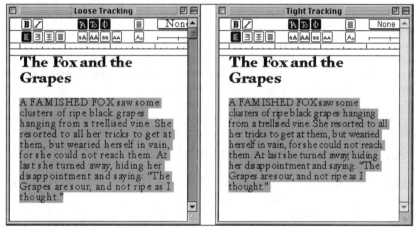

Figure 13-22: Text with loose tracking (left) has more space between characters than text with tight tracking (right).

The capability to change tracking can be handy when you're trying to fit text into a space that's a little too big or too small. You can also adjust tracking to improve the appearance of the text in headlines, script typefaces, or logos, or to create arty effects.

Kerning

Sometimes, particularly in large sizes, letters that are supposed to look like they're part of the same word have too much space between them. For example, a capital *T* at the beginning of a word may not be close enough to the lowercase *r* that follows, making the word harder to read. Correcting the spacing between letter pairs is called *kerning*.

Many fonts include kerning information for letter pairs that commonly need closer spacing for legibility, but you may find cases that are not covered by a font's built-in kerning. In QuickDraw GX-compatible programs, you can just select the two letters that need closer spacing and adjust the spacing (kerning) until it satisfies you. Figure 13-23 is an example of kerning.

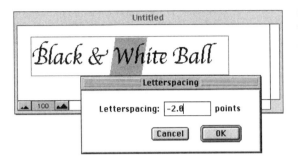

Figure 13-23: Kerning brings together pairs of letters that are too far apart, such as the *W* and *h* in this figure.

Subscript and superscript

For years, some programs have made it possible to insert subscript and superscript numbers and text, such as footnote references in text and elements of formulas. Any program that takes advantage of QuickDraw GX enables you to easily insert subscript or superscript that's properly positioned and in a size that's in scale with the nearby text. Figure 13-24 shows examples of superscript and subscript text from a QuickDraw GX demonstration program.

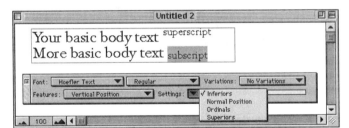

Figure 13-24: With QuickDraw GX and a compliant program, you can format subscripts and superscripts in one step.

Obtaining Fonts

The Mac OS comes with a standard set of TrueType fonts: Times, Helvetica, Palatino, Courier, Symbol, Chicago, Geneva, Monaco, and New York. Mac OS 8–8.1 also include Charcoal. Mac OS 8.5 comes with all these fonts plus Capitals, Gadget, Sand, Techno, and Textile. You can get more fonts from many sources.

Noncommercial fonts

You can get additional TrueType and PostScript fonts at nominal cost from sources of shareware and freeware (see "Where to Get Utility Software" in Chapter 26). Figure 13-25 shows examples of freeware and shareware TrueType fonts.

Figure 13-25: Some freeware and shareware TrueType fonts.

Commercial fonts

Many type companies make TrueType and PostScript fonts, including these companies:

Active Images
1-310-458-9094
http://www.comicbookfonts.com

Adobe Systems, Inc.
1-800-833-6687
http://www.adobe.com

Agfa Division, Bayer Corp.
1-978-508-5600; 1-800-424-8973
http://www.agfahome.com/
agfatype/pstype/main.html

Bitstream, Inc.
1-617-497-6222; 1-800-522-3668
http://www.bitstream.com

Casady & Greene, Inc.
1-408-484-9228; 1-800-359-4920
http://www.casadyg.com

Castle Systems Design
1-415-459-6495
http://www.castletype.com

Deniart Systems
1-416-941-0919; 1-800-725-9974
http://www.deniart.com

dincTYPE
1-973-472-8765
http://www.girlswhowearglasses.
com

Emigre
1-916-451-4344; 1-800-944-9021
http://www.emigre.com

The Font Bureau, Inc.
1-617-423-8770
http://www.fontbureau.com

FontShop International
(FontFont)
http://www.fontfont.de

Font World, Inc.
1-716-686-1099
http://www.fontworld.com

Hoefler Type Foundry Inc.
1-212-777-6640
http://www.typography.com

International Typeface Corp.
1-212-949-8072
http://www.itcfonts.com

Letraset
1-201-845-6100
http://www.esselte.com/letraset/
index.html

Linotype Library GmbH
49 (0) 06172 484 401
http://www.linotypelibrary.com

Monotype Typography Inc.
1-847-718-0400; 1-800-666-6897
http://www.monotype.com

P22 Type Foundry
1-716-885-4482; 1-800-722-5080
http://www.p22.com

T-26
1-773-862-1201; 1-888-T26-FONT
http://www.t26font.com

Tangram Studio
1-519-369-3898
http://www.bmts.com/~tangram/

Treacyfaces, Inc.
1-203-389-7037; 1-800-800-6805
http://www.treacyfaces.com

URW++ Design & Development
GmbH
49 (40) 60 60 50
http://www.urwpp.de

Summary

In this chapter, you learned that fixed-size (bitmap) fonts look good only at installed sizes, but that the Mac OS can smoothly scale TrueType fonts to any size for the display screen or any type of printer. PostScript fonts look good at any size on PostScript printers. With the addition of Adobe Type Manager (ATM) software, PostScript fonts also look good on the display screen and non-PostScript printers. You also learned that all three types of fonts are kept in the Fonts folder, although PostScript fonts can also be kept in the Extensions folder or System Folder. For convenience, TrueType and fixed-size fonts are often kept in font suitcases. You can add and remove fonts by dragging their icons to and from the Fonts folder. The Mac OS handles font display and printing automatically, but you can configure font smoothing in Mac OS 8.5. If you use ATM with any Mac OS version, you can adjust how it scales PostScript fonts.

This chapter also explained how the Mac OS chooses between fixed-size, TrueType, and PostScript versions of the same font. The priorities are different for the display screen, PostScript printers, and non-PostScript printers.

This chapter also gave an overview of how outline fonts (TrueType and PostScript) work.

In addition, this chapter described QuickDraw GX typography, which is an option with Mac OS 7.6–8.5. You learned about TrueType GX fonts, ligature substitution, swashes, numeral and fraction options, font variations, letter-spacing controls, and subscript and superscript options.

✦   ✦   ✦

Get Ready to Print

✦ ✦ ✦ ✦

✦ ✦ ✦ ✦

With the Mac OS, no matter what type of printer you
have, you set up and control printing the same basic
way in almost every application. The Mac OS enforces this
consistency by providing complete printing services to
applications. All applications use the same piece of software
to prepare the page description for, and communicate with, a
particular type of printer. This software, called a *printer driver*,
resides in the Extensions folder inside the System Folder.

You can choose a printer with the standard Chooser desk
accessory, which comes with the Mac OS, and that choice
persists among all applications and through restarts until you
choose again. Apple's Desktop Printing software improves the
administration of background printing and allows you to print
documents by dragging their icons to a printer icon on the
desktop. Desktop printing also allows you to choose a printer
from a universal Desktop Printer menu or a Control Strip
module, which bypasses the Chooser and gives you complete
control of the printing process without leaving your application.

You control the rest of the printing process with your
application's Page Setup and Print commands; the standard
options for these commands are the same in all applications.
Alternatively, you can select one document or a group of
documents (created by one application or several) and
then give the command to print the selected documents
from the Finder.

You don't have to wait for documents to finish printing before
continuing with other work. With many printer models, the
Mac OS can manage printing in the background, so you can
continue working on other tasks.

This chapter tells you how to set up for the specific printer or printers you use and how to manage background printing. You learn how to use the desktop printer methods included with Mac OS 7.6–8.5, and you also learn how to use printers that don't show up as desktop printers. (For instructions on setting up and printing documents, see Chapter 15.)

The software and methods described here don't apply if you have installed the optional QuickDraw GX software versions 1.0–1.1.5. Those versions of QuickDraw GX, which can't be used with Mac OS 8–8.5, provide alternative printing methods. (For a discussion of QuickDraw GX printing, see Appendix A.) If you use QuickDraw GX 1.1.6, which is included with Mac OS 8–8.5, you use the printing methods that are described in this chapter and the next.

Comparing Printer Driver Software

For each type of printer you use, your computer needs printing software in the Extensions folder. That software is called a *printer driver*. A printer driver prepares a complete description of each page to be printed in a format that the printer can interpret, and then sends the page descriptions to the printer. Figure 14-1 displays the icons of the printer drivers that come with Mac OS 7.6–8.5.

Figure 14-1: The Mac OS printer drivers.

Your application prints by sending a description of your document to the printer driver software. The printer driver translates the description into data that the printer can use.

Many printers work with Macs, and each type of printer requires its own printer driver software. Printers made for the Macintosh market come with printer drivers. If you can't find the printer driver for your printer, contact its maker for replacement software.

In general, you should use the latest version of a printer driver available. For example, if you buy an Apple printer after upgrading to Mac OS 8.5 and the printer comes with older driver software than the driver that came with Mac OS 8.5, use the driver that came with Mac OS 8.5. The latest versions of printer drivers are usually available at low cost or for free from printer makers' Web sites. The latest drivers for Apple printers are available from Apple's Software Updates library (http://www.apple.com/swupdates/).

If you're not sure which version of a printer driver you have, select its icon in the Extensions folder and choose Get Info from Finder's File menu. The driver's Info window reports the version number.

PostScript printer drivers

Printers that interpret PostScript commands to create printable images are called *PostScript printers*. Examples include most Apple LaserWriter models (but not the Personal LaserWriter LS, Personal LaserWriter 300, or LaserWriter Select 300), the Hewlett-Packard LaserJet series, Texas Instruments' MicroLaser series, GCC Technologies' Elite series, and NEC's SilentWriter and ColorMate series. Although some of these printers come with proprietary driver software, most of the printers also work with Apple's LaserWriter 8 drivers or Adobe's AdobePS drivers.

Apple's LaserWriter 8 drivers

The LaserWriter 8 driver versions that come with Mac OS 7.6–8.5 have numerous improvements over earlier LaserWriter 8 driver versions. Beginning with LaserWriter 8 version 8.4.2 in Mac OS 7.6, if you have access to more than one PostScript printer, you can choose the one you want when you print a document. (With earlier LaserWriter 8 drivers, you must choose the printer before printing.) When you print a document, you can also schedule when you want it to print, either relative to other documents waiting to be printed or at a specific time. Moreover, with LaserWriter 8 version 8.4 and later you don't have to worry about running out of disk space when printing a large document, as you do with earlier LaserWriter 8 drivers.

LaserWriter 8 version 8.5.1 allows you to print multiple collated or uncollated copies of a document. You can "print to" Acrobat PDF files directly if Adobe Acrobat Distiller is installed on your Mac. You can define custom page sizes for printers that can accommodate them. You have more control over color matching with ColorSync. In addition, you can use the included Desktop Printing Utility to create more kinds of desktop printers than the Chooser can create. LaserWriter 8 version 8.5.1 is part of a standard installation of Mac OS 8.1.

LaserWriter 8 version 8.6 includes a version of the desktop printing software that is open to all types of printers. Previously, only PostScript printers and Apple printers could show up as desktop printers. In addition, LaserWriter 8 version 8.6 supports the Unicode method of encoding text and the Euro currency symbol. LaserWriter 8 version 8.6 is part of a standard installation of Mac OS 8.5.

CAUTION

68030 and 68040 Macs with Mac OS 7.6

A computer with a 68030 or 68040 processor can't use LaserWriter 8 version 8.4 or later with Mac OS 7.6 unless the computer also has the CFM-68K Runtime Enabler version 4.0 or later installed. The easiest way to get this required file is to upgrade to Mac OS 7.6.1–8.5. The CFM-68K file is not required with any PowerPC computer.

Adobe's AdobePS and PSPrinter drivers

Apple developed LaserWriter 8 in collaboration with Adobe Systems (creator of PostScript) to take advantage of PostScript Level 2. Adobe distributes a driver similar to LaserWriter 8 version 8.5.1 under the name AdobePS 8.5.1. If you buy a PostScript printer made by a company other than Apple, the printer may come with the AdobePS driver. Prior to AdobePS, Adobe made the PSPrinter 8.3.1, which was similar to a version of LaserWriter 8 earlier than 8.4. Until the release of AdobePS 8.5.1, Adobe did not have a version of PSPrinter similar to Apple's LaserWriter 8 version 8.4–8.5.1. Most PostScript printers that work with PSPrinter 8.3.1 and AdobePS 8.5.1 also work with LaserWriter 8 version 8.4.3–8.6.

CAUTION

Using AdobePS with LaserWriter 8

It's a coincidence that LaserWriter 8 version 8.5.1 and AdobePS 8.5.1 have the same version number. This coincidence causes a problem if you install AdobePS 8.5.1 on a computer that already has LaserWriter 8 version 8.5.1. Both drivers use a common file named PrintingLib (it's in the Extensions folder). When you install AdobePS 8.5.1, the Adobe PrintingLib file replaces the Apple PrintingLib file, and LaserWriter 8 version 8.5.1 stops working. The solution is to reinstall LaserWriter 8 version 8.5.1 or later. This replaces the Adobe PrintingLib file with the Apple PrintingLib file, which both drivers can use. To reinstall LaserWriter 8 version 8.5.1 or 8.6, do a custom installation of Mac OS 8.1 or 8.5. For Mac OS 8.5, click the Customize button in the last step of the Mac OS Install program, select the Mac OS 8.5 module, and choose Customized Installation from its pop-up menu. In the dialog box that appears, select the LaserWriter 8 component (not LaserWriter 8f) and click OK. Then click Start. For Mac OS 8.1, click Customize in the last step of the Mac OS Install program, select the Mac OS 8.1 module, and click Start. When the Mac OS Installer window appears, choose Custom Install from the pop-up menu. Then select the LaserWriter 8 component (not LaserWriter 8f), which is part of the Printing component group, and click Install. Note that selecting the LaserWriter 8f component in a custom installation of Mac OS 8.1 or 8.5 would install the LaserWriter 8.2.3f driver for LaserWriters with faxing capabilities, and would not update the PrintingLib file. (For more information on custom installations, see Chapters 31 and 32.)

PostScript Printer Description (PPD) files

The LaserWriter 8, AdobePS, and PSPrinter drivers let you configure specific features of a particular printer, such as its *resolution* (the number of dots it can print per inch) and the size and capacity of its paper trays. These PostScript drivers get a printer's optional features from a special file called a *PostScript Printer Description (PPD)* file. A set of PPD files comes with the LaserWriter 8 driver. The PPD files reside in a folder named Printer Descriptions inside the Extensions folder (which is in the System Folder). In addition, printer manufacturers include the appropriate PPD with each printer that has PostScript Level 2 or 3. If you don't go through the setup process with your printer, the LaserWriter 8, AdobePS, and PSPrinter drivers use generic settings based on the page sizes and features of the original Apple LaserWriter. (The setup process is described in "Choosing the Default Printer" later in this chapter.)

Non-PostScript printer drivers

Many printers do not use PostScript to create page images. Examples from Apple include all the various StyleWriter printers, the ImageWriter II, the Personal LaserWriter 300, and the Personal LaserWriter LS. Non-PostScript printers from other companies include Hewlett-Packard's DeskWriter and DeskJet series, the Epson Stylus models, and GCC Technologies' PLP II.

Each type of non-PostScript printer has its own printer driver software. With few exceptions, your Extensions folder must include a different driver for each non-PostScript printer that you use. Notable exceptions:

✦ StyleWriter (original) can use the Color StyleWriter 1500, StyleWriter 1200, StyleWriter II, or StyleWriter drivers

✦ StyleWriter II can use the Color StyleWriter 1500, StyleWriter 1200, or StyleWriter II drivers

✦ StyleWriter 1200 can use the Color StyleWriter 1500, StyleWriter 1200 drivers

✦ Color StyleWriter 2400 can use Color StyleWriter 2500 driver

✦ Color StyleWriter 2200 can use Color StyleWriter 2500 driver

✦ Personal LaserWriter LS can use LaserWriter 300 driver

Other output device drivers

Other types of output devices, although not technically printers, also have printer driver software. These devices include fax/modems, plotters, and portable document makers such as Adobe Acrobat and Common Ground. If you have any of these devices, each must have a driver in your Extensions folder.

Choosing the Default Printer

The Mac OS can print to any printer, fax modem, or other output device for which you have a driver in your Extensions folder. Because you can use more than one printer or output device with your computer, you need to designate which one you want to make the default, or active, printer or device. Designating a default printer or device is a two-step process. First you select the driver that the printer or device uses, and then you select a specific printer that uses the driver. You can do both steps with the Chooser accessory program, as described in this section.

Selecting a printer driver

In the Chooser, you begin the process of designating the default printer or other device by selecting its driver. The left side of the Chooser displays an icon for each printer driver in your Extensions folder, each of which corresponds to the types of printers or other output devices you can use. To select a driver, you click the appropriate icon or type the first part of that icon's name. Figure 14-2 shows an example of the Chooser ready for selecting a printer driver.

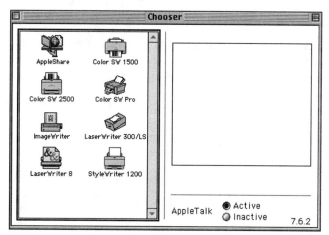

Figure 14-2: Select a printer driver on the left side of the Chooser.

Selecting a specific printer

After you select a printer driver you want to begin using on the left side, you select a specific printer on the right side of the Chooser window. The procedure is somewhat different for selecting a networked printer, a personal printer, or someone's shared printer.

Selecting a networked printer

If you select the driver for a networked type of printer, such as LaserWriter 8, the right side of the Chooser displays the names of all available printers that use the selected driver. You select the printer you want to make the default printer by clicking its name. You can also select a listed printer by typing the first part of its name. (To select by typing, a heavy border must surround the list of printer names. If it isn't, press Tab until it is.) Close the Chooser after you select the name of the networked printer that you want to make the default printer. Figure 14-3 shows an example list of printers that use the LaserWriter 8 driver.

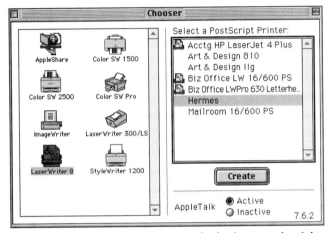

Figure 14-3: Select a specific networked printer on the right side of the Chooser.

If your network has zones, you see a list of network zones in the lower-left corner of the Chooser, and the right side of the Chooser displays printer names only for the currently selected zone. You can select a different zone to see the printers available in it. (If you don't see a list of zones, your network has no zones.)

If there are no names listed on the right side of the Chooser when a networked type of printer driver is selected on the left side of the window, then there are no printers of that type available on the network (in the currently selected zone, if your network has zones). If you want to begin using a printer that isn't available now, you may be able to create a desktop printer for it as described in "Using the Desktop Printer Utility" later in this chapter.

Selecting a personal printer

If the printer driver you select on the left side of the Chooser is for a personal printer, such as Color SW 2500, the right side of the Chooser displays the ports to which it could be connected. A personal printer connects directly to your computer. Your computer may have a choice of ports or only one port. You select a port by clicking it in the Chooser. Figure 14-4 shows an example list of ports for a personal printer.

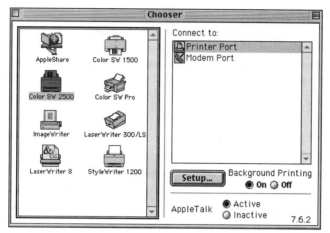

Figure 14-4: Select a port for the personal printer on the right side of the Chooser.

You may not be able to select a port for your personal printer unless you set the AppleTalk option to Inactive in the Chooser. If you don't want to make AppleTalk inactive, you can use the AppleTalk control panel to set the AppleTalk connection to something other than the port you want to use for your printer. For example, you can set the AppleTalk control panel's Connect Via option to Remote Only if it is installed on your computer. (For more information on the Remote Only option, see "Configuring an AppleTalk Connection" in Chapter 19.)

Turning off AppleTalk may not release the port you want to use for a personal printer. If you have trouble printing to a personal printer connected to a port that was used previously for an AppleTalk network, restart the computer after making AppleTalk inactive.

Selecting a shared printer

If you select the driver for a personal printer on the left side of the Chooser, you may see more than ports on the right side. You may also see the names of shared printers listed there. Each shared printer is a personal printer connected to someone else's computer on your network. The names of shared printers appear only if other people on your network have made their personal printers available for sharing, as described later in this chapter. Additionally, you can only see the name of a shared printer when the computer to which it's connected is turned on. You select a shared printer by clicking or typing its name. Figure 14-5 shows a shared StyleWriter printer in the Chooser.

After selecting a shared printer, you can get information about it by clicking the Get Info button in the Chooser. The dialog box that appears reports the Mac OS version installed on the printer's computer, the name of that computer, and the fonts installed on your computer that are missing on the shared printer's computer. Documents containing fonts that are not installed on the shared printer's computer will print slowly or may not print correctly.

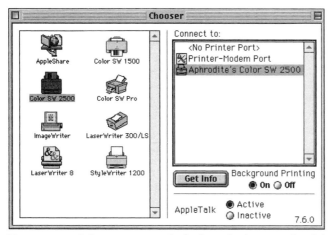

Figure 14-5: Select someone else's shared printer on the right side of the Chooser.

Setting up the selected printer

After selecting a specific printer, you may need to set it up. You need to set up a printer that uses the LaserWriter 8 or PSPrinter driver. You may be able to set up a personal printer to let other people on your network share it and to keep a log of its usage.

To set up a printer you have selected in the Chooser, click the Create button or the Setup button on the right side of the Chooser window. When you click the Setup or Create button, the printer driver either displays status messages describing its automatic setup process or it displays a dialog box with setup options for you to choose.

If no Setup or Create button appears on the right side of the Chooser, or if the button is dimmed (grayed out), then there is nothing to set up. This will be the case if you have not selected a specific printer on the right side of the Chooser.

LaserWriter 8 or PSPrinter setup

The first time you select a printer that uses the LaserWriter 8 driver or the PSPrinter driver, a Create button appears on the right side of the Chooser. When you click this button, the Mac OS determines the correct PPD file for the printer. If the printer can have optional equipment such as extra paper trays or a RAM upgrade, the Mac OS determines the printer's configuration.

At the conclusion of this process, the Create button changes to a Setup button. If you click this button, a dialog box appears with additional buttons that you can click to change the printer's setup.

Personal printer setup

If your computer has a personal printer directly connected to one of its ports, you may be able to make the printer available for other people on your network to share. Your computer acts as a host for your personal printer on the network. This means that your hard disk must store all the print requests waiting to be printed by everyone who's using your printer, and that your computer must print those files in the background. If you continue working while your computer handles all that background printing, you may notice a performance slowdown.

You can share a personal printer that uses any Color StyleWriter driver, the StyleWriter 1200 driver, or the LaserWriter 300 driver. When you select a port for a personal printer that uses one of these drivers, a Setup button appears on the right side of the Chooser. Clicking this button displays the sharing setup dialog box for the printer. Figure 14-6 shows the sharing setup dialog for a personal printer that uses the Color StyleWriter 2500 driver.

Figure 14-6: Setting up a personal printer for sharing.

In the printer's sharing setup dialog box, turn on the Share this Printer option. Give the printer a distinctive name by which it will be known on the network. You also can specify a password that anyone who wants to use the printer will have to enter. You have the option of keeping a log of printer activity. Click OK to dismiss the dialog box.

Closing the Chooser

After selecting a driver, selecting a specific printer or device, and setting it up, you should close the Chooser. The printer or device you selected is now the default printer and you can print on it by using the Page Setup and Print commands in any application (as described in the next chapter).

SECRETS

What Makes Desktop Printers Appear

Mac OS 7.6–8.5 normally creates a desktop printer after you select an eligible printer with the Chooser. Yet there may be a desktop printer icon on your desktop even if you have never used the Chooser. A desktop printer normally appears after you select an eligible printer with the Mac OS Setup program, which runs automatically when you first start your computer after installing Mac OS 8–8.5. In addition, if you upgrade to Mac OS 7.6–8.5 from System 7.5.5 or earlier, a desktop printer may appear automatically for the printer you used most recently before upgrading.

If a desktop printer already exists for the printer you want to use, and its icon has a heavy black border, you don't have to select the same printer again with the Chooser. The heavy black border indicates the default printer. If the desktop printer doesn't have a heavy black border, then it isn't currently the default printer. You need to select the printer again in the Chooser as described earlier. Alternatively, you can use Finder's Printing menu as described in "Working with Desktop Printers" later in this chapter.

Only some of the printers you select in the Chooser can become desktop printers. Any printer that uses one of the Apple LaserWriter, StyleWriter, or ImageWriter printer drivers will become a desktop printer. Don't expect to see desktop printers for printers, fax modems, or devices that use other drivers that were released prior to Mac OS 8.5. Companies that create printer drivers must enhance the drivers so they create desktop printers, and this capability first became available with Mac OS 8.5.

Desktop printers require two extensions in your Extensions folder: Desktop Printer Spooler and Desktop PrintMonitor. Both are part of a standard installation of Mac OS 7.6–8.5. If you remove these extensions or disable them with the Extensions Manager control panel, you won't be able to use desktop printers.

If a specific printer has been selected for the first time, the Mac OS may create a *desktop printer* for it. When this happens, an icon representing the printer appears on the desktop. (You may have to wait several seconds before the desktop printer icon appears.) You can use desktop printers to change the default printer and to manage printing, as described in "Working with Desktop Printers" and "Managing Background Printing" later in this chapter.

Using the Desktop Printer Utility

In addition to creating desktop printers with the Chooser, you can use the Desktop Printer Utility program. It can create regular desktop printers and three other kinds of desktop printers based on the LaserWriter 8 driver version 8.5.1 and later and the AdobePS driver version 8.5.1 and later. If you want to create desktop printers that use other printer drivers, use the Chooser as described in the previous section, "Choosing a Printer to Use."

You'll find the Desktop Printer Utility in the Apple LaserWriter Software folder within the Apple Extras folder. The Desktop Printer Utility is part of a standard installation of Mac OS 8.1–8.5. You can use the Desktop Printer Utility in Mac OS 7.6–7.6.1 by installing the latest LaserWriter driver, which is available from Apple's Software Updates library (http://www.apple.com/swupdates/). The Desktop Printer Utility is not compatible with Mac OS 8.

Types of desktop printers

You can create these four types of desktop printers with the Desktop Printer Utility:

✦ **Regular desktop printers**, which are the same as the desktop printers created by selecting the LaserWriter 8 driver and a particular networked printer in the Chooser (as described in the previous section, "Choosing the Default Printer)".

✦ **LPR (TCP/IP) desktop printers**, which use the cross-platform LPR (Line Printer Remote) protocol and connect via a TCP/IP network such as an intranet or the Internet.

✦ **Hold desktop printers**, which keep print requests on hold until you connect your computer to a printer and can resume printing. You may find a hold desktop printer convenient while using a PowerBook away from your printer.

✦ **PostScript Translator desktop printers**, which are not actually connected to printers. Instead, they always create PostScript files that can be sent to a PostScript printer later.

In addition to these four types of desktop printers, the Desktop Printer Utility can be customized by software developers to create custom desktop printers that send PostScript files to a particular application for processing. For example, a custom desktop printer could be created to send PostScript files to a program that displays pages onscreen rather than printing them on paper, in essence providing a print preview.

Creating a new desktop printer

To create a desktop printer, open the Desktop Printer Utility. The program displays its New dialog box, in which you select the type of desktop printer you want to create. If the Desktop Printer Utility is already open, you can display the New dialog box by choosing New from the File menu. Figure 14-7 shows the Desktop Printer Utility's New dialog box.

Choosing a printer driver

At the top of the New dialog box, choose the printer driver that you want the new desktop printer to use. The pop-up menu that lists your choices includes only Desktop Printer Utility-compatible PostScript drivers. The LaserWriter 8 driver is the only compatible driver that comes with the Mac OS. In addition, the AdobePS driver that you can get from Adobe (see "Comparing Printer Driver Software" earlier in this chapter) is also compatible with the Desktop Printer Utility.

Figure 14-7: Create several types of desktop printers with the Desktop Printer Utility.

Selecting the kind of desktop printer

In the middle of the New dialog box, select the kind of desktop printer you want to create and click OK. For the LaserWriter 8 driver, you can select any of these kinds of desktop printers:

✦ **Printer (AppleTalk)**, which creates a regular desktop printer.

✦ **Printer (LPR)**, which creates a desktop printer for a printer connected to your computer via a TCP/IP network such as the Internet or an intranet. When communicating with this printer, the Mac OS uses the standard LPR protocol. Several newer Apple LaserWriter models — 8500, 16/600PS, 12/640PS, 12/600PS, 12/660PS, and Pro 810 — can use LPR and a TCP/IP network as well as the traditional PAP protocol (Printer Access Protocol) and an AppleTalk network common to all LaserWriter models.

✦ **Printer (no printer connection)**, which creates a desktop printer that you can use when your computer is not connected to an actual printer. Printed documents are held in the desktop printer for later printing, as discussed in "Managing Background Printing" later in this chapter.

✦ **Translator (PostScript)**, which creates a desktop printer that always saves printed pages as a PostScript file. (For more information on saving printed pages as PostScript files, see "Setting LaserWriter 8 Options" in Chapter 15.)

Specifying a PPD file and printer

After you select the kind of desktop printer you want and click OK in the New dialog box, the Desktop Printer Utility program displays an untitled window. This window shows the PPD file selected for the desktop printer as well as an additional setting for some kinds of desktop printers. You can change settings shown in a desktop printer window by clicking Change buttons in the window. Figure 14-8 shows an example of an untitled desktop printer window.

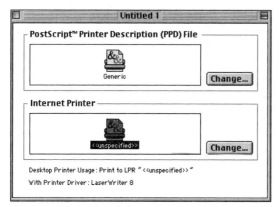

Figure 14-8: See and change the PPD file and other settings for a desktop printer.

To change a desktop printer's PPD file, click the Change button next to the PPD icon at the top of the Desktop Printer Utility window. This brings up a standard Open dialog box in which you can select a different PPD file from the Printer Descriptions folder within your Extensions folder.

To change a desktop printer's additional settings, click the Change button next to its icon in the Desktop Printer Utility window. This brings up a dialog box in which you can change the settings. For a regular desktop printer connected to an AppleTalk network, you can choose a networked printer by zone and name, in much the same way as you can with the Chooser. For a desktop printer connected to a TCP/IP network such as the Internet, you can enter the printer's network address and queue. For a desktop printer that creates PostScript files, you can select a folder in which the files are saved. For a desktop printer with no connection to an actual printer, there are no additional settings besides the PPD file.

When you finish changing a desktop printer's settings, choose Save from the Desktop Printer Utility's File menu. In the standard Save dialog box that appears, name the desktop printer and select a folder location for it. Desktop printers do not have to live on the desktop.

Changing a desktop printer

You can use the Desktop Printer Utility to change the PPD file and other settings of any desktop printer based on the LaserWriter 8 driver. To change a desktop printer's settings, open the desktop printer with the Open command in the Desktop Printer Utility's File menu. The program displays the desktop printer's settings in a titled window like the untitled window of a new desktop printer (review Figure 14-8). Change the settings in this window by clicking the Change buttons in it, as previously described.

SECRETS

PPD File Confusion

You may encounter a problem when trying to select a PPD file for a printer that uses the LaserWriter 8 driver. This problem occurs when you try to select a PPD file after having recently upgraded your computer to QuickTime 3.0. A dialog box appears saying the PPD file wasn't created by the application you're using and asking you to select an alternate program to open the PPD file. Your options will include the program you're using (Desktop Printer Utility, Chooser, Finder, or System) and the same program "with QuickTime translation." If you select the application alone (not with QuickTime translation), Mac OS Easy Open remembers your choice and doesn't ask you about PPD files again. If you choose the program "with QuickTime Translation," you will get an error message that mentions error –2048. This same message appears again every time you try to configure a printer. To clear this problem, open the Mac OS Easy Open control panel and turn on its "Always show dialog box" option. This forces the Easy Open dialog box to appear the next time you configure a printer, so you can override your previous choice for opening PPD files. Once you have changed your PPD preference, you can turn off the "Always show dialog box" option.

This problem can occur when you create a desktop printer or change its setup with the Desktop Printer Utility, the Chooser, or Finder's Printing menu.

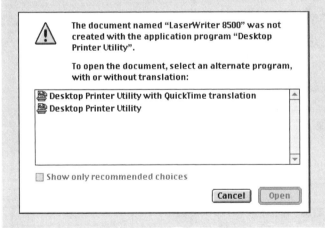

Working with Desktop Printers

You can handle desktop printers as you would a folder in the Finder. You can rename desktop printers, move them from the desktop to a folder, create aliases for them, and drag them to the Trash.

When you select a desktop printer in the Finder, a Printing menu appears in the menu bar next to the Special menu. You can use other menu commands in the Finder to change the default printer, check printer status, and change printer setup. You may also be able to change the default printer using other techniques.

Changing the default printer

If you have more than one desktop printer, you choose one that represents the printer that you want to use by default. The Finder indicates which desktop printer is the default printer by drawing a heavy black border around its icon. You can choose the default printer by using the Printing menu in the Finder. Alternatively, you may be able to use a universal Desktop Printer menu or a Control Strip module. You can also use the Chooser to change the default printer.

Printing menu

To set a default printer using the Finder's Printing menu, select the desktop printer that you want to become the default. When the Printing menu appears, choose Set Default Printer from it. The Printing menu is only available in the Finder. Figure 14-9 shows a couple of desktop printer icons and the Printing menu in Mac OS 8.5.

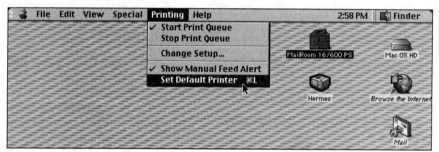

Figure 14-9: Setting a default printer with Finder's Printing menu.

Desktop printer menu and Control Strip module

There are even more convenient methods than the Finder's Printing menu for changing the default printer. You can choose a desktop printer while using any application—no need to switch to the Finder and use the Printer menu. If the Control Strip is installed on your computer, you can choose a printer from it. You can also choose a printer from a universal Desktop Printer menu in Mac OS 7.6–7.6.1 and Mac OS 8.1–8.5. The Desktop Printer menu has a printer icon as its title and appears near the right end of the menu bar. The Desktop Printer menu isn't available in Mac OS 8. Figure 14-10 shows an example of the Printer Selector module in the Control Strip.

The Printer Selector control strip module and the Desktop Printer menu are not part of a standard installation on every Mac, but you can install them separately. For instructions on installing the Control Strip, see "Control Strip Adjustments" in Chapter 11. The Printer Selector module is installed with the Control Strip.

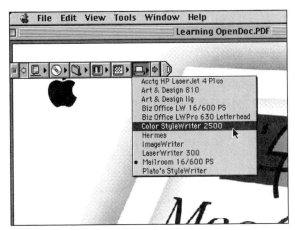

Figure 14-10: Choosing a default printer from the Control Strip.

The method of installing the Desktop Printer menu is different in Mac OS 8.5, Mac OS 8.1, and Mac OS 7.6–7.6.1. To install the Desktop Printer menu in Mac OS 8.5, do a custom installation with the Mac OS Install program. In the last step of the program, click the Customize button, select the Mac OS 8.5 module, and choose Customized Installation from its pop-up menu. In the dialog box that appears, select Desktop Printing and click OK. Then click Start. (Chapter 31 has detailed instructions for doing a custom installation of Mac OS 8.5.)

To install the Desktop Printer menu in Mac OS 8.1, you must do a custom installation of the LaserWriter 8.5.1 or 8.6 installation software, which is available from Apple's Software Updates library (http://www.apple.com/swupdates/). Run the Installer program and when you get to its main window, choose Custom Install from the pop-up menu. Then select the Desktop Printer Menu component and click Install. (Chapter 32 has detailed instructions for installing Mac OS enhancements such as an upgrade of the LaserWriter software.)

You can install the Desktop Printer menu in Mac OS 7.6–7.6.1 by doing a custom installation of the Mac OS. In the last step of the Install Mac OS program, select the Mac OS module and click Start. When the Mac OS Installer window appears, choose Custom Install from the pop-up menu. Then select the Desktop Printing component, which is part of the Printing component group, and click Install. (Chapter 32 has detailed instructions for doing a custom installation of Mac OS 7.6–7.6.1.)

Chooser

Although the Chooser is less convenient than the methods already described for designating the default printer, it works for all printers and output devices including those that can't have desktop printers. Just select the printer or other device in the Chooser as described in "Choosing the Default Printer" earlier in this chapter. If the printer that you select in the Chooser already has a desktop printer, the Chooser makes the selected printer the default printer without creating another desktop printer for it.

Checking a desktop printer's status

You can use menu commands in the Finder to check the current status, configuration, and installed font information for a desktop printer that is based on the LaserWriter 8 driver. This information appears in two views of a desktop printer's Info window. You can switch between viewing status and configuration information and viewing a list of installed fonts by choosing the view you want from the pop-up menu near the top of the desktop printer's Info window. Figure 14-11 shows examples of both views of a desktop printer Info window.

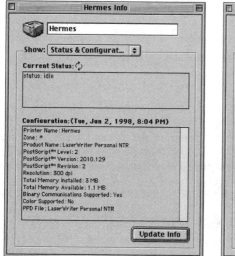 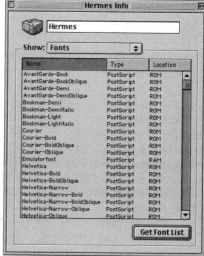

Figure 14-11: Viewing a desktop printer's current status, configuration, and fonts.

To display a desktop printer's Info window in Mac OS 8.5, select the desktop printer and choose Status & Configuration or Fonts from the Get Info submenu. (This submenu appears in the Finder's File menu and in a desktop printer's contextual menu.) In Mac OS 7.6–8.1, select the desktop printer and choose Get Printer Info from the Finder's Printing menu. If none of these menu commands is available, you can't get status, configuration, or installed font information for the selected desktop printer.

Changing a desktop printer's setup

Change Setup, which is another command in the Finder's Printing menu, lets you change the PPD file and reconfigure any installed options of a desktop printer that is based on a LaserWriter 8 driver. Selecting a printer icon and choosing Change Setup brings up a dialog box that displays the current setup. The dialog box contains a button for changing the PPD file, other controls for changing the settings of options installed in the printer, and an Auto Setup button that has the printer driver interrogate the printer to configure those settings automatically. Figure 14-12 shows an example of the Change Setup dialog box.

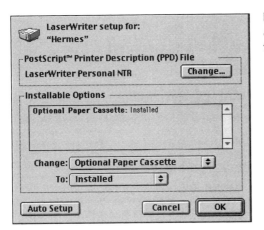

Figure 14-12: Changing a desktop printer's setup from the Finder.

Managing Background Printing

When you print a document (as described in the next chapter), the printer driver creates page descriptions for each page to be printed. The driver may send the page descriptions to the printer immediately, forcing you to wait until the document finishes printing before you can do anything else. Alternatively, many printer drivers can save the page descriptions in a file for later automatic printing in the background, while you do other work in the foreground. A file of page descriptions is called a *print request,* a *print job,* or a *spool file.*

In the short time it takes to save a print request, the printer driver has control of the computer. You regain control as soon as a driver finishes saving. While you work (or not), the Desktop PrintMonitor application opens automatically in the background and handles the waiting print request by sending the saved page descriptions to the printer a bit at a time during the slices of time it gets to work in the background. (Instead of the Desktop PrintMonitor, the PrintMonitor application handles all waiting print requests for printers without desktop icons.) The background printing activity may make the computer feel less responsive, especially on a slow computer.

While a document is printing in the background, you can queue additional print requests by using the Print command in one or more applications. The Desktop PrintMonitor application (or PrintMonitor, for printers without desktop icons) normally handles the queued print requests in the order they were saved. You can override this sequence by setting a specific print time or a special priority, as described later in this section. You can also stop and start the print queue whenever you want.

The rest of this section tells you how to turn background printing on and off and then explains how to manage a queue of waiting print requests. You'll find separate explanations for managing a print queue with desktop printers and without them, because the methods are different.

Turning background printing on and off

You can turn background printing on or off separately for each printer that can print in the background. With most printers, you can set background printing in the Chooser before you print documents. You can set background printing each time you print to a desktop printer that uses any of these drivers: LaserWriter 8 version 8.4 and later, PSPrinter, or AdobePS.

Setting background printing before printing

To use the Chooser to turn background printing on or off for a printer, you must first select the printer in the Chooser window (as detailed earlier in this chapter in "Choosing the Default Printer"). To recap, first you select the printer driver on the left side of the Chooser. Next, on the right side of the Chooser window, you select the specific printer by its name or by the port it connects to. Now you can set the Background Printing option in the lower right area of the Chooser. Figure 14-13 shows the Background Printing option in the Chooser.

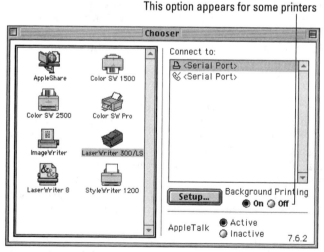

Figure 14-13: With some printer drivers, you turn background printing on or off in the Chooser.

Setting background printing when you print

You do not need to set background printing in the Chooser before printing to a desktop printer that uses any of these drivers: LaserWriter 8 version 8.4 and later, PSPrinter, or AdobePS. Instead you can turn background printing on or off whenever you use the Print command to print a document. In the Print command's dialog box, you choose the Background Printing group of options, and set the Print In option for background or foreground printing. Figure 14-14 shows the Print In option of the Print command for LaserWriter 8 version 8.6.

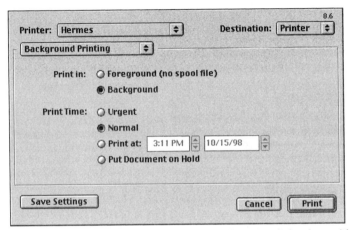

Figure 14-14: Set background printing in the Print dialog box with LaserWriter 8 version 8.4 and later.

Managing a desktop printer's queue

You can view and manage the queue of waiting print requests for each desktop printer individually. If your Mac doesn't create a desktop icon for a printer when you choose it with the Chooser, then you must use the methods described later for managing the print queue without desktop printers.

Viewing the print queue

At any time, you can see the queue of print requests waiting for a particular desktop printer by opening the desktop printer in the Finder. You open a desktop printer like a folder. Opening a desktop printer icon displays its window. At the top of the window are buttons for managing the queue of print requests and general information about the print queue. A box below the buttons identifies the print request now being printed (if any) and reports the status of that print job. Below that is a list of waiting print requests. You can sort the list of waiting print requests by name, number of pages, number of copies, or print time. Choose a sort order by clicking a column heading in the desktop printer's window. With Mac OS 7.6–7.6.1, you can also choose a sort order from the View menu. Figure 14-15 shows a desktop printer's window.

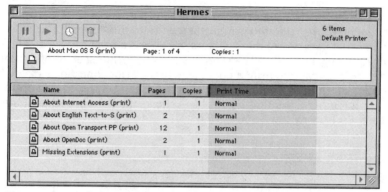

Figure 14-15: View queued print requests in a desktop printer's window.

Redirecting a print request

You can redirect a waiting print request by dragging it from its current desktop printer window to the icon or window of a compatible desktop printer. In general, desktop printers that use the same driver (they have the same icon selected on the left side of the Chooser) are compatible.

Changing the printing order

Print requests in a desktop printer's window print in the listed order when the list is sorted by print time. You can change the order of print requests by dragging them up and down in the window. You can drag a print request by its icon, name, or any other text on the same line in the desktop printer's window. Figure 14-16 shows an example of changing a print request's order in the queue.

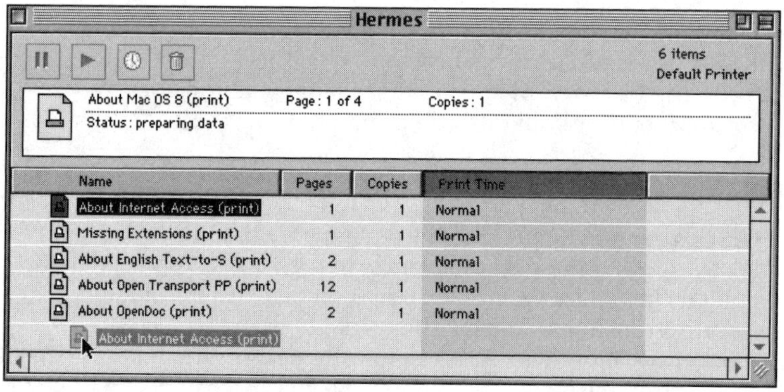

Figure 14-16: Change the order of print requests by dragging them in the desktop printer's queue.

Scheduling print requests

You can also change a print request's place in line by setting its priority to urgent, normal, or scheduled for a specific time and date. To set a print request's priority, select it and click the Set Print Time button (the one with the clock icon) in the desktop printer's window. Figure 14-17 shows the dialog box in which you set a print request's priority.

A print request's priority changes automatically if you drag it to a place among print requests of a different priority. For example, dragging a scheduled print request above an urgent print request makes the scheduled print request urgent.

Placing a print request on hold

You can postpone a print request indefinitely, even if the print request is currently being printed. Select a print request in the desktop printer's window and click the Hold button, which looks like a VCR's Pause button. To take a print request off hold, select it and then click the Resume button, which looks like a VCR's Play button. Clicking the Resume button displays the Resume Print Request dialog box, in which you can specify the page from which you want printing to resume.

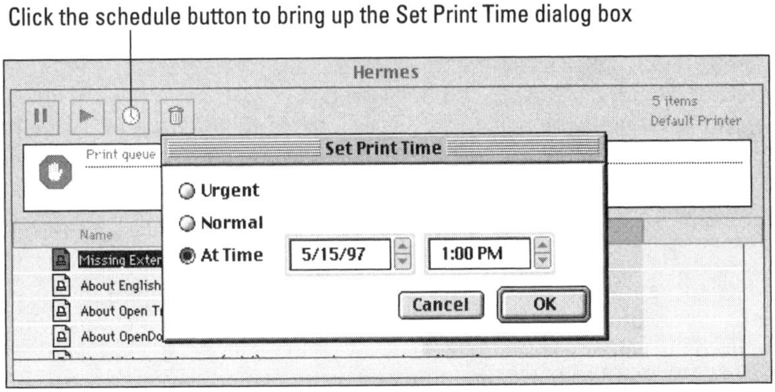

Click the schedule button to bring up the Set Print Time dialog box

Figure 14-17: Schedule a priority or a specific time for a print request.

Stopping or removing a print request

You can stop a print request by dragging it out of the desktop printer's window. To get rid of a print request altogether, either drag it to the Trash or select it and click the Remove button, which has a trash can icon.

Managing multiple print requests

You can schedule or resequence more than one print request at a time in a desktop printer's window. To select multiple print requests, press the Shift key while clicking them or drag across them.

Stopping and starting printing

To stop all printing on a particular desktop printer, select it and then choose Stop Print Queue from the Printing menu. A small stop sign appears on the desktop printer's icon.

To start printing again, select the desktop printer and then choose Start Print Queue from the Printing menu.

Manual paper feed notification

If you print a document using a printer's manual feed tray, you normally receive a notification alert when the printer is waiting for you to manually feed paper. The Printing menu makes it easy to turn off this notification. Just select the relevant desktop printer and choose Show Manual Feed Alert from the Printing menu so that there is no check mark next to it in the menu.

QUICK TIPS

Instant Reprints (Well, Almost)

It takes quite a while to save background print requests for some documents, and that's on top of the time it takes to open the application and the document before you can begin printing. For example, it may take several minutes to save a print request for a Photoshop image to be printed on a Color StyleWriter. You don't have to repeat that wait each time you reprint the image in the future if you can spare the disk space to store a copy of the print request. (Yes, you could print multiple copies of the image at one time and hand them out as needed — it doesn't take any longer to save a print request for multiple copies than for a single copy — but then you may end up with extra copies that you have to throw away, thus wasting ink and expensive special paper.)

Here is a procedure for reprinting without the delay of saving a new print request each time: Before printing a document for the first time, select the desktop printer and choose Stop Print Queue from the Finder's Printing menu. Then print the document, causing a print request to be created for the desktop printer. If you forget to stop the print queue before printing, immediately go to the Finder and stop the print queue or open the desktop printer and put the print request on hold. Next, open the desktop printer and drag the print request to any folder. When you're ready to make a print, hold down the Option key and drag the print request from that folder to the desktop printer. By holding down the Option key, you make a copy of the print request for the desktop printer and leave the original print request untouched for future reprints. If necessary, use the Finder's Start Print Queue command to start background printing. Et voilà! Reprints without saving new print requests or opening a document and its application!

Managing the print queue without desktop printers

You can use the PrintMonitor application to view and manage the queue of waiting print requests for some printers that don't have desktop icons. The PrintMonitor application handles printing of waiting print requests while you continue working with other applications. PrintMonitor opens in the background automatically whenever there are print requests in the PrintMonitor Documents folder (inside the System Folder), deletes each print request that it prints, and quits automatically when the PrintMonitor Documents folder is empty.

Some printers made by companies other than Apple come with their own applications for managing the queue of waiting print requests. For instructions on using one of these applications, check the documentation that came with your printer.

Viewing the print queue

While PrintMonitor is open in the background, you can make it the active application by choosing it from the Application menu. You also can open it at any time by double-clicking its icon, which is located in the Extensions folder. Making PrintMonitor active or opening it displays its window. The PrintMonitor window identifies the print request that is printing, lists the print requests waiting to be printed, and displays the status of the current print request. Figure 14-18 shows the PrintMonitor window.

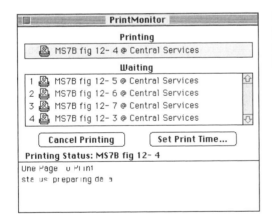

Figure 14-18: View queued print requests (without desktop printers) in the PrintMonitor window.

PrintMonitor automatically hides its window when you switch to another application, but PrintMonitor remains open in the background as long as it has print requests to process.

Changing the printing order

PrintMonitor ordinarily processes print requests in chronological order, oldest first. You can change the order by dragging print requests in the PrintMonitor window. You drag a print request by its icon, not by its name or sequence number. While you drag, an outline of the print request follows the mouse pointer, as shown in Figure 14-19.

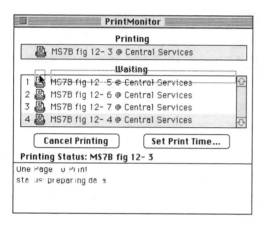

Figure 14-19: Change the order of print requests (without desktop printers) by dragging them in the PrintMonitor queue.

Scheduling printing requests

You can schedule when PrintMonitor will process a print request, or you can postpone a print request indefinitely. In the PrintMonitor window, you first select the print request you want to schedule (by clicking it). You can select the print request being printed or any print request waiting to be printed. Then click the Set Print Time button. Figure 14-20 shows the dialog box in which you set a time and date for processing a print request or postpone it indefinitely.

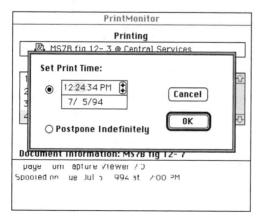

Figure 14-20: Scheduling a specific time for a print request (without desktop printers).

A print request scheduled for later printing appears in PrintMonitor's waiting list with an alarm-clock icon in place of a sequence number. A print request postponed indefinitely appears in the waiting list with a dash in place of a sequence number, and it will not be printed until you schedule a print time for it.

Stopping and starting printing

You can suspend all background printing by choosing Stop Printing from PrintMonitor's File menu. Before PrintMonitor stops printing, it finishes the print request that it is currently printing. To resume printing, choose Resume Printing from the File menu.

Setting PrintMonitor preferences

PrintMonitor can notify you when something happens that requires your attention during background printing. For example, PrintMonitor can notify you when you need to manually feed paper for background printing. An alert box, a blinking PrintMonitor icon in the menu bar, or both, can notify you. To specify how you want to be notified, you use the Preferences command in PrintMonitor's File menu. Note that if you turn off notification of manual paper feed and forget to feed paper when the printer needs it, the printer eventually cancels the print request automatically. Figure 14-21 shows the Preferences dialog box for PrintMonitor.

QUICK TIPS

Print Later

If you want to print to a printer that doesn't have a desktop icon and that isn't connected to your Mac now, you can delay printing. Turn on background printing in the Chooser and print the desired documents. Then open PrintMonitor and use its Stop Printing command to suspend printing. Now any documents that you print wait in PrintMonitor's queue until you connect to a printer and begin printing with PrintMonitor's Resume Printing command. To avoid PrintMonitor's nagging alert messages and blinking icon in the menu bar, use PrintMonitor's Preferences to suppress notification of printing errors.

To shut down your Mac while it is not connected to a printer and background printing is turned on, you must respond correctly to two PrintMonitor alerts that appear during the shutdown process. The first alert tells you that something is being printed and asks whether you want to finish printing or print later; you must click the Print Later button. Then another alert tells you that the printer can't be found; click the Cancel Printing button to conclude the shutdown process without losing any queued print requests. (If you click Try Again instead, you abort the shutdown process, and PrintMonitor tries again to find the missing printer.) This process is somewhat confusing, because clicking Cancel Printing under other circumstances actually deletes the print request that is being printed.

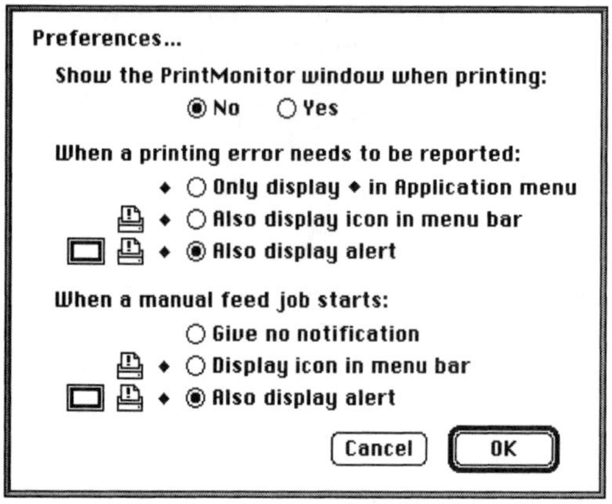

Figure 14-21: Setting PrintMonitor preferences.

You can also use the Preferences command to specify how you want to be notified about printing errors, such as PrintMonitor not being able to locate a printer that is supposed to print a print request. PrintMonitor can just display a diamond symbol next to its name in the Application menu at the right end of the menu bar; it can display the symbol and blink its icon in the menu bar; or it can do both of those things and display an alert as well. You can turn off everything except the diamond in the Application menu.

Summary

In this chapter, you learned that every printer you use must have a printer driver in your Extensions folder. A printer driver prepares a complete description of each page to be printed in a format that the printer can interpret, and then sends the page descriptions to the printer. To begin using a printer, you use the Chooser to select a driver and the specific printer. With Mac OS 7.6–8.5, selecting a printer in the Chooser normally creates a desktop printer. Once you have created desktop printers, you can use the Finder's Printing menu, the optional universal Desktop Printer menu, or the optional Printer Selector module in the Control Strip to select the printer that you want to use. You don't have to use the Chooser again for desktop printers.

You can usually continue working while the Mac OS prints in the background. You can view queued print requests by opening desktop printers. You can change the order of queued print requests, set their priorities or print times, put them on hold, or delete them. You can also stop and start any desktop printer's queue. If you have printers without desktop icons, you can manage their queued print requests with the PrintMonitor program or another program supplied by the printer maker.

✦   ✦   ✦

Print Your Documents

You're ready to print. You've made the printer you want to use the default printer, as described in the Chapter 14. Now it's time to set page-formatting options, specify how many pages and copies to print, and actually start printing. You can do all this from the Finder or from the applications that created the documents you want to print.

This chapter begins by introducing the Page Setup and Print commands you use to set page formatting and printing options. Next, this chapter explains how to print from the Finder and other applications. The bulk of the chapter details the page-formatting and printing options for printers that use Apple printer driver software.

Introducing the Print and Page Setup Commands

Almost every Mac OS application has the same commands for printing documents — Page Setup and Print — and those commands are usually in the File menu. Some applications give you other methods of printing, such as a Print button in a toolbar, but most alternate methods are based on the standard Page Setup and Print commands. Learn how to use the standard commands, and you know how to print most documents. (A few applications, such as FoxBase, can be programmed to bypass these commands completely, and this chapter does not cover printing from them.)

The Page Setup command is used to specify how the document pages are to be formatted. You need to set the paper size (such as letter or legal size), a page orientation (horizontal (landscape) or vertical (portrait)), a reduction or enlargement factor, and other options that affect how the document is to be arranged on the page. With some printers, you also can turn optional printer effects on and off.

The Print command is used to specify a range of pages, a number of copies, and a paper source. You may have additional options, depending on the type of printer driver you have chosen.

With both the Page Setup command and the Print command there may be additional options that are not described in this chapter because some applications and utility software add their own options to those commands. For example, the existence of a Page Setup option labeled ClickBook means the ClickBook utility from Blue Squirrel (801-523-1063, http://www.bluesquirrel.com) is installed for printing double-sided pages or booklets on regular printers. For explanations of Print or Page Setup options not described in this chapter, check the documentation for the application you're using and for any printing utility software installed on your computer.

This chapter tells you how to set up and print pages on printers that use the following Apple printer driver software, which is included as part of a standard installation of Mac OS 7.6–8.5:

✦ LaserWriter 8

✦ Color StyleWriter 2500, Color StyleWriter 1500, and Color StyleWriter Pro

✦ StyleWriter 1200

✦ LaserWriter 300/LS

✦ ImageWriter

Your printer may use a different driver. In that case, the procedures for setting up and printing will be similar to the ones described in this chapter, but the specific options will be different. For details, refer to the documentation that came with the printer.

You use the Chooser or desktop printers to select a printer driver for your printer, as described in Chapter 14. That chapter also explains how to manage a queue of documents waiting to print in the background while you continue working on other tasks.

The Print and Page Setup commands described here don't apply if you have installed the optional QuickDraw GX software versions 1.0–1.1.5. Those versions of QuickDraw GX, which can't be used with Mac OS 8–8.5, provide alternative printing methods. (For a discussion of QuickDraw GX printing, see Appendix A.)

Printing from the Finder

If all you need to do is print a document — that is, you don't need to open it, review it on screen, or edit it first — you can print it directly from the Finder. You don't even have to open the application that created the document.

To print a document from the Finder, drag the document icon to a desktop printer icon. Some desktop printers send all documents to the applications that created them for printing, as described in the next paragraph. But desktop printers that use the LaserWriter 8 version 8.6 driver (included with Mac OS 8.5) can print certain types of documents directly. These include PostScript, Encapsulated PostScript (EPS), PICT, and JPEG documents. The part of the LaserWriter 8 version 8.6 driver that sends documents directly to the printer is called the Download Manager. Programmers can extend it to handle more types of documents by creating plug-in software modules.

If a desktop printer can't print your document directly, it sends a request to the application that created the document, telling the application to print the document. The application opens, or becomes active if it's already open in the background, and displays the dialog box of its Print command so you can set options. Some applications also display the Page Setup dialog box so that you can set page layout options. The specific options you can set are somewhat different for each printer driver, as detailed later in this chapter. When you finish setting options, the application prints the document. If the application was not open when you started the printing process in the Finder, the application quits automatically. (Some applications stay open.)

If you don't want to use a desktop printer, select the document that you want to print and choose Print from the Finder's file menu. The Finder tells the application that created the document to print it, as described in the previous paragraph for desktop printers.

If you try to print a document but don't have the application that created it, you will see a list of alternative applications in an alert box the same as if you were trying to open the document. The File Exchange control panel in Mac OS 8.5 or the Mac OS Easy Open control panel in Mac OS-7.6–8.1 displays this alert box. You see a different dialog box if you have turned off automatic document translation. For more information on these dialog boxes, see "Opening Programs, Documents, and More" in Chapter 7.

You can use the Finder to print several documents just as easily as to print one. You simply select the documents you want to print and either drag them as a group to the desktop printer icon or choose the Print command from the Finder's file menu. The documents can be created by different applications, but they must all be in the same window or on the desktop. If the documents are in different folders, you can drag the documents to the desktop, select and print them, and then use the Finder's Put Away command to return them to the folders they came from. You can also print documents from different expanded folders that you can see in a list view of an enclosing folder or disk.

In addition to a Print command, the Finder's File menu also has a Page Setup command and a Print Window command (or a Print Desktop command if no folder or disk window is active). You do not use these commands to print documents from the Finder. These commands are for printing the Finder windows or the desktop. In fact, they have the same function in the Finder as the Page Setup and Print commands have in any other application.

Printing from Other Applications

In addition to printing from the Finder, you can print from within applications that can open the documents you want to print. You have to open the document you want to print, and the document window must be in front of other document windows. Then you use the Page Setup and Print commands from the application's File menu to set options and actually start printing. The specific options you can set are somewhat different for each printer driver, as detailed later in this chapter.

You don't have to set the Page Setup options every time you print a document. You can simply choose the Print command, and your previous Page Setup settings are used again. If you use the Print command without ever setting Page Setup options for a particular document, the application supplies its standard Page Setup options.

In addition to a regular Print command, some applications also have a Print One Copy command. This alternative command streamlines printing by foregoing the usual Print dialog box. The application supplies its standard settings for the options in the Print dialog box.

In some applications, you can print the document in the front window by clicking a Print button in a toolbar. This action generally has the same effect as choosing Print from the File menu. In a few applications, the Print button displays the Page Setup dialog box before the Print dialog box.

A few applications can be set up to bypass the Print and Page Setup commands. For example, a FileMaker Pro database can be programmed to print a report using preset Page Setup and Print options. All you do is click a button in the database window or choose a command from the Script menu, and the report prints according to the preset options.

Setting LaserWriter 8 Options

This section describes how to set up and print documents on printers that can use the versions of Apple's LaserWriter 8 printer driver that are included with Mac OS 7.6–8.5. All Apple LaserWriter printers with PostScript can use LaserWriter 8, and so can most PostScript printers made by other companies.

Specifically, this section describes how to use versions 8.4 and later of the LaserWriter 8 driver. These versions have a different interface than earlier versions. Mac OS 8.5 includes LaserWriter 8 version 8.6. Mac OS 8.1 includes LaserWriter 8 version 8.5.1. Mac OS 7.6–8 includes LaserWriter 8 version 8.4.2 or 8.4.3.

Setting LaserWriter 8 Page Setup options

When you choose the Page Setup command for a printer that uses the LaserWriter 8 driver, you see a dialog box with settings for page attributes, including paper type, orientation, and scale. You can switch to settings for PostScript Options by choosing that category from the unlabeled pop-up menu at the top of the dialog box. With a few kinds of PostScript printers, you can also switch to settings for Custom Page Size by choosing from this pop-up menu. Figure 15-1 shows the pop-up menu for switching among groups of options in the Page Setup dialog box for LaserWriter 8 version 8.4 and later.

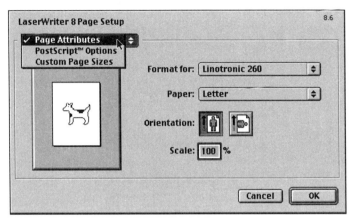

Figure 15-1: Choosing a group of options for LaserWriter 8 page setup.

Instead of choosing a group of options from the pop-up menu at the top of the Page Setup dialog box, you can move from group to group by pressing ⌘-Down Arrow(↓), ⌘-Up Arrow(↑), Page Up, or Page Down.

Page Attributes

When you choose Page Attributes from the unlabeled pop-up menu near the top of the Page Setup dialog box (LaserWriter 8 version 8.4 and later), these options are displayed, as shown in Figure 15-2:

- ✦ **Format for** lets you choose which of your Mac OS desktop printers to format. The pop-up menu lists your desktop printers that use the LaserWriter 8 driver. The setup of the printer you choose here (in particular its PPD file) can affect the page format.

- ✦ **Paper** lets you choose a paper size such as US Letter ($8\frac{1}{2}$ x 11 inches), US Legal ($8\frac{1}{2}$ x 14 inches), and A5 and B5 (European standard sizes). There are two variations of some sizes, such as US Letter and US Letter Small. The Small variation has a larger unprintable area at the edges of the paper that matches the US Letter size of older LaserWriter drivers. The regular variation gives you the maximum printable area for your printer (as specified by the printer's PPD file). If you see the size Other listed for the Paper option, it means the document was previously printed using a paper size that is not available on the currently selected printer. If you choose another Paper setting, the Other choice will no longer be available.

✦ **Orientation** determines whether the top of the printed page will be on the short edge or long edge of the paper.

✦ **Scale** reduces or enlarges the printed image according to the percentage you enter. Full size is 100 percent, the minimum reduction is 25 percent, and the maximum enlargement is 400 percent.

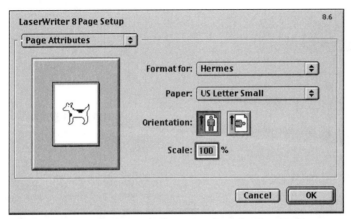

Figure 15-2: Setting Page Attributes options for LaserWriter 8 page setup.

PostScript Options

When you choose PostScript Options from the unlabeled pop-up menu near the top of the Page Setup dialog box, the following options are displayed, as shown in Figure 15-3:

✦ **Flip Horizontal** and **Flip Vertical** create mirror images of your document. You can see the result in the illustration in the dialog box when you click the checkbox. The Flip Horizontal option flips the image right to left, which is useful if you are creating a film image on a Linotronic imagesetter for a transparency or if the pages have to be emulsion side down. Flipping the image vertically (upside down) has no apparent use because turning the paper around has the same effect.

✦ **Invert Image** makes all the black parts of a page print white, and vice versa. You probably won't have much use for this parlor trick unless you create film negatives on a slide printer that has no method of its own for creating negative images.

✦ **Substitute Fonts** substitutes PostScript fonts for any fixed-sized screen fonts for which no PostScript or TrueType equivalent is available (as described in Chapter 13). For example, Geneva becomes Helvetica, Monaco becomes Courier, and New York becomes Times. The one drawback of font substitution is that although the variable-size font is substituted for its fixed-sized cousin, the spacing of letters and words on a line does not change, and the printed results often are remarkably ugly. For the best results, do not use fixed-size fonts that lack TrueType or PostScript equivalents (such as Venice or London), and leave the Substitute Fonts option off.

✦ **Smooth Text** smoothes the jagged edges of fixed sizes for which there are no matching PostScript fonts or TrueType fonts (such as Venice 14 and London 18). For best results, avoid such fonts, and leave the Smooth Text option off.

✦ **Smooth Graphics** smoothes the jagged edges of bitmap graphic images created with painting programs. Smoothing improves some images but blurs the detail out of others. Try printing with Smooth Graphics set both ways, and go with the one that looks best to you. This option has no effect on graphics that are created with drawing programs such as FreeHand and Illustrator.

✦ **Precision Bitmap Alignment** reduces the entire printed image to avoid minor distortions in bitmap graphics. The distortions occur because of the nature of the dot density of bitmap graphics. For example, 72 dpi (dots-per-inch), which is the standard screen-image size, does not divide evenly into 300 dpi, 400 dpi, or 600 dpi (the dot density of many laser printers). When you are printing to a 300-dpi printer, for example, turning on this option reduces page images by four percent, effectively printing them at 288 dpi (an even multiple of 72 dpi). The reductions align the bitmaps properly to produce crisper output.

✦ **Unlimited Downloadable Fonts** allows you to use more fonts than your printer's memory can hold at one time by removing fonts from the printer's memory after they are used, making way for other fonts. Be aware that the constant downloading and flushing of font files takes time and thus slows printing. EPS (Encapsulated PostScript) graphics that use fonts that are not present elsewhere on the page will not print correctly because the printer will substitute Courier for those orphan fonts. If you see Courier in a graphic where you did not want it, make sure that this option is turned off.

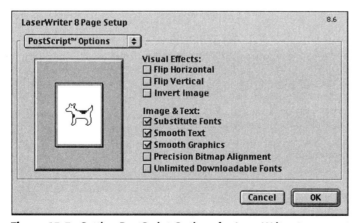

Figure 15-3: Setting PostScript Options for LaserWriter 8 page setup.

Custom Page Sizes

You can define and use custom page sizes if your printer allows them and your Mac has LaserWriter 8 version 8.5.1 or later. In this case, you will be able to choose Custom Page Sizes from the unlabeled pop-up menu near the top of the Page Setup dialog box. When you make this choice, you see a list of custom page sizes that are already defined. If you select a custom size, you see a preview of it in the dialog box. You can delete the selected size, edit it, or create a new custom size by clicking buttons in the dialog box. Figure 15-4 is an example of the Custom Page Sizes options in LaserWriter 8 version 8.6.

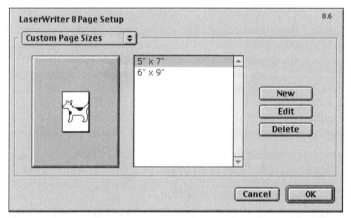

Figure 15-4: Setting Custom Page Sizes options for LaserWriter 8 page setup.

Click the New or Edit button to display a dialog box in which you enter or change the paper size height and width. You can also specify the top, bottom, right, and left margins. In addition, you may need to specify a width or height offset for the custom page. For example, a printer that uses a roll of film or paper will print a custom page that's smaller than the roll. The offsets tell the printer where to position the page on the larger media. For cut sheets of paper or other media, the page size is usually the same as the sheet size and there are no offsets.

All custom page sizes appear as choices for the Paper option in the Page Attributes section of the Page Setup command. Every custom page size is available with every printer that allows custom sizes and uses LaserWriter 8 version 8.5.1 and later. In other words, none of the custom page sizes is unique to a particular printer.

Saving custom Page Setup settings

If you don't like the Page Setup settings that LaserWriter 8 version 8.2 or later uses by default, you can have it use your settings instead. After making your changes in the Page Setup dialog box, press Option while clicking OK to dismiss the dialog box. An alert asks you to confirm whether you want to save the current Page Setup settings as the default settings.

You have to perform this exercise separately in each application that has its own Page Setup settings. You may be able to tell whether a particular application has its own Page Setup settings by looking for the application's name in the pop-up menu at the top left of the Page Setup dialog box. If that pop-up menu doesn't list the current application's name, the application may use the generic Page Setup default settings. Changing the generic Page Setup defaults in one application affects all applications that use them (but doesn't affect applications with their own Page Setup settings).

Setting LaserWriter 8 Print options

When you choose the Print command for a printer that uses the LaserWriter 8 driver, you see a dialog box with settings for the number of copies, page numbers to print, paper source, output destination, and more. You can switch among several groups of options by choosing a group from the unlabeled pop-up menu near the top of the dialog box. Figure 15-5 shows the pop-up menu for switching among groups of options in the Print dialog box for LaserWriter 8 version 8.4 and later.

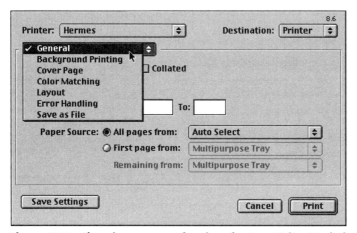

Figure 15-5: Choosing a group of options for LaserWriter 8 printing.

Instead of choosing a group of options from the pop-up menu at the top of the Print dialog box, you can move from group to group by pressing ⌘-Down Arrow(↓), ⌘-Up Arrow(↑), Page Up, or Page Down.

The remainder of this section describes the Print command's options in more detail. The descriptions are organized according to the Print option groups used in LaserWriter 8 version 8.4 and later — all, general, background printing, cover page, color matching, layout, error handling, save as file, imaging options, and printer specific options.

Universal options

No matter which group of options you choose in the Print dialog box for LaserWriter 8 version 8.4 and later, these options are always available at the top and bottom of the dialog box (as shown previously in Figure 15-5):

✦ **Printer** lets you choose which of your desktop printers that you want to print your document. The pop-up menu lists your desktop printers that use the LaserWriter 8 driver.

✦ **Destination** specifies whether the driver sends page descriptions to the chosen printer or to a file. The options for the latter setting are described later in this section under the heading "Save as File options."

✦ **Save Settings** makes the settings you have made in the Print dialog box the ones used by default for the currently chosen desktop printer.

General options

When you choose General from the unlabeled pop-up menu near the top of the Print dialog box for LaserWriter 8 version 8.4 and later, these options are displayed, as shown in Figure 15-6:

✦ **Copies** specifies the number of copies to print.

✦ **Collated**, when selected, specifies that multiple copies each print in correct page sequence. If unselected (or unavailable), all copies of one page print, then all copies of the next page, and so on. Collated printing may take longer than uncollated printing. Because each collated copy is sent to the printer as a separate print request, print requests from other computers may be interspersed between the collated copies. (This option is not available in LaserWriter 8 versions prior to 8.5.1.)

✦ **Pages** specifies the range of pages to print.

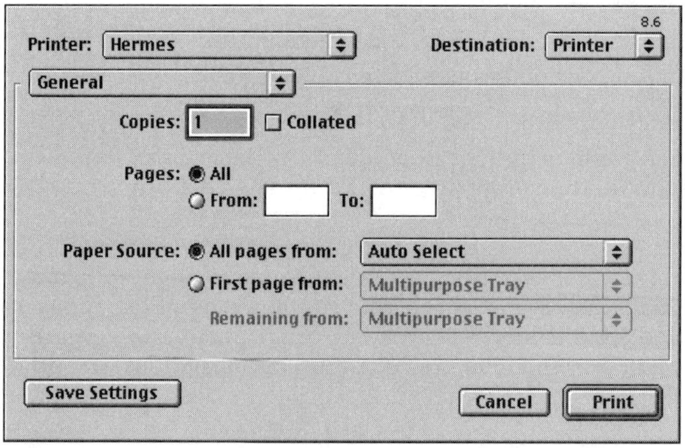

Figure 15-6: Setting General options for LaserWriter 8 printing.

✦ **Paper Source** specifies from where the chosen printer should get the paper to print your document — multipurpose tray, envelope feeder, paper cassette, manual feed, and so forth. You can choose one paper source for all pages or a separate source for the first page and for remaining pages.

Background Printing options

When you choose Background Printing from the unlabeled pop-up menu near the top of the Print dialog box for LaserWriter 8 version 8.4 and later, these options are displayed, as shown in Figure 15-7:

✦ **Print in** specifies whether you want your document to print in the foreground or background. Foreground printing requires less disk space than background printing and may cause your document to start printing faster, but does not let you use the computer for anything else until printing stops. Background printing lets you work on other tasks while printing continues, but requires extra disk space for temporary spool (page description) files. Foreground printing is not available in some applications.

✦ **Print Time** specifies a priority for printing a document in the background — urgent, normal, or hold — or a specific time and day when you want your document printed. You can change this setting for a document waiting to be printed in the background by opening the desktop printer icon (as described in "Managing Background Printing" in Chapter 14). The Print Time option is disabled if you set the Print in option for foreground printing, which is always immediate.

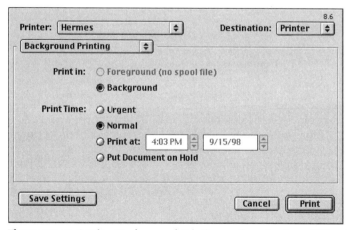

Figure 15-7: Setting Background Printing options for LaserWriter 8 printing.

Cover Page options

When you choose Cover Page from the unlabeled pop-up menu near the top of the Print dialog box for LaserWriter 8 version 8.4 and later, these options are displayed, as shown in Figure 15-8:

✦ **Print Cover Page** specifies whether to print a cover page before printing your document, after printing your document, or not at all. A cover page reports the document's name, the owner name of the computer that printed it, and when it was printed.

✦ **Cover Page Paper Source** specifies where the chosen printer should get paper to print a cover page. This option is disabled if you set the Print Cover Page option to None.

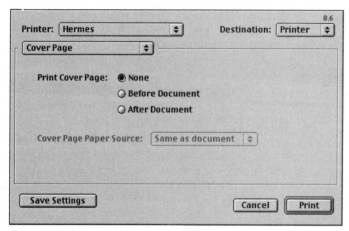

Figure 15-8: Setting Cover Page options for LaserWriter 8 printing.

Color Matching options

When you choose Color Matching from the unlabeled pop-up menu near the top of the Print dialog box for LaserWriter 8 version 8.4 and later, these options are displayed, as shown in Figure 15-9:

✦ **Print Color** lets you choose to print your document in black and white or in color on a color printer, or in shades of gray on a monochrome printer. If your computer has ColorSync 2.0 or later and the files folder contains printer profiles, you can choose to have ColorSync or PostScript match the printed grays and colors to the displayed colors as closely as possible. The PostScript setting for this option requires a printer with PostScript Level 2 capability.

✦ **Intent** (LaserWriter 8 version 8.5.1 and later and ColorSync 2.1 or later required) lets you choose a method of matching the gamut of colors in the document to the gamut of colors that the printer can reproduce. The methods are:

  • **Perceptual matching** scales all colors in the document to fit within the printer's color gamut. This method gives good results for photographs and other bitmap graphics. All colors in the document change, even those that the printer can reproduce, but they all change by the same amount so everything looks pretty good.

- **Relative colorimetric matching** doesn't change colors in the document that the printer can reproduce. Colors that the printer can't reproduce change to the closest reproducible color having the same lightness (but different saturation). Colors that are different from each other in the document may look the same as each other when printed.

- **Saturation matching** doesn't change colors in the document that the printer can reproduce. Colors that the printer can't reproduce change to the closest reproducible color having the same saturation (but different lightness). This is appropriate for charts and graphs, where you care more about keeping colors different than preventing perceptible color shifts.

- **Absolute colorimetric matching** doesn't change colors in the document that the printer can reproduce. Colors that the printer can't reproduce are not printed. This may result in some loss of detail and sparseness in the printed document.

- **Auto selection matching** uses the Saturation matching method on text and line drawings but the Perceptual matching method on bitmap graphics.

✦ **Printer Profile** specifies the color profile to use for color matching. You choose a profile from the pop-up menu, which lists all the appropriate printer profile files in the ColorSync Profiles folder (which is in the Preferences folder inside the System Folder). Additionally, if the Print Color setting is PostScript Color Matching, you can choose Printer Default to use the profile currently stored in the printer. The Printer Profile setting is disabled if you set the Print Color option to Black & White or Color/Grayscale.

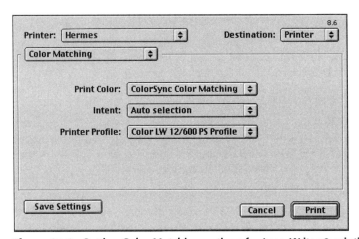

Figure 15-9: Setting Color Matching options for LaserWriter 8 printing.

Layout options

When you choose Layout from the unlabeled pop-up menu near the top of the Print dialog box for LaserWriter 8 version 8.4 and later, these options are displayed, as shown in Figure 15-10:

✦ **Pages per sheet** lets you choose a number of minipages to print on each sheet of paper. Each minipage is a full-page image reduced in size so that two, four, or more minipages fit on a sheet of paper.

✦ **Layout Direction** specifies whether the minipages are arranged from left-to-right or right-to-left. This option is available if you set the "Pages per sheet" option to more than one minipage per sheet of paper.

✦ **Border** lets you choose the type of borderline to print around each reduced minipage. This option is available if you set the "Pages per sheet" option to more than one minipage per sheet of paper.

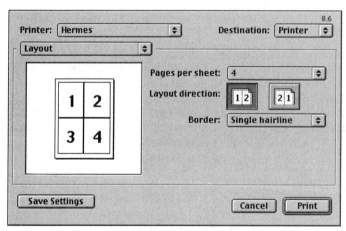

Figure 15-10: Setting Layout options for LaserWriter 8 printing.

Error Handling options

When you choose Error Handling from the unlabeled pop-up menu near the top of the Print dialog box for LaserWriter 8 version 8.4 and later, one or both of the following options are displayed, as shown in Figure 15-11:

✦ **If there is a PostScript error** specifies how the LaserWriter 8 driver handles PostScript errors: no special error reporting, display a summary of PostScript errors onscreen, or print detailed descriptions of PostScript errors.

✦ **If the cassette is out of paper** specifies what the LaserWriter driver should do if the paper source runs out of paper: either automatically look for the same size paper in another paper tray or display an alert onscreen. (This option is not available on all types of laser printers.)

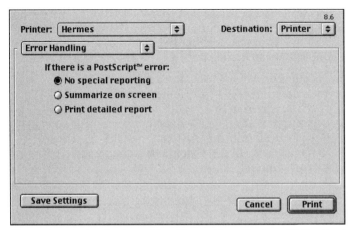

Figure 15-11: Setting Error Handling options for LaserWriter 8 printing.

Save as File options

When you choose Save as File from the unlabeled pop-up menu near the top of the Print dialog box for LaserWriter 8 version 8.4 and later, these options are displayed, as shown in Figure 15-12:

✦ **Format** specifies the kind of file to save. Choose one of the following:

• **PostScript Job** creates a standard PostScript file for later printing.

• The three **EPS** (Encapsulated PostScript) formats create a one-page graphic for placement in another document. The EPS Mac Standard Preview includes a black-and-white 72-dpi bitmap image for previewing onscreen. The EPS Mac Enhanced Preview includes a color PICT preview image, which can be smoothly reduced or enlarged on the screen display. The EPS Mac No Preview takes the least amount of disk space because it has no preview image. Without a preview image, you can't see the file onscreen, but this option prints just like the other EPS formats.

• **Acrobat PDF** creates a PDF (Portable Document File) file that can be read by Acrobat Reader. This setting is available only with LaserWriter 8 version 8.5.1 and later and requires that Acrobat Distiller be installed on your Mac. Distiller is not included with the free Acrobat Reader — it's part of the full $295 version of Acrobat, which you can buy through retailers. It's also bundled with recent versions of Adobe PageMaker.

✦ **PostScript Level** specifies PostScript compatibility. Choose the Level 1 Compatible option for a file that can be used on printers with PostScript Level 1, 2, or 3. If you are using only PostScript Level 2 and 3 printers, choose the Level 2 and 3 option (LaserWriter 8.5.1 and later) or the Level 2 Only option (LaserWriter 8 version 8.4–8.4.3).

✦ **Data Format** specifies whether to use text characters or binary data in the PostScript file. Choosing the ASCII option creates a more widely compatible PostScript file than the Binary option, but the Binary option can speed printing on a printer that can handle it.

✦ **Font Inclusion** specifies how many fonts to embed in the PostScript file. The None setting, which does not embed any fonts, uses the least disk space but prints correctly only on a system that has all needed fonts. The All option, which embeds every font used in the document, may use a great deal of disk space, but all fonts will print from any system. The All But Standard 13 option embeds all the fonts used except the 13 fonts that commonly are factory-installed in PostScript printers.

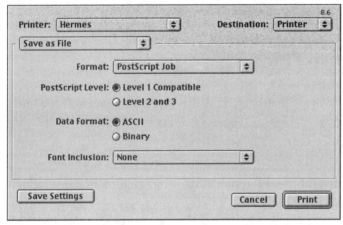

Figure 15-12: Setting options for saving PostScript files with LaserWriter 8.

If you choose Acrobat PDF as the Format option, these options replace the PostScript Level, Data Format, and Font Inclusion options, as shown in Figure 15-13:

✦ **Compress Text and Line Art** specifies whether to compress text and graphics using the LZW method in the PDF file.

✦ **Embed All Fonts** specifies whether to embed all fonts used in the document as part of the PDF file.

✦ **ASCII Format** specifies whether to use ASCII85 encoding for the document, which will result in a PDF file that is almost pure ASCII.

✦ **Compression and Downsample** controls the type of compression and the final resolution of bitmap graphics in the PDF file. You set these options separately for color, grayscale, and monochrome bitmap images.

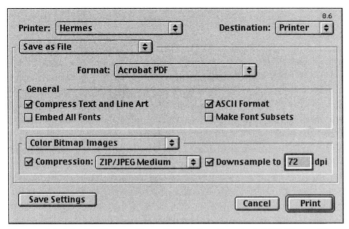

Figure 15-13: Setting options for saving Acrobat PDF files with LaserWriter 8.

Imaging Options

When you choose Imaging Options from the unlabeled pop-up menu near the top of the Print dialog box for LaserWriter 8 version 8.4 and later, one or more of the following options are displayed, as shown in Figure 15-14:

✦ **Resolution** specifies the granularity of the printed image in dots or pixels per inch.

✦ **FinePrint**, if on, specifies that the printer should smooth jagged edges of text and graphic objects. Bitmapped images may print better with this option off. This option is only available with printers that have Apple's FinePrint technology.

✦ **PhotoGrade**, if on, specifies that the printer should enhance the shading and contrast of graphics. Text quality may be better with this option off. This option is only available with printers that have Apple's PhotoGrade technology.

✦ **Image for Paper Type** adjusts brightness for the selected type of paper.

The Imaging Options choice does not appear in the pop-up menu if none of these options apply to the current printer.

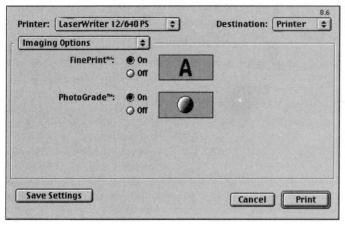

Figure 15-14: Setting Imaging options for LaserWriter 8 printing.

Printer Specific Options

When you choose Printer Specific Options from the unlabeled pop-up menu near the top of the Print dialog box for LaserWriter 8 version 8.4 and later, options that are specific to the current printer appear. For example, a LaserWriter Pro 630 printer has a Choose Resolution option in the Printer Specific Options group (rather than a Resolution option in the Imaging Options group). The Printer Specific Options choice does not appear in the pop-up menu if the current printer has no special options.

Setting Color StyleWriter Options

This section describes how to set up and print documents on printers that can use the three Color StyleWriter drivers included with Mac OS 7.6–8.5. The included drivers are Color StyleWriter 2500, Color StyleWriter 1500, and Color StyleWriter Pro. All Apple Color StyleWriter printers except the 4100, 4500, and 6000 can use one of these drivers. If you have a Color StyleWriter 2200 or 2400, you can use the Color StyleWriter 2500 driver instead of the driver that came with the printer.

Setting Color StyleWriter Page Setup options

When you choose the Page Setup command for a printer that uses a Color StyleWriter 1500, 2500, or Pro driver, you see a dialog box with settings for various page attributes. In addition, a Watermark button in the Color StyleWriter 1500 and 2500 dialog boxes lets you select a graphic to be printed lightly as a page background, like a watermark. Figure 15-15 shows the Page Setup dialog box and the Watermark dialog box for Color StyleWriter 2500.

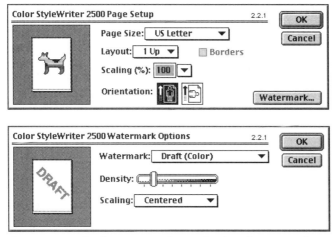

Figure 15-15: Setting page attributes (top) and watermark options (bottom) for Color StyleWriter page setup.

Page attribute options

The Page Setup dialog box for the Color StyleWriter 1500, 2500, and Pro drivers has these page attribute options:

✦ **Page Size** lets you choose a paper size such as US Letter ($8\frac{1}{2}$ x 11 inches), US Legal ($8\frac{1}{2}$ x 14 inches), and #10 Envelope.

✦ **Layout** (not present with Color StyleWriter Pro) lets you choose a number of minipages to be printed per sheet of paper.

✦ **Borders** (not present with Color StyleWriter Pro) controls the printing of borders around minipages. This option becomes available if you set the Layout option to print more than one minipage per sheet of paper.

✦ **Scaling** reduces or enlarges the printed image according to the percentage you enter. You can either type a percentage or choose one from the pop-up menu. Full size is 100 percent, the minimum reduction is 5 percent, and the maximum enlargement is 999 percent.

✦ **Orientation** determines whether the top of the printed page will be on a short edge or a long edge of the paper.

Watermark options

The Watermark dialog box appears when you click the Watermark button in the Page Setup dialog box of the Color StyleWriter 1500, 2500, or Pro drivers. The Watermark dialog box has these options:

✦ **Watermark** specifies the graphic to be printed as a watermark. You choose one of the graphics listed in the Watermark pop-up menu, and a thumbnail preview of the watermark you chose appears in the dialog box. (You choose

None if you no longer want a watermark.) The pop-up menu lists all graphics files of type PICT contained in the Printing Prefs folder, which is in the Preferences folder inside the System Folder. You can move files in and out of that folder with the Finder. In addition, you can create and edit watermark images with graphics programs such as ClarisWorks, Adobe Photoshop, and Macromedia FreeHand. If a watermark file contains text, make sure the fonts it uses are installed in your Fonts folder so the text looks its best.

✦ **Density** adjusts the darkness of the watermark image. The thumbnail preview of the watermark image does not reflect changes to the Density setting.

✦ **Scaling** adjusts the size and placement of the watermark image on the page. You set this option by choosing from the Scaling pop-up menu. Your choices include:

  • **Centered** resizes the watermark to fill the center of the page without changing the watermark's original proportions.

  • **Align Top Left** places the watermark in its original size at the upper-left corner of the page.

  • **Stretch to Fit** resizes the watermark to fill the page from top-to-bottom and side-to-side, even if the watermark's proportions change.

Setting Color StyleWriter Print options

When you choose the Print command for a printer that uses a Color StyleWriter 1500, 2500, or Pro driver, you see a dialog box with settings for number of copies, page numbers to print, print quality, and more. A Color button lets you specify a color blending method and an optional color matching method. A Utilities button lets you specify that you want the printer to clean the ink cartridge or perform other available self-maintenance. Figure 15-16 shows the main and secondary Print dialog boxes for Color StyleWriter 2500.

Main Print options

The Print dialog box for the Color StyleWriter 1500, 2500, and Pro drivers has these main options:

✦ **Copies** specifies the number of copies to print.

✦ **Pages** specifies the range of pages to print.

✦ **Print Quality** offers a trade-off between appearance and speed, with Best quality the slowest and the best looking.

✦ **Paper Type** adjusts the printer for the selected type of paper.

✦ **Image** lets you choose the amount of color appropriate for your document. For color graphics or photos, choose Color or Grayscale. For text or line drawings without color or shades of gray, choose Black & White.

✦ **Notification** specifies a sound or message to use to notify you when your document finishes printing. You can choose any available system alert sound. (You can add or remove alert sounds with the SimpleSound program as described in Chapter 25.)

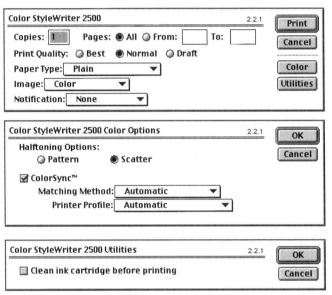

Figure 15-16: Setting options for Color StyleWriter printing (top), color printing (middle), and printer utilities (bottom).

Color Options

The Color Options dialog box appears when you click the Color button in the Print dialog box for the Color StyleWriter 1500, 2500, and Pro drivers. The Color Options dialog box has these options:

✦ **Halftoning Options** specifies whether to blend colors and gray tones using a pattern of dots or a random scattering of dots.

✦ **ColorSync**, if on, specifies that Apple's ColorSync should match printed colors to displayed colors as closely as possible. This option is disabled unless the ColorSync software is installed and you set the Image option in the main Print dialog box to Color.

✦ **Matching Method** lets you choose the color matching method that's best for the content of your document. The Photographic method reduces color saturation, and the Business Graphics method increases color saturation. The Automatic method picks the Photographic method if the page contains mostly bitmap images or the Business Graphics method if the page contains mostly graphic objects.

✦ **Printer Profile** specifies the color profile to use for color matching. You choose a profile from the pop-up menu, which lists all the appropriate printer profile files in the ColorSync Profiles folder (which is in the Preferences folder inside the System Folder). This option is disabled unless the ColorSync option is turned on.

Utilities options

The Utilities dialog box appears when you click the Utilities button in the Print dialog box for the Color StyleWriter 1500, 2500, and Pro drivers. The Utilities dialog box has one or more options for cleaning the ink cartridge before printing. With the Color StyleWriter Pro driver, there are also options for preparing a new print head and checking the printer alignment.

Setting StyleWriter Options

This section describes how to set up and print documents on printers that can use the StyleWriter 1200 driver included with Mac OS 7.6–8.5. The Apple StyleWriter 1200, StyleWriter II, and original StyleWriter can use this driver.

Setting StyleWriter Page Setup options

When you choose the Page Setup command for a printer that uses the StyleWriter 1200 driver, you see a dialog box with settings for various page attributes. In addition, a Watermark button lets you select a graphic to be printed lightly as a page background, like a watermark. Figure 15-17 shows the Page Setup dialog box and the Watermark dialog box for StyleWriter 1200.

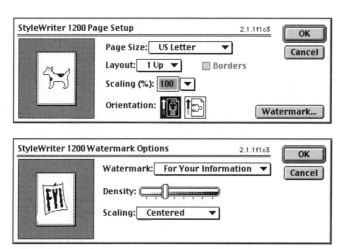

Figure 15-17: Setting page attributes (top) and watermark options (bottom) for StyleWriter page setup.

All the Page Setup settings for the StyleWriter drivers are explained fully in the preceding section, "Setting Color StyleWriter Options."

Setting StyleWriter Print options

When you choose the Print command for a printer that uses the StyleWriter 1200 driver, you see a dialog box with settings for number of copies, page numbers to print, print quality, and more. An Options button lets you specify other options. Figure 15-18 shows the main Print dialog box and the Print Options dialog box for StyleWriter 1200.

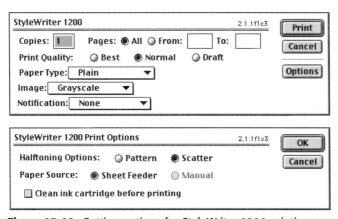

Figure 15-18: Setting options for StyleWriter 1200 printing.

The Print options for the black-and-white StyleWriter drivers are similar to the options for Color StyleWriter drivers. For descriptions of the options, see the preceding section, "Setting Color StyleWriter Options."

Setting LaserWriter 300/LS Options

This section describes how to set up and print documents on printers that use the LaserWriter 300/LS driver included with Mac OS 7.6–8.5. These drivers are for Apple laser printers that don't have PostScript and that don't connect to a network, including the Personal LaserWriter 300, LaserWriter Select 300, and Personal LaserWriter LS.

Setting LaserWriter 300/LS Page Setup options

When you choose the Page Setup command for a printer that uses a LaserWriter 300/LS driver, you see a dialog box with settings for page size, scaling, and page orientation. An Options button gives you access to printer effects. Figure 15-19 shows the Page Setup dialog box and the Options dialog box for LaserWriter 300/LS.

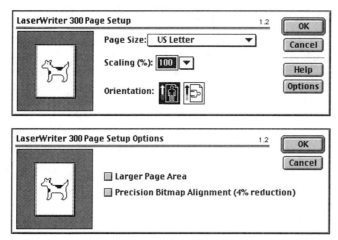

Figure 15-19: Setting page attributes (top) and printer effects (bottom) for LaserWriter 300/LS page setup.

Page attribute options

The Page Setup dialog box for the LaserWriter 300/LS driver has these page attribute options:

✦ **Page Size** lets you choose a paper size such as US Letter ($8^1/_2$ x 11 inches), US Legal ($8^1/_2$ x 14 inches), and #10 Envelope.

✦ **Scaling** reduces or enlarges the printed image according to the percentage you enter. You can either type a percentage or choose one from the pop-up menu. Full size is 100 percent, the minimum reduction is 5 percent, and the maximum enlargement is 999 percent.

✦ **Orientation** determines whether the top of the printed page will be on a short edge or a long edge of the paper.

Page Setup Options

The Page Setup Options dialog box appears when you click the Options button in the Page Setup dialog box for the LaserWriter 300/LS driver. The Page Setup Options dialog box has these options:

✦ **Larger Page Area** lets you print closer to the edges of legal-size paper.

✦ **Precision Bitmap Alignment** reduces the entire printed image to avoid minor distortions in bitmap graphics. The distortions occur because of the nature of the dot density of bitmap graphics. For example, 72 dpi, which is the standard screen-image size, does not divide evenly into 300 dpi (the dot density of laser printers that use the LaserWriter 300/LS driver). Turning on this option reduces page images by four percent, effectively printing them at 288 dpi (an even multiple of 72 dpi). The reductions align the bitmaps properly to produce crisper output.

Setting LaserWriter 300/LS Print options

When you choose the Print command for a printer that uses the LaserWriter 300/LS driver, you see a dialog box with settings for number of copies, page numbers to print, paper source, and more. You can click the Options button to bring up a Print Options dialog box. Figure 15-20 shows the main Print and secondary Print Options dialog boxes for LaserWriter 300.

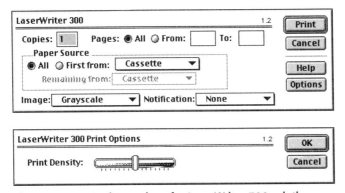

Figure 15-20: Setting options for LaserWriter 300 printing.

In the main Print dialog box, you can set all pages to come from one paper source — paper cassette or manual-feed tray — or you can set the first page to come from one source and the remaining pages to come from another source. The LaserWriter 300/LS driver is not for PostScript printers and it cannot save page descriptions as a PostScript file.

The Image option lets you choose Grayscale for printing shades of gray, Black & White for fastest printing, or PhotoGrade (if the current printer is equipped with it) for enhanced grays. The Notification option specifies the sound or message to be used to notify you when your document finishes printing. You can choose any available system alert sound. (You can add or remove alert sounds with the SimpleSound program as described in Chapter 25.)

In the Print Options dialog box, you can set the print density by adjusting a slider. Moving the slider to the left makes printing lighter, thereby saving toner. Moving it to the right makes printing darker and uses more toner.

Setting ImageWriter Options

This section describes how to set up and print documents on printers that use the ImageWriter driver included with Mac OS 7.6–8.5. The ImageWriter II and the original ImageWriter can use this driver.

Setting ImageWriter Page Setup options

When you choose the Page Setup command for an ImageWriter II or original ImageWriter printer, you see a dialog box with settings for paper size, orientation, and special effects. Figure 15-21 shows the Page Setup dialog box for ImageWriter.

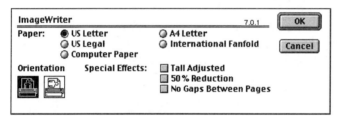

Figure 15-21: Setting page attributes and special effects for ImageWriter page setup.

The Page Setup dialog box for the ImageWriter driver has these options:

✦ **Paper** lets you choose a paper size: single sheets of US Letter ($8^1/_2$ x 11 inches), US Legal ($8^1/_2$ x 14 inches), or A4 Letter ($8^1/_2$ x $11^2/_3$ inches); or continuous, sprocket-fed International Fanfold ($8^1/_4$ x 11 inches).

✦ **Orientation** determines whether the top of the printed page will be on a short edge or a long edge of the paper.

✦ **Tall Adjusted** correctly proportions graphics or text. Turning on this option prints graphics with correct proportions but widens individual text characters. Turning off this option prints text with correct proportions but elongates graphics.

✦ **50% Reduction** prints page images half their actual size.

✦ **No Gaps Between Pages** eliminates top and bottom margins, primarily for printing continuously on fanfold paper.

Quick Tips

Hints for Better ImageWriter Printing

If pictures printed on an ImageWriter look vertically stretched, as though El Greco had drawn them, choose the Page Setup command's Tall Adjusted option. This option adjusts the computer output from 72 dpi to the 80-dpi vertical resolution of the printer, thus generating a proportional image.

To avoid the irregular word spacing that occurs in draft mode, change your document's font to a monospaced font, such as Monaco or Courier, for printing out a draft. The fixed-spaced font on the screen then will match the spacing of the printer's internal font, making the draft easier to read. Change your document to a more professional variable-sized font, such as Helvetica or Times, when you are ready to print your final copy.

Always install bitmap fonts in pairs—9-point with 18-point, 10-point with 20-point, and so on—so that the Font Manager portion of the Mac OS has the larger font available for scaling in Best mode. The best way to avoid spacing problems is to use TrueType fonts (or PostScript fonts and Adobe Type Manager software) and let the computer do the scaling for you.

A very clear font for use with the ImageWriter family is Boston II, a shareware font that is available from user groups and online information services.

Best quality looks clearest with a slightly used printer ribbon, not with a brand-new ribbon, because there is less smudging of characters from high levels of ink on the ribbon.

Do not stockpile ribbons for an ImageWriter; buy them one or two at a time. The ink in the ribbons dries out over time.

Setting ImageWriter Print options

When you choose the Print command for an ImageWriter II or original ImageWriter printer, you see a dialog box with settings for print quality, page numbers to print, number of copies, and paper source. Figure 15-22 shows the Print dialog box for ImageWriter.

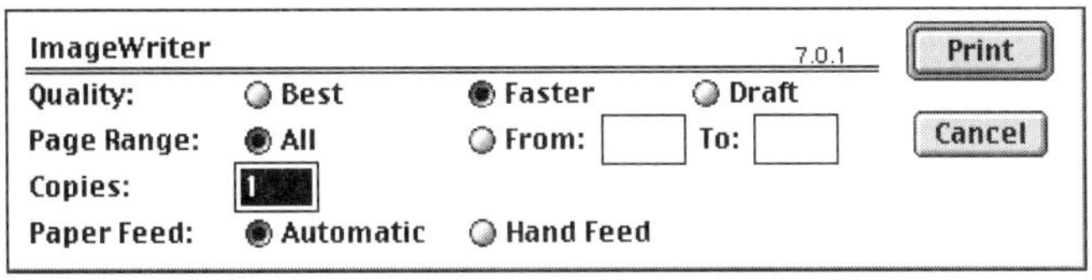

Figure 15-22: Setting options for ImageWriter printing.

Choosing the Best quality option prints your document at 144 dpi, which is twice the screen resolution. Best quality is slower than Faster quality, which prints at 72 dpi. Draft quality prints text only (no pictures) with a font built into the printer. The built-in font's spacing matches the spacing of Monaco 10-point and other 10-point monospaced fonts. Printing proportionally spaced fonts in Draft quality results in poorly spaced letters and words that may be hard to read.

Summary

This chapter described how you print a document from the Finder using desktop printers or the Print command. You can also print a document from an application that can open it by using the application's Page Setup and Print commands. You use the same commands for all printers, but the options available in the Print and Page Setup dialog boxes depend on the printer driver for the printer. This chapter detailed the Page Setup and Print options for printers that use these drivers:

✦ LaserWriter 8

✦ Color StyleWriter 2500, Color StyleWriter 1500, and Color StyleWriter Pro

✦ StyleWriter 1200

✦ LaserWriter 300/LS

✦ ImageWriter

✦   ✦   ✦

Interact with Multimedia

The Mac OS gives you many ways to enjoy audio and video. The QuickTime system extension lets you watch digital movies, including MPEG video. You can also use QuickTime to listen to digitized sound and synthesized music. With QuickTime VR, you can view "virtual reality" panoramas and objects interactively. If your computer has a PowerPC processor, you can use the QuickDraw 3D system extension to display and manipulate three-dimensional objects. If your computer has a CD-ROM drive, you can use the AppleCD Audio Player program to control playback of audio CDs from your computer's CD-ROM drive, using simple push buttons or sophisticated programming of tracks by name. If your computer has video-input ports or a TV tuner expansion card, you can use the Apple Video Player program to view videos from video equipment such as a camcorder, VCR, or television, and to capture that video input digitally on disk.

This chapter explains how to use all this audio and video software.

Introducing QuickTime Movies

Apple's QuickTime software enables your computer to work with data that changes over time, or *time-based data,* such as motion pictures with sound. In other words, it lets you store and watch movies on your computer. In fact, just about all Macintosh computers can play QuickTime movies. QuickTime doesn't require any special equipment, although faster computers generally play movies more smoothly than slower computers.

Apple's QuickTime software not only makes it possible to play movies on your computer, QuickTime makes movies ubiquitous! You don't need a special program to watch QuickTime movies. Most applications let you copy and paste movies as easily as you copy and paste graphics, and you can play a QuickTime movie wherever you encounter one. For starters, you can watch QuickTime movies from — and paste them into — SimpleText and the Scrapbook. Figure 16-1 is an example of a QuickTime movie in a SimpleText window.

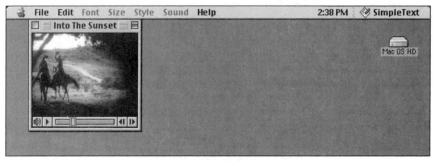

Figure 16-1: Watching a QuickTime movie in SimpleText.

There's more to QuickTime movies than a motion picture and a soundtrack. Recent versions of QuickTime expand the definition of *movie* considerably to include all kinds of interesting data that change or move over time. With QuickTime 2.5 and later, "movies" can include any combination of:

✦ **Motion pictures** — such as what you watch on TV or at the movies

✦ **Digitized sound recordings** — music and other sounds — that play in CD-quality sound (44.1kHz, 16-bit stereo) on PowerPC computers

✦ **Synthesized music** based on MIDI (Musical Instrument Digital Interface), which takes far less disk space to store than digitized sound, yet sound realistic and play in CD-quality sound on PowerPC computers

✦ **Text** for closed-caption viewing, karaoke sing-a-longs, or text-based searches of movie content

✦ **Three-dimensional graphics**, drawn live by QuickDraw 3D as they spin and move across the screen

✦ **Sprites**, which move independently like actors moving on a stage with a motion-picture backdrop

✦ **MPEG movies** that use the common MPEG-1 video and audio standard

✦ **Panoramas and objects** that you can view in 360 degrees using QuickTime VR methods

✦ **Timecode information**, which displays elapsed hours, minutes, seconds, and frames at the bottom of a playing movie

✦ **Functional information**, such as information that tells QuickTime how other tracks interact

What's in a movie

The motion pictures, sound, and other types of time-based data in a QuickTime movie exist in separate tracks. A simple movie might consist of one video track and one sound track. A more complex movie may have several video tracks, several audio tracks, and closed-caption text tracks for text subtitles. Each video track could be designed specially for playback with a certain number of available colors (for example, 256 colors, thousands of colors, and millions of colors), each audio track could provide dialog in a different language (English, Spanish, Japanese, and so on), and each closed-caption text track could provide subtitles in a different language.

If a QuickTime movie contains MIDI-synthesized music, sprites, QuickDraw 3D graphics, or a QuickTime VR scene or object, then each is in a separate track. QuickTime takes care of synchronizing all of the tracks so that they play at the right time.

QuickTime magic

A computer shouldn't be capable of playing digital movies any more than a bumblebee should be able to fly. A single full-screen color picture on a 14-inch monitor takes a megabyte of disk space. To show 30 pictures, or *frames,* per second, which is what you see on TV, a computer has to store, retrieve, and display 30MB per second. Only the fastest computers and hard disk drives are that fast. Even if you have a fast computer, storage space is still a problem for movies. For example, a 1-minute video clip requires 1,800MB of disk space.

QuickTime pulls every trick in the book to play movies. Most movies are smaller than the full 640 x 480 pixels available on a 14-inch color monitor. In QuickTime's early days, when PowerPC processors didn't exist and single-speed CD-ROM drives were state-of-the-art, QuickTime movies were the size of a large postage stamp (160 x 120 pixels). Today, quarter-screen movies (320 x 240 pixels) play back smoothly from a CD-ROM and fast PowerPC computers can play full-screen movies from a hard disk.

Furthermore, QuickTime movies may play back fewer frames per second than TV or movies. You see 30 *fps* (frames per second) on TV or videotape in the United States and other countries that use the NTSC standard (25 fps in Europe and other places that use the PAL or SECAM standards). By comparison, many QuickTime movies are designed to play at 15 fps from a CD-ROM. QuickTime is certainly capable of playing full-motion movies from a hard disk on a PowerPC computer.

Showing small pictures at slow frame rates reduces the amount of data to be stored, retrieved, and displayed, but not nearly enough. So QuickTime compresses movies, throwing out the redundant parts. A compressed move contains less data to store on disk. Just as importantly, a compressed movie contains less data to be transferred each second from hard disk, CD-ROM, or the Internet.

SECRETS

Compressed Images
QuickTime not only handles time-based and interactive media, but it also extends the standard graphics format PICT to handle compressed still images and image previews. An application that recognizes QuickTime can compress a graphic image using any QuickTime-compatible software or hardware compressor that is available on your computer. All applications that can open uncompressed PICT images are also capable of opening compressed PICT images. QuickTime automatically decompresses a compressed PICT image without requiring changes to the application program.

Getting QuickTime software

You get the QuickTime software as part of a standard installation of Mac OS 7.6–8.5. The version of QuickTime depends on the version of Mac OS. With Mac OS 8.5, you get QuickTime 3.0. This is a basic edition of QuickTime 3.0. You can upgrade to QuickTime Pro for $29.95 by phone (1-888-295-0648) or from Apple's QuickTime site on the Web (http://www.apple.com/quicktime/). You can obtain a free upgrade to QuickTime Pro 3.0 if you purchase a retail package of Mac OS 8.5 and register it through Apple's registration Web site (http://www.applereg.com).

Mac OS 7.6–8.1 includes QuickTime 2.5. You can get QuickTime 3.0 separately from Apple's QuickTime site on the Web. QuickTime 3.0 incorporates QuickTime VR and QuickDraw 3D, which are described in later sections of this chapter.

Some applications replace QuickTime with an earlier version than what was installed on your computer. All kinds of problems may ensue as a result of installing an earlier version of QuickTime, some of which seem unrelated to QuickTime. Not only may some QuickTime movies no longer play, but you may not be able to open as many different types of graphics and audio files as you could before the earlier version was installed. To fix these problems, install QuickTime 3.0 from the Mac OS 8.5 CD or from software you get from Apple's QuickTime Web site and do not replace it with earlier versions.

BACKGROUNDER

What's in QuickTime 3.0 Pro
What do you get when you plunk down $29.95 to upgrade from the basic edition of QuickTime 3 to QuickTime 3 Pro? The upgrade enables the PictureViewer application to save still images (in BMP, JPEG, Photoshop, PICT, or QuickTime Image format). The upgrade similarly enables the QuickTime plug-in for Web browsers to save movies from the Web. Moreover, the upgrade brings many improvements to the MoviePlayer application. Here's what MoviePlayer 3 Pro can do that the basic MoviePlayer 3 cannot:

✦ Create new movies

✦ Open a sequence of still images as a movie

✦ Import these media formats: 3DMF 3D image, regular and karaoke MIDI music, PICS animation, PICT image, System 7 Sound, and text

✦ Export movies to these media formats: BMP image, DV stream, PICT image, and QuickTime movie

✦ Export sound tracks to these sound formats: AIFF, System 7 Sound, Wave, and µLaw

✦ Apply video and audio compression

✦ Edit movies by drag-and-drop and with Cut, Copy, and Paste commands

✦ Extract individual tracks from a movie

✦ Show and set the movie poster frame

✦ Present a movie centered on a black screen

✦ Play a movie at half size and full-screen size

✦ Play a movie in a continuous loop

✦ Play only the selected part of a movie

✦ Adjust the size and orientation of each video track in the movie frame

✦ Show and set the following additional movie information: Colors, Controller, Files, General, and Preview

✦ Show and set the following additional video track information: Alternate Language, Format, Frame Rate, Gamma, General, Graphics Mode, High Quality, Layer, Mask, and Preload

✦ Show and set the following additional sound track information: Alternate Language, Files, General, High Quality, Preload, and Volume

Actually, you can tap most of these features without upgrading to QuickTime 3.0 Pro. Instead, use MoviePlayer 2.5–2.5.1 (plus the Goodies and Authoring Extras that come with it) with the basic edition of QuickTime 3.0. The combination of MoviePlayer 2.5–2.5.1 with the basic edition of QuickTime 3.0 lacks only these MoviePlayer 3.0 Pro capabilities:

✦ Open a sequence of still images as a movie

✦ Apply video compression

✦ Automatically save fast-start movies for the best playback on the Web

✦ Open and export DV Streams format

✦ Adjust the size and orientation of each video track

✦ Edit movies by drag-and-drop

Playing QuickTime Movies

QuickTime makes it possible to play movies in all kinds of applications and it establishes standard methods for controlling playback in all applications. There is a standard QuickTime movie controller, and there are standard methods for controlling play back when the controller is absent. The MoviePlayer application included with QuickTime has additional features that you can use to play movies. If you play movies that contain MIDI-synthesized music, you may be able to affect how they sound by setting some options in the QuickTime Settings control panel.

The QuickTime movie controller

You usually control playback of a QuickTime movie with a standard collection of buttons and sliders along the bottom edge of the movie. With this controller, you can play, stop, browse, or step through the movie. If the movie has a soundtrack, you can use the controller to adjust the sound level. The controller also gauges where the current scene is in relation to the beginning and end of the movie. By pressing certain keys while operating the controller, you can turn the sound on and off, copy and paste parts of the movie, play in reverse, change the playback rate, and more. Figure 16-2 summarizes the functions of a standard QuickTime movie controller. (Some applications have variants of the standard controller and may put the controller in a palette that floats above the document window.)

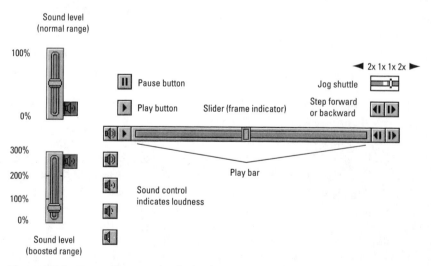

Figure 16-2: Controlling movie playback.

Playing and pausing

To start a movie playing, click the play button. This button has a right-pointing triangle like the play button on a tape recorder or VCR. While a movie is playing, this button becomes a pause button.

Stepping forward and backward

The two step buttons at the right of the play bar step backward and forward at the rate of one frame per click. The step buttons have different effects on movies that don't have frames. For example, in a movie that has only sound or music tracks, each click of a step button skips ahead or back a quarter of a second.

Going to another part of the movie

The gray play bar in the middle of the movie controller shows the position of the currently playing frame relative to the beginning and end of the movie. To go to a different place in the movie, you can drag the frame marker in the play bar or simply click the play bar.

You can go immediately to the beginning or end of the movie. To go the beginning, Option-click the forward-step button. To go to the end, Option-click the backward-step button.

Adjusting the sound

To adjust the sound level, you use the button labeled with the speaker. Click and hold down this button to pop up a slider that you can use to raise or lower the sound level. You can turn the sound off and on by Option-clicking the speaker button. You can set the sound level to up to three times louder than its normal maximum by holding down the Shift key while adjusting the level with the slider. If the speaker button is absent, the movie has no sound.

Changing playback direction and speed

To play the movie backward, ⌘-click the reverse-step button. Control-click either step button to reveal a jog shuttle that controls the direction and playback rate. Dragging the jog shuttle to the right gradually increases the forward playback rate from below normal to twice normal speed. Dragging the jog shuttle to the left has the same effect on playback speed, but makes the movie play backward.

QUICK TIPS

QuickTime Controller Shortcuts

The QuickTime movie controller responds to all kinds of keyboard shortcuts. Pressing the Return key or spacebar alternately starts and pauses play forward. Pressing ⌘-period(.) also pauses playing. You can press ⌘-right arrow(→) to play forward and ⌘-left arrow(←) to play backward. Press the right arrow (→) to step forward and left arrow (←) to step backward. To raise or lower the sound level, press the up arrow (↑) or down arrow (↓). Shift-up arrow(↑) raises the sound level beyond its normal maximum.

Choosing a chapter

A text area appears to the left of the step buttons in the movie controller for some movies. This *chapter list button* lets you go to predetermined points in the movie, much as index tabs let you turn to sections of a binder. Pressing the chapter list button pops up a menu of chapter titles, and choosing a chapter title takes you quickly to the corresponding part of the movie. If the chapter list button is absent, the movie has no chapters defined.

Playback without controllers

Applications may display movies without controllers. In this case, a badge in the lower-left corner of the movie distinguishes it from a still graphic. To play a movie that has a badge and no controller, you double-click the movie. If you press the Shift key while double-clicking the movie, it plays backward. Clicking a playing movie stops it. You can also display a standard movie controller by clicking the badge. Figure 16-3 shows a QuickTime movie with a badge.

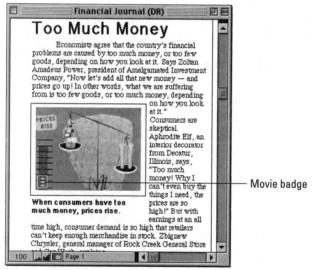

Figure 16-3: Identifying a movie without a controller.

The MoviePlayer application

Although you don't need a special application to view QuickTime movies, Mac OS 7.6–8.5 includes one called MoviePlayer. With the MoviePlayer menu commands, you have more control over playing a movie.

Many MoviePlayer commands are not available in the basic edition of MoviePlayer 3.0, which comes with the free version of QuickTime 3.0. These commands become available when you upgrade to QuickTime 3.0 Pro. In addition, most of these commands are available in MoviePlayer 2.5–2.5.1 no matter which version of QuickTime you have — 2.5, 3.0 basic, or 3.0 Pro. This means that you can use MoviePlayer 2.5–2.5.1 with the basic edition of QuickTime 3.0 to get most of the benefits of MoviePlayer 3.0 Pro. For a detailed comparison of features in the various versions of MoviePlayer, see the sidebar "What's in QuickTime 3.0 Pro" earlier in this chapter.

The following descriptions of MoviePlayer commands indicate the MoviePlayer versions in which the described command is available.

Changing the window size

Unlike most other applications that can show QuickTime movies, every version of the MoviePlayer application displays QuickTime movies in windows with size boxes. If you resize a movie window, QuickTime resizes the movie to fill the window. A resized movie generally plays less smoothly if you change its proportions. As a precautionary measure, QuickTime 3.0 normally forces movie windows to maintain their original proportions. To resize without this constraint, press the Shift key while dragging the size box. (QuickTime 2.5 and earlier do not constrain the movie window size in this way.)

A movie looks best at an even multiple of its original size, such as half-size or double-size. MoviePlayer (all versions) will constrain a movie to an optimal multiple of its original size if you press the Option key while dragging the movie window's size box. To quickly shrink a window to the nearest even multiple of its original size, Option-click its size box.

In addition to dragging a movie window's size box, you can use MoviePlayer menu commands to resize it. The basic edition of MoviePlayer 3.0 has Double Size and Normal Size commands. Movie Player 3.0 Pro and MoviePlayer 2.5–2.5.1 have two more commands: Half Size and Fill Screen.

Presenting a movie

Instead of displaying a movie in a window, you can present it centered on a completely black screen. In MoviePlayer 3.0 Pro or MoviePlayer 2.5–2.5.1, choose Present Movie from the File menu. (The Present Movie command is not available in the basic edition of MoviePlayer 3.0.)

The Present Movie command displays a dialog box in which you can set the movie size and specify whether you want to play the movie normally or slide show fashion (i.e., one frame at a time). If your computer has more than one monitor, this dialog box lets you select the monitor on which you want the movie presented. Setting a movie's presentation size in this dialog box to Double or Full Screen usually produces better results than resizing the movie manually before presenting it.

If your monitor is capable of displaying several screen resolutions, such as 640 x 480 and 832 x 624, MoviePlayer may force it to switch temporarily before presenting a movie. MoviePlayer switches to the resolution that is closest to but not smaller than the movie's size switch before presenting a movie at normal size, double size, or half size. After presenting the movie, MoviePlayer switches back to the resolution you were using. As a side effect of this resolution switching, windows in other open programs and desktop icons may be repositioned. You may have to spend several minutes moving icons and windows back to their former positions.

To stop a movie presentation, press the Esc key or ⌘-period(.). You can also stop the presentation of a normal movie by clicking the mouse button. With a slide show presentation, clicking the mouse button advances to the next movie frame; double-clicking goes back one frame.

Searching for a text track

While viewing a movie that contains a text track, you can search for specific text in the movie. In MoviePlayer 3.0 Pro or MoviePlayer 2.5–2.5.1, choose Find from the Edit menu. (Text searching is not available in the basic edition of MoviePlayer 3.0.)

The Find command displays a dialog box in which you enter the text you want to find and specify whether you want to search forward or backward. If MoviePlayer finds the text you're looking for, it immediately shows the corresponding part of the movie and highlights the found text. You can search for another occurrence of the same text by choosing Find Again from the Edit menu. Figure 16-4 shows an example of a movie with found text highlighted.

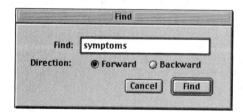

Figure 16-4: Specify text to find (left) to see the where it appears in a movie's text track (right).

If the Find command is disabled (grayed out), the movie doesn't have a text track.

Choosing a language

QuickTime movies can have sound tracks in several languages. To select the language you want to hear, choose the Choose Language command from the Movie menu. MoviePlayer displays a dialog box that lists the available languages. If the Choose Language command is disabled (grayed out), the movie doesn't have sound tracks in multiple languages. Figure 16-5 displays the dialog box in which you choose a language.

Figure 16-5: Choosing a language in a movie that has more than one language available.

Playing continuously (looping)

You can set MoviePlayer 3.0 Pro or MoviePlayer 2.5–2.5.1 to play a QuickTime movie in a continuous loop, either always playing forward or playing alternately forward and backward. Choose Loop or Loop Back and Forth from the Movie menu. (These commands are not available in the basic edition of MoviePlayer 3.0.)

Playing part of a movie

In MoviePlayer 3.0 Pro or MoviePlayer 2.5–2.5.1, you can select part of a movie and then play only the selected part. (You can't select part of a movie in the basic edition of MoviePlayer 3.0.)

To select part of a movie, go to the place in the movie where you want to begin selecting. Then Shift-click the play button to start the movie and begin selecting. Release the Shift key to end the selection and stop playing. The selected part of the movie appears black in the play bar. Figure 16-6 shows a movie that has been partly selected.

Figure 16-6: Selecting part of a movie with the Shift key makes the play bar turn black.

To play the selected part of a movie, choose Play Selection Only from the Movie menu and then click the play button. When there is a check mark next to Play

Selection Only in the Movie menu, all the movie controls and MoviePlayer commands apply only to the selected part. For example, the Loop command causes only the selected part to play continuously. You can go immediately to the beginning or end of the selection by Option-clicking the appropriate step button.

Instead of selecting part of a movie while it plays, you can move the slider in the play bar to the beginning of the part you want to select. Then hold down the Shift key and move the slider to the end of the part you want to select. As long as you hold down the Shift key, you can drag the slider to adjust the end of the selection.

You can extend or reduce a selection by holding down the Shift key and dragging the slider or clicking in the play bar. To adjust the end point of a selection precisely, Shift-click the step buttons. To begin selecting at a precise point, use the step buttons to go there before holding down the Shift key. You can make a selection from left to right or from right to left in the play bar. To cancel a selection, ⌘-click anywhere in the play bar.

Playing every frame

In MoviePlayer 3.0 Pro or MoviePlayer 2.5–2.5.1, you can prevent QuickTime from dropping any video frames to keep the video and audio tracks synchronized. If you want to see every frame even if it means playing the movie more slowly and without sound, choose Play All Frames from the Movie menu. (The Play All Frames command is not available in the basic edition of MoviePlayer 3.0.)

Playing all movies

You can have MoviePlayer 3.0 Pro or MoviePlayer 2.5–2.5.1 play all movies that are currently open by choosing Play All Movies from the Movie menu. (This command is not available in the basic edition of MoviePlayer 3.0.)

Interacting with QuickTime VR Scenes

You can do more with QuickTime than play linear movies. Apple's QuickTime VR software lets you explore places as if you were really there and examine objects as if they were with you. When you view a QuickTime VR panorama of a place, you can look up, look down, turn around, zoom in to see detail, and zoom out for a broader view. When you view a QuickTime VR object, you can manipulate it to see a different view of it. As you explore a panorama, you can move from it into a neighboring panorama or to an object in it. For example, you could move from one room to another room and then examine an object there.

You can interact with a QuickTime VR panorama or object from any application in which you can view a linear QuickTime movie. You can use SimpleText, the Scrapbook, MoviePlayer, or any other application that can play QuickTime movies.

When you view a QuickTime VR panorama or object, a QuickTime VR controller usually appears at the bottom of the window. It's in the same place as the controller for a regular QuickTime movie, but you don't use the QuickTime VR controller as the primary means of interacting with a QuickTime VR scene. You simply drag the mouse pointer to explore a QuickTime VR panorama or investigate a QuickTime VR object. The remainder of this section describes how to use the mouse pointer and the VR controller to interact with a QuickTime VR scene.

Exploring VR panoramas

To look around a QuickTime VR panorama, you click the picture and drag left, right, up, or down. The picture moves in the direction that you drag, and the pointer changes shape to indicate the direction of movement. Figure 16-7 shows a QuickTime VR panorama being moved to the right. The pointer in the center foreground indicates the direction of the pan.

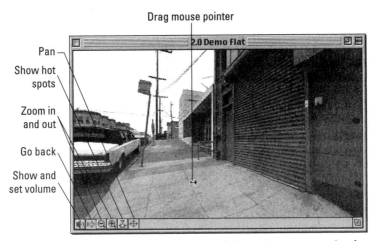

Figure 16-7: Moving the picture in a QuickTime VR panorama (to the right).

Investigating VR objects

To manipulate a QuickTime VR object, you click it and drag left, right, up, or down. As you drag, the object or some part of it moves. For example, it may turn around so that you can see all sides of it, or it may open and close. The author of the VR picture determines the effect.

When viewing a QuickTime VR object, you can also place the pointer near an inside edge of the VR window and press the mouse button to move the object continuously. Figure 16-8 shows several views of a QuickTime VR object.

The QuickTime VR controller

As you probably noticed, there is a controller at the bottom of a QuickTime VR window, but you don't use it to move the picture. The controller has buttons for controlling the sound level, zooming in and out, and interacting with hot spots in the picture. As you move the pointer over each control, a text description of its function appears in the VR controller. Figure 16-9 summarizes the functions of a QuickTime VR controller.

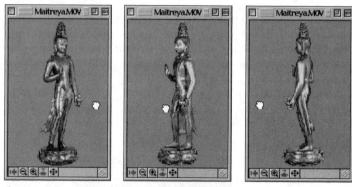

Figure 16-8: Manipulating a QuickTime VR object.

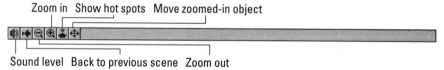

Figure 16-9: Controlling movie playback.

The VR controller does not include a sound control if the panorama or object does not have a sound track.

Zooming in and out

While viewing a QuickTime VR panorama or object, you can zoom in or out. To zoom in, click the VR controller button that looks like magnifying glass with a plus sign. To zoom out, click the button that looks like a magnifying glass with a minus sign. You can also press the Shift key to zoom in or press the Control key to zoom out.

As you zoom in on an object, it eventually becomes too large to see all at once in the QuickTime VR window. There are two ways you can see another part of a zoomed-in object. You can click the controller button labeled with two crossed arrows and then drag the object. Alternatively, you can press the Option key while dragging the object. Either way, the object holds its pose as it moves around in the window. To resume normal operation, click the button again or release the Option key.

Interacting with hot spots

A QuickTime VR panorama or object can contain *hot spots*. These are areas of the picture that you click to cause some action to occur. Typically, the action involves going to another panorama or object. A hot spot can trigger another kind of action, such as displaying text in the empty area of the VR controller or taking you to a Web page.

Hot spots are normally unmarked. One way to find them is to move the pointer around the panorama or object. When the pointer is over a hot spot, its shape changes. A variety of different pointer shapes may indicate a hot spot. One common shape is a large white arrow pointing up.

You can also have QuickTime VR show the hot spots in the picture. To highlight the hot spots with translucent rectangles, click the VR controller button labeled with an up arrow (↑) and question mark. If you double-click this button, it stays down and you can see all hot spots as you drag the pointer to move the picture. Figure 16-10 is an example of an outlined hot spot in a QuickTime VR panorama.

Click to outline hot spots

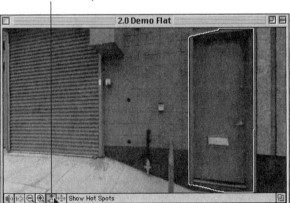

Figure 16-10: Hot spots revealed in a QuickTime VR panorama (around the door).

If clicking a hot spot takes you to another panorama or object, you can go back to your previous location by clicking the Back button, which is labeled with a left arrow (←) in the VR controller. If you've progressed through several hot spots, you can retrace your steps by clicking the Back button repeatedly.

Getting QuickTime VR software

QuickTime VR is part of a standard installation of Mac OS 8–8.5. You can add QuickTime VR to Mac OS 7.6.1 and earlier by installing QuickTime 3.0, which is available from Apple's QuickTime site on the Web (http://www.apple.com/quicktime/).

Viewing QuickDraw 3D Objects

There's more to QuickTime than interacting with VR panoramas and objects or playing regular movies. QuickTime incorporates Apple's QuickDraw 3D software, which renders three-dimensional images in real time. You don't need any special equipment, just a Mac with a PowerPC processor and at least 16MB of RAM. The PowerPC processor does not have to be original factory equipment — it can be on an upgrade card. QuickDraw 3D works best on a monitor that is set to display thousands or millions of colors.

Interacting with QuickDraw 3D objects

You can view and manipulate QuickDraw 3D graphics in any application designed to take advantage of it, such as the versions of SimpleText and Scrapbook that come with Mac OS 7.6–8.5. In participating applications such as these, QuickDraw 3D provides a viewer with buttons for changing the view of the image, as shown in Figure 16-11.

The QuickDraw 3D viewer's buttons let you move the image closer or farther away, rotate and tilt the image, move the image in the viewer frame, and restore the original view. In some applications, you get a five-button viewer, whereas other applications provide a four-button viewer. Here's how the buttons work:

+ **Camera**. Choose a view from the menu that pops up when you click this button. Choices typically include Fit To View, Front View, Back View, Left View, Right View, Top View, and Bottom View.

+ **Distance**. Click inside the frame and drag toward the bottom of the frame to move the image closer, or drag toward the top of the frame to move the image farther away.

+ **Rotate**. Click the image and drag to rotate it, or click outside the image and drag to tilt it.

+ **Move**. Drag the image to move it vertically or horizontally in the frame.

+ **Restore**. Click the button to restore the initial viewing distance, rotation, and position in the frame. This button is not present in some applications.

QuickDraw 3D also establishes a common file format for 3D graphics, called 3DMF (for "3D metafile"). The 3DMF format for 3D graphics is analogous to the PICT format for 2D graphics.

You don't always interact with QuickDraw 3D graphics. QuickTime movies can show animated QuickDraw 3D graphics together with video and audio tracks.

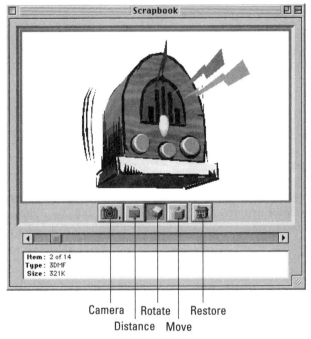

Camera | Rotate | Restore
Distance | Move

Figure 16-11: A QuickDraw 3D viewer has buttons for changing the view.

Getting QuickDraw 3D software

On a Mac with a PowerPC processor and at least 16MB of RAM, QuickDraw 3D is part of a standard installation of Mac OS 8.5. Mac OS 7.6–8.1 includes QuickDraw 3D as an optional part of a standard installation. QuickDraw 3D is also available as part of the latest QuickTime software, which you can get from Apple's QuickTime Web site (http://www.apple.com/quicktime/).

Basic QuickTime Movie Editing

If you have MoviePlayer 3.0 Pro or MoviePlayer 2.5.1, you're not limited to playing movies. You can also copy, paste, and otherwise edit movies. This section describes basic editing tasks that you can perform. (The free, basic edition of MoviePlayer 3.0 doesn't include editing capabilities — you have to use MoviePlayer 2.5–2.5.1 or upgrade to QuickTime 3.0 Pro, as described in "Introducing QuickTime Movies" earlier in this chapter.)

Selecting and copying a movie clip

You can copy all or part of a movie and copy it to the Clipboard so that you can put it in another movie. First you must select the part of the movie that you want to copy. Move the slider in the play bar until you see the beginning of the part that you want to select. Then hold down the Shift key and drag the slider until you see the end of the part that you want to select. As you drag, the play bar turns black to indicate the selected part. Alternatively, you can Shift-click near the end of the part that you want to select and then, while continuing to hold down the Shift key, drag the slider to the exact end of the selection. You can make a selection from right to left, as well as from left to right. Figure 16-6, shown previously, illustrates a movie that has been partly selected.

If you have trouble moving the slider to exactly the right place, try using the step buttons while pressing the Shift key. You can also make a selection by holding down the Shift key while playing a movie.

Whatever way you make a selection, it includes the frame you start with but does not include the last frame you see when you stop selecting. In other words, a selection ends with the frame before the last frame you see. To check the first or last frame of your selection, Option-click the appropriate step button. To check the entire selection, choose Play Selection Only from the Movie menu and then play the movie. Only the selection plays when there is a check mark next to Play Selection Only.

To select a whole movie, choose Select All from the Edit menu. You can cancel a selection by ⌘-clicking anywhere in the play bar. Alternatively, you can choose Select None from the Edit menu.

To place the selected part of a movie on the Clipboard, choose Copy from the Edit menu. You can choose Cut instead, but this, of course, deletes the selected part of the movie in addition to placing it on the Clipboard.

Pasting a movie clip

After copying or cutting a movie clip to the Clipboard, you can paste it anywhere in the same movie or another movie. Simply move the slider to the place where you want to insert the movie clip, and choose Paste from the Edit menu. If the slider is anywhere except the end of the movie, MoviePlayer inserts the pasted clip before the slider position. If the slider is at the end of the movie, MoviePlayer inserts the pasted clip after the slider position.

If you want to review a clip after pasting it, use the Play Selection Only command or Option-click the step buttons as described previously in "Playing QuickTime Movies."

Replacing part of a movie

You can replace part of a movie with a movie clip on the Clipboard. After copying the replacement clip, select the part of the movie you want to replace. Then hold down the Shift key and choose Replace from the Edit menu. While the Shift key is down, Replace appears in the Edit menu instead of Paste.

Deleting part of a movie

You can delete the selected part of a movie by choosing Clear from the Edit menu. Pressing the Delete key also deletes the selected part of a movie.

Instead of deleting the selected part of a movie, you can trim away everything that's not selected. Hold down the Option key and choose Trim from the Edit menu. While the Option key is down, Trim replaces Clear in the Edit menu.

You can use the Undo command in the Edit menu to restore a movie if you change your mind about clearing or trimming.

Deleting movie tracks

Rather than delete a selected part of a movie, you may want to delete an entire track. For example, you could delete the sound track to make a silent movie or you could delete the video track to make an audio-only movie. To delete tracks, choose Delete Tracks from the File menu. MoviePlayer displays a dialog box that lists the movie's tracks by name. You can select one or more tracks and click Delete to delete them. To select multiple tracks individually, ⌘-click each one. To select several adjacent tracks, click the first one and then Shift-click the last. Figure 16-12 shows an example of the Delete Tracks dialog box.

Figure 16-12: Deleting tracks from a movie.

Adding movie tracks

Instead of inserting a movie clip with the Paste command, you can add it to a movie as an overlaid track or tracks. The tracks you add play at the same time as the other tracks in the same part of the movie. For example, you can add a sound track to a silent movie, and both video and sound will play at the same time.

STEP-BY-STEP

Adding an Echo Effect

You can add a nifty echo effect to a QuickTime movie by adding a copy of its own sound track slightly offset in time. To do so, open the movie in MoviePlayer and follow these steps:

1. Use MoviePlayer's Delete Tracks command to delete all tracks except the sound track.

2. Use the Select All command (⌘-A) to select the entire movie, which is now just a sound track.

3. Use the Copy command (⌘-C) to copy the selection to the Clipboard.

4. Use the Undo Delete Tracks command (⌘-Z) to undo the track deletion.

5. Use the Select None command (⌘-D) to cancel the selection.

6. Move the slider to the beginning of the play bar.

7. Click the Step Forward button once to advance to the second frame of the movie.

8. Use the Add command (Option-⌘-V) to add the copied sound track.

To add a track to a movie, you must copy it from another movie. However, the Copy command copies all the tracks from a movie. If you want to copy only one track from a movie, you must temporarily delete all the other tracks in the movie. Then select and copy all or part of the movie. Immediately after copying you can restore the deleted tracks by choosing Undo Delete Tracks from the Edit menu. Next, switch to the movie in which you want to add the copied track, and move the slider on its play bar to the place where you want the new track to start playing. Now hold down the Option key and choose Add from the Edit menu. While the Option key is down, Add replaces Paste in the Edit menu.

If the track you add is longer than the existing tracks, MoviePlayer automatically makes the whole movie longer. You may want to delete the added length from the end of the movie, especially if the track you added was a sound track. When you add a long sound track, MoviePlayer pads the end of the video track with white.

Making a new movie

To make a new QuickTime movie with nothing in it, choose New from MoviePlayer's File menu. MoviePlayer displays an untitled movie window with a controller but no content. You can copy clips from other movies and paste or add them to your new movie.

You can also make a new QuickTime movie by importing another media file, such as a sound file or an animation file. Choose Import from the File menu and in the standard Open dialog box that appears, select the media file you want to import.

QuickTime converts the media file to a movie and MoviePlayer opens the converted movie. You can now copy a clip from this movie and paste, replace, or add the clip to any other movie.

Setting a movie poster

You can designate a picture from a QuickTime movie to represent the movie in various circumstances. This picture is called the movie's *poster.* For instance, you see a movie's poster when the movie is selected in an Open dialog box or another file-related dialog box that shows previews. MoviePlayer displays the poster in the Movie Information window that appears when you choose Show Copyright from the Movie menu. Figure 16-13 illustrates a poster in an Open dialog box.

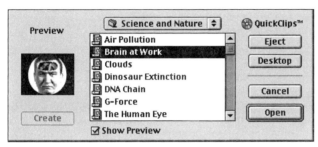

Figure 16-13: Some applications display a movie's poster as a preview.

To set a movie's poster, go to the place in the movie that you want to use as the poster. Then choose Set Poster Frame from the Movie menu. This command works for QuickTime VR scenes and QuickDraw 3D objects, as well as linear QuickTime movies.

Saving a movie

After editing a movie, be sure to save it by choosing Save or Save As from the File menu. The size of a movie when you save it is the size it will be when it is opened subsequently. Also, the current states of the Loop, Loop Back and Forth, and Play All Frames commands are saved with the movie and will apply when the movie is opened again.

Dependent and self-contained movies

When you save a movie, you can make it a self-contained file or dependent on other files. A movie with file dependencies doesn't contain all the data for the movie. Instead, some of the movie data is saved in separate files that may be used by other movies. You conserve disk space by having several movies dependent on the same files. However, QuickTime can't play a movie if its dependent files are missing. For example, if you copy part of a movie from a CD-ROM and paste it into a new movie that you save on your hard disk with file dependencies, you won't be able to play the movie unless the CD-ROM is inserted. This situation doesn't exist with a self-contained movie — it has no file dependencies because it contains a copy of all its data.

Saving for the Web

When saving a QuickTime movie for playback in a Web browser, make the movie self-contained. In addition, you must end the movie file name with the suffix ".mov". Web browsers know that a file name with this suffix contains a QuickTime movie. If you omit the suffix, Web browsers won't play your movie.

If you save a QuickTime movie for the Web with MoviePlayer 2.5–2.5.1, you must turn on the option "Playable on non-Apple computers" in the Save dialog box. (MoviePlayer 3.0 Pro doesn't have this option because it automatically saves movies in a format that's compatible with non-Apple computers.)

Audio CDs

If your computer has a CD-ROM drive, you can listen to audio CDs with it. This section tells you how to play an audio CD automatically and how to control it with the Control Strip. This section also explains how to control the playing of audio CDs with the AppleCD Audio Player application, how to adjust the cable connections and control panel settings to hear audio CD sound on your computer, and how to have a CD play automatically when it is inserted it or when your computer starts. This section also describes how you can record passages from audio CDs as sound files.

If you play an Enhanced CD from your CD-ROM drive and open a program, access a file, or use the Finder, the Enhanced CD may stop playing. Enhanced CDs contain audio and other types of media such as text, movies, or multimedia software. This problem does not occur when playing regular audio CDs, which contain only audio.

The AppleCD Audio Player

The AppleCD Audio Player application plays audio CDs from your CD-ROM drive. It has buttons that correspond to all the tangible push-button controls you'd expect to find on a machine that plays CDs. Many of the Audio Player's onscreen buttons have keyboard equivalents. What sets the Audio Player apart from an ordinary CD player is its program mode. You can program a custom play list for every CD, and Audio Player remembers each play list you create. You can also enter CD and track titles, which Audio Player remembers as well. Figure 16-14 shows the AppleCD Audio Player and identifies its basic controls.

The Audio Player program has an Options menu that you can use to change the window color and the number-display color. You also can use this menu to play back the left channel or right channel only. In addition, if your computer has more than one CD-ROM drive, the Startup CD Drive submenu lets you choose the drive you want the

Audio Player to control by selecting its SCSI ID number. After changing the Startup CD Drive, you have to quit the Audio Player and open it again to enforce the change.

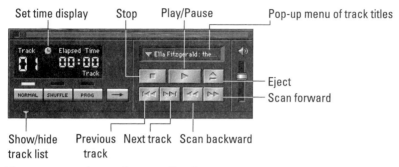

Figure 16-14: The AppleCD Audio Player program.

Using control panel buttons

You can play, pause, stop, skip backward, skip forward, scan backward, and scan forward by clicking the buttons on the right side of the control panel. Here's how the buttons work:

✦ Clicking the Normal button plays the CD tracks sequentially.

✦ Clicking the Shuffle button plays the tracks in random order. Each time you click Shuffle, the order changes.

✦ Clicking the Prog button plays the tracks in an order that you specify (as described in "Programming CD playback," later in this section).

✦ Clicking the arrow button next to the Prog button alternates between playing the CD one time or continuously in the mode that you've selected (normal, shuffle, or program).

✦ Clicking the small down arrow (▼) above the Stop button displays a pop-up menu that lists the tracks on the CD. Use this menu to play a specific track.

✦ Clicking the clock icon near the time display also displays a pop-up menu. Use this menu to set the display to show elapsed or remaining time on the current track or on the entire disc.

Using keyboard controls

You can also operate many of Audio Player's controls from the keyboard. These keyboard shortcuts work when the Audio Player is the active application:

✦ Press the left-arrow (←) and right-arrow (→) keys to scan backward or scan forward track by track.

✦ Press the space bar or the Enter key to alternately play and pause the CD.

✦ Press the Delete key or the Clear key to stop playing the CD.

✦ Press ⌘-E to eject the CD.

✦ Press the up-arrow (↑) and down-arrow (↓) keys to operate the volume control, if the Audio Player includes one. (The presence of a volume control depends on the capabilities of the CD-ROM drive.)

Naming CDs and tracks

When you insert an audio CD, the Audio Player pulls the track times off the CD, but not the track titles. It displays generic titles (Track 1, Track 2, and so forth), but you can replace them with the real track and CD titles. It takes only a couple of minutes to enter the titles for a typical CD, and you only have to do it once—the Audio Player remembers the titles permanently. Once you enter the titles, they reappear every time you pop the CD back into the CD-ROM drive. Figure 16-15 is an example of track titles in the Audio Player.

Although it doesn't take long to enter titles for one CD, it will take hours to enter titles for 100 or more CDs. You can spare yourself this effort by using the TitleTrack CD Player from RiverSong Interactive (http://www.titletrack.com). This $15 shareware program downloads titles from a huge database on the Internet, and the titles appear in the AppleCD Audio Player as well as the TitleTrack CD Player.

QUICK TIPS

Audio CD Control

Want to control audio CD playback with keystrokes or a pop-up remote control from any application? Try the $15 PopupCD shareware by John Brochu. It can also record audio clips directly from CD to hard drive. The figure below shows the PopupCD control panel with its keystroke configuration dialog box and the pop-up remote control.

 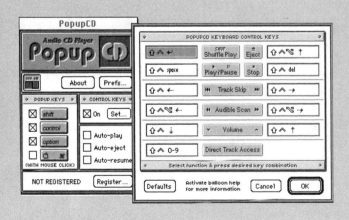

Figure 16-15: The AppleCD Audio Player remembers track titles you enter for each CD.

If you want to enter titles, the Audio Player must be in Normal mode or Shuffle mode (not Prog mode). Click the tiny Edit List button (the small triangle located below the Normal button) to show the CD title and below it a track list. To enter track titles, press Tab to move through the track list, typing the titles as you go. To enter a CD title, click the CD title at the top of the play list and type the new title.

You can enter up to 62 characters for each track title. Although the track list itself can't display full titles that long, you can see full titles in a pop-up menu by clicking the CD title in the top right part of the Audio Player. To see more tracks, you can enlarge the window by dragging its size box.

The Audio Player stores the titles that you enter for each CD in the CD Remote Programs file in the Preferences folder (inside the System Folder).

Programming CD playback

To program the order in which the AppleCD Audio Player plays the tracks of a CD, click the Prog button. Then click the Edit List button (the small triangle below the Normal button) to display the track list and play list at the bottom of the Audio Player window. The track list appears on the left side of the window and lists all tracks sequentially. The play list appears on the right side of the window and you build it by dragging tracks from the track list to slots in the play list. The play list can include up to 99 tracks.

You can mix up the order of tracks on the play list any way you like, put the same track on the play list more than once, and leave tracks out of the play list altogether. You can rearrange tracks in the play list on the right by dragging them up or down. You can remove a track from the play list by dragging it back to the track list.

The Audio Player stores all your custom play lists in the CD Remote Programs file together with the CD and track titles you have entered. Figure 16-16 shows an example of a custom play list being built.

Figure 16-16: Drag track titles to program a play list in the AppleCD Audio Player.

Hearing Audio CD sound

To hear audio CDs on your computer, you may need to set some sound input options in the Monitors & Sound control panel or the Sound control panel. If you want to play audio CDs from an external CD-ROM drive, you first need to connect the drive's sound output either to the computer's input, to amplified speakers, or to a stereo system.

Playing CDs from an external CD-ROM drive

You may be able to play audio CDs from an external CD-ROM drive through your computer's low-fidelity internal speaker or through externally powered speakers that are connected to the computer's sound output port. Be sure to use magnetically shielded speakers near a monitor or disk. If you want to hear the computer's sounds and the audio CD sound through the same speakers, get a pair of powered speakers with mixed dual inputs (one input for the computer and the other for the CD-ROM drive), such as the AppleDesign Powered Speakers I or II.

External speakers are easy to hook up to an external CD-ROM drive, but you can't control their volume with the Audio Player or your computer's control panels. Furthermore, connecting external speakers to an external CD-ROM drive precludes recording CD sound from the drive (as described later in this section). To control the volume of an external CD-ROM drive from your computer or record sound from the external drive, you need to connect the external drive's sound output jacks to your computer's sound input port with a stereo patch cord (available wherever stereo accessories are sold). Your patch cord must have a plug or plugs that fit the sound output jacks on your CD-ROM drive, as well as a plug or plugs that fit the microphone port on your computer. Most external CD-ROM drives have a headphone jack on the front, and many drives also have RCA-style jacks on the back. Your computer probably has a stereo minijack for its microphone input, like the kind used for cassette player headphones. Some computers also have RCA-style jacks for alternate sound input. By examining the output jacks on your CD-ROM drive and the input port on your computer, you should be able to figure out the kind of patch cord plugs that are required for your equipment.

With some Mac models and versions of the Mac OS, you must also move the External CD Sound file from the Apple Extras folder to the Extensions folder. According to Apple, the only Macs that require that extension are the 630 series and the Power Mac and Performa 5200 and 6200 series. If your Apple Extras folder doesn't contain the External CD Sound extension, you probably don't need it. Apple includes the extension with all computers that need it. Apple doesn't distribute the extension through its online Software Updates library or on Mac OS CDs. If you use powered speakers or a stereo system, you don't need the External CD Sound file.

Changing sound input options

To hear an audio CD, you may need to change a couple of sound input settings in the Monitors & Sound control panel (in Mac OS 8–8.5) or in the Sound control panel (in Mac OS 7.6–7.6.1). You may have to make these changes whether you're using an internal CD-ROM drive or an external drive whose sound output is connected to your computer's microphone port (as described previously). You'll also have to turn off speech recognition, as described in Chapter 21. However, if you're playing audio CDs on an external CD-ROM drive that's connected to powered speakers or a stereo system, you can play and listen to audio CDs without making any of the control panel changes described here. In this case, you can even listen to an audio CD and use speech recognition at the same time, as long as the CD sound doesn't confuse the speech recognition software.

The settings you need to check are slightly different in each version of the Mac OS.

SECRETS

The Power Mac Microphone Port

Although a Power Mac's microphone port is designed for the extralong plug of Apple's PlainTalk speech recognition microphone, you can use an ordinary patch cord to connect an audio source to the microphone port. The PlainTalk microphone's plug reaches deep inside the Power Mac's microphone port to draw power for the microphone's internal preamplifier. A patch cord doesn't need electricity, so its regular $1/_8$-inch stereo miniplug need not reach the port's power lead. The Quadra 660AV and 840AV have the same type of microphone port.

BACKGROUNDER

Sound Input Levels

When you connect an audio source such as an external CD-ROM drive to your computer, you must make sure it delivers a signal at the right level. If the level is too high, you will hear distorted sound. If the level is too low, the sound may be noisy or inaudible. You can connect a line-level audio source such as a VCR, cassette deck, or audio CD player to any of these Macs, which have a line-level sound input (2 volts maximum, 8 KΩ impedance): all PowerPC computers; the Quadra 605, 630, 660AV, and 840AV; the LC 475, 575, and 630; and the PowerBook 500 series. All other Macs have a microphone-level sound input (20 millivolt, 600Ω). To avoid overloading the microphone-level sound circuitry with a line-level source—which would distort recorded sound but cause no damage—you should use a special cable that attenuates the high-level signal (for example, Sony part number RK-G128 or Radio Shack part number 42-2461-A).

If you're using Mac OS 8.5, open the Monitors & Sound control panel and click the Sound button to see the sound options. Set the Sound Input option to Microphone for an external CD-ROM drive or to Internal CD for an internal drive, and turn on the Listening option. While looking at the Sound options, make sure the Computer System Volume option is not turned all the way down or muted. You should now hear the audio CD.

If you're using Mac OS 8.1, open the Monitors & Sound control panel and click the Sound button to see the sound options. Set the Sound Monitoring Source option to Sound In for an external CD-ROM drive or to CD for an internal drive. While looking at the Sound options, make sure the Computer System Volume option is not turned all the way down or muted. You should now hear the audio CD.

If you're using Mac OS 8, open the Monitors & Sound control panel and click the Sound button to see the sound options. Set the Sound Input option to Microphone for an external CD-ROM drive or Internal CD for an internal drive, and turn on the Listening option. While looking at the Sound options, make sure the Sound Out Level and Computer Speaker Volume options are not turned all the way down or muted. You should now hear the audio CD.

If you're using Mac OS 7.6–7.6.1, open the Sound control panel and turn on the Playthrough option by clicking the Options button in the Sound In section of the Sound control panel. On Macs that normally use the Monitors & Sound control panel with Mac OS 7.6–7.6.1 (such as Macs with PCI slots) the Sound control panel is in the Apple Extras folder, not the Control Panels folder. Also, make sure the levels are not turned all the way down or muted in the Volumes section of the Sound control panel. You should now hear the audio CD.

On some older computers, such as the Mac LC III, you must use the free PlayThrough application by Andreas Pardeike to hear audio CDs from an external CD-ROM drive that's connected to the computer's microphone port. You enable play-through by launching PlayThrough and leaving it open, but to put it in the background you must click outside its window (for some reason the Application menu doesn't work). To disable play-through, choose Ablage, which is German for Quit, from PlayThrough's File menu. This menu also contains German commands for setting the volume (Lautstärke 0 through 7).

Recording Audio CD sound

You can record sound from an audio CD using the SimpleSound application, newer versions of the Monitors & Sound control panel, or the Sound control panel. In all cases, you control the CD with the AppleCD Audio Player program. For more control over recording short segments from an audio CD, use the freeware utility program GrabAudio by Theo Vosse. You can record long segments of an audio CD as a sound-only movie by using QuickTime.

Before you can record from an audio CD, you may have to set the computer's sound input source using the Monitors & Sound control panel or the Sound control panel (as described previously).

Some older Macs can't record directly from an audio CD in the internal CD-ROM drive if anything is plugged into the sound input (microphone) port. Affected models include Quadra or Centris 610 or 650, Quadra 800, Mac IIvx or IIvi, and Performa 600CD.

Recording system alert sounds

If you're tired of the standard system alert sounds, you can record a new alert sound from your own audio CD using the AppleCD Audio Player program and one of the following: the Monitors & Sound control panel, the Sound control panel, or the SimpleSound program. At least one of these comes with every version of the Mac OS.

The Monitors & Sound control panel, the Sound control panel, and the SimpleSound program all display a standard dialog box for recording an alert sound. This dialog box contains buttons that resemble the controls on a conventional tape recorder. There are buttons to record, stop, pause, and play. In addition, there are buttons for canceling and saving a recording you have made. Figure 16-17 shows the standard dialog box for recording an alert sound.

Figure 16-17: The standard dialog box for recording a system alert sound.

Before recording an alert sound from a CD, observe the Audio Player program while listening to the passage you want to record and note the track and time where the passage starts. Then use the Audio Player's controls to pause the CD a few seconds before the start of the passage. Make sure the Audio Player's volume control is all the way up.

To record using the Monitors & Sound control panel or the Sound control panel, open either control panel and display its Alert Sounds settings. Switch back to the Audio Player, start the CD playing and, without hesitation, switch back to the control panel and click the Add button. You will see the standard dialog box for recording an alert sound (previously shown in Figure 16-17). Click the Record button a split second before the beginning of the passage that you want to record, and click the Stop button when you want it to finish (a second or two for an alert sound). Then click the Save button to save the alert sound with a name that you want.

To record an alert sound using the SimpleSound program, choose Alert Sound from SimpleSound's Sound menu. This displays the Alert Sounds window. Switch to the Audio Player and start the CD playing a few seconds before the start of the sound that you want to record. Immediately switch back to SimpleSound and click the Add button in the Alert Sounds window to display the standard dialog box for recording sound (previously shown in Figure 16-17). Click the Record button a split second before the beginning of the passage that you want to record, and click the Stop button when you want it to finish. Then click the Save button to save the new alert sound.

CAUTION

Can You Copy That?

Be careful what you copy. Sound and video recordings and broadcasts are protected by copyright just like printed materials. Before capturing part of an audio CD, audiotape, phonograph record, radio broadcast, videotape, videodisc, television broadcast, or other recorded pictures and sound, you may need to get the copyright owner's permission. It's best to get permission in writing. You don't need permission to copy from works in the public domain, such as works created by United States government agencies. Works of state and local governments, as well as other national governments, may be protected by copyright. You also don't need permission if your copying comes under the doctrine of *fair use* as defined by the U.S. Copyright law. The law doesn't precisely define fair use, but does specify four criteria that must be considered:

1. The purpose and character of the use, including whether such use is of commercial nature or is for nonprofit educational purposes

2. The nature of the copyrighted work

3. The amount and substantiality of the portion used in relation to the copyrighted work as a whole

4. The effect of the use upon the potential market for or value of the copyrighted work

Recording AIFF sound files

In addition to recording alert sounds, the SimpleSound program can capture part of a CD as an AIFF digital sound file. First, use the AppleCD Audio Player program to start the CD playing about 15 seconds before the start of the section you want to capture. Without hesitation switch to SimpleSound and choose the New command (or press ⌘-N) to bring up the standard Mac OS sound recording controls. Click the Record button a split second before the beginning of the passage that you want to record, and click the Stop button when you want it to finish. Then click the Save button to save the digital sound file in the AIFF format.

Recording QuickTime sound movies

Any program that can open QuickTime movies can record a passage from an audio CD as a QuickTime sound-only movie. SimpleSound, SimpleText, and MoviePlayer can all do this. To begin, choose Open from the program's File menu. In the Open dialog box, open the audio CD, select the track that you want to record, and click the convert button. This displays a Save dialog box. Click the Options button in this Save dialog box to display the Audio CD Input Options dialog box. Adjust the slider controls in this dialog box to specify which part of the audio track to include. Set the sound quality here as well. Dismiss this dialog box and click Save in the previous dialog box. QuickTime copies the audio data from the CD to the movie file. Figure 16-18 is an example of the Audio CD Input Options dialog box.

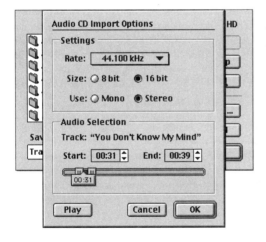

Figure 16-18: Selecting part of an audio CD track to save as a sound-only QuickTime movie.

This procedure requires at least a 2X CD-ROM driver.

Playing audio CDs automatically

You can have your computer play an audio CD when the computer starts. Putting an alias of Track 1 from any audio CD into the Startup Items folder has the Finder automatically launch AppleCD Audio Player during startup and begin playing whatever CD is in the drive. The Track 1 alias works with any audio CD, not just the one used to make the alias. If there's no CD in the drive, the Mac OS requests one during startup. To make the alias, insert any audio CD, open its icon, select Track 1, and use the Make Alias command.

It's also possible to have your Mac automatically play an audio CD any time you insert one. Just turn on the Enable Audio CD AutoPlay option in the AutoPlay section of the QuickTime Settings control panel, as shown in Figure 16-19.

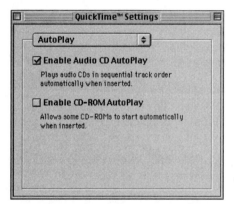

Figure 16-19: Setting the AutoPlay options in the QuickTime Settings control panel.

The AutoPlay feature starts playing the CD earlier in the startup process than the Startup Items method and doesn't require the AppleCD Audio Player application. However, you do have to open AppleCD Audio Player (or its equivalent) if you want to control playback of an autoplaying CD while it's playing. (Of course, you can always just stop the autoplaying CD by ejecting it.) The AutoPlay feature does not work with some CD-ROM drives that are not sold by Apple.

Apple Video Player

If your computer has video inputs, chances are you can use the Apple Video Player application to play video and audio from a VCR, camcorder, or other video equipment on your computer screen. If your computer has a TV tuner installed, you can use the Video Player to tune in and watch TV shows. In addition, the Video Player can capture the video and audio and save it in a movie file on disk. You can use the Apple Video Player with the following Apple video input equipment:

✦ Apple Audio/Video card installed in a Power Mac G3 computer

✦ Built-in video ports on Power Mac 7500, 7600, 8500, and 8600 computers

✦ Apple Video System card or Apple TV/Video System card in these series of computers:

- Power Mac and Performa 5200, 5300, 5400, 5500, 6300, 6400, and 6500

- Quadra and Performa 580 and 630

✦ Power Mac AV card in Power Mac 6100AV, 7100AV, and 8100AV computers

If your computer doesn't have video input capability, you may be able to add it by installing a video card made by Apple or another company such as ATI Technologies (905-882-2600, http://www.atitech.ca) or IXmicro (408-369-8282, http://www.ixmicro. com). If you get a video card made by a company other than Apple, the card may use its own video player application instead of the Apple Video Player. For example, video cards from ATI Technologies use the Xclaim Video Player.

You can also buy more sophisticated video software that works with most major brands of video input equipment, including the Apple video input equipment listed previously and video cards from ATI Technologies, IXmicro, and Radius. Video editing and composing software such as Adobe Premiere and Avid Cinema can both capture movies like the Apple Video Player, and they can also slice, dice, chop, mix, combine, and bake new movies from pieces of captured movies.

CAUTION

AutoStart Worms

There are two options in the AutoPlay section of the QuickTime Settings control panel, Enable Audio CD AutoPlay and Enable CD-ROM AutoPlay. Both seem harmless, but the second one opens the door for a malicious program called AutoStart 9805 Worm. If the Enable CD-ROM AutoPlay option is turned on, QuickTime looks for an AutoStart program on every disk you insert into your computer (not just on CD-ROMs), and automatically launches this program if it exists. The point of this mechanism is to allow programs on CD-ROMs to start themselves automatically. For example, a game CD-ROM could start itself as soon as you insert the CD-ROM.

The AutoStart 9805 Worm is the type of program that QuickTime will launch automatically, but this program makes an extension in your System Folder so that it can get control every time you start your computer. The program also reproduces itself on all your disks. (It can't spread to uninfected CD-ROMs because they are locked.) This program is a *worm* because it reproduces itself but does not infect other files. (A program that reproduces itself by infecting other files is a *virus*.) If a Zip disk or other removable disk becomes infected with the worm on your computer and you insert this disk in another computer that has the Enable CD-ROM AutoPlay option turned on, the worm spreads to that computer also.

You can significantly reduce the chance of your system being infected by the AutoStart 9805 Worm or similar programs by turning off the Enable CD-ROM AutoPlay option in the QuickTime Settings control panel. You do not need to turn off the Enable Audio CD AutoPlay option. If you're concerned that your computer may already be infected, you can detect and eradicate this worm by using the free EarlyBird 1.1 program from Lineaux (http://www.lineaux.com/notes/worm_intro.htm) or the free WormScanner program by James W. Walker (http://members.aol.com/jwwalker/pages/worm.html).

This section explains how to connect your video source to your computer and watch and capture video input with the Apple Video Player.

Connecting a video source

Before you can watch or capture video from a VCR or other video equipment outside your computer, you need to connect the video equipment to your computer. This involves connecting a cable from the video output jack of the video source to the video input port on your computer, and connecting another cable from the audio output jack (or jacks, for stereo) of the video source to the computer's audio input port or microphone port.

The type of video cable you use depends on the type of output jack on the VCR or other video equipment. If the video equipment has an S-video output jack (which looks like a keyboard port or serial port on your computer), use an S-video cable. If the video equipment has a *composite* output jack (which looks like the RCA jacks on many stereo components), use a composite cable. Most consumer-grade camcorders, VCRs, and TVs have composite output jacks. High-end video equipment use S-video jacks.

You can use an adapter to connect a composite cable to an S-video port on your computer. If your computer has only an S-video input port, it probably came with a composite cable adapter.

The video cable doesn't carry sound, so you have to connect a separate audio cable from the VCR or other video equipment to your computer. The plug at one end of the audio cable must fit the type of audio output jack on the video equipment, which is usually one or two RCA jacks. The plug at the other end of the audio cable must fit the computer's audio input port. Your computer may have a pair of RCA jacks for audio input or a stereo minijack (the microphone port).

Because the details of connecting video equipment to a computer vary according to the type of video input, you should consult the manual that came with your computer or video card for specific instructions.

Watching video

The Apple Video Player has a window for viewing video from an external video source or an internal TV tuner (if your computer has one). You select the video source and adjust the picture with controls in a separate Controls window. To see the controls for video source and picture, click the video screen icon on the left side of the Controls window. Figure 16-20 shows the main Video Player window and the Controls window.

Capturing video

While watching video through the Apple Video Player, you can save a single frame as a picture file, copy a frame to the Clipboard, or save a video sequence as a QuickTime movie. You capture a single frame with the Copy Video Display command in the Edit menu, and you capture SimpleText picture files or QuickTime movie files with controls in the Controls window. To see the capture controls, you click the video camera icon on the left side of the Controls window. Figure 16-21 shows the capture controls.

Figure 16-20: Selecting a video source and adjusting the picture in the Apple Video Player.

Figure 16-21: Capturing single-frame or movie files with the Apple Video Player.

To successfully capture a still picture or a movie, you may need to increase the memory size of the Apple Video Player using the Get Info command in the Finder. The memory requirements depend on the size of the Video window and on the complexity of the image. If the Video Player runs out of memory while attempting to capture an image, it displays a vaguely worded alert notifying you that an error occurred.

Capturing a still picture

To capture a still picture, click the Freeze button in the Controls window when you see an image in the Video window that you want to save. The picture in the video window stops (although the video input continues unseen unless you pause or stop the VCR or other video source). If you like the still picture in the Video window, you can save it as a SimpleText picture file (a PICT file) by clicking the Save button in the Controls window. If you don't like the still picture, click the Freeze button again to resume viewing the video input.

The size of the Video window directly affects the size of the captured picture. Making the window smaller reduces the amount of disk space required to store the picture. To use the least amount of disk space, choose Smallest Size from the Video Player's Window menu.

Capturing a movie

To capture a video sequence as a movie, click the Record button in the Controls window as you see the sequence begin in the Video window. Recording begins, the Record button changes to a Stop button, and the Pause button becomes functional. Click the Pause button if you want to suspend the recording process while the incoming video continues playing. When you click the Pause button, it changes to a Resume button, and clicking the Resume button resumes recording with the sequence then playing in the Video window. To end the recording, click the Stop button. The Video Player then uses QuickTime to compress the movie so that it takes up less disk space (unless you turned off compression as described later), and displays a Save As dialog box so that you can name the movie file and select a folder for it.

While recording is in progress, the motion you see in the Video window may become more jerky than usual. This does not mean the recorded movie will be as jerky. The computer optimizes the number of video frames it can record per second by devoting less processing power to displaying the incoming video. You want the computer to record as many frames per second as it can, because a higher frame rate produces smoother motion. The computer can record video at a higher frame rate if you eliminate background-processing tasks that sap its performance. For example:

✦ Turn off the menu bar clock (see "Date, Time, and Location Settings" in Chapter 11).

✦ Turn off virtual memory and restart the computer to make virtual memory changes take effect (see "Increasing Total Memory" in Chapter 18).

✦ If you use RAM Doubler instead of virtual memory, turn it off.

✦ Make sure file sharing is off and make AppleTalk and TCP/IP inactive (see "Configuring an AppleTalk Connection" and "Configuring a TCP/IP Connection" in Chapter 19).

✦ Insert a floppy disk, a CD-ROM, and any other type of removable disk you have so the computer doesn't have to periodically check to see if you've inserted one.

Another factor that affects frame rate is the size of the Video window. The window size also affects the picture quality and file size of a captured movie. For the best quality movie in the least amount of disk space, choose Smallest Size from Video Player's Window menu. This sets the movie frame size to 160 x 120 pixels. Choosing Normal Size from the Windows menu sets the frame size to 320 x 240 pixels.

You can also increase a movie's frame rate and reduce its file size by having the movie compressed. Unfortunately video compression degrades picture quality. You can adjust the amount of compression or completely turn off compression by choosing Preferences from the Video Player's Setup menu and setting the Movie Compression option to None, Normal, or Most. The Normal setting reduces file size by 12 to 50 percent. The Most setting reduces file size up to 50 percent more than the Normal setting. The compression method that the Video Player uses, known as Apple Video, works best when the number of colors is set to thousands (not 256 or millions) in the Monitors & Sound control panel or the Monitors control panel (whichever your computer has).

Frame rate is also affected by the speed of the hard disk. You need a fast hard disk to record at high frame rates. To achieve the optimum frame rate of 30 fps (frames per second) with a normal frame size (320 x 240 pixels), your hard disk should be capable of sustained writes at 5MB per second or more. That rate is the maximum throughput of a regular external SCSI port, so you should connect your fast hard disk to a SCSI-2 port (10MB per second) or SCSI-3 port (20MB per second). Some Macs, such as the Power Mac 8500 and 8600, come with internal SCSI-2 ports. You can also install expansion cards with fast SCSI ports.

Frame rate and picture quality are irrelevant if your hard disk doesn't have enough space to record the movie. Capturing a normal frame size requires 2MB to 4MB per second, depending on the frame rate. That much disk space must be available to initially capture the movie; that is, when the Video Player automatically saves the uncompressed captured video in a temporary file. This temporary file is normally on the same disk as the Video Player program. If that disk becomes full and your computer has other hard disks, the Video Player looks for more temporary storage space on them. After recording the movie, the Video Player has QuickTime compress it and then releases the temporary storage space.

Summary

In this chapter, you learned that QuickTime pulls every trick in the book to play digital movies on your computer. It plays movies at reduced frame sizes and at slower than normal frame rates, and that it works with compressed movies to reduce the amount of data it has to transfer from disk.

This chapter told you how to play a QuickTime movie with and without the VCR-like movie controller. With the controller, you can play and pause, step forward or backward, go to any part of the movie, adjust the sound level, change playback direction and speed, and more. This chapter also explained how to interact with QuickTime VR panoramas and objects. You can change your view of a VR panorama by panning, tilting, zooming, and clicking hot spots. You can manipulate a VR object to see a different view of it. You also learned how to manipulate 3D graphics displayed by the QuickDraw 3D system extension.

This chapter explained the basic ways that you can edit QuickTime movies with MoviePlayer 3.0 Pro or MoviePlayer 2.5–2.5.1. You can select and copy a movie clip and paste it elsewhere in the same movie or another movie. You can delete or replace part of a movie. You can delete and add tracks in a movie. You can set a movie's poster. When you save your edits, you can make a movie self-contained or dependent on other files.

This chapter also explained how to play audio CDs with your computer's CD-ROM drive. You can use the AppleCD Audio Player application to control playing with all the push-button controls you'd expect to find on a CD player, and to program playback in ways few CD players can match. To hear audio CD sound on your computer, you may have to set some options in the Monitors & Sound control panel or the Sound control panel. To use an external CD-ROM drive, you have to connect it to your computer with an audio patch cord. You can also use the control panels or the SimpleSound application together with the Audio Player application to record parts of CDs as sound files.

Finally, this chapter described how to watch video on a computer with video-input equipment, and how to capture still pictures or QuickTime movies from incoming video. You have to connect cables from the video equipment to your computer's video and audio ports. Then you can use the Apple Video Player application (if your computer has Apple video input) to watch and capture incoming video.

✦   ✦   ✦

Explore the Internet

The Internet is an amazing resource that's just become popular in the past few years. Using the Internet, you have access to an incredible variety of information and entertainment resources, from online newspapers and encyclopedias to the latest research data to stage and film reviews, and much more. Electronic mail (e-mail) connects people all around the world, bringing words from far away lands to your screen just seconds after they're sent. Mac OS 8–8.5 makes it easy to get on the Internet; it includes a setup assistant to get you connected easily and many applications that help you surf the Net.

Setting Up an Internet Connection

Before you can tap the wealth of information and services on the Internet, you need to set up your computer so that it can make an Internet connection. To assist you in configuring an Internet connection, Mac OS 8–8.5 includes a special program which is aptly named the Internet Setup Assistant. It leads you step-by-step through a series of decisions and questions to gather your Internet information, and it enters that information into the various control panels and applications that the Mac OS uses for Internet access. You'll find an alias to the Internet Setup Assistant in the Assistants folder on your startup disk. In Mac OS 7.6–7.6.1, you can set up an Internet connection using various control panels, as described later in this chapter in "Managing Internet Settings."

Getting started

You can use the Internet Setup Assistant any time you want to configure a new Internet connection. In Mac OS 8–8.1, you can also use this assistant to change an existing configuration. You automatically get an opportunity to use the Internet Setup Assistant when you first start your computer after installing Mac OS 8–8.5. At other times, you can double-click the Internet Setup Assistant's alias — or choose it from the Internet submenu of the Apple menu in Mac OS 8.5 — to begin the setup process. When you open the Internet Setup Assistant in Mac OS 8.5, it immediately asks you to confirm that you want to set up your computer to use the Internet. If you click the Yes button, the Internet Setup Assistant then asks whether you already have an Internet account. This decision point is where the Internet Setup Assistant begins in Mac OS 8–8.1. Figure 17-1 shows the windows where the Internet Setup Assistant asks whether you want to sign up for a new Internet account or set up an existing account.

Figure 17-1: Specify whether you want to configure a new or existing Internet account in Mac OS 8.5 (left) or Mac OS 8–8.1 (right).

Signing up for a new account

If you don't already have an Internet account, click No in Mac OS 8.5 or Register in Mac OS 8–8.1. Then the Internet Setup Assistant helps you get a new account with an *Internet Service Provider (ISP)*, which is the company that provides you with modem access to the Internet. The Internet Setup Assistant makes a toll-free call through your modem to a registration service and gives you the opportunity to sign up with an ISP. You'll need a credit card to use this service, and it's only available in the United States and Canada. Be aware that this service offers only a fraction of the ISPs that are doing business in metropolitan areas. For more options, check your Yellow Pages or the file named International Internet Access in the Internet Extras folder on the Mac OS 8.5 CD. Remember also that signing up with an ISP generally does not involve a long-term commitment. You can always switch to a different ISP if you find a deal you like better. However, if you change ISPs then you will probably have to change your e-mail address and have to notify all your e-mail correspondents of your new address. If you receive lots of e-mail, you will probably need to keep your old account open for a while so that you don't miss any e-mail from people who don't send to your new address right away.

Configuring an existing account

If you already have an Internet account with an ISP or via a network at work or school and you just need to set up Mac OS 8–8.5 for that account, click the Yes button (Mac OS 8.5) or the Update button (Mac OS 8–8.1) in the Internet Setup Assistant. You'll see an introduction that explains what you need to know to configure an Internet connection. Read the information and then click the right arrow (→) at the bottom of the Internet Setup Assistant window to add an Internet configuration.

In Mac OS 8–8.1, the next step is to tell the Assistant whether you want to add, modify, or remove an Internet configuration. The Assistant displays these three options. To add an Internet configuration, click "Add Internet configuration" and then click the right arrow (→) at the bottom of the window.

In Mac OS 8.5, you can only add a new Internet configuration using the Internet Configuration Assistant. Therefore the Assistant does not give you a choice of adding, modifying, or removing configurations.

You begin a new configuration in Mac OS 8–8.5 by giving the configuration a name. The name of your ISP is a good choice. If you're going to connect to an ISP via a modem or an ISDN modem (technically, an ISDN terminal adapter), select the Modem setting at the bottom of the window and continue at the next heading, "Setting Up a Modem Connection." If you have an Internet connection through a network, select the Network setting (Mac OS 8.5) or the LAN setting (Mac OS 8–8.1) and skip to the subsequent heading, "Setting Up a Network Connection." Note that a cable modem, despite its name, demands a network connection because the cable modem connects to your Mac's Ethernet network port. An ISDN router also connects via Ethernet and requires a network connection. Figure 17-2 shows the settings for a configuration name and type of connection.

Figure 17-2: Enter the name and type of connection in Mac OS 8.5 (left) or Mac OS 8–8.1 (right).

Setting up a modem connection

If you're setting up a connection to an ISP via modem, the Internet Setup Assistant next asks what kind of modem you're using. In Mac OS 8.5, choose your modem model from the Modem pop-up menu. In Mac OS 8–8.1, select your modem model in the scrolling list. Use the Port pop-up menu to choose the port to which your modem is connected (probably the modem port). You'll most likely want to set the Tone/Pulse option to Tone, which most phone lines in the United States and Canada use. Figure 17-3 shows the modem settings.

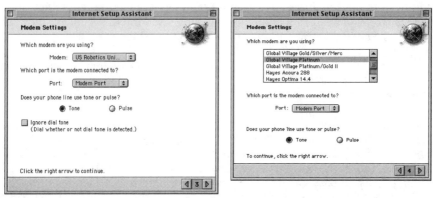

Figure 17-3: Enter your modem settings in Mac OS 8.5 (left) or Mac OS 8–8.1 (right).

The next step is especially important because it's where you enter the phone number for your ISP, your account name, and your password. Your account name is usually the same as the first part of your e-mail address. Figure 17-4 shows these settings.

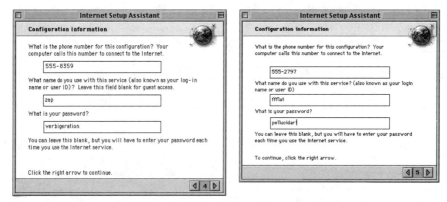

Figure 17-4: Enter your ISP account phone number, your name, and your password in Mac OS 8.5 (left) or Mac OS 8–8.1 (right).

BACKGROUNDER

Connecting via Modem and Network

You might reasonably think that if you connect to the Internet via modem, you should invariably select the Modem setting in the Internet Setup Assistant. In fact, you can also use a modem to connect to a local area network (LAN) that provides your Internet access. In this case, you must select the Network setting (Mac OS 8.5) or LAN setting (Mac OS 8–8.1). If you use a modem, how do you know which setting to select? If you use a modem to connect to an Internet Service Provider, select the Modem setting. If you use a modem to connect to a network at work, school, or other organization, and you get your Internet access via that network, select the Network or LAN setting.

On a technical level, each setting connects to the Internet using a different *protocol,* or language. The Modem setting uses PPP, the de facto standard protocol for dial-up connections to TCP/IP networks like the Web. The Network or LAN setting uses the ARAP protocol to make a dial-up connection to an AppleTalk network, and then uses the MacIP protocol to make a connection to the Internet over the AppleTalk network. For more information on configuring your computer for a remote connection to an AppleTalk network or the Internet, see Chapter 19.

In Mac OS 8.5, the Assistant next asks whether your computer must use a PPP Connect Script to establish a connection with your ISP. This script specifies a conversation your computer must have with the ISP's computer, in which the ISP's computer prompts your computer to send items of information in a prescribed order. Your ISP will probably provide a PPP Connect Script file if it requires one. If you select Yes in this step, you then get to choose a PPP Connect Script from a pop-up menu. This pop-up menu lists all the PPP Connect Script files in the PPP Connect Scripts folder inside your Extensions folder. This pop-up also has a Select Other choice, which displays a standard Open dialog box where you can select a PPP Connect Script from a different folder. If you select a PPP Connect Script file from outside the PPP Connect Scripts folder, the Assistant puts a copy of the file in the folder and actually chooses this copy.

Next, the Assistant asks whether you have been assigned your own permanent IP address, which is a numerical address such as 206.117.213.011 that identifies one machine on the Internet. Because you're connecting by modem, you probably don't have a permanent IP address; instead, your ISP assigns your computer an IP address dynamically, which is to say, temporarily, and only for the length of time you're connected. Don't confuse IP addresses, which identify machines, with e-mail addresses, which identify people. If you don't have a permanent IP address, select No and click the right arrow (→) to move on.

The remaining steps in configuring an Internet connection are the same for a modem connection and a network connection. If you aren't connecting to the Internet via a local network, skip the next heading, which describes the initial steps for setting up a network connection, and continue at the subsequent heading, "Finishing Setup," to finish setting up your Internet connection.

Setting up a network connection

If you have an Internet account at work, school, or other organization rather than through an ISP, your computer is probably connected to a local area network (LAN) such as Ethernet. You may also be able to connect to the Internet by calling a remote LAN via modem. In either case, your computer connects to the Internet via a local network, not through an ISP. You also connect via network if you have a cable modem.

Some of the steps for configuring a network connection to the Internet are different than for configuring an ISP connection. The first part of the configuration is the same, and is described under the heading "Getting Started" earlier in this section. When you come to the step where you indicate how you'll be connecting to the Internet, select the Network setting (Mac OS 8.5) or LAN setting (Mac OS 8–8.1) and forge on by clicking the right arrow (→) at the bottom of the window.

If your computer can connect to the Internet by calling a network via modem, the Assistant asks if you want to do this. Select No if your computer is wired directly to an Ethernet network, LocalTalk network, or other local network that provides your Internet access. Select Yes if your computer connects via modem to a local network located somewhere else. Click the right arrow (→) to continue.

Next, the Internet Setup Assistant may ask whether you've been assigned a permanent IP address such as 206.117.213.011. An IP address uniquely identifies your computer on the Internet. Because your computer is connected to a network, it may well have a permanent IP address. If so, select Yes and click the right arrow (→). The Assistant asks you to enter the numerical IP address that your network administrator gave you. Figure 17-5 shows the IP address setting.

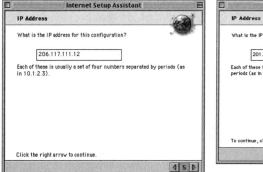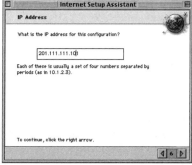

Figure 17-5: Enter your computer's IP address in Mac OS 8.5 (left) or Mac OS 8–8.1 (right).

After the Assistant asks for an IP address, it asks for a subnet mask and router address. You don't need to know what these settings mean — just enter the numbers exactly as your network administrator gives them to you. Figure 17-6 shows the subnet mask and router address settings.

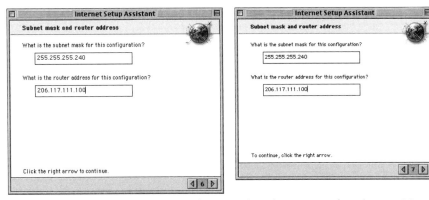

Figure 17-6: Enter the mysterious subnet mask and router numbers in Mac OS 8.5 (left) or Mac OS 8–8.1 (right).

Finishing setup

The remaining steps are the same for setting up a modem connection through an ISP or a local area network connection to the Internet. The next information you must supply is the addresses of your Domain Name Service (DNS) server. A DNS server converts the hard-to-remember numerical IP addresses such as 17.254.3.62 into something easier for humans to remember such as www.apple.com. Every ISP or local area network has a DNS server, and whenever you enter any kind of Internet address, the DNS server converts it into its numerical equivalent and sends the address on its way (and in the right direction, too). Your ISP or network administrator will probably give you the IP addresses of two DNS servers (primary and secondary). Enter these numerical addresses in the space provided, pressing the Return key after each address to separate them. You can skip the DNS addresses if your ISP or network supplies them automatically each time you connect. You can skip the host name for this configuration. Figure 17-7 shows the DNS settings.

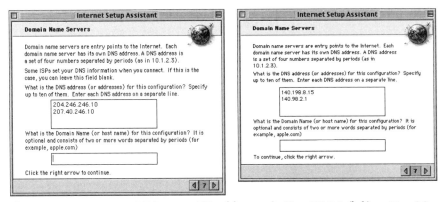

Figure 17-7: Enter your DNS servers' IP addresses in Mac OS 8.5 (left) or Mac OS 8–8.1 (right).

In the next step, the Internet Setup Assistant asks for the e-mail address and e-mail password that your ISP or network administrator has given you. In Mac OS 8.5, you can also enter a character or symbol that your e-mail program will use to mark text that you quote from an e-mail message in your reply to the message. The standard character for marking quotes in e-mail is a greater-than symbol (>). Figure 17-8 shows the e-mail address and password settings.

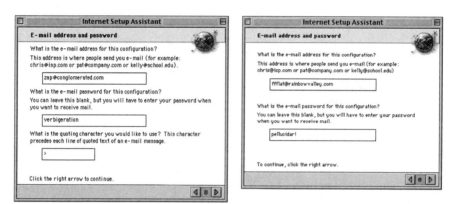

Figure 17-8: Enter your e-mail address and password in Mac OS 8.5 (left) or Mac OS 8–8.1 (right).

The next step asks for additional information about your e-mail account. You need to enter the e-mail account (sometimes called the POP account). This is different from your e-mail address in that it includes both your user name and the name of the mail server, as in zap@pop.conglomerated.com. You also need to enter the mail server name (also known as the SMTP host), as in mail.conglomerated.com. Figure 17-9 shows the e-mail account and mail server settings.

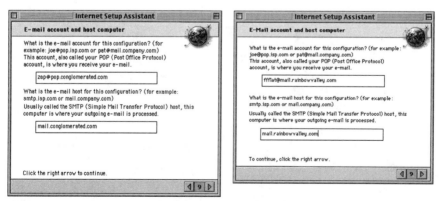

Figure 17-9: Enter your e-mail (POP) account and e-mail server (SMTP host) in Mac OS 8.5 (left) or Mac OS 8–8.1 (right).

Next, the Assistant asks you to specify the name of the host computer for newsgroups, which provides access to discussion groups on the Internet. The newsgroup host is also known as the Usenet host or NNTP (Network News Transfer Protocol) host. If you're connecting through an ISP, it probably has a newsgroup host whose name is the ISP's domain name preceded by the word "news," as in news.conglomerated.com. Figure 17-10 shows the newsgroup host setting.

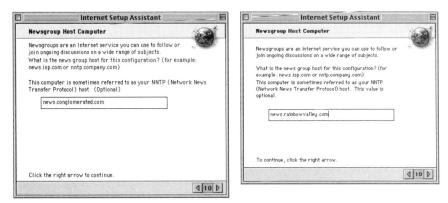

Figure 17-10: Enter your news server address in Mac OS 8.5 (left) or Mac OS 8–8.1 (right).

In Mac OS 8.5, the Assistant next asks whether your connection to the Internet goes through proxy servers. Your company, school, or organization may use proxy servers to provide security. If you select Yes, then the Assistant asks you to enter the host and port for each proxy server you use: HTTP (the Web), Gopher, FTP, or SOCKS. Don't worry about what these acronyms stand for. Just get this information from your network administrator.

The last step in setting up an Internet connection gives you an opportunity to review the settings you've entered before the Assistant puts them into effect. To review, click the Show Details button. If any of the settings are wrong, you can click the left arrow (←) to go back to the steps where you entered them, make corrections, and then click the right arrow (→) to get back to this step. To make the settings effective, click the Go Ahead button and wait a few minutes while the Assistant stores your settings in various control panels. You also have the option of clicking the Cancel button to quit the Internet Setup Assistant without making any of your settings effective. Figure 17-11 shows the last step in setting up an Internet connection.

After finishing the last step in the Internet Setup Assistant, you can make a connection in a variety of ways, as described later in "Making an Internet Connection."

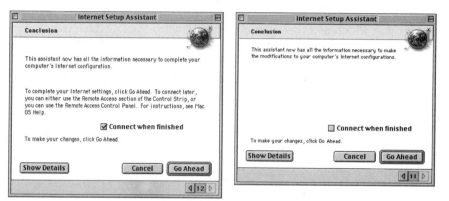

Figure 17-11: Decide whether to make the Internet configuration effective in Mac OS 8.5 (left) or Mac OS 8–8.1 (right).

Managing Internet Settings

Although the Internet Setup Assistant helps you set up a connection to the Internet in Mac OS 8–8.5, you may need to set additional options or change settings later. If you use Mac OS 7.6–7.6.1, which don't include the Internet Setup Assistant, you need some other means to set up an Internet connection. The Mac OS comes with an assortment of software for managing your Internet settings.

Adjusting network settings

When you connect your computer to the Internet, you are actually connecting it to a very large TCP/IP network. The Internet Setup Assistant gets basic network settings from you and places them in several control panels: TCP/IP, Modem, and Remote Access or PPP. You can work directly in these control panels to modify existing settings and to set additional options that the Internet Setup Assistant ignores. You can also use these control panels to set up an Internet connection from scratch. These control panels have these settings:

✦ **TCP/IP** has settings for the method of connecting to the Internet (such as PPP or Ethernet); your computer's permanent IP address, subnet mask, and router address if it has these; the DNS addresses; and the domain name.

✦ **Modem** has settings for the type of modem, the port it's connected to, and the type of phone line (tone or pulse). An additional option that you can't control via the Internet Setup Assistant is whether the modem makes audible dialing and connecting sounds.

✦ **Remote Access** or **PPP** has settings for your Internet account name, password, and phone number. If you use a PPP Connection Script, you set it here. Other options you can set here that you can't set with the Internet Setup Assistant include redialing of the phone number or an alternate number; connection reminders and provisions for automatic disconnection; whether to connect automatically when starting an Internet application; and more. If your computer has Mac OS 7.6–8.1, you may have both PPP and Remote Access control panels. If so, you use the PPP control panel to configure your Internet account. In this case, your version of Remote Access is used only for connecting to a remote AppleTalk network. Remote Access 3.0, which comes with Mac OS 8.5 and can be installed separately in earlier Mac OS versions, combines the functions of the PPP and older Remote Access control panels.

For detailed information on all these control panels, see Chapter 19.

Adjusting Internet application preferences

The variety of application programs that you use to get information and services on the Internet have many preference settings in common. For example, your e-mail application certainly needs to know your e-mail address, but so do your Web browser and the application you use to participate in newsgroups. The makers of many Internet applications have agreed to share common preference settings so that you don't have to enter or change them redundantly in each application. You set some of these common preferences when the Internet Setup Assistant is used. You set all the common preferences and many more using the Internet control panel in Mac OS 8.5 or the Internet Config program in Mac OS 7.6–8.1. The Internet control panel comes with Mac OS 8.5. Internet Config 1.3 comes with Mac OS 8–8.1 and can also be used with Mac OS 7.6–7.6.1. A later version, Internet Config 2.0, can be used with Mac OS 7.6–8.5 and is available free on the Internet from Stairways Software (http://www.stairways.com/ic/).

The Internet control panel and the Internet Config program store preference settings in the Internet Preferences file in the Preferences folder inside the System Folder. Your Internet applications may also let you change some of the same preference settings. For example, you can change your e-mail password in your e-mail application, the Internet control panel, or the Internet Config program. The most recent change takes precedence.

The Internet control panel

With Mac OS 8.5, you get the Internet control panel for changing common Internet preferences shared by many Internet applications. You can also use the Internet control panel to save all the current settings as a group, and you can choose a saved group that you want to be in effect. Figure 17-12 is an example of the Internet control panel.

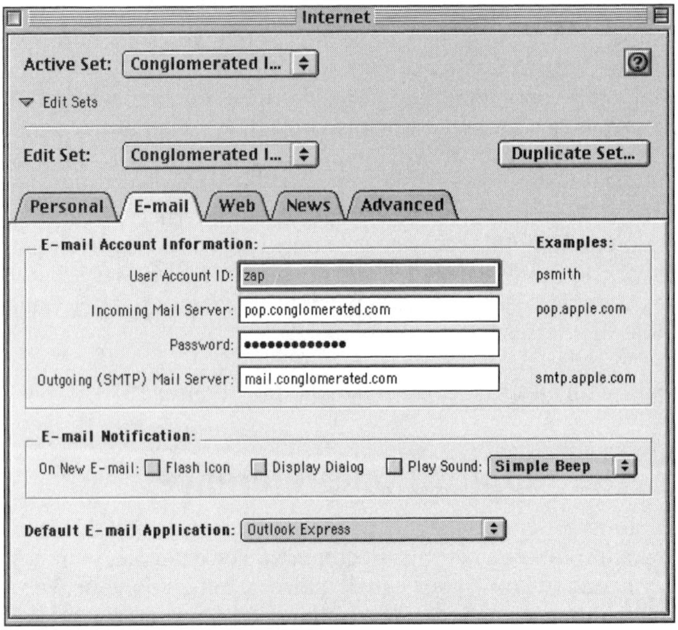

Figure 17-12: Use the Internet control panel to change shared Internet preferences in Mac OS 8.5.

Basic settings

The Internet control panel organizes preference settings by category. To see the settings for each category, click its tab in the control panel. The Internet control panel has four basic categories: Personal, E-mail, Web, and News. These categories have settings as follows:

✦ **Personal** has settings for your name, e-mail address, and organization. You can add information that you want displayed by a Finger server, such as your title, mailing address, and phone number. You can also enter the signature text you want added to the bottom of e-mail messages and newsgroup messages that you create.

✦ **E-mail** has settings for your account name, the server names for mail you receive (POP server) and send (SMTP server), and e-mail password. You can also select how you wish to be notified when you receive e-mail. In addition, you can choose a default e-mail application.

✦ **Web** has settings for home page, search page, and the folder for files you download. You can also set the color of linked text, whether it should be underlined, and the color of the background. In addition, you can choose a default Web browser.

✦ **News** has the name of your news server. In addition, you can select whether to connect to the news server as a guest or with a name and password that is set here. You can also choose your default newsgroup application.

Advanced settings

Besides the basic categories, the control panel has seven advanced categories that are normally hidden. To see them, choose User Mode from the Edit menu and select Advanced mode in the dialog box that appears. You can also select Administration mode, which reveals the same settings and lets you lock settings individually. When you select Advanced or Administration mode, an Advanced tab appears in the Internet control panel.

A scrolling list of seven categories appears on the left side of the control panel when you click the Advanced tab. Figure 17-13 shows one of the categories in the Advanced section of the Internet control panel.

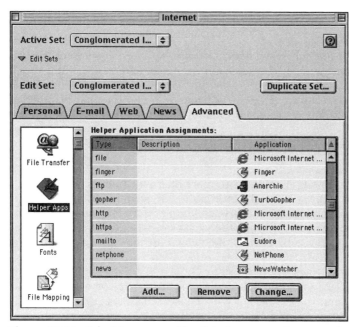

Figure 17-13: Select from a scrolling list of seven preference categories in the Advanced section of the Internet control panel.

The advanced categories have these settings:

✦ **File Transfer** has settings for the default FTP servers and an option to use passive mode for file transfers. Passive mode doesn't work with all FTP servers, but may be required if you connect through a *firewall,* which is part of a local area network designed to prevent Internet users from getting into the local network and to stop local network users from sending sensitive information out.

✦ **Helper Apps** assigns each type of URL to an application that can handle it. For example, "http" is assigned to a Web browser and "mailto" is assigned to an e-mail application.

✦ **Fonts** has settings for the font and size of text displayed in a list, displayed in a message, and printed in a message.

✦ **File Mapping** specifies which Mac applications open various types of Internet files. A table maps each type of Internet file to a Mac application that can open it. The type of file is determined by its file name extension, which is the last part of its name following a period.

✦ **Firewalls** has settings for a SOCKS firewall and for proxy servers for Web, Gopher, and FTP. These settings are required by some organizations to shield their local networks from intrusion by Internet users. You can also list domain names of servers that you do not want to access through a firewall.

✦ **Messages** specifies the character or symbol that marks quoted text in e-mail reply messages. You can also enter text that you want added at the top of outgoing e-mail and text that you want added at the top of outgoing newsgroup messages.

✦ **Hosts** specifies default servers for the following Internet services: Ph (finds e-mail addresses inside an organization), Finger (finds information about a specific user on the Internet), Whois (finds e-mail addresses on the Internet), Telnet (remote terminal), FTP (file transfer), Gopher (menu-based information retrieval), WAIS (query-based information retrieval), and LDAP server and search base.

Groups of settings

If you use your Internet applications with more than one Internet connection, you may need different settings for each connection. For example, you may need one group of settings when you connect through your personal ISP and another group of settings when you connect through the local area network at work. You can save groups of settings and switch between them using the Internet control panel.

To save the current settings as a new group, choose New Set from the File menu. To make a copy of the current group, click the Duplicate Set button or choose Duplicate Set from the File menu. To rename a group, choose Rename Set from the File menu. To delete a group, choose Delete Set from the File menu.

To switch groups, choose one from the Active Set pop-up menu at the top of the control panel.

Using Internet Config

With Mac OS 8–8.1, you get the Internet Config application for changing common Internet preferences shared by many Internet applications. Internet Config 1.3 comes with Mac OS 8–8.1 and can also be used with Mac OS 7.6–7.6.1. As mentioned earlier, Internet Config 2.0 is now available and can be used with Mac OS 7.6–8.5.

When you open Internet Config, it displays an Internet Preferences window that contains buttons for ten categories of settings. Clicking a category button displays a window in which you can change preference settings for that category. For example, to change your e-mail settings, click the Email button in the Internet Preferences window. This brings up the Email preferences window, where you can enter your e-mail address, account, password, and so on. Figure 17-14 shows the Internet Preferences window and the Email preferences window.

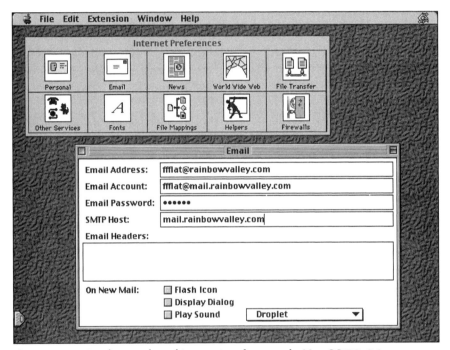

Figure 17-14: To change shared Internet preferences in Mac OS 7.6–8.1, use Internet Config.

Internet Config 1.3, which you get with Mac OS 8–8.1, does not let you save groups of Internet preference settings or switch between groups of settings. Internet Config 2.0 does let you work with groups of settings. You can duplicate, rename, delete, and switch groups of settings by choosing commands from the Sets menu.

You don't have to set all or even most of the Internet Config preferences at once. Set the ones you need now, and return to set more at another time. When you have set all of the Internet preferences you need for now, quit the Internet Config program, saving the changes you made when asked if you wish to do so.

Making an Internet Connection

Setting up your computer to connect to the Internet makes it ready to access e-mail, Web pages, and other Internet services. If you have a network connection to the Internet, you can access its services at any time by using the applications described in subsequent sections of this chapter. A network connection gives you full-time access to the Internet.

A modem connection generally does not give you full-time access to the Internet. When you want to use Internet services through a modem, you must make a connection to your ISP. You can make a manual connection or an automatic connection. When you finish using Internet services, you can disconnect from the ISP. You'll probably want to disconnect if your ISP charges for the amount of time you are connected or the phone company charges for the time you use the phone line. You'll have to disconnect if you need to use the phone line or the modem for something else.

Connecting manually

You can connect to your ISP manually through a modem with the Remote Access control panel or PPP control panel, whichever your computer has. If your computer has both Remote Access and PPP control panels, you use the PPP control panel to connect to your ISP. In this case, your version of Remote Access is used for connecting to a remote AppleTalk network. In addition, with Mac OS 8–8.5 you can use the Internet Dialer program to connect to an ISP.

Connecting with the Remote Access or PPP control panel

To make an Internet connection with the Remote Access control panel or the PPP control panel, all you need to do is open it, make sure that the information entered there is correct, and then click its Connect button. Your modem will dial your ISP and the control panel will negotiate a connection with your ISP by supplying your account name and password. When a message tells you the connection is OK, you can use an Internet application such as Netscape Navigator or Microsoft Internet Explorer (as described later in this chapter). Figure 17-15 shows the Remote Access and PPP control panels.

Connecting with the Internet Dialer

If you have Mac OS 8–8.1, you can use the Internet Dialer program to connect to your ISP for Internet access. The Internet Dialer has a Connect button for initiating a connection and a timer that shows how long you have been connected. Internet Dialer also has a pop-up menu that lists all the ISP accounts you have configured using the Internet Setup Assistant or the TCP/IP, Modem, and PPP control panels. You'll find an alias of the Internet Dialer in the Internet folder on the Mac OS 8–8.1 startup disk. Figure 17-16 shows the Internet Dialer window.

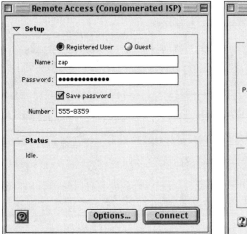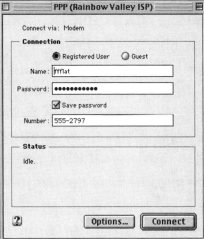

Figure 17-15: Manually connecting to the Internet with the Remote Access control panel (left) or PPP control panel (right).

Figure 17-16: Manually connecting to the Internet with the Internet Dialer in Mac OS 8–8.1.

For the Internet Dialer to use configurations that you have made directly in the TCP/IP, Modem, and PPP control panels, each of the three control panels must have a configuration with the same name. For example, if you have a configuration named Rainbow Valley in the PPP control panel, there must also be a configuration with that name in the Modem and the TCP/IP control panels. These naming requirements are taken care of automatically when you use the Internet Setup Assistant to configure an Internet connection.

Connecting automatically

You can have the Remote Access or the PPP control panel automatically dial and connect to the Internet whenever you open an application that requires an Internet connection. For example, when you open Netscape Navigator and it looks for the home Web page, Remote Access or PPP will dial the modem and connect to your ISP; then Navigator can go to the home Web page. To make automatic connections happen, you turn on the "Connect automatically when starting TCP/IP applications" option in the Options dialog box of the Remote Access or the PPP control panel. You get at this dialog box by clicking the Options button in the control panel. Then to see this option, click the Protocol tab and choose PPP from the pop-up menu in the Remote Access Options dialog box, or click the Connection tab in the PPP Options dialog box, as shown in Figure 17-17.

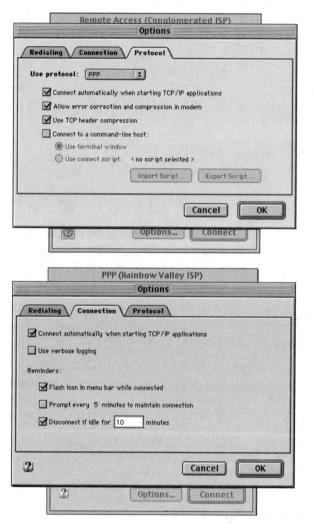

Figure 17-17:
Turn on automatic
Internet connection
in the Remote Access
control panel (top) or
the PPP Options control
panel (bottom).

Disconnecting

To disconnect from your ISP, click the Disconnect button in the Remote Access, the
PPP control panel, or the Internet Dialer program. After a moment, your modem will
hang up and the connection will end.

You can also set Remote Access control panel or the PPP control panel to
disconnect automatically. You can have it disconnect after a period of inactivity you
specify. In addition, you can have the control panel prompt you periodically with a
dialog box and disconnect if you fail to respond to the dialog box (because you
have left your computer and forgotten to disconnect manually). You set up these
options in the Connections section of the control panel's Options dialog box.

Sending and Receiving E-mail

Although not as flashy as the Web, electronic mail is the most popular reason people use the Internet. E-mail lets you communicate with people all over the world. Unlike regular mail, your correspondents can be reading your messages within minutes after you send them, no matter whether the recipients are across the street or halfway around the world.

Using Microsoft Outlook Express

Microsoft Outlook Express is set to be the default e-mail application in Mac OS 8.5. Outlook Express handles multiple Internet e-mail accounts. If you have more than one e-mail account, you can see mail from all of them in one place, organize all your mail in one set of folders, and use one unified address book. Another feature is the capability to set up rules that automatically process your mail. For example, you can set up rules that look at the sender of a message and label the message with a color, move it to a specific mail folder, and send a reply, all automatically.

SECRETS

Choosing an E-mail Application

If you use Mac OS 8–8.5, your Mac is preset to use a particular e-mail application, called the *default e-mail application,* but you can use another one instead. The default e-mail application is the one that opens when you double-click the Mail icon on the desktop. Choosing Mail from the Internet submenu of the Apple menu in Mac OS 8.5 also opens the default e-mail application.

The default e-mail application in Mac OS 8.5 is Microsoft Outlook Express; it's also available free on the Internet (http://www.microsoft.com/ie/mac/oe/) for separate installation in Mac OS 7.6–8.1. The default e-mail application in Mac OS 8–8.1 is Claris Emailer Lite. Besides the default e-mail application, you get Cyberdog with Mac OS 8; Netscape Navigator 3.01 with Mac OS 8–8.1; and America Online with most Macintosh computers. Cyberdog and the OpenDoc software it requires are both available for separate installation in Mac OS 7.6–7.6.1 and Mac OS 8.1–8.5 from Apple's Cyberdog Web site (http://cyberdog.apple.com). Navigator 3.01 or its successor, Communicator 4, is available for separate installation in Mac OS 7.6–8.5 from the Netscape Web site (http://www.netscape.com). Eudora is another popular e-mail program but it is not included with the Mac OS. A free basic edition, Eudora Lite, is available for the Mac OS from the Qualcomm Web site (http://eudora.qualcomm.com/eudoralight/).

If you don't want to use the default e-mail application, you can make another application the default. To change the default e-mail application in the Internet control panel, click the E-mail tab and use the Default E-mail Application pop-up menu. To change the default browser in Internet Config, click the Helpers button. In the Helpers window, select the "mailto" helper and click the Change button. In the Add Helper dialog box, click Choose Helper and select the e-mail application you want to use.

Outlook Express preferences

The first time you open Microsoft Outlook Express, it gives you the opportunity to import from an e-mail program that you used previously. If you want Outlook Express to import your mail, addresses, and settings from another e-mail program, click Yes. If you haven't used any other e-mail program or you don't want to import from another e-mail program, click No. In this case, Outlook Express picks up some of the e-mail settings that you made previously with the Internet Setup Assistant, the Internet control panel, or the Internet Config program. Whether you import from another e-mail program or not, Outlook Express displays its preference settings so that you can make any changes necessary, as shown in Figure 17-18.

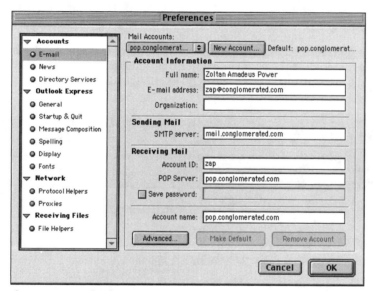

Figure 17-18: Check your e-mail settings in the Outlook Express Preferences dialog box.

The first time you open Outlook Express, it may change some of the settings that you made previously in the Internet Setup Assistant, the Internet control panel, or Internet Config program. It may clear the e-mail password, which is in the E-mail section of the Preferences dialog box. It also may change the newsgroup server setting (which is in the News section of the Preferences dialog box) to msnews.microsoft.com. Change these settings to your liking and click OK to dismiss the Preferences dialog box.

Outlook Express main window

The main Outlook Express window has buttons across the top, a list of mail folders on the left, and a list of messages and a message preview on the right. You can hide any of these windowpanes, except the list of messages, by clicking the small icons in the lower-left corner of the window or choosing from the View menu. Figure 17-19 is an example of the Outlook Express main window.

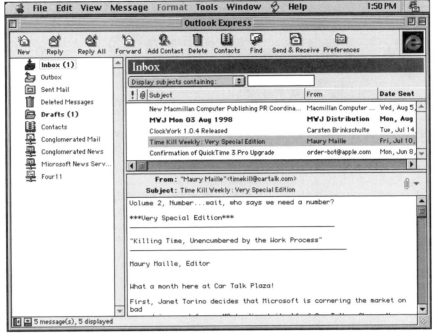

Figure 17-19: See a list of mail folders, a list of messages in the selected folder, and a preview of the selected message in Outlook Express.

To see a list of the messages in any folder, select it by clicking its icon on the left side of the window. Most people prefer to have mail sorted by Date or Subject. To see a preview of a listed message, select it by clicking it in the list. You can also open mail folders and messages in separate windows by double-clicking them.

You can sort the messages in a mail folder by clicking a column heading in the folder's list of messages. Option-click a column heading to sort in reverse order.

You can rearrange and resize the headings in a list of messages. To move a column left or right, drag its headings. To resize a column, drag the borderline of its heading. To add or remove columns, use the Columns submenu of the View menu.

Receiving mail

To get your mail, click the Send & Receive button at the top of the Outlook Express window or choose a command from the Send & Receive submenu of the Tools menu. A progress window appears to show messages being received. Received mail goes into the In Box. The number of unread messages appears in parentheses after the In Box (or other folder) name on the left side of the window, and unread messages are also listed in bold. Although you can read a message in the preview pane of the main Outlook Express window, you won't have to scroll as much if you open the message in its own window. To read a message in its own window, double-click it in the list of messages. Figure 17-20 shows an example of an e-mail message window.

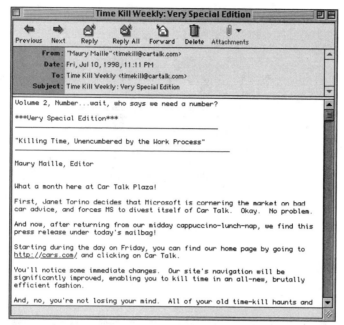

Figure 17-20: Read an e-mail message in its own window in Outlook Express.

The row of buttons atop the message window let you act on the message. Most of the buttons are self-explanatory. The Previous and Next buttons display the message that comes before or after the one you're reading. The Reply and Reply All buttons both create a new message, but Reply addresses the new message only to the sender while Reply All also addresses the new message to everyone else who received the original message.

You can adjust the amount of space used to display the message header below the buttons. Simply drag the border that separates the header from the body up or down.

If Outlook Express does not connect to your ISP and get your mail when you click the Send & Receive button or choose from the Send & Receive submenu, then you may not have set the Remote Access or the PPP control panel for automatic connection (as described in "Making an Internet Connection" earlier in this chapter). In this case, you must first make an Internet connection manually and then use the Send & Receive button or submenu.

After getting your mail, you need to disconnect from the Internet if you connect via modem. You can disconnect manually or set the Remote Access or the PPP control panel to disconnect automatically after a period of inactivity. Alternatively, you can use AppleScript to automate connecting, getting and sending mail, and disconnecting (as described in "Using AppleScript with Applications" in Chapter 23).

Replying to and sending mail

Clicking the Reply button in a message window brings up a new message window with the subject and the recipient already entered. If you select some text in the message window before you click Reply, Outlook Express copies the text into the new message window and normally marks all this quoted text with a > symbol at the beginning of each line. This is the standard e-mail convention for marking quoted text. Figure 17-21 is an example of the Outlook Express reply message window.

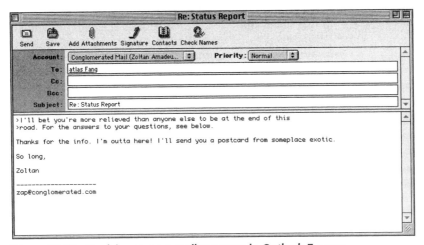

Figure 17-21: Replying to an e-mail message in Outlook Express.

After typing the text of your reply, click the Save button or the Send button. The Save button places the message in the Drafts folder. The Send button either sends the message immediately or places it in the Out Box depending on the setting of the option "Send messages immediately" in the General section of the Preferences dialog box.

To start an entirely new message, click the New button in the main Outlook Express window or choose Mail Message from the New submenu of the File menu. For a new message, you have to type a subject and specify one or more recipients in the spaces provided.

When you're ready to send all of your replies and new messages, click the Send & Receive button or choose a command from the Send & Receive submenu of the Tools menu. If Outlook Express does not connect to your ISP and send your mail, then you may not have set the Remote Access or the PPP control panel for automatic connection (see "Making an Internet Connection" earlier in this chapter). In this case, you must first make an Internet connection manually and then use the Send & Receive button or submenu. After Outlook Express sends your mail, you should disconnect from your ISP using the Remote Access or the PPP control panel. (See "Making an Internet Connection" earlier in this chapter for more information on modem connections.)

Using Claris Emailer Lite

Claris Emailer is a terrific e-mail program and a lite version is included with Mac OS 8–8.1. Actually, it's both a lite and an older version, as Emailer has since been updated to version 2.0. Emailer Lite handles only one Internet e-mail account, whereas the full version can get e-mail from any number of Internet, America Online, CompuServe, and Radiomail accounts. The real advantage of the full version is that if you have more than one e-mail account, you can manage all of your e-mail with one program and with one unified address book. You can also get all of your mail from all of your accounts with a single phone call. Another feature the full version sports that is missing in the lite version is the capability to set up Mail Actions, which automatically process your mail according to rules you set up. For example, you can set up a mail action that looks at the sender of a message and assigns the message a priority, files it in a specific mail folder, and sends a reply—all automatically.

Emailer setup

When you first open Claris Emailer Lite, you are presented with a personalization dialog box. Enter your name and, optionally, your company name. (You don't need a serial number.) Click the OK button to display Internet Service Entry dialog box. Figure 17-22 shows this dialog box.

If you've already entered your e-mail information in the Internet Setup Assistant or directly into Internet Config (as described earlier in this chapter), the information appears in this dialog box and all you need to do is enter the account name (usually the name of your Internet Service Provider). If you haven't entered your e-mail information in the Internet Setup Assistant or Internet Config, you'll need to enter the following information in Emailer's dialog box:

✦ **User name** is your name as you wish it to appear in the header of your e-mail messages. (It's usually better to put your real name in here, rather than a handle such as "Galactic Hero.")

✦ **Email address** is the address assigned to you by your ISP, in the form name@domain (for example, zap@conglomerated.com).

✦ **Email account** may be the same as your e-mail address or it may require a slightly different form of address. Your ISP will tell you what information goes here when you sign up for your Internet account.

✦ **Email password** is the secret password that you gave your ISP when you signed up. It's best to use some combination of letters and numbers, and you should make your password more than five characters long. (Don't use easily guessed passwords such as your name, your spouse's or kids' names, your dog's name, or the words "secret," "password," or any other obvious password.) You should also consider changing your password from time to time.

✦ **SMTP host** is the name of the incoming mail server machine at your ISP. This is usually the word "smtp" or "mail," followed by a period, and then followed by your ISP's domain name (as in "mail.conglomerated.com"). Again, your ISP should provide you with this information.

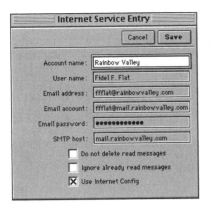

Figure 17-22: Set up your e-mail account in Emailer Lite's Internet Service dialog box.

When you've entered the required information, click the Save button. A dialog box appears that asks if you want to connect now to your ISP and pick up your mail. Unless there is some reason you don't want to get your mail, click the Yes button. Emailer will connect to your ISP (dialing the modem if necessary) and get your incoming mail, displaying it in the Browser window. Emailer can connect automatically through a modem only if you have set Remote Access or the PPP control panel to make automatic connections (as described in "Making an Internet Connection" earlier in this chapter). Figure 17-23 shows a sample Browser window with received mail.

As you can see, the Browser has four tabs, representing the In Box for received mail, the Out Box for mail you have written, the Filing Cabinet where you can store mail in folders you create, and the Address Book for keeping the e-mail addresses of your correspondents.

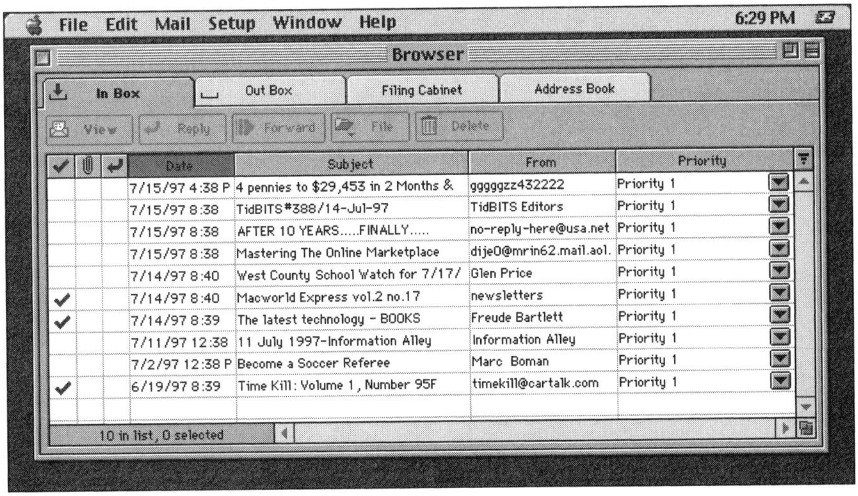

Figure 17-23: Viewing the list of received e-mail in Emailer Lite's In Box.

Receiving mail

To get your mail, choose Connect Now from the Mail menu. A dialog box appears with options for sending mail, receiving mail, or both. Make sure the Get option is turned on and click the Connect button to have Emailer retrieve your mail from your Internet mail server. The Connect Again command in the Mail menu repeats the mail connection without bringing up the dialog box again. If you connect to the Internet through a modem and have set the Remote Access or the PPP control panel for automatic connection, Emailer's Connect Now and Connect Again commands make an automatic Internet connection. If you haven't set the Remote Access or the PPP control panel for automatic connection, you have to connect to the Internet manually (as described earlier in this chapter) before using Emailer's Connect Now or Connect Again commands. Either way, you'll have to disconnect manually after receiving your mail, because the version of Emailer included with the Mac OS can't tell Remote Access or PPP to disconnect. Emailer 2.0v3 can disconnect automatically. Alternatively, you can use AppleScript to automate connecting, getting and sending mail, and disconnecting with any version of Emailer (as described in "Using AppleScript with Applications" in Chapter 23).

Received mail appears in the Emailer In Box. To sort messages by any of the columns, click the column name. Most people prefer to have mail sorted by Subject or Date. To read a message, double-click it in the In Box or select it and click the View button. Figure 17-24 is an example of an e-mail message window.

In the message window is a row of buttons that let you act on the message; a header where the sender's name and e-mail address is displayed; and the message body. The buttons are self-explanatory, except for the File button, which is a pop-up menu that lets you put the message into any of your mail folders. The other button that might puzzle you is the button with a plus (+) sign next to the sender's e-mail address. Clicking this button lets you easily add the sender to Emailer's address book.

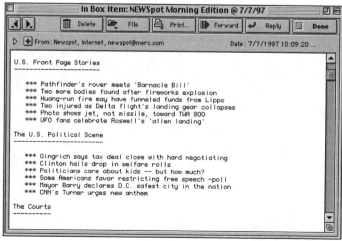

Figure 17-24: Viewing an e-mail message in Emailer Lite.

Emailer has keyboard equivalents for many of its buttons. To see the keyboard equivalents displayed on the buttons, hold down the ⌘ key for a few seconds.

Replying to and sending mail

Clicking the Reply button in a message window brings up a new message window with the subject and the recipient already entered. If you select some text in the message window before you click Reply, Emailer copies the text into the new message window with a > symbol at the beginning of each line. This is the standard e-mail convention for marking quoted text. Figure 17-25 shows an example of the Emailer reply message window.

Type in your message and then click the Save button or press the Enter key to put the message in your Out Box for later transmission. You can then continue working your way through your received messages, replying as needed.

To start an entirely new message, choose New from the Mail menu, or use its keyboard equivalent, ⌘-N. For a new message, you have to type a subject and specify one or more recipients in the spaces provided.

When you're ready to send all of your replies and new messages, choose Connect Now from the Mail menu. In the Connect Now Setup dialog box, be sure the Send option is turned on before clicking the Connect button. If this option was turned on the last time you connected to your Internet mail server, you can use Emailer's Connect Again command instead of its Connect Now command. If you connect to the Internet through a modem, you must either make a manual connection or set the Remote Access or the PPP control panel to make automatic connections before using Emailer's Connect Now or Connect Again commands. Furthermore, you must manually disconnect from the Internet after Emailer has sent your outgoing mail. (See "Making an Internet Connection" earlier in this chapter for more information on modem connections.)

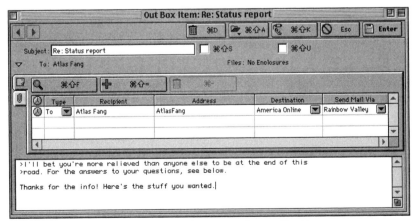

Figure 17-25: Replying to an e-mail message in Emailer Lite.

Using Cyberdog

You can use Cyberdog to work with your e-mail, although it isn't as full-featured as Outlook Express or Emailer. Setup is easy, however. Just choose Mail & News Setup from the Mail/News menu. If you've previously entered your mail information in the Internet Setup Assistant or Internet Config, it will automatically be set up in Cyberdog. Both Cyberdog and the OpenDoc software it requires come with Mac OS 7.6–8 and are available separately through Apple's Cyberdog Web site (http://cyberdog.apple. com). Figure 17-26 shows Cyberdog's Mail & News Setup dialog box with the preferences provided by Internet Config.

If you haven't already set your mail preferences in the Internet Setup Assistant or Internet Config, you can enter them in this dialog box. Select the Mail icon in the scrolling list on the left and enter your e-mail address and SMTP host (mail server) information. You can set preferences in the other areas of this dialog box by clicking the other icons, but all that Cyberdog requires is the address and host. Feel free to explore the rest of the icons, especially the Handlers icon, which you can use to automatically process your incoming mail. Also check out the Mail Trays icon, which allows you to set up multiple mail accounts if you have them. Click the OK button when you're done setting preferences.

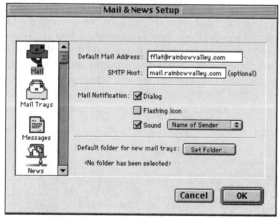

Figure 17-26: Setting your mail preferences in Cyberdog.

Checking mail

To get your mail, choose Check Mail in the Mail/News menu and enter your mail password when prompted to do so. Cyberdog connects, gets your incoming mail, and displays a list of received messages in a Mail Trays window. Double-click a listed message to open it. Like any other address in Cyberdog, you store your mail addresses in the Notebook and you can drag e-mail addresses from incoming messages to the Notebook.

Creating and sending mail

To make a new message, choose New Message from the Mail/News menu. A dialog box appears, asking which letterhead you want to use. If you choose one of the supplied letterheads that includes a picture, be aware that recipients will only be able to see the picture if they, too, are using Cyberdog; most other people will get an annoying file enclosure with your message. For maximum readability, it's best to choose the "Blank Document – Plain Text" letterhead. In the message form that appears, fill in the Subject line and then press the Tab key to get to the To: field. You can type in the recipient's address or you can click the Addresses button on the form to use an address from your Notebook. When you're done writing your message, click the Send Now button to dispatch your mail immediately or the Send Later button to schedule delivery for a later time.

Browsing the World Wide Web

The World Wide Web is the 800-pound gorilla that shook the Internet into prominence with the public, so much so that many people think that the Web is the Internet. Not so; the Web is just one of the many services available over the Internet. It happens to be the most interesting because it lets you easily access text and pictures from places all over the world. You access the Web with a program called a *Web browser,* and at least one Web browser is installed with Mac OS 8–8.5. You can open this Web browser by double-clicking the Browse the Internet icon on the desktop or by choosing it from the Internet Access submenu of the Apple menu in Mac OS 8.5.

To use the Web, you first need to know a bit of the terminology. Web browser programs display information in *Web pages,* which can contain text, pictures, animation, and even audio and video clips. On a Web page, there is usually underlined text known as *links* or *hyperlinks.* Clicking one of these links takes you to another Web page. The machines that store all of this information and that serve it to you on request are called *Web servers.* The intriguing thing about hyperlinks is that the Web page that they take you to can be another page on that same server or a page on any other Web server on the planet. So, it's possible to click your way around the world and not even know it!

Using Netscape Navigator or Internet Explorer

When Netscape Navigator or Internet Explorer opens, it displays a browser window and goes to a Web page that has been previously designated as the *home page.* With Mac OS 8–8.5, the home page is initially set to the Apple Live page (http://livepage. apple.com). Figure 17-27 shows the Apple Live home page in Navigator 4.05, and Figure 17-28 shows the same page in Internet Explorer 4.01.

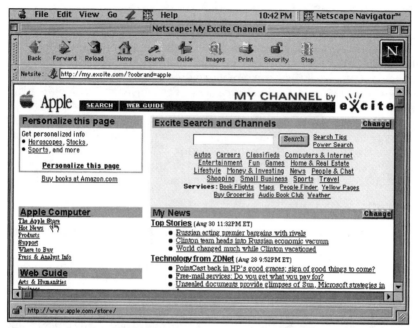

Figure 17-27: Browsing the Web with Netscape Navigator (*Web page courtesy of Apple Computer, Inc.*).

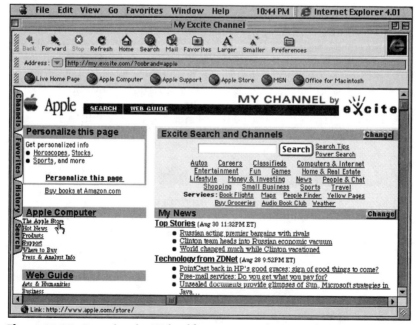

Figure 17-28: Browsing the Web with Internet Explorer (*Web page courtesy of Apple Computer, Inc.*).

SECRETS

Choosing a Web Browser

Although your Mac is preset to use a particular Web browser, called the *default browser*, you can use another or even a couple others. The default Web browser is the one that opens when you open Browse the Internet by double-clicking its icon on the desktop or choosing it from the Apple menu. Which browser is the default browser on your Mac depends on the Mac OS version and its history. In general, Internet Explorer is the default browser for Macs with Mac OS 8.1–8.5, and Netscape Navigator is the default browser for Macs with Mac OS 8. However, Navigator is usually the default browser on an older Mac that has been upgraded from Mac OS 8 or earlier to Mac OS 8.1–8.5. Your Mac may not follow these generalizations, regardless of the Mac OS version, if you have installed a replacement Web browser.

The easiest way to use a different Web browser is to install it and open it by double-clicking its icon. But you can also change the default browser using the Internet control panel that comes with Mac OS 8.5 or the Internet Config program that comes with Mac OS 7.6–8.1.

To change the default browser in the Internet control panel, click the Web tab and use the Default Web Browser pop-up menu. Technical note: this pop-up menu changes the assignment of the "http" helper application, but not the "https" or "file" helpers. To change these as well, click the Advanced tab and then click the Helper Apps icon on the left side of the control panel. In the scrolling list of helper application assignments, select one that is still assigned to the old default browser and click the Change button. In the Edit Helper dialog box, click the Select button and select the new default browser. Repeat this procedure for all other helper assignments that need updating. (If you don't see the Advanced tab in the control panel, choose User Mode from the Edit menu and select Advanced mode.)

To change the default browser in Internet Config, click the Helpers button. In the Helpers window, select any helper that is still assigned to the old default Web browser and click the Change button. In the Add Helper dialog box, click Choose Helper and select the new browser. Repeat this procedure for all the helper assignments that need updating.

If you have a Mac OS 8.5 CD, you can install Netscape Navigator by doing a custom installation of the Mac OS. In the last step of the Install Mac OS 8.5 program, click the Customize button, select the Internet Access module, choose Customized Installation from its pop-up menu, and select the Netscape Navigator component. You could also install Navigator from a Mac OS 8.1 CD or Internet Explorer from a Mac OS 8 CD, but the browser versions on these CDs are out of date. The latest version of Internet Explorer is available from the Microsoft Web site (http://www.microsoft.com/ie/Mac/), and the latest version of Netscape Navigator is available from the Netscape Web site (http://www.netscape.com).

Besides the mainstream browsers, Cyberdog is included for optional installation with Mac OS 8. It's also available free from Apple's Cyberdog Web site (http://cyberdog.apple.com) for installation with Mac OS 7.6–8.5. Cyberdog requires Apple's OpenDoc software, which is included with Mac OS 8–8.1 and is available free from the OpenDoc Web site (http://opendoc.apple.com) for Mac OS 7.6–7.6.1 and 8.5.

You can change the home page setting to a different Web page or to no page at all. In Internet Explorer, you set the home page in the Home/Search section of the Preferences dialog box (accessed from the Edit menu). In Navigator 4, you set the home page in the Navigator section of the Preferences dialog box (accessed from the Edit menu). In Navigator 3, you set the home page in the Appearance section of the General Preferences dialog box (accessed from the Options menu).

From the home page, you can go to other places on the Web by clicking one of the underlined links on the page. Graphics on the page can also be links. To determine if something is a link on a Web page, move the mouse over the area; if the pointer turns from an arrow into a pointing hand, it's a link.

Clicking links is a good way to get used to browsing the Web, but you should also know how to use the browser's other navigation features, which include toolbar buttons, location or address box, Bookmarks or Favorites menu, Go menu, and multiple browser windows. Internet Explorer 4 also has Favorites buttons and a tabbed Explorer bar.

Toolbar buttons

The toolbar at the top of the browser window contains a set of buttons that you can use to navigate the Web. These navigation buttons help you move from one page to the next, move to your home page, or get around on the Web page that you're currently viewing. Each browser has a slightly different complement of navigation buttons; the buttons may even vary from one version of a browser to the next. Here's what the most common toolbar buttons do:

✦ **Back** takes you to the page you were just viewing. You can keep clicking the Back button to go to previous pages. This is useful when you're browsing and want to get back to a place that you want to read again. In Internet Explorer 4 and Navigator 4, a pop-up menu of recently visited Web pages appears when you click the Back button and hold the mouse button.

✦ **Forward** returns you to a subsequent page after you've used the Back button. Most times, this button is grayed out (which means it's unavailable) because you are at the front of your browsing session.

✦ **Stop** tells the browser to stop loading a page and display as much of the page as it has loaded.

✦ **Home** takes you back to the home page—the page that loads automatically when the browser starts up.

✦ **Reload** or **Refresh** tells the browser to get the current Web page from the Internet again and redisplay it. This reloading is useful with pages that have constantly changing content, such as online news.

✦ **Search** takes you to a page that helps you locate Web pages that contain information that you want to see. The browsers installed with Mac OS 8–8.5

go to an Apple-sponsored search page that uses the Excite search engine. For another way to search the Web in Mac OS 8.5, see "Searching the Internet" later in this chapter.

✦ **Favorites** displays a window of links to Web pages that you have added to your Favorites list in Internet Explorer.

✦ **Larger** and **Smaller** increase and decrease the size of text in the Internet Explorer window.

✦ **Images** tells Navigator to reload all the graphics on a page (unlike Reload, which reloads the entire page). People with slow connections seem to use this the most, because they don't always let all the graphics from a page finish loading before they press the Stop button.

✦ **Print** prints the current Web page on the printer you have selected. Be aware that many Web pages are wider or taller than real sheets of paper, so one Web page may take any number of pages to print out. You may be able to make a Web page fit on one sheet of paper by using the Page Setup command to change the page orientation or reduction factor.

As useful as the toolbar buttons are, they take up a fair amount of space. You can make them smaller by eliminating their icons and displaying just their text labels. In Internet Explorer, you change the toolbar settings in the Browser Display section of the Preferences dialog box. In Navigator, you change the toolbar settings in the Appearance section of the Preferences dialog box (Navigator 4) or the General Preferences dialog box (Navigator 3). You can alternately hide and show the toolbar altogether by choosing from the View menu in Internet Explorer or Navigator 4 or from the Options menu in Navigator 3.

BACKGROUNDER

Understanding URLs

You've probably seen Web addresses in advertisements—they're the ones that look like http://www.paramount.com. These Web addresses are one example of a type of address called a *URL*, which stands for Universal Resource Locator. The nice part about URLs is that they can point you directly to any Web page, or any file on an FTP site. In fact, there's a URL for everything you can get to on the Internet.

A URL begins with a code that specifies a kind of Internet location. The remainder of the URL specifies a location in terms of a server or account name, a *domain name* (the name of the organization or company that owns the server), and, in some cases, a file directory. In the http://www.paramount.com example, the http:// part specifies that the address is for a Web page, the www portion is the name of a computer that serves Web pages, and paramount.com is the domain name.

Address or location box

Below the toolbar buttons is a box labeled Address, Netsite, or Location. You can use it to identify the URL of the current page and to enter the URL of a page you want to see. To go to another page whose URL you know, click the old URL to select it, type the new URL, and press the Return key. You can also select all or part of the URL and copy it to the Clipboard.

When you type a URL in the address box or location box, you don't have to type in the entire URL of a site you want to visit. You can omit the http:// part of the URL, because the browser assumes it and puts it in for you when you press the Enter or Return key. In fact, you don't even have to type in the www. or .com parts of a URL that has them. Because most of the places on the Web start with www. and end with .com, if you type a one-word URL in the location box, the browser adds www. to the beginning and .com to the end. For example, if you type *apple* into the location box and press Enter or Return, you'll end up at http://www.apple.com, the main Apple Web site.

Bookmarks or Favorite menu

Rather than remembering the URL for a page, you can add a *bookmark* for it to the Favorites menu in Internet Explorer or the Bookmarks menu in Navigator. A bookmark keeps track of the URL and the name of a Web page.

To create a bookmark for the current Web page, choose Add Bookmark from the Bookmarks menu or Add Page to Favorites from the Favorites menu. The browser adds the name of the page to the bottom of the menu. You can go back to that Web page later by choosing its name from the Bookmarks menu or Favorites menu.

Go menu

The Go menu keeps a list of the recently visited pages in the current browsing session. To go back to a page, choose it from the Go menu.

Internet Explorer keeps a record of pages that you have visited, including pages from previous browsing sessions. To see this list, choose History from the Go menu. You can revisit a page by double-clicking it on the list. The number of pages that Internet Explorer remembers is set in the Advanced section of the Preferences dialog box.

Opening multiple browser windows

You can have more than one browser window open at a time. This is useful because sometimes you want to read one page while another page loads from the Internet. Browser windows are independent, and you can have as many Web pages open as the browser program has the memory to handle. To open another browser window, choose New Window (New Web Browser in Navigator 3) from the File menu. If you regularly keep many browser windows open, it's a good idea to increase the browser program's memory size by 2,000K or more with the Finder's Get Info command (see "Adjusting Application Memory Use" in the next chapter).

Using Cyberdog

Apple's Cyberdog offers a decidedly different way to browse the Web. Unlike Internet Explorer and Netscape Navigator, you don't invariably see a Web browser window when you open Cyberdog. What you see are the unique contents of a Cyberdog document, which can include *cyberbuttons* that you click to go to Web sites, one or more Web browsers displaying live Internet pages, notebooks that list favorite Web sites, your e-mail, and other Internet items. In addition to Internet items, a Cyberdog document can contain ordinary contents such as text, graphics, movies, and sound. Of course, no one document contains all these elements, but you can combine them freely in any document. Figure 17-29 is an example of a Cyberdog document that contains cyberbuttons, a Web browser, and a notebook that lists favorite Web sites, as well as some text and graphics.

Cyberdog is not a conventional application. It is a collection of OpenDoc plug-in software components that you can mix and match any way you like in a document. Unfortunately, Apple has decided not to develop Cyberdog beyond version 2.0, which has started to get long of tooth compared to recent versions of Navigator and Internet Explorer. That doesn't mean that you can't take advantage of Cyberdog in its current incarnation, but don't expect its Web browser to get any better than it is.

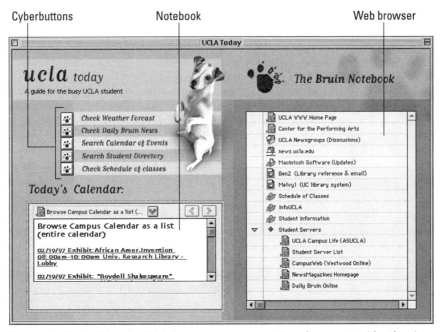

Figure 17-29: A Cyberdog Web browser can appear in a document with other items.

You can create Cyberdog documents by double-clicking the Cyberdog DocBuilder stationery pad, which is found in the Samples & Tools folder inside the Cyberdog 2.0 folder. When you open the Cyberdog DocBuilder stationery pad, you get an empty Cyberdog document. Content is added to it as content is added to any OpenDoc document, by dragging in Cyberdog objects (cyberbuttons, a Web browser, and so on) or other OpenDoc objects (text, graphics, and so on). For more information on working with OpenDoc documents, see "OpenDoc Compound Documents" in Chapter 24.

Cyberdog's Web browser

Although Cyberdog as a whole is unconventional, browsing the Web with it isn't too much different from using a conventional application such as Navigator or Internet Explorer. One difference is that you use a Cyberdog notebook instead of a Bookmarks or Favorites menu to keep track of your favorite Internet locations. Each entry in a Cyberdog notebook consists of an address icon and a name. A notebook can be in a window by itself or it can be embedded in a larger document. Figure 17-30 is an example of a Cyberdog notebook in a window by itself (review Figure 17-29 for an example of a notebook in a larger document).

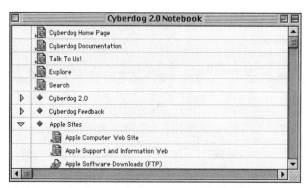

Figure 17-30: Keep favorite Internet locations in a Cyberdog notebook.

You go to a Web page listed in a Cyberdog notebook by double-clicking the address icon of that page. Cyberdog displays the page in a separate Web browser window.

You can also have Cyberdog go to a Web page and display it in a separate browser window by clicking a cyberbutton or by choosing Connect To from the Cyberdog menu and typing a URL in the resulting dialog box. Cyberdog's Web browser has a number of other navigation features. They include the current page's address icon, navigation buttons, and a location box. Figure 17-31 shows the navigation features in a Cyberdog Web browser.

Address button
for current page   Location box   History button   Web page   Forward and
                                                                     Backward buttons

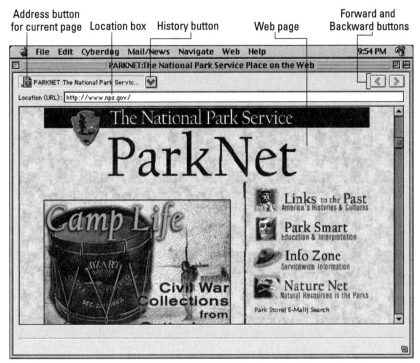

Figure 17-31: Cyberdog's Web browser provides several navigation features.

Current address icon

In Cyberdog, you can drag the address icon of the current Web page from the upper-left corner of a browser window to a notebook, making it easy to keep track of places you like. If you prefer, you can add the page location to your notebook by choosing Add Window to Notebook from the Cyberdog menu. This is especially useful if you happen to have more than one notebook open because a dialog box appears in which you can choose the notebook to use. Figure 17-32 shows the Add to Notebook dialog box.

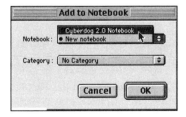

Figure 17-32: Choose a Cyberdog notebook for the current Web page's address.

Navigation buttons

Here's how the Cyberdog navigation buttons work:

✦ **History**, which is labeled with a large down arrow (↓), keeps a running log of the pages that you've visited in the current surfing session. It displays a pop-up menu that lets you easily return to a prior page.

✦ **Back**, which is labeled with a large left arrow (←), brings you back to the page you were last viewing.

✦ **Forward**, which is labeled with a large right arrow (→), returns you to the page you came from if you've used the Back button.

Location box

The location box at the top of a Cyberdog Web browser tells you the URL of the page you're currently viewing. You can also use the location box to go to a different URL. Simply type the URL in the location box and press the Return key.

Using Connect To

The simple Connect To application takes you to any Internet address whose URL you know, automatically using the appropriate Internet application. Connect To is listed in the Apple menu in Mac OS 8–8.1 and the Internet submenu of the Apple menu in Mac OS 8.5. When you choose Connect To, it displays a dialog box where you enter a URL. Connect To then routes your request to an application that handles that kind of URL. For example, if you enter a Web URL (that is, a URL beginning with http://), Connect To tells Finder to open your default Web browser (or switch to it, if it's already open), and then tells the browser to open the Web page at the URL. If you enter an e-mail URL (that is, a URL beginning with mailto:), Connect To has Finder open (or switch to) your default e-mail program and then sends the URL to the e-mail program, which enters it in the address field of a new message.

Connect To determines which application to use for each kind of URL by looking at the preferences set in the Helper Apps section of the Internet control panel or the Helpers section of the Internet Config program. These preferences are preset during the installation of Mac OS 8–8.5, but you can change them at any time (see "Managing Internet Settings" earlier in this chapter).

Searching the Internet

As mentioned previously, you can search for specific information on the Web by clicking the Search button at the top of a browser window in Netscape Navigator or Microsoft Internet Explorer. This button takes you to one of many Internet search sites, which are also known as *search engines*. You can go to another search site by typing its URL in the address box or location box in the Web browser window. Here are the URLs of several popular Web search sites:

✦ Yahoo! — http://www.yahoo.com

✦ Excite — http://www.excite.com

✦ InfoSeek — http://infoseek.com

✦ HotBot — http://www.hotbot.com

✦ Lycos — http://www.lycos.com

✦ AltaVista — http://www.altavista.digital.com

Each Internet search site has its own unique index of the Web, so an identical search at each site could produce different results. It stands to reason the most comprehensive search would entail using several of the search sites. In fact, there are Web sites such as the Search-It-All site (http://www.search-it-all.com) that enable you to do this.

In Mac OS 8.5, you can conduct a comprehensive search of the Web with the Sherlock program. After opening the Sherlock program (by choosing it from the Apple menu), click the Search Internet tab at the top of its window. In the space provided, type words that you expect to be on the Web pages that you want to find. Then in the scrolling list, select the search sites that you want to use. Click the Search button to begin. The Sherlock program sends your search request to each of the search sites you selected and waits for the results from them. Figure 17-33 is an example of a Web search using the Search Internet section of the Sherlock program.

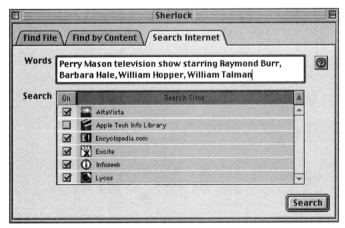

Figure 17-33: Search the Web with multiple search engines using the Sherlock program in Mac OS 8.5.

The Sherlock program begins displaying search results as soon as one of the search sites returns them. As other search sites return their results, the Sherlock program merges them in its Items Found window. For each Web page that matches your search request, the Items Found window lists the name, address, and relevance. You can sort the list by clicking a column heading in the Items Found window. To sort in reverse order, click the triangular sort direction indicator at the right end of the column headings. If you select one of the listed items, a summary appears at the bottom of the Items Found window. To see the whole page in your Web browser, double-click its name in the Found Items window. Figure 17-34 is an example of an Items Found window for a Web search.

If the Sherlock program does not connect to your ISP when you click the Search button, then you may not have set the Remote Access or the PPP control panel for automatic connection. In this case, you must first make an Internet connection and then connect the Search button. (See "Making an Internet Connection" earlier in this chapter for more information.)

Storing Internet Locations

When you see a Web page or a link that you want to keep track of, you can add it to the Bookmarks or Favorites menu in Netscape Navigator or Microsoft Internet Explorer. You can also drag a link to the Scrapbook or to a text document to put its URL there. Later, you can drag a URL from a text document or the Scrapbook to a Web browser window to see the Web page at that location.

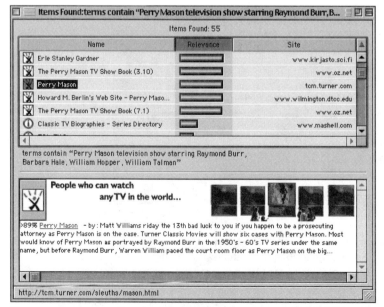

Figure 17-34: A search using all search engines may take a while.

You can also keep track of Internet locations in Mac OS 8.5 by dragging URLs to the desktop, a folder, or a disk. The Finder creates an Internet location file, which points to the URL you dragged. When you open an Internet location file, your Web browser or other Internet application opens and connects to the URL specified by the document.

You can make Internet location files for several types of locations on the Internet or your local area network, and each type of location file will have a unique icon. Figure 17-35 shows examples of several kinds of location files.

Figure 17-35: Each type of location file has a unique icon in Mac OS 8.5.

You can create these kinds of location files:

✦ Web page location such as http://www.conglomerated.com

✦ E-mail address such as mailto:zap@conglomerated.com

✦ Newsgroup location such as news:news.conglomerated.com

✦ FTP location such as ftp://ftp.conglomerated.com

✦ AppleShare file server location such as afp:/at/Silver Server:White Zone

✦ AppleTalk network zone such as at://White Zone

✦ File location such as file:///Mac%20OS%20HD/Web%20Pages/default.html

Sharing Your Own Web Site

Ever wanted to host your own Web site? Mac OS 8–8.5 have a Web server built in. The Web Sharing control panel is a snap to set up and use and lets you put a Web site on the Internet or on your company's intranet in about a minute (not counting the time it takes you to actually create your Web pages). There are, however, some limitations.

A Web server needs a fixed IP address and name so that people can point their browser to the Web site. If you connect to the Internet by modem, your ISP assigns your computer a temporary IP address, also called a dynamic address, which isn't very useful for a Web server. Because a dynamic address changes every time you connect to the Internet other people won't be able to find the address of your Web server. But if your computer happens to have a fixed IP address, which is likely if you have a network connect to the Internet, then you can take advantage of Web Sharing to make Web pages and files on your computer available to any other computer with a Web browser and an Internet connection. (Other computers connecting to your Web site do not need fixed IP addresses.)

Because Web Sharing is intended for personal use, it's not especially high-powered. On the one hand, you shouldn't try to use Web Sharing to host a Web site getting thousands of hits per day. On the other hand, it's perfect for sharing information within your company with your coworkers. And it can even run CGIs (Common Gateway Interfaces), which are scripts (usually written in AppleScript or UserLand Frontier) that can do things such as take the output from a Web form and send it to a database like FileMaker Pro.

You use the Web Sharing control panel to specify which folder contains your Web pages and to specify which of those pages is your site's home page. You also use the control panel to select the type of security you want and to start or stop Web sharing. Figure 17-36 shows the Web Sharing control panel.

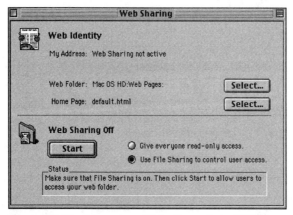

Figure 17-36: Set up your Web site and start Web sharing in the Web Sharing control panel.

In the control panel, you use the first of two buttons labeled Select to specify the folder that contains your Web pages. Initially, this is set to the Web Pages folder on the startup disk. You use the second Select button to bring up a dialog box that lists the Web pages in that folder and you select one to be your Web site's home page. Figure 17-37 shows the dialog box in which you select a home page.

Figure 17-37: Choosing your home page.

In the home page dialog box, you can click the None button (instead of selecting a home page and clicking the Select button). This turns on an interesting feature called Personal NetFinder. When Personal NetFinder is active, visitors to your Web site don't see a regular home page; instead, they see a listing of the files and folders that are found in the Web Pages folder (similar to the list view of a folder window). Figure 17-38 is a sample of a Personal NetFinder listing as viewed in Netscape Navigator.

After specifying the folder that contains your Web pages and selecting a home page (or not), all you need to do to get your server on the air is to click the Start button. You can also use the two radio buttons to the right of the Start button to allow all users read-only access, or to have Web Sharing apply the security and require passwords that you've set up using the Users & Groups control panel (as described in "Identifying Who Can Access Your Shared Items" in Chapter 21).

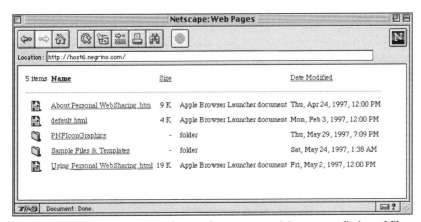

Figure 17-38: If your Web site has no home page, visitors see a listing of files that are found in your Web Pages folder.

When Web Sharing is on, your Web site's address appears in the Web Sharing control panel next to the heading My Address. Your Web site has a numeric IP address such as http://192.0.0.2. Depending on the type of Internet connection you have, your Web site may also have a name address such as http://host6.conglomerated.com. Give this name or number to people who want to connect to your Web site so that they can type the name into their Web browsers.

If your network only assigns numeric IP addresses, put a note on your home page telling people who connect to add a bookmark for your page so that they don't have to type in those numbers again.

Participating in Newsgroups

Besides e-mail and the Web, there's another part of the Internet that is called Usenet. You can think of Usenet as a worldwide bulletin board system, where people from everywhere can post messages and join discussions about subjects that interest them. Each subject is called a *newsgroup*. There are more than 25,000 newsgroups covering virtually every subject you can imagine. To find a newsgroup that interests you, you have to know a little about the structure of newsgroup names. A newsgroup name has several parts separated by periods. The first part specifies the general subject, the next part narrows the subject, and subsequent parts narrow the subject still further. Table 17-1 shows the most common top-level newsgroup names and Table 17-2 shows examples of full newsgroup names.

Using Outlook Express to read news

You can find the newsgroup of your dreams using a variety of programs. In addition to sending and receiving e-mail, Microsoft Outlook Express can read and post messages to newsgroups. Outlook Express lists news servers among the folders in the left pane of the main window. Click a news server to see a list of available newsgroups in the right pane of the main window. The first time you do this, don't be surprised if it takes several minutes to retrieve all the newsgroup names from the news server. Outlook Express remembers the newsgroup names, so the next time you click the same news server the names appear right away. You can check for new newsgroups by choosing Get New Newsgroups from the View menu.

Table 17-1 Common Top-Level Newsgroup Names	
Identifier	*Included Subjects*
biz	Business
comp	Computers

Identifier	Included Subjects
news	News and other topical information
rec	Recreational hobbies and arts
sci	Scientific
soc	Social
talk	Debates
misc	Miscellaneous subjects
alt	Subjects that don't fit into one of the other "official" categories

Table 17-2
Sample Full Newsgroup Names

Newsgroup Name	Subject
alt.fan.gill-anderson	The pictures are out there
comp.sys.lang.java	Java programming language
rec.arts.music.folk	Folk music and musicians
sci.nanotech	Nanotechnology discussions

You can scroll through groups to find the ones that interest you. When you see a likely group, you can subscribe to it to make it easier to find again. To subscribe to a newsgroup, select it and choose Subscribe from the Tools menu. After subscribing to all of the groups that look good to you, choose Subscribed Only from the View menu to list only your groups. To see all groups, choose Subscribed Only again so there is no check mark next to it in the View menu.

To see a list of messages in a newsgroup, double-click its title. The list of messages appears in the top pane of a new window. If no messages are listed, click the More button at the top of the window. Select a listed message to see a preview of it in the bottom pane of the same window. You can also open the message in its own window by double-clicking its title in the list. If there are replies to a message, you can see them by clicking the disclosure triangle next to the original message title.

If you wish to reply to a message and join the discussion, click the Reply To Newsgroup button above the list of messages, and type your message in the new message form that appears. Click the Post button to send your message.

Using other news clients

Besides Outlook Express, you can use Netscape Navigator 3 or Netscape Communicator 4 to read and post Usenet messages. Navigator 3 is installed with Mac OS 8 and Communicator is available from the Netscape Web site (http://www.netscape. com). Note that Navigator 4 does not include a newsgroup reader; the newsgroup reader and Navigator 4 are part of the Communicator 4 package. You can also read and post newsgroup messages with Cyberdog. There are also several other Usenet client programs available.

The best news newsgroup client of them all is NewsWatcher, a free program that you can get from various Internet locations (see "Where to Get Utility Software" in Chapter 26). NewsWatcher has many tools to make subscribing to newsgroups, as well as reading and replying to messages, easy. It is much more flexible than the other programs. If you get serious about Usenet, be sure to check out NewsWatcher.

Summary

After reading this chapter you know how to set up an Internet connection using the Internet Setup Assistant program that comes with Mac OS 8–8.5. You can adjust the settings that govern the network connection to the Internet using the TCP/IP, Modem, and Remote Access or PPP control panels. You can set common preferences for your Internet applications using the Internet control panel that comes with Mac OS 8.5 or the Internet Config program that comes with Mac OS 7.6–8.1.

You know how to connect to and disconnect from the Internet. While connected, you can send and receive e-mail with Microsoft Outlook Express, Claris Emailer, Cyberdog, or another e-mail program. You know how to browse the Web with Microsoft Internet Explorer, Netscape Navigator, or Cyberdog. You can use the Connect To program to get to any Internet location whose URL you know. You know how to search the Web using the Search Internet section of the Sherlock program in Mac OS 8.5. In addition, you know how to set up your own Web site with the Web Sharing control panel. Finally, you know how to participate in Usenet newsgroup discussions.

✦   ✦   ✦

Beyond the Basics of the Mac OS

Manage Your Memory

If you never open more than one program at a time and don't care about your computer's performance or effectiveness (not to mention your own), you can ignore the topic of memory management. But to get the most from your computer, you must pay attention to how you use its memory.

This chapter explains how to find out the amount of memory each open program is using. It tells you how to adjust the amount of memory your application programs use, and how to reduce the amount of memory the Mac OS uses. This chapter also describes several ways to increase the amount of memory available for opening programs.

Gauging Memory Use

Computers use memory like a large company might use office space (though on a very different time scale). Just as each department needs office space, each computer program needs a memory partition. Departments come in all sizes and so do computer programs. Over the years a company may eliminate some departments and use their space for new ones. Similar events take place on a computer but in a much shorter time. In a matter of hours, you may quit some programs and use their memory space to open others. Figure 18-1 diagrams how programs share a computer's memory space at one point in time.

To use your computer's memory most effectively, you need to know the total memory available, which programs are open, how much memory they use, and how much memory is currently unused. You also need to know roughly how much memory each program uses, because you may have to quit one or more open programs to make space for another one that you want to open.

BACKGROUNDER

Memory Compared with Hard Disk Space

Note that memory management does not involve disk space. The amount of disk space reported available at the top of your hard disk's window indicates how much space you have to store programs and documents when they are not open. When you open a program, the Mac OS allocates some memory space for the program, copies part of the program into that memory space from disk, and starts running the part copied into memory. Programs usually require much less memory space than they do disk space because the entire program file is not generally loaded into memory all at once. Rather, a program's memory space contains just the portion of the program that you need now.

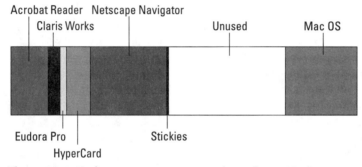

Figure 18-1: Each open program gets a piece of your Mac's memory.

About This Computer

For information on the condition of your Mac's memory, switch to the Finder and choose About This Computer from the Apple menu. The Finder displays a window that reports the total amount of memory installed in your computer and the largest amount available for opening another program. It also graphs the amount allocated to and currently used by the Mac OS and each open program. In Mac OS 7.6–7.6.1, the About This Computer Window refers to the Mac OS as System Software. Figure 18-2 is an example of the About This Computer window in Mac OS 8.5.

To learn the exact amount the Mac OS or an open program is using at the moment, turn on Balloon Help and point at the item's memory-use bar in the About This Computer window.

The About This Computer window reports the size of the largest unused block of memory. There may be other unused blocks as well, each smaller than the largest block. This condition, known as *fragmented memory,* can make it difficult to open a large program. You'll find techniques for recognizing fragmented memory and dealing with it in "Adjusting Application Memory Use" later in this chapter.

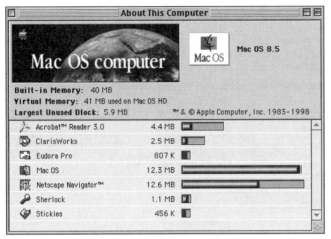

Figure 18-2: Gauging memory usage in the About This Computer window.

What's more, the Mac OS may not report every bit of memory that's in use. For example, built-in video uses 40K to 600K on various computer models but some versions of the Finder do not include that amount in the Mac OS size. There may be an additional discrepancy of several K (kilobytes) due to rounding errors.

Memory-mapping utilities

For a more precise report of memory use than you get in the Finder's About This Computer window, use a utility such as Memory Mapper from Jintek (http://www.street-logic.com/freeware.html#memory). It shows not only how much memory each open application uses, but where the applications are in relation to each other and to blocks of unused memory. Figure 18-3 is an example of Memory Mapper's window, although the graph it displays is color-coded to the list of programs and is much easier to decipher on a color monitor than in this black-and-white reproduction.

You don't see one number for Mac OS size in the Memory Mapper window. Instead of reporting an aggregate amount as in the About This Computer window, Memory Mapper breaks out Mac OS memory use into several individual items, including:

✦ **High Memory**, which is used for video, sound, and disk cache

✦ **Finder**

✦ **Desktop PrintMonitor, File Sharing, QuickTime, Speech Recognition,** and other system extensions that are actually programs open in the background

✦ **System Heap**, which is used for fonts, icons, sounds, and other system resources

✦ **Low Memory Globals,** which is used for many system parameters

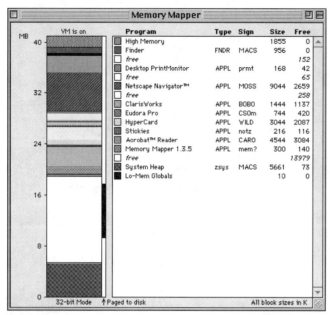

Figure 18-3: Checking memory use with Memory Mapper.

Adjusting Application Memory Use

Each program that you open gets a piece of memory called a *memory partition* for its exclusive use. This section tells you how to change the size of an application's memory partition with the Finder's Get Info command, increasing the partition size to help the application perform better or decreasing the size so that you can open additional programs. This section also tells you how to avoid fragmenting unused memory as you quit some programs to free memory for opening others, and how to fix memory fragmentation if it does happen.

Application memory size

You can change how much memory an application program gets by setting the memory sizes in its Info window, which the Finder's Get Info command displays, or with the AppSizer utility program (described in Chapter 26). You must quit an open application before changing its memory-size setting. If an application is open, its Info window shows the memory-size settings but won't let you change them. You can't ever change the memory size of some kinds of programs such as desk accessories. If a program's size is permanently set, its Info window doesn't show any memory sizes. Figure 18-4 shows sample Info windows of an application that is not open.

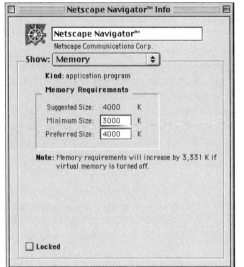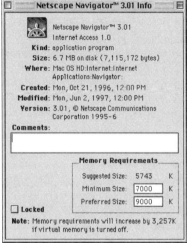

Figure 18-4: Use the Get Info command to set memory sizes for an application in Mac OS 8.5 (left) or Mac OS 7.6–8.1 (right).

Memory information is displayed in a separate section of a program's Info window in Mac OS 8.5. To see a program's memory information when its Info window is closed, select the program and choose Memory from the Get Info submenu of the File menu. The Get Info submenu also appears in a program's contextual menu. To see memory information in an open Info window, choose Memory from the pop-up menu near the top of the window.

In Mac OS 7.6–8.1, memory information appears at the bottom of a program's Info window. To see a program's memory information, select the program and choose Get Info from the File menu. The Get Info command also appears in the program's contextual menu in Mac OS 8–8.1.

Suggested, Minimum, and Preferred sizes

An application's Info window shows three memory sizes: Suggested, Minimum, and Preferred. The system won't open a program unless there is a block of available memory at least as large as the Minimum size. The system allocates more memory, if available, but never more than the Preferred size. The Suggested size, which you can't change, is the amount of memory the program's developer recommends for standard program performance.

Setting the Preferred size higher than the Suggested size may improve performance or enable you to open more documents or larger documents. Setting the Preferred size below the suggested size usually has the opposite effect. For example, setting HyperCard's Preferred size below the Suggested size reduces the number of stacks that you can have open simultaneously, limits your access to painting tools and scripting, and prevents opening some stacks altogether.

CAUTION

Going Below the Minimum

Every application has a memory size that's not listed in its Info window. This fourth memory size, which is set by the program developer, specifies the least amount of memory in which a program will work without crashing. Most programs use this safe minimum size for the initial setting of the Minimum size in the Info window. Setting the Minimum size lower than the safe minimum may cause the program to crash. For example, HyperCard 2.3 does not work properly if you set its Minimum size below Apple's recommended minimum of 800K. The Finder warns you when you close an Info window if you have set the Minimum size lower than the safe minimum recommended by the developer.

You can see the safe minimum size with a resource-editing program such as Apple's ResEdit. Use ResEdit to open the application's SIZE -1 resource. The minimum size listed there is the application's safe minimum size in bytes; divide by 1024 for the size in K (kilobytes). ResEdit is available from Apple's Software Updates library (http://www.apple.com/swupdates/).

Some programs require more memory with Mac OS 8–8.5 than with Mac OS 7.6–7.6.1. If a program refuses to open after you upgrade to Mac OS 8–8.5, try increasing its minimum memory size by 200K or 300K and opening it again.

Virtual memory's effect

A note at the bottom of some Info windows advises that turning on virtual memory changes the memory requirements. This note appears in the Info window of a program that is designed to allow the Mac OS to use part of the program's file on disk as if it were additional memory. All programs optimized for the PowerPC processor and some other programs are designed this way. This type of program requires less memory when virtual memory is turned on or the RAM Doubler utility software is installed and turned on (as described in the section "Increasing Total Memory" later in this chapter).

Memory fragmentation

As you open and quit a series of programs, the unused portion of your computer's memory tends to become fragmented into several noncontiguous blocks. You may find yourself unable to open a program because it needs a memory partition bigger than the biggest unused block (the Largest Unused Block amount displayed in the About This Computer window). The total of all unused blocks may be large enough to open the program, but the Mac OS cannot consolidate fragmented memory nor open a program in multiple blocks of memory. It's like looking for a parallel parking space on a street with several half spaces between parked cars. A small car wouldn't fit in any of the spaces, but if you could put the half spaces together you'd have enough room to park a truck. Figure 18-5 illustrates fragmented memory (compare Figure 18-5 to Figure 18-1).

QUICK TIPS

Is Your Memory Fragmented?

To check for memory fragmentation, add up the memory sizes of all the open programs and the Mac OS as listed in the About This Computer window. (Mac OS is called System Software in Mac OS 7.6–7.6.1.) Then subtract the total from the total memory reported in the About This Computer window. Also subtract 300K to 600K (depending on monitor resolution and number of colors) if your computer doesn't have dedicated video memory known as VRAM (Video Random Access Memory). In this case, your computer uses its main memory, sometimes called DRAM (Dynamic Random Access Memory), for the screen image. Examples of Macs that do this include a Power Mac 6100, 7100, or 8100 with a monitor connected to the system board video port.

If the number you come up with is substantially less than the largest unused block, your unused memory is probably fragmented into two or more blocks.

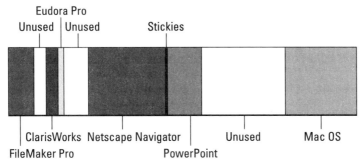

Figure 18-5: Opening and quitting programs haphazardly may fragment unused memory.

Avoiding fragmented memory

You can avoid memory fragmentation by planning the order in which you open and quit programs. First, open the programs you're least likely to quit and then open the programs that are the most expendable in your work session, starting with the most important of them and finishing with the least important. When you need more memory to open another program, quit the most recently opened program. If that doesn't free enough memory, quit the next most recently opened program, and so on. This method frees up a contiguous block of memory. Quitting programs helter-skelter leads to memory fragmentation.

QUICK TIPS

Arranging Startup Items for Optimal Memory Use

If you open several application programs during startup, you may have to quit some of them later to free memory for opening another. Naturally, you want to quit the applications least important to you. You free the most memory by quitting the applications opened last during startup. To make that easy, rename the items in your Startup Items folder so that the most important application comes first alphabetically, the next most important comes second, and so on. One way to do that is by putting a sequence number (01, 02, 03, and so on) at the beginning of the startup item name. This trick works only for ordering items of the same kind — aliases, application programs, control panels, documents, and so forth — because the Finder opens all of one kind of an item before opening any of another kind.

The Finder sometimes hastens memory fragmentation in low-memory situations. If you try to open an application that needs more memory than is available, the Finder suggests quitting all programs with no open windows — or the largest open program, if all have open windows. Accepting the Finder's suggestion can fragment memory. To avoid memory fragmentation, you must quit programs in the reverse of the order in which they were opened.

Fixing fragmented memory

To consolidate fragmented memory, quit all open programs and then open them again. This method isn't completely foolproof. You may have a program that doesn't release all of its memory when you quit it. This error is called a *memory leak*. A program that makes use of shared library extensions may also leave memory fragmented after you quit it, in this case because the shared library continues to occupy memory after the program has quit. Restarting your computer fixes fragmentation and may reduce the amount of memory used by the Mac OS as well.

If you don't want to restart or even quit all open applications, you can use the Memory Mapper utility to identify the applications that are open between blocks of unused memory and quit only those applications to consolidate memory. You can actually send a Quit message from Memory Mapper to any open program. To do that, select the program in Memory Mapper's window and choose Send Quit Event from the File menu.

Adjusting Mac OS Memory Usage

The Mac OS gives itself a big memory partition when you start your computer, shown by the length of the bar labeled Mac OS in the About This Computer window. This section explains how you can reduce the size of the Mac OS by disabling marginally useful system extensions and control panels, turning off expendable system options, reducing the disk cache, and reducing or eliminating a RAM disk.

Minimum Mac OS size

Just how small can the Mac OS be? You can reduce its memory size to the minimum by pressing Shift while restarting your computer. Look for the message "Extensions Off" (Mac OS 8.5) or "Extensions Disabled" (Mac OS 7.6–8.1) during startup. It confirms that you have suppressed loading of all items in the Extensions folder, Control Panels folder, and System Folder that would increase the Mac OS memory size. You have also bypassed opening items in the Startup Items folder, forced virtual memory off, and prevented file sharing from starting.

None of these changes persist when you restart without pressing Shift. To make changes stick, you must remove items from the special folders and change settings in the Memory and other control panels.

Startup items

Many of those lovely little icons that march across your screen during startup are chewing up memory as they go. They're not alone. Lots of other startup software that doesn't display icons also increases the Mac OS memory partition.

Many items identified as system extensions in a list view of the Extensions folder or System Folder increase the Mac OS memory size during startup. So do some other types of items besides extensions. But some items in the Extensions folder do not increase memory size. Chooser extensions for printers (LaserWriter, StyleWriter, ImageWriter, and so on), communications tools, MNPLinkTool documents, Finder Help, and the PrintMonitor application fall into this category.

Control panels that display an icon at the bottom of the screen during startup (or offer the option of doing so) have system extensions built in and most of them increase the Mac OS memory size. Control panels that don't display startup icons generally don't increase the Mac OS memory size, though there are exceptions such as Easy Access.

The easiest way to manage extensions and control panels is with the Extensions Manager control panel (see "Managing Startup Items" in Chapter 10). There are also commercial alternatives that provide more information and control than Extensions Manager. For example, Conflict Catcher from Casady & Greene, Inc. (408-484-9228, http://www.casadyg.com) tells you how much memory each startup item uses and when it was installed.

The key to adjusting memory size is to compare the Mac OS memory size before and after removing an item and weigh the potential memory savings against the benefit the item provides. It's a trial-and-error process unless you have Conflict Catcher or another utility that can determine the memory sizes of startup items.

To see the effect of removing startup items, you have to restart the computer.

Expendable options

You can reduce the Mac OS memory size by turning off a handful of system options that you might not be using. For example, if you're not using file sharing, you can recover 200K to 300K by turning it off in the File Sharing control panel (Mac OS 8–8.5) or the Sharing Setup Control panel (Mac OS 7.6–7.6.1). If you're not using speech recognition, turn it off in the Speech control panel. You can also save some memory by turning off AppleTalk in the Chooser.

Disk cache

A portion of the Mac OS memory partition always goes to the disk cache, which improves system performance by storing recently used information from the disk in memory. When the information is needed again, it can be copied from memory instead of from disk. Copying from memory is much faster than copying from disk.

You can use the Memory control panel to adjust the amount of memory allocated for the disk cache. Be aware that setting the disk cache very low will degrade performance in many applications, particularly the Mac OS 8–8.5 Finder. The usual rule of thumb is to set the disk cache to 32K times the amount of your computer built-in memory in MB (megabytes). Virtual memory and RAM Doubler don't count in this calculation, but a RAM disk does. For example, if your computer has 32MB of built-in memory, the standard disk cache size would be 1,024K ($32 \times 32 = 1,024$). If your computer has 48MB of built-in memory and 16MB RAM disk, the standard disk cache size would also be 1,024K ($32 \times (48 - 16) = 1,024$). Figure 18-6 shows examples of the disk cache setting in the Memory control panel.

Changing disk cache size in Mac OS 8.5

To change the disk cache size in Mac OS 8.5, select the Custom Setting option at the top of the Memory control panel. When you do this, an alert appears warning you not to change the cache size unless you know what you're doing. Click the Custom button in this alert box to proceed. You can now change the cache size by clicking up (↑) and down (↓) arrows at the top of the Memory control panel. The minimum disk cache size is 128K in Mac OS 8.5.

You can set the disk cache size according to the rule of thumb described previously by selecting the Default Setting option at the top of the Memory control panel in Mac OS 8.5.

Changing disk cache size in Mac OS 7.6–8.1

To change the disk cache size in Mac OS 7.6–8.1, click the up (↑) and down (↓) arrows at the top of the Memory control panel. The minimum disk cache size is 96K in Mac OS 7.6–8.1.

You can set the disk cache according to the rule of thumb described previously by clicking the Use Defaults button at the bottom of the Memory control panel.

SECRETS

Disk Cache and IIsi or IIci Performance

If you have a Mac IIsi, and you set the number of colors or grays for a monitor attached to the built-in video port to four or more, you can improve system performance by setting the disk cache to 768K. Then the disk cache and the built-in video circuitry together use all the memory that's soldered to the main circuit board. This forces the Mac OS and your programs into the part of memory found in the four SIMM sockets, which may help the programs run much faster than they would if they shared the soldered-on memory with the built-in video circuitry.

The same trick works on a Mac IIci with four 256K SIMMs installed in the four sockets nearest the disk drive. If the IIci has larger SIMMs in those four sockets, you would have to set the disk cache size higher to achieve the performance increase. For example, on a IIci with four 1MB SIMMs in the sockets nearest the disk drive, you would need to set the disk cache to 3,328K (3.25MB). A setting this high is wasteful unless the other four SIMMs were each 8MB or larger.

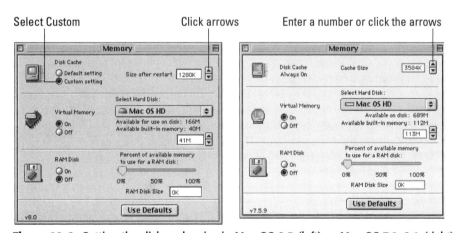

Figure 18-6: Setting the disk cache size in Mac OS 8.5 (left) or Mac OS 7.6–8.1 (right).

RAM disk

While the disk cache is always on and the Mac OS manages it automatically, you can use another option in the Memory control panel to dedicate more memory to speeding up disk-related tasks. The RAM Disk option uses part of your computer's memory as if it were a hard disk. This disk is called a *RAM disk* because it exists in the computer's *RAM (Random Access Memory)*, which is also known as built-in memory. You determine the size of the RAM disk by setting the amount of memory used by it. This amount is added to the Mac OS size in the About This Computer window. Figure 18-7 shows the RAM Disk option in the Memory control panel.

Turn on RAM disk

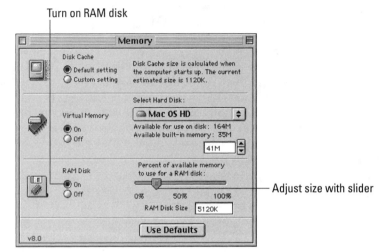

Adjust size with slider

Figure 18-7: Setting up a RAM disk.

When you restart after turning on the RAM Disk option, the Mac OS creates a disk whose contents are stored in the computer's high-speed memory, not on a relatively slow, mechanical disk mechanism. A RAM disk has an icon that appears on the desktop, and you manipulate folders and files on a RAM disk the same as on any other disk. A RAM disk works much faster than a hard disk, but does not store items permanently.

The RAM Disk option is not available on all computers. If it is available on your computer, your Memory control panel will include it. If the RAM Disk option disappears from the Memory control panel after upgrading the Mac OS, try restarting the computer with the Shift key held down. Then restart again, and the RAM Disk option may reappear.

The RAM Disk option is dimmed if your computer does not have enough unused memory for the minimum RAM disk size. The minimum size for the RAM Disk option is 448K in Mac OS 7.6–7.6.1 and 480K in Mac OS 8–8.5.

RAM disk permanence

The contents of a RAM disk are preserved when you restart most Macs. This is true even if you use the emergency restart keys (⌘-Control-power button) or the Reset button that some Mac models have.

Macintosh G3 models, however, do not preserve a RAM disk across a restart. The Grackle memory controller chip in these models doesn't reliably maintain the contents of memory during a restart. The Grackle chip enables the G3 models to use SDRAM memory, which provides higher performance but is more volatile than the fast-page mode memory used on older Mac models.

You lose the contents of a RAM disk when you shut down your computer or after a power failure, unless your computer is a PowerBook. To preserve a RAM disk under these conditions on a PowerBook, you must turn on the Save on Shut Down option in the Memory control panel. During shutdown of a PowerBook with this option turned on, Mac OS 7.6–8.5 saves the RAM disk's contents in a file in the Preferences folder and uses that to restore the RAM disk the next time you start up. In the event of a power failure on a PowerBook with a depleted battery, Mac OS 7.6–8.5 will restore the RAM disk to its state as of the last time that you shut down.

You can make a RAM disk as persistent on a desktop Mac as it is on a PowerBook. Install John Rethorst's free utility John's RAM Disk Backup to have your RAM disk automatically backed up during shutdown and restored on startup. The ramBunctious shareware alternative to the Memory control panel's RAM Disk option can also preserve the contents of a RAM disk. These utilities are described in Chapter 26.

Resizing or removing a RAM disk

To resize or remove a RAM disk, first copy the files that you want to save from it to another disk. Then drag everything from the RAM disk to the Trash and empty the Trash. Finally, use the Memory control panel to turn the RAM disk off or change its size. Restart your computer to make the changes take effect.

RAM disk alternatives

Instead of creating a RAM disk with the Memory control panel, you can use a shareware application such as ramBunctious, which is described in Chapter 26.

The advantage to creating a RAM disk with an application is that you don't have to restart the computer to remove the RAM disk and recover the memory it used. The disadvantage to creating a RAM disk with an application is that you can't use it as a startup disk. You can restart your computer from a RAM disk created with the Memory control panel.

CAUTION

RAM Disk Is Not Permanent

You can make a good effort to preserve a RAM disk, but its contents can easily be lost. If you use a RAM disk, observe these precautions:

✦ Don't store a file exclusively on a RAM disk. Copy documents from RAM disk to another disk frequently.

✦ Copy files from the RAM disk to another disk before shutting down.

✦ Don't use a program for the first time on a RAM disk. Test it on another disk first.

Increasing Total Memory

Enjoy whatever unused memory you have while it lasts. Software developers see unused memory as a vacuum to be filled with new programs and new features for old programs. Before long, you will want and then need more memory for new software and upgrades.

When you find yourself invariably quitting programs in order to open others, it's time to increase your computer's memory. As this section explains, you can increase memory by turning on or increasing virtual memory, by adding more memory modules, or by using a memory enhancement program such as RAM Doubler.

Virtual memory

You may be able to increase the total memory available for opening applications without upgrading your computer's built-in memory (RAM). The Mac OS can transparently use part of a hard disk as additional memory. This extra memory, called *virtual memory,* enables you to get by with less built-in memory. You buy and install only as much built-in memory as you need for average use, not for peak use.

Virtual memory has other benefits with many application programs. All programs that are optimized for the PowerPC processor (programs that use only native PowerPC instructions) require less memory when virtual memory is turned on. The same is true of some other programs. You can see the difference virtual memory makes for a program by using the Finder's Get Info command, as described in the previous section of this chapter.

In addition, the Mac OS may use less memory when virtual memory is turned on. This is particularly true on the iMac and other models that have a Mac OS ROM file in the System Folder. On these models, the Mac OS may use as much as 4MB less memory when virtual memory is turned on.

The downside to virtual memory is that it can slow the system, especially if you set it up wrong.

Configuring virtual memory

The Memory control panel is used to turn virtual memory on and off. At the same time, you can set the size of total memory. If you have more than one disk volume with enough space to be used for virtual memory storage, you can choose one. The amount of disk space required equals the amount of built-in memory installed in your computer plus the amount of memory you want to add with virtual memory. Removable disks cannot generally be used for virtual memory storage in Mac OS 7.6–8.1, but this restriction does not apply in Mac OS 8.5. A disk that uses the Mac

OS Extended format (also known as HFS Plus) can't be used for virtual memory storage on a Mac with a 68040 processor; this restriction does not apply to Macs with PowerPC processors. After setting up virtual memory, you must restart your computer for changes to take effect. Figure 18-8 shows the virtual memory options in the Memory control panel.

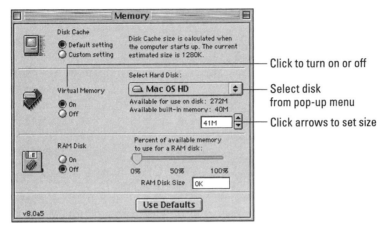

Figure 18-8: Setting up virtual memory.

With virtual memory on the About This Computer window normally reports the total amount of memory and the amount of built-in memory. It also tells you how much disk space is used for virtual memory storage. In Mac OS 8.5, application programs can suppress the display of virtual memory information in the About This Computer window.

After turning on virtual memory there is a noticeable a reduction in the amount of space available on the disk volume used for virtual memory storage. (The amount of available space is displayed at the top of the disk window in the Finder.) An invisible file named VM Storage accounts for the reduction in disk space.

The higher you set virtual memory in the Memory control panel, the more it slows the system. If you use virtual memory mostly to reduce the memory requirements of PowerPC applications, set the virtual memory size to 1MB more than the amount of built-in memory. If you use virtual memory to make more memory available for opening programs, set it no higher than double the built-in memory. Use the additional memory for opening multiple small programs, not for opening one huge program.

The limit on total memory (virtual memory plus built-in memory) is one gigabyte (1,024MB) with Mac OS 7.6–8.5.

SECRETS

Virtual Memory Turn-Off

Virtual memory users, do you hate having to open the Memory control panel when you occasionally have to turn virtual memory on and off? For instance, you must turn off virtual memory for maximum performance with QuickTime movies and multimedia applications. Sure, holding down the Shift key during startup turns it off — and all your system extensions as well. But by holding down the ⌘ key during startup, you can disable virtual memory and still keep all your extensions. Restarting without the ⌘ key restores virtual memory with its previous settings. No more trips to the Memory control panel.

How virtual memory works

Virtual memory gives you more memory for opening programs by keeping only the most active program segments in the computer's built-in memory. Less-used segments of open programs are kept in the invisible VM Storage file on the hard disk. When a program needs a segment not currently in built-in memory, the virtual memory system automatically swaps the least-used segment in built-in memory with the needed segment on disk. For example, a swap might occur when you switch programs. However, no swapping occurs unless you are trying to use more memory than your computer has built-in memory.

Virtual memory's capability of loading program pieces on demand is also responsible for reducing a PowerPC application's memory requirements. What makes PowerPC applications need more memory when virtual memory is off is how the Mac OS loads a PowerPC application into memory. Apple designed the Mac OS to load PowerPC applications in bigger pieces, called *code fragments,* than other applications' smaller pieces, called *segments.* Larger pieces should require more memory for the same reason that you need a bigger ferryboat to carry busses than cars. That's exactly the case with virtual memory turned off. A PowerPC application needs at least enough space for its largest code fragment, and usually more, when virtual memory is turned off.

In designing the system around large PowerPC code fragments, Apple planned to compensate by having the virtual memory system load and unload portions of code fragments on demand. With virtual memory turned on, code fragments don't have to be loaded whole and an application can get by with less memory.

How virtual memory affects performance

Because a hard disk is much slower than built-in memory, using virtual memory can degrade system performance. The performance penalty is barely noticeable if a swap between built-in memory and disk happens when you switch programs. The slowdown may be severe if you use virtual memory to open a program that's bigger than the amount of built-in memory left after Mac OS gets its share. The disk may thrash for several minutes as it tries to swap segments back and forth.

QUICK TIPS

Hiding from Virtual Memory

With virtual memory turned on, you can often improve system performance by using the Hide Others command in the Application menu. Hidden windows of background applications don't need updating, which may require disk access when virtual memory is on. However, some programs continue working in the background even with their windows hidden. For example, a database program might generate a report in the background. But the Hide Others command usually reduces the amount of background work going on.

The performance of code fragment management on PowerPC computers is actually better than the performance of virtual memory in general. That's because code fragments are never written to the VM Storage file. In fact, the VM Storage file is not involved at all in managing a PowerPC application's code fragments. The application file itself is the storage file. Using a technique called *file mapping,* the Mac OS loads code fragments directly from the application file into built-in memory. This technique eliminates the delay that sometimes occurs if a program's code is loaded into memory and then immediately written out to the VM Storage file. That thrashing never happens with file mapping.

File mapping benefits performance in another way. The Mac OS never writes code fragments back to the application file as it would if the code fragments went through the VM Storage file. The Mac OS assumes code fragments never change. So when part of a code fragment is no longer needed, a needed part can replace it right away. The Mac OS doesn't take the time to write the disused piece back to the disk because it can always read an identical copy that's still there in the application file.

Installing more memory

Virtual memory has its uses, but it can't take the place of built-in memory, which is also known as RAM. If you're not sure how much built-in memory your computer has, look in the About This Computer window. In that window, the Built-in Memory is the amount of memory installed in the form of RAM chips. You won't see an amount labeled Built-in Memory if you use Mac OS 7.1–7.6.1 and virtual memory is turned off. In this case, the amount reported as Total Memory is the amount of built-in memory. If the amount is reported in K (kilobytes), you can convert the amount to MB (megabytes) by dividing the number of K by 1,024. For example, $32,768K \div 1,024 = 32MB$.

Do-it-yourself memory upgrade

If your computer needs more built-in memory, you may be able to upgrade it yourself. Upgrading involves opening the computer (tricky on some PowerBook models) and either installing or replacing some small, plug-in circuit board modules.

Each computer model has specific memory-configuration rules. Some Macs use *DIMMs* (dual in-line memory modules) and some use *SIMMs* (single in-line memory modules). Both DIMMs and SIMMs come in various capacities, measured in MB (megabytes), and speeds, measured in ns (nanoseconds). PowerBooks use special memory modules. You can install memory modules only in certain combinations on each model. To find out which type of memory modules your computer uses, consult the latest free GURU (Guide to RAM Upgrades) application from the NewerRAM division of Peripheral Enhancements Corp. (316-943-0222, http://www. newerram. com). Another source of information is the electronic document Apple Memory Guide from Apple's Software Updates library (http://www.apple.com/ swupdates/). You can also get advice from dealers and companies that sell memory.

Although you may be perfectly capable of installing SIMMs or DIMMs in your computer, Apple recommends that only an Apple-certified technician install them. Apple's warranty does not cover any damage that you or a noncertified technician causes when installing or removing SIMMs and DIMMs. Proceed with caution, but know that many computer owners install their own memory boards. The more paranoid owners may also remove what they install before taking their computers in for warranty service. Most technicians won't bother to ask unless they see damage or oddball parts, such as composite SIMMs or DIMMs.

Buying memory

You can order memory by mail from a plethora of companies that advertise in *Macworld* and other Macintosh magazines. Memory prices are highly competitive. When shopping for a memory upgrade, look for a lifetime warranty from a reputable company that as best as you can tell will be around to honor the warranty. RAM chips are very reliable, but they can fail.

Buy your memory from a company that includes illustrated installation instructions for your make and model. Pay a little extra to get the instructions if you have to. A grounding wrist strap is a good precaution against unlikely damage due to static electricity discharge during installation. If the memory seller doesn't include one, you can buy one for a few dollars from an electronics store (Radio Shack part no. 276-2397).

Steer clear of composite SIMMs and DIMMs. They may work on one computer, but on another they may cause sporadic startup failures, system errors, or mysterious crashes. You may have no trouble with one composite SIMM or DIMM, but install another and watch your computer have fits. You can spot a composite SIMM or DIMM by the large number of chips on it. For example, a regular 16MB SIMM uses 8 16-megabit chips, but a composite SIMM might use 32 4-megabit chips. The best way to avoid composite SIMMs and DIMMs is to buy from a reputable source.

Memory upgrade by a technician

If you don't want to upgrade the memory yourself, you can take your computer and your mail order SIMM or DIMM to an Apple dealer or other computer service center. An experienced technician should be able to install more memory in well under 30 minutes, so you shouldn't have to pay for more than a half-hour of labor. Some stores charge less to install memory they sell to you, so investigate that angle before bringing in your own memory that you "got for your birthday."

Memory optimizing software

You can get twice as much from your computer's built-in memory with very little performance penalty by using one or two software products — RAM Doubler and RAMCharger. You can use either product alone or use them together.

RAM Doubler

RAM Doubler from Connectix (800-950-5880, 650-571-5100, http://www.connectix. com) can actually triple the amount of total memory as reported in the About This Computer window. If you prefer, you can set RAM Doubler to extend memory by a lesser amount. You can even set RAM Doubler to not extend memory at all, but just to provide file mapping and code fragment management for PowerPC applications.

Compared with the Memory control panel's virtual memory, RAM Doubler is faster, more efficient, and uses very little hard disk space. It's great for older PowerBooks that can only have 8MB of RAM, because it doesn't use the power-draining hard disk like virtual memory does. Virtual memory's strengths are that it's free and is somewhat more reliable.

RAM Doubler accomplishes its magic by reallocating built-in memory automatically behind the scenes while you work. It takes over the memory reserved but not used by open applications (the lighter portion of the bars graphed in the About This Computer window) and temporarily reallocates the unused memory to applications that need it. RAM Doubler also compresses parts of programs in memory that probably won't be used again, such as parts that initialize a program when you open it. Also, RAM Doubler may store infrequently used areas of memory to disk, just like conventional virtual memory, especially if your computer has less than 8MB of built-in memory. RAM Doubler reduces overall system performance slightly, but you may not notice the difference in normal operations. However, it's not suitable for time-critical operations such as video digitizing.

You can't use RAM Doubler in combination with virtual memory. You can't set the memory size of any application higher than the amount of your computer's built-in memory; Connectix recommends leaving your programs set at their usual memory sizes.

RAMCharger

The benefits of RAMCharger from Jump Development (412-681-2692, http://www. jumpdev.com) can't be stated precisely. RAMCharger doesn't literally double the total available memory, but it does allow you to keep more programs open at the same time. In addition, it allows open programs to use more memory than the Preferred sizes set in their Info windows.

RAMCharger takes a different approach to memory optimization than RAM Doubler. RAMCharger opens a program in its Minimum memory size, not its Preferred memory size, as specified in the program's Info window. If a program needs more memory, RAMCharger gives it more from the unused portion of your computer's built-in memory. When the program no longer needs the extra memory, RAMCharger reclaims it for future reallocation. You may not notice any performance degradation in normal operations.

You can use RAMCharger with virtual memory on or off. RAMCharger also works in combination with RAM Doubler.

Summary

In this chapter, you learned that the About This Computer window shows you the total memory available, which programs are open, how much memory each uses, and how much memory is currently unused. The Memory Mapper utility shows you a more detailed picture of this information.

This chapter also told you how to set an application's minimum and preferred memory sizes with the Finder's Get Info command. You learned what causes memory fragmentation, how to fix it, and how to avoid it. You learned how to determine the minimum Mac OS size on your computer by holding down the Shift key during startup. You read about four ways to reduce the Mac OS size: disable nonessential startup items, turn off expendable options, reduce disk cache size, and reduce or eliminate a RAM disk.

In this chapter, you also learned how to increase the total memory available for opening programs. Options include turning on virtual memory, installing more RAM, and using RAM Doubler or RAMCharger.

✦   ✦   ✦

Set Up a Network

I f you have more than one computer in your office or home, you can benefit by connecting them in a network. The idea may seem intimidating, but a simple Mac OS network is easy to set up and doesn't cost much. Some of the things that you can do with a simple Mac OS network are:

✦ Share one Internet connection among several computers

✦ Share printers, including printers without network ports

✦ Share files from other computers in your company or home as if their files were on your desktop, and share files from your computer with other computers

✦ Access a central database while other computers do likewise

✦ Maintain a group schedule or calendar

✦ Back up hard disks of all networked computers on a central tape drive

✦ Access your hard disk from a remote location over a telephone line

This chapter focuses on setting up a network so that you can use some of those services. The first section discusses hooking up a *local area network (LAN)* using either LocalTalk or Ethernet, the two most common types of network wiring for Mac OS computers. You can skip that section if your computer is already hooked to a network. The next two sections discuss configuring the Mac OS for AppleTalk and TCP/IP, the two most common kinds of Mac networks. The remainder of this chapter explains how you can connect your computer to a remote computer or network by modem.

This chapter does not describe how to use network services once your network is set up. For information on printers and printing, see Chapters 14 and 15. For information on Internet services such as global e-mail and the World Wide Web, see Chapter 17. For information on accessing shared files and network equipment, see Chapter 20. For information on sharing your files with other computers, see Chapter 21.

Hooking Up a Network

The first step in setting up a local network is hooking up lines of communication between the computers and printers that you want on the network. Basically that involves running a cable to each computer and printer. You may also need a cable connector box for each computer and a central junction box. If your computer is already connected to a network, you can skip this section.

This section describes how to hook up a LocalTalk network using inexpensive LocalTalk connector boxes and either Apple's LocalTalk cables or an ordinary telephone cord. This section also describes how to hook up an Ethernet network using 10Base-T parts, which are the lowest in cost of the many Ethernet cabling alternatives. In addition, this section discusses how you can bridge a LocalTalk network and an Ethernet network.

Besides Ethernet and LocalTalk, Macs can be connected using other types of network wiring such as Token Ring. Because Mac OS computers don't come with token ring network ports, one must be added in the form of a network interface card. If your organization has a Token Ring network, you undoubtedly have a network administrator or other expert who has already connected your computer to it or will do so for you. Setting up a Token Ring network or any network other than Ethernet or LocalTalk is not something that you want to attempt on your own. At any rate, it's outside the scope of this book.

Wiring a LocalTalk network

The simplest and cheapest type of Mac OS network wiring is LocalTalk. Many Mac OS computers have a LocalTalk network port, and so do most printers that can be connected to a Mac OS network. It costs less than $20 per computer and printer (for a network cable and connector box) to set up a small LocalTalk network. All the software you need is built into all versions of the Mac OS. LocalTalk performance is generally suitable for networks of a couple dozen or fewer computers and printers, although performance depends greatly on how much the computers use the network. LocalTalk wiring is primarily for Mac OS-only networks, although it is possible to buy LocalTalk expansion cards to hook up Windows and DOS PCs.

To hook up a LocalTalk network, you simply plug a small network connector box into the printer port of each computer and into the LocalTalk port of each network printer or other network device (such as a network modem) and run wires between the connectors. There are two types of LocalTalk connectors. In some cases, you can network two devices without connectors.

PhoneNet-style LocalTalk

The most common type of LocalTalk connector box has a modular phone jack. You link the connector boxes with an ordinary telephone cord, the kind used to connect a telephone to a modular wall socket. Be sure to use a four-wire cord, not two-wire (look for four colored wires showing through the clear RJ-11 modular plugs). In many homes and small businesses you can use the existing telephone wiring and jacks in the walls to extend your network from room to room. With the four-wire cables common in homes, for example, the telephone uses the red and green wires and the network can use the yellow and black wires.

This type of connector was pioneered and patented under the PhoneNet brand name by Farallon Communications (510-814-5000, http://www.farallon.com). Many other companies now license the technology from Farallon and sell compatible connectors at lower cost. Some of the cheaper connectors use less durable parts.

For networking only two devices — for example, two computers or one computer and one printer — you can save money by using Farallon's one-jack PhoneNet pocket connectors. Later you can add to this minimal network with dual-jack connector boxes.

Apple-style LocalTalk

Instead of phone cords and PhoneNet connector boxes, you can use Apple's proprietary LocalTalk connector boxes and cables. However, this stuff costs more and doesn't offer any advantage over PhoneNet. If you already have some Apple LocalTalk supplies, you can get adapters from Farallon to mix them with phone wiring.

Serial-cable LocalTalk

If your network has only two computers or one computer and a printer, you don't have to use LocalTalk connectors. You can connect the two devices with a serial printer cable, such as the one you would use to connect a StyleWriter to a computer. This is the cheapest way to network two devices, but they must be near each other because the cable is not very long.

Wiring an Ethernet network

An Ethernet network is significantly faster than a LocalTalk network, but Ethernet costs somewhat more. The cost to set up a small Ethernet network starts at $20, $50, or $120 per computer or printer, depending on the type of built-in port (if any). The cost and performance of Ethernet scales up to accommodate networks of all sizes. The software for accessing an Ethernet network is included with the Mac OS, although you may have to do a custom installation to get it installed. An Ethernet network can include computers using Mac OS, Windows, Unix, and other operating systems. They can use commonplace application software — for example, Internet applications — to communicate and share services (see Chapter 17 for more information on Internet applications).

Ethernet cables

Ethernet networks may be wired with several types of cable. The most popular is 10Base-T or 100Base-T cable, also known as *unshielded twisted-pair (UTP)* cable. It looks like telephone cable and uses RJ-45 connectors that look like big modular phone connectors. Other kinds include thinnet, thick coax, and fiber-optic Ethernet cables.

UTP cable is graded according to how well it protects against electrical interference. Category 3 cable is adequate for 10Base-T networks. Category 5 offers more protection, but it costs more. The additional cost for Category 5 is insignificant when compared to the cost of installation. Furthermore, properly installed Category 5 cable can also be used for a 100Base-T Ethernet network, which is ten times faster than a 10Base-T network. This means that you could upgrade a 10Base-T network to a 100Base-T network without any rewiring. The only caveat is that 100Base-T has more stringent rules about cable installation than 10Base-T. For example, sharp bends are not allowed in 100Base-T cables.

Ethernet ports

Even if you use UTP cable, hooking up an Ethernet network is more complicated than hooking up a LocalTalk network. For starters, you can't count on every computer having a built-in Ethernet port.

Some computers have a built-in RJ-45 port for 10Base-T Ethernet. In a few cases, such as the iMac, this port can also be used for 100Base-T Ethernet. Other Mac OS computers have an AAUI (Apple attachment unit interface) port to accommodate any kind of Ethernet cable. An AAUI port requires a connector box, called a *transceiver,* designed for the particular type of Ethernet cable in your network. A few Mac models have both 10Base-T and AAUI ports; you plug in a 10Base-T cable directly or use a transceiver for another kind of Ethernet cable.

Computers without built-in Ethernet need an Ethernet adapter to connect to an Ethernet network. There are internal adapter cards for the various kinds of expansion slots found in Mac OS computers: PCI, NuBus slot, Comm, and PDS (processor direct slot). Internal Ethernet adapters are sometimes called *network interface cards (NIC),* although this term is more common with Windows PCs.

For computers without internal expansion slots, there are external Ethernet adapters. A PowerBook that accepts PC cards (also known as PCMCIA cards) can use an Ethernet adapter on a PC card. Computers and printers that have only a LocalTalk port can use a LocalTalk-to-10Base-T adapter. There are also 10Base-T adapters that connect to a Mac's SCSI port. All these Ethernet adapters are available from many manufacturers, including 3Com, Farallon, Asanté, and Dayna.

Ethernet connections

Ethernet networks that use 10Base-T or 100Base-T cable usually have junction boxes called *hubs.* You connect each computer, Ethernet-capable printer, or other Ethernet device to a hub with a length of UTP cable. Each computer or other device plugs into a different port on the hub. Hubs come in many different sizes, although 5-port, 8-port, and 16-port hubs are the most common. Prices start around $50 for a generic 5-port 10Base-T hub and go up for more ports and a name brand. 100Base-T hubs cost more than 10Base-T hubs.

If you use up all the ports on one hub, you can connect another hub to it. This is called *daisy chaining.* You can daisy chain up to three hubs with UTP cable. This limit does not apply to daisy chaining with thinnet cable, and many 10Base-T and 100Base-T hubs have thinnet ports for this purpose.

It's actually possible to construct a small 10Base-T Ethernet network without a hub. You can use Farallon's EtherWave family of transceivers and adapter cards to daisy chain up to eight computers and printers with 10Base-T cable. EtherWave transceivers cost more than ordinary transceivers, but wiring costs are usually lower and you don't have to buy a hub.

You can also directly connect two computers equipped with 10Base-T Ethernet ports by using a crossover cable—you don't need a hub or special transceivers. Global Computer Supplies (800-845-6225) carries these cables in 3-foot, 12-foot, and custom lengths for less than $10. When using a 10Base-T crossover cable to connect two computers without a hub, you must start up both computers before changing the connection to Ethernet in the AppleTalk control panel or Network control panel. If the Mac OS doesn't see another device on the Ethernet network, it won't let you set the AppleTalk connection to Ethernet. After successfully setting the AppleTalk connection to Ethernet, a similar problem occurs if you subsequently start one computer while the other is off. An alert explains, "An error occurred while trying to start up your AppleTalk connection. The built-in LocalTalk port will be used instead." If this happens, you have to reset the AppleTalk connection to Ethernet after starting up the other computer. (The AppleTalk control panel is covered in "Configuring an AppleTalk Connection," later in this chapter.)

Bridging Ethernet and LocalTalk

Sometimes a hybrid network, part Ethernet and part LocalTalk, makes sense. For example, you might have a printer with a LocalTalk port (and no Ethernet port) that you want to use with an iMac, which has no LocalTalk port, or with several computers that have Ethernet ports. Or you might have some older computers connected in a LocalTalk network that you'd like to connect to an iMac or to several computers on an Ethernet network. Fortunately you can interconnect the dissimilar networks with a *bridge.*

LaserWriter Bridge

Apple's free LaserWriter Bridge 2.1 software lets you use a LocalTalk printer from a computer that's connected to an Ethernet network, such as an iMac. In fact, if more than one printer is connected to the LocalTalk network, you can use any of them. The theoretical maximum is 32 printers, but Apple recommends 8 or fewer. You install LaserWriter Bridge 2.1 on the computer to which a LocalTalk printer (or a network of printers) is connected. You can allow other computers on the Ethernet network to use the LocalTalk printer or printers, or you can designate the bridge to be private. LaserWriter Bridge is available from Apple's Software Updates library (http://www.apple.com/swupdates/).

LaserWriter Bridge works only one way: It allows computers on an Ethernet network to see printers on a LocalTalk network. It doesn't allow computers on a LocalTalk network to see printers or computers on an Ethernet network.

LocalTalk Bridge

Apple's full-featured bridge software, LocalTalk Bridge 2.1 (order part no. M3246Z/A), creates a two-way connection between a LocalTalk network and an Ethernet network. The LocalTalk computers can use printers, shared files, and other network services on the Ethernet network. Computers on the Ethernet network can use printers, shared files, and other network services on the LocalTalk network. You install LocalTalk Bridge 2.1 on the computer that is connected to both the Ethernet network and the LocalTalk network. If you prefer, you can make the connection private, so that only the computer with the LocalTalk Bridge can use network services on both networks.

The LocalTalk Bridge software tends to sap the performance of the computer it's installed on. Moreover, this product has become hard to find and expensive compared to other products, which may indicate that Apple intends to discontinue it.

Farallon EtherMac iPrint Adapter LT

You can avoid all the shortcomings of bridge software with a separate device such as the $99 EtherMac iPrint Adapter LT from Farallon Communications (510-814-5000, http://www.farallon.com). Although this device is marketed specifically as a means of connecting an iMac to a LocalTalk printer such as a LaserWriter, it has broader applications. You can use the iPrint to connect a single iMac or an entire Ethernet network to up to eight LocalTalk printers and computers. After you connect a LocalTalk network and an Ethernet network to the iPrint, the computers on either network can use printers, file servers, and other services on the other network.

There are a couple of network connection options if you want to use an iPrint to connect an iMac to an older Mac and a LocalTalk printer. One option is to leave the old Mac on a LocalTalk network with the laser printer, connect them to the iPrint with a LocalTalk cable, and connect the iMac to the iPrint with an Ethernet cable. This way you save the cost of an Ethernet hub and an Ethernet transceiver or adapter card for your old Mac. The other option is to connect the computers to an Ethernet hub, connect the hub to the iPrint with an Ethernet cable, and connect the iPrint to the laser printer with a LocalTalk cable. This costs more money, but your computers share files over Ethernet, which is much faster than LocalTalk.

Configuring an AppleTalk Connection

To use network services on your computer, the Mac OS must be configured to get network services from the port that is physically connected to the network. You can configure the Mac OS for more than one kind of network, with each kind of network providing a specific set of services. The most common kinds of Mac OS networks are AppleTalk and TCP/IP. Apple Talk and TCP/IP are *protocols,* which are "languages" that computers speak to each other over a network. All the computers on a network that use the same protocol (i.e., speak the same language) can exchange information over the network. On an AppleTalk network, computers speak the AppleTalk protocol. On a TCP/IP network, they speak the TCP/IP protocol.

An AppleTalk network provides Mac-oriented services such as printer sharing, file sharing, data sharing, and program sharing. Apple designed AppleTalk to be easy to use and reliable. AppleTalk has been built into every version of the Mac OS. Until the advent of Open Transport networking software in 1995, AppleTalk was the primary kind of Mac OS network and all other kinds of networks were subordinate.

Note that connecting to a network does not necessarily make specific network services available. For example, connecting to an AppleTalk network makes it possible to use a network printer, but you can't actually print to a network printer unless one is connected to the network and set up as described in Chapter 14. Likewise, connecting to an AppleTalk network makes it possible to share files with other computers on the network, but to actually share files the computers must have file sharing set up as described in Chapter 21.

This section describes how to configure an AppleTalk network connection with the AppleTalk or Network control panel and how to turn an AppleTalk connection on and off.

To use TCP/IP network services such as the Internet, the Mac OS on your computer must be configured for a TCP/IP network as described in "Configuring a TCP/IP Connection" later in this chapter.

Specifying an AppleTalk connection

By default, the Mac OS connects to an AppleTalk network at the printer port. If your AppleTalk network is connected to an Ethernet port or the modem port, you need to make that setting in the AppleTalk control panel. Figure 19-1 shows an AppleTalk control panel with several port choices.

AppleTalk ports and zones

The AppleTalk control panel lists the available network ports in a pop-up menu. You choose the one through which your computer connects to an AppleTalk network. If your computer is connected to an AppleTalk network that's divided into multiple zones, the AppleTalk control panel also specifies the zone in which your computer resides. Depending on the characteristics of your computer and network, you may be able to change the network connection port, the zone, or both. If your computer has only one network connection port, you won't be able to change the port. If your computer is connected to a network with only one zone, there won't be any zones available to choose from. If someone else sets up your computer's AppleTalk network connection, the port and zone settings may be locked so that you can't change them.

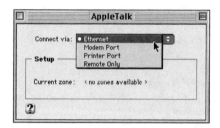

Figure 19-1: Choose a connection port for an AppleTalk network in the AppleTalk control panel.

If you change the connection port in the AppleTalk control panel, a message warns that you'll lose any network services that you're using with your current AppleTalk connection. This is because you can maintain a connection to only one AppleTalk network at a time. When you switch to a different network port, you can no longer access any printers, shared files, file servers, or other AppleTalk network services on the former AppleTalk connection port. Changing the AppleTalk connection port does not affect network services on other kinds of networks, such as Internet services on a TCP/IP network.

AppleTalk user modes

You can see more settings or fewer settings in the AppleTalk control panel by changing the user mode. There are three modes: Basic, Advanced, and Administration. To change the user mode, choose User Mode from the Edit menu, and select the mode in the dialog box that appears. If you select Administration mode, you can set a password that protects Administration mode settings. Figure 19-2 shows the User Mode dialog box.

In the Advanced mode, you see the network address that was dynamically assigned to your computer when it connected to the network. By selecting the "User defined" checkbox, you can assign a fixed address to your computer. If you assign a fixed address, you must be sure that no other computer on the network has the same address. Clicking the Options button brings up a dialog box in which you can turn AppleTalk on and off. Figure 19-3 shows the AppleTalk control panel's Advanced mode.

In the Administration mode, you can assign a fixed network address as in the Advanced mode. In addition, you can lock each of the three AppleTalk settings independently — port, zone, and AppleTalk network address. Locked settings can't be changed in Basic or Advanced modes. Figure 19-4 shows the control panel's Administration mode.

Figure 19-2: Select a user mode for the AppleTalk control panel.

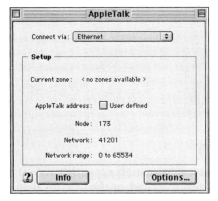

Figure 19-3: The AppleTalk control panel's Advanced mode.

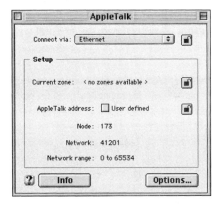

Figure 19-4: The AppleTalk control panel's Administration mode.

AppleTalk configurations

Rather than setting options in the AppleTalk control panel directly, you can configure them as a group for a particular network or location. You do this with the Configurations command in the File menu. This command displays a dialog box that lists groups of settings by name and has buttons for acting on the group that's selected in the list. There are buttons for making the selected group active, creating a new group by duplicating the selected group, renaming the selected group, and deleting the selected group. Other buttons let you export the selected group as a file and import a group that someone else has exported. Figure 19-5 shows an example of the Configurations dialog box.

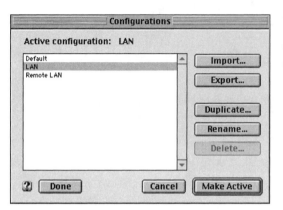

Figure 19-5: The Configurations dialog box lets you work with named groups of settings for different networks or locations.

Turning AppleTalk off and on

If you're not using an AppleTalk network, you can turn it off altogether with the Chooser accessory program, the AppleTalk control panel, or the Control Strip. Turning off AppleTalk saves power on a PowerBook. If AppleTalk is set to connect via the printer port or another serial port, turning off AppleTalk also frees this port for another purpose such as connecting a serial printer. However, it's not necessary to turn off AppleTalk just to free the printer port, as detailed in the sidebar "AppleTalk Without a Serial Port."

QUICK TIPS

AppleTalk Without a Serial Port

You may need to turn off AppleTalk so that you can print to a StyleWriter or other serial printer through the printer port while using the modem port for a modem. If your computer has only one serial port, you may need to turn off AppleTalk so that you can use the port with an external modem. The trouble is, however, that if you turn off AppleTalk, you won't be able to use applications such as NetPresenz that require AppleTalk. Furthermore, if your computer has Open Transport networking software 1.1.2 or earlier, turning off AppleTalk may cause it to crash. This crashing condition does not occur with Mac OS 8–8.5, which includes Open Transport 1.2 or later.

You can keep AppleTalk turned on and still use a serial printer and a modem by installing the Remote Only extension and then selecting Remote Only in the AppleTalk control panel. The Remote Only extension comes with Mac OS 8–8.5. It's also available as part of Open Transport 1.1.2 and later from Apple's Software Updates library (http://www.apple.com/

swupdates/). Remote Only is also part of the ARA Client software, which is described later in this chapter.

If you use Mac OS 7.6–7.6.1, access the Internet with FreePPP or MacPPP, and turn off AppleTalk, your computer may crash when you try to open a PPP connection a second time. The crash doesn't happen when AppleTalk is active and it shouldn't happen if you use Apple's Open Transport/PPP software to access the Internet.

Turning AppleTalk off and on with the Chooser

To turn off AppleTalk, open the Chooser (under the Apple menu) and in the lower-right corner of its window set the AppleTalk option to Inactive. If you turn off AppleTalk, it remains off until you turn it on again by selecting the Activate option in the Chooser. Figure 19-6 shows the AppleTalk option in the Chooser.

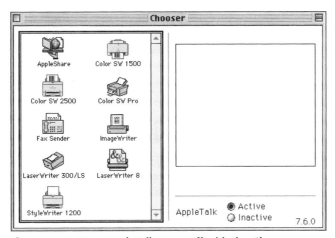

Figure 19-6: Turn AppleTalk on or off with the Chooser.

If you attempt to turn off AppleTalk while you are using a network service such as file sharing, you get a warning message that current services will be disconnected.

Turning AppleTalk off and on with the AppleTalk control panel

If your computer has an AppleTalk control panel (not a Network control panel), you can use it to turn AppleTalk off and on. With the AppleTalk control panel set to Advanced or Administration mode, click the Options button to bring up the AppleTalk Options dialog box. There you can select Inactive to turn off AppleTalk or select Active to turn on AppleTalk. Figure 19-7 shows the AppleTalk control panel's Options dialog box.

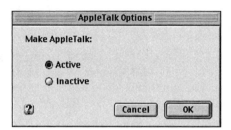

Figure 19-7: Turn AppleTalk on or off via the AppleTalk control panel's Options dialog box.

Turning AppleTalk off and on with the Control Strip

If the Control Strip is available on your computer, you can use it to turn AppleTalk off and on. Turn off AppleTalk by choosing AppleTalk Inactive from the pop-up menu of the AppleTalk Switch control strip module. Turn AppleTalk on by choosing AppleTalk Active from this menu. Figure 19-8 shows the AppleTalk Switch control strip module.

Figure 19-8: Turn AppleTalk off and on with the Control Strip.

Configuring a TCP/IP Connection

To use TCP/IP network services such as the Internet, the Mac OS must be configured to connect to a TCP/IP network through one of your computer's ports. Naturally, that port must be physically connected to a network that provides TCP/IP services. The port may be wired to an Ethernet or LocalTalk network, or a modem plugged into the port may provide a dial-up connection.

This section describes how to configure a TCP/IP network connection with the TCP/IP control panel. If you want to set up a TCP/IP network just to access the Internet and you have Mac OS 8 or later, you should consider using the Internet Setup Assistant program instead of the control panels described here. (The Internet Setup Assistant is described in "Setting Up an Internet Connection" in Chapter 17.)

To use Mac OS-oriented network services such as printer and file sharing, you need to configure an AppleTalk network connection as described in the previous section, "Configuring an AppleTalk Connection."

Preparing for a TCP/IP connection

Before setting up a TCP/IP connection, you need to know some facts about the network. You may have to get the facts from an expert such as your local network administrator or your Internet service provider (ISP). Here is what you need to know:

✦ Type of network connection: is it PPP, Ethernet, MacIP, or some other

✦ Your TCP/IP configuration method such as manual, PPP Server, BootP Server, DHCP Server, RARP Server, or MacIP Server

✦ Domain name server (DNS) address or addresses, each being a set of four numbers separated by periods similar to 192.14.59.10 (provided automatically by some configuration methods)

✦ IP address of your computer, which is a set of four numbers separated by periods similar to 192.14.59.35 (provided automatically by most configuration methods)

✦ Subnet mask (provided automatically by most configuration methods)

✦ Router address (provided automatically by most configuration methods and not applicable for some networks)

✦ Phone number your computer calls to connect to the Internet (needed only for PPP or other dial-up connection)

Specifying a TCP/IP connection

You specify a TCP/IP network connection by entering the information obtained from your Internet service provider or network administrator into the TCP/IP control panel. If someone else sets up your computer's TCP/IP network connection, the connection and configuration settings may be locked so you can't change them. Figure 19-9 shows a TCP/IP control panel configured for a typical dial-up (telephone) connection.

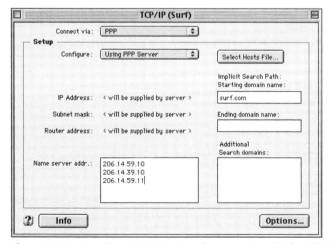

Figure 19-9: Specify a TCP/IP network connection in the TCP/IP control panel.

TCP/IP user modes

You can see more settings or fewer settings in the TCP/IP control panel by changing the user mode. There are three modes: Basic, Advanced, and Administration. To change the user mode, choose User Mode from the Edit menu and select the mode in the dialog box that appears. Figure 19-10 shows this dialog box.

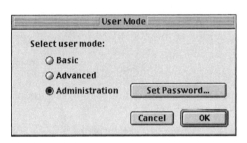

Figure 19-10: Select a user mode for the TCP/IP control panel.

The Basic user mode shows the settings that most people need. The Advanced mode shows additional settings for special situations. The Administration mode provides control over which settings can be changed. If you select Administration mode, you can set a password that protects Administration mode settings. In the Administration mode, you can lock several TCP/IP settings independently. Locked settings can't be changed in Basic or Advanced modes.

TCP/IP configurations

Instead of setting individual options in the AppleTalk control panel, you can configure them as a group for a particular network or location. You do this with the Configurations command in the File menu. This command displays a dialog box that lists groups of settings by name and has buttons for acting on the group that's selected in the list. There are buttons for making the selected group active, creating a new group by duplicating the selected group, renaming the selected group, and deleting the selected group. Other buttons let you export the selected group as a file and import a group that someone else has exported. Figure 19-11 is an example of the Configurations dialog box.

Introducing Remote Network Connections

Your computer can connect remotely to another computer, an AppleTalk or TCP/IP network, or an ISP. Your computer makes remote connections through its modem and a telephone line. The remote computer, network, or ISP must have a compatible modem.

When connected to a remote computer, you can access its shared files. You can also access shared files, file servers, network printers, and other network services on the network that the remote computer is connected to. You access all the remote services exactly as though you were connected locally to the computer or network (as described in Chapter 20). Their owners or network administrators may restrict your access to shared files, file servers, and so forth. Conversely, no one using a remote computer or network can take advantage of your remote connection to access files you are sharing on your local network (as described in Chapter 21). You must run a file server program on your computer to make your files available to remote network users.

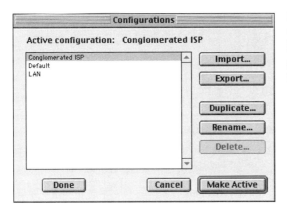

Figure 19-11: The Configurations dialog box lets you work with named groups of settings for different networks or locations.

Remote network only

When you set up your computer for a remote connection, you can disconnect your local AppleTalk network. There are two reasons you may need to do this. For one, you may be unable to see remote printers or file servers that have the same names as printers or file servers on your local network unless you disconnect the local network. (Local services have priority over remote services.) You may also want to disconnect your local AppleTalk network so that you can use your serial ports for other purposes. For example, you may want to use the printer port for a StyleWriter printer and use the modem port for a modem that connects you to a remote AppleTalk network.

To disconnect your local AppleTalk network, set the AppleTalk connection to Remote Only in the AppleTalk control panel.

Remote access speed

Several factors affect the speed of a remote connection, including the software, the computer's serial port, and the modem or other connection equipment. The Remote Access control panel, Remote Access Client program, and PPP control panel can connect at speeds up to 230Kbps (230,400 bits per second). No modem can transfer data over a regular phone line at these speeds, but a two-channel ISDN terminal adapter can connect at 112Kbps or 128Kbps over an ISDN phone line. This is half the speed of a LocalTalk network, but only a small fraction of a 10Base-T Ethernet network's speed.

If you have a modem with built-in data compression hardware, you may still be able to benefit from speeds up to 230Kbps. In this case, your modem transfers data to and from your computer several times faster than it transfers data over the phone line. Your modem makes up the speed differential by reducing the amount of data it transfers over the phone line by compressing data before sending it and decompressing it after receiving it over the phone line.

The built-in serial ports are not capable of 230Kbps on all Mac OS computers. These Apple computers have high-speed serial ports:

✦ Centris and Quadra 660AV and 840AV

✦ Performa 6100 series

✦ Power Mac 6100, 7100, 7200, 7300, 7500, 7600, 8100, 8500, 8600, 9500, 9600, and G3 series

✦ PowerBook 3400 and PowerBook G3 series

✦ Workgroup Server 6150, 7250, 8150, 8550, and 9150 models

The Power Mac 5200, 5300, 6200, 6300 series do not have high-speed serial ports. Neither do the PowerBook 1400, 2300, and 5300 models. Older Mac and PowerBook models that were not originally equipped with PowerPC processors do not have high-speed serial ports. Maximum serial-port speed on these computers is 57.6Kbps (57,600 bits per second or bps).

Making a Remote Network Connection in Mac OS 8.5

On all Macs with Mac OS 8.5 and on some Macs with Mac OS 7.6 –8.1, connecting to a remote network involves several different pieces of software. This section describes how to set up and establish a remote connection using the following software:

✦ **Modem** control panel, which you use to set up your computer's modem for remote access

✦ **DialAssist** control panel, which you can use to simplify remote access calls that involve long distance, credit card, international, or private PBX phone numbers

✦ **Remote Access** control panel, which you use to configure all remote connections and that you can use to start, stop, and monitor a connection

✦ **Remote Access Status** program, which you can use to start, stop, and monitor a connection

✦ **Control Strip,** which you can use to start, stop, and monitor a connection

You should have all this software if you use Mac OS 8.5. You probably have all this software if you use Mac OS 8.1 on a Mac manufactured during the middle of 1998. In addition, you should have all this software if upgraded Mac OS 7.6–8.1 by buying and installing Apple Remote Access 3.0 or later.

If you use Mac OS 7.6–8.1, you may have the Modem and DialAssist control panels. Both of these control panels are part of a standard installation of Mac OS 8–8.1. In Mac OS 7.6–7.6.1, the Modem control panel is part of the optional Open Transport PPP module and the DialAssist control panel is part of the optional Apple Remote Access 2.1 module. You can select these modules when you install Mac OS 7.6–7.6.1, as described in Chapter 32.

If you use Mac OS 7.6–8.1, you may also have the Control Strip. The Control Strip is normally installed on all PowerBooks and can be custom installed on desktop Macs.

Using the Modem control panel

You use the Modem control panel to specify the port to which modem is connected and to identify the type of modem you have. You can also set several dialing options. Figure 19-12 is an example of the Modem control panel.

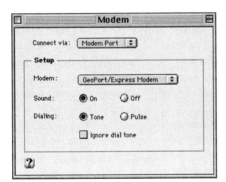

Figure 19-12: The Modem control panel sets up your modem to make a remote connection.

These settings apply to all remote connections in Mac OS 8.5. These settings also apply to all remote connections in Mac OS 7.6–8.1 if Apple Remote Access 3.0 or later is installed. Otherwise, the Modem control panel applies only to ISP or remote TCP/IP network connections in Mac OS 7.6–8.1, in which case the Remote Access Setup control panel governs connections to a remote Mac or AppleTalk network (as described in "Making a Remote Network Connection in Mac OS 7.6–8.1," later in this chapter).

Modem user modes

You can see more settings or fewer settings in the Modem control panel by changing the user mode. The two modes are Basic and Administration. To change the user mode, choose User Mode from the Edit menu and select the mode in the dialog box that appears. Figure 19-13 shows this dialog box.

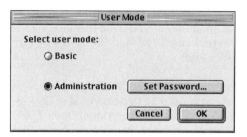

Figure 19-13: Select a user mode for the Modem control panel.

The Basic user mode shows the settings that most people need. The Administration mode provides control over which settings can be changed. If you select Administration mode, you can set a password that protects the Administration mode settings. In the Administration mode, you can lock several Modem settings independently. Locked settings can't be changed in Basic mode.

Modem configurations

Rather than setting options in the Modem control panel directly, you can configure them as a group for a particular network or location. You do this with the Configurations command in the File menu. This command displays a dialog box that lists groups of settings by name and has buttons for acting on the group that's selected in the list. There are buttons for making the selected group active, creating a new group by duplicating the selected group, renaming the selected group, and deleting the selected group. Other buttons let you export the selected group as a file and import a group that someone else has exported. Figure 19-14 is an example of the Configurations dialog box.

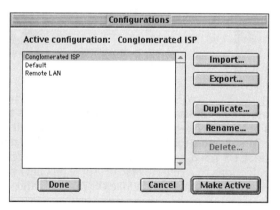

Figure 19-14: The Configurations dialog box lets you work with named groups of settings for different networks or locations.

Modem scripts

You identify the type of modem you have by choosing a modem script for it from the Modem pop-up menu in the Modem control panel. A *modem script* contains the sequence of modem commands needed to start and stop remote connections with a particular type of modem. In some cases, the Modem pop-up menu lists more than one modem script for a modem. Each of the alternatives makes a different kind of connection, typically a connection at a different speed.

The remote access software included with Mac OS 7.6–8.5 comes with over 30 modem scripts. In addition, modems usually come with modem scripts that need to be installed on the computer. If your modem is not listed in the Modem pop-up menu, make sure your modem software is installed properly. Modem scripts go in Modem Script folder within your Extensions folder. You can also check with the modem manufacturer to see if a modem script is available for use with Apple Remote Access.

Using the DialAssist control panel

The DialAssist control panel simplifies making long distance, credit card, international, and private PBX phone calls for a remote network connection. You enter the area or city code you're calling from and choose other dialing codes from four pop-up menus — DialAssist modifies the phone number accordingly. You see the results of the DialAssist control panel in the Remote Access control panel (described next) and Remote Access Client program (described in the next section, "Making a Remote Network Connection in Mac OS 7.6–8.1"). Figure 19-15 shows the DialAssist control panel.

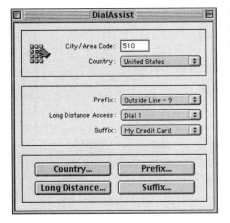

Figure 19-15: The DialAssist control panel simplifies complicated phone numbers for remote access.

The DialAssist control panel comes preconfigured with the most common dialing codes. You can add, change, or remove codes by clicking the buttons at the bottom of the control panel. Click Country to change codes for incoming and outgoing calls for any country. Click Prefix to change codes for getting an outside line from a PBX. Click Long Distance to change access codes for long distance service providers. Click Suffix to change credit card, calling card, or other suffix codes.

Using the Remote Access control panel

The Remote Access control panel is used to configure a remote connection to a computer, network, or ISP. Once you have entered the necessary connection information, you connect by clicking the control panel's Connect button. You can also connect automatically by using an application that accesses the Internet or a remote TCP/IP network. You can change this behavior and set a variety of other options that affect the connection by clicking the Options button in the control panel. Figure 19-16 shows the Remote Access control panel.

Figure 19-16: The Remote Access control panel configures all remote connections in Mac OS 8.5.

Remote Access configuration

To configure the Remote Access control panel, you specify whether to connect as a registered user or as an anonymous guest. To connect as a registered user, you must provide a user name or account ID, a password, and the phone number to call to make a connection. As a guest, all you need to provide is the phone number.

If there is a Use DialAssist option visible above the phone number in the Remote Access control panel, you can turn it on to have the DialAssist control panel help you dial complicated phone numbers. The DialAssist option appears only if the user mode is set to Advanced or Administration, as described later in this section under the heading "Remote Access User Modes." The DialAssist control panel is described earlier in this section under the heading "Using the DialAssist Control Panel." Figure 19-17 shows the Remote Access control panel with the DialAssist option in use.

If you turn on the Use DialAssist option, the Remote Access control panel provides two spaces for the phone number you are calling, one labeled Number and the other labeled Area Code, and a pop-up menu labeled Country. Do not include an area code or city code in the space labeled Number. Enter the area code or city code for the number you are calling in the space labeled Area Code. In addition, you need to indicate which country you are calling by choosing it from the Country pop-up menu. When you enter the Area Code and Country, the Remote Access control panel has the DialAssist control panel use this information to construct the number that will be dialed. The full number that will be dialed appears in the Remote Access control panel next to the Preview label.

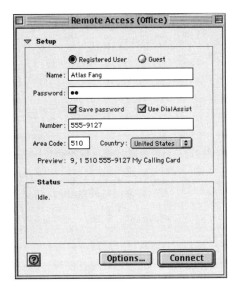

Figure 19-17: The DialAssist option, if present and selected, provides a separate space for entering an area code or city code and a pop-up menu for choosing a country to call.

If you do not turn on the Use DialAssist option or it is not present, then you need to enter the full phone number in the space labeled Number. For a long distance number, you must include the long-distance access code and area code prefixes, such as 1-800-. For an international call, you must include the international access code and the country code prefixes. For a credit card or calling card call, you must include the card number as a suffix.

When you enter a phone number, you can include hyphens, spaces, parentheses, and slashes for readability. The Remote Access control panel ignores them in the phone number. Commas in the phone number instruct the modem to pause during dialing. Most modems pause two seconds for each comma.

Rather than setting options in the Remote Access control panel directly, you can configure them as a group for a particular network or location. You do this with the Configurations command in the File menu. This command displays a dialog box that lists groups of settings by name and has buttons for acting on the group that's selected in the list. There are buttons for making the selected group active, creating a new group by duplicating the selected group, renaming the selected group, and deleting the selected group. Other buttons let you export the selected group as a file and import a group that someone else has exported. Figure 19-18 is an example of the Configurations dialog box.

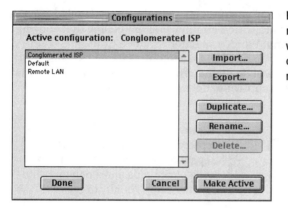

Figure 19-18: The Configurations dialog box lets you work with named groups of settings for different networks or locations.

Remote Access connection status

At the bottom part of the Remote Access control panel status information is displayed during a connection. You can reduce the size of the control panel to show only the status information by clicking the disclosure triangle in the top-left corner of the control panel. Figure 19-19 shows the reduced view of the Remote Access control panel.

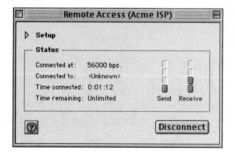

Figure 19-19: The Remote Access control panel displays the connection status.

While connected, the Remote Access control panel has a Disconnect button. You can terminate the connection by clicking this button.

Remote Access manual dialing

If you're calling from a place where you must dial the number yourself (such as when making an operator-assisted call), don't click the Connect button in the Remote Access control panel. Instead, choose Dial Manually from the Remote Access menu and follow the instructions on the screen.

Remote Access options

Clicking the Options button in the Remote Access control panel brings up a dialog box in which you can set options that affect the connection. The options are organized into three groups: Redialing, Connection, and Protocol. You display a group of options by clicking its tab at the top of the dialog box. Figure 19-20 shows the Redialing options of the Remote Access control panel.

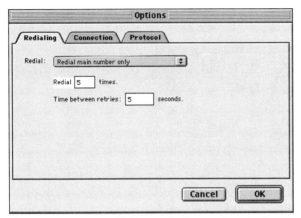

Figure 19-20: Set redialing and other options in the Remote Access Options dialog box.

The Redialing options determine whether the Remote Access control panel redials when the phone number is busy and whether it dials an alternate number if there is no answer on the main number. You can specify the number of times to redial before giving up and how long to wait between attempts. This interval should be at least five seconds so that your modem has time to reset itself between dialing attempts. If you specify an alternate phone number, the Remote Access control panel tries it once if the main number doesn't answer.

The Connection options control the amount of detail in the connection log and the behavior of connection reminders. Figure 19-21 shows the Connection options of the Remote Access control panel.

You should leave verbose (detailed) logging turned off unless you need details to troubleshoot connection problems. A detailed log uses up more disk space.

The Reminders options, which are under the Connections tab, determine how Remote Access reminds you of a connection and whether it automatically terminates the connection under certain circumstances. These options are useful if you pay for the amount of time you are connected. You can have the Remote Access icon flash above the Apple menu icon to remind you that you are connected. You can have a dialog box appear periodically and automatically stop the connection if no one responds to it. If you turn on this option, you can specify how often this dialog box appears. In addition, you can have Remote Access automatically disconnect when the connection has been idle for the number of minutes you specify. If you turn on this option but Remote Access never disconnects automatically, then some application is continuing to use the connection. You may be able to set application preferences to prevent continuous or periodic use of the connection. For example, set your e-mail program so that it does not check for mail every five minutes. Also note that some Web pages contain items that continuously access the Internet. If you suspect this is happening, go to another Web page, close the Web browser window, or quit the Web browser application.

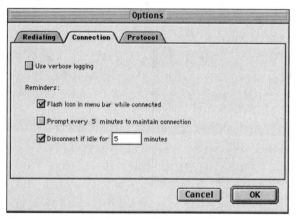

Figure 19-21: Set connection options in the Remote Access Options dialog box.

The Protocol option lets you choose a network protocol for the connection. Choose Automatic to let Remote Access pick an appropriate protocol. Choose PPP for a connection to an ISP or remote TCP/IP network. Choose ARAP for a connection to a network server that uses the Apple Remote Access Protocol (ARAP), such as a Mac that is running Remote Access Personal Server 1.0–2.1. If you're connecting to a Mac that is running Remote Access Personal Server 3.0 or later, you can choose PPP or ARAP. PPP gives you faster access, but is more complicated to set up. Figure 19-22 shows the Protocol options with PPP chosen.

If you choose the PPP protocol, you can set several additional options. One PPP option controls whether you can make an automatic connection. If you turn on automatic connection, the Mac OS makes a connection whenever an application accesses the Internet or remote TCP/IP network. The wording of this option suggests that the automatic connection happens the moment you open the application. In fact, the automatic connection may happen some time later when you do something in the application that causes it to access the Internet or remote network. For example, you can set a Web browser's preferences so that it will not access the Internet until you choose a bookmark, click a link, or otherwise specify a Web location that you want to see.

Another PPP option determines whether to allow your modem's hardware to do data compression and error checking. If your modem has these capabilities, turning on this option may improve the performance of the connection.

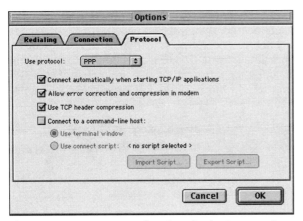

Figure 19-22: Set protocol options in the Remote Access Options dialog box.

A third PPP option determines whether the Mac OS will try to compress TCP headers for efficiency. You should leave this option turned on because the ISP or remote network server can refuse header compression without causing a problem.

A fourth PPP option enables you to connect to an ISP or remote network that requires you to enter specific information such as your account name and password while connecting. If you turn on this option, you can then select a method for entering the information. One method is to type the information in a terminal window. The other method is to specify a connection script that enters the necessary information for you. You can create a connection script by clicking the Settings button in the terminal window to record your typing while you make a connection.

Remote Access user modes

The Remote Access control panel has three modes, Basic, Advanced, and Administration. The Basic mode shows the settings most people need. The Advanced mode includes an additional option that determines whether the DialAssist control panel automatically modifies the phone number for long distance, credit card, international, or PBX dialing. In the Administration mode, you can lock several settings independently. Locked settings can't be changed in Basic or Advanced modes. You can also set a password that protects Administration mode settings.

To change the user mode, choose User Mode from the Edit menu, and select the mode in the dialog box that appears. Figure 19-23 shows this dialog box.

Using the Remote Access status program

Once you have configured a remote connection with the Remote Access control panel, you can use the smaller Remote Access Status program to start, stop, and monitor remote connections. The Remote Access Status program is normally listed in the Apple menu. While disconnected, this program has a very small window with a Connect button. When you click this button to start connecting, the window expands to show connection status information. During a connection, the window has a Disconnect button. Clicking this button stops the connection. Figure 19-24 shows the expanded and contracted window of the Remote Access Status program.

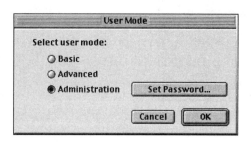

Figure 19-23: Select a user mode for the Remote Access control panel.

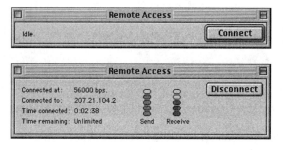

Figure 19-24: Use Remote Access Status to start a remote connection (top) and to monitor or stop it (bottom).

Using the Remote Access control strip module

If your computer has a Control Strip, you can use it to start, stop, and monitor a remote connection in Mac OS 8.5. You can also use the Control Strip to choose a different named configuration of the Remote Access control panel and to open this control panel. Figure 19-25 is an example of the Remote Access control strip module.

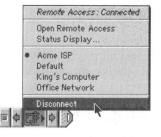

Figure 19-25: Use the Control Strip to control and monitor a remote connection.

Remote Access configuration

The Remote Access pop-up in the Control Strip lists names of all configurations saved in the Remote Access control panel. The configuration marked with a bullet in the pop-up is the active configuration that is used the next time you make a connection. To make a different configuration active, press the Remote Access icon in the Control Strip and choose the configuration from the pop-up menu. To open the Remote Access control panel so that you can change configuration settings, choose Open Remote Access from the pop-up menu.

Remote Access connect and disconnect

You can start a remote connection by choosing Connect from the bottom of the Remote Access pop-up menu in the Control Strip. During a connection, Connect changes to Disconnect in the pop-up menu. Choosing Disconnect stops the connection.

Remote Access connection status

You can see the connection status by looking at the Remote Access icon or at the top of the Remote Access pop-up menu. During a connection, you see a line representing a network wire at the bottom of the icon. This line flashes while a connection is starting up or stopping. When the connection is idle, you do not see this line.

The Remote Access control strip module can also report the duration of the current connection or the amount of time remaining. This statistic appears next to the Remote Access icon in the Control Strip. To specify which statistic you would like to see, press the icon and choose Status Display from the pop-up menu. A dialog box appears in which you can select the type of status information you want to see in the Control Strip. Figure 19-26 shows this dialog box.

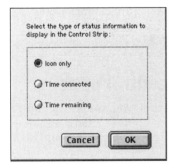

Figure 19-26: Select the type of connection information to display in the Remote Access control strip module.

Making a Remote Network Connection in Mac OS 7.6–8.1

On Macs with Mac OS 7.6–8.1, a variety of software is used to make a remote network connection. This section describes how to set up and establish a remote connection using the following software:

✦ **Remote Access Setup** control panel, which you use to set up your modem for a remote connection to a Mac or an AppleTalk network

✦ **Remote Access Client** program, which you use to start, stop, and monitor a remote connection to a Mac or an AppleTalk network

✦ **PPP** control panel, which you use to start, stop, and monitor a connection to an ISP or a remote TCP/IP network

In addition to these three items, you also use the Modem control panel to set up your modem for a connection to an ISP or a remote TCP/IP network. Because this control panel is also used in Mac OS 8.5, it is described in the previous section "Making a Remote Network Connection in Mac OS 8.5."

All this software is part of a standard installation of Mac OS 8–8.1. In Mac OS 7.6–7.6.1, the Modem and PPP control panels are part of the optional Open Transport 1.0 module, and the Remote Access Setup control panel and the Remote Access Client program are part of the optional Remote Access Client 2.1 module. You can select these modules when you install Mac OS 7.6–7.6.1, as described in Chapter 32.

If you have the Remote Access control panel, you use it and the Modem control panel for all remote connections (see the previous section "Making a Remote Network Connection in Mac OS 8.5"). These two control panels replace the Remote Access Setup control panel, Remote Access Client program, and PPP control panel if you buy and install the Apple Remote Access 3.0 software (or Mac OS 8.5). This software was factory-installed with Mac OS 8.1 on some Macs manufactured during the middle of 1998 (prior to the release of Mac OS 8.5).

Using the Remote Access Setup control panel

If your Mac has the Remote Access Setup control panel, you use it to set up your modem for a remote connection to a computer or an AppleTalk network. This control panel specifies the port for your modem, the type of modem, and dialing options, as shown in Figure 19-27.

The Remote Access Client program connects using the Apple Remote Access Protocol (ARAP). If you want to connect to a remote computer, it must be running the Apple Remote Access Personal Server program, which uses ARAP. The Remote Access Personal Server program is not included with the Mac OS. You can buy this server program from software resellers.

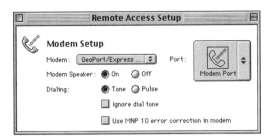

Figure 19-27: Configure a remote AppleTalk connection in the Remote Access Setup control panel.

If you want to connect to a remote AppleTalk network, it must have some kind of server that uses ARAP. The server can be a program running on a computer connected to the remote network or a separate device connected directly to the network.

Using the Remote Access Client program

If your Mac has the Remote Access Client program, you use it to establish a remote connection to a computer or an AppleTalk network. All you need to make a connection is your registered name and password on the remote computer or network (as described in "Using Shared Folders and Disks" in Chapter 20) and the phone number of the remote computer or network server. You can save this information as a Remote Access Client document, which you can later open to make the same connection again. An Options button in the Remote Access Client window lets you specify how to redial if the number is busy. You have the option of entering an alternate number to call if the main number is busy or doesn't answer. There is also the option of being reminded by a flashing icon in the menu bar or an alert message that you must periodically acknowledge in order to maintain your connection. Figure 19-28 is an example of the Remote Access Client window and its Options dialog box.

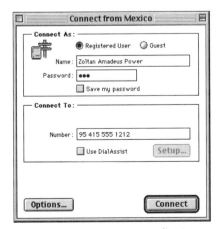
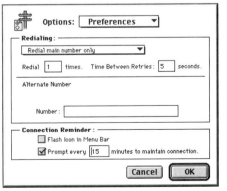

Figure 19-28: Connect to a distant network with the Remote Access Client program (left) and its Options dialog box (right).

Using the PPP control panel

If your Mac has the PPP control panel, you use it to connect to an ISP or to a remote TCP/IP network. Once you have entered the necessary connection information, you can make a connection by clicking the control panel's Connect button. You can also connect automatically by using an application that accesses the Internet or a remote TCP/IP network. You can change this behavior and set a variety of other options that affect the connection by clicking the Options button in the control panel. At the bottom of the Remote Access control panel status information is displayed during a connection. While connected, the Remote Access control panel has a Disconnect button. You can terminate the connection by clicking this button. Figure 19-29 shows the PPP control panel.

Figure 19-29: The PPP control panel connects to an ISP or to a remote TCP/IP network.

PPP configuration

To configure the PPP control panel, you specify whether to connect as a registered user or as an anonymous guest. To connect as a registered user, you must provide a user name or account ID, a password, and the phone number to call to make a connection. As a guest, all you need to provide is the phone number.

Rather than setting options in the PPP control panel directly, you can configure them as a group for a particular network or location with the Configurations command in the File menu. This command displays a dialog box that lists groups of settings by name and has buttons for acting on the group that's selected in the list. There are buttons for making the selected group active, creating a new group by duplicating the selected group, renaming the selected group, and deleting the selected group. Other buttons let you export the selected group as a file and import a group that someone else has exported. Figure 19-30 is an example of the Configurations dialog box.

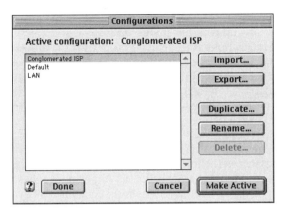

Figure 19-30: The Configurations dialog box lets you work with named groups of settings for different networks or locations.

PPP manual dialing

If you're calling from a place where you must dial the number yourself (such as when making an operator-assisted call), don't click the Connect button in the PPP control panel. Instead, choose Dial Manually from the PPP menu and follow the instructions on the screen.

PPP options

Clicking the Options button in the PPP control panel brings up a dialog box in which you can set options that affect the connection. The options are organized into three groups: Redialing, Connection, and Protocol. You display a group of options by clicking its tab at the top of the dialog box.

The Redialing options determine whether the PPP control panel redials when the phone number is busy and whether it dials an alternate number if there is no answer on the main number. You can specify the number of times to redial before giving up and how long to wait between attempts. This interval should be at least five seconds so that your modem has time to reset itself between dialing attempts. If you specify an alternate number, the PPP control panel tries it once if the main number doesn't answer.

The Connection options control automatic connection, the amount of detail in the connection log, and the behavior of connection reminders. If you turn on automatic connection, the Mac OS makes a connection whenever an application accesses the Internet or a remote TCP/IP network. The wording of this option suggests that the automatic connection happens the moment you open the application. In fact, the automatic connection may happen some time later when you do something in the application that causes it to access the Internet or remote network. For example, you can set a Web browser's preferences so that it will not access the Internet until you choose a bookmark, click a link, or otherwise specify a Web location that you want to see.

The Reminders options, which are under the Connections tab, determine how the Mac OS reminds you of a connection and whether it automatically disconnects under certain circumstances. These options are useful if you pay for the amount of time that you are connected. You can have the Remote Access icon flash above the Apple menu icon to remind you that you are connected. You can have a dialog box appear periodically and automatically stop the connection if no one responds to it. If you turn on this option, you can specify how often this dialog box appears. In addition, you can have the Mac OS automatically disconnect when no program has accessed the Internet or remote network for a number of minutes you specify. If you turn on this option but the Mac OS never disconnects automatically, then some application is continuing to access the Internet or remote network. You may be able to set application preferences to prevent continuous or periodic access; for example, you can set your e-mail program so that it does not check for mail every five minutes. Also note that some Web pages contain items that continuously access the Internet. If you suspect this is happening, go to another Web page, close the Web browser window, or quit the Web browser application.

There are three Protocol options in the PPP control panel's Options dialog box. One option determines whether to allow your modem's hardware to do data compression and error checking. If your modem has these capabilities, turning on this option may improve the performance of the connection. Another Protocol option determines whether the Mac OS will try to compress TCP headers for efficiency. You should leave this option turned on because the ISP or remote network server can refuse header compression without causing a problem. The third Protocol option enables you to connect to an ISP or remote network that requires you to enter specific information, such as your account name and password, while connecting. If you turn on this option, you can select a method for entering the information. One method is to type the information in a terminal window. The other method is to specify a connection script that enters the necessary information for you. You can create a connection script by clicking the Settings button in the terminal window to record your typing while you make a connection.

PPP user modes

You can see more settings or fewer settings in the PPP control panel by changing the user mode. There are two modes, Basic and Administration. To change the user mode, choose User Mode from the Edit menu, and select the mode in the dialog box that appears. Figure 19-31 shows this dialog box.

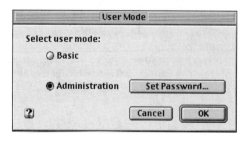

Figure 19-31: Select a user mode for the Modem control panel.

The Basic user mode shows the settings most people need. In the Administration mode, you can lock several settings independently. Locked settings can't be changed in Basic mode. You can also set a password that protects Administration mode settings.

Summary

In this chapter, you learned how to hook up a simple local area network (LAN). You can create a LocalTalk network with inexpensive connector boxes and either Apple's LocalTalk cables or ordinary telephone cords. For a better performing (though more expensive) LAN, you can create an Ethernet network using 10Base-T, which is the lowest in cost of the many Ethernet cabling alternatives. You can also create both LocalTalk and Ethernet networks and bridge them with Apple's LaserWriter Bridge 2.1 or LocalTalk Bridge 2.1 software.

This chapter told you how to configure the Mac OS for network connections. You use the AppleTalk control panel to configure an AppleTalk network connection. You use the TCP/IP control panel to configure a TCP/IP network connection.

In addition, this chapter explained how to connect to a remote computer, remote network, or an Internet service provider (ISP) by modem. To connect to a remote computer or AppleTalk network, you use the Modem and Remote Access control panels or the Remote Access Client program. To connect to an ISP or remote TCP/IP network, you use the Modem control panel and either the Remote Access control panel or the PPP control panel.

✦   ✦   ✦

Access Shared Files and Network Services

Just as you may have books of your own but expand your reading by going to the community library, you can work with more files than you have on your local hard disk by working with shared folders and disks from your local network. What's more, you can go beyond the limits of your local network and use the Internet to obtain files from all over the world.

This chapter explains how to gain access to files from your local network, a remote computer, a remote network, or the Internet. If your computer is not already on a network, Chapter 19 explains how to hook it up to a local network, a remote computer, or a remote network. If your computer is not set up to use the Internet, Chapter 17 tells you how to do it. The same chapter describes a way to make a folder from your computer available as a Web site on the Internet. Chapter 21 explains how to share your folders and disks with other people whose computers are connected to your network.

Using Shared Folders and Disks

If your computer is on a local network, you can connect to shared folders and disks on the network and work with files from them. In addition, you can connect to shared folders and disks on a remote computer or network by modem and phone line.

SECRETS

Mac and Windows File Sharing

If you use a Mac and a Windows PC, you probably need to transfer files back and forth. For small files, you can use floppy disks (if both computers have floppy disk drives). For large files or frequent file transfers, it makes sense to share files over a network.

To use Mac file servers from a Windows PC, you need software that adds AppleTalk protocols to Windows. PC MacLAN for Windows lets a PC use shared Mac folders, disks, and printers as if they were on a Windows network. Conversely, a PC can share selected folders with Macs on the network. The Windows user simply clicks a folder with the right mouse button, selects AppleTalk Sharing from the pop-up menu that appears, and enters the name to use for the shared folder and who has permission to use it. Up to ten Macs can connect to a PC's shared folders at the same time. PC MacLAN is from Miramar Systems (805-966-2432, http://www.miramarsys.com). Instead of PC MacLAN, the Windows PCs on your network could install COPSTalk from CoOperative Printing Solutions (770-840-0810, http://www.copstalk.com). COPSTalk lets a PC see shared Mac folders but not vice versa.

If Macs are in the minority on your network, you may need to install software that enables your Mac to use Windows networking protocols. Dave, from Thursby Systems (817-478-5070, http://www.thursby.com), enables you to use shared folders from Windows PCs and to share your folders and disks with PC users. You can connect to shared Windows folders using the Chooser by clicking the Dave Client icon instead of the AppleShare icon. Alternatively, you can connect using Dave Access. Once you have connected to a shared Windows folder, you can make an alias of it to simplify future connections. To share your folders with Windows PCs, you use the Dave Sharing control panel. Your shared folders show up on Windows PCs in their Network Neighborhood.

For a network between Macs and Windows PCs, Ethernet works great. Many Macs have built-in Ethernet capability and need only a transceiver for a particular type of Ethernet cable, with 10Base-T cable the most popular by far. Some Macs even have a built-in 10Base-T port and don't require a transceiver. Macs without any kind of built-in Ethernet need an Ethernet adapter, and a variety of adapters are available from many manufacturers. Most PCs need an Ethernet network interface card (NIC). There are several options for connecting computers with Ethernet (as discussed in "Hooking Up a Network" in Chapter 19).

This section explains how to connect to shared folders and disks and how to work with them on your computer. In Mac OS 8.5, you can connect to shared folders and disks using the Chooser, the Network Browser, a Navigation Services dialog box, or aliases. In Mac OS 7.6–8.1, you use the Chooser or aliases to connect to shared folders and disks. When you work with a shared folder or disk, the person who owns it may restrict your access to its contents. Subject to these restrictions, you can transfer items between your local disks and the shared folder or disk. You may also be able to open documents and applications directly from the shared folder or disk.

Identifying yourself to a file server

Shared folders and disks are located on computers that are connected to the network. Computers that share folders and disks are known as *file servers*. A file server can be a computer whose principal job is sharing disks for the network at-large. In addition, people can make their personal computers into part-time file servers by using Mac OS file sharing (as described in Chapter 21). The same procedure is followed to connect to shared folders and disks on either kind of file server.

Before you can connect to shared folders and disks on a file server, you need to know the name of the file server. If your network has zones, you also need to find out the name of the zone in which the file server is located. This information is all you need to know to connect to shared folders and disks that allow guest access. Some shared folders and disks may require you to connect as a registered user to work with their files. In this case, you must know your registered name and password on the file server where the shared folders or disks are located. You may have a different registered name and password on each file server. The owner of each file server assigns you a registered name and password, and may allow you to change your password.

Connecting with the Chooser

To make a connection to a shared folder or disk, open the Chooser (under the Apple menu). Look at the bottom right corner of the Chooser and make sure that AppleTalk is active (so that you can use your local network). Next, select the AppleShare icon on the left side of the Chooser to display a list of file servers on the right side of the Chooser. If you see a list of zones on the left side of the Chooser, your network contains zones; you may need to select a different zone to see the file server you want listed on the right side of the Chooser. (If you don't see a list of zones in the Chooser, your network has only one zone.) From the list of file servers, select the one that has the shared folder or disk you want to use. Figure 20-1 shows the Chooser with a file server selected in a network without zones.

Some file servers that use the TCP/IP network protocol instead of AppleTalk are not listed in the Chooser when you click the AppleShare icon. To connect to shared folders and disks on one of these servers, click the Server IP Address button in the Chooser. In the dialog box that appears, enter the file server's IP address (a four-part number such as 198.162.2.100) or its URL (such as afp://server-name/volume-name/folder-path). You can get a server's IP address or URL from the server's owner.

Identifying yourself

When you have selected the file server that has the shared folder or disk that you want to use, click the OK button in the Chooser. A dialog box appears, allowing you to identify yourself as a registered user or guest of the file server. Figure 20-2 is an example of this dialog box.

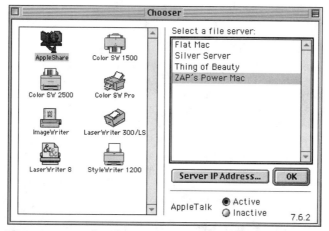

Figure 20-1: In the Chooser, you can select the file server that has a shared folder or disk you want to use.

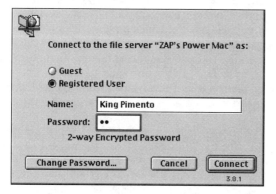

Figure 20-2: Identify yourself as a guest or registered user of a file server.

To connect as a registered user, select the Registered User option, and enter your registered name and password in the spaces provided. The owner of the file server that you want to access must have assigned this name and password. If your own computer is set up as a file server (using Mac OS file sharing) and you're connecting to it from another computer, enter the owner name and password. When you enter your password, you must type it exactly right, including uppercase and lowercase letters (it's case-sensitive). Then click the OK button.

If you're not a registered user and the Guest option isn't dimmed, you can connect to shared folders and disks on a file server that allows guest access. If the Guest option is dimmed, guests are not permitted to access any shared folders or disks on the selected file server. Ask the owner of the file server to give you a registered name and password.

Before connecting to a file server, you may be able to change your password on it. Click the Change Password button, and a series of dialog boxes leads you through the process of changing your password. If you get a message saying that your password couldn't be changed, you probably don't have permission to change your password on the file server you're about to connect to. Contact the owner of that file server to find out.

Selecting network volumes

After connecting you as a registered user or guest of a file server, the Chooser displays a dialog box that names the a file server and lists its shared folders and disks. You select the names of items that you want to use now and the check boxes of items that you want to use each time you start your computer, and then click the OK button. To select more than one item name, Shift-click each name. You can scroll through the list or type the first few letters of a shared item's name to find it. If a listed item is dimmed, either you're already using that folder or disk or the owner of that folder or disk hasn't granted you access privileges to see it. Figure 20-3 is an example of the Chooser's dialog box that lists a file server's shared items.

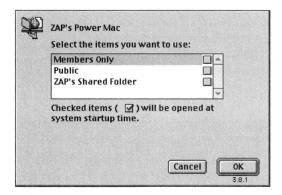

Figure 20-3: Select shared folders and disks from a file server.

If you mark a checkbox and are a registered user, two options appear in the dialog box below the list of items. Select the option Save My Name Only if you want the system to ask for your password before opening the shared folder or disk during startup. Use this option to prevent unauthorized people from accessing the shared folder or disk from your computer by restarting it. If you select the option Save My Name and Password, your computer automatically supplies your password when it opens the checked items during startup.

An icon appears on your desktop for each shared folder or disk you connect to. The icon for a shared folder looks the same as the icon for a shared disk. The Mac OS considers all shared folders and shared disks to be a kind of disk.

Connecting with the Network Browser

Instead of connecting to shared folders and disks using the Chooser in Mac OS 8.5, you can use the Network Browser (under the Apple menu). When you open the Network Browser, it displays a list of file servers on your network. (Some file servers that use the TCP/IP network protocol instead of the AppleTalk network protocol do not appear in the list.) If your network has multiple zones, they appear in the Network Browser as well. To connect to a shared folder or disk on a file server, you must open the file server in the Network Browser. Figure 20-4 is an example of the Network Browser.

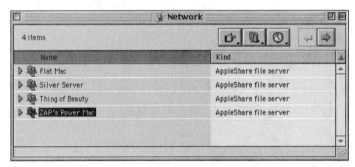

Figure 20-4: In the Network Browser, you can connect to shared folders and disks from any file server on your network.

To open a file server in the Network Browser, do one of the following:

✦ Double-click the file server's name or icon. A list of shared folders and disks from the file server will replace the list of file servers in the Network Browser.

✦ Click the disclosure triangle to the left of the file server's icon so that it points down. The shared disks and folders from the file server will be listed below it in the Network Browser.

✦ Select the file server (by clicking it once) and choose Open in Place or Open in New Window from the File menu. The Open in Place command will replace the list of file servers with a list of shared folders and disks from the file server you open. The Open in New Window will display the list of shared folders and disks in a new window, leaving the list of file servers displayed in a background window.

✦ Choose a file server or a shared disk from the pop-up menu of the Favorites button or the Recent button. These pop-up menus are described in more detail later in this section.

✦ For a file server that uses the TCP/IP network protocol, choose Connect to Server from the pop-up menu of the Shortcuts button. In the dialog box that appears, enter the file server's IP network address (a four-part number such as 198.162.2.100) or its URL (such as afp://server-name/volume-name/folder-path).

Identifying yourself

When you open a file server or shared disk in the Network Browser, a dialog box appears asking you to identify yourself as a registered user or guest of the file server. Figure 20-5 is an example of this dialog box.

```
Connect to the file server "Flat Mac" as:

  ○ Guest
  ● Registered User

  Name:      Zoltan Amadeus Power

  Password:  •••
             2-way Encrypted Password

  [ Change Password... ]      [ Cancel ]  [ Connect ]
```

Figure 20-5: Identify yourself as a guest or registered user of a file server.

To connect as a registered user, select the Registered User option, and enter your registered name and password in the spaces provided. The owner of the file server that you want to access must have assigned this name and password. If your own computer is set up as a file server (using Mac OS file sharing) and you're connecting to it from another computer, enter the owner name and password. When you enter your password, you must type it exactly right, including uppercase and lowercase letters (it's case-sensitive). Then click the OK button.

If you're not a registered user and the Guest option isn't dimmed, you can connect to shared folders and disks on a file server that allows guest access. If the Guest option is dimmed, guests are not permitted access to any shared folders or disks on the file server. Ask the owner of the file server to give you a registered name and password.

Before connecting to a file server, you may be able to change your password on it. Click the Change Password button, and a series of dialog boxes leads you through the process of changing your password. If you get a message saying your password couldn't be changed, you probably don't have permission to change your password on the file server you're about to connect to. Contact the owner of that file server to find out.

Opening shared folders and disks

After connecting you as a registered user or guest of a file server, the Network Browser displays a list of the shared folders and disks that the file server allows you to see. In this list, the icon for a shared folder looks the same as the icon for a shared disk, because the Mac OS considers all shared folders and shared disks to be a kind of disk. You can open the shared folders and disks using any of these methods:

✦ Double-click a shared folder or disk. Its icon appears on the desktop and opens in the Finder.

✦ Select a shared folder or disk and choose Open in New Window from the File menu. An icon for the shared folder or disk appears on the desktop and opens in the Finder.

✦ Choose a shared folder or disk from the pop-up menu of the Favorites button or the Recent button. These pop-up menus are described in more detail under the next four headings.

Note that you can open only one folder or disk at time with the Network Browser. In contrast, the Chooser lets you select multiple shared items on the same file server and connect to them all at once.

Using the Shortcuts button

The Network Browser's Shortcuts button (the pointing-finger icon) provides quick access to the file servers on your AppleTalk network and a means of connecting to file servers on a TCP/IP network. Clicking this button displays a pop-up menu, as shown in Figure 20-6.

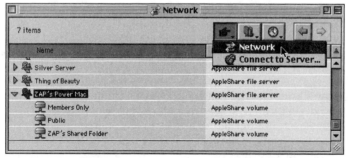

Figure 20-6: The Shortcuts menu provides quick access to file servers on your AppleTalk network and lets you connect to a file server on a TCP/IP network.

Choosing Network from the Shortcuts pop-up menu takes the Network Browser back to a list of file servers (and zones, if your network has them).

Choosing Connect to Server from the Shortcuts pop-up menu allows you to connect to a file server by entering an IP network address (such as 192.168.1.254) or a URL (such as afp://server-name/volume-name/folder-path). The file server must be one that uses the TCP/IP network protocol instead of the AppleTalk network protocol. You can get a server's IP address or URL from the server's owner.

Using the Favorites button

The Network Browser's Favorites button (the bookmarked-folder icon) lists your favorite shared folders, shared disks, file servers, and zones in a pop-up menu when you click it. Figure 20-7 is an example of this pop-up menu.

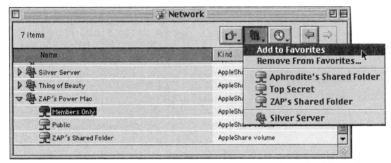

Figure 20-7: The Favorites menu lists your favorite shared folders, disks, file servers, and zones.

When you choose an item from the Favorites pop-up menu, the Network Browser displays it. If you're not already connected to a shared folder or disk from the same file server, the Network Browser asks you to identify yourself as a registered user or guest (as described previously).

You can add items displayed in the Network Browser to the Favorites pop-up menu. To add an item, select it and choose Add to Favorites from the Favorites pop-up menu. Alternatively, you can drag the item to the Favorites button. Note that in the Network Browser, only your favorite shared folders, shared disks, and file servers appear in the Favorites pop-up menu. Other kinds of favorites, such as regular folders and files that are in shared folders and disks, appear in Favorites pop-up menus in other contexts.

All your favorite items have aliases in the Favorites folder inside the System Folder. This folder is normally listed in the Apple menu.

You can remove items from the Favorites pop-up menu using the Remove Favorites command. This command displays a dialog box that lists all items in the Favorites folder, including items that don't appear in the Network Browser's Favorites pop-up menu. To delete a favorite, select it in the Remove Favorites dialog box and click Remove. You can select multiple favorites to remove by Shift-clicking and Command-clicking them.

To rename a favorite, change the name of its alias in the Favorites folder. You can also add and remove favorites by adding and removing aliases in the Favorites folder.

Using the Recent button

The Network Browser's Recent button (the clockface icon) lists your most recently used shared folders and disks in a pop-up menu when you click it. Figure 20-8 is an example of this pop-up menu.

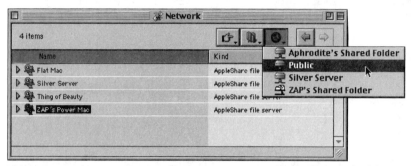

Figure 20-8: The Recent menu lists your most recently used shared folders and disks.

When you choose an item from this menu, the Network Browser displays it. If you're not already connected to a shared folder or disk from the same file server, the Network Browser asks you to identify yourself as a registered user or guest (as described previously).

The number of items listed in the Recent pop-up menu is controlled by options in the Apple Menu Options control panel. To change the number of items, enter a different number for the Servers option. If you enter zero for the Servers option or turn off the "Remember recently used items" option, the Recent pop-up menu will be inactive the next time you open the Network Browser.

Some items listed in the Recent pop-up menu have aliases in the Recent Servers folder inside the Apple Menu folder. Other items listed in the Recent pop-up menu have aliases in the Recent folder that is in the Network Browser folder inside the Preferences folder within the System Folder. You can edit the Recent pop-up menu by renaming, adding, and removing items in these two folders. The Recent Servers folder gets moved to the Trash if you turn off the "Remember recently used items" option in the Apple Menu Options control panel.

Using the Back and Forward buttons

You can go back to see the last item you opened in the Network Browser window by clicking the Back button (the left-arrow (←) icon). After going back, you can go forward by clicking the Forward button (the right-arrow (→) icon).

Connecting with Navigation Services

In Mac OS 8.5, you can connect to shared folders and disks directly from the Navigation Services dialog box that some applications use for opening and saving files. To have the Navigation Services dialog box display a list of the file servers on your network, press the Shortcuts button (with the pointing-hand icon) and choose Network from its pop-up menu. If your network has multiple zones, they appear in the Navigation Services dialog box as well. Figure 20-9 is an example list of file servers in a Navigation Services dialog box.

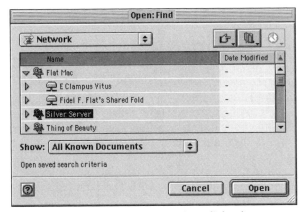

Figure 20-9: In a Navigation Services dialog box, you can connect to shared folders or disks from any file server on your network.

Once you see the list of file servers in a Navigation Services dialog box, follow the same procedure as previously described for the Network Browser to connect to a shared folder or disk. After connecting to a shared folder or disk, you browse it in the Navigation Services dialog box as if it were a local hard disk (for more information, see "Opening Programs, Documents, and More" in Chapter 7).

Connecting with aliases and network locations

You don't have to go through the Chooser or the Network Browser to use a shared folder or disk again. Connect once as described previously and while the shared item's icon is on your desktop, make an alias of it. You can also make an alias of a file or folder contained in the shared folder or disk. If you open the alias of something located on a file server, the Mac OS connects to the file server and opens the alias's original item for you. You have to enter your password again unless you were connected as a guest when you made the alias.

In Mac OS 8.5, you can use the Network Browser to make an alias of any item you can see in it. One method is to select the shared item and choose Make Alias from the Network Browser's File menu. An alert message advises you that the alias must be created on the desktop; click OK to do this or Cancel to call it off. You can also make an alias by dragging an item from the Network Browser to the desktop.

When you make an alias of a file server in Mac OS 8.5, the file that is created is not actually an alias. It is a *network location.* Opening a network location (for example, by double-clicking its icon) opens the Network Browser and displays a list of the file server's shared folders and disks that you are allowed to see. (When you make an alias of a shared folder, shared disk, folder, or file, you get an alias.)

Recognizing your access privileges

Connecting to a shared folder or disk doesn't necessarily give you unlimited access to its contents. Access to the contents can be restricted on a folder-by-folder basis. What you can do with a folder depends on the access privileges that its owner has granted you. You may be allowed to open a folder, or confined to putting things into it, or forbidden from using it at all. If you can open a folder, you may be allowed to see only files, only folders, or both files and folders inside it. The Finder indicates your access privileges to folders inside a shared folder or disk with special folder icons and small icons in folder and disk windows. You can also determine your privileges by displaying a folder's Info window (Mac OS 8.5) or sharing window (Mac OS 7.6–8.1).

Ascertaining privileges from folder icons

Often you can ascertain your privileges for a folder by looking at the folder's icon. A folder icon with a belt around it indicates that you don't have any access privileges. A belt-strapped folder icon with an accompanying down arrow (↓) is a drop box; you can drop items into the folder but cannot open it or use anything inside it. In Mac OS 8.5, a small padlock appears on the icon of a folder that is locked. A locked folder can't be renamed, moved to a different folder, or put in the Trash. Figure 20-10 shows examples of the special folder icons.

Privilege icons in window headers

When you open a folder that belongs to someone else, look for one or two small icons just below the window's close box. The icons indicate any privileges that the folder's owner has denied you. A pencil with a line through it means that you can't make changes to items in the window. A document with a line through it means that you can't see files in the window. A folder with a line through it means that you can't see folders in the window. Figure 20-11 shows examples of the privilege icons in Mac OS 8–8.5.

You can
open these
folders

You can only
drop things
into these folders

You can't use
these folders
at all

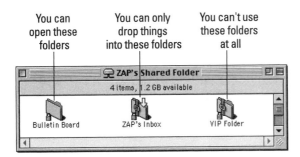

Figure 20-10: Special folder icons indicate access privileges in Mac OS 8.5 (top), Mac OS 8–8.1 (middle), and Mac OS 7.6–7.6.1 (bottom).

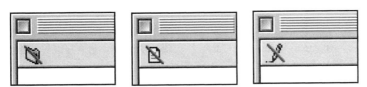

Figure 20-11: Identifying denied privileges in windows: can't see folders (left), can't see files (middle), and can't make changes (right).

Privileges in an Info window or sharing window

In addition to interpreting access privileges from icons, you can look at the Info window (Mac OS 8.5) or the sharing window (Mac OS 7.6–8.1) of a shared folder or disk you're using. For an item shared from another computer, the Info window or sharing window tells where the item is, the name under which you're connected, and your access privileges for that item. Table 20-1 shows the access privileges that you need in order to perform common tasks with a shared folder or disk. Figure 20-12 shows examples of the Info window and the sharing window.

Table 20-1
Access Privileges for Common Tasks

To do this with a shared folder or disk:	You need these privileges: Mac OS 8–8.5	Mac OS 7.6–7.6.1
Open a file from it	Read Only or Read & Write	See Files
Save changes to a file in it	Read & Write	See Files, Make Changes
Drag something to it	Write Only or Read & Write	Make Changes
Copy a file from it	Read Only or Read & Write	See Files
Copy a folder from it	Read Only or Read & Write	See Folders
Discard a file from it	Read & Write	See Files, Make Changes
Discard a folder from it	Read & Write	See Folders, Make Changes
Create a file in it Make Changes	Read & Write	See Folders, See Files,
Create a folder in it	Read & Write	See Folders, Make Changes

To view sharing information in Mac OS 8.5, select the shared folder or disk and choose Sharing from the Get Info submenu of the File menu. You can also choose this command from the folder or disk's contextual menu. If an item's Info window is open but is not displaying its sharing information, choose Sharing from the Show pop-up menu near the top of the Info window.

To view sharing information in Mac OS 7.6–8.1, select the shared folder or disk and choose Sharing from the File menu. You can also choose this command from the folder or disk's contextual menu in Mac OS 8–8.1.

Unless you're the owner of the item, you can only view the privileges. Only the item's owner can change its privileges (as described in Chapter 21).

An owner's special privileges

If you connect to a file server as its owner, you can see and use everything on that file server's disks. In other words, you have full access privileges to all items, whether or not they have been designated for sharing. This feature is handy if you need copies of files from your computer while you're not at your desk. If you leave file sharing turned on (as described in the next chapter), you can connect to your computer from another computer on your network. Then you can copy your files to the computer you're using. From there you can read, change, or print the files you copied. However, other people can also access all your files if they learn your owner name and password. You can reduce this risk at the expense of convenience, as discussed in "Controlling Security Risks" in Chapter 21.

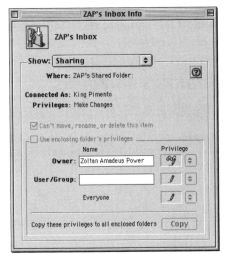

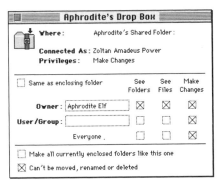

Figure 20-12: See access privileges in Mac OS 8.5 (top left), Mac OS 8–8.1 (top right), or Mac OS 7.6–7.6.1 (bottom).

Transferring network files

The most common use of shared folders and disks is to transfer files or folders between your computer and a shared folder or disk. For the most part, you transfer files and folders to and from a shared folder or disk just as you would copy files to and from a floppy disk.

Opening network files

When you open a shared document, Finder searches your local disks for the application needed to open the document. If you don't have the necessary application, Finder opens the application across the network. Running applications over a network is usually slower than running an application on your computer. To give you a rough idea of network activity, the Mac OS displays a small double-arrow in the upper left corner of the menu bar while it is sending or receiving anything over the network.

Disconnecting from shared folders and disks

In general, you remain connected to a shared folder or disk until you deliberately disconnect from it. You disconnect from a shared folder or disk by removing its icon from your desktop. You can drag the desktop icon to the Trash, or you can select it and use the Finder's Put Away or Eject commands. Restarting or shutting down your computer also disconnects you from all shared folders and disks, although you may be reconnected to individual shared folders or disks automatically on startup if you selected this option in the Chooser (see "Connecting with the Chooser" in the previous section of this chapter). Putting a PowerBook to sleep disconnects all shared folders and disks. Putting a desktop Mac to sleep does not disconnect shared folders and disks.

There are a couple of ways that you can be disconnected involuntarily from a shared disk. For one, the owner of a shared folder or disk can summarily disconnect you. If you are connected to a shared folder or disk on a remote computer or network, the duration of your connection may be limited. When your time runs out, you are automatically disconnected. You can usually reconnect if a timed connection expires or a file server's owner disconnects you.

Of course, you will be disconnected without warning if the file server shuts down or if some problem arises with the network equipment. In addition, you will be disconnected from shared folders and disks on a PowerBook if it goes to sleep. In contrast, you generally will not be disconnected from shared folders and disks on a desktop computer that goes to sleep.

Disconnecting a shared folder or disk may not disconnect your computer from its file server. Your computer remains connected to a file server as long as any of its shared folders or disks are on your desktop. While your computer is connected to a file server, you don't have to enter your user name or password to connect to any shared folders or disks that the owner has given you access privileges to see. In other words, you can reconnect to a shared folder or disk without entering your password if you are still connected to another of the file server's shared folders or disks. The file server's security can be breeched by this convenience if you're not careful.

To keep file servers secure, you should disconnect from all shared folders and disks before leaving your computer unattended. If you leave shared folders and disks on your desktop when you step away, anyone who can use your computer can connect to other shared items that you have access privileges to see on the same file server. Removing all shared folder and disk icons from your desktop means you must enter your name and password again to reconnect, but so must anyone else.

Obtaining Files from the Internet

In addition to using files from shared folders and disks on your network, you can obtain useful (and sometimes, absolutely frivolous) files on the Internet from other computers all over the world. The process of copying files from the Internet to your computer is called *downloading.* Similarly, if you send a file from your computer, you are *uploading* the file.

On the Internet, files are sent using a protocol (network language) called *FTP* (File Transfer Protocol). A computer can make files available using this protocol by running a type of program called an *FTP server.* This term also refers to the combination of the server program and the computer that's running it. You may sometimes hear people refer to an *FTP site,* which is a collection of files on an FTP server that are available for downloading. An FTP site has the same function on the Internet as a shared disk on your network.

To receive or send files using this protocol, you use a program called an *FTP client* on your computer. The FTP client connects your computer to an FTP server and handles downloading and uploading (receiving and sending) the files. An FTP client has the same function on the Internet as the Chooser or Network Browser and Finder on a local network.

There are FTP clients built into Internet Explorer, Netscape Navigator, and Cyberdog, the Web browser programs that come with Mac OS 7.6–8.5. In addition, there are independent FTP client programs such as the low-cost shareware Fetch and Anarchie (more about these later). They are available from FTP sites on the Internet.

Getting ready to download

Before downloading any files, you should specify where to put them. The best place to do this in Mac OS 8.5 is the Internet control panel. If necessary, click the Edit Sets disclosure triangle to expand the control panel and see its individual preference settings. From the Edit Set pop-up menu, choose the set of preferences that you want to edit. Next, click the Web tab to see Web and FTP options. Then, in the area labeled Download, click the Select button. This brings up a Navigation Services dialog box, in which you select the folder that you want to use for downloaded files. Figure 20-13 shows the Web and FTP preferences in the Internet control panel.

In Mac OS 7.6–8.1, the best place to specify a folder for downloaded files is in the Internet Config program. You click the File Transfer button in Internet Config's Internet Preferences window to bring up the File Transfer window. At the bottom of this window, click the button next to the label Download Folder. This brings up an Open dialog box, in which you select the folder you want to use for downloaded files. Finally, quit Internet Config and save the changes you made when asked if you wish to do so. Figure 20-14 shows the File Transfer window in Internet Config.

Click here to select a folder for downloaded files

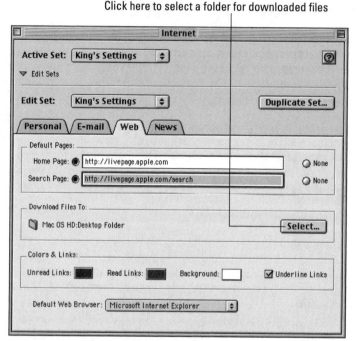

Figure 20-13: Set the folder for downloaded files in Mac OS 8.5 with the Internet control panel.

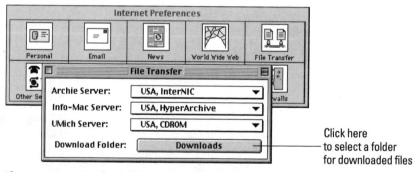

Click here to select a folder for downloaded files

Figure 20-14: Set the folder for downloaded files in Mac OS 7.6–8.1 with Internet Config.

If you don't use the Internet control panel or Internet Config, you should set the destination folder in your Web browser or FTP client. Using Netscape Navigator 4.05 as an example, choose Preferences from the Edit menu, select the Advanced tab in the resulting dialog box, and then click the Browse button next to the text that begins Downloads Directory. This brings up an Open dialog box, in which you select the folder you want to use for downloaded files. After selecting a downloads folder, the path to it appears in the General Preferences dialog box.

Downloading files

Here's how most FTP file transfers work: While browsing a Web page, you come across a description of a file that interests you, with a link to download the file. You click the link, and the browser opens a file-transfer progress window and downloads the file to your hard disk. Pretty easy, right? That's because browsers understand how to handle URLs that begin with ftp:// — they route them to their built-in FTP client programs. Figure 20-15 shows how this works in Netscape Navigator 4.05.

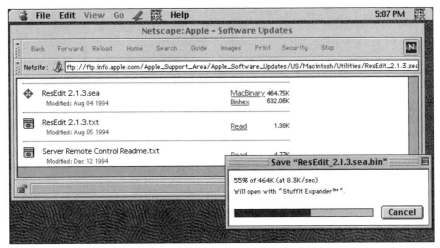

Figure 20-15: Using Netscape Navigator to download a file. Note the small progress window at the lower right.

Downloading with FTP client programs

Sometimes you want to download a file from an FTP site but you don't want or need to fire up a Web browser. Or perhaps you want to upload a file, which most Web browsers can't do. Instead, you can use one of the independent FTP client programs that are available for the Mac OS. Of these, the two most popular are Anarchie and Fetch. Both are shareware, but ask your Internet service provider if they have a license to distribute Fetch free. (For information on obtaining shareware, see "Where to Get Utility Software" in Chapter 26.)

Anarchie

Anarchie is a terrific FTP program written by the Australian author Peter Lewis. Anarchie lets you work with files on FTP servers in much the same way that you work with files in Finder. Some other FTP programs make you deal with files in directory dialog boxes (similar to the Open and Save dialog boxes). With Anarchie, if you want to download a file from an FTP server, you go to that server and double-click a folder icon that represents one of the file directories on the FTP server. A window opens with the contents of the directory (as it might if you had a Finder window open to a list view). To download a file or group of files from the open directory, you can simply select them and drag them to your Mac OS desktop. Uploading is as simple as dragging files from your desktop to a directory window. Anarchie also keeps a handy set of bookmarks with pointers to useful FTP sites of interest to Mac OS users. Figure 20-16 shows the Mac OS desktop with an FTP server's Internet folder open to display the Anarchie files.

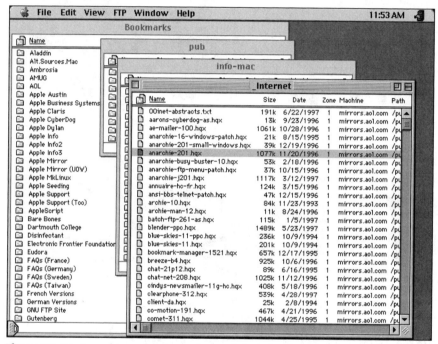

Figure 20-16: Anarchie makes browsing and downloading files from FTP servers easy.

Fetch

Fetch was developed by Dartmouth University and was one of the earliest FTP programs available for the Mac OS. Working with files in Fetch 3.0.3 isn't quite like working with files in the Finder. After connecting to a server, you can double-click a folder to see its contents, but the folder's contents don't appear in a new window. Instead, the folder opens in the same window. So, you can only see one folder at a time. To see a previous folder, you choose it from a pop-up menu at the top of the Fetch window. You can download files by dragging them to your desktop, and you can upload files by dragging from your desktop to the Fetch window. Fetch also lets you keep a list of shortcuts for fast access to favorite FTP sites.

Decoding and decompressing files

Files that you download from the Internet must be converted into a form that your Mac can use. The reason that this is necessary has to do partly with the Internet and partly with the Mac OS. First, the Internet is pretty much a plain-text environment; it sends streams of text across the phone lines. But pictures, formatted text, sounds, application programs, and most other kinds of Mac files aren't plain-text files; they're a kind of file called a *binary file*. For binary files to be sent over the Internet, they must be converted into text files.

There are several standards for encoding binary files as plain text. The two most commonly used for Mac files are called *BinHex* and *MacBinary*. In general, MacBinary produces smaller encoded files, which take less time to download. However, BinHex-encoded files download somewhat more reliably than MacBinary-encoded files.

Besides being encoded as plain text, files that you download from the Internet are usually compressed. This is a scheme where a binary file is run through a compression program before it is encoded with BinHex or MacBinary. The resulting compressed binary file is considerably smaller in size than the uncompressed file and, as a result, it takes less time to upload and download.

There are many methods for compressing files. With Mac files, the most common compression method is the one used by the Stuffit family of programs from Aladdin Systems (408-761-6200, http://www.aladdinsys.com). *Stuffed* files are compressed with this method. With Windows and DOS files, the most common compression method is called *ZIP*, after the PKZip DOS program that originated it. *Zipped* files are compressed with this method.

You can usually tell what type of file you're downloading by looking at the series of letters after the period at the end of the file's name. This part of the name is called the *extension*. Table 20-2 deciphers the extensions of encoded and compressed files that you're likely to encounter while cruising the Internet.

Using file converter software

When you receive a file that has been encoded and possibly compressed as well, software on your computer must decode and decompress the file before you can use it. First, the software decodes the BinHex or MacBinary file and saves a decoded version of the file. Then the software decompresses this file and saves yet another file. The last file is the one you can actually use. You end up with two or three files: the encoded version (typically with an extension of .hqx or .bin), the compressed version (usually with the extension .sit or .sea), and the binary file. You'll probably want to throw away the encoded and compressed versions once you have the decoded binary file.

Table 20-2
File Name Extensions for Encoded and Compressed Files

File Name Extension	What It Means
.bin	Encoded in MacBinary format (also known as BinHex5)
.gz	Compressed with Unix *GNU Zip* program
.hqx	Encoded in BinHex4 format
.img	Encoded as a disk image
.sea	Self Extracting Archive — compressed with StuffIt or another program, but no separate decompression utility needed
.sit	Compressed with StuffIt
.smi	Encoded as a self-mounting disk image
.tar	Multiple files combined into one with the Unix tar program
.uu or .uue	Encoded in UUencode format
.z or .Z	Compressed with Unix *compress* program
.zip	Compressed with the DOS or Windows PKZip program

The application programs that handle decoding and decompressing are sometimes called *helper* applications because they work in conjunction with FTP clients, Web browsers, and other Internet programs that receive and send files on the Internet. The Web browser or FTP client inspects a downloaded file's extension and tells the appropriate helper application to decode or decompress a file. The helper opens (usually into the background), does its job, and quits. Often, you won't even be aware that the process has taken place.

StuffIt Expander

A pair of helper applications that come with Mac OS 8–8.5 will handle virtually all of your decoding and decompressing needs. The first member of this matched pair is called StuffIt Expander, and it's free from Aladdin Systems. StuffIt Expander can decode and decompress most Mac files you find on the Internet. It can decode BinHex (.hqx or .hex) or MacBinary (.bin) files, and it can decompress StuffIt (.sit) and Compact Pro (.cpt) files. StuffIt Expander is incredibly easy to use; if your Internet applications don't open it automatically as needed, you can simply drag-and-drop files onto the StuffIt Expander icon. You can also set StuffIt Expander preferences to automatically decode and decompress all files that show up in a particular folder that you choose.

StuffIt Expander can handle many more encoding and compression methods if you install the $30 shareware package called DropStuff with Expander Enhancer, also from Aladdin Systems. The Expander Enhancer part of this package enables StuffIt Expander to expand files compressed with virtually every compression format found on Mac OS, Unix, Windows, and DOS computers. These include ZIP (.zip),

ARC (.arc), gzip (.gz), Unix Compress (.Z), UUencode (.uu), and StuffIt SpaceSaver files. It will also join files that were segmented with another StuffIt product. The programs are accelerated on PowerPC computers, though they'll work fine (albeit a bit slower) on other Macs.

The DropStuff part of the shareware package enables you to compress and encode files that you want to send on the Internet. You can have your Internet applications open it automatically, and you can compress and encode files by dragging them to the DropStuff icon.

The really great thing about the StuffIt Expander package is that it operates transparently. When you click an FTP link in your Web browser, the browser downloads the file from the FTP server, then hands off the file to StuffIt Expander, which decodes the file (converting it back into a binary file), decompresses the file further if necessary, and automatically quits. StuffIt Expander can also handle batches of files to be decoded and decompressed at the same time, and (if you prefer) it's smart enough to automatically delete the BinHex-encoded files once it finishes decoding them.

ZipIt

If you need to compress files that you want to send to a Windows PC on the Internet, there are two choices. If you want to compress files using the ZIP method, which is the standard method on PCs, you can run the ZipIt program on your Mac. This program can also decompress ZIP files on your Mac. ZipIt is $15 shareware.

Instead of using the ZIP format, you can compress using the StuffIt format that's commonly used on Macs. You can compress files in this format with the DropStuff program that's part of the DropStuff with Expander Enhancer shareware just described. PC users who want to expand your compressed files will need the free StuffIt Expander for Windows program from Aladdin Systems.

Summary

In this chapter, you learned how to connect to and work with shared folders and disks from file servers on your local network. The file servers can be computers that specialize in sharing folders and disks, or they can be personal computers using Mac OS file sharing. The basic means of connecting to shared folders and disks is the Chooser. In Mac OS 8.5, you can also connect using the Network Browser and Navigation Services dialog boxes. You can streamline subsequent connections to a shared folder or disk by opening an alias of it or of any item in it.

This chapter also explained that the owner of a shared folder or disk can restrict your access to it. To determine your access privileges to a folder, you can look at its icon, open it, and look for small icons in the header of its window, or inspect the Sharing section of its Info window (Mac OS 8.5) or sharing window (Mac OS 7.6–8.1).

This chapter also discussed transferring and opening files on the network. In addition, you learned how to disconnect from shared folders and disks.

Besides sharing folders and disks on your local network, you can download and upload files on the Internet. This chapter told you about downloading with a Web browser or an FTP client. You also learned about decoding and decompressing downloaded files so you can use them.

✦   ✦   ✦

Share Your Files

Just as you can share books with people who live and work near you, the Mac OS allows you to share disks, folders, and the files in them with people whose computers are on the same network as your computer. You control who can connect to your shared folders and disks, and you determine what other people can do with the contents of your shared folders and disks.

This chapter explains how to share some of your folders or disks with other people on your network. First you plan for file sharing and identify your computer on the network. Next you start the Mac OS file-sharing feature on your computer and designate which disks or folders contain files that you want to share. Then you can identify who you want to let access your shared items. For each of your shared folders you can restrict the type of access some people have. At any time you can monitor file-sharing activity to see who is connected to your computer and how much of its processing power is consumed by file sharing.

Other people connect to and work with your shared folders and disks using the same procedures that you use with theirs. Chapter 20 describes how you can gain access to other peoples' shared files on your local network, a remote computer, a remote network connect, or the Internet. If your computer is not already on a network, Chapter 19 explains how to hook it up to one.

Planning for File Sharing

The personal file-sharing capabilities of the Mac OS make sharing items across a network surprisingly easy, but not without some cost. This section discusses the capabilities and limitations of Mac OS file sharing so that you can decide in advance whether it meets your needs. The alternative to file sharing is a dedicated, centralized file server.

Distributed or centralized file sharing

Your network can implement file sharing in a distributed or centralized fashion. With distributed file sharing, which is also known as *peer-to-peer file sharing,* each computer makes files, folders, and disks available to other computers on the network. While your computer shares your files with other computers, you are free to use your computer for other tasks. Reduced performance of your computer while other computers are accessing it is the price you pay for making files from your computer available for people using other computers to share. In addition, the Mac OS file sharing limits the number of people that can share the same folder or disk at the same time, which makes file sharing unsuitable for serving files to large numbers of computers on a network.

By contrast, a network with centralized file sharing dedicates one computer (or more) to providing file-sharing services. That computer runs file server software, such as Apple's AppleShare IP software, which enables the computer to serve files to a large number of other computers. Other computers on the network get shared files from the dedicated *file server* (or file servers) rather than from each other. Usually, a computer that acts as a dedicated file server needs to be fast and to have one or more large hard disks. The Mac OS does not include file server software; you must purchase it separately.

Although the Mac OS file-sharing capabilities are designed for distributed file sharing, you can use file sharing on a dedicated computer to create an ersatz dedicated file server for a small network. Folders or entire hard disks on that file-server computer can be made available to other computers on the network as described in the remainder of this chapter.

The problem with an ersatz file server is its performance. The Mac OS assumes somebody is using the dedicated computer for more than sharing files and reserves about 50 percent of the dedicated computer's processing power for nonfile-sharing tasks. A utility called Nok Nok 2.0 from PB Computing (512-378-4444, http://www.pbcomputing.com), which sells for $25, can adjust the amount of processing power reserved for file sharing, greatly improving file-sharing performance. Apple's AppleShare IP 6.0 provides even faster file service, and other services to boot, but it costs $499 to $1599, depending on the number of users.

Limitations on file sharing

With personal file sharing you can designate up to ten disks or folders whose contents you want to share (as described later in this chapter). Only the disks and folders you designate count toward the limit of ten shared items; folders inside the designated disks and folders don't count toward the limit.

Up to ten other computers can be connected to your shared folders and disks at one time, but only five can access files at once. This limit applies only to file sharing, not necessarily to other network activity such as using a multiuser database file located on your computer.

BACKGROUNDER

AppleShare IP 6.0 File Server

A network with more than ten people actively sharing files needs a dedicated file server administered by software such as Apple's AppleShare IP 6.0 software. The AppleShare IP software extends network file-sharing and background-printing services beyond what the Mac OS provides. Installing AppleShare IP turns a computer into an efficient centralized file server capable of sharing the files and folders on its hard disk (or disks) among up to 500 simultaneous users (10,000 registered users) of Mac OS, Windows 95–98, and Windows NT computers. In addition to being a Mac OS file and printer server, AppleShare IP provides Internet services such as e-mail, Web, and FTP.

Centralized disk storage reduces the amount of local disk storage required by each networked computer, while providing a way for people who work together to share information. People can store files on the server's disks, where other people can open or copy them. Many people can access the server's disks and folders simultaneously, and new files become available to everyone instantly. Unlike the file sharing provided by the Mac OS, no one uses the server's computer to do personal work because it is dedicated to providing network services. Conversely, your computer is not burdened when someone else on the network accesses one of your shared items on the AppleShare server's disks.

A centralized file server is set up and maintained by a trained person called a *network administrator*. The AppleShare IP software includes organizational, administrative, and security features to manage file access on the network. The network administrator does not control access to folders and files on the server's disks; that is the responsibility of each person who puts items on the disks.

AppleShare's file server is compatible with the Mac OS file sharing. You use the methods described in this chapter to make your files available for sharing whether those files are on your computer's hard disk or the file server's hard disks. You also access files on the file server's hard disks using the methods described in Chapter 20.

The AppleShare IP print server supports up to 30 AppleTalk PostScript printers, 10 queues, and 32 simultaneous print sessions so users don't have to wait for print jobs to finish or have their computers bogged down by background printing. It can balance the total printing load among all available printers, so that faster printers do more of the work. The printer server is available to Mac OS and Windows computers on the network.

AppleShare IP 6.0 software runs on a Mac computer with a PowerPC G3, 604e, 604, or 601 processor; it also runs on a Power Mac 6500 (which has a PowerPC 603e processor). AppleShare IP 6.0 requires 48MB of RAM (64MB with virtual memory turned off) and Mac OS 8.1–8.5.

You can identify registered users and groups of users and specify which of them can connect to your shared folders and disks. In addition, you can restrict who can access each folder and what kind of access is allowed: reading, writing, both, or neither. You'll find more on identifying who can access your shared items and on controlling access to your shared items later in this chapter.

If you need to exceed the limitations described here, your network needs a dedicated file server such as AppleShare IP 6.0.

You cannot use Mac OS file sharing and Apple's At Ease software at the same time. If you turn on file sharing while using At Ease, your computer may freeze. (At Ease provides a simplified desktop for children and novices; a restricted Finder desktop for limiting experienced users to folders and applications you designate; and a normal Finder interface for authorized users. At Ease is not included with the Mac OS; you purchase and install it separately.)

Guidelines for file sharing

These guidelines and tips for sharing folders and disks help to optimize file sharing and prevent potential problems:

✦ Share from the highest level of your disk and folder structure. For example, a disk can't be shared if it contains an already-shared folder (no matter how deeply nested in the unshared disk). If you attempt to share a disk or folder that contains an already-shared folder, you get a message telling you that the disk or folder cannot be shared because it contains a shared folder. To work around this situation, identify the shared items (as explained in "Monitoring File Sharing Activity" later in this chapter), unshare it, and then share the enclosing disk or folder.

✦ Share as few folders as possible. The more shared folders being accessed, the greater the memory and processing demands on your computer. Sharing too many folders can slow your system to a crawl.

✦ Check any applicable licensing agreements before sharing folders that contain programs, artwork, or sounds. Often, licensing agreements or copyright laws restrict use of these items to a single computer.

✦ Set up a dedicated computer to act as a dedicated file server for the shared information. This method is often the most efficient way to share numerous files or to share folders with several users simultaneously.

Identifying Your Computer

Before you can begin sharing files, you must give your computer a network identity. Identifying your computer involves entering the name of its owner, a password to prevent other people from connecting to your computer as its owner, and a name for your computer. With Mac OS 8–8.5, you specify those facts when you go through the Mac OS Setup Assistant program. The Assistant comes up automatically the first time you restart the computer after installing Mac OS 8–8.5. You can run it again at any time; it's located in the Assistants folder on the startup disk.

You can also specify your computer's network identity with the File Sharing control panel or the Sharing Setup control panel, whichever your computer has. The File

Sharing control panel is part of Mac OS 8–8.5, and the Sharing Setup control panel is part of Mac OS 7.6–7.6.1. Figure 21-1 shows the File Sharing and Sharing Setup control panels.

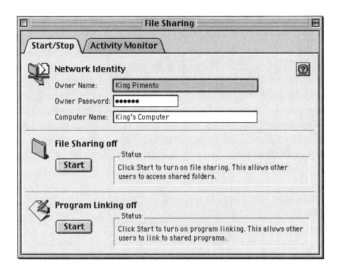

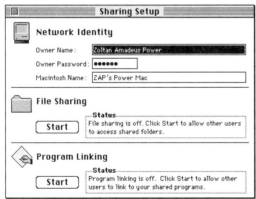

Figure 21-1: Specify a Mac's network identity in the File Sharing control panel (top) or the Sharing Setup control panel (bottom).

The Owner Password can be up to eight characters long. A password is *case sensitive,* meaning that if you create a password that includes uppercase and lowercase letters, you must always type that password with the same uppercase and lowercase letters to gain access. Select a password that is easy for you to remember but difficult for others to guess. Mix letters with numbers; try replacing the letters *I* and *O* with the numbers 1 and 0 (for example, "brownie" becomes "br0wn1e"). You must know the Owner Password to access your computer from another computer on the network. For privacy, the system displays bullets in place of the actual password characters in the File Sharing or Sharing Setup control panel.

The computer name that you enter should be one that other people will easily recognize when they see it in the Chooser among the list of AppleShare file servers. The name must be unique on your network. If you enter a name that another computer is already using, the system displays an alert telling you to use a different name.

Turning File Sharing Off and On

Once your computer's network identity is set in the File Sharing or Sharing Setup control panel, you can use the same control panel to turn file sharing on and off at any time. You must turn on file sharing when you want to make your shared folders and disks available to people using other computers on the network. You do not need to turn on file sharing to connect to shared folders and disks from file servers on the network.

Turning on file sharing increases the Mac OS memory size by 200K to 300K. Also, your computer is theoretically more vulnerable to invasion while file sharing is on, although you can institute effective security measures (lock the door, so to speak) as described in "Controlling Access to Your Shared Items" later in this chapter. All in all, it's a good idea to leave file sharing turned off unless other people need to access your shared files over the network.

When you turn off file sharing, other computers on the network cannot connect to your shared folders or disks. Turning off file sharing does not change which folders and disks you have designated for sharing (as described in the next section) or the access privileges you have set for your shared items (as described in the subsequent section "Controlling Access to Your Shared Items"). With file sharing turned off, other computers simply can't connect to your computer for file sharing. They may still be able to connect to your computer if it provides other network services, such as access to a multiuser database file.

Turning on file sharing

To turn on file sharing, click the Start button in the File Sharing section of the File Sharing control panel or the Sharing Setup control panel, whichever your computer has. The Start button's label changes to Cancel, and the status message next to the button describes what is happening while file sharing is starting up. It may take anywhere from several seconds to several minutes for file sharing to start up, depending on the number of disk volumes and shared items on your computer. You can close the control panel anytime after clicking the Start button, but you won't know precisely when file sharing is enabled if you do. Your computer is ready to share its files when the button's label changes to Stop and the File Sharing control panel reports "File Sharing on" or the Sharing Setup control panel's status message reads "File sharing is now on." Figure 21-2 shows how the File Sharing control panel and the Sharing Setup control look when file sharing is turned on.

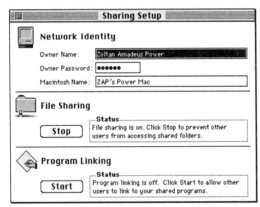

Figure 21-2: File sharing is turned on in the File Sharing control panel (top) or the Sharing Setup control panel (bottom).

There are other ways to turn on file sharing. You can use the Control Strip if it's installed on your computer. Or you can speak the command "Start file sharing" if speech recognition is installed on your computer. (For more information on the Control Strip, see Chapter 11. For more information on speech recognition, see Chapter 22.) Figure 21-3 shows the File Sharing control strip module in Mac OS 8.5.

Figure 21-3: Turn on file sharing in the File Sharing control strip module.

If you shut down or restart your computer after turning on file sharing in Mac OS 8.1–8.5, the Mac OS automatically starts file sharing the next time the computer starts up. This is also true in Mac OS 7.6–8 if you turn on file sharing with the File Sharing or Sharing setup control panel or by spoken command. When you turn file sharing on with the Control Strip in Mac OS 7.6–8, the Mac OS does not automatically turn it on again when you restart the computer.

Turning off file sharing

To turn off file sharing, click the Stop button in the File Sharing section of the File Sharing control panel or the Sharing Setup control panel. A dialog box appears, asking you to specify the number of minutes' warning to be given to anyone who is sharing items from your computer. (Allow enough time for people sharing items from your computer to close any shared items.) Every computer that's connected to yours displays a message indicating that access to your computer is going to be disconnected at the end of the time you specified. The same events happen when you shut down or restart your computer with file sharing on. Figure 21-4 shows the dialog box in which you specify how much time remains until file sharing stops and the message box that appears on other computers that are connected to your computer for file sharing.

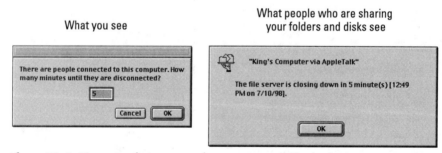

Figure 21-4: Messages that appear when you turn off file sharing.

Designating Your Shared Items

After identifying your computer and turning on file sharing, you can designate the folders and disks that contain files that you want to share. You can share up to ten folders and disks (including CDs and removable hard disks) at a time. To share just one file, you must drag it into a folder and share the folder.

When you share a folder or disk, every item it contains is shared, including enclosed folders. You can't share a document by itself (outside a folder) or a folder located on a floppy disk. After you share a folder or disk, you can drag items into the shared folder or disk to share them as well.

Aliases in shared folders or disks are shared, but their original items are shared only if they are in shared folders or disks. If network users try to use a shared alias whose original item is not in a shared folder or disk, the Mac OS tells them the original item can't be found.

Making an item shared

You make a folder or disk a shared item and see its sharing information by using the Sharing command. In Mac OS 8.5, the Sharing command is in the Get Info submenu, which is in the File menu and in the contextual menu of folders and disks that can be shared. In Mac OS 7.6–8.1, the Sharing command is in the File menu. In Mac OS 8–8.1, the Sharing command is also in the contextual menu of folders and disks that can be shared. Figure 21-5 shows a shared folder's sharing information.

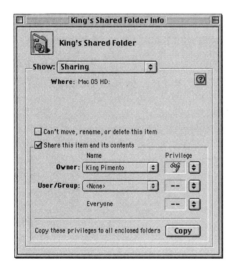

Figure 21-5: The Sharing command displays sharing information for the selected folder or disk in Mac OS 8.5 (top left), Mac OS 8–8.1 (top right), and Mac OS 7.6–7.6.1 (bottom).

To share one of your folders or disks, select it and use the Sharing command. This displays the item's sharing information in its Info window (Mac OS 8.5) or sharing window (Mac OS 7.6–8.1). In this window, turn on the option "Share this item and its contents." The other sharing options in this window establish which users can access the shared item and what privileges they have (as explained in "Controlling Access to Your Shared Items" later in this chapter). The initial settings for a shared item depend on the version of Mac OS you're using. With Mac OS 8–8.5, a folder's initial settings allow only the item's owner to access the folder; the owner can add items, delete items, and save changes to files in the folder. With Mac OS 7.6–7.6.1, a folder's initial settings enable anyone on the network to access the folder and its contents and make any changes he or she wants.

The settings that you make in an item's sharing information persist until you use the Sharing command again to change them. Shutting down or restarting your computer does not affect sharing settings; neither does turning off file sharing.

Recognizing your shared items by their icons

The icon of a shared folder on your computer appears with network cables, which indicate its shared status. When someone is using your shared folder, the folder icon has faces on it. Unlike folder icons, disk icons don't change when you share them. Figure 21-6 shows how shared folders look.

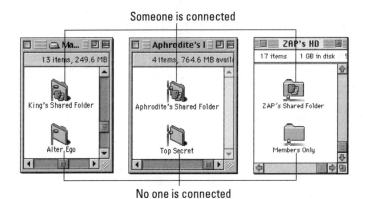

Figure 21-6: Shared folders have distinctive icons in Mac OS 8.5 (left), Mac OS 8–8.1 (middle), and Mac OS 7.6–7.6.1 (right).

You can't rename a folder or disk that you have shared nor can you drag it to the Trash. Also, you can't eject and put away a removable disk or CD that contains shared folders. To do any of these things, you first must turn off file sharing or turn off the option "Share this item and its contents" in the item's Info window (Mac OS 8.5) or sharing window (Mac OS 7.6–8.1).

SECRETS

Network Trash

If someone drags a file or folder from your computer to the Trash on his or her desktop, the Finder creates an invisible folder on your computer with the name Network Trash Folder. As long as the user doesn't empty the Trash, the items thrown away appear inside the Network Trash Folder in folders labeled Trash Can #1, Trash Can #2, and so on — one for each computer with something of yours in its Trash. To restore an item that someone else has trashed, use a utility program such as ResEdit (described in Chapter 26) to make the Network Trash Folder visible. Then find the item that you want to rescue and drag it out of the Trash Can folder it's in. You can set access privileges to prevent others from trashing your shared items (as described in "Controlling Access to Your Shared Items" later in this chapter).

Identifying Who Can Access Your Shared Items

You could let everyone access your shared folders and disks (as happens by default if you're using Mac OS 7.6–7.6.1) or you could let no one but yourself access your shared items (as happens by default if you're using Mac OS 8–8.5). But you don't have to take an all-or-nothing approach. This section explains how to use the Users & Groups control panel to identify individuals and groups of people who you want to grant or deny access to your shared items. The next section, "Controlling Access to Your Shared Items," tells you how to specify which of those people or groups has privileged access to a shared folder or disk and its contents.

Users & Groups

The Users & Groups control panel displays named icons for people and groups who can access your shared items. There's always an icon for the computer's owner. The owner icon is marked with a clipboard if you're using Mac OS 8–8.5, or it has a bold outline if you're using Mac OS 7.6–7.6.1. There's also always an icon for guests — that is, any unidentified person using a computer on your network. The guest icon is marked with a suitcase if you're using Mac OS 8–8.5, or its name is enclosed in angle brackets if you're using Mac OS 7.6–7.6.1. You create additional icons for registered network users to whom you want to grant greater access privileges than guests have. You can also create groups of registered users. You can create any number of registered users and groups in the Mac OS 8–8.5 Users & Groups control panel. With Mac OS 7.6–7.6.1, you're limited to 100 users and 100 groups, but for optimal performance, you shouldn't name more than 50. Figure 21-7 shows examples of the Users & Groups control panel.

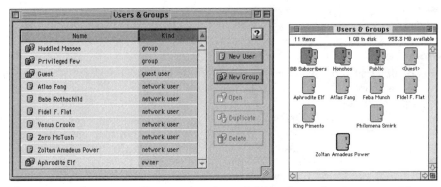

Figure 21-7: The Users & Groups control panel determines who can connect to your shared folders and disks in Mac OS 8–8.5 (left) and Mac OS 7.6–7.6.1 (right).

Sorting users and groups

When working in the Users & Groups control panel, it can be helpful to sort the Users & Groups list by kind so that all groups are listed together alphabetically and all network users are listed together alphabetically. If you're using Mac OS 8–8.5, click the column heading to sort the list by that heading. If you're using Mac OS 7.6–7.6.1, choose the sort order from the View menu.

Selecting multiple users or groups

You can perform some operations in the Users & Groups control panel on more than one user or group at the same time. With Mac OS 8–8.5, you ⌘-click to select multiple icons one by one, or Shift-click to select a range of icons. With Mac OS 7.6–7.6.1, you Shift-click to select multiple icons one by one, or drag a selection rectangle to select a range.

The owner

The owner icon controls your ability to access your computer when you connect as its owner from another computer. The owner can have the unique ability to access all disks whether they're designated for sharing or not. The owner icon bears the name of the computer's owner and looks different from other icons in the Users & Groups control panel. In Mac OS 8–8.5, it looks like a face next to a clipboard. In Mac OS 7.6–7.6.1, the owner icon has a heavy black outline.

You change the owner's access privileges in the owner window, which you display by opening the owner icon. You can also change the owner's name and password in the owner window if you're using Mac OS 8–8.5. With Mac OS 8–8.5, the owner name and password in the owner window and in the File Sharing control panel always match; if you make a change one place, the Mac OS updates the other place. With Mac OS 7.6–7.6.1 you must use the Sharing Setup control panel to change the owner's name and password. Figure 21-8 shows the two views you can see of the owner window in Mac OS 8–8.5 and the one view you see in Mac OS 7.6–7.6.1.

 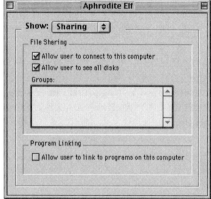

Figure 21-8: The owner's file sharing privileges in Mac OS 8–8.5 (top) and Mac OS 7.6–7.6.1 (bottom).

Turning on the "Allow user to connect" option gives you access to your computer from another computer connected to the network. Turning on the "Allow user to change password" option enables you to change the owner password remotely. The option "Allow user to see entire disk" enables you to see and use any items on any disk attached to your computer. This setting gives you access to all disks and folders on your computer (while you are connected to your computer from another computer), whether they are shared or not. When you connect as the computer owner you have unlimited access whether or not you're named the owner of a shared folder and regardless of the privileges assigned to shared disks and folders.

Guests

The Guest icon controls the ability of any unidentified network user to connect to your shared folders and disks. You can deny guests any access or you can allow guests to connect to your shared folders and disks and restrict guest access to shared folders and disks individually (as described in the next section, "Controlling Access to Your Shared Items").

To disable all guest access, open the Guest icon in the Users & Groups control panel to display the Guest window, and turn off the "Allow guests to connect" option. Now only registered users are allowed to connect to your shared items. Figure 21-9 shows the two views you can see of the Guest window in Mac OS 8–8.5 and the one view you see in Mac OS 7.6–7.6.1.

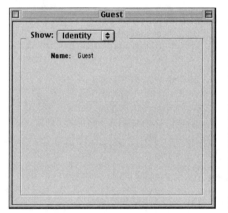
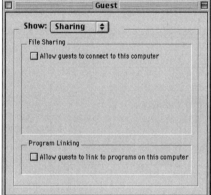

Figure 21-9: Guests' file sharing privileges in Mac OS 8–8.5 (top) and Mac OS 7.6–7.6.1 (bottom).

Registered network users

Registering network users helps secure your shared items from unauthorized access. You can specify whether each registered user can connect to your shared folders and disks, as described in this section. You can also give a registered user special access privileges to shared folders as described in the next section, "Controlling Access to Your Shared Items."

Creating a new network user

To register a network user, first open the Users & Groups control panel. Next, click the New User button or choose New User from the File menu to create a new user icon in the Users & Groups control panel. (The New User button doesn't exist in Mac OS 7.6–7.6.1.) An icon named New User appears in the Users & Groups control panel, and if you're using Mac OS 8–8.5, the icon opens to display the user window for that new network user.

Rather than create a new user, you can duplicate one or more existing users in the Users & Groups control panel by selecting one or more user icons and clicking the Duplicate button or choosing Duplicate from the File menu. (The Duplicate button doesn't exist in Mac OS 7.6–7.6.1.)

Identifying a network user

When you create a new user, the new user name is selected and you can replace it by typing the name of the network user who you want to register. After duplicating a selection of multiple users, you have to select and rename the duplicates one by one.

You should ask a network user what name he or she would like to use when connecting to your computer to share your files, and suggest he or she use the owner name in his or her File Sharing or Sharing Setup control panel. If you devise the name yourself, you must tell the network user his or her registered name because the user must type the exact name to connect to your shared folders and disks. Network user names are not case sensitive, so a user doesn't have to match your use of uppercase and lowercase letters when connecting to your computer. As soon as you give a network user a name, he or she is registered on your computer.

You can add another level of security by assigning to a registered user a password that he or she needs to type to access your shared items. You assign a password in the user window, which you display by opening the user icon. Enter a password up to eight characters long. Remember that the user must type the password exactly as you type it here, including uppercase and lowercase letters. Figure 21-10 shows the two views you can see of a user window in Mac OS 8–8.5 and the one view you see in Mac OS 7.6–7.6.1.

Setting a network user's privileges

Additional options in a user window let you specify whether a registered user can connect to your shared folders and disks and whether the user can change his or her password. If the "Allow user to connect" option is turned on, the network user name can be used to connect to your shared folders and disks. Turn off that option to deny access to anyone using that registered name. If you want to let this user change the password at will, turn on the "Allow user to change password" option. When you finish setting the registered user's access privileges, close the user window to make your changes take effect.

Remember that access privileges are associated with a registered user name, not with a particular person. Any person who connects to your computer with a valid user name (and password, if any) has the privileges you set for that registered user name. If you're concerned about the security of your shared items, you can tell your registered users not to divulge their passwords and periodically ask them to change their passwords.

Figure 21-10: A registered user's file sharing privileges in Mac OS 8–8.5 (top) and Mac OS 7.6–7.6.1 (bottom).

Changing a network user's privileges

You can modify a registered user's name, password, and access privileges, or remove the user from your set of registered users at any time.

To remove a registered user, drag its icon from the Users & Groups control panel to the Trash. Alternatively, you can select one or more user icons and click the Delete button or choose Delete from the File menu. (The Delete button doesn't exist in Mac OS 7.6–7.6.1.)

Remote access privileges

If you have purchased and installed the Remote Access Personal Server software, then the owner, guest, and user windows include additional options. (These additional options do not appear if you have installed only the Remote Access or Remote Access Client software. This software is part of a standard installation of Mac OS 8–8.5 and is included for optional installation with Mac OS 7.6–7.6.1.) Figure 21-11 shows the remote access privileges.

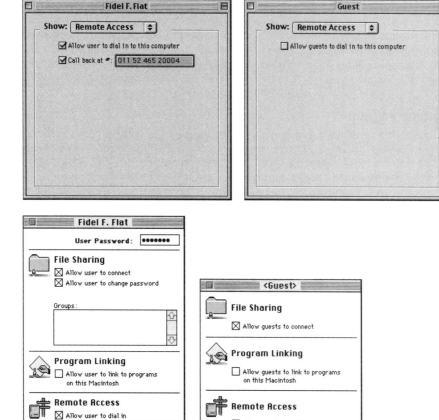

Figure 21-11: Remote access privileges for registered users (including the owner) and guests in Mac OS 8–8.5 (top) and Mac OS 7.6–7.6.1 (bottom).

The remote access options let you allow or deny remote access to the owner, to guests, and to each registered user individually. You can specify a callback phone number for the owner and for each registered guest. When Apple Remote Access Personal Server gets a call from a user who has a callback number, the program hangs up and calls the user back at the specified number. This procedure prevents an unauthorized person from gaining access to your shared folders and disks by learning a registered user's password and trying to call from an unauthorized location. When you specify a callback number, you have to pay the cost of the phone call for the connection, but you know that the person connecting to your shared folders and disks has the correct password and is calling from the registered user's computer.

Groups of users

Office or work environments usually consist of groups of people, such as departments or project teams, who need to share certain items. With Mac OS file sharing, you can specify special access privileges for groups as well as for individual users. Groups simply are collections of individual registered users, and you can grant specific access privileges for a shared folder or disk to a group instead of to a single user. (The procedures for setting access privileges of shared folders and disks are covered in the next section, "Controlling Access to Your Shared Items.")

Creating a group

To establish a group of users, open the Users & Groups control panel and click the New Group button or choose New Group from the File menu. (The New Group button doesn't exist in Mac OS 7.6–7.6.1.) An icon named New Group appears in the Users & Groups control panel, and if you're using Mac OS 8–8.5, the icon opens to display the group window for that new group. The group icon looks different than a single-user icon.

Rather than create new groups, you can duplicate one or more existing groups in the Users & Groups control panel by selecting one or more group icons and clicking the Duplicate button or choosing Duplicate from the File menu. (The Duplicate button doesn't exist in Mac OS 7.6–7.6.1.)

Right after you create a new group, the new group name is selected and you can replace it by typing a name you make up. If you duplicate a selection of multiple groups, you have to select and rename them one by one.

Don't invent group names that might offend someone who uses your shared files. Your group names are not private if you use them to set specific access privileges to shared items. At least some people who connect to your computer will be able to see some of your group names.

Adding users to a group

To add registered users to a group, drag their user icons to the group icon or group window. You can also add a user to a group by dragging the group icon to the user icon. To speed the process of adding users to groups, select multiple users and drag them to the group icon together. You don't need to include the owner icon in groups because the owner always has full access to everything on all disks.

To see the members of the group, open the group icon. The group window shows a user icon for every user in the group. (If you're using Mac OS 7.6–7.6.1, user icons look different in group windows than in the Users & Groups control panel.) If you want to see or change information for a registered user, you can open the user icon wherever you see it — in a group window or in the User & Groups window. You cannot create a new user directly in a group window, however. Figure 21-12 is an example of a group window.

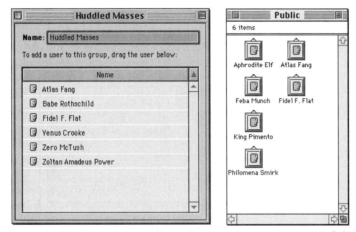

Figure 21-12: See the members of a group in Mac OS 8–8.5 (left) and Mac OS 7.6–7.6.1 (right).

Removing users from a group

To remove users from a group, open the group icon to display its window, and drag the user icons that you want to remove from the group window to the Trash. If you're using Mac OS 8–8.5, you can also remove users from a group by selecting the user icons in the group window and choosing Remove from the File menu. Users are removed right away; they don't wait in the Trash until you empty it.

Seeing the groups a user belongs to

To see all the groups to which a registered user belongs, open the user icon. If you're using Mac OS 8–8.5, you also need to choose Sharing from the pop-up menu at the top of the user window. The user window displays a list of groups to which the registered user belongs, as shown in Figure 21-13.

Controlling Access to Your Shared Items

Even if you allow guests and registered users to connect to your shared folders and disk, by default Mac OS 8–8.5 doesn't permit them to see or change the contents of any shared items. Mac OS 7.6–7.6.1 take the opposite approach; by default they let everyone who connects to your shared folders and disks see and change anything in them. Besides those extremes, you can grant full or partial access to each shared folder independently. Moreover, each shared folder can have different access privileges for three categories of users: the owner, one user or group, and everyone. For example, you might want to ensure that a user or group of users has access to a folder of templates on your computer but cannot modify the templates. Access privileges also enable you to selectively share a folder of confidential documents, such as new product plans.

Figure 21-13: See the groups to which a registered user belongs in Mac OS 8–8.5 (left) and Mac OS 7.6–7.6.1 (right).

This section explains how you use the Finder's Sharing command to set separate access privileges for the owner, one registered network user or one group, and everyone else. (The previous section, "Identifying Who Can Access Your Shared Items," tells you how to identify network users and groups of users to whom you want to grant or deny access to your shared folders.)

Setting specific access privileges

You set the access privileges of a folder or disk in its Info window (Mac OS 8.5) or sharing window (Mac OS 7.6–8.1). This window appears when you select the folder or disk and choose the Sharing command from the Get Info submenu of the File menu (Mac OS 8.5), the File menu (Mac OS 7.6–8.1), or the contextual menu of the folder or disk (Mac OS 8–8.5). The access privileges you can set and the methods you use for setting them are different in Mac OS 8–8.5 than in Mac OS 7.6–7.6.1.

Access privileges in Mac OS 8–8.5

An Info window in Mac OS 8.5 or a sharing window in Mac OS 8–8.1 displays icons to indicate the access privileges of each user category. You set access privileges by choosing from pop-up menus. Figure 21-14 shows a pop-up menu for setting access privileges in Mac OS 8–8.5.

You can set one of these four privilege levels for each user category in the access privileges pop-up menus displayed by Mac OS 8–8.5:

✦ **Read & Write** lets users open the folder and see enclosed folders; see, open, and copy enclosed files; and create, delete, move, and change enclosed files and folders.

✦ **Read only** lets users open the folder and see enclosed folders, and see, open, and copy enclosed files.

✦ **Write only** lets users drag files and folders into the folder, but does not allow users to open the folder. Note that this privilege makes sense only for folders enclosed by a shared folder or disk. Users can't access any write-only disk or a write-only folder that's not enclosed in a shared folder.

✦ **None** denies users access to the folder.

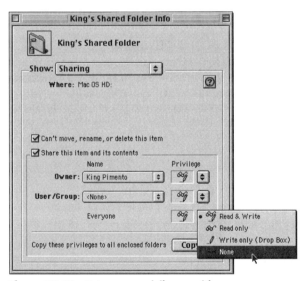

Figure 21-14: Set access privileges with pop-up menus in Mac OS 8–8.5.

Access privileges in Mac OS 7.6–7.6.1

In Mac OS 7.6–7.6.1, a sharing window displays access privileges of each user category with checkboxes, and you set access privileges by turning the checkboxes on or off. Figure 21-15 shows the checkboxes you use to set access privileges in Mac OS 7.6.1.

In this sharing window, you can grant or deny any combination of these three access privileges for each user category:

✦ **See Folders** lets users open the folder and see folders inside it.

✦ **See Files** lets users see, open, and copy files inside the folder.

✦ **Make Changes** lets users create, delete, move, and change files (if the See Files privilege is granted) and folders (if the See Folders privilege is granted) that are inside the folder. By itself (without See Files or See Folders), Make Changes lets users drag files and folders into the folder, but not open the folder.

Figure 21-15: Setting access privileges with checkboxes in Mac OS 7.6–7.6.1.

Correlation between old and new access privileges

Each access privilege level in Mac OS 8–8.5 corresponds to a combination of access privileges in Mac OS 7.6–7.6.1. For example, setting the Read Only privilege in Mac OS 8–8.5 corresponds to the See Folders and See Files privileges in Mac OS 7.6. Table 21-1 lists all the newer privilege levels and the equivalent combinations of older privilege settings.

Table 21-1 Mac OS 8–8.5 Privileges Compared with Mac OS 7.6–7.6.1 Privileges	
Privilege set in Mac OS 8–8.5	*Privileges set in Mac OS 7.6–7.6.1*
Read & Write	See Folders, See Files, and Make Changes
Read Only	See Folders and See Files
Write Only	Make Changes
None	None

Not all combinations of access privileges in Mac OS 7.6 and earlier correspond to privilege levels in Mac OS 8–8.5. Mac OS 8–8.5 honors all combinations of access privileges set on computers that use Mac OS 7.6 and earlier. Mac OS 8–8.5 displays a question mark in an Info window or a sharing window for a combination of privileges that doesn't match one of the privilege levels it knows about. The following combinations of access privileges have no corresponding privilege level in Mac OS 8–8.5:

✦ See Folders and Make Changes

✦ See Files and Make Changes

✦ See Folders alone

✦ See Files alone

Selecting specific or adopted access privileges

By default, folders inside a shared disk or shared folder adopt the access privileges of the enclosing folder or disk. Instead, you can set specific access privileges for any enclosed folder. An option in an enclosed folder's Info window or sharing window controls whether the folder has specific access privileges or adopts the privileges of its enclosing folder. The option is labeled "Use enclosing folder's privileges" in Mac OS 8–8.5. With Mac OS 7.6–7.6.1, the option is labeled "Same as enclosing folder." This option appears only for folders that are inside a shared folder or shared disk.

A folder with adopted privileges that is moved to a new folder takes on the privileges of its new enclosing folder. In contrast, a folder with specific access privileges keeps its specific privileges when moved to a different enclosing folder.

Setting specific privileges for an enclosed folder

To set specific access privileges for an enclosed folder, display the enclosed folder's Info window or sharing window, turn off the option labeled "Use enclosing folder's privileges" or "Same as enclosing folder," and set the specific access privileges you want the enclosed folder to have. Figure 21-16 is an example of an enclosed folder's Info window or sharing window with specific, not adopted, privileges set.

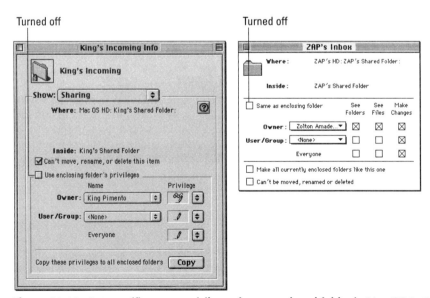

Figure 21-16: Set specific access privileges for an enclosed folder in Mac OS 8–8.5 (left) and Mac OS 7.6–7.6.1 (right).

Adopting the enclosing folder's privileges

To make an enclosed folder adopt the access privileges of its enclosing folder, bring up the enclosed folder's Info window or sharing window and turn on the option labeled "Use enclosing folder's privileges" or "Same as enclosing folder." When you turn on that option, the Mac OS dims the controls for setting access privileges. Figure 21-17 is an example of an enclosed folder's Info window or sharing window with adopted privileges set.

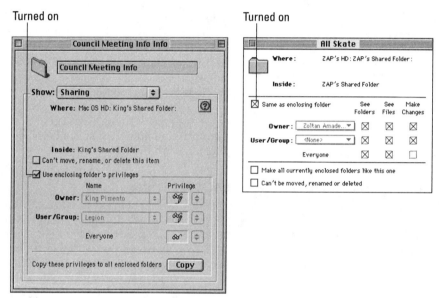

Figure 21-17: An enclosed folder with adopted access privileges in Mac OS 8–8.5 (left) and Mac OS 7.6–7.6.1 (right).

Changing all enclosed folders' privileges

In Mac OS 8–8.5, if you change a folder's privileges and want to force all enclosed folders to have the same privileges, click the Copy button in the enclosing folder's Info window or sharing window. In Mac OS 7.6–7.6.1 (which doesn't have the Copy button), you turn on the option "Make all currently enclosed folders like this one" and close the sharing window. Folders inside enclosed folders are also affected.

Think twice before clicking a Copy button in Mac OS 8–8.5 or turning on the option "Make all currently enclosed folders like this one" in Mac OS 7.6–7.6.1. Forcing enclosed folders to use the privileges of their enclosing folder turns off the option labeled "Use enclosing folder's privileges" or "Same as enclosing folder" in all enclosed folders. Henceforth none of the enclosed folders will be updated automatically when you change the enclosing folder's privileges. You'll have to click the Copy button or turn on the option "Make all currently enclosed folders like this one" every time you change the enclosing folder's privileges, or else laboriously go through all enclosed folders and turn on the option labeled "Use enclosing folder's privileges" or "Same as enclosing folder."

You don't need to (and generally shouldn't) click the Copy button or turn on the option "Make all currently enclosed folders like this one" when you first make a disk or folder available for sharing. At that time all the enclosed folders automatically adopt the privileges of the enclosing folder or disk. Any new enclosed folders that you create also automatically adopt the privileges of the enclosing folder.

Specifying who has access privileges

The Info window or sharing window displays these three categories of users for whom you can set access privileges:

✦ **Owner** names the owner of the computer from which the folder was created (not necessarily your computer) or a registered user or group to whom the current owner assigns ownership.

✦ **User/Group** names one registered user or one group of users with special access privileges to the shared folder or disk.

✦ **Everyone** refers to anyone who connects to the computer as a guest or as a registered user.

The three categories of users are dimmed if the "Share this item and its contents" option is off, or for enclosed folders if the option labeled "Use enclosing folder's privileges" or "Same as enclosing folder" is on.

Owner privileges

Ownership of a folder or disk gives you the right to modify its access privileges. You can transfer ownership of a folder or disk to a registered user, to a group, or to all network users that you allow to connect to your computer. If the folder or disk is on your computer, you choose a new owner from the Owner pop-up menu in the folder or disk's Info window or sharing window. If the folder or disk you own is on someone else's computer, you type the name of the new owner in the space provided. Figure 21-18 shows both procedures in Mac OS 8.5 (the only differences in Mac OS 7.6–8.1 are cosmetic).

On your own computer,
use the pop-up menu

On someone else's computer,
type the new owner's name

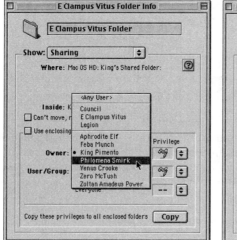

Figure 21-18: Change the owner of a shared folder or disk.

The Owner pop-up menu lists the registered users and groups to whom you can transfer the ownership of the folder. If you have added a new user or group that doesn't appear in the pop-up menu, close the Info window or sharing window and then reopen it to make the new name appear.

No pop-up menu appears for a shared folder or disk that you own on someone else's computer, so you must type the new owner's name. The name you type must match the name of a registered user or a group in the Users & Groups control panel of the computer where the folder or disk is located. Leave the Owner name blank if you want to transfer ownership to everyone.

Remember that after you transfer ownership of a folder or disk, the new owner can restrict your access to that item and its contents — but only when you try to access the folder from another computer on the network. Giving away ownership of a folder or disk on your computer doesn't take away your ability to open, use, or modify it from your own computer. In effect, an item can have dual ownership, giving two users ownership privileges. If you make another user the owner of an item on your computer, both you and that other user have ownership privileges. You can reclaim sole ownership at any time by making yourself the owner in the item's Info window or sharing window.

User/Group privileges

You can give one registered user or a group of registered users greater access privileges than other network users to a shared folder or disk. If the folder or disk is on your computer, you choose a registered user or group from the User/Group pop-up menu in the folder or disk's Info window or sharing window. If the folder or disk you own is on someone else's computer, you type the name in the space provided. Figure 21-19 shows both procedures in Mac OS 8.5 (the only differences in Mac OS 7.6–8.1 are cosmetic).

On your own computer,
use the pop-up menu

On someone else's computer,
type the name of the
new registered user or group

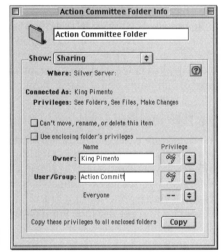

Figure 21-19: Changing the user or group that has special access privileges to a shared folder or disk.

The User/Group pop-up menu lists all the registered users and groups in your Users & Groups control panel. If you have added a new user or group that doesn't appear in the pop-up menu, close the Info window or sharing window and then reopen it to make the new name appear.

QUICK TIPS

Giving Rank Its Privileges

If you're using Mac OS 7.6–7.6.1, you should make the Everyone category's access privileges less than or the same as those of the User/Group category. Likewise, you should make the User/Group category's privileges less than those of the Owner. Mac OS 8–8.5 won't let you do otherwise, but Mac OS 7.6–7.6.1 will. No one can actually get lesser privileges than the Everyone category, because everyone who connects is part of that category. Even registered users designated as the User/Group or the Owner are part of the Everyone category. Just remember: rank has its privileges.

The pop-up menu doesn't appear for a shared folder or disk that you own on someone else's computer, so you must type the name of a registered user or group in the space provided. The name you type must match the name of a registered user or a group in the Users & Groups control panel of the computer where the folder or disk is located. If you want to change the User/Group to none, delete the User/Group name and leave it blank.

The Everyone category

The Everyone category includes all registered users that you let connect to your computer. This category also includes guests (unregistered users) if you let them connect. If you want registered users but no one else to have access to the shared folders on your computer, disable Guest access in the Users & Groups control panel (as described in "Identifying Who Can Access Your Shared Items" earlier in this chapter). Then set the Everyone category to the privileges you want all registered users to have.

A registered user or group of users that is specified for the User/Group or Owner category can have greater privileges than those that are granted by the Everyone category.

Common access-privilege scenarios

Controlling who can do what with files in shared areas opens new possibilities for working in groups. Using access-privilege settings, you can keep folders private between two users, make the folders accessible to everyone on the network, or assign combinations between these extremes. The remainder of this section describes setting access privileges for five interesting file-sharing scenarios.

Universal access

Allowing everyone on the network access to a shared item and its contents is easy: just set the Everyone category to Read & Write in Mac OS 8–8.5 or grant the Everyone category the See Files, See Folders, and Make Changes privileges in Mac OS 7.6–7.6.1. You don't actually have to set the User/Group and Owner categories. Figure 21-20 shows the access privileges for universal access.

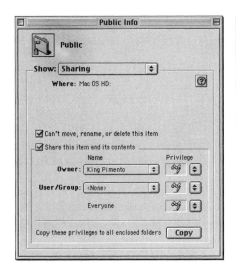

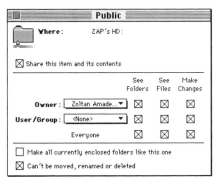

Figure 21-20: Access privileges for universal access in Mac OS 8.5 (top left), Mac OS 8 (top right), and Mac OS 7.6–7.6.1 (bottom).

Restricted access

If you want to give one registered user or one group access to a shared item but deny access to guests, name that user or group in the User/Group category and set the User/Group privileges as you like. Be sure the Everyone category has no privileges (you'll have to turn them all off if you're using Mac OS 7.6–7.6.1). Figure 21-21 shows the access privileges for restricted access.

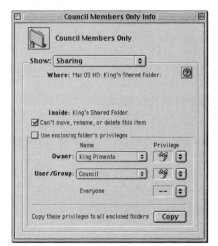

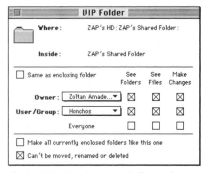

Figure 21-21: Access privileges for restricted access in Mac OS 8.5 (top left), Mac OS 8 (top right), and Mac OS 7.6–7.6.1 (bottom).

Private access

If you own a folder on someone else's computer, you can keep that folder private by setting the User/Group and Everyone categories to have no privileges. Only you and the user of that computer can access your folder. Figure 21-22 shows the necessary settings.

To keep a folder or disk on your own computer private, make sure that its "Share this item and its contents" option is off; use Finder's Sharing command to verify its status.

You'll still be able to access that folder when you use another computer to connect to your computer as its owner. Remember, a computer's owner normally has full access privileges to every disk and folder when connecting over the network.

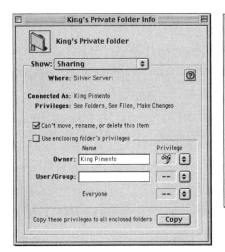

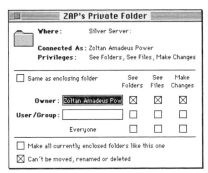

Figure 21-22: Access privileges for private access in Mac OS 8.5 (top left), Mac OS 8 (top right), and Mac OS 7.6–7.6.1 (bottom).

A private in-box folder

Setting up a folder to act as an in-box (or in-basket) enables other network users to deposit documents, folders, and other items in that folder. In-box folders sometimes are referred to as *drop boxes,* meaning that other users can drop in items, but only you can take those items out. A drop box must be inside another shared folder to enable network users to access it.

You prevent all other people from seeing, removing, or changing your folder's contents by setting the User/Group and Everyone categories to Write Only in Mac OS 8–8.5 or granting only the Make Changes privilege in Mac OS 7.6–7.6.1. Figure 21-23 shows the privilege settings for a private in-box folder.

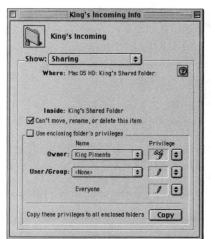

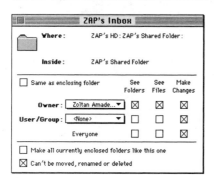

Figure 21-23: Access privileges for an in-box folder in Mac OS 8.5 (top left), Mac OS 8 (top right), and Mac OS 7.6–7.6.1 (bottom).

A bulletin board

Another useful configuration of access privileges is setting up a folder to act as a bulletin board, enabling other users to open and read documents but preventing them from adding or changing documents. They could submit items for posting to the bulletin board by dropping them in an in-box folder (as described previously).

To establish a bulletin-board folder, set the Everyone category to Read Only in Mac OS 8–8.5 or grant only the See Folders and See Files privileges in Mac OS 7.6–7.6.1. If you don't want to share your bulletin-board folder with everyone, set the Everyone category to have no privileges. Then specify a user or group for the User/Group category and set the User/Group access privileges to Read Only in Mac OS 8–8.5 or grant only the See Folders and See Files privileges in Mac OS 7.6–7.6.1. You might want to name a small group as the owner of the folder so that members of the owner group could help with bulletin-board administration. Figure 21-24 shows the settings for a bulletin board folder.

Controlling Security Risks

File sharing poses a security risk, especially if you make an entire hard disk available for sharing and if you allow guests to connect to it. When you make an entire hard disk available for sharing, you either have to trust everyone you let access it or you have to go to a lot of trouble to set specific access privileges for various folders that you want to keep network users out of. There's always the risk of forgetting to deny access to a folder that you don't want network users to share.

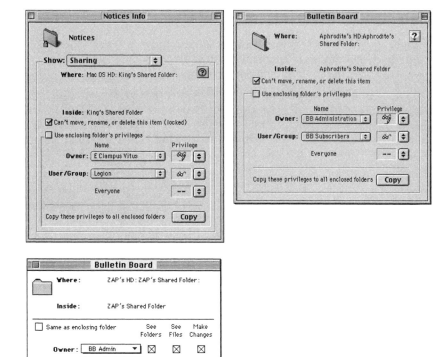

Figure 21-24: Access privileges for a bulletin-board folder in Mac OS 8.5 (top left), Mac OS 8 (top right), and Mac OS 7.6–7.6.1 (bottom).

Guests pose a particular security risk because they can connect without a password. By disabling guest access in the Users & Groups control panel, you can require everyone who connects to your computer to enter a password. Although passwords can be divulged, stolen, or guessed, requiring passwords is still more secure than not requiring passwords.

The computer owner's special ability to connect to all disks and work without restrictions also threatens the computer's security. Anyone who can learn or guess your owner name and password can crack your computer from another computer on your network.

Controlling access to disks, folders, and files

Here are some ways you can improve file-sharing security:

✦ Share folders, not entire disks.

✦ Register users and give them passwords.

✦ Organize registered users into groups. Make a folder for each group and put in it files and folders for group members to share. You can make a registered user a member of more than one group.

✦ For each group folder you create, set its User/Group to be the group for which you created the folder. Also set the User/Group privilege level that you want group members to have. Be sure to set the Everyone privileges to none. If you want group members to have less access to some items, put those items in a folder inside the group's folder and set specific lesser privileges for that enclosed folder.

✦ If you decide to allow guests, let them connect to one shared folder and put files and folders you want them to share in this folder. If you want to let guests use additional folders, put them inside this one shared folder. Your registered users will also have access to this folder. Of course, you can also let registered users connect to additional shared folders.

✦ Set a privilege level for your guest folder's Everyone category. If you want guests to have less access to some items, create a folder inside your main guest folder and set specific access privileges for the enclosed folder. For all shared folders outside your guest folder, make sure that the Everyone category has no privileges.

✦ Do not overvalue the security of registered users and passwords. An authorized person may connect to one of your shared folders from any computer on the network and then leave this computer without disconnecting. Someone else can then come along and use this computer to access all your shared files (subject to the access privileges you have set). Remind people who connect to your shared folders that they must put away all your shared folders (by dragging them to the Trash) when they finish using them.

✦ Consider removing the owner's special access to all folders and disks, essentially treating the owner like an ordinary registered user. This makes your computer more secure. This also makes file sharing less convenient because you have to assign access privileges to the owner for every disk or folder that you want to access (as owner) over the network. To remove the owner's special access privileges, open the owner in the Users & Groups control panel. In the owner window, turn off the option labeled "Allow user to see all disks" (in Mac OS 8–8.5) or "Allow user to see entire disk" (in Mac OS 7.6–7.6.1).

QUICK TIPS

Coping with Network Insecurity

Can crackers invade your network? Mac OS file sharing puts your disks at risk if your computer is connected to a network. The risk of invasion exists even if you normally have file sharing turned off. Someone who spends 40 seconds at your keyboard can open your File Sharing control panel or Sharing Setup control panel, change your owner password (without knowing your current password), start file sharing, and close the control panel, leaving no sign of these activities. Then, at his or her leisure, the cracker can use another computer on the network to connect to your computer as its owner and snoop through everything on your disks without leaving any electronic footprints.

You eventually would notice if someone changed your files, of course, and you would see that your password had been changed if you tried to connect to your computer from another computer. But a less easily detectable invasion involves altering access privileges with the Users & Groups control panel and the Finder's Sharing command; this procedure could take less than 10 minutes.

Apple could make your system more secure by adding password access to the File Sharing control panel and the Users & Groups control panel. In the meantime, you can password-protect your disks or folders by using software such as Folder Bolt from Kent-Marsh. Another approach is to encrypt sensitive files with Private File from Aladdin Systems (408-761-6200, http://www.aladdinsys.com). If you want to go to great lengths, you can encrypt your entire disk with PGPdisk from Network Associates (408-988-3832, http://www.nai.com/default_pgp.asp) or the CryptDisk shareware by Will Price. Otherwise, you must either remove the File Sharing extension from your Extensions folder or trust everyone who has access to a Mac on your network.

Locking folders

To prevent anyone from renaming a folder, deleting it, or moving it into another folder, bring up the folder's sharing window and turn on the option labeled "Can't move, rename, or delete this item" (in Mac OS 8–8.5) or "Can't be moved, renamed, or deleted" (in Mac OS 7.6–7.6.1). This option works like the Locked option in the Info windows of files. It affects you or anyone else using your computer as well as network users who access the folder from another computer. This option affects a folder even if you don't make the folder available for sharing. This option is not available for disks, although they are always locked when they are shared.

Monitoring File-Sharing Activity

When Mac OS file sharing is on, you can see who is connected to your computer and list your shared folders and disks. To monitor file-sharing activity, open the File Sharing control panel and select its Activity Monitor view (in Mac OS 8–8.5) or open the File Sharing Monitor control panel (in Mac OS 7.6–7.6.1). You see a list of your shared folders and disks (enclosed folders are not listed). You also see a list of the network users currently connected to your computer. An activity indicator shows you how much of your computer's total processing time is being spent handling file sharing. Figure 21-25 shows how all this looks.

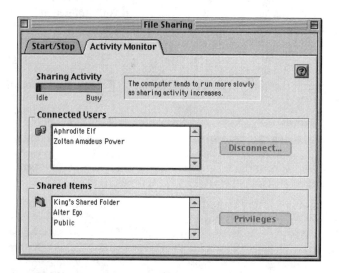

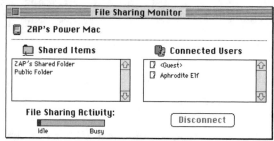

Figure 21-25: Seeing who is connected and what you are sharing in Mac OS 8–8.5 (top) and in Mac OS 7.6–7.6.1 (bottom).

If any guests are connected to your computer, each one that is currently connected is listed as <Guest>. Because guests are anonymous, there's no way to tell which guest is which.

You can disconnect one or more users by selecting them in the list of connected users and clicking the Disconnect button. You select multiple users by ⌘-clicking or Shift-clicking in Mac OS 8–8.5, or by Shift-clicking in Mac OS 7.6–7.6.1. When you click the Disconnect button, the system asks you to specify the number of minutes you want to elapse before the disconnection occurs. It's good networking etiquette to give people enough time to save any changes they have made to the files before you disconnect them. To disconnect a user immediately, specify 0 minutes. This disconnection doesn't turn off file sharing.

QUICK TIPS

Send Secret Messages

If you use Mac OS 8–8.5, you can send a message to anyone connected to your shared folders or disks. Open the File Sharing control panel and click the Activity Monitor tab. Then Option-double-click the name of any user (even <Guest>) displayed in the Connected Users list. This displays a dialog box in which you type your message. When you click OK in this dialog box, the message appears on the other user's screen in a small dialog box. If you want to send the same message to more than one user, Shift-click or ⌘-click to select their names before you Option-double-click one of them and type the message.

Bear in mind that this procedure disconnects a user only temporarily. The same user can connect again and access your shared folders. To keep a user from connecting again, use the Users & Groups control panel to deny that user access to your computer.

You can also review and change the access privileges of items in the shared items list of the File Sharing control panel in Mac OS 8–8.5. You select one or more items in the list and click the Privileges button to bring up the sharing windows of the selected items. (The Privileges button does not exist in the File Sharing Monitor control panel of Mac OS 7.6–7.6.1.)

Summary

In this chapter, you learned that the peer-to-peer (distributed) file sharing provided by the Mac OS is great for a small group, but a dedicated file server like AppleShare IP is generally better for a large group. You read about Mac OS file sharing's limitations: 10 shared items, 10 computers connected to yours, 5 computers accessing your files, and with Mac OS 7.6–7.6.1, 100 registered users and 100 groups. You also read some guidelines for file sharing.

You learned how to use the File Sharing control panel in Mac OS 8–8.5 or the Sharing Setup control panel in Mac OS 7.6–7.6.1 to identify your computer with a name, an owner, and an owner password; and to turn file sharing on and off.

You learned how to use the Finder's Sharing command to designate which folders and disks are available for sharing. This chapter also told you how to use the Users & Groups control panel to register network users with names and passwords; how to create groups of registered users; and how to set general access privileges for each registered user, the owner, and guests.

Then you learned how to set access privileges for your shared folders and disks. You can set each folder and disk's privileges separately for three categories of network users: all network users (everyone), one registered user or group of your choosing, and the owner. The owner can be any registered user or group you choose. You can set specific privileges for an enclosed folder, or it can adopt the privileges of the folder that encloses it.

Although file sharing poses risks to your computer's security, you learned some strategies for controlling the risks. You also found out how to monitor the file sharing activity on your computer.

✦   ✦   ✦

Master Speech

✦ ✦ ✦ ✦

In This Chapter

Determining
requirements and
sources for speech

Hearing text read
aloud by any
computer that has
text-to-speech
software

Speaking commands
to PowerPC
computers that have
speech recognition
software

✦ ✦ ✦ ✦

Keyboarding and mousing are not particularly natural
ways to communicate. For years, computer designers
have looked for a more natural way to operate computers. One
of the most compelling ways to work with a computer is simply
to talk to it. Present-day Mac OS computers have taken the first
steps toward achieving the science fiction of *Star Trek,* when
people of the future speak naturally and conversationally with
their computers. When the crew of the spaceship *Enterprise*
traveled back in time to a mid-1980s San Francisco in the movie
Star Trek IV, chief engineer Scotty tried to use a Mac SE by
speaking into the mouse. Of course it was a big joke. Macs
have been able to speak text out loud since 1985, but it wasn't
until 1993 that Apple introduced speech recognition.

Apple calls its speech technology PlainTalk. You don't
always see that name in Apple's documentation or product
descriptions because the company now distributes the text-to-
speech and speech recognition parts of PlainTalk separately.
Apple generally identifies the separate parts of PlainTalk as
English Text-to-Speech, Mexican Spanish Text-to-Speech, and
English Speech Recognition.

This chapter describes how to use the speech software
that may be installed on your computer, beginning with a
discussion of speech software versions and requirements.
After that, the chapter tells you how to use text-to-speech
capabilities and speech recognition capabilities.

Speech Requirements and Sources

This section tells you which processor your computer must
have for various levels of speech software. This section also
tells you where to find speech installation software.

Speech requirements

All Macs OS computers from the Mac Plus on up are capable of basic speech. Computers with 68030 processors running at 33MHz or better are capable of more sophisticated speech. Computers with 68040 and PowerPC processors have the power to synthesize quite natural sounding speech.

Speech recognition has more stringent requirements than speech synthesis, and they prevent the popular iMac, as well as older Macs, from using Apple's English Speech Recognition software version 1.5.3 and earlier. Your computer must have a PowerPC processor (except as noted in the next paragraph) and an Apple PlainTalk microphone or its equivalent. The microphones built into Apple audiovisual monitors work for speech recognition, as do the microphones built into the PowerBook 2300, 5300, 3400, and G3. In addition, your computer must be capable of 16-bit, 22kHz sound input. This is the requirement that excludes the iMac, which has 16-bit, 44kHz sound input. Although 44kHz sound input is better than 22kHz, the higher rate inputs too much data for English Speech Recognition software to process. The sound input requirement also rules out early production units of the Performa 5200 and 5200 LC that have 8-bit sound input. You can determine whether a 5200 has 16-bit sound input by looking at the Sound Out settings in the Sound control panel. If the 16-bit option is grayed out, the 5200 has 8-bit sound and speech recognition won't work.

Among the Macs that don't use PowerPC processors, only the Centris and Quadra 660AV and the Quadra 840AV have sufficient processing power to recognize speech while you continue working. The 660AV and 840AV have a special coprocessor, an AT&T 3210 digital signal processor (DSP), that handles speech recognition; therefore, speech recognition does not burden the 68040 central processor in the 660AVs and 840AVs. The DSP handles speech recognition while the 68040 processor does other work. The 660AV and 840AV require an older version of speech recognition software that is not covered in this chapter.

Sources of speech software

Apple includes English Text-to-Speech software with Mac OS 7.6–8.5. It is part of a standard installation of Mac OS 8.5, but you must explicitly choose to install it in Mac OS 7.6–8.1 (as described in Chapters 31 and 32). In addition, Mac OS CDs include extra installation software for Mexican Spanish Text-to-Speech.

English Speech Recognition software comes with Mac OS 8.5, but it is not part of a standard installation. You must do a custom installation of Mac OS 8.5 (as described in Chapter 31) and select the Speech Recognition module. English Speech Recognition software is also included on the CD-ROM that comes with a Power Mac capable of using it. English Speech Recognition 1.5.3 is for Mac OS 8.5. Use English Speech Recognition 1.5 with Mac 7.6–OS 8.1 (unless you have a Centris or Quadra 660AV or 840AV, which work only with English Speech Recognition 1.3).

The current versions of Apple's speech software are available free from Apple's PlainTalk Web site (http://www.speech.apple.com/ptk/).

Text-to-Speech

There are several ways to get a Mac OS computer to speak. You can use an application that has commands for speaking the text in a document. You can program the computer to speak. And you can have the computer automatically read out the text of alert messages. Regardless of what your computer speaks, it can speak in different voices, and with later versions of speech software you can choose the voice. This section tells you how to choose a voice and make your computer speak. There's also a discussion of speech quality at the end of the section.

Choosing a voice

The PlainTalk Text-to-Speech software can talk in different voices. You choose a voice for the system as a whole. Each application can use the system voice, pick its own voice, or let you choose a voice for that application's speech. However, not all applications give you a voice choice.

Choosing a system voice

You can choose your computer's voice and set a speaking rate with the Speech control panel. A pop-up menu lists the available voices, a slider adjusts the speaking rate, and a button lets you hear a sample using the current settings. Figure 22-1 shows the Speech control panel's Voice settings.

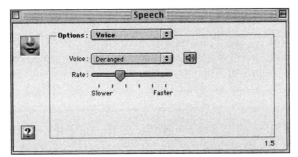

Figure 22-1: Set the computer's speaking voice and speaking rate.

Choosing an application voice

The method for choosing an application's speaking voice varies among applications. For instance, in SimpleText you choose a voice from the Voices submenu of the Sound menu. Figure 22-2 is an example of SimpleText's Voices submenu.

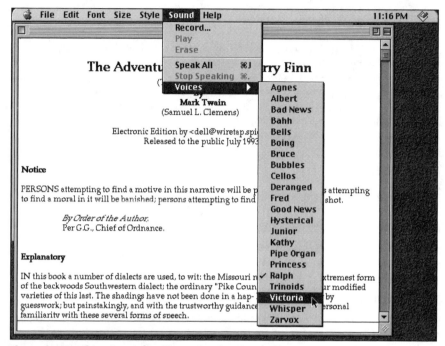

Figure 22-2: Choosing a speaking voice for SimpleText.

Where voices are installed

For each speaking voice available on your computer there is a voice file in the Voices folder, which is inside the System Folder. (With Mac 7.6–OS 7.6.1 the Voices folder is in the Extensions folder.) You get several male, female, and robotic voices when you install English Text-to-Speech. The exact assortment depends on the capabilities of your computer model, as explained in detail at the end of this section.

You can remove voices by dragging their files out of the Voices folder. If you obtain additional voices from a source such as Apple's Speech Web site (http://www. speech.apple.com), you can make them available by dragging them into the Voices folder.

Talking alerts

You can use the Speech control panel to set up the manner in which the computer announces its alert messages. There's an option for having the computer read the text of alert messages aloud, a slider for adjusting how long the computer waits after it displays an alert message before it speaks, and an option for having the computer speak a phrase such as "Excuse me!" when it displays an alert. There's also a button that lets you hear a sample alert using the current settings. Figure 22-3 shows the Speech control panel's Talking Alert settings.

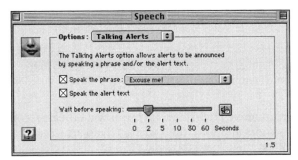

Figure 22-3: Set the computer to announce alert messages.

If you select the option to have the computer speak a phrase when it displays an alert, you choose the phrase you want from a pop-up menu. The pop-up menu includes a choice that tells the computer to use the next phrase listed in the menu each time it speaks an alert. The pop-up also includes a choice that tells the computer to pick a phrase at random from the list each time it speaks an alert. There's also a choice that lets you edit (change, add, or delete) phrases.

If you set the time the computer waits before speaking an alert to more than two seconds, the computer plays the alert sound as soon as it displays an alert and then waits to speak. If you set the time to wait before speaking to less than two seconds, the computer does not play the alert sound when it displays an alert message.

Reading documents aloud

To have your computer speak the text in a document, you need one of the many applications that include commands for speaking. SimpleText is one, and ClarisWorks, FileMaker Pro, and WordPerfect are others. Various applications have different methods for initiating speech. For example, SimpleText has a Speak command in its Sound menu, whereas ClarisWorks has a Shortcut button. Most applications that can speak text will speak the currently selected text or all text in the active document if no text is selected.

Text-to-speech also augments other types of software. Here are some examples:

✦ outSPOKEN from ALVA Access (510-923-6280, http://www.aagi.com) uses text-to-speech software to read out the text and the graphics of standard Mac OS applications such as word processors, spreadsheets, communications programs, and more.

✦ Talk:About by Don Johnston Inc. (847-526-2682, http://www.donjohnston.com) lets individuals who don't speak participate in conversations.

✦ eText by META Innovation (61 3 9439 6639, http://www.meta-inn.com) uses text-to-speech to teach typing for computers (not for typewriters).

✦ NetMeter by The AG Group, Inc. (510-937-7900, http://www.aggroup.com) monitors network traffic and can vocally announce network traffic conditions and warnings.

✦ Storybook Weaver Deluxe from The Learning Company (617-494-5700, http://www.learningco.com) can read aloud storybooks that kids write in English or Spanish.

✦ Hollywood by Theatrix Interactive (800-795-8749, http://www.theatrix.com) lets kids become screenwriters and have their written dialogue, character actions, and stage directions performed on screen by any of ten characters.

✦ MacYack Pro from Scantron Quality Computers (800-966-1508, http://www.lowtek.com/macyack/) lets you add speech to any word processor, hear dialog boxes, see and hear customized messages at startup and shutdown, hear calculations instantly, correct pronunciation errors, create double-clickable speech files, have speaking alert sounds, add speech to HyperCard stacks, and use AppleScript to add speech to other programs.

Speaking on command

In addition to having documents and alerts read to you, you can program your computer to speak on command. One way to accomplish this is with AppleScript (which is described in Chapter 23). Alternatively you can use a macro utility such as QuicKeys from CE Software (515-222-1801, http://www.cesoft.com). The QuicKeys Speak Ease shortcut speaks text you enter in its text window or text you copy from a document (up to 32K) to the Clipboard. Whenever you type the shortcut's keystroke, the computer speaks the text that you entered or copied. You also can set up a timer so that the computer speaks the text at specified intervals. Figure 22-4 shows the QuicKeys dialog box in which you specify text-to-speech.

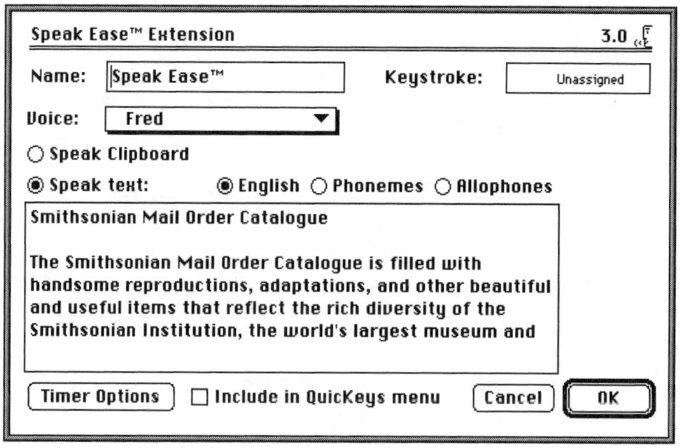

Figure 22-4: The QuicKeys Speak Ease shortcut allows you to enter text you want spoken.

Speech quality

Several factors affect the quality of computer-generated speech. Clarity of intonation obviously affects how easily you can understand your computer's speech. Less obvious factors include handling contractions, sequencing words idiomatically, avoiding robotic cadence, and generating the sounds of speech.

For natural-sounding speech, the text-to-speech system needs to compensate for idiomatic differences between written and spoken text. This includes expanding contractions, changing word order, and making substitutions. For example, when the system sees "$40 billion" it should not say "dollars forty billion." The system also has to deal with ambiguous abbreviations such as "St. Mary's Church is on St. Mary's St."

Besides saying the right words in the right order, the text-to-speech system has to pronounce them correctly. Consider how many ways "ough" is pronounced in the words enough, ought, slough, dough, through, and drought. Pronunciation also depends on sentence structure, as in "A strong wind can wind a kite string around a tree." Moreover, the system has to avoid putting the emPHASis on the wrong sylLAble. Names pose a special problem because their spelling is even less reliable a guide to pronunciation than ordinary English words.

Getting the words and pronunciation right isn't enough. Without the right cadence, spoken words may sound robotic. Beyond just sounding unnatural, the wrong phrasing may convey the wrong meaning. Compare the meaning of "Atlas already ate, Venus" to "Atlas already ate Venus."

The most computationally intensive part of speech synthesis is producing the sound of a human voice speaking the text. Each moment of speech requires many mathematical calculations and ample memory. The higher the quality of speech, the greater the computational and memory demands. In other words, a higher-performance computer is capable of higher quality speech.

Apple's text-to-speech software has three levels of speech quality, each demanding a different level of computer performance. The levels are known as MacinTalk 2, MacinTalk 3, and MacinTalk Pro. Each consists of a system extension and a set of voices. When you install text-to-speech software, the Installer program gives you the parts that are appropriate for your computer. For example, a PowerPC computer gets MacinTalk Pro and MacinTalk 3. (You can get MacinTalk 2 on a PowerPC computer by doing a custom installation of the text-to-speech software.)

MacinTalk 2

The least demanding speech synthesizer is MacinTalk 2. It generates an audio signal the same way as music synthesizers, with a technique known as wave table synthesis. MacinTalk 2 has ten voices that you can use on any Mac OS computer from a Mac Plus up. However, MacinTalk 2 and its ten voices are not included with and can't be used with English Speech Recognition 1.5.3, which is the version you must use with Mac OS 8.5.

Quick Tips

Making Speech Sound More Natural

The Mac does a pretty good job of speaking text, but you can adjust the cadence and pronunciation of the speech to make it sound more natural. You make these adjustments by adding punctuation and emphasis codes.

When the Mac reads text, it tends to pause less often than a person would. You can make the Mac pause more often by inserting extra commas where you want pauses. For example:

```
"You have a lunch date, at 12:30, on Tuesday, at the Sam & Ella
Cafe."
```

To insert a brief pause, put single quotation marks around a phrase. For example:

```
"Exclusive to the 'Coast Starlight' is the 'Pacific Parlour
Car.'"
```

You may also notice that the Mac tends to emphasize too many words, making it hard to tell which are important. You can insert a code before a word you want to have less emphasis. The code you insert is *[[emph -]]*. This code must have exactly one space before the hyphen, and none anywhere else. Here is an example:

```
"The shuttle bus runs every half [[emph -]] hour, on the half
[[emph -]] hour."
```

If you need to add emphasis, insert the code *[[emph +]]*. This code also has exactly one space in it. Here is an example:

```
"Food and drink are [[emph +]] not allowed, in the museum."
```

MacinTalk 3

The mid-level speech synthesizer, MacinTalk 3, sounds less robotic than MacinTalk 2 because it's based on an acoustic model of the human vocal tract. MacinTalk 3 has 19 voices, including several novelty voices (robots, talking bubbles, whispering, and singing) that you can use on a computer with a 33MHz 68030 processor or better.

MacinTalk Pro

The best synthesizer, MacinTalk Pro, bases its audio signal on samples of real human speech. It sounds more like a human voice than the other synthesizers, especially when synthesizing a female voice. To assist with pronunciations, MacinTalk Pro has a dictionary of 65,000 words plus 5,000 common U.S. names. To generate cadence, it uses a sophisticated model of the acoustic structure of human speech that resulted from many years of research. MacinTalk Pro has three English voices that require a 68040 or PowerPC processor. It also has two Mexican Spanish voices that require a 68020 processor or better. All the voices are available in three quality levels, with each level striking a different balance between memory requirements and speech quality.

Speech Recognition

Apple made headlines in 1992 when it began touting its speech recognition technology, which was then called Casper. Now called English Speech Recognition, the technology enables many Mac models to take spoken commands from anyone who speaks North American English. You don't have to train the computer to recognize your voice. You just speak normally, without intense pauses, unnatural diction, or special intonation.

English Speech Recognition is designed to understand a few dozen commands for controlling your computer. You can add to and remove some of the commands that the speech recognition system understands, but you can't turn it into a general dictation system.

This section explains how to configure speech recognition and how to speak commands. It tells you what commands the speech recognition system understands and how you can add your own speakable commands. The section concludes by describing some applications that make special use of speech recognition.

Configuring speech recognition

You configure speech recognition with the Speech control panel. You can turn speech recognition on and off, make limited adjustments to what is recognized, and specify the kind of feedback you get when you speak commands.

On and off

You turn speech recognition on or off in the Speakable Items section of the Speech control panel. You can also specify whether the computer should listen for the names of buttons such as OK and Cancel when speech recognition is on. Figure 22-5 shows the Speakable Items section of the Speech control panel.

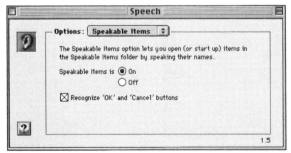

Figure 22-5: Turn speech recognition on and off and set it to listen for button names.

Feedback

Turning on speech recognition brings up a feedback window, which floats above all other windows. At the left side of the feedback window, an animated cartoon character indicates whether the computer is standing by, is listening for a command, is hearing sounds, recognizes your spoken words as a command, or doesn't recognize your spoken words. Beneath the character, some italicized text reminds you what you must do to make the computer listen for a command: press the named key or speak the indicated code name (as described later in this section). The feedback window can also display your voice commands in writing along with a written response. You can hide and show the text by clicking the feedback window's zoom box. Figure 22-6 is an example of the speech recognition feedback window.

Figure 22-6: Getting feedback on your spoken commands.

You determine how the computer lets you know whether it heard and recognized your spoken commands by setting options in the Feedback section of the Speech control panel. You can choose the feedback window's cartoon character from a pop-up menu. You can turn the "Speak text feedback" option on or off to control whether the computer speaks its response to your commands in addition to displaying them in writing in the feedback window. You can also choose a sound from a pop-up menu that lists the sounds in the System file, and the computer will play that sound when it recognizes what you said. Figure 22-7 shows the Feedback section of the Speech control panel.

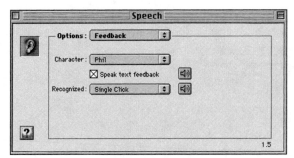

Figure 22-7: Specify how you want the computer to respond to your spoken commands.

Speaking commands

You don't want the computer listening to every word you say, or it might try to interpret conversational remarks as commands. There are basically two methods for controlling when the computer listens for commands: the push-to-talk method and the code name method. The push-to-talk method is the most reliable method because the computer listens for commands only while you are pressing a key you designate. With the other method, the computer listens for its code name and tries to interpret the words that follow it as a command.

Push-to-Talk method

To use the push-to-talk method of signaling the computer that you are speaking a command, bring up the Listening section of the Speech control panel and set the Method option to "Listen only while key(s) are pressed." The Key(s) option specifies the key or keys you must hold down to make the computer listen for a spoken command. You can change the setting of the Key(s) option by pressing a different key or combination of keys. Generally you must use the Esc key, Delete key, a symbol key, or any key on the numeric keypad either alone or together with any one or more of the Shift, Option, and Control keys. You can't use letter keys or number keys on the main part of the keyboard. Figure 22-8 shows the Speech control panel set for the push-to-talk method with the Esc key, which is the initial setting.

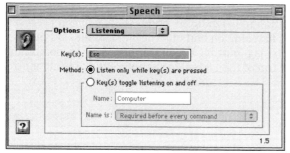

Figure 22-8: Setting speech recognition for push-to-talk listening.

Code Name method

If you prefer to have the computer listen for a code name that you say before speaking a command, bring up the Listening section of the Speech control panel and set the Method option to "Key(s) toggle listening on and off." Then you can type a name for the computer in the space provided. You can use the nearby pop-up menu to specify when you must speak the name. You can make the code name optional, but not without risk: the computer could interpret something you say in conversation as a voice command. Figure 22-9 shows the Speech control panel set for the code name method.

You can configure speech recognition so that you don't have to speak the code name if you spoke the last command less than 15 seconds ago (or another interval that you specify). The idea is that when you have the computer's attention, you shouldn't have to get its attention all the time. You can tell whether you need to speak the code name by looking at the speech recognition feedback window. If you see the code name beneath the feedback character, you have to speak the name before the next command.

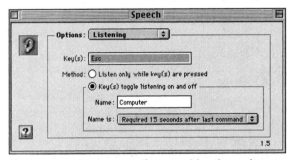

Figure 22-9: Setting speech recognition for code name listening.

Attention key

When you set speech recognition to listen for its code name, you can press a key or a combination of keys to turn listening on and off. Turning listening off puts speech recognition on standby, which may improve the performance of the computer. You specify the key or keys at the top of the Listening section of the Speech control panel.

Speakable commands

After setting up and turning on speech recognition, you are ready to speak commands (such as "Make this speakable"), with the expectation that the computer will carry out your order. But what commands will the computer obey? The answer is pretty simple: items in the Speakable Items folder and some buttons in dialog boxes.

Speakable Items folder

Speech recognition recognizes the names of items in the Speakable Items folder (which you can access from the Apple menu) as commands. Saying the word "open" before the name of an item in the Speakable Items folder is generally optional unless the item name begins with the word "open." For example, if you had a speakable item named "ClarisWorks," you could open it by saying "open ClarisWorks" or "ClarisWorks."

Speech recognition is similarly liberal about the use of *a, an, the, and,* and *or* in spoken commands. For instance, you can say "close window" or "close the window." Moreover, you can often substitute *these* for *this,* as in "Make this speakable" and "Make these speakable." The computer is somewhat more likely to recognize a phrase that exactly matches a speakable item. If the computer has trouble recognizing a spoken command, try saying the exact name of the speakable item.

When speaking a command, you should not pause between words, but you should pause slightly when saying a command with initials or an acronym, as if you were spelling it out for someone. For example, if you had a speakable item named "open PPP control panel" you should say "open P P P control panel."

If a name includes an ampersand, a slash, or another symbol, speech recognition ignores it. For example, if you had a speakable item named "open Monitors & Sound" you could say "open Monitors Sound" or "open Monitors and Sound."

Speech Recognition 1.5 ignores numbers and punctuation. For example, if you had a speakable item named "Web Browser 3.1" you could say "Open Web Browser three point one," or "Open Web Browser three one," or simply "Open Web Browser."

Menu items

If you want Speech Recognition to recognize menu commands, you will have to create an AppleScript application for each menu command. This works only for scriptable applications. (For more information on AppleScript, see Chapter 23.)

More speakable commands

You make the computer understand more spoken commands by adding items to the Speakable Items folder. Anything that you can open in the Finder becomes a speakable command when you add it to the Speakable Items folder.

Aliases

If there are documents, applications, folders, control panels, or any other items that you want to open by spoken command, simply put aliases of them in the Speakable Items folder. You can do this very easily by selecting the items in the Finder and speaking the command "Make this speakable." The result is an alias in the Speakable Items folder for every item you originally selected, and the aliases have exactly the same names as the original items. If the computer doesn't recognize the name of an item you add to the Speakable Items folder, try restarting the computer.

You can change the speakable command that opens an alias by editing the name of the alias. You should remove the word *alias* from any alias names that include it, although speech recognition usually ignores *alias* at the end of a speakable item's name. If the computer doesn't respond when you say "open" followed by the name of a speakable item, change the item's name so that it begins with "open."

If speakable items have names that sound similar, the computer may have trouble distinguishing them. If the computer frequently mistakes one speakable item for another, try changing the name of one or both so they don't sound alike. Also, the computer has more trouble identifying short names than long ones. To prevent these problems, make the names of your speakable items as long and unique sounding as possible.

AppleScript and the Script Editor

To make a multistep speakable command, use the Script Editor program to create an AppleScript application that you put in the Speakable Items folder. With some applications you can record an AppleScript application of a procedure while you carry it out. Another way to create your own AppleScript application is to base the new script on an existing one. However, you can create AppleScript applications only to control applications that respond to Apple events. (For more information on AppleScript and Apple events, see Chapter 23.)

Speech recognition applications

It would be very difficult if not impossible to add enough items to the Speakable Items folder to gain anything approaching complete control of an application. Yet applications have access to the speech recognition infrastructure behind the Speakable Items folder, and an application developer can use that infrastructure to give you extensive spoken control of an application. These applications offer enhanced control through speech recognition:

✦ SurfTalk by Digital Dreams (http://www.surftalk.com) is an add-on for Netscape Navigator or Microsoft Internet Explorer that lets you control the Web browser with spoken commands. You can follow hot links on a Web page, go to bookmarks, and use common navigational commands such as "Go back," "Reload," and "Add Bookmark."

✦ Speech Typer by Michael F. Kamprath (http://www. kamprath.net/claireware/) takes speech recognition beyond speakable commands into the realm of data entry. It lets you type any predefined phrase into any application you may be using. Because you must predefine spoken phrases, Speech Typer doesn't turn speech recognition into a full-fledged dictation system, but it does allow you to dictate commonly used words and phrases.

✦ MT-NewsWatcher by Simon Fraser (http://www.best.com/~smfr/mtnw/) is a speech-controlled Internet newsreader.

✦ Dynamic English by DynEd International (650-578-8067 http://www.dyned. com) teaches English as a second language by using speech recognition to improve articulation and fluency and to reinforce language structure and vocabulary.

✦ Hearts Deluxe 4.4 by Free Verse Software (212-929-3549, http://www.freeverse. com) lets you play the classic card game of hearts against Winston Churchill, Alice in Wonderland, or a bunch of dogs, using only your voice.

✦ IndyCar Racing II by Sierra On-Line (425-649-9800, http://www.sierra.com) is a car racing game in which you can call out commands to your crew over your radio so they'll be ready for time-critical servicing as soon as you roll into the pit.

Summary

In this chapter, you learned the requirements and sources for Apple's PlainTalk text-to-speech and speech recognition software. You found out there are several ways to get a Mac OS computer to speak. You can use an application that has commands for speaking the text in a document. You can program the computer to speak. And you can have the computer automatically read out the text of alert messages. Regardless of what your computer speaks, it can speak in different voices, and with later versions of speech software you can choose the voice. The quality of the speech depends on which speech synthesizer your computer has the power to use: MacinTalk 2, MacinTalk 3, or MacinTalk Pro.

You also learned how to use speech recognition software. You use the Speech control panel to turn recognition on and off and to specify how you want the system to respond when it recognizes a spoken command. You learned the push-to-talk method of speaking commands and the code name method. Finally, you found out what spoken commands the computer understands and how you can add more with aliases and AppleScript.

✦   ✦   ✦

Automate with Scripts

People have worked together for thousands of years, and nowadays personal computer programs can too. The key to working together is communication, for both people and programs.

The Mac OS technology that enables Mac programs, called *interapplication communication* (IAC), was first implemented system-wide in System 7.0. The publish and subscribe capabilities described in the next chapter, together with the Copy and Paste commands, are one part of IAC. The other part of IAC enables programs to share services.

Apple Events

Programs can share services behind the scenes by sending and receiving messages called *Apple events*. When an application receives Apple event messages sent by another program, the receiving application, also known as the *server application*, does something. The action that the server application takes depends on the contents of the Apple event messages. This action can be anything from executing a particular command to taking some data, working with it, and then returning a result to the program that sent the Apple events, known as the *client application*.

When you choose Shut Down or Restart from the Special menu, for example, the Finder sends the Apple event Quit to every open program. When you drag and drop icons into an application, the Finder sends the Apple event Open Documents, which includes a list of all the items that you dragged into the icon. Programs that make aliases or shut down your machine for you accomplish these tasks by sending Apple events to the Finder.

A program, however, does not automatically send or receive Apple events; the developer must build in the capability to receive and act on Apple events. More and more developers are putting Apple-event capability in their applications. Most applications introduced or revised since the middle of 1991 can receive and act on at least the four basic Apple events: Open Application, Open Documents, Print Documents, and Quit Application, each of which are defined in Table 23-1.

Table 23-1
Basic Apple Events Messages

Message Sent to Application	What Happens
Open Application	The application opens
Open Documents	The application opens the specified documents
Print Documents	The application prints the specified documents
Quit Application	The application quits

The Finder uses the basic Apple-events messages to open programs, open documents, print documents, and quit programs. When you double-click a program icon, the Finder sends the program an Open Application message. When you double-click a document, the Finder sends the program that created the document an Open Application message and an Open Documents message with the name of the document you double-clicked. When you select one or more documents and choose Print from the Finder's menu, the Finder sends the application an Open Application message, a Print Documents message with the identity of the documents you selected, and a Quit Application message. When you choose the Shut Down or Restart command, the Finder sends a Quit Application message to each open program. For programs that don't understand the basic Apple events, the Finder uses its traditional means of opening, printing, and quitting.

Programs that go beyond the four basic Apple-events messages understand another two dozen core Apple-events messages. These messages encompass actions and objects that almost all programs have in common, such as the Close, Save, Undo, Redo, Cut, Copy, and Paste commands. Programs with related capabilities recognize still more sets of Apple-events messages. Word processing programs understand messages about text manipulation, for example, and drawing programs understand messages about graphics manipulation. Program developers can also define private messages that only their own programs know.

The Mac OS provides the means of communicating Apple-events messages between programs. The programs can be on the same computer or on different computers connected to the same network. A program doesn't have to be open or even accessible to receive messages; the Mac OS stores messages and forwards them when the program becomes available. Only application programs can send and receive Apple events; "true" control panels and desk accessories cannot. Control panels that are actually applications (they are listed in the Applications menu when open) are not subject to this limitation. And a desk accessory can work around this limitation by sending and receiving through a small surrogate application program that is always open in the background. This background application does not have to appear in the Application menu, and the computer user does not have to know that the application is open.

To understand how Apple events work, think of them as a telephone system. The Mac OS furnishes a "telephone" and "voicemail" for each program, as well as the wires that connect them. For messages sent across a network, the Mac OS uses the built-in AppleTalk networking software and LocalTalk, Ethernet, or other networking connectors and cables (described in Chapter 19). Application programs talk on the telephones and leave Apple-events messages for each other. Desk accessories aren't capable of talking on the phone, but some of them have agents that forward incoming and outgoing messages.

Apple events offer many intriguing possibilities for the world of personal computing. No longer does one application need to handle every possible function; instead, it can send messages to helper applications. For example, the Sherlock program in Mac OS 8.5 and the Find File program in Mac OS 7.6–8.1 handle some commands from their File menus, such as Get Info and Open Enclosing Folder, by sending Apple-events messages to the Finder, which actually carries out the commands.

Introducing AppleScript

Apple events aren't just for professional software engineers. Mac enthusiasts who have little technical training can use Apple events to control applications by writing commands in the *AppleScript* language. For example, suppose you want to quit all open applications so you can open one really big application. The Mac OS doesn't have a Quit All command, but you can create one with an AppleScript command. You can use AppleScript commands to automate simple tasks such as this one, as well as more complex tasks, as you'll see in the following sections.

AppleScript Language

AppleScript is a user-oriented programming language that allows end users to send Apple events to programs. With AppleScript, you write your own programs, called *scripts*, to perform complex tasks easily. You can use AppleScript to move data between applications. You can develop your own tools to accomplish exactly what you need.

Because AppleScript is aimed at users, Apple has made the scripting language as easy as possible to understand and use. The language is very natural and English-like. You can look at scripts and know right away what they're supposed to do. Also, AppleScript removes the need for you to decipher the codes that make up Apple events. Instead, you get information from the application itself about what words to use to represent the Apple events that the program understands. Inside an application, a Get Data event is represented by codes like "core" and "getd," but with AppleScript you may see only "get." This way, even novice users can understand AppleScript. Finally, AppleScript can actually watch you as you work with an application and write a script for you behind the scenes. This process is called *script recording*.

Although AppleScript is designed for end users, it offers all the capabilities of a traditional programming language and won't frustrate programmers and more advanced users. You can store information in variables for later use; write if–then statements to execute different commands, depending on some condition that you specify; or repeat a set of commands as many times as you want. AppleScript also offers error checking and object-oriented programming.

AppleScript pieces

Several pieces make up a complete AppleScript setup. Perhaps most noticeable is the Automated Tasks folder listed in your Apple menu. Initially this folder contains sample scripts that Apple includes with the Mac OS. You can add and remove scripts from the Automated Tasks folder as you wish. You can open the folder by choosing it from the Apple Menu because the folder has an alias in the Apple Menu Items folder. The Automated Tasks folder is actually located in the AppleScript folder (inside the Apple Extras folder on your startup disk). The AppleScript folder also contains additional sample scripts from Apple in the More Automated Tasks folder.

In addition to the sample scripts, there are several AppleScript items in the System Folder or the Extensions folder. Chief among these is the AppleScript extension, which contains the actual AppleScript language. Another important AppleScript item is a folder named Scripting Additions. This folder contains special files, called *scripting additions,* which add commands to the AppleScript language, much as plug-in files add capabilities to Photoshop or a Web browser. In Mac OS 8–8.5, there can be two Scripting Additions folders: one in the System Folder and another in the Extensions folder. However, if there are any duplicate items in the two Scripting Additions folders, the one in the System Folder takes precedence. In Mac OS 7.6–7.6.1, the Scripting Additions folder must be in the Extensions folder.

AppleScript also includes a simple application, Script Editor, for creating and editing scripts. You can use the Script Editor to record, write, and edit scripts for any application that is compatible with AppleScript. A prime example of a scriptable application (an application that you can control with AppleScript) is the Finder. In Mac OS 7.6–7.6.1, the Finder is only scriptable if the Finder Scripting Extension file is in the Extensions folder. The Finder in Mac OS 8–8.5 does not require or use the Finder Scripting Extension.

If you do a lot of scripting, you may want to replace the Script Editor with a more capable application such as Scripter from Main Event Software (202-298-9595, http://www.mainevent.com) or Script Debugger from Late Night Software (604-929-5578, http://www.latenightsw.com).

Introducing the Script Editor

Script Editor is the program that you use the most when you use AppleScript. This simple program allows you to write and run scripts. Find the Script Editor icon on your hard drive and open it.

When you open Script Editor, an empty window appears. This *script window* can contain one script. The bottom pane of the script window is the *script editing area*, where you type and edit the text of the script. The top pane of the window is the *script description area*. You use this area to type a description of what the script does. Figure 23-1 shows an empty script window.

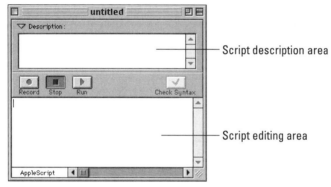

Figure 23-1: The new script window that appears when Script Editor opens.

The middle area of the window contains four buttons. The first button puts you in Record mode. When you click this button, AppleScript begins watching you as you work with applications. If you are working in an application that accepts recording, AppleScript writes out the script commands that correlate to the things that you do with the application. Pressing ⌘-D also starts recording.

Clicking the Stop button takes you out of recording mode or stops a script that is running, depending on which action is relevant at the time. Pressing ⌘-period(.) is the same as clicking the Stop button.

The Run button starts running the script in the script editing area. You also can press ⌘-R to run the script.

Finally, the script window contains a Check Syntax button. Clicking this button compiles the script. *Compiling* a script means putting it in a format that AppleScript recognizes as a script. While AppleScript compiles your script, it checks your script for things that it doesn't understand. For example, if you forget a parenthesis where AppleScript expects to find one, it lets you know. After you fix any syntax errors, AppleScript compiles the script.

Recording a Script

One of the easiest ways to see how AppleScript looks is to record your actions and let AppleScript write a script for you. You cannot record scripts for every scriptable program because software developers must do more work to make an application recordable than to make it scriptable.

One recordable application is the Finder. You can experiment with it to see how script recording works. To do this, open the Script Editor and click the Record button in a new script window. A tape cassette icon flashes over the Apple menu while you are recording a script to remind you that AppleScript is recording your actions. Now switch to the Finder, make a new folder, set its label, open it, move its window, and set its view options. When you finish, switch back to Script Editor and click the Stop button. AppleScript displays a script that when run will mimic all your actions. (Some Finder actions can't be recorded in Mac OS 7.6–7.6.1.) Figure 23-2 is an example of a script you might record in the Mac OS 8–8.1 Finder.

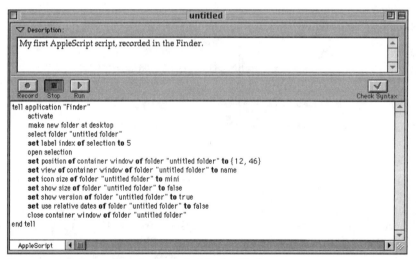

Figure 23-2: A sample script recorded in the Finder.

To test the script, go back to the Finder and delete the new folder you created. (This ensures that the Finder starts out the same way as when you recorded your script.) Now switch back to Script Editor and click the Run button in your recorded script's window. AppleScript plays back everything you did. When the script finishes running, there should be a new folder set up exactly as when you finished recording your script. Now switch to Script Editor again and examine the script. You'll find the script to be fairly understandable — it may not be fluent English, but many of the commands will make sense as you read them.

Analyzing a Script

Having looked through the script that AppleScript wrote in the previous Finder example, you may be surprised to learn that AppleScript doesn't know anything about the Finder operations. AppleScript doesn't know how to set an icon's label, how to move windows, or how to do any of the things that your script did in Finder. In fact, AppleScript knows how to perform only five commands: Get, Set, Count, Copy, and Run. AppleScript learns how to perform other commands in a script from the application controlled by the script. Each scriptable application contains a dictionary that defines the AppleScript commands that work with the application. In technical discussions of AppleScript, you may hear a scriptable application's dictionary of AppleScript commands referred to as the application's "aete" resource.

Look at the sample script you recorded. The first line says "tell application 'Finder'." To AppleScript, this means "start working with the application named Finder." When a script is compiled, AppleScript looks at the application you specified. By looking at the program's dictionary, AppleScript figures out what Apple events the program understands. AppleScript learns, for example, that the Finder understands the "make" Apple event. The dictionary also tells AppleScript what kind of information, or *objects*, the application knows how to work with, such as files, folders, and disks. Finally, the dictionary tells AppleScript what words to use as AppleScript commands instead of the codes that the application understands.

When you run your sample script and AppleScript reaches the "tell application 'Finder'" line, AppleScript starts sending Apple events to the application program named in that line. AppleScript translates every command it encounters in your script into an Apple event code based on the program's dictionary, and it sends that code to the application. The application receives the Apple event and takes the appropriate action.

When AppleScript hits the End Tell command that appears at the bottom of the script you recorded, it stops sending messages to the Finder. If you are working with several applications, you may have another Tell command that names a different application, in which case AppleScript starts talking to this application, sending it Apple event codes.

You can look at the dictionary of an application to see what commands the application understands. In Script Editor, choose Open Dictionary from the File menu. A standard Open dialog box appears. Select the Finder and click the Open button. The Script Editor displays a dictionary window for the Finder, as shown in Figure 23-3.

The left side of the dictionary window displays a list of commands, classes of objects, and suites that the application recognizes. A *suite* is a group of commands and other items for a related activity, but you don't have to worry about suites when you're scripting.

Describes the command or object classes selected in the list to the left

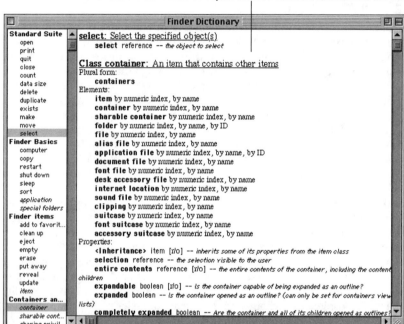

Figure 23-3: A scriptable application's AppleScript dictionary defines commands the application understands.

You can select one or more terms listed on the left side of a dictionary window to see detailed descriptions of the terms on the right. Just as you can get more information about a command from a program's dictionary, so can AppleScript.

Because AppleScript gets all the relevant information from the application itself, you never have to worry about controlling a new application. As long as the application has a dictionary, AppleScript can work with it.

Scripting additions also have dictionaries, which you can open the same way as you open applications' dictionaries. In fact, in the Open Dictionary dialog box, Script Editor provides a button that takes you directly to the Scripting Additions folder.

Saving Your Script

The Script Editor allows you to save your scripts in three distinct forms. You choose the form from a pop-up menu in the Script Editor's Save dialog box, as shown in Figure 23-4.

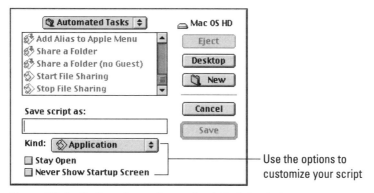

Figure 23-4: Options for saving an AppleScript script.

The pop-up menu contains three options:

✦ **Application** saves the script as an application, complete with an icon. Opening the icon (by double-clicking it, for example) runs the script. You must have AppleScript installed to open a script application.

✦ **Compiled Script** saves the script in a compiled form that you can open with the Script Editor and run or change from there.

✦ **Text** saves the script as a plain text document, which you can open in Script Editor, in any word processing program, and in many other applications.

If you choose Application from the pop-up menu in the Save dialog box, two checkboxes appear in the dialog box. The Stay Open checkbox, if checked, causes the script application to stay open after its script finishes running. If the Stay Open checkbox is not checked, the script application quits automatically after running its script. Checking the Never Show Startup Screen checkbox suppresses the display of an identifying "about" window when the script application is opened.

Creating a Script from Scratch

You now know how to use Script Editor to record your actions and write an AppleScript script. This type of script, however, has limited value. A recorded script is not much more intelligent than a simple macro because the script doesn't take advantage of AppleScript's full programming language. Furthermore, not all applications that work with AppleScript permit recording, so you can't always rely on being able to record.

More frequently, you'll use AppleScript to create complex scripts from scratch. This section shows that you can create a full-blown script quickly and use the resulting custom utility to augment a program's capabilities.

Making a Finder utility

One of the nice features of the Mac OS is that it enables you to drag files into the System Folder and have the Finder figure out where those files should go. Control panels are stored in the Control Panels folder, Fonts go in the Fonts folder, Desk Accessories are placed in the Apple Menu Items folder, and so on.

This capability, however, is limited to whatever the people at Apple provide. For example, if you drag an After Dark module into the System Folder, the Finder won't put the module in the After Dark Files folder. You must dig your way through the System Folder hierarchy to get to the relevant folder.

You can, however, write a simple script that uses the Finder and mimics the System Folder's behavior, but moves files to the folders in which you want those files to go. As you'll see, the script is more powerful than the System Folder, because the target folder can be anywhere. For example, you can make your QuickTime movies find their way into a folder that's nowhere near your System Folder.

Beginning the script

Open Script Editor or create a new window if Script Editor is already open. This blank window is where you'll write your script.

You can change the default size of a new script window. First, make the script window the size you want, and then choose Set Default Window Size from the File menu in Script Editor.

The first thing this script must do is provide a way to select the file you want to move. One of the scripting additions that comes with AppleScript, Choose File, allows you to bring up a dialog box for selecting a file from within the script.

In the script editing area of the window, type:

```
choose file
```

and then click the Check Syntax button. AppleScript changes the text fonts as it compiles the script, using different type styles to show different kinds of words. Geneva 10-point Bold, for example, represents words that are native to AppleScript, whereas Plain Geneva 9-point represents words that come from another application. (If you don't like these typestyles, you can change them via the AppleScript Formatting command in Script Editor's Edit menu.)

Click the Run button to run the script you wrote, selecting any type of file and clicking the Open button. AppleScript shows you the result of the script in a window named, appropriately enough, "the result." (If this window isn't open, choose Show Result from the Controls menu.) The window contains the word "alias" and the path through your folders to the file you selected. Notice that this word does not mean that the file is an alias — in the context of a script, *alias* means the same thing as *file path*. Figure 23-5 shows an example of the result window.

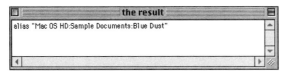

Figure 23-5: Checking a file specification in Script Editor's "the result" window.

The result of the Choose File command is called a *file specification* or *file spec*. A file spec tells the Mac OS exactly where to find a file or folder. You will need the file spec later in the script, so you must put it in a *variable,* which is a container for information. You can place data in a variable and then retrieve it whenever you want before the script finishes running. You can also place new data in a variable during the course of the script.

On the next line of the script, type:

```
copy the result to filePath
```

This line places the result of the Choose File command in a variable named filePath. To access the information, type the name of the variable in your script; AppleScript understands this name as a representation of the file spec you got from the first command.

You may notice the capital *P* in the filePath and wonder whether capitalization is important when entering AppleScript commands. In general, you can capitalize any way that makes commands easier to read. Many AppleScripts authors adopt the convention of capitalizing each word except the first word in a variable name, hence filePath.

When you run the script, you'll see that the Copy command doesn't change the result of the script. The result of copying information to a variable is the information itself.

Working with the Finder

Ultimately, the script you are creating decides where to move a file you select, based on the file's four-letter file type. That means you have to get the file type of the file you selected. You can use the Finder to get this information. Enter these commands in the script, starting on the third line of the script:

```
tell application "Finder"
copy the file type of file filePath to fileType
end tell
```

The first of these lines tells AppleScript to start using the Finder. Remember that after encountering this Tell command, AppleScript knows all the commands and objects from the Finder's AppleScript dictionary.

The second line asks the Finder for the file type of the file you selected and then copies that information into the variable named fileType. Even though the word "Finder" doesn't appear in this line, the Tell command in the preceding line tells AppleScript to direct these requests to the Finder.

Finally, the End Tell command tells AppleScript to stop working with the Finder for now.

Run the script, select a file, and look at the result. The result window contains the four-letter file type of the file you selected, displayed as a piece of text.

Executing script commands conditionally

For the next part of the script, you have to provide the information—you can't get it from the Finder. You need to write the commands that will move the file to the folder you want, based on the file type of the file (stored in the variable fileType).

To accomplish this task, you write a series of conditional statements, or *conditionals* for short. A conditional is a command or set of commands that AppleScript runs only when a certain condition is met. AppleScript evaluates the condition you set forth, and if the condition is true, AppleScript runs the specified commands.

The condition you will set up for each conditional is whether the information in the variable fileType is equal to a four-letter string that you will provide. You attach to the conditional a command that moves the file to a designated folder. In other words, if the information in the variable fileType is equal to a particular four-letter string, AppleScript moves the file to a certain folder. In AppleScript, the conditional looks like this:

```
if fileType is "sfil" then move file filePath to folder
"Sounds" of startup disk
```

In this example, the condition is whether the information in fileType is "sfil," which is the four-letter type of sound files. If it is, AppleScript moves the file specified by the variable filePath to the folder named Sounds on the hard drive named Mac OS HD.

Include as many of these conditionals as you want. In each conditional, use a different four-character file type for the type of file you want to move, and specify the path of the folder to which you want AppleScript to move files of that type. A quick way to enter several conditionals is to select one conditional, copy it, paste it into the script, and change the relevant pieces of information. You can repeat this for each conditional you want to include.

When you type a long command, notice that the Script Editor never breaks it automatically (as a word processor would). You can break a long line manually by pressing Option-Return. (Do not break a line in the middle of a quoted text string, however.) AppleScript displays a special symbol (¬) to indicate a manual line break. Here's an example:

```
if fileType is "sfil" then move file filePath ¬
to folder "Sounds" of startup disk
```

Figure 23-6 shows an example of a script with three conditional statements that move a selected file depending on its file type.

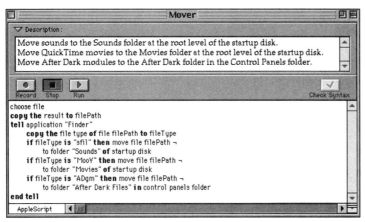

Figure 23-6: A sample script with conditional statements.

Trying out your script

After creating a new script, you must run it and test it thoroughly. To test the script that moves files according to their type, run the script. When the dialog box appears, select a file that is of a type your script should recognize but that is not in the destination folder, and click the Open button. Switch to the Finder, and make sure that the file you selected moved from the source folder to the destination folder. Then repeat the test, selecting a different file type that your script should recognize.

Quick Tips

Finding a Folder Path

If you don't know the full path of a folder, you can use a script to get this information. Open a new window in Script Editor and type the following script in the script editing area:

```
choose folder
```

Run the script and select a folder. The result is a file spec for the folder you selected. You can copy only the text and paste it in any script.

Finding a File's Type

You may not know the file type of the files that you want to move. For example, you may know that you want to put After Dark modules in the After Dark Files folder, but you may not know that the four-letter file type of After Dark modules is "ADgm." To make a script that reports the file type, copy the following five-line script into a new Script Editor window:

```
choose file
copy the result to filePath
tell application "Finder"
copy the file type of file filePath to fileType
end tell
```

Run this five-line script, and select a file whose four-character file type you need to learn. If the result window is not visible, choose Show Result from the Controls menu. The result of the script is the file type of the file you selected. You can copy and paste the result from the result window into a conditional statement in any script window.

It's even easier to determine a file's type using the Find File section of the Sherlock program in Mac OS 8.5 or the Find File program in Mac OS 7.6–8.1. In Sherlock or Find File, choose File Type from the left-most pop-up menu and Is from the adjacent pop-up menu. Now drag any file from the Finder to the middle of the Sherlock or Find File window, and you will see the file's type displayed there.

Creating a drag-and-drop script application

Although the sample script you created is useful, it would be more useful as an icon on your desktop to which you could drag files and have them move to their appropriate spots, just as you can with the System Folder. You wouldn't have to run Script Editor every time you want to move files, and you could move more than one file at a time. AppleScript gives you this capability.

You already know that AppleScript can make standalone applications from your scripts. With a little extra work, you can make an application with drag-and-drop capability so that you can simply drag files to it.

Remember that when you drag and drop a set of icons into an application on the desktop, the Finder sends that application an Open Documents message that includes a list of the files you dragged to the icon. This message is sent to all applications, even to ones that you make with AppleScript.

You need to tell your script to intercept that Apple event and run the appropriate commands. Place the following line at the beginning of your script:

```
on open (itemList)
```

Now enter the following line at the end of your script:

```
end open
```

The first line tells the script to intercept the Open Documents message and to put the list of files in a variable named itemList. The End Open command helps AppleScript know which commands to run when the open message is received. Any lines between the first and second lines are run when the script receives an Apple-event Open Documents.

Save this script by choosing the Save As command from the File menu. From the pop-up menu in the Save As dialog box, choose the Application option. If you switch to the Finder and look at the icon of the application you just created, you'll notice that the icon contains an arrow that indicates that this application is a drag-and-drop application. Script Editor knows how to use this kind of icon because it sees that the application's script intercepts the Apple-event Open Documents. (You can give the application a custom icon, as described in Chapter 8.)

The script won't be fully operational until you make a few more changes. As the script stands, it places the list of files in a variable, but it doesn't do anything with that information. If you dragged several files to the application now, the script would merely bring up a dialog box asking you to pick a file and then quit, having accomplished nothing.

First, delete what now are the second and third lines of the script (the ones beginning with the words "choose" and "copy"), and replace them with the following:

```
repeat with x from 1 to the number of items in itemList
copy item x of itemList to filePath
```

Between the End Tell and End Open commands, enter the following:

```
end repeat
```

Figure 23-7 shows the complete sample script modified for drag-and-drop operation.

In the modified script, AppleScript repeatedly executes the commands between the Repeat and End Repeat commands for the number of times specified in the Repeat command. This arrangement is called a *repeat loop*. The first time AppleScript executes the Repeat command, it sets variable x to 1, as specified by "from 1." When AppleScript encounters the End Repeat command, it loops back to the Repeat command, increments the variable x by 1, and compares the new value of x with the number of items that were dragged to the icon ("the number of items in itemList"). If the two values are not equal, AppleScript sequentially executes the command following the Repeat command. If the two values are equal, AppleScript goes to the command immediately following End Repeat. The End Open command ends the script.

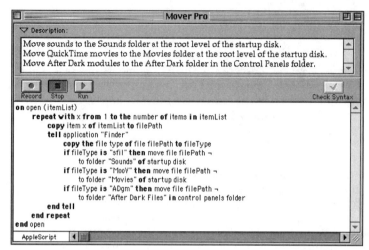

Figure 23-7: A sample script ready to be saved as a drag-and-drop script application.

The first command in the repeat loop that you just created takes item x of the variable itemList (where, once again, x is a number ranging from 1 to the number of items in itemList) and then copies that information to the filePath variable.

Save the script, and switch back to the Finder. You now have a drag-and-drop application that you can use to move certain types of files to specific folders. Anytime you want to add a file type, use Script Editor to open the script, add a conditional that covers that file type, and save the script. You can have the script move several different types of files into a single folder, if you want, but you can't have the script move different files of the same type in different folders.

If you want to edit a script application, you can drag its icon to the Script Editor icon, and Script Editor will open the script for you. (Remember that double-clicking a script application runs it.)

Creating a folder action script

Mac OS 8.5 introduces another use for AppleScript in the Finder: *folder-action scripts*. You attach folder-action scripts to folders and the Finder runs the scripts automatically under certain circumstances. The Finder will run folder-action scripts that are attached to a folder when you open the folder or close its window, add or remove items in the folder, or change the folder window's size or position. These scripts run only if the folder is open (its window is displayed) or the folder is expanded in the list view of a folder that encloses it. (For more information about folder actions, see "Working with Folder Actions" in Chapter 6.)

You can easily modify the drag-and-drop script application you just created so that it becomes a folder-action script. Once you attach the script to a specific folder, you can simply drag items to the open folder, and the items will be routed automatically to the appropriate locations.

Instead of beginning the script with an On Open command, use an On Adding Folder Items To command, as follows:

```
on adding folder items to this_folder after receiving added_items
```

In this line, the variable this_folder will contain the path of the folder that is associated with the script. The variable added_items serves the same function as itemList in the drag-and-drop application script — it will contain the list of items that were dragged to the folder.

You need to balance the new first line of the script by replacing the End Open command at the end of the script with this line:

```
end adding folder items to
```

After the On Adding Folder Items To command, the script needs to tell the Finder to determine how many items were dragged to the folder. The script must activate the Finder to get this information from it. Place these two lines after the On Adding Folder Items To command:

```
tell application "Finder"
activate
```

Next add the following line, which saves the number of items that were dragged to the folder in the variable item_count:

```
set the item_count to the number of items in the added_items
```

You can now start a repeat loop as before, but you must modify it to read as follows:

```
repeat with x from 1 to item_count
copy item x of added_items to filePath
```

Now delete the Tell Application "Finder" command that follows the Repeat command and move the End Tell command after the End Repeat command. The final script is shown in Figure 23-8.

Save the script as a compiled script (not as a script application). To attach your script to a specific folder, simply Control-click the folder to display its contextual menu, and choose Attach a Folder Action from it. In the standard Open dialog box that appears, select the script you saved. Once you have attached the folder action script to a folder, a distinctive badge appears on the folder's icon. Remember, the folder must be open (or expanded in a list view of an enclosing folder) for the attached folder action script to run.

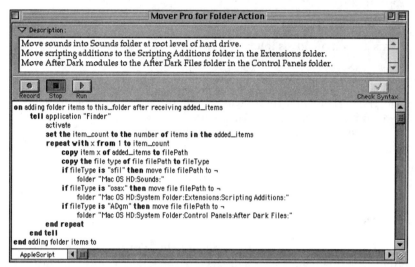

Figure 23-8: A folder-action script to route files of particular types to specific folders.

To learn more about creating folder action scripts, study the sample folder-action scripts supplied with Mac OS 8.5. They are located in the Folder Action Scripts folder within the Scripts folder in the System Folder. You may also want to check out the AppleScript Help that comes with Mac OS 8.5. To see it, choose Help Center from the Help menu and then click AppleScript Help in the Help Center window.

Caution

Changes to Scripting in Mac OS 8.5

Mac OS 8.5 brings many improvements and changes to the AppleScript commands for the Finder and the standard scripting additions files. In addition, many more control panels, extensions, and applications are scriptable. The following are scriptable in Mac OS 8.5: Appearance, Apple Help Viewer, Apple Menu Options, Apple System Profiler, Application Switcher, ColorSync Extension, Desktop Printer Manager, File Exchange, Location Manager, Network Setup Scripting, and Sherlock.

The changes to the Finder are not supposed to affect the operation of existing scripts. Nevertheless, you should carefully test any existing scripts that contain Finder-related commands. If you open existing scripts in the Script Editor or another script-editing program, you may see some changes in wording. Some terms may have the word "deprecated" or the word "obsolete" added. For example, the term "file type" may be changed to "file type obsolete." You can usually update obsolete and deprecated terms by deleting the words "obsolete" and "deprecated," and then compiling the script again. If this method isn't successful, check the Finder's dictionary to see if the spelling of the term has changed slightly. For example, the "show kind" property of container windows has changed to "shows kind" in Mac OS 8.5. There are also many more ways to control the Finder in Mac OS 8.5 than in previous Mac OS versions. Investigate them in the Finder's AppleScript dictionary.

Mac OS 8.5 consolidates a plethora of scripting additions into one file, improves some of them, and adds to them. The Standard Additions file contains these formerly separate additions: Beep, Choose, Application, Choose File, Current Date, Display Dialog, File Commands, Load Script, Numerics, String Commands, Read/Write Commands, Run Script, Store Script, and Time To GMT. The Standard Additions file also contains new scripting additions that delay for a fixed amount of time, speak text, summarize text, and more. For details, check the AppleScript dictionary for the Standard Additions file.

For more information on these and other AppleScript changes in Mac OS 8.5, check the AppleScript Web site (http://applescript.apple.com).

Using AppleScript with Applications

The Finder is only one application that you can use with AppleScript; more and more vendors are including AppleScript capability in their applications. This section provides a few examples of scripts that use some popular scriptable programs. These scripts are reasonably small, so you can type them quickly. The scripts also give you an idea of other things that AppleScript can do.

ShrinkWrap and a Web browser

Many people find that a Web browser performs better if its cache is on a RAM disk. But if you use the Memory control panel to create the RAM disk, it's always there using up memory even if you're not browsing the Web. One solution is to use the ShrinkWrap utility from Aladdin Systems (http://www.aladdinsys.com) to create a RAM disk.

ShrinkWrap can create a file that contains an image of the browser's cache disk. You can mount the disk image file as a RAM disk on demand, and you can put away the RAM disk whenever you want, freeing the memory it used. To use the RAM disk, you can double-click the disk image file to mount the RAM disk just before you open the browser. Alternatively, you can put an alias of the disk image file into the Startup Items folder so that ShrinkWrap will mount the disk image as a RAM disk at startup.

A more elegant solution is to create a small script application that mounts the RAM disk and then opens the browser. You would open this script application in lieu of opening the browser directly. For quick access to this script application, you could name it "Browse the Internet RDC" (where *RDC* stands for "RAM disk cache") and put it or an alias of it on the desktop. The script requires ShrinkWrap 2.0 or later, because earlier versions do not allow setting ShrinkWrap preferences with

AppleScript commands. To avoid compatibility problems, you should use ShrinkWrap 3.0 or later with Mac OS 8–8.5. Figure 23-9 shows the script.

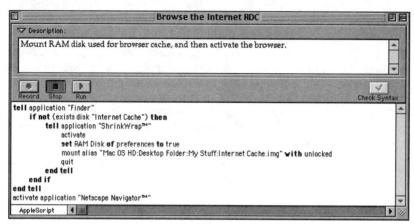

Figure 23-9: A script application that mounts a RAM disk that is used for a browser cache and then activates the browser.

Before creating the script application, you must open ShrinkWrap and create the Internet Cache disk image file, or you won't be able to save the script application successfully. Before running the script application for the first time, you must mount the disk image, open your Web browser, and change the location of its cache to the mounted disk image. If you open the Web browser directly without first mounting the disk image, the browser resets the cache to its default location, and you have to set it back to the mounted disk image again.

When you type the script from Figure 23-9 into a Script Editor window, be sure you replace "Internet Cache" with the actual name of your RAM disk, and replace "Mac OS HD:Internet Cache" with the path to your ShrinkWrap disk image file. Also, put the exact name of your browser in the last statement of the script.

Another short script application can automate the process of quitting the Web browser and putting away the RAM disk. The same script can also disconnect a dial-up Internet connection. For easy access to this script application, you could name it "Quit Browsing the Internet RDC" and put it or an alias of it in the Apple menu. Figure 23-10 shows this script.

When you type the script from Figure 23-10 into a Script Editor window, be sure you replace "Internet Cache" with the actual name of your RAM disk. Also, put the exact name of your browser in the first line of the script.

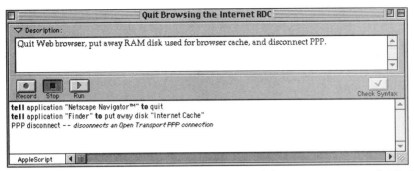

Figure 23-10: A script application that quits a Web browser, puts away the RAM disk that is used for its cache, and disconnects the dial-up Internet connection.

The last line of the script disconnects a dial-up Internet connection made with Open Transport PPP, which is a standard part of Mac OS 8–8.5. If you use MacPPP or FreePPP for dial-up Internet connections, replace the last line with "closePPP." To control MacPPP or FreePPP with AppleScript, you must put the MacPPP Control scripting addition file in your Scripting Additions folder. MacPPP Control is available from sources of freeware and shareware (see "Where to Get Utility Software" in Chapter 26). If you use MacPPP or FreePPP version 2.5 or later, you must also use MacPPP Control version 1.5 or later.

Notice that the script in Figure 23-10 does not modify the browser's Quit command so that it also removes the RAM disk. Unfortunately, few applications allow attaching an AppleScript script to their menu commands. There is a way to seamlessly integrate an AppleScript script that automatically puts away the RAM disk when you quit the browser. You can do this by modifying the AppleScript application that mounts the RAM disk and launches the browser in the first place. You add some script commands that periodically check to see if the browser is still open and put away the RAM disk if it's not. To make the AppleScript application stay open in the background so it can monitor the browser's status, you must turn on the Stay Open option when you save it. Figure 23-11 shows an example of this script with Netscape Navigator as the browser.

This script could also include a command that disconnects your PPP connection after you quit the browser. For example, inserting the PPP Disconnect command before the Put Away command would disconnect an Open Transport PPP connection before putting away the RAM disk. If you use the Control PPP for AppleScript control of FreePPP or MacPPP, the disconnect command is ClosePPP.

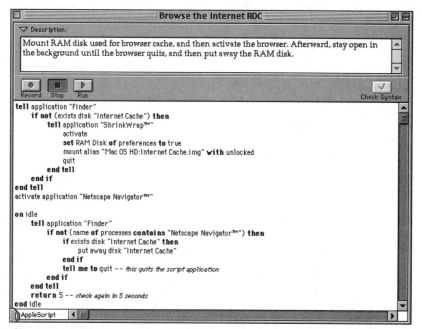

Figure 23-11: The last 11 lines of this stay-open script application put away the RAM disk that is used for a Web browser's cache after you quit the browser.

Outlook Express and Claris Emailer

Microsoft Outlook Express and Claris Emailer Lite are powerful programs in themselves, but thanks to AppleScript, you can make them even more powerful. Outlook Express is part of a standard installation of Mac OS 8.5, and is also available free from Microsoft's Web site (http://www.microsoft.com/ie/mac/oe) for installation with other Mac OS versions. Emailer Lite is part of a standard installation of Mac OS 8–8.1.

Both Outlook Express and Emailer Lite send and receive e-mail, but like many Internet applications, they rely on other software such as Open Transport PPP (via the PPP or Remote Access control panels), MacPPP, or FreePPP to open and close dial-up Internet connections. You can automate your Internet e-mail with a script. First the script dials through Open Transport PPP or through MacPPP/FreePPP. Then the script accesses your mail through Outlook Express or Emailer. Finally, the script hangs up through Open Transport PPP or through MacPPP/FreePPP. Here are some of the options available:

✦ **Outlook Express** does not come with a script for establishing and disconnecting from dial-up connections, but you can get one from the "Unofficial" Microsoft Outlook Express Web site (http://www.macemail.com/oe/pages/applescript.shtml). In particular, try the item "OT/PPP scripts" by Omar Shahine.

✦ **Emailer 1.0v2–2.0v3** come with an AppleScript script and instructions for using it, but Emailer Lite does not. (Emailer is the commercial version of the product that has more features than the free Lite version.) Moreover, the included script does not work reliably unless you bring Emailer or the AppleScript script to the front while PPP is making a connection. You can get improved AppleScript scripts from the Fog City Web site (http://www.fogcity. com). In particular, check the Emailer Utilities page on this Web site for the item "Internet and Email Scripts" by W. John Carlsen. Both Emailer and Emailer Lite allow you to use scripts with their automatic scheduling features.

Outlook Express 4.01 and Emailer 2.0 are not only scriptable but also attachable. This means that you can execute AppleScript scripts directly from the application itself — you don't have to switch to Script Editor or choose script applications from your Apple menu. Outlook Express and Emailer 2.0 have an AppleScript menu that lists compiled scripts (not script applications) that you have added to a special folder. In Outlook Express, you add scripts to the Script Menu Items folder in the Outlook Express folder. In Emailer 2.0, you add scripts to the AppleScripts folder in the Claris Emailer Files folder within the Claris Emailer folder. The AppleScript menu in Outlook Express or Emailer 2.0 is very handy for small utility scripts that augment the e-mail application's capabilities.

Although Outlook Express comes with scripts for tasks such as changing the color of message headings in mailboxes, inserting text files into messages, and saving selected text of a message, there are also many other freely available scripts that you can get from the Internet. For example, there are scripts to have Outlook Express read your e-mail messages aloud to you using the Mac OS text-to-speech software (see Chapter 22), forward messages as attachments, count words in messages, and delete old sent messages. The AppleScript Archive on the "Unofficial" Microsoft Outlook Express Web site, mentioned previously, is an excellent source for scripts for Outlook Express.

Likewise, numerous scripts are freely available for Emailer users. For example, you can get scripts that change the status of currently selected incoming or outgoing messages, forward all selected messages to a single address, save the currently selected messages in a text file, permanently delete the selected messages and move their enclosures to the Trash, and so on. Check for scripts on the Emailer Utilities page and the Emailer 2.0 Utilities page of the previously mentioned Fog City Web site.

QuarkXPress

QuarkXPress guides are great, but that doesn't mean you want them around forever. You could delete the guides manually, page by page, but it's easier to run the script shown in Figure 23-12.

When you run this script, you will be asked to locate your copy of QuarkXPress if its name does not exactly match the name in quotes in the first line of the script.

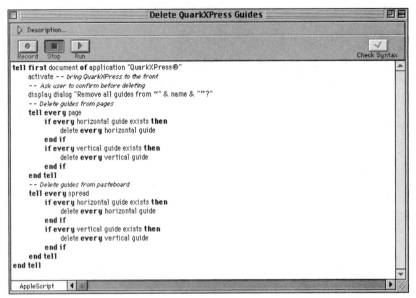

Figure 23-12: This script deletes all guides in the front-most QuarkXPress document.

Linking Programs

You have seen how AppleScript can automate tasks on your own machine. You can also send Apple events to open applications on other machines in a network. As a result, you can use AppleScript to control applications on other people's machines. Sharing programs by sending and receiving Apple events across a network is called *program linking*.

Program linking adds tremendous potential to AppleScript. If you are in charge of a network, you can use AppleScript to perform network installations or backups. If you have a script that uses many applications, you can speed up the script by sending a command to a remote application and retrieving the data later. You send only a blip across the network; the remote application does the work while other parts of your script are running, and you get the results later. In addition, this capability can help you get around memory problems that might arise from opening several applications from a script.

Setting up program linking

Program linking can be controlled much like file sharing. You can turn program linking on and off, can control who on the network is allowed access to your programs, and can deny access to specific programs.

Starting and stopping program linking

If you want to allow other network users to link to programs on your computer, you must activate program linking. To do this, click the Start button in the Program Linking section of the File Sharing control panel (Mac OS 8–8.5) or the Sharing Setup control panel (Mac OS 7.6–7.6.1). Your computer is ready for program linking when the button's label changes to Stop and the File Sharing control panel reports "Program Linking on," or the Sharing Setup control panel's status message reads "Program linking is on." Figure 23-13 shows how the File Sharing control panel and the Sharing Setup control look when program linking is turned on.

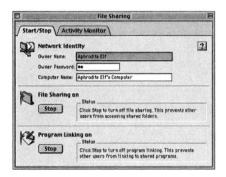

Figure 23-13: Program linking is turned on in Mac OS 8–8.5 (top) and Mac OS 7.6–7.6.1 (bottom).

To turn off program linking, click the Stop button in the Program Linking section of the File Sharing control panel or the Sharing Setup control panel, whichever the computer has. Clicking the Stop button prevents all programs on the computer from receiving Apple events from any other computer on the network.

Authorizing access to shared programs

You control which network users can link to programs on your computer with the Users & Groups control panel. To allow everyone on the network to link to your programs, open the Guest icon in the Users & Groups control panel, and turn on the "Allow guests to link to programs on this computer" option. (This option is called "Allow guests to link to programs on this Macintosh" in Mac OS 7.6–7.6.1.)

To prevent unidentified network users from linking to your programs, turn off this option. Figure 23-14 shows the guest window.

If you don't give guests program-linking privileges, you need to designate which registered users in your Users & Groups control panel can link to your programs. To allow a registered user to link to your programs, open that user's icon in your Users & Groups control panel. In the user's window, turn on the "Allow user to link to programs on this computer" option ("Allow guests to link to programs on this Macintosh" in Mac OS 7.6–7.6.1). (For information on registering users, see "Identifying Who Can Access Your Shared Items" in Chapter 21.) Figure 23-15 shows a user window.

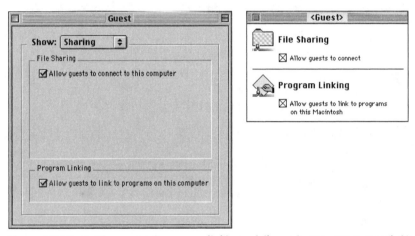

Figure 23-14: Setting guests' program-linking privileges in Mac OS 8–8.5 (left) and Mac OS 7.6–7.6.1 (right).

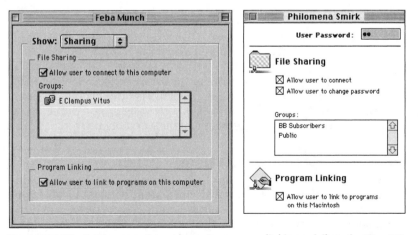

Figure 23-15: Setting a registered user's program linking privilege in Mac OS 8–8.5 (left) and Mac OS 7.6–7.6.1 (right).

You can block any registered user from linking to your programs by turning off that user's "Allow user to link to programs on this computer" option ("Allow guests to link to programs on this Macintosh" in Mac OS 7.6–7.6.1).

Denying access to specific programs

Even though you may allow certain network users to link to your programs, you may want to specifically deny access to a particular application, just as you may want to prevent someone from seeing a particular folder inside a shared folder. You control program linking for each application in its sharing window, which appears when you select the program in Finder and choose Sharing from the Get Info submenu of the File menu in Mac OS 8.5 or choose Sharing from the File menu in Mac OS 7.6–8.1. Figure 23-16 is an example of a program's sharing window.

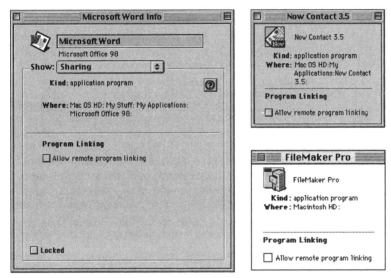

Figure 23-16: Preventing other users from sharing a specific program in Mac OS 8.5 (left), Mac OS 8–8.1 (top right), and Mac OS 7.6–7.6.1 (bottom right).

To prevent an application from receiving Apple events sent by another computer, turn off the "Allow remote program linking" option in its sharing window and then close the window. If the option is dimmed, the program is open; you must quit a program before changing its program-linking option.

Scripting across a network

Using AppleScript to run a program across the network doesn't take much more work than writing a script to use a program on the same computer. Start program linking on a networked computer. Now go to another computer on the network. Open the Script Editor and type this command:

```
choose application
```

This command brings up a dialog box in which you select an application on your computer or on the network. On the left side of this dialog box, select the computer you set up (you may need to select a zone if your network has zones and the computer is in a different zone). The applications that are running on the selected computer are displayed on the right side of the dialog box. One application is the Finder. Select it and click OK. Figure 23-17 shows the dialog box with a computer and its Finder application selected.

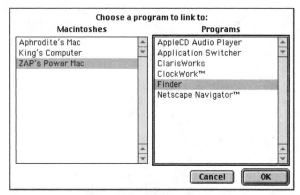

Figure 23-17: Choosing a program to link to.

Open the result window in Script Editor, if it's not open already. You see that the result of this short script is the network path of the application you selected: the name of the application, the name of the computer, and the name of the zone (if your network has more than one zone).

Enter the following line below the first one and then run the script, selecting the same application on the same computer:

```
copy the result to netpath
```

This script places the path to the application in a variable named netpath. To send Apple events to this application, enter the next two lines in the script:

```
tell netpath
end tell
```

This Tell command specifies the name of the application with the netpath variable instead of with the word "application" and the literal name of the application. The effect is the same: AppleScript starts sending Apple events to the application, which in this case happens to be on a different computer.

Enter these command lines between the Tell and the End Tell command lines:

```
activate
beep
say "Your computer is under my control. Resistance is futile."
```

```
set windowList to windows whose closeable is true
set nbrWindows to count of windowList
if nbrWindows > 0 then
   set openItemsList to item of every window whose closeable is
true
   say "I will now close all your windows."
   repeat with aWindow in windowList
        close aWindow
   end repeat
   say "I will now open them again."
   if nbrWindows > 1 then open reverse of openItemsList
   if nbrWindows = 1 then open openItemsList
end if
get count of every item of font
set fontCount to count of items in font
set half to round (fontCount / 2)
open font
say "You have " & fontCount & ¬
   " fonts. That is too many. Get rid of " & half & ¬
        ", or I will call the font [[emph -]] police."
say "I now return control to [[emph +]] you. Have a nice day!"
```

The Say command causes an error if the target computer does not have a scripting addition to handle it. If the target computer has Mac OS 8.5, the Standard Additions file handles the Say command. If the target computer has Mac OS 7.6–8.1, it must have the Say scripting additions file in its Scripting Additions folder (either the one in the System Folder or the one in the Extensions folder). The Say scripting addition is available free from Apple's Speech Technology site on the Web at http://speech. apple.com/dev/ssscript.hqx.

To make matters worse, the scripting addition for the Say command that comes with Mac OS 8.5 is not compatible with the Say scripting addition that you get separately for Mac OS 7.6–8.1. If the target computer does not have the same scripting addition for the Say command as your computer — because your computer has Mac OS 8.5 and the other computer has an earlier Mac OS version, or vice versa — then the Say command will not work. If the Say command does not work for any reason, the script abruptly stops working with an error alert on your computer.

There is a way to work around the incompatibility between the two versions of the scripting addition for the Say command. If you know the target computer has Mac OS 8.5 and your computer has Mac OS 7.6–8.1, replace the Say commands in the foregoing script with «event sysottos» (you type the symbols surrounding this text by pressing Option-\ and Option-Shift-\). This hieroglyphic replacement text is the Apple-event code that underlies the Say command in Mac OS 8.5. Conversely, if you know the target computer has Mac OS 7.6–8.1 and your computer has Mac OS 8.5, you can replace the Say command with «event aevtSAY». This is the Apple-event code for the Say command as implemented by the Say scripting addition. These shenanigans with the Say command illustrate how knotty AppleScript problems can get. As your scripts get more complex, you can expect to spend more time carefully testing them and fixing bugs. Scripts take time to develop, but if you use them frequently, the effort pays off.

If you can't install the Say scripting additions file or Mac OS 8.5 on the target computer, you can make the foregoing script work by removing the Say commands from it. Note that you cannot replace the Say commands with Display Dialog commands, because AppleScript does not allow Display Dialog commands to be sent to a linked computer.

When you run the script, it displays a dialog box in which you select the Finder that is running on another computer. Before the script can send Apple events to that Finder, however, the script must connect your computer to the other computer. To do this, the script displays a connection dialog box like the ones you use to connect to other computers for file sharing, as shown in Figure 23-18.

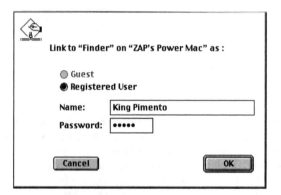

Figure 23-18: Linking to another machine as a registered user.

In the connection dialog box, you specify whether you want to connect as a guest (if the other computer allows guests) or as a registered user. To connect as a registered user, enter your name and password as they were set up in the other computer's Users & Groups control panel. If you connect successfully, the script runs.

Before going over to the other computer to check the results, try running the script again. This time, you don't have to go through the logon process. Once you connect to another application, you don't have to go through the connection dialog every time you want to send an Apple event. You have to reenter your password if someone quits the application you're linked to or turns off program linking on the target computer.

Now go to the other computer and look at the Finder. You should see the Fonts folder opened, as your script directed.

That's all the work you have to do if you want to script a remote application. You don't have to use the Choose Application command, either. You can simply write the network path of the application, as in this example:

```
tell application "Finder" of machine "Fang's 8600"
...
end tell
```

Program linking offers many possibilities for scripters. For example, you could use a script to create a large catalog by farming out different sections of that catalog to several networked computers. Each machine could work on its section and the script could pick up the resulting file via file sharing from the computers as they finish their individual sections. As another example, a network administrator could backup crucial documents from computers across the network onto a central tape drive and then shutdown the individual computers.

Quick Tips

Working Around Program-Linking Barriers

One of the biggest problems with using Apple events over a network is that some applications do not accept Apple events that come from a remote computer. There is a way around this problem, however. Script applications — that is, scripts you save as applications from the Script Editor — accept Apple events from across a network. When a script application runs a script, the application acts as though the script is on the local computer. If you're trying to control a remote application that does not allow networked Apple events, you can send a message to a script application on the remote computer. The script application in turn executes a script to control other applications on the same computer.

To see how this process works, create this simple script application on a networked computer:

```
on netMessage()
tell application "Finder"
    open about this computer
end tell
end netMessage
```

This script has a handler for netMessage, just as the earlier drag-and-drop script had a handler for open. This netMessage handler tells the Finder to display the About this Computer window. (If you create this script on a computer with System 7.5.5 or earlier, replace the second line with "open about this Macintosh.") This script has no problem sending Apple events to the Finder on the same computer because no network is involved.

When you save this script as a script application, be sure to turn on the Stay Open option in the Save dialog box. With this option checked, the script stays open once you open it, rather than quitting after the script runs.

Open the script application and go to another networked computer that has AppleScript installed. On that computer, write this script:

```
choose application
copy the result to netPath
tell netPath to netMessage()
```

Run the script, and use the dialog box to select the name of the script application that you left open on the other computer. The script gets the result and tells the script application to "netMessage." The script application on the other computer receives this message and runs the commands in the netMessage handler, showing the About this Computer window on that computer. (If the other computer has System 7.5.5 or earlier and you modified the script running on it as instructed in the previous paragraph, that computer displays the About This Macintosh window.)

Summary

In this chapter, you learned how applications can communicate by sending each other messages called Apple events. When an application receives an Apple event, it performs a task specified by the event. You can use the Apple-event mechanism to automate tasks involving one or more applications. You do this with AppleScript scripts. AppleScript is a programming language designed with everyday users in mind, but with enough power for advanced users and programmers.

You learned how to create scripts with the Script Editor application. An easy way to create scripts for some applications is to have AppleScript record your actions as a script. You then save the recorded script and run it again to repeat the same actions.

You also learned that a recorded script has limited value. To take full advantage of AppleScript, use the Script Editor or another script-editing program to create scripts from scratch. You type AppleScript statements into a new Script Editor window, check the syntax for errors, and run the script to test it. Your script might use conditional statements to perform some operations only when the specified conditions are met. You'll probably use repeat loops to execute a group of statements over and over. When you're done, you may save the script as a script application. In Mac OS 8.5, you can attach a script to a folder to define a folder action.

This chapter described several examples of how to use scripts to control applications other than the Finder. A script can mount a RAM disk and then the Web browser that uses the RAM disk for its cache. Another script can dial-up a PPP connection to the Internet and then send and receive e-mail with Outlook Express or Claris Emailer. Yet another script can remove all guides from a QuarkXPress document automatically, saving the drudgery of doing the job with the mouse.

And finally, this chapter showed how AppleScript can control applications over a network on computers that have program linking set up and turned on. You turn on program linking with a computer's File Sharing or Sharing Setup control panel. You use the Users & Groups to designate which users can link to programs on your computer. And you use Finder's Sharing command to designate which programs other computers can link to. Once your computer is connected to another computer for program linking, you can use AppleScript to control applications on the other computer.

✦   ✦   ✦

Create Compound Documents

In This Chapter

Introducing OpenDoc parts, editors, and stationery

Creating OpenDoc documents from stationery and from existing documents

Creating new OpenDoc stationery based on your own documents

Working with OpenDoc parts

Using publish and subscribe

Don't limit yourself to copy and paste whenever you want to create a compound document containing various types of material or material from several sources. The Mac OS offers two more powerful methods: OpenDoc and publish and subscribe.

OpenDoc makes it possible for you to include any type of material in a document. Unlike copy and paste you're not limited to the types of material allowed by the application you're using. Every OpenDoc document can contain standard text and graphics as well as spreadsheets, graphs, database records, QuickTime media, sounds, styled text, live Web pages, and so forth. It may sound like OpenDoc is a superintegrated, does-it-all behemoth, but it's not. OpenDoc by itself can't work with any kind of material. Instead it provides an endless number of software sockets for a kind of general purpose plug-in software, and each plug-in software part gives you the capability to work with a particular type of material.

Publish and subscribe is like copy and paste, but where copy and paste is static, publish and subscribe is dynamic. Copied material that you paste into a document doesn't change unless you replace it by pasting a newer copy. Compare that to publish and subscribe, which places a dynamically linked copy of material from one document into another document, so that if the material changes in the source document, the linked copy changes automatically.

This chapter describes OpenDoc and publish and subscribe in more detail. You'll learn how to create and work with OpenDoc documents and how to create publishers, subscribe to editions, set publisher and subscriber options, update editions, and more.

OpenDoc Compound Documents

OpenDoc lets you create documents in an old-fashioned way. Rather than emphasizing applications, as personal computers have always done, OpenDoc puts the focus where it was before personal computers came along—on documents. With OpenDoc you don't have to switch applications to work on a different kind of content. You just select the content you want to work on and the appropriate menus appear automatically in the menu bar, and you use the menu commands to work with the selected content.

The OpenDoc software is part of a standard installation of Mac OS 7.6–8.1. It's not part of a standard installation of Mac OS 8.5, but you can install OpenDoc separately from the CD Extras folder on the Mac OS CD. You can also get the OpenDoc software from Apple's OpenDoc site on the Web (http://opendoc.apple.com).

Although OpenDoc is an interesting technology with a lot of promise, Apple has decided not to develop it any further. You should not expect to see any OpenDoc improvements in the Mac OS after Mac OS 8.1.

Introducing OpenDoc parts

An OpenDoc document can include any kind of content for which an appropriate OpenDoc plug-in software component, called a *part,* is installed on your computer. In general, each OpenDoc part lets you work on one type of document content— text, graphics, spreadsheets, charts, database information, sound, movies, Web pages, e-mail, and so on. You can drag any combination of OpenDoc parts into an OpenDoc document. Mix and match OpenDoc parts to create any document you can think of. If you want to use a new kind of content, you simply plug in an OpenDoc part that can handle it. Figure 24-1 shows an OpenDoc document with several parts.

Parts can't function independently like applications and desk accessories can. Parts rely on an infrastructure that OpenDoc provides. Installing OpenDoc software provides the infrastructure. To do anything with the OpenDoc infrastructure, however, you have to install parts. OpenDoc is like the electrical outlets in a house: They make it possible to have light, music, TV shows, hot and cold food, and so forth, but the appliances you plug in actually provide those things.

When you give your OpenDoc documents to other people, they need OpenDoc parts that handle the kinds of content found in your document. That doesn't mean another person's OpenDoc parts have to be exactly the same as yours. For example, you might use the Brand X graphics part while someone else uses the Brand Y graphics part. As long as recipients of your documents have OpenDoc graphics parts with the same basic capabilities as yours, they will be able to view graphics in OpenDoc documents you send them. If you don't have the necessary OpenDoc part for a kind of content in an OpenDoc document you receive, OpenDoc displays a gray box in place of the content and tells you the name of the missing part.

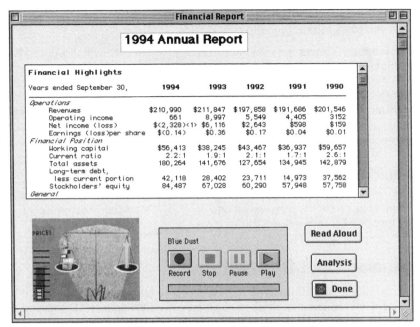

Figure 24-1: OpenDoc documents can include all kinds of content.

Cyberdog

One source of OpenDoc parts is the Mac OS installation software. Mac OS 7.6–8 include Cyberdog, which is a collection of OpenDoc parts, for optional installation. In addition to parts for accessing Internet services such as the Web and e-mail, Cyberdog has parts for basic text editing, and for viewing graphics and QuickTime movies. (For specific information on using Cyberdog to access the Internet, see "Sending and Receiving E-mail" and "Browsing the World Wide Web" in Chapter 17.) You can also get Cyberdog from Apple's Cyberdog Web site (http://cyberdog. apple.com).

OpenDoc Essentials Kit

In addition to Cyberdog, Apple distributes a collection of basic OpenDoc parts known as the OpenDoc Essentials Kit, which contains:

✦ **Apple Draw** for creating and editing basic graphics

✦ **Apple 3DMF Viewer** for viewing and manipulating 3D shapes created with QuickDraw 3D (does not work with QuickDraw 3D version 1.5 or later)

✦ **Apple Audio** for recording and playing back sound or playing a sound file saved in a variety of formats

✦ **Apple Button** for adding buttons that can play sounds, start AppleScripts, or take you to an Internet location

✦ **Apple Image Viewer** for viewing pictures saved in GIF, TIFF, JPEG, or PICT format

The OpenDoc Essentials Kit comes with Mac OS 7.6–7.6.1 for optional installation. The OpenDoc Essentials Kit is not included with Mac OS 8–8.5, but you can get it from Apple's OpenDoc DR Live site on the Web (http://www.opendoc.apple.com/dr-live/OpenDocParts/byName.html).

Apple QuickTime Viewer

Another OpenDoc part from Apple, the Apple QuickTime Viewer, plays QuickTime movies and QuickTime VR panoramas and objects. It's available separately from Apple's OpenDoc DR Live site on the Web.

Introducing OpenDoc editors

Installing OpenDoc parts puts items called *editors* in an Editors folder, which is in the System Folder. You can think of an OpenDoc editor as a small, focused application that specializes in a particular kind of data. Editors are like the items in the Extensions folder in that you don't open or use an editor directly. You can get access to a part editor's functionality through the corresponding stationery files (described later).

Some editors, called viewers, allow you to see, hear, or otherwise experience a type of content, but do not allow you to change the content. For example, the Apple QuickTime Viewer lets you watch QuickTime movies and manipulate QuickTime VR panoramas and objects, but the viewer does not let you change the movies, panoramas, or objects. Figure 24-2 shows the contents of the Editors folder after installing Mac OS 8, Cyberdog, the OpenDoc Essentials Kit, and the Apple QuickTime Viewer.

Some editors exist as separate files, and other editors exist together in a conjoint file. The Editors folder contains items that OpenDoc uses besides editors.

You should leave all OpenDoc editors, including viewers, in the Editors folder, and leave the Editors folder in the System Folder, so that OpenDoc can find the editors. Editor files do not have to be directly in the Editors folder — they can be in folders within the Editors folder — but Apple warns that if you move an editor file so that it is no longer in the Editors folder, OpenDoc will not be able to find it.

Introducing OpenDoc stationery

You don't open an OpenDoc editor to create a new document. Instead, you open a stationery document. OpenDoc stationery works much like stationery documents of conventional applications. When you open a stationery document, you get a new document. With OpenDoc, you also get the functionality of an OpenDoc editor. For example, if you open an Apple Draw stationery document, you get a new document and the ability to create and edit basic graphics in it. Besides opening stationery to create a new document, you can drag OpenDoc stationery to an existing OpenDoc document to add a new part to the document.

Editors		
18 items, 265.5 MB available		
Name	**Size**	**Kind**
▽ 🗀 Cyberdog Libraries	–	folder
🗐 Cyberdog Data	33K	library
📄 Cyberdog DocBuilder Editor	462K	library
🐕 Cyberdog Editors	3.8 MB	library
▽ 🗀 OpenDoc	–	folder
▽ 🗀 OpenDoc Shell Plug-Ins	–	folder
❓ AppleGuidePlugIn	83K	library
🗐 About the ShellPlugIns Folder	33K	SimpleText read-only document
🖥 OpenDoc Editor Setup	99K	library
▽ 🗀 OpenDoc™ Essentials Kit	–	folder
🔲 Apple 3DMF Viewer	396K	library
🔊 Apple Audio	413K	library
⬜ Apple Button	413K	library
📐 Apple Draw	693K	library
🖼 Apple Image Viewer	545K	library
📄 Apple QuickTime™ Viewer	611K	library
🗐 ODFLibrary	561K	library
🗐 About the Editors Folder	33K	SimpleText read-only document

Figure 24-2: Some part editors, part viewers, and other OpenDoc items in an Editors folder.

There's a Stationery folder at the root level of the startup disk, where stationery may be installed initially when you install OpenDoc parts. But some part installers don't put stationery in the Stationery folder. For example, Cyberdog puts stationery in a Samples & Tools folder inside the Cyberdog folder. You can move stationery anywhere you like; it doesn't have to remain where you initially find it. In fact, you can create your own OpenDoc stationery (more on that later). Figure 24-3 shows the contents of the Stationery folder after installing the OpenDoc Essentials Kit.

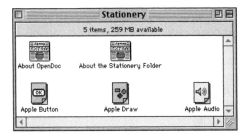

Figure 24-3: OpenDoc part stationery in the Stationery folder.

Creating an OpenDoc document

You can create an OpenDoc document from stationery or from another OpenDoc document. Regardless of the method you use to create an OpenDoc document, OpenDoc opens the new document and immediately saves the document on disk with a temporary name. You can change the name and location when you save the document. In addition, the new document is listed in the Applications menu at the right end of the menu bar.

Creating a document from stationery

To create a document from stationery, find the stationery for the part that you want to use as your document's root part and open the stationery. OpenDoc creates a new copy of the stationery and opens this new copy. OpenDoc gives the new document a temporary name based on the stationery name and initially saves the new document in the same folder as the stationery. The new document may be empty, or it may have some initial content. Figure 24-4 shows a new empty document created from the Apple Draw stationery that's part of the OpenDoc Essentials Kit.

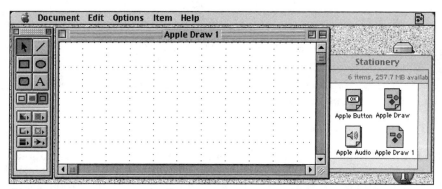

Figure 24-4: A new OpenDoc document has a temporary name and is saved to disk automatically.

Creating a document from another document

There are several ways to create a new document from an existing OpenDoc document. You can create a new document based on parts in the existing document or on the part that contains all the other parts, which is called the *root part*.

To create a new document based on the root part of an existing document, open the document and choose New from the Document menu. OpenDoc gives the new document a temporary name based on the name of the root part and initially saves the new document in the same folder as the existing document.

To create a new document based on a part in an existing document, first select the part and then choose New from the Document menu. You can create a new document by dragging a part from an existing document to the desktop, a folder, or a disk. You can also create a new document by selecting multiple parts, content from a part, or content that includes one or more parts, and then dragging the selection to the desktop, a folder, or a disk.

Note that some OpenDoc documents (notably Cyberdog documents) have a File menu instead of a Document menu. In those documents, the New command is in the File menu.

Saving a document

Anytime after making changes to a new document you can save it. Use the Save command (not Save a Copy) in the Document menu or File menu. The Save command displays a standard Save dialog box in which you can specify a name and location for the document if you don't want to use the ones proposed by OpenDoc.

Creating new OpenDoc stationery

After creating a new document, you can make changes to it, and if you'd like to be able to create more documents like the changed one, you can make your own stationery from the changed document. To make new stationery from an open document, use the Save a Copy menu command to bring up the standard Save dialog. In addition to typing a name and selecting a location for the stationery, select the Stationery option. Figure 24-5 shows the Save a Copy command's dialog box with the Stationery option selected.

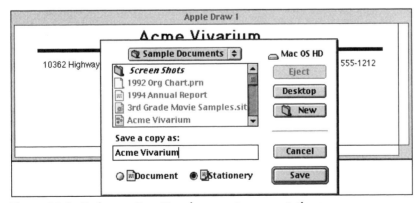

Figure 24-5: Saving an OpenDoc document as new stationery.

Introducing the Document and Edit menus

When working on most OpenDoc documents, you see Document and Edit menus next to the Apple menu instead of the File and Edit menus that you see when working in conventional applications. The Document menu contains commands that affect the whole document. The Edit menu contains commands that you can use to change a document's contents. OpenDoc provides the Document and Edit menus and most of the commands in them. The part editor provides the rest of the menus. Figure 24-6 shows examples of the Document and Edit menus.

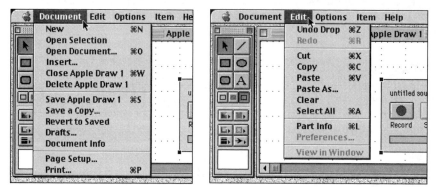

Figure 24-6: Most OpenDoc documents have similar Document and Edit menus.

The Document menu does not have a Quit command. None is needed because OpenDoc automatically quits an editor when you switch to another editor. When you close the last OpenDoc window, OpenDoc itself quits automatically.

The Document menu isn't universal. When working with some OpenDoc documents, notably Cyberdog documents, there is a File menu with a Quit command. Cyberdog has added this command so it looks more like a conventional application.

Adding parts to OpenDoc documents

You can add parts to some OpenDoc documents and to some parts inside OpenDoc documents. To add a part to an OpenDoc document, you can drag the part's stationery icon into the document window, or you can drag a part from one OpenDoc document to another. Either way, a copy of the part you dragged is placed in the destination window. To add a part to another part that's inside an OpenDoc document, drag the part you want to add to the part inside the document window. Figure 24-7 shows part stationery being dragged into an OpenDoc document.

You can also add a part to a document or to a part in a document with the Insert command in the Document menu. First you make the document active (bring its window to the front). If you want to add a part to a part that's already in the document, select the part you want to add to. Then choose Insert from the Document window. In the Open dialog that appears, select the stationery for the part you want to add. For example, to add a drawing part, you could select the Apple Draw stationery.

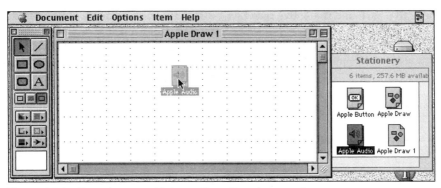

Figure 24-7: Dragging a part into an OpenDoc document.

Instead of adding a part directly, you can add a part indirectly by adding a file whose content the part handles. Either drag the file to the OpenDoc document window, or use the Insert command and select the file. For example, you could add an Apple Audio part to an OpenDoc document by dragging a sound file to the document window or by choosing the Insert command and selecting a sound file.

Not all OpenDoc documents and parts can contain other parts. A part that can contain other parts is called a *container*. An OpenDoc document can contain other parts only if its root part (the part you used to create the document) is a container. You don't do anything to make a part a container. Software engineers determine whether a part is a container when they design it. For example, Apple engineers made the Apple Draw part a container but did not make the Apple Button part a container.

Working with parts

Once a part is in an OpenDoc document, you can edit its content, move it, resize it, copy it, delete it, or get information about it. Before moving, resizing, copying, deleting, or getting information about a part, you must select it.

Adding content

You can add content to a part in an OpenDoc document by dragging a file onto the part. The file must contain something the part can handle. If a file's content is compatible with a part, the part becomes highlighted when you drag the file to the part. Some parts can handle more than one type of content. For example, you can drag a sound file or a QuickTime movie but not a text file to an Apple Audio part because a sound file and a QuickTime movie contain sound but a text file does not. Figure 24-8 shows a sound file being added to an Apple Audio part.

Editing content

If a part has content, you can edit the content by making the part active and making your changes. To make a part active, you click anywhere inside it. There can be only one active part, and the active part has a distinctive border made of two dotted lines. Clicking the background of the document window makes the document's root part active, although no border appears around the root part when it is the active part. Figure 24-9 shows the border around an active part in an Apple Draw container.

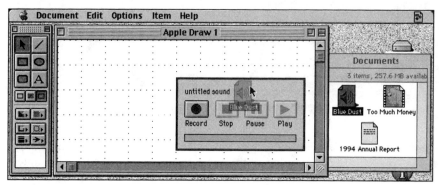

Figure 24-8: Adding content to an OpenDoc part by dragging a compatible file to it.

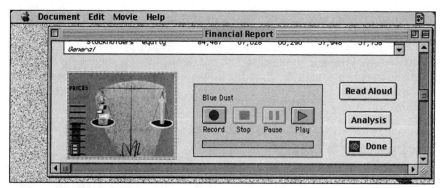

Figure 24-9: A distinctive border made of two dotted lines indicates the active part (here it is the QuickTime movie on the left that is the active part).

When you activate a part, the part editor's menus appear in the menu bar. You can use the menu commands to edit the part.

Selecting a part

Before you can move, resize, copy, delete, or get information about a part, you must select it. Remember that clicking a part makes it active so you can work with the part's content. When you want to work with a whole part and not its content, you must select the part, not activate it. Where the active part has a dotted-line border, a selected part has small, black square handles at its corners. Figure 24-10 shows a selected part in the Apple Draw container.

You can't select a part while another part is active. First, you must click the background of the document window to make the root part active. Then you press the Shift key or the ⌘ key and click the part you want to select. To select more than one part in the same container, click the container's background to make the container active and press the Shift key while you click each part. Some kinds of containers also allow you to select one or more parts by dragging a selection rectangle around the part or parts.

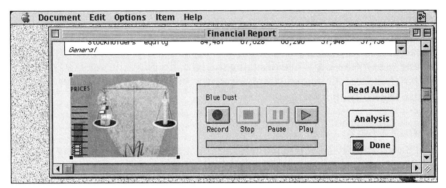

Figure 24-10: Small black handles at the corners of a part indicate it is selected.

If you want to select the active part, you don't have to make it inactive first. You can just click its border. In a container where the active part has a dotted-line border, such as the Apple Draw container, you should be able to tell where to click by watching for the pointer to change to a hand as you place it on the border. However, not all containers change the pointer to a hand when you place it on the border.

When you select a part, the part's container becomes active. You will see the menus change when the container becomes active (unless the selected part and the container are the same kind of part).

You can deselect a selected part by Shift-clicking it. If more than one part is selected in a container, you can deselect them all by clicking the background of the container.

Some parts can only be selected by pressing the Shift key or the ⌘ key and clicking the part while it is inactive. For example, an Apple Button part might play a sound when clicked unless you Shift-click or ⌘-click it to select it for editing.

Moving a part

You can move a part by selecting it and dragging it to a new location in the document. To move the selected part to another OpenDoc document, press the Control key and drag. (If you drag to another document without pressing the Control key, you add a copy of the selected part to the other document.) You can also use the Cut and Paste commands to move the selected part to another document.

In some types of OpenDoc containers, you can move the selected part by pressing the arrow keys. The characteristics of the container part determine whether the arrow keys work. For instance, the arrow keys work in a document whose root part is an Apple Draw part.

Resizing a part

You change the size or shape of a part by selecting it and dragging one of its small black handles. Some kinds of containers do not allow resizing of parts in them.

Copying a part

You can make a copy of a part in the same document by selecting the part and pressing the Option key while dragging the part. To copy the selected part to another OpenDoc document, simply drag it without pressing any keys. You can also use the Copy and Paste commands to copy the selected part.

Deleting a part

You delete a part by selecting it and dragging it to the Trash, choosing Clear from the Edit menu, or pressing the Delete key.

Getting part information

You can get information about a part and change some of its properties by selecting it and choosing Part Info from the Edit menu. In addition to the standard properties shown in the Part Info window, some editors make additional properties accessible through a Settings button at the bottom of the Part Info window. Figure 24-11 is an example of a Part Info dialog box.

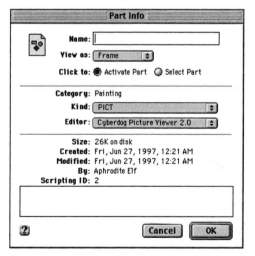

Figure 24-11: Getting information about an OpenDoc part.

The standard properties that can be changed are:

✦ **Name**, which can be anything you want to type, but it's not displayed for many parts (the Apple Audio part is one that does display its name).

✦ **View as**, which can be Frame (a bounded rectangle, oval, or irregular shape that contains the part), Large Icon or Small Icon (like in the Finder, but not named), or Thumbnail (usually a miniature picture that represents the part). To view or edit a part represented by an icon or a thumbnail, you double-click the icon or thumbnail.

✦ **Click to**, which can be Activate Part, meaning the part becomes active when you click it (as described previously), or Select Part, meaning the whole part is selected when you click it (you don't have to Shift-click as described previously).

✦ **Kind**, which is the format of the part's content. The pop-up menu lists different formats that the part may be able to use, but the part's editor can't necessarily work with all the choices listed in the pop-up menu.

✦ **Editor**, which is the software you use to view the part's content and edit the content if the editor allows editing. If more than one editor is available for the kind of data specified by the Kind property, a pop-up menu lists all the editors in your Editors folder that can handle the kind of data specified by the Kind property. But if only one editor can handle the part's kind of data, the Editor pop-up is replaced by the name of the editor as static text. Sometimes changing the Kind property makes more editors available.

In addition to these standard properties, the editor for the part may add more properties such as a script or a printing option. Other properties may be accessible through a Settings button at the bottom of the Part Info window. Clicking the Settings button brings up a dialog box that contains the additional properties. You may also be able to bring up the same Settings dialog box for a part by activating the part and choosing a Settings command from one of the part editor's menus. Figure 24-12 shows the Settings dialog box for the Apple QuickTime Viewer part.

You can also get product information about a part by activating it (not selecting it) and choosing the first command in the Apple menu, which begins with "About."

Setting document memory size

Each OpenDoc document has a memory size, much the way conventional applications have memory sizes. If you get a message saying memory is running low, you can increase the document's memory size. To change the active (front-most) document's memory size, you choose Document Info from the Document window. The Document Info dialog box appears, and in it you click the Size button to bring up the Memory Requirements dialog box. In that dialog box, you select the option Use Document Preferred Size and click the nearby up arrow(↑) or down arrow(↓) to increase or decrease the amount of memory the document uses. Then click OK to dismiss the Memory Requirements dialog box, and click OK again to dismiss the Document Info dialog box. Finally, close the document and reopen it. The new memory size takes effect when you reopen the document. Figure 24-13 shows the Memory Requirements and Document Info dialog boxes.

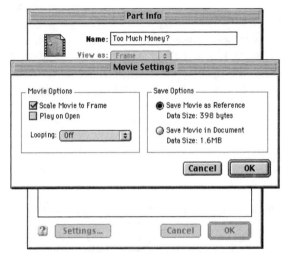

Figure 24-12: Some parts have additional settings accessible through the Part Info dialog box.

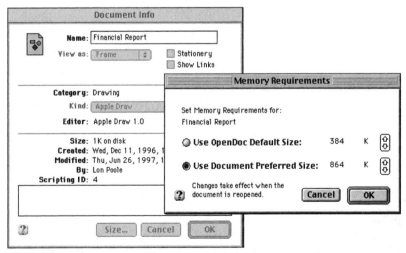

Figure 24-13: Adjusting an OpenDoc document's memory size.

Setting up editors

It's very likely that you have two or more OpenDoc part editors that handle a particular kind of content, yet it's also possible that you may receive an OpenDoc document that someone else created with a different part editor for the same kind of content. To cope with those situations, you use the Editor Setup control panel to specify a preferred editor for each kind of content. If you open a document that contains a part created by an editor that you don't have, OpenDoc uses the preferred editor for the kind of content in that part.

To specify a preferred editor for a kind of content, open the Editor Setup control panel. In its list, select a kind of content and click the Choose Editor button (or double-click the kind) to see a list of editors available on your computer for that kind of content. Select an editor to be the preferred editor for that kind of content and click OK (or simply double-click the editor). Figure 24-14 shows the Editor Setup control panel with the Choose Editor dialog box open.

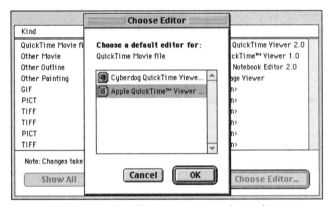

Figure 24-14: Use the Editor Setup control panel to set your preferred editor for a kind of content.

Publish and Subscribe

The United States Constitution is often referred to as a living document because it has the capability to change with the times. You can create your own living documents, albeit of a type different from the United States Constitution, using applications that have adopted the publish and subscribe capabilities of the Mac OS. The Create Publisher and Subscribe To commands enable you to share information between documents dynamically.

Think of the Create Publisher and Subscribe To commands as being live Copy and Paste commands. You can use these commands to copy a group of cells or a chart from a spreadsheet and paste it into a word processing report. Anytime the selected information in the spreadsheet changes, the report is updated automatically.

In this section, you learn how to breathe life into your documents by using the Create Publisher, Subscribe To, and other related commands.

Introducing publishers, editions, and subscribers

The Mac OS borrows concepts and terminology from the publishing industry for its publish and subscribe technology. A selected area of a document becomes a *publisher* when you make a live copy of it available to other documents. The publisher can include any information that you can select within a document.

Publishing material from a document creates a live copy of the material in a separate file, which is called an *edition*. You include a copy of an edition in another document by subscribing to the edition. The area of the document that contains a copy of an edition is called a *subscriber*. A document can contain any number and combination of publishers and subscribers. Figure 24-15 diagrams the relationship between publisher, edition, and subscriber.

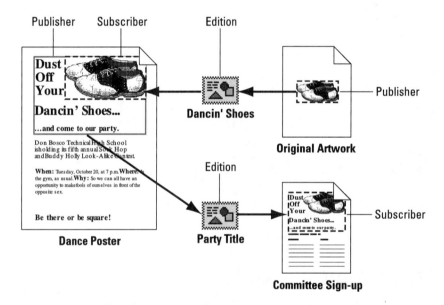

Figure 24-15: This flowchart shows the relationship between publisher, edition, and subscriber.

Saving a document after changing a publisher in it can update the publisher's edition automatically (or you can update the edition manually). When an edition is updated, the Mac OS notifies all subscribers to that edition that a new edition is available. The subscriber can automatically reflect the latest information from the edition, or you can update it manually.

Documents containing subscribers do not have to be open for the subscribers to receive edition updates. The Mac OS stores notices of edition updates destined for closed subscribers. When you open documents containing subscribers, most applications automatically check for notices of new editions. Some applications make you choose a command to update subscribers. Information always flows from the publisher to an edition and then to the edition's subscribers.

Publish and subscribe work across a network just as well as they work locally on your computer. You can subscribe and get updates to editions that are on any shared disk or folder from someone else. Likewise, other people can subscribe and get updates to editions on shared disks or folders from you. If you update an edition that someone has subscribed to on another computer, their edition will be updated the next time they connect to your shared disk or folder that contains the updated edition. (For more information on file sharing, see Chapter 21.)

The publish and subscribe process works only in programs that are designed to take advantage of it. Such programs contain publishing commands in the Edit menu or in a submenu of the Edit menu. If you have a program that lacks those commands, check with the program's developer to see whether an upgraded version is available.

Creating a publisher

You create a publisher by selecting the information that you want to share and then choosing Create Publisher from the Edit menu of your program. Many programs put the Create Publisher command in a Publishing submenu or an Editions submenu of the Edit menu. Figure 24-16 is an example of creating a publisher.

In most programs, you need to select text or graphics in your document to create a publisher. If you haven't selected anything, the Create Publisher command is dimmed. In a few programs, such as Adobe Photoshop, you can publish an entire document by choosing Create Publisher without selecting anything.

After you choose the Create Publisher command, the Publisher dialog box appears. A thumbnail view of the material that you selected appears in the Preview area of the dialog box. Figure 24-17 is an example of the Publisher dialog box.

Usually, the folder in which you saved the last edition is open in the dialog box. The Mac OS knows which folder to open because it keeps an alias of the most recently saved edition in the Preferences folder inside the System Folder. You can go to a different folder by using the same methods you would use with the Save As command. If you want to make the edition available to other users on your network, be sure to save the edition in a folder or disk that you allow those users to share.

To keep a new publisher, you must save the document that contains it. If you close the document without saving, the program asks whether you want to save changes. You lose the publisher if you decline to save.

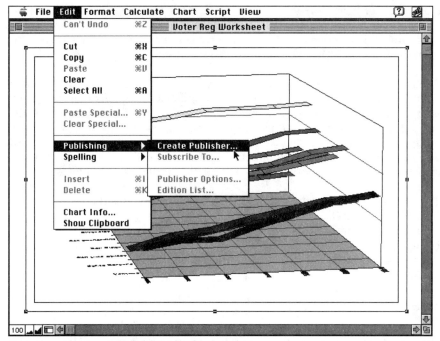

Figure 24-16: Creating a publisher.

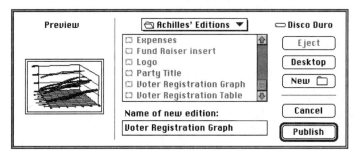

Figure 24-17: Saving an edition.

You can create as many independent publishers in a document as you want. Some programs permit publishers to overlap partially or completely; that is, one publisher can include all or part of the information contained in another publisher. Apple's guidelines suggest that word processing programs permit nested publishers but not overlapping publishers. Spreadsheet programs and graphics programs should permit both nesting and overlapping publishers. A program that does not allow overlapped or nested publishers dims the Create Publisher command when you select any part of a document that already is part of an existing publisher.

BACKGROUNDER

Smart Multiformat Editions

An edition's format—plain text, styled text, paint-type picture, object-type graphic, and so on—is determined by the program that created the publisher. Some programs save information in several formats in an edition file. When you have a program subscribe to a multiformat edition, the program uses the most appropriate format for its documents. Microsoft Excel, for example, saves spreadsheet cells as a picture, as a text table, and as a range of formatted Excel cells. A graphics document subscribing to an Excel edition uses the picture format; a word processor probably uses the text table (although Microsoft Word uses the formatted cells to create a formatted Word table); and another Excel worksheet uses the formatted cells.

Subscribing to an edition

You subscribe to an edition to incorporate live information from another document into the document on which you're working. To subscribe to an edition, select a place in your document for the edition and then choose Subscribe To from the Edit menu. Some programs put the Subscribe To command in a Publishing submenu of the Edit menu. Figure 24-18 is an example of subscribing to an edition.

The place you select for the edition depends on the type of document that's subscribing to it. In a word processing document, you click an insertion point. In a spreadsheet document, you select a cell or range of cells. You do not have to select a place in most graphics documents because you can move the subscriber after placing it in the document.

Choosing Subscribe To from the Edit menu displays the Subscribe To dialog box. The dialog box displays the highlighted name of the last edition that you published or subscribed to, and you can select a different edition as though you were using an Open command. When you select an edition, a thumbnail view of its contents appears in the Preview area of the dialog box. Clicking the Subscribe button places a copy of the selected edition in your document. Figure 24-19 is an example of the Subscribe To dialog box.

A document can subscribe to any number of editions. The editions can be on a disk directly connected to your computer, or on a disk or folder that you're sharing from another computer on the same network.

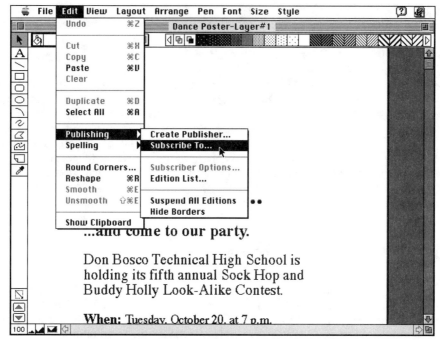

Figure 24-18: Subscribing to an edition.

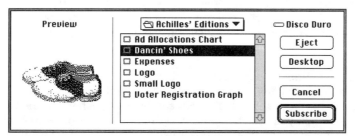

Figure 24-19: Selecting an edition to subscribe to.

Controlling publisher and subscriber borders

Most programs display a gray border around a publisher or subscriber when
you click or select something inside the publisher or subscriber. The border also
appears if you select part of a document that contains a publisher or subscriber. The
standard borderlines, which are three pixels thick, are medium gray (50 percent gray)
for publishers and dark gray (75 percent gray) for subscribers. Clicking outside the
publisher or subscriber makes the border disappear. Figure 24-20 shows examples of
the publisher and subscriber borders.

Figure 24-20: Borders around publishers and subscribers.

An optional Edit menu command, Show Borders, displays borders around all publishers and subscribers in the active document. After you choose the Show Borders command, it becomes the Hide borders command, which (surprise!) hides all borders except the one for the subscriber or publisher that you clicked.

Some programs, including Microsoft Excel 4, 5, and 98, don't show publisher or subscriber borders. Excel's Edit Links command (Links command in Excel 4–5) can select a publisher's range of cells (but not a chart, another type of publisher, or a subscriber). In the Links dialog box, you select the name of the publisher that you want from a list of publishers in the document, and then you click a Select button. Excel selects the range of cells and scrolls the document window so that you can see it.

Setting publisher and subscriber options

The Mac OS provides several options for working with publishers and subscribers. You can *adorn* a subscriber (change its formatting), locate and open a subscriber's publisher, control edition updates, and cancel or suspend a publisher or subscriber.

Application programs use different methods to make publisher and subscriber options available. Some programs place a Publisher Options command in the Edit menu when a publisher is selected in the active window, and they place a Subscriber Options command in the menu when a subscriber is selected. Choosing one of those commands brings up a dialog box in which you set the publisher or subscriber options. Figures 24-21 and 24-22 are examples of the Publisher Options and Subscriber Options dialog boxes.

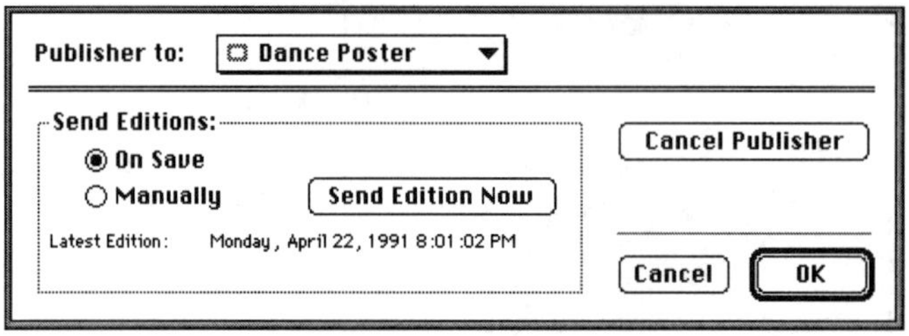

Figure 24-21: A Publisher Options dialog box.

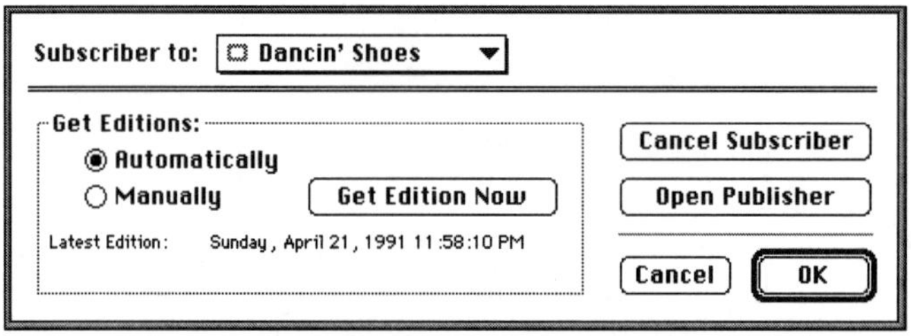

Figure 24-22: A Subscriber Options dialog box.

Other programs put the Publisher Options and Subscriber Options commands in a Publishing submenu or an Editions submenu of the Edit menu. As a shortcut, many programs bring up the appropriate options dialog box when you double-click a publisher or subscriber while pressing Option.

Microsoft Excel 4, 5, and 98 have their own eccentric methods. In Excel 98, you choose Edit Link from the Edit menu (choose Links from the File menu in Excel 4–5) to display the Links dialog box. In that dialog box, you select the publisher or subscriber whose options you want to see, and click an Options button. Excel's eccentric methods for publish and subscribe have their origins in Microsoft's own data-sharing technology called OLE (Object Linking and Embedding). Excel has a hybrid of OLE and publish and subscribe.

Adorning a subscriber

Most programs do not permit you to change the contents of a subscriber directly, because your changes would disappear the next time the subscriber was updated. Many programs do, however, permit you to adorn a subscriber in ways that the program can reapply to a new edition. For example, you may be able to resize or crop an entire subscriber as you would resize or crop a graphic in a word processing document. You may be able to change all the text in a subscriber to a different font, style, or size.

Programs that allow adornment generally have an option in the Subscriber Options dialog box that you can set to maintain or cancel adornments. When this option is on, the program reapplies the changes that you made to the subscriber the next time the subscriber is updated. Figure 24-23 is an example of a Subscriber Options dialog box with an option for maintaining subscriber adornment.

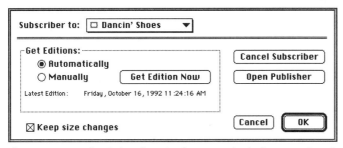

Figure 24-23: The Subscriber Options may include an option that maintains subscriber adornment.

Opening a subscriber's publisher

Generally, you make changes to a subscriber by opening its publisher and changing the publisher. To help you open a publisher the Subscriber Options dialog box includes an Open Publisher button. Clicking this button is supposed to open the document that contains the subscriber's publisher (and the program that created the publisher's document, if it's not already open), scroll the publisher into view, and select the publisher. Some programs also open a publisher when you press Option while double-clicking a subscriber. In practice, however, clicking the Open Publisher button and Option-clicking the subscriber do not always open the publisher.

Sometimes you can open a publisher by opening its edition icon in the Finder. When you do, an edition window appears. The window contains a miniature view of the publisher and an Open Publisher button. Clicking this button is supposed to open the publisher's original document, just as the Open Publisher button does in the Subscriber Options dialog box, but the Open Publisher button doesn't always work. Figure 24-24 is an example of an edition window.

Figure 24-24: You may be able to open a publisher from its edition window.

QUICK TIPS

Suspend Before You Amend

In programs that permit you to modify a subscriber, you should suspend or cancel automatic edition updating before you begin editing the subscriber. This action preserves your changes until you update the subscriber manually by clicking the Get Edition Now button in the Subscriber Options dialog box. When a subscriber is updated, changes you have made directly to it (not to the corresponding publisher) may be lost. Some programs warn you before automatically updating a subscriber that you have modified, but many automatically update without warning.

You can see the last edition that you used by opening the Preferences folder in the System Folder. Opening the alias named Last Edition Used displayed the edition window of the last edition you saved.

Making changes to a publisher

Because a publisher is just part of an ordinary document, you can modify a publisher within a document the way you would any other part of a document. You can add material to a publisher or delete material from it, making the publisher larger or smaller. You can cut an entire publisher and paste it in a different place in the document. Copying and pasting or otherwise duplicating a publisher, however, isn't a good idea. If you do, all duplicates of the publisher share one edition, making the contents of subscribers to that edition seem to be unpredictable. (The edition reflects the contents of the most recently updated duplicate publisher.)

Each time you save a document that contains a revised publisher, the application program automatically updates the publisher's edition. You can turn off automatic updating and update only manually, however, as described next.

Updating editions

The Subscriber and Publisher Options dialog boxes enable you to control whether edition updates are sent or received automatically or manually. Various programs label these dialog-box options differently. You can set update options individually for each publisher and subscriber. For example, you may want one subscriber in a document (such as a logo) to be updated on request and another subscriber (such as daily sales figures) to be updated automatically.

A publisher's Publisher Options dialog box (refer to Figure 24-21) controls when new editions of the publisher are sent. If you select the On Save option, the program automatically sends a new edition the next time you save the document (if you modified the publisher). Selecting the Manually option suspends sending new editions of the publisher until you click the Send Edition Now button in the Publisher Options dialog box.

The subscriber can receive new editions automatically or manually. If the Automatically option is selected in the subscriber's Subscriber Options dialog box (refer to Figure 24-22), the subscriber gets updated as soon as the program receives a new edition. You can suspend automatic subscriber updating by selecting the Manually option in the subscriber's Subscriber Options dialog box. To get a manual update, click the Get Edition Now button in the Subscriber Options dialog box.

You can cancel a publisher or subscriber by clicking the Cancel Subscriber or Cancel Publisher button in the Publisher Options or Subscriber Options dialog box. Canceling a publisher or subscriber permanently breaks the link between the publisher and the subscriber.

Some programs enable you to suspend all updating activity temporarily by providing a Suspend All Editions command (or its equivalent) in the Edit menu. When this command is activated, a check mark appears next to it in the menu and the program blocks all publishers from sending new editions and all subscribers from receiving new editions. Turning off the command removes the check mark from the menu and updates, with any new editions, all subscribers that are set to receive new editions automatically. The Stop All Editions command affects only publishers and subscribers in documents created by the program in which you use the command.

Summary

In this chapter, you learned that OpenDoc provides an infrastructure for plug-in part software, and that each plug-in part gives you the capability to work with a particular type of content. Installing parts puts editors in the Editors folder. Editors are like small, focused applications that specialize in particular kinds of data. You don't open an OpenDoc editor to create a new document. Instead, you open a stationery document. You can also create a new OpenDoc document from an existing document by using the New command or by dragging parts to the desktop. To create your own stationery, you can use the Save a Copy command.

Some OpenDoc parts can contain other parts. You can add a part by dragging its stationery to a container. Another way to add a part is to drag a file whose content the part can handle. Once a part is in an OpenDoc document, you can edit its content, move it, resize it, copy it, delete it, or get information about it. To view or work with the content of a part, you make the part active. To work with the part itself, you select the part as a whole.

Another way to create compound documents is with publish and subscribe—the dynamic alternatives to copy and paste. You select part of a document that you want to include in another document, but instead of copying it to the Clipboard, you publish a live copy of the selection in an edition file. Then in the other document, you subscribe to the edition. Thereafter, the subscriber is updated automatically whenever the publisher changes. (You usually have the option of making the updates happen manually instead of automatically.)

You want to avoid making substantive changes to subscribers, because your changes would disappear the next time the subscriber was updated. Many programs do let you resize or otherwise adorn a subscriber in ways that the program can reapply to a new edition.

✦   ✦   ✦

Making the Most of the Mac OS

Put Accessory Programs to Work

Apple has always included accessory programs with the Mac OS. Accessory programs enhance the features and capabilities of the Mac OS. Each accessory is a small, focused program that provides a narrowly defined set of features and capabilities. Some are indispensable, such as the Chooser, which you use to set up or select a printer and to access files over a network. Others are more diversionary, such as the Jigsaw Puzzle or the AppleCD Audio Player, which plays music CDs. Some you will use all the time, such as Sherlock or Find File, which quickly search your disks for items that you can't find by browsing. Others you hardly ever use, but will be mighty glad to have when you need them, such as Disk First Aid.

Introducing Accessory Programs

In the old days, accessory programs were all desk accessories and you could open them only from the Apple menu. These days some accessories are application programs and others are desk accessories, and very little differentiates them. You can put both kinds of programs in folders, on the desktop, or in the Apple menu. Each desk accessory can have its own unique icon, although some use the generic desk accessory icon, which looks like a backward generic application icon.

You move and copy desk accessories by dragging their icons in the Finder, just as you would with an application. If you want to install a desk accessory in the Apple menu, simply drag it to the System Folder icon. The Finder recognizes desk accessories and puts them in the Apple Menu Items folder. For historical reasons, desk accessories can also exist in suitcase files, like fonts.

You can open a desk accessory in every way but one that you can open an application program. For example, you can open a desk accessory by double-clicking it or by choosing it from the Apple menu. But unlike an application program, you can't open a desk accessory by opening one of its documents because desk accessories don't have documents. Thus, you can't open a desk accessory by double-clicking a document or by dragging a document to the desk accessory icon.

Another difference between most desk accessories and applications is the way you quit them. Like application programs, desk accessories have a Quit command in the File menu. In addition, most desk accessories quit automatically when you close their windows.

Accessory Program Encyclopedia

Each accessory program has a unique set of features and capabilities that enhance the Mac OS. This section describes the features and capabilities of the accessory programs that come with the Mac OS. The accessory programs are discussed here in alphabetical order.

As you go through this section, note that most accessory programs have detailed descriptions but a few have only brief descriptions. Accessory programs that are covered in depth elsewhere in this book have brief descriptions here that refer you to another chapter for details. The detailed descriptions here, which tell how to use the programs, are for accessory programs that are not covered elsewhere in this book.

Apple Applet Runner

Java is a programming language that has received a lot of attention. The reason for this is that Java makes it easy to create small applications, called applets, that can be automatically received by your browser from a Web page, and that extend the functionality of the page. For example, if you have a Java-enabled browser (Netscape Navigator 3.0 or later, Microsoft Internet Explorer 3.0 or later, and Cyberdog 2.0 are all Java-enabled) you could go to a stock page and have continually updated stock quotes scroll in ticker-tape fashion across your screen. Netscape and Microsoft provide their own implementations of Java along with their browsers. Cyberdog uses the Mac OS Runtime for Java (MRJ), a system component which is installed with Mac OS 8–8.5. Optionally, Microsoft Internet Explorer can use MRJ instead of its own version of Java.

Okay, so being able to run applets inside Web pages is a nice feature, but other than that, how important is Java? For the near term, not very. Sun Microsystems, the company that invented Java, is still inventing it, and as the language changes, it is moving away from its original selling point to software developers, which was that it was completely cross-platform. This meant that a programmer using Java could theoretically write a program once, then run it on Macs, Windows machines, or UNIX systems. But as Sun has released new versions of Java that are incompatible with previous versions, and Microsoft has created other incompatible Java versions, that dream seems to be fading. In the meantime, Apple has committed to supporting Java in its system software, both on Mac OS 8–8.5 and in the forthcoming Mac OS X operating system.

Different versions of MRJ support different aspects of Sun's Java language. MRJ 2.0 supports all of the features of Sun's Java 1.1.3, which allows developers to create applets that look very much like Macintosh applications. The supported features of Java 1.1.3 include security and signed applets; JavaBeans component software; enhancements to most existing Java packages (including AWT, the Application Windowing Toolkit, networking, and I/O); Java Database Connectivity (JDBC); inner classes; reflection; and the Java Native Interface. Mac OS 8.5 includes MRJ 2.0; Mac OS 8.1 may include MRJ 2.0 or 1.0.2; Mac OS 8 includes MRJ 1.0.2.

If you want to try some Java applets, you can do it with the Apple Applet Runner, a program that lets you run Java applets outside of a browser. You'll find the Apple Applet Runner and a folder of sample applets inside the Mac OS Runtime for Java folder, which is installed inside the Apple Extras folder when you do a standard installation of Mac OS 8–8.5. Just double-click the Apple Applet Runner to open it, and then choose one or more of the sample applets from the Applets menu. Figure 25-1 shows some sample Java applets in the Apple Applet Runner.

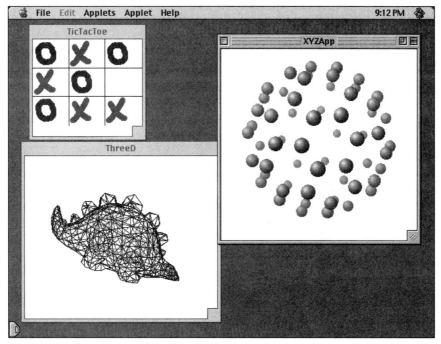

Figure 25-1: Run Java applets with the Apple Applet Runner.

BACKGROUNDER

In Case You've Heard of JavaScript

Despite the similar names and the fact that they're both associated with Web browsers, Java and JavaScript are almost completely unrelated. JavaScript is a scripting language developed by Netscape to help Web page developers automate the Netscape Navigator browser. JavaScript was originally called LiveScript, but when Java became "The Next Big Thing," Netscape changed LiveScript's name to try to ride Java's marketing coattails.

In Mac OS 8–8.1, you can also include Java applets in an OpenDoc document by using the Apple Applet Viewer. It is part of the Mac OS Runtime for Java package installed with Mac OS 8–8.1. You'll find OpenDoc stationery for the Apple Applet Viewer in the Stationery folder on the startup disk. This folder has an alias named OpenDoc Stationery in the Apple menu. You won't get the Apple Applet Viewer if OpenDoc is not already installed when you install Mac OS Runtime for Java. After installing OpenDoc, reinstall MRJ to get the Apple Applet Viewer.

AppleCD Audio Player

The AppleCD Audio Player application plays audio CDs in your CD-ROM drive. You can play, pause, stop, skip back, skip forward, scan back, and scan forward by clicking the buttons on the right side of the control panel. What's more, you can program a custom play list for every CD, and Audio Player remembers each play list you create. You can also enter CD and track titles, which Audio Player remembers as well. See "Audio CDs" in Chapter 16 for more details on using this accessory. Figure 25-2 shows the AppleCD Audio Player program.

Figure 25-2: The AppleCD Audio Player program plays audio CDs in your CD-ROM drive.

Apple System Profiler

If you ever need to call Apple for technical support for your computer, you may be asked all kinds of questions you don't know the answer to. What's your processor type? Exactly which version of the system are you running? Which SCSI bus is your startup drive on? And so on.

The Apple System Profiler answers these questions and more. Just by running this program you can find out the details of your computer's setup in several categories. The way System Profiler organizes information into categories depends on which version you have. Version 2.1 comes with Mac OS 8.5; version 1.3.2 comes with Mac OS 8.1; version 1.2.1 comes with Mac OS 8; version 1.1.4 comes with Mac OS 7.6.1; and version 1.1.2 comes with Mac OS 7.6.

Apple System Profiler 2.1

System Profiler 2.1, which comes with Mac OS 8.5, offers system information in six categories. A tab at the top of the application's window represents each category. Figure 25-3 shows some of what you see in the first category.

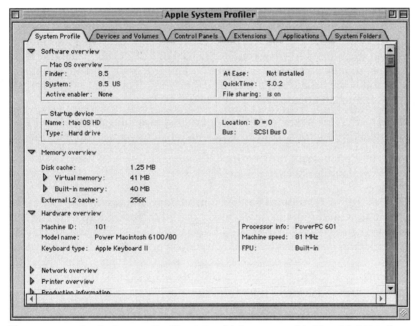

Figure 25-3: Apple System Profiler 2.1, which comes with Mac OS 8.5, tells you more than you ever wanted to know about your hardware and software.

To see another category of system information, you click its tab in the application window or choose the category you want from the Commands menu. You can choose from among these categories:

✦ The **System Profile** category provides details about your system's software, memory, hardware, network, printer, and production information. This category has six subcategories, which you can show or hide by clicking the disclosure triangle next to the subcategory name in the application window. You can see these subcategories:

- The **Software overview** subcategory provides information about the Mac OS running on your computer: which version of the Finder and System you're using, whether an enabler is active, if At Ease is installed, what version of QuickTime is installed, and whether file sharing is on or off. The software overview also profiles your startup device, listing name, type of device, SCSI ID number, and SCSI bus number.

- The **Memory overview** subcategory provides details about disk cache, virtual memory, built-in memory, and external caches.

- The **Hardware overview** subcategory identifies the machine ID, model name, keyboard type, processor type, machine speed, and FPU type.

- The **Network overview** subcategory displays details about networking options that are installed and active, and what versions of Open Transport, AppleTalk, and TCP/IP are in use. Under AppleTalk you can find out about file sharing, AppleTalk zones, active network ports, what network this computer is part of, what its node number and hardware address are, and what router it uses. For TCP/IP, you can determine if personal Web sharing and multihoming are on or off and get information about the broadcast, netmask, IP address, default gateway address, domain, and name server address.

- The **Printer overview** subcategory displays information about the desktop printer's name, driver, version, icon name, and location.

- The **Production information** subcategory tells you which ROM revision the computer is using.

✦ The **Devices and Volumes** category provides a hierarchical chart of information about all the devices connected to your computer. The highest level of the hierarchy is the type of device: SCSI bus, PCI slot, floppy drive, network, and so on. As you read across you see more detailed information about each type of device. For example, for SCSI devices, you see a list of all devices attached to the SCSI bus in order by SCSI ID number. For each device, you can see what type of device it is, what driver it's using and the vendor, revision number, product ID, and serial number. For a removable-media drive, you can see if a disk is currently inserted. For a storage device, you can see information about all the volumes on it; for each volume, you can check the format, size, space available, percent full, and whether the volume is write protected or file sharing is on. You determine the level of detail you see by clicking disclosure triangles that hide or reveal more details about each device.

✦ The **Control Panels** category lists all of the control panels currently in the System Folders of your choice, displaying the name, version, and file size of each control panel. This feature also tells you if a control panel is from Apple and if it's enabled. Selecting a control panel brings up more information such as where the control panel is located and its creation and modification dates. Some control panels also display a brief description of their functions when selected.

✦ The **Extensions** category lists all of the extensions currently in the System Folders of your choice, displaying the name, version, and file size of each extension. This feature also tells you if an extension is from Apple and if it's enabled. Selecting an extension from the list brings up more information such as where the extension is located and its creation and modification dates. Some extensions also display a brief description of their functions when selected.

✦ The **Applications** category lists all of the application programs on your disks. This feature displays the name, version number, memory size, file size, and whether it's an Apple application. Selecting an application from the list brings up information about where the application is located and its creation and modification dates. Some applications also display a brief description of their functions when selected.

✦ The **System Folders** category displays a list of system folders on the startup disk (and any other selected volume) on your computer.

Each time you open System Profiler, it gathers information for the System Profile category. You can also set up System Profiler to gather information for any other category at the same time. To do this, choose Preferences from the Edit menu and then select the categories you want.

You can also create reports of System Profiler information by choosing New Report from the File menu. A dialog box in which you select the categories of information you want in the report appears. Reports can be in Apple System Profiler format or in text format. You select the report format you want at the top of the report window. In addition, you can set a standard report format with the Preferences command.

The Commands menu allows you to update a system profile at any time. For the Control Panels, Extensions, Applications, and System Folders sections of the Apple System Profiler, you determine which volumes the Apple System Profiler searches by choosing Search Options in the Commands menu and then selecting the volumes you want in the dialog box that appears.

Apple System Profiler 1.2.1–1.3.2

System Profiler 1.2.1–1.3.2, which comes with Mac OS 8–8.1, offers eight categories of information. Figure 25-4 shows what you see in the first category.

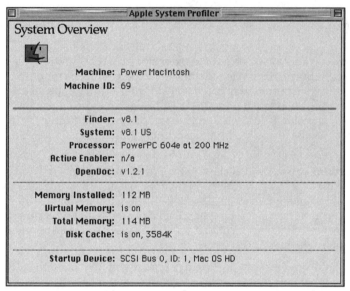

Figure 25-4: Apple System Profiler 1.3.2, which comes with Mac OS 8.1, divulges the intimate details about your hardware and software.

To see another category of system information, choose it from the Select menu. You can choose among these categories:

✦ **System Overview** displays basic information about your computer; including your personal customer number for the computer; the name and identification number of your computer model; the Finder and System versions; the type of processor and its speed; the active system enabler version (if any); the OpenDoc version; the amount of RAM installed; virtual memory status; the total amount of memory; the size of the disk cache; and the SCSI ID of the startup disk.

✦ **Network/Communication Overview** displays file sharing status; the name of the AppleTalk network zone (if any); the chosen printer's name, software version, and network location (if it's on a network); the active network port; a list of the networking software currently installed; and the current TCP/IP address information if you're connected to the Internet or another TCP/IP network.

✦ **Volume Information** displays a list of hard disk, shared disk, and other storage volumes. For a volume you select from the list, you see the volume's name and kind (such as hard disk); its capacity and space available; its SCSI ID and bus number; whether the volume is mounted on the desktop and write-protected (locked); and where the volume is located.

✦ **Device Information** displays a list of SCSI devices connected to the computer. For a device you select from a list, you see the device type; SCSI ID and bus number; make and model; version of the device's read-only memory (ROM);

the type of SCSI interface; whether the device has removable media; and the number of volumes on the device.

✦ **Control Panel Information** displays a list of control panels in the System Folder, both enabled and disabled, and the folder location of the one currently selected in the list. You can restrict the list to show only Apple control panels or only non-Apple control panels.

✦ **Extension Information** displays a list of extensions in the System Folder, both enabled and disabled, and the folder location of the one currently selected in the list. You can restrict the list to show only Apple extensions or only non-Apple extensions.

✦ **System Folder Information** displays a list of System Folders on the startup disk.

✦ **Application Information** displays a list of application programs on the startup disk and the folder location of the one currently selected in the list.

Sometimes it's easier to get a report that has all of the system information in a single file. You can use the Create Report item in the File menu to do just that. When selected, Create Report asks you for a file name and saves a complete listing of your system details to it. You can examine reports you have previously saved with the Open Report command.

Apple Video Player

The Apple Video Player application plays video and audio from a VCR, camcorder, or other video equipment on a computer with video inputs. The application can also display TV shows on a computer with a TV tuner installed. In addition, the Video Player can capture the video and save it in a movie file on disk. For detailed information, see "Apple Video Player" in Chapter 16. Figure 25-5 shows the Apple Video Player's main window and its Controls window.

Figure 25-5: The Apple Video Player plays and captures TV and video on a computer with video inputs.

Calculator

The Calculator desk accessory adds, subtracts, multiplies, and divides numbers that you enter. You can type numbers and operation symbols, or click the keys in the desk accessory. In addition, you can copy the text of a calculation — for example, 69.95+26.98+14.99*.0725 — and paste it into the Calculator. Figure 25-6 shows the Calculator desk accessory.

Figure 25-6: The Calculator desk accessory does simple arithmetic.

The Chooser

The Chooser desk accessory enables you to select a printer or other output device and to create desktop printer icons, as described in Chapter 14. You also use the Chooser to connect to shared folders and disks from other computers on the same network as your computer; for more information, see "Choosing the Default Printer" in Chapter 20. Figure 25-7 shows the Chooser desk accessory.

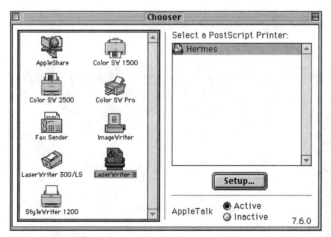

Figure 25-7: The Chooser desk accessory lets you select a printer and connect to shared folders and disks.

Connect To

The Connect To program quickly connects you to any Internet location whose URL (Uniform Resource Locator) you know. You enter the URL in the space provided, and Connect To sends the URL to the appropriate Internet application. For example, Connect To sends a URL that begins with http:// to your Web browser application. For more details, see "Using Connect To" in Chapter 17. Figure 25-8 shows the Connect To program.

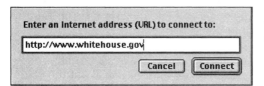

Figure 25-8: The Connect To program connects you to any Internet URL.

Desktop Printer Utility

Desktop printing allows you to print a file by dragging its icon directly to the desktop printer icon on your desktop. With this method of printing, you don't need to open the document or the application that created it, and you don't need to go through the Chooser to select a new printer if its icon is already on your desktop.

The Desktop Printer Utility, which is part of the standard installation of Mac OS 8.1–8.5, is an application for making desktop printer icons for PostScript printers. You'll find it in the Apple LaserWriter Software folder inside the Apple Extras Folder. The Desktop Printer Utility works with printers using the LaserWriter 8 driver version 8.5.1–8.6 as well as the AdobePS driver version 8.5.1. The Desktop Printer Utility creates desktop icons that let you choose a connected printer and print to it immediately. In addition, this utility creates desktop icons for printing to PostScript files, for holding files to print at a later time, for sending files over the Internet for printing, and for translating files into PostScript for printing by specific applications. Figure 25-9 shows the Desktop Printer Utility.

Figure 25-9: The Desktop Printer Utility creates desktop printers for PostScript printers.

For a full description of the Desktop Printer Utility, see "Using the Desktop Printer Utility" in Chapter 14.

DigitalColor Meter

If you work with color images, you may need to know precisely what color is displayed at a point on the monitor. You can use the DigitalColor Meter application to measure and record the RGB values of colors on your monitor. If you have an Apple ColorSync or AppleVision monitor, DigitalColor Meter can also translate displayed colors to industry-standard color standard such as Pantone and CIE. DigitalColor Meter may be in your Apple menu. If not, look for it in the Monitors Extras Folder, which is inside the Apple Extras folder.

Opening DigitalColor Meter brings up a window that displays a magnified view of the area around the mouse pointer, together with information about the color value at or near the mouse pointer. Figure 25-10 is an example of DigitalColor Meter displaying RGB values.

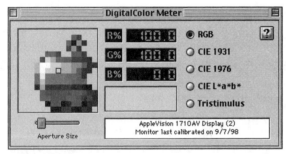

Figure 25-10: DigitalColor Meter measures the color at or near the mouse pointer.

The Aperture Size slider lets you adjust the size of the area under scrutiny. At the smallest aperture setting, DigitalColor Meter measures the single pixel lying directly beneath the pointer. At larger aperture settings, DigitalColor Meter determines the average color of the pixels inside the aperture.

You can hold a sample of the color you're pointing to — so that you don't lose the color as you move the pointer — by pressing ⌘-H. While a color is on hold, you can see its value in any of the available color standards by selecting the color standard in the DigitalColor Meter window. If you select the RGB standard, the Meter menu lets you choose whether DigitalColor Meter displays the color measurement as percentages of red, green, and blue; as values between 0 and 65535 for red, green, and blue; or as Hex values between 00 and FF for red, green, and blue. The Hex measurement is useful for specifying a color in the HTML code of a Web page. The other values are useful for specifying a color in a graphics or publishing application. If your graphics program expects RGB values between 0 and 255, you can convert

DigitalColor Meter's higher values by dividing each value by 256 and rounding up to the nearest whole number.

An easy way to enter the DigitalColor Meter's measurement into another program is with the Copy and Paste commands in the Edit menu. While pointing at a color in DigitalColor Meter, press ⌘-C to copy the color measurement to the Clipboard. Then switch to your other program and enter the color values there by choosing Paste from the Edit menu.

Disk First Aid

The Disk First Aid program checks the condition of a disk's directory, which keeps track of where files are stored on the disk, and can often repair any problem it finds. A directory can become damaged when the computer crashes or freezes. To use Disk First Aid, select one or more disks in its window and click the Verify button or the Repair button. Figure 25-11 shows the Disk First Aid window for the version of Disk First Aid that comes with Mac OS 8.5.

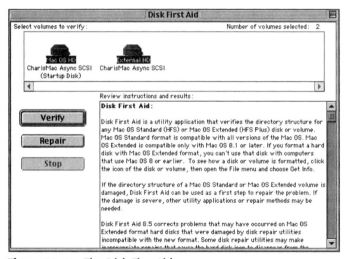

Figure 25-11: The Disk First Aid program.

If you want to verify or repair a Mac OS Extended (HFS Plus) disk, you need to use Disk First Aid version 8.1 or later. Disk First Aid 8.1 comes with Mac OS 8.1 and can be used with earlier Mac OS versions.

You can repair the current startup disk using Disk First Aid version 8.2 and later. Disk First Aid 8.2 shipped with some new Macs that were manufactured during the four or five months before Mac OS 8.5 became available. Disk First Aid 8.5 comes with Mac OS 8.5, and can be used with earlier Mac OS versions. If you need to repair the startup disk using Disk First Aid 8.1 or earlier, you must start up from a Mac OS installation CD-ROM or from a Disk Tools floppy disk.

Disk First Aid is in the Utilities folder on the startup disk. (For more information on Disk First Aid, see "Troubleshooting Tools" in Chapter 29 and "Preparing for Installation" in Chapter 30.)

Find File

The Find File utility program that comes with Mac OS 7.6–8.1 finds files, folders, and disks that match up to specified criteria. There are 16 criteria to choose among and you can combine up to 8 criteria in a single search. Find File is described fully in "Finding Items" in Chapter 6. Figure 25-12 shows the Find File program.

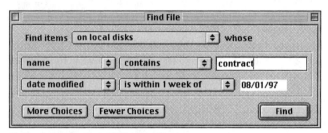

Figure 25-12: The Find File program.

Graphing Calculator

PowerPC computers come with the Graphing Calculator, which is a special calculator program to show off PowerPC's processing power. It can graph an equation in the same time that it takes the ordinary Calculator to perform arithmetic on a lesser Mac. Figure 25-13 shows the Graphing Calculator and its full keypad.

You can enter equations in the Graphing Calculator and it will draw the graph the equation represents. For example, enter "$z = x^2 + y^2$" into the space above the graph. For exponents, type a caret symbol (^) by pressing Shift-6 to move the cursor up above the line; when you're done entering an exponent, press the right arrow($\rightarrow$) key to return to normal.

You will see the graph of this equation — a three-dimensional parabola — drawn. Using the mouse, you can spin the graph about an axis and see it from another angle. Hold down the mouse over the image and move left or right. The graph will spin in the direction you move the mouse.

The Graphing Calculator knows how to draw in two or three dimensions and knows about the variables x, y, and z. You can use these variables in your equations. You can also use constants like pi, infinity, and e.

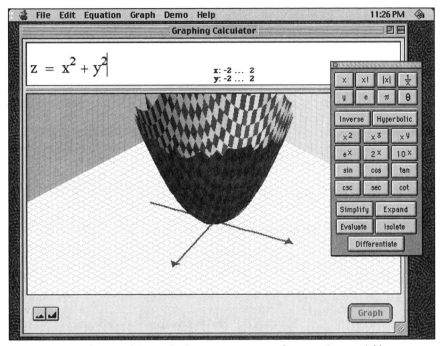

Figure 25-13: The Graphing Calculator program graphs equations quickly on PowerPC computers.

Unlike many calculators, the Graphing Calculator understands equations as you've learned them in math class. If you need help entering parts of your equation, use the Full Keypad or Small Keypad from the Equation menu. Both provide a floating window with buttons for sine, cosine, exponents, and other commonly used functions. Other useful functions, such as Square Root and Derivative, are also available in the Equation menu.

The Edit menu lets you copy the graph to the Clipboard so that you can paste it into other documents — very handy for school reports. You can also use standard Cut, Copy, and Paste commands to bring equations into word processors. And you can use the Preferences menu item to change the size of the graph grid, or the font and size of the typefaces used.

The Demo menu steps through the graphing of a set of equations. It's useful when trying to learn all that the Graphing Calculator can do, but it's probably best used to impress folks with the power and speed of your PowerPC computer.

Jigsaw Puzzle

The Jigsaw Puzzle program can create endless numbers of jigsaw puzzles with large, medium, or small pieces from any graphics file that is compatible with SimpleText (that is, in a format that QuickTime can open). You can have the program show the picture on which the puzzle is based (like the box top of a conventional puzzle), and you can also have it solve the puzzle for you. Figure 25-14 shows the Jigsaw Puzzle program with a puzzle made from one of the pictures from the Extra Desktop Pictures folder in the CD Extras folder on the Mac OS 8 installation CD-ROM.

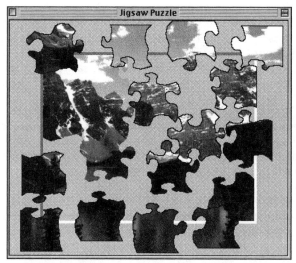

Figure 25-14: The Jigsaw Puzzle program with medium-size pieces.

Key Caps

The Key Caps program shows all the characters that you can type in any font installed in your system. You choose the font from the Key Caps menu, which appears to the right of the Edit menu when the Key Caps desk accessory is active. Key Caps changes to show the effect of pressing Shift, Option, or Control separately or in combination. Figure 25-15 is an example of the Key Caps program.

Figure 25-15: The Key Caps program shows the effect of pressing any combination of keys in any font you have.

In Key Caps, pressing Option outlines the keys that, when pressed along with Option, don't directly produce a character. Each of those Option-key combinations, which are called *dead keys*, adds an accent or other diacritic to certain subsequently typed keys. Pressing a dead key — for example, Option-E for an accent — outlines the keys that can have that diacritic added. Figure 25-16 shows how dead keys appear in Key Caps.

Pressing Option outlines keys that
can add a diacritic, and pressing one
of them while pressing Option . . .

. . . outlines the keys that can have
a diacritic added

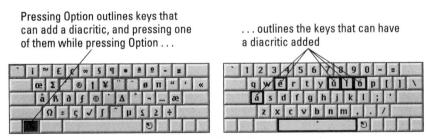

Figure 25-16: Reviewing dead keys and their effects.

QUICK TIPS

Printing Key Caps

You may want to print Key Caps as a handy reference, but it has no Print command. To work around this situation, follow these steps to take a picture of the screen and print that picture:

1. Open Key Caps, choose the font that you want it to show, and press any modifier keys (Shift, Option, Control, or ⌘) that you want to be in effect. Move the mouse pointer to an empty area of the menu bar; hold down the mouse button; temporarily release the modifier keys; press Caps Lock-⌘-Shift-4; again press the modifier keys that you released temporarily; and, finally, release the mouse button. Your gyrations should be rewarded by the sound of a camera shutter as the system snaps a picture of the Key Caps window.

2. Now open your startup disk and look for a document named Picture 1. (If you take additional snapshots, those snapshots are numbered sequentially.)

3. Print this document using SimpleText or any graphics program.

MoviePlayer

MoviePlayer specializes in QuickTime movies. While you may be able to play movies in SimpleText and other ordinary applications, MoviePlayer gives you more control over the movie. For example, you can change the size of a movie window and you can view detailed information about a movie in a separate window. You can even edit movies with some versions of MoviePlayer. Figure 25-17 shows the Movie Player information window for a movie.

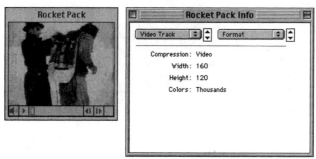

Figure 25-17: MoviePlayer can display detailed information about QuickTime movies.

When Apple split QuickTime 3.0 into two editions, regular and Pro, it did the same with MoviePlayer. The regular edition of MoviePlayer 3.0 has fewer playback options than MoviePlayer 2.5.1. For instance, MoviePlayer 2.5.1 can present a movie centered on a completely black screen and can play a movie continuously.

In addition, MoviePlayer 2.5.1 can edit movies. You can use it to cut, copy, and paste parts of movies, create new movies, and import and export individual movie tracks. MoviePlayer 3.0 Pro can do everything that MoviePlayer 2.5.1 can do and more, such as applying filters and special effects.

If you have Mac OS 8.5 or have installed QuickTime 3.0 with Mac OS 7.6–8.1, you'll find MoviePlayer 3.0 inside the QuickTime folder on your startup disk. If you have Mac OS 8–8.1 and have not installed QuickTime 3.0, Movie Player 2.5.1 is located in the Applications folder on the startup disk. With Mac OS 7.6–7.6.1, it's in the Apple Extras folder on the startup disk. For more information on Movie Player, see "Playing QuickTime Movies" and "Basic QuickTime Movie Editing" in Chapter 16.

Note Pad

The Note Pad saves brief messages that you type or paste into it. You can print notes, go to any note by number, and find text in one note or all notes. Each note can contain up to 32K (about 32,000) characters. You can drag text between the Note Pad and another application that has adopted Mac OS drag-and-drop editing, such as ClarisWorks, the Scrapbook, and SimpleText (see "Moving Document Contents Around" in Chapter 7). You can scroll and resize the Note Pad window. In addition, you can set the font and size of the text in the notes by choosing Preferences from the Edit menu. Figure 25-18 shows the Note Pad.

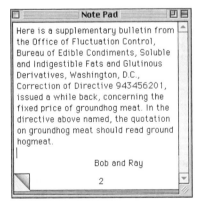

Figure 25-18: Keep brief notes in the Note Pad program.

To create a new Note, use the New command from the File menu, or press ⌘-N. Click the dog-ear in the lower-left corner to flip forward or backward through the notes.

PictureViewer and PictureViewer Pro

PictureViewer is a simple application for viewing and making minor changes to still images; it comes as part of QuickTime 3.0. PictureViewer Pro is an enhanced version that you get if you upgrade to QuickTime 3.0 Pro. You'll find PictureViewer in the QuickTime folder inside the Applications folder on your startup disk. (QuickTime is discussed in more detail in Chapter 16.)

PictureViewer lets you open and view images in several image formats, among them, BMP, GIF, JPEG, MacPaint, PICT, PNG, Photoshop, QuickTime Image, SGI, Targa, TIFF, and QuickDraw GX Picture. You can also use PictureViewer to view other image formats for which you have installed graphics importers.

To open an image file in PictureViewer, you can drag the file's icon to the PictureViewer icon. Alternatively, you can choose Open from PictureViewer's File menu. The Open dialog box lets you see a preview of the image if one already exists, or create a preview if none exists. To create the preview, click the Create button in the Open dialog box, as shown in Figure 25-19.

Once an image is open, you can resize it and change its orientation.

After opening an image in PictureViewer, you can resize the image window by choosing Half Size, Normal Size, Double Size, or Fill Screen from the Image menu. Although the image window has no grow box, you can, nevertheless, drag the bottom-right corner of its window to resize it. PictureViewer normally constrains the window to an optimal size. To resize freely, you must Shift-drag. Option-dragging resizes the image in preset percentages (100%, 75%, 50%, 25%, and 10%).

Figure 25-19: QuickTime 3.0's PictureViewer application previews images in its Open dialog box.

To change an image's orientation in the window, choose Rotate Right, Rotate Left, Flip Horizontal, or Flip Vertical from the Image menu. Once you've made changes, your can print it or copy it to the Clipboard. If you have PictureViewer Pro, you can save your changes to the image by choosing Export from the File menu.

Scrapbook

The Scrapbook stores and retrieves text, pictures, sounds, movies, and other types of information that you paste into it, one item at a time. You can copy an item to or from the Scrapbook by dragging from or to another application that has adopted Mac OS drag-and-drop editing, such as ClarisWorks, SimpleText, or the Finder (see

"Moving Document Contents Around" in Chapter 7 for details). Figure 25-20 shows a movie pasted into the Scrapbook.

Figure 25-20: The Scrapbook stores all kinds of clippings pasted into it.

As you scroll through items, the Scrapbook reports the number of the item, the type of the item, and its size. For picture items, the Scrapbook also reports the item's dimensions and the amount (if any) by which the item is reduced for display in the Scrapbook. The Scrapbook also reports the duration of sounds and movies.

Script Editor

The Script Editor is used to write, record, and edit AppleScript scripts. You'll find it in the AppleScript folder inside the Apple Extras folder on the startup disk. For more information on AppleScript and Script Editor, see Chapter 23. Figure 25-21 is an example script in a Script Editor window.

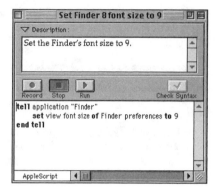

Figure 25-21: Write and edit AppleScript scripts in the Script Editor program.

Sherlock

In Mac OS 8.5, the Sherlock program enhances and extends the Find File application found in earlier versions of the Mac OS. Sherlock provides a window with tabs for three different types of searches: Find File, Find by Content, and Search Internet. Figure 25-22 shows the Sherlock window in Mac OS 8.5.

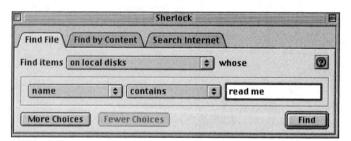

Figure 25-22: The Sherlock program finds files, document content, and Internet content in Mac OS 8.5.

The Find File section of Sherlock lets you search for files, folders, and disks on your system. There are 15 criteria by which you can search, and you can combine up to 10 in a single search. For more detailed instructions, see "Finding Items" in Chapter 6.

The Find by Content section of Sherlock extends the search function to allow you to search not only for the name of a file, disk, or folder, but to search for content within files. To be able to search for words within a file, you must have indexed the disk on which the file resides. To access the indexing function, click the Index button in the Find by Content section of the Sherlock application. For more detailed instructions, see "Finding Documents by Content" in Chapter 7.

The Search Internet section of Sherlock allows you to find files on the Internet through the auspices of such well-known search engines as AltaVista, Infoseek, and Lycos. The results of your search appear in the Sherlock application's results list. You can connect to any of these sites by double-clicking the name in the list. For more detailed instructions, see "Searching the Internet" in Chapter 17.

SimpleSound

SimpleSound is a small application that you can use to record sound. You can record sound files and new system alert sounds. The Alert Sounds window shows a list of all alert sounds currently in your System file. You can also open sound files, each in its own window. Figure 25-23 shows the Alert Sounds window and the windows of two sound files.

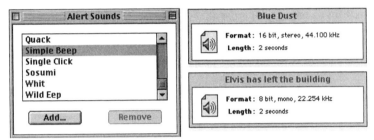

Figure 25-23: Record system alert sounds and individual sound files in the SimpleSound program.

Playing sounds

You can play an alert sound by clicking its name in the Alert Sounds window. Selecting an alert sound in the Alert Sounds window also makes it the system alert sound, just like selecting it in the Monitors & Sound control panel or the Sound control panel (see "Sound Adjustments" in Chapter 11).

To play an open sound file, make its window active and use the Play command in the Sound menu, or double-click the icon in the sound's window. You can stop a playing sound with the Stop command in the Sound menu, by clicking the icon in the sound's window once or by pressing ⌘-period(.).

Making sounds

Before making a new sound, you can set the sound quality by choosing a quality level from the Sound menu. Higher quality sound requires more storage space on disk. There are four sound quality level choices:

✦ **CD Quality** records in stereo with 16-bit samples and a 44.1kHz sampling rate.

✦ **Music Quality** records in mono with 8-bit samples and a 22kHz sample rate.

✦ **Speech Quality** records in mono with 3-to-1 compression and a 22kHz sampling rate.

✦ **Phone Quality** records in mono with 6-to-1 compression and a 22kHz sampling rate.

To make a new alert sound, click the Add button in the Alert Sounds window. To make a new sound file, use the New command in the File menu. Either action brings up a dialog box with buttons that work like a traditional tape recorder. The dialog box also shows the elapsed recording time and the remaining time available. Click the Record button to record or rerecord sound from the computer's microphone or from another audio source. (You set the sound input source in the Sound section of the Monitors & Sound control panel or the Sound In section of the Sound control panel, as described in Chapter 11.) Then click the Play button to hear your recording. When you're satisfied with your recording, click the Save button, and type a name for the new sound when you're asked. Figure 25-24 shows the dialog box in which you record a sound.

Figure 25-24: The SimpleSound program's dialog box for recording a new sound.

New alert sounds are saved in the Finder sound format (also known as the snd format) and are put in the System file. You can open the System file and drag sounds to the desktop.

New sound files are saved in the audio interchange file format (AIFF), and each sound goes in the folder that you select when you save the sound.

SimpleText

SimpleText is often thought of as just a tool for opening Read Me files, but it can do more. SimpleText can read text aloud as well as open graphics files and copy selected portions of an image to the Clipboard. Furthermore, unless you have removed QuickTime, you can use SimpleText to play QuickTime movies and open and manipulate QuickDraw 3D graphics.

Text editing

The text-editing features of SimpleText are not fancy. You have no control over paragraph formatting. The paragraph width changes as you resize the SimpleText document's window. Line spacing and tab stops are fixed.

In plain-text documents, you can make selections and cut, copy, and paste text. You can change the font, size, and style, but you must apply each attribute separately. (You cannot create styles that assign font, size, and style all in one operation.) If you want to search or search and replace, you must have SimpleText 1.4 (which comes with Mac OS 8–8.5); earlier versions can't search. Moreover, the text-editing capabilities described in this paragraph do not work in read-only SimpleText documents — the kind with an icon that looks like a newspaper.

Speech and sound

To make SimpleText read aloud, select some text in a SimpleText document and then choose Speak Selection (⌘-J) from SimpleText's Sound menu. If you make no selection, the Sound menu offers the command Speak All. Choose a voice from the Voices menu. Some voices simulate realistic humanlike speech, others are mechanistic, humorous, or musical.

You can also record a voice annotation or other sound and attach it to a plain-text document for later playback. Choosing Record from the Sound menu brings up a dialog box for recording up to 25 seconds of sound. Clicking Save in this dialog box saves the sound in the current SimpleText document. To play a saved sound, choose Play from the Sound menu.

Graphics and other media

SimpleText can also open graphics files, 3D objects, and QuickTime movies. You can drag a multimedia file to the SimpleText icon to open it, or use the Open command in SimpleText's File menu. SimpleText can open PICT files directly. If you have QuickTime installed, SimpleText uses it to convert other graphics files to PICT. Depending on the version of QuickTime, you may be able to open and convert BMP, GIF, JPEG, MacPaint, PICT, PNG, Photoshop, QuickTime Image, SGI, Targa, TIFF, and QuickDraw GX Picture files.

Once SimpleText has opened a graphics file, the mouse pointer appears as a cross hairs pointer, which you can use to select a portion of the image and copy it to the Clipboard. When you use SimpleText to open a QuickDraw 3D graphic, you can manipulate the 3D graphic using the standard QuickDraw 3D controller. When you use SimpleText to open QuickTime movies, the movie appears in a window with a standard QuickTime movie controller at the bottom. (For more information on these multimedia controllers, see "Viewing QuickDraw 3D Objects" and "Playing QuickTime Movies" in Chapter 16.)

Stickies

The Stickies application displays notes similar to Post-it Notes on your screen. You can set the color and the text font, size, and style for each note. You can drag selected text to move it within a note, copy it between notes, or copy it between a note and another application that has adopted Mac OS drag-and-drop editing, such as SimpleText and the Note Pad. Stickies windows have no scroll bars, but you can scroll by pressing the arrow keys or by dragging inside the note. Figure 25-25 displays several examples of Stickies notes.

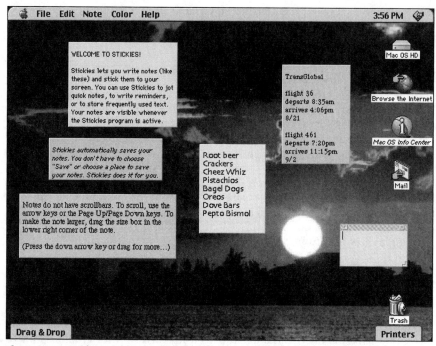

Figure 25-25: The Stickies application displays notes similar to Post-it Notes.

Summary

After reading this chapter, you know that a number of accessory programs come with the Mac OS. Each is a small, focused program that provides very specific features and capabilities. Accessory programs range from the indispensable Chooser, which you use to set up or select a printer and to access files over a network, to the diversionary Jigsaw Puzzle. You'll use some of them such as Sherlock or Find File, which quickly search disks for items you can't seem to find, regularly. Others, such as Disk First Aid, you'll use only in case of trouble. Some accessory programs are desk accessories and others are application programs, although the difference between the two types is minimal.

✦   ✦   ✦

Enhance with Utility Software

In This Chapter

Obtaining utility software online from user groups and from Apple

Checking out the alphabetical listing of utility programs

Every system software upgrade, including Mac OS 8.5, offers significant enhancements in performance and ease of use over older Mac system software. However, even Mac OS 8.5 can stand some assistance in performing its disk and file management, alias management, networking, and other duties. Software that enhances the Mac OS to even further increase your productivity is the subject of this chapter.

Many programmers have developed small accessory applications, control panels, and system extensions that enhance the performance of the Finder and other system software. Mac OS users are an idiosyncratic lot and like to personalize their systems. These shareware, freeware, and commercial software utilities personalize the activities of the Finder and other system software so that the computer does exactly what you need it to do, when you need it to do it. With these programs, you can open specific files directly without having to know where they are located. You can also throw away files while using an application without going to the Finder, create aliases in new ways, and make using your Mac much more fun.

The software items described in this chapter are listed alphabetically, with a short description of each of their features, and with the names of their authors, their system requirements, and prices. Software is updated often, especially noncommercial software, and you may find that newer versions of programs have features not described here.

Where to Get Utility Software

You can use several avenues to acquire the software listed in this chapter. All the software is available from some software library on the Internet or from a commercial online information service. Much of the software is available on CD-ROM from user groups. And some of the software is available from Apple. Start with the following sources.

✦ **Macworld's Macdownload** software library (http://www.macdownload.com) has much of the software listed in this chapter, plus many more shareware, freeware, and Apple utilities. All are available for the cost of downloading.

✦ **America Online** (800-827-6364) has a large collection of shareware, freeware, and Apple utility software, all available for the cost of downloading.

✦ **Info-Mac Archive** is a major storehouse of shareware, freeware, and demo versions of retail software. All software is submitted to a central location and redistributed to mirror sites throughout the world, such as AOL's FTP mirror site (ftp://mirrors.aol.com/pub/info-mac/) and Apple's FTP mirror site (ftp://mirror.apple.com/mirrors/Info-Mac.Archive/). At most mirror sites, you browse for files by category. MIT's HyperArchive mirror has an Info-Mac search facility (http://hyperarchive.lcs.mit.edu/HyperArchive.html), and so does the University of Illinois (http://uiarchive.cso.uiuc.edu/pubindex/info-mac/wgindex.html).

✦ **Umich mac.archive** is another major storehouse of shareware, freeware, and demo versions of retail software. Like Info-Mac, Umich has mirror sites throughout the world, such as AOL's FTP mirror site (ftp://mirrors.aol.com/pub/mac/) and Apple's FTP mirror site (ftp://mirror.apple.com/mirrors/mac.archive.umich.edu/). There's a list of mirror sites at the main Umich mac.archive site (http://www-personal.umich.edu/~sdamask/umich-mirrors/).

✦ **Filez** (http://www.filez.com) and **Shareware.com** (http://www.shareware.com) have extensive, searchable directories of shareware and freeware.

✦ **Berkeley Macintosh Users Group (BMUG)** (510-549-2684, http://www.bmug.org), **Arizona Macintosh Users Group (AMUG)** (602-553-8966, http://www.amug.org), and other **user groups** sell collections of shareware and freeware on CD-ROM. Apple will refer you to the user group nearest you (800-538-9696).

✦ **Apple's Software Updates library** (http://www.apple.com/swupdates/) has all Apple utility software and much of, but not all of, Mac system software. Everything in the library is available for the cost of downloading.

✦ **Apple's Developer FTP site** (ftp://ftp.apple.com/devworld/Utilities/) offers a number of utilities.

✦ The **Apple Order Center** (800-293-6617) supplies some Apple utility software on floppy disk and CD-ROM for a nominal fee, usually $10 to $20.

How to use utility software

This chapter describes utility software but does not include detailed operating instructions. Because noncommercial software is usually distributed online or on disk, it doesn't come with printed manuals. Instead, noncommercial software usually comes with a documentation file, frequently called "Read Me." You should also check for onscreen help in the Help menu or at the top of the Apple menu.

About shareware and freeware

The software described in this chapter is not available in any store. This software is distributed on the Internet, through online information services, by user groups, and person-to-person. Whatever you pay for an online connection or a user group's CD-ROM goes strictly to the online service or user group; none of that money goes to the authors of the software. That's fine with some authors, who distribute their products as *freeware* and don't expect to be paid.

Authors of *shareware* encourage you to try their software and to share copies with friends and coworkers. Each person who decides to keep a shareware product sends payment directly to the author. Many shareware authors also accept payment through Kagi Software (http://www.kagi.com), which is a clearinghouse on the Internet.

It's important to understand that freeware and shareware are not in the public domain. Most freeware authors and all shareware authors retain the copyrights to their work. You can use it and you can generally pass it around, but you can't sell it.

Shareware and freeware programs typically are written by enthusiasts who can't afford to provide technical support by telephone, as the developers of commercial programs can. Moreover, shareware and freeware authors can't afford to thoroughly test their software with many combinations of computer models, Mac OS versions, and other software.

Much shareware and freeware is not as stable as commercial software. Be sure to follow the instructions and discussions provided by the authors in their Read Me or Help files before using any of these programs. Be forewarned: You use shareware and freeware at your own risk.

QUICK TIPS

Support Shareware Authors

Shareware depends on the honor and honesty of the people who use it. If you decide to keep shareware installed on your disk, the Honorable Society of Civilized People politely insists that you immediately send payment to the author. The fees that you pay for the shareware you use today (generally $5 to $50) help fund development of more great shareware. For detailed information about the amount of payment requested for a particular shareware product and where to send payment, check the product's Read Me file, About command (in the Apple menu), or onscreen help.

System Utilities Listing

Apple, commercial developers, and shareware and freeware authors offer thousands of utility programs. Many new programs become available each day. The software listed in this chapter has been culled from the pack based on its usefulness, ease of use, completeness, and reliability. This list is not meant to be all-inclusive, but rather to be an example of the types of software that are available to enhance the performance of your computer with the Mac OS. The great variation in computer models, Mac OS versions, and configurations makes it impossible to predict accurately whether a utility will work on your system. Some Read Me files and documentation mention the systems and configurations required and known conflicts, but others do not. Most of the utilities listed here should work with Mac OS 7.6–8.1. Many will probably work with Mac OS 8.5 as well, but at the time this book went to press compatibility with Mac OS 8.5 was unknown for most of these utilities.

A few of the programs listed here are redundant or partially redundant with Mac OS 8–8.5 features, but are still beneficial to users of earlier Mac OS versions. The individual program descriptions in this section tell you about redundancies.

Authors of noncommercial software don't typically have the facilities to test their programs with a variety of software combinations and computer models. Instead, they fix problems reported by people who try out the utility programs. If you decide to try a program, check the Read Me file or other included documentation for compatibility information of the version you get. If the compatibility information doesn't assure you that the utility program you want to try is compatible with your computer model and Mac OS version, you should take the precaution of making a backup of your hard disk before trying the utility program.

The Web has additional information about some shareware and freeware programs. The program descriptions in this chapter include URLs of Web pages wherever possible. When you use these URLs, remember that Web pages come and go. If you try a URL cited here and it doesn't work, look for the program in the Info-Mac Archive and other places mentioned in the previous section.

Aaron

Aaron gives a Mac OS 8 look to Mac OS 7.6–7.6.1 by replacing dialog boxes, pop-up menus, scroll bars, folders, windows, and other interface elements. This extension by Gregory Landweber and Edward Voas requires a color-capable computer and costs $10.

Aaron Light

Aaron Light patches third-party applications to give them a more consistent Mac OS 8 appearance by, for example, giving progress bars Mac OS 8's rounded 3D look. Aaron Light also substitutes the font Espi Sans Bold 10 point for Chicago 12 point as the system font. This extension by Gregory Landweber (http://www.kaleidoscope. net/greg/) requires Mac OS 8–8.1 and costs $5.

Agent Audio

Agent Audio lets you replace the "snd" resources (sounds) of any file or application that already contains them. Select the program you wish to customize and Agent Audio lets you view and edit the available sounds or extract and archive the sounds into playable "snd" files. This application by Clixsounds (http://www.clixsounds.com) requires a color monitor and 2MB of RAM and costs $12.

a.k.a.

Drag a file onto a.k.a. to create or rename aliases and place the newly created aliases anywhere on any mounted volume or in user-specified folders. This extension by Fred Monroe is free.

Alias Crony

Alias Crony can scan all of your online volumes to create lists of attached and unattached aliases; retrieve aliases and originals; and link, update, delete, and move aliases (some of these functions are redundant with Mac OS 8.5). It also creates "SuperAliases" of applications that can reside on separate volumes and still possess drag-capability, enabling you to drag items onto the alias to launch the application. This application by Rocco Moliterno of Yellowsoft (http://users .iol.it/yellowsoft), costs $10.

AliasZoo

AliasZoo is a quick and easy way to get control over the mountain of alias files living on your hard drive. It searches a hard drive or folder and displays a report listing details on the aliases it finds, deletes orphaned aliases quickly and easily, and includes Apple Guide support. This application by Cliff McCollum (http://www. islandnet.com/~cliffmcc/) of Blue Globe Software costs $15.

AMICO (Apple Menu Items Custom Order)

AMICO lets you change the order of items in the Apple menu without renaming them. You can also add gray divider lines and divider titles between groups of items. This extension by Dennis Chronopoulos costs $10.

Apple Data Detectors

Apple Data Detectors allows you to scan selected text for certain types of information and then perform actions on that information from within a contextual menu. Apple Data Detectors includes Apple Internet Address Detectors, which allows you to gather all of the URLs and e-mail addresses in a selection into a list on the contextual menu and then choose from a list of actions to perform on one or more of the addresses, such as adding an e-mail address to your address book, addressing a new e-mail message to a selected address, opening a browser and connecting to a selected site, adding a bookmark, or connecting to a remote computer. Internet Address Data Detectors is not compatible with Mac OS 8.5 unless you remove the file Contextual Menu Enabler from the Extensions folder. With this file removed, the Internet Address Detectors will work only in applications that have been revised to support Apple Data Detectors. The Apple Data Detectors extension, control panel, and contextual menu plug-in set is free from Apple Computer (http://applescript.apple.com/data_detectors/detectors.00.html).

Apple Geographic Detectors

Apple Geographic Detectors works in conjunction with Apple Data Detectors, and allows you to scan selected text for U.S. cities, states, and protectorates. The geographic data appears on a contextual menu where you can choose to perform one of two actions on it: you can connect to Yahoo's map site for that geographical area or look up a zip code for the area on the U.S. Postal Service Web site. This detector add-on is free from Apple Computer (http://applescript.apple.com/data_detectors/detectors.00.html).

AppSizer

AppSizer enables you to change the amount of memory allocated to applications (the suggested size in the Info window) as you launch them. This control panel from Peirce Software (http://www.peircesw.com) costs $19.95.

ARACommander

The ARACommander control panel is an adjunct to the Remote Access software included with Mac OS 7.6–8.1. ARACommander automates dialing into remote networks by creating connectors that contain the telecommunications and network configuration information necessary to complete the transaction. The device requires less disk space and less RAM than the Apple Remote Access client and server software (see "Introducing Remote Network Connections" in Chapter 19). This control panel by Trilobyte Software requires Apple Remote Access and costs $25.

BatteryAmnesia

BatteryAmnesia provides a safe, fast, and automatic way to deep discharge a PowerBook's (NiCad) or nickel-hydride (NiMH) battery, bypassing the low-battery warning messages, and preventing the sleep state normally brought on by those messages. It runs your PowerBook's battery down until a hardware shutdown occurs, which is at a lower voltage, providing the best discharge possible without an expensive external battery conditioner. This application by Jeremy Kezer (http://www.kezer.net/shareware.html) requires a PowerBook and costs $10.

Blitz

The Blitz file management utility can catalogue hard disks and large removable drives such as CD-ROMs when volumes are dragged and dropped onto its application. Blitz records large catalogues using very little disk space, while providing extremely fast search functionality. This application by Matthew Bickham (http://yoyo.cc.monash.edu.au/~bickham/) requires a computer with a color monitor (256 colors or better) and costs $10.

BunchOApps

BunchOApps lists your most recently run applications and installed applications and launches them when selected. You can specify how many applications to remember (up to 25). This Control Strip module by Patrick McClaughry requires Apple's Control Strip or Men & Mice's Desktop Strip and is free.

Carpetbag

Carpetbag allows various system resources, such as fonts, sounds, and FKeys, to be kept outside your System file. Place PostScript fonts in one specified folder outside the System Folder and ATM and the LaserWriter driver will see them. This control panel by James W. White costs $5.

ClickTyper

ClickTyper offers key-free typing to people with limited ability to use their hands. ClickTyper creates a virtual onscreen keyboard where you enter text, navigate a document, and perform other operations, such as printing and shutting down. The application's two modes — Mouse Mode and Click Mode — allow you to choose the amount of movement you must make. In Click Mode, ClickTyper highlights areas of the keyboard; clicking anywhere confirms that the desired "key" is in the highlighted area. ClickTyper highlights smaller and smaller areas until you identify the precise key. This application by Ivan Gobbo (http://www.kagi.com/inai/ct/) costs $20.

Clock Synch

Clock Synch synchronizes the clocks between two or more computers on an AppleTalk network, by setting the clocks of the servant computers to that of a master computer. This application by Jeremy Kezer (http://www.kezer.net/shareware.html) requires an AppleTalk network and costs $15.

CMScript

CMScript allows you to run AppleScripts related to the "context" — the application that you are currently in — from Mac OS 8–8.5's Contextual Menus. CMScript comes with Context Grabber, a plug-in that aids in script creation by determining the current context, copying the appropriate Apple event for the current context to the clipboard (for pasting into a script), and/or creating template scripts that are preconfigured for the current context. This extension by Michael Schürig (http://www.uni-bonn.de/~uzs90z/) is free.

Coloristic

Coloristic opens a window that magnifies the area around the cursor. As you move the cursor, the contents of the window change. The window also displays the color value for the pixel directly under the cursor. (This capability duplicates the function of the DigitalColor Meter program included with Mac OS 8–8.5.) One preference setting allows you to scale the pixels as you resize the window to make selecting individual pixels easier. Another setting lets you display color values as Decimal, Hexadecimal, or Internet. You can copy these values to the clipboard. This application from Bubble Pop Software (http://www.bubblepop.com) is free.

CoolViews

The CoolViews control panel allows you to customize the Finder windows, determine which columns appear, how wide they are, and their order (these functions are redundant with Mac OS 8.5). You can also reveal a hidden feature of Mac OS 8–8.1: columns for Creator and Type. CoolViews lets you set preferences for the list views of all folders on your system and lets you modify other aspects of the Finder windows such as background color and date formats. This control panel by Graham Herrick, Quadratic Software (http://www.quadratic.com) requires Mac OS 8–8.1 and a monitor with 256 colors or grays. CoolViews costs $20.

CopyPaste

CopyPaste enhances the Mac OS clipboard functionality by remembering the last ten items copied and keeping them accessible via menu or key commands and includes hot keys for switching between applications you're copying and pasting between. It can also append the Clip Sets to text files or save the clipboards on shutdown or restart. This extension from ScriptSoftware (http://www.scriptsoftware.com) costs $20.

Default Folder

Default Folder enhances Open and Save dialog boxes, making file management easier by letting you specify where files should always be saved by certain applications, providing a pop-up menu of recently used folders, moving items to the Trash from within dialog boxes, and adjusting multiple save options. This control panel by St. Clair Software (http://www.stclairsoft.com) costs $25.

Desktop Gallery

Desktop Gallery puts an automated slide show on the Mac desktop. You select a folder that contains GIF, JPEG, PICT, or MacPaint images, and Desktop Gallery displays each image in the folder (and any subfolders), either in order or randomly, at the interval you specify. The images are sized and positioned according to the settings in Apple's Desktop Pictures control panel (which must be installed). Desktop Gallery version 1.1 does not work with Mac OS 8.5, which has no Desktop Pictures control panel. The Desktop Gallery control panel from Digital Native (http://www.pex.net/~DigitalNative/) costs $15 and requires Mac OS 8–8.1.

Desktop Resetter

Desktop Resetter lets you define preferred locations for desktop icons and restore icons to these positions easily when they get rearranged by other users or when you change monitor resolutions. Resetter can remember different icon setups for different monitor resolutions. This application by Nick D'Amato (http://members. home.net/goddfadda/resetter.html) costs $10.

Dialog View

Dialog View lets you enlarge Open and Save dialog boxes so that you can see more files and folders with less scrolling. It also lets you choose a font for the file list in these dialog boxes (a condensed font will show longer file names). This control panel from James W. Walker (http://members.aol.com/jwwalker/) costs $10.

Discolour

Discolour enables Mac OS 7.6–7.6.1 computers to display full-color floppy disk icons instead of the black-and-white system default. This extension by Ambrosia Software (http://www.ambrosia.com) requires a color computer and is free.

Disk Copy

Disk Copy will mount disk images on your desktop, make exact copies of floppy disks from a disk image, convert disk images from one format to another, and create a disk image from a mounted volume or individual folder. In conjunction with DiskScripts and AppleScript, it can be used to automate software installations and disk image manipulation. This application by Apple Computer is free; it's included on the Mac OS installation CD.

Disk Rejuvenator

Disk Rejuvenator addresses problems of hard disks becoming inaccessible from the standard Open dialog boxes and of custom icons disappearing (which can be caused by the Finder information for the root of the disk becoming corrupted). It corrects the problems by examining your disk's attributes and correcting those that are in need of correction. This application by Aladdin Systems (http://www.aladdinsys.com) is free.

DiskSurveyor

DiskSurveyor provides a graphical display of the files and folders that reside on your hard drive and shows the amount of space these individual items are taking up. You can open and manage folders from within the display and create disk summary files that list all the files found on CD-ROMs or any other volume. This application by Tom Luhrs, Twilight Software, requires a monitor set to display at least 256 colors or grays and costs $10.

Download Deputy

Download Deputy lets you queue a number of remote files for batch downloading. You create lists of URLs by typing them into a URL window; by dragging them to the window from your browser; or by activating the URL Grabber, which keeps track of every FTP address you click on as you browse. You can start a batch download manually or schedule downloads for a later time. Download Deputy can perform a number of actions once download is complete: It can close your PPP connection, expand files with Stuffit Expander, quit, and shut down. The URL Grabber feature requires Netscape Navigator 3.0 or later. The Download Deputy application, from ilesa Software (http://www.ilesa.com), costs $21.

DragThing

DragThing is an application dock designed to tidy up the icons littering your desktop. Simply drag an application from the Finder onto an empty square in a dock and then drag documents onto the application to open them. Double-click a docked application to launch it or bring it to the front. In addition, the docks can contain files, folders, disks, and servers, and there is also an option to display the name of the active application in a special dock. This program by James Thomson (http://www.dragthing.com) costs $15.

Drop Slot

Drag and drop unsorted files onto the Drop Slot application icon and they are automatically stored in folders on your hard drive in the same way the System Folder automatically moves its items to the correct folder. Drop Slot stores files by type, prompting you for destinations and storing types it recognizes in folders you designate. This application by Rick Christianson costs $10.

Drop*PS

Drop*PS sends text files containing PostScript code to any PostScript printer, independently of installed printer drivers. This application by Bare Bones Software (http://www.barebones.com) is free.

Drop-Rename

Drop-Rename enables you to search for and rename files or folders with a variety of options, such as changing name cases and file extensions, changing specified search strings under certain conditions, and more. Multithreading lets it run easily in the background. You can also create "Renamelets," which are customized self-running applications for operations you perform regularly. This application by Chaotic Software (http://www.chaoticsoftware.com) costs $10.

DropStuff with Expander Enhancer

DropStuff with Expander Enhancer creates compressed StuffIt archives when you drag your files and folders onto the DropStuff icon. With Expander Enhancer installed, the StuffIt Expander program is capable of decompressing archived files in a wide variety of formats. DropStuff with Expander Enhancer by Aladdin Systems (http://www.aladdinsys.com) is included with Mac OS 8–8.5 in the Internet Utilities folder (inside the Internet folder on the startup disk) and has a shareware fee of $30.

Easy Errors

Easy Errors enables you to quickly access the meanings of particular errors reported by the Mac OS (or the Newton OS, if you happen to have a Newton device) by selecting the appropriate system and entering the error number. Easy Errors displays a result code and, in most cases, a more useful description. This application by Dave Ribinic is free.

EMMpathy

EMMpathy fixes PowerBook 520 and 540 Smart Battery memory-related errors and includes VST's Smart Battery Probe, an advanced smart-battery diagnostic. This application by Bill Steinberg and VST Technologies is free.

Fat Cursors

Fat Cursors installs slightly larger arrow and I-beam pointers and features a "find pointer" function. This is particularly handy for PowerBook users. This control panel by Robert Abatecola costs $10.

File Buddy

File Buddy enhances file management. You can obtain a wide set of file and folder information using extensive search criteria; find files containing specified resources and delete or modify these resources; modify batches of file names and extensions; create aliases; find and delete duplicates, unattached aliases, and old preferences files; rebuild the desktop; and more. This application by Laurence Harris costs $25.

File eXpress

Drop files on the File eXpress FXPackager's mailbox icon and you can send them to any other machine running File eXpress on your AppleTalk or TCP/IP network. The program places a FXInBox folder on your desktop for your incoming files. This application by Ruskin Group is free for noncommercial use.

FileLock

Big Al FileLock is a simple password-protection program that lets you place a password on any file. Users will then be forced to enter the correct password to open the file. This application by Al Staffieri, Jr. costs $10.

FileTyper

Drop files on FileTyper's icon to quickly change types, creators, attribute flags, and date stamps on files. It also supports processing batches of files, filtering, and directory searches. This application by Daniel Azuma (http://www.ugcs.caltech.edu/~dazuma/) costs $10.

FinderNote

FinderNote is a simple text editor whose documents are saved as clippings and can be read in the Finder (on the desktop) without needing to run any application. This application by Jae Ho Chang (http://www.xs4all.nl/~jaeho) is free.

Finder Options

Finder Options lets you selectively enable these hidden options in Mac OS 7.6–7.6.1: Control-drag to make aliases; add a Reveal Original item (⌘-R) to the File menu for finding an alias's original item; ⌘-Delete to move to the Trash; disable zoom rectangles; and disable translucent dragging. Most of these features are redundant with Mac OS 8–8.5. This control panel by Rolf Braun is free.

FinderPop

FinderPop extends the capabilities of Mac OS 8–8.5's contextual menus. You can access contextual menus simply by clicking and holding down the mouse button. FinderPop submenus let you peek into closed folders and disks; view all open the Finder windows or everything that's located on the desktop; and switch between currently running programs. You can also add aliases to a special FinderPop folder; these items then appear in the contextual menu (or in a submenu) for easy access. For example, you can select several files, Control-click one of the selected icons, and then choose an application from the FindPop menu to open the files with that application. This control panel by Turlough O'Connor (http://www.geocities.com/SiliconValley/Bay/2573/) is free.

The Finder View Settings

The Finder View Settings gives you the ability to apply folder-view settings globally to all folders in Mac OS 8–8.1, and to apply settings to individual folders selectively. You can determine which information to display in the folder window, whether or not to calculate folder sizes, what format to display dates in, and whether to show icons in lists as large, small, or miniature. Many of these functions are redundant with Mac OS 8.5. You can also accelerate or eliminate the Finder's zoom rectangles in Mac OS 8. This control panel by Alessandro Levi Montalcini (http://www.montalcini. com) costs $10.

Folder Icon Maker

Folder Icon Maker creates folders with custom icons when you drag an application or document onto the FIM application. A new folder will be created in the directory containing the file. FIM also supports PICT data as a source for custom folders and works with folder resource files. This application by Gregory Robbins is free.

Font Book

Font Book creates overviews of a font that can be printed and used as quick reference materials. There are a dozen ways to set up the sample pages, including an ASCII reference sheet, a layout that uses the font in standard type styles, several layouts showing the font in various sizes, one layout showing the font in a long piece of text, and several design layouts. This application by Matthias Kahlert (http://www.kagi.com/mkahlert/fb/default.html) costs $10.

!ForceQuit

!ForceQuit enhances the conventional Force Quit (Option-⌘-Escape) feature of the Mac OS. You can either totally enable or disable forced quits or disable forced quits only for selected applications. This extension by Daffy Software is free.

GifConverter

GifConverter does more than its name implies. It handles a variety of file formats, including TIFF, RIFF, PICT, JPEG, PNG, MacPaint, and Thunderscan. It reads and writes all those formats plus it can create startup screens and black-and-white EPS files. GifConverter provides image-editing tools that let you scale and rotate an image, change its resolution, change color palettes, and dither colors. GifConverter is AppleScript-compatible and comes with several batch-conversion scripts. This application by Kevin A. Mitchell (http://www.kamit.com/gifconverter/) costs $30.

GoMac

GoMac behaves like the Windows 95 task bar and includes a Program Bar that displays open applications and a Start menu that lists all installed applications, recently accessed servers, files and folders, other easy navigation tools, and a small pop-up calendar. This control panel by Proteron, L.L.C is free.

GrabAudio

GrabAudio lets you record any part of an audio CD quickly and easily using simple digital-audio marking features. This application by Theo Vosse requires an Apple CD300 CD player or better and the Apple CD software (which is included with the Mac OS). GrabAudio is free.

GraphicConverter

GraphicConverter converts an amazing number of graphics file formats found not only on Mac and Windows, but Amiga and Atari computers as well. GraphicConverter imports 100 different file formats and exports 40 different file formats. In addition, the program has tools and filters for editing pictures. This application by Thorsten Lemke (http://www.lemkesoft.de) costs $35.

GURU

GURU provides information concerning memory upgrades for every model of Mac OS computer ever made by Apple and other companies. GURU is updated regularly. It also includes memory information on all Apple LaserWriter printers. Memory information includes RAM, DRAM, VRAM, EDO, SDRAM, PSDRAM, Static RAM, and FRAM. This application from the NewerRAM division of Peripheral Enhancements Corp. (http://www.newerram.com) is free.

Helium

Helium enhances the Mac OS balloon-help feature, by enabling you to use key commands to make help balloons appear and disappear automatically or to toggle balloon help on and off, as well as setting a more legible font size for the help text. This control panel by Tiger Technologies (http://www.tigertech.com) costs $7.

HourWorld

HourWorld Lite displays a map of the world that indicates where the sun is currently shining and where it has set, and allows you to display five clocks set to the local time of cities around the world. The full version offers more clocks, the capability to print almanacs of sunrise and sunset times, phone call coordination and global positioning features, plus an editable database. The lite version of this application by Paul Software Engineering (http://www.hourworld.com/prod01.htm) costs $15 and the full version costs $29.95.

Icon Archiver

The Icon Archiver is a database utility that can quickly scan whole disks or folders for icons and icon archives and can create archives of compressed icons. It filters icons by size and color depth, provides a wide variety of icon views, removes duplicate icons, and sorts icons using multiple criteria. This application by Alessandro Levi Montalcini (http://www.montalcini.com) costs $25.

I Love Native!

I Love Native! enables you to check whether an application, control panel, system extension, shared library, or code resource file is written in PowerPC, 68K, or fat (both PowerPC and 68K) code. It allows you to create either a PowerPC-only or a 68K-only application from a fat application to reduce the application's file size. It also allows you to combine a PowerPC-only and a 68K-only application into a fat application (both 68K and PowerPC applications must be the same program). This application by Jerry Du is free.

The InformINIT

The InformINIT is a regularly updated guide for information on extensions and control panels, listing almost every system extension Apple has ever produced with information on what they do, who needs them, version numbers, RAM consumption, and tips and tricks. This application by Dan Frakes (http://cafe.AmbrosiaSW.com/DEF/InformINIT.html) costs $15.

IPNetRouter

IPNetRouter lets you share one dial-up Internet account among any number of computers on a local network (Ethernet, LocalTalk, or both). In addition to this feature, which is known as IP masquerading, IPNetRouter offers IP multihoming (using multiple IP interfaces simultaneously) and IP forwarding (routing IP traffic between network interfaces). This application from Sustainable Softworks (http://www.sustworks.com) requires Open Transport 1.1.1 or later, which is included with Mac OS 7.6–8.5, and costs $89.

John's RAM Disk Backup

John's RAM Disk Backup is a pair of utilities that allow you to save the contents of any disk named RAM Disk when you shut down the Mac and restore them when you restart. You place the Backup RAM Disk utility in the Shutdown Items folder. It copies the RAM Disk contents to a folder in the System Folder on shutdown. Restore RAM Disk goes in the Startup Items folder and copies items from the System Folder copy to your RAM disk. This application duo (search for it as RAM Disk Backup) by John C. Rethorst is free.

Jon's Commands

Jon's Commands is an AppleScript addition that provides a number of useful AppleScript commands. There are commands for deleting, renaming, or moving a file or folder; retrieving data from and posting data to the Clipboard; getting a list of keys that are currently being pressed; getting information about an alias; and more. This extension from Jon Pugh (http://www.seanet.com/~jonpugh/#Software/) is free.

Kaleidoscope

Kaleidoscope completely overhauls the Mac OS interface using plug-in Color Scheme files that are fairly simple to create using another program called "Kaleidoscope for Laymen." It includes an Aaron plug-in (described earlier in this chapter), a WindowShade widget, dynamic draggable windows, customizable Finder window backgrounds, and much more. This control panel by Greg Landweber (http://www.kaleidoscope.net/greg/) costs $20.

KeyQuencer Lite

KeyQuencer Lite is a powerful keyboard-shortcut utility with several dozen ready-to-play macros. One keystroke flips your monitor to a different color setting. Another lets you take a screen shot (a captured PICT file) of anything you rope off with the selection rectangle. Other KeyQuencer Lite macros do things such as type the date, move a window, adjust the speaker volume, or switch to the next open program. You must build every KeyQuencer Lite macro manually; however, the task is made simpler with built-in menu commands. This control panel from Binary Software (http://www.binarysoft.com/kqmac/kqmac.html) costs $30.

The Lightsaver

The Lightsaver changes the Mac's clock to adjust to daylight savings time on the appropriate date. (This capability is redundant with Mac OS 8.5.) It comes with predefined settings for the United States and the European Union, but users can also define their own rules and have The Lightsaver apply them instead. This control panel by Francesco Meschia costs $9.

MacErrors

MacErrors helps you decipher those mysterious Macintosh system errors. You can enter the error ID and press Return to display the error's result code and description, or move through the list of errors using the arrow keys. This application by Marty Wachter costs $10.

Mac Identifier

When the Mac OS is unable to provide model or icon information about the computer that it is running on, Mac Identifier provides the information from a special database of stored model names. This is useful for network administrators and users who need to share other's disks. This control panel by Maurice Volaski (http://www.fluxsoft.com) costs $5.

Mac OS Purge

Mac OS Purge optimizes the Mac OS memory very quickly. It's especially useful under tight memory conditions, such as when running with small amounts of RAM or when run between launching memory-intensive applications. It runs, purges, and returns to the Finder. This application by E. Kenji Takeuchi is free.

MacSlack

MacSlack lets you determine how much space is wasted on your hard drive due to "slack space" (the space left over when a file doesn't completely fill a cluster on the hard drive). It calculates how much of that space is reclaimable if you partition the drive, thereby reducing cluster size. MacSlack also calculates how much space is reclaimable if you reformat the entire drive using the Mac OS Extended format (also known as HFS+), which is available in Mac OS 8.1–8.5. This drag-and-drop application by Eric Bennett (http://biochem.bio.cornell.edu/emb22/software/macslack/) is free.

Memory Mapper

Memory Mapper creates a precise report of current memory use on your computer. It graphically displays how much memory each open application uses and where the applications are in relation to each other and to blocks of unused memory. Memory Mapper provides detailed information about the Mac OS memory use, breaking it into several items, including High Memory (video, sound, and disk cache), the Finder, system extensions that are actually programs open in the background, System Heap (fonts, icons, sounds, and other system resources), and Low Memory Globals (system parameters). This application from Jintek (http://www.street-logic.com/freeware.html#memory) is free.

Memory Minder

Memory Minder's interface lets you examine how much memory your open applications are actually using and lets you adjust the preferred memory size while an application is open (changes take effect the next time you launch the application). This type of management should enable you to keep more applications open simultaneously. This application by Andrew S. Downs costs $10.

Mt. Everything

The Mt. Everything enhanced hard disk management application is most beneficial for users with multiple drives. It displays the types, manufacturers, and partition maps of devices connected to your SCSI bus; mounts partitions and drives without the necessity of restarting; supplies its own driver software; and supports removable media. This control panel by Horst H. Pralow is yours to use for the cost of a postcard sent to the author as specified in the program's documentation.

MultiTimer Pro

MultiTimer Pro compiles autosaved data logs of the time you spend on your computer, including time spent in specific applications, online time, and other tasks. MultiTimer Pro lets you create special modules to represent each project, which ensures accurate records of your sessions. You can record multiple projects simultaneously using MultiTimer Pro, and you can paste log files with MultiTimer Pro module data into spreadsheets. This application by Karl Bunker (http://users. aol.com/karlbunker/) costs $15.

MyBattery

MyBattery shows the voltage levels for three different PowerBook batteries. The program also lets you enable and disable AppleTalk and turn your modem on and off. This application by Jeremy Kezer costs $10.

MyEyes

MyEyes draws a pair of eyes on the menu bar that constantly follow the pointer's movement. MyEyes helps PowerBook users who have trouble seeing the pointer find it more quickly. This extension by Federico Filipponi costs $10.

Neatnik

Neatnik sends Apple events to the Finder to manage window view options in Mac OS 8–8.1. You apply the settings that you want to the parent folder for position, size, and view options; Neatnik then applies those settings to folders nested within the parent folder. These functions are redundant with Mac OS 8.5. This application by Karl Bunker (http://users.aol.com/KarlBunker/Neatnik.html) costs $35.

NetCD

NetCD creates a controller window for playing audio CDs on the Mac. In addition, the program can download the title and track list for each of your audio CDs from the CDDB database on the Internet to your computer. Whenever you insert the same CD again, its track and title information appears in NetCD or in the AppleCD Audio Player or the audio CD control strip module that come with Mac OS 7.6–8.5. This application by Toby Rush (http://members.xoom.com/tobyrush/software/programs/netcd.html) is free.

Net-Print

Net-Print prints or saves text from the Internet or any application. You can combine text selections from multiple sources on a single page or in a single file. In addition, you can include source information such as URL, title, and date. This control panel by John Moe (http://www.macinsearch.com/users/johnmoe/) costs $10.

NetStickies

NetStickies adds AppleTalk network functionality to the Stickies application that comes with Mac OS 7.6–8.5. You can send and receive sticky notes from other users who have NetStickies installed, send text clippings from a text drag-and-drop, and send clipboard text. The target user receives the text as a sticky note that is immediately visible onscreen. This extension by Ron Duritsch (ftp://ftp.one.net/trilobyte) is free.

Newer Technology Gauge Series

The Gauge Series profiles and measures the performance of various hardware components in your computer, including Level-2 cache, CPU, RAM, SCSI devices, and PCI Slots. This set of applications from Newer Technologies, Inc. (http://www.newertech.com/software/newertools.html) is free.

Open with Process

Open with Process adds a command to the Finder's contextual menus in Mac OS 8–8.5. This command allows you to open a file in an application other than the one that created it. In the Finder, select the items you want to open, Control-click to display the contextual menu, and choose Open with Process. This command sends an Open Document event to any currently running application you choose. This contextual menu plug-in by George Temple (http://www.monmouth.com/~ttempel) costs $1.

OSA Menu

OSA Menu adds an icon to the menu bar that gives you access from within applications to scripts written with an OSA-compliant script editor. You can start and stop recording a script directly from the OSA Menu, run scripts, and access the script folders for the current application as well as for universal scripts. This extension by Leonard Rosenthol (http://www.netreach.net/~leonardr/) is free.

Path

Path adds a command to the Finder's contextual menus in Mac OS 8–8.5. This command enables you to copy the full path names of selected files and folders to the Clipboard. You choose whether to include the AppleTalk zone and server in the path name. This contextual menu plug-in by George Tempel (http://www.monmouth.com/~ttempel) costs $1.

PlugAlert

PlugAlert detects when the power adapter has become unplugged from the wall or your PowerBook and also indicates when the wall outlet isn't supplying electricity. This extension by Sean Hummel is free.

PopChar Pro

PopChar Pro simplifies "typing" of unusual characters. Pull down the PopChar menu and select the character you want; PopChar Pro automatically inserts it in the current document as if you had typed the proper key combination on the keyboard. This control panel from Uni Software Plus (http://www.unisoft.co.at/products/popchar.html) costs $39.

PopupCD

PopupCD provides a pop-up remote control for quick and easy access to your audio CDs through your CD-ROM drive. The remote control has all the functions normally used with conventional CD players, as well as a playing time indicator and a pop-up track menu. You can access all functions with configurable keyboard hot keys as well through the onscreen remote. If you're tired of launching or switching applications just to control your CDs, PopupCD can be an elegant and unobtrusive alternative. PopupCD can also record audio clips directly from CD to hard drive. This control panel by John Brochu (http://www.tiac.net/users/jbrochu/) requires the Apple CD-ROM software version 5.0.1 or later, which is included with the Mac OS. It costs $15.

PowerBar Pro

PowerBar Pro is an application launcher featuring handy Finder-action tiles, such as Move to Trash, Empty Trash, and Restart. Tiles can launch QuicKeys macros, Control Strip modules, or other PowerBar palettes. When you hold the mouse down on a folder tile, a pop-up menu shows everything inside. This application by Scott Johnson, Trilobyte Software (ftp://ftp.one.net/trilobyte), costs $25.

PowerMenu

PowerMenu adds contextual menu capabilities to Mac OS 7.6, and extends the capabilities of Mac OS 8's contextual menus. These menus make it easy to launch applications, open documents, and open files in programs other than the creating program. You can manipulate the Finder files from the contextual menu; for example, copying and moving files between folders without dragging and dropping, or copying multiple files from various locations and then pasting them all in one location with a single command. This control panel, extension, and CMM plug-in by Mark Aiken (http://www.kagi.com/authors/marka/pm.html) costs $15.

PowerSaver Tweak

PowerSaver Tweak provides more control over power-conservation settings than the standard Energy Saver and PowerBook control panels. It lets you configure the conservation settings for specific applications, screen dimming, drive spindown, system sleep, and CPU cycling for up to 50 applications (unregistered copies allow for up to 4 applications). For example, you can prevent your PowerBook from cycling while you are playing a particular game. Or use PowerSaver Tweak so that your hard drive never spins down while using Microsoft Word. This control panel by Jeremy Kezer (http://members.aol.com/jbkezer/shareware.html) requires a PowerBook or a computer with PCI expansion slots and costs $10.

Power Speed Mouse

Power Speed Mouse allows you to speed up your mouse. It's particularly beneficial if you're using a large monitor, because the mouse speeds up over long distances but otherwise moves normally. The application has options for speeding up the mouse and returning the mouse to normal. Speeds must be reset across restarts. This application by Alamo Computer is free.

Printdesk Lite

Printdesk Lite is print server software. It allows users on a network to access shared printers and image setters at any time; there is no need to wait for prior jobs to finish printing. This application from Nine Bits (http://www.ninebits.com) is free.

Program Switcher

Program Switcher allows you to switch between the running programs on your computer via a simple two-key keystroke (this function is redundant with Mac OS 8.5). You can also assign keystrokes to the Finder-related functions for rapid desktop shortcuts, such as showing and hiding applications. This control panel by Michael F. Kamprath (http://www.leonardo.net/kamprath/) costs $10.

QuickNailer

QuickNailer displays thumbnail previews of your graphics and movie files, and saves the previews in a catalog or in Web pages (HTML files). This utility can also display full-size images, present slide shows, and show file information. It uses QuickTime for file-format translation. This application by Stephen Baber (http://www.amug.org/~sbaber/) costs $18.

RamBunctious

RamBunctious creates RAM disks with a variety of user-configurable options. You can create RAM-only or disk-based volumes. For disk-based volumes, a write-through option saves data to a disk image file for added security. RamBunctious carries out the write-through operations at user-specified intervals or when the disk is put away; you can initiate a write-through at any time by clicking a button in the control window. This window also enables you to change a disk's settings at any time. RamBunctious can be controlled with AppleScript and comes with several example scripts. This application by Elden Wood and Bob Clark (http://www.kagi.com/authors/rambunctious/) costs $12.

ReminderPro

ReminderPro lets you schedule one-time or repeating reminders as you work on your computer. The package includes a Control Strip module for scheduling reminders instantly, and the ReminderPro system extension, which works continuously in the background to display reminders at the appropriate times as well as automating tasks like scheduled launching of applications, opening of documents, and automatically running AppleScripts at designated times. This extension by Manoj Patwardhan of Crystal Software, Inc. costs $18.

ResEdit

Apple's ResEdit enables you to edit system and application resources, such as icons, menus, and the text of alert messages. You can do many fun things with ResEdit but beware — only work on copies of the files that you are editing. This application by Apple Computer (http://swupdates.info.apple.com/cgi-bin/lister.pl?Apple.Support.Area/Apple.Software.Updates/US/Macintosh/Utilities) is free.

SCSI Probe

SCSI Probe identifies and mounts SCSI devices connected to your Mac. SCSI Probe displays device type, vendor, product, and version information for any device connected to the SCSI bus. An included startup extension lets you mount volumes without going through the control panel. This control panel by Robert Polic is free.

Sesame

Sesame prevents unauthorized access to your computer by requesting a password whenever the Sesame application is running. This application by Bernard Frangoulis costs $10.

ShrinkWrap

ShrinkWrap creates disk image files similar to Disk Copy (which was described earlier in this chapter) when you drag-and-drop floppy drive icons onto the ShrinkWrap icon. It also opens Disk Copy disk images and automatically compresses and decompresses archived image files on-the-fly with Aladdin's StuffIt Expander (described in "Obtaining Files from the Internet" in Chapter 20). ShrinkWrap 3.0, distributed by Aladdin Systems (408-761-6200, http://www.aladdinsys.com), costs $29.95.

Shutdown Delay

Shutdown Delay displays a dialog box at restart or shutdown time that allows you to complete the original command, return to the desktop, restart, shut down, or force quit and return to the Finder. This control panel by Alessandro Levi Montalcini (http://www.montalcini.com) costs $10.

Sleeper

Sleeper conserves energy when you're away from your computer and quiets your disk drive. After periods of inactivity, Sleeper will dim the screen on your desktop computer and spin down SCSI disk drives; at separate times if you prefer. Sleeper will also let your current screen saver work while handling the disk drives. This control panel by St. Clair Software (http://www.stclairsoft.com) costs $25.

Sloop

Sloop adds pointer focusing to the Mac OS: whatever window the pointer is over automatically moves to the front (acquires focus) — which is a navigational strategy that is popular in X Windows, which provides windows for the Unix OS. You can configure Sloop to operate exclusively in specific applications or as a general desktop feature. This extension from Quadratic Software (http://www. quadratic.com) costs $20.

Snitch

Snitch extends the capabilities of the Finder's Get Info window through a set of plug-ins, allowing you to see and change a variety of information about files and folders. Plug-in capabilities include letting you see and change creator and type codes, see preview information, preview the first 100 bytes of a file's data and resource forks, and update aliases. A batch info window allows you to edit several items at once. This control panel from Nifty Neato Software (http://www.niftyneato.com) costs $20.

SoftwareFPU

SoftwareFPU allows most applications expecting an FPU (floating-point unit) to work properly on a computer that does not have one, as is the case on some older Mac models, in particular those with 68LC040 processors). Because of a bug in the 68LC040 chip, this program may or may not work with individual applications running on Macs with this processor; more information is provided in the program's documentation. The author also makes PowerFPU, a commercial version with twice the performance on PowerPC computers. This control panel by John M. Neil requires a 68030 or 68LC040 processor without FPU or a PowerPC processor and costs $20.

SoundApp

SoundApp is a sound playback and conversion utility for the Mac OS. Use it as a sound-playing helper application with Web browsers. In addition to managing a collection of play lists, SoundApp can play or convert files dropped onto it in a variety of formats and sample rates. This application by Norman Franke III is free.

SoundMaster

SoundMaster makes your computer play sounds when you perform various tasks on your system such as inserting a disk, emptying the trash, shutting down, or performing keyboard functions such as tabbing, deleting, and scrolling (some of these functions are redundant with Mac OS 8.5). This control panel by Bruce Tomlin costs $15.

SpeedShare and SpeedShare Pro

SpeedShare and SpeedShare Pro allow you to share files on a remote Mac over the Internet even without a permanent Internet address. When you run the SpeedShare server software, you make all or some of the items on your Mac available by setting up a server name and password and connecting to the Internet. Users who have installed the SpeedShare Client software can now access the SpeedShare Server via QDEA's Rendezvous or through a direct TCP/IP address. (Rendezvous keeps track of the dynamic addresses of the Macs currently using SpeedShare on the Internet so that they can connect to each other.) Clients can browse, move, and copy files on connected SpeedShare servers. The Pro version is enhanced for professional environments and offers features such as very fast transfer of files over LANs and multiple simultaneous connections from many users. Both client applications from Qdea (http://www.qdea.com) are free; SpeedShare Server costs $49.95 and SpeedShare Pro Server costs $129.95.

StickyClick

StickyClick simulates the sticky menus feature of Mac OS 8–8.5 on computers that have Mac OS 7.6–7.6.1. This extension by Steve Zellers is free.

Super Comments

Super Comments permits comments to be viewed in Open dialog boxes and edited in Save dialog boxes. It can also save Get Info comments when you rebuild the desktop (this feature is redundant with Mac OS 8–8.5). This control panel by Maurice Volaski (http://www.fluxsoft.com) costs $10.

SuperTools

SuperTools is three applications that speed the launching, printing, and erasing of documents. SuperPrint is a dropbox desktop printer that prints a document on a currently selected printer when you drag and drop the document's icon onto SuperPrint. SuperLaunch lets you bundle a series of documents to create workbooks by dragging the collection on top of the SuperLaunch icon. SuperTrash permanently erases a document by writing zeroes on top of its data before deletion. This application by Pascal Pochet costs $25.

SwitchBack

SwitchBack synchronizes two folders on the same volume, on two different volumes, or on two different computers connected by a network so that copies of the most recent versions of files are found in both places. It works with all Mac OS computers and also backs up DOS disks. This application by Glendower Software Ltd. costs $30.

System Picker

System Picker lets you keep more than one valid System Folder on a single disk volume and choose the folder that will be the active System Folder on restart. It scans all volumes to create a list of usable System Folders that are accessible via a pop-up menu. System Picker 1.1 or later is required for Mac OS 8–8.5. This application by Kevin Aitken is free. Apple distributes System Picker as unsupported software on its FTP site at ftp://ftp.apple.com/devworld/utilites/.

TechTool

TechTool performs various simple diagnostic and repair operations, such as analyzing your system file for damage, cleaning the floppy drive, deleting and rebuilding the desktop, resetting PRAM, and displaying the date the computer was manufactured and the number of hours it has been used. This application from Micromat Computer Systems (http://www.micromat.com/micromat/software.html) is free.

Tex-Edit Plus

Tex-Edit Plus is a small, fast text editor that offers a number of word-processing features, including find and replace, change case, block formatting, customizable tabs, and line spacing. Tex-Edit is scriptable. You can access scripts from the menu bar. Scripts included with the program offer quick document modifications; for example, changing text to HTML, switching between smart and dumb quotes, and formatting for Mac e-mail messages that were created in Windows and vice versa. This application from Tom Bender, Trans-Tex Software (http://members.aol.com/tombb/), costs $10.

TimeSlice

The TimeSlice time-tracking program logs timed tasks you perform on your computer, including time spent in particular applications. You can use it to run multiple time sessions at once; search and sort time records; set time and money budgets; and start, stop, pause, resume, and restart time records. This application by Maui Software (http://www.mauisoftware.com) costs $49.

TitlePop

The TitlePop extension turns a document window's title into a pop-up menu that lists items for windows that belong to the current program and an item for background programs, which are shown in hierarchical menus below their respective program items. You can bring any window to the front by selecting it from the TitlePop menu. This extension by Jouko Pakkanen is free.

TomeViewer

TomeViewer lets you view the contents of tome files on a Mac OS installation disk without actually going through the installation process. You can also expand and extract items within a tome and get detailed information about the type, creator, full size, compressed size, percent saved, and version number of each item. You can also use TomeViewer to install items for which there is no separate installation routine. This unsupported application from Apple Computer (ftp://ftp.apple.com/devworld/Development_Kits/Installer_SDK_Cornucopia/Tools.sit.hqx) is free.

Trash It!

The Trash It! Control Strip module can empty the Trash without warnings about locked or busy files. It accepts drag-and-drop multiple file and folder deletions and can delete the desktop on mounted volumes and floppies. This control strip module by Ammon Skidmore, Skidperfect Software, requires the Extensions Strip, Control Strip, or Desktop Strip software. It is free.

TypeIt4Me

TypeIt4Me works inside any application that allows text-entry, letting you type small abbreviations for predefined strings like names, addresses, and difficult-to-type phrases. It's similar to the commercial program QuicKeys; however, instead of assigning key commands, you assign your own special abbreviations. This control panel by Ricardo Ettore costs $30.

UltraFind

UltraFind quickly searches any mounted media on your desktop or network, including remote volumes via modem using ARA, provides detailed information about items, copies or moves them across the network, performs backups, or deletes selected items. It can also extract information from damaged files. This application by UltraDesign Technology (http://www.ultradesign.com) costs $39.

Virtual

Virtual, an adaptation of Sun Microsystems' window manager, "olvwm," enables you to simulate more than one monitor on your desktop, drawing as many virtual screens as you like, as well as the windows of open applications inside them. You can create windows' representations in Virtual, place them in different virtual screens to organize them in workgroups, make some windows sticky, or assign whole applications to a particular virtual screen. This application by Pierre-Luc Paour (http://www.kagi.com/paour) costs $10.

Window Picker

Window Picker lets you find any open window in the Finder and bring it to the front using Mac OS 8–8.5's contextual menus. This contextual menu plug-in from Hi Resolution is free.

WrapScreen

WrapScreen implements a wraparound mouse pointer: instead of stopping at the right edge of the screen, for example, the pointer appears at the left edge. This control panel by Eric Arbourg is yours to use for the cost of a donation.

Yank

Yank uninstalls an application and files created by the application by moving them to the Trash. It also detects and moves outdated preferences folders, also moving them to the Trash. Yank does not automatically delete anything. This application by Maui Software (http://www.mauisoftware.com) costs $15.

Summary

In this chapter, you learned that shareware and freeware is available from many Internet sites, America Online, user groups, and Apple Computer. You can distribute copies of most shareware and freeware, but authors generally retain copyrights to their software. Shareware authors ask you to send payment for products you decide to keep, but freeware authors don't ask for payment. The utilities listed in this chapter are a representative sample of the shareware and freeware that's available to enhance the Mac OS.

✦   ✦   ✦

Discover Tips and Secrets

Scattered throughout the previous chapters of this book
are scores of tips and secrets for getting more out of Mac
OS 7.6–8.5. For your convenience, this chapter and the next
chapter contain a digest of the most useful tips and secrets
plus some tips that don't appear elsewhere in this book. In
this chapter, are tips for the desktop: icons, folders and
windows, the Trash, the Apple Menu, and fonts. Chapter 28
concentrates on system-related tips: dialog boxes, file sharing,
system utilities, control panels and extensions, applications,
and memory and system performance.

To use some of these tips, you need a copy of ResEdit, Apple's
no-cost resource editor. You can get ResEdit from Apple's
Software Updates library (http://www.apple.com/swupdates/),
online services such as America Online (keyword: filesearch),
and Macintosh user groups. You can also get a copy of ResEdit
from Macworld's Macdownload software library (http://
macdownload.com). For more sources of shareware and
freeware, see "Where to Get Utility Software" in Chapter 26.

Icons

This section contains tips for saving time and effort while
editing icon names, for making and using aliases on the
desktop, and for getting icons to look the way you want.

Spotting a name selected for editing

For a visual cue that you have selected the name of an icon on
a color or grayscale monitor, use the Appearance control panel
(Mac OS 8–8.5) or the Color control panel (Mac OS 7.6–7.6 1) to
set the text-highlight color to something other than black and

white. Then you'll know that a name highlighted in color (or gray) is ready for editing, whereas a name highlighted in black and white is not. Figure 27-1 is an example of a file name highlighted in gray and ready for editing and a file that has been merely selected and is therefore not editable.

Figure 27-1: A distinctive highlight color makes it easy to spot an icon whose name is ready for editing (left).

Edit, don't open

If you have trouble editing icon names without opening the item, remember to click the item *name,* not the icon. Keep the pointer over the item name and wait for the name to highlight automatically. (The lag time between your click and the name highlighting depends on the double-click speed you've chosen in the Mouse control panel: a slower double-click speed means a longer wait for the name to highlight.)

Undoing an accidental name change

If you rename an icon by mistake, choose Undo from the Edit menu (or press ⌘-Z) to restore the original name. Another way to restore the icon's original name is to press Backspace or Delete until the name is empty and then press Return or click outside the icon. (You cannot undo your changes to a name after you finish editing it, only while it is still selected for editing.)

Copy/paste icon names

While editing a name, you can use the Undo, Cut, Copy, Paste, and Select All commands in the Edit menu. You can also copy the entire name of any item by selecting its icon (or its whole name) and then choosing the Copy command from the Edit menu. This capability is handy when you're copying a disk and want to give the copy the same name as the original.

You can copy the name of a locked item — select the item and use the Copy command — but you can't change the name of a locked item. (Unlock a file by using the Get Info command (⌘-I), a folder by using the Sharing command, or a floppy disk by sliding its locking tab.)

The Mac OS doesn't limit you to copying one icon name at a time. If you select several items and then use the Copy command, the names of all the items are put on the Clipboard (up to 256 characters total in Mac OS 7.6–8.1, or an unlimited number in Mac OS 8.5), one name per line.

Removing the "alias" from alias names

When you use the Finder's Make Alias command, the resulting alias has the word *alias* at the end of its name. To remove the word *alias* from the end of an icon name, select the name for editing, press the right-arrow (→) or down-arrow (↓) key to move the insertion point to the end of the name, and press Delete five or six times. Pressing Delete five times leaves a blank space at the end of the alias name to distinguish it from the original name; pressing Delete six times removes this space.

Aliases where you want them

Making an alias of an item that's not on the same disk as the alias is a three-step process if you use Finder's Make Alias command: first, make the alias on the same disk as its original item; second, copy the alias to the destination disk; and third, delete the first alias. A better way is to make an alias exactly where you want it in the first place. In Mac OS 8–8.5, simply hold down ⌘-Option while dragging the original item to the disk where you want an alias. In Mac OS 7.6–7.6.1, get ready by adding Rolf Braun's freeware Finder Options to the Extensions Control Panels folder and restarting. You can then make an alias by pressing the Control key and dragging the original item where you want an alias of it.

Desktop aliases

Rather than drag frequently used programs, control panels, documents, and folders themselves onto the desktop, make aliases of those items and place the aliases on the desktop. You get quick access to the original items through their desktop aliases. Also, you can open several related items at the same time by opening aliases on the desktop, even if the original items happen to be in different folders or on different disks.

If your desktop becomes too cluttered with aliases, you can store related aliases together in a desktop folder and tuck the folder conveniently out of the way at the bottom of your screen. In Mac OS 8–8.5, you can open the folder and make it a pop-up window. Figure 27-2 shows aliases on the desktop and in a pop-up window.

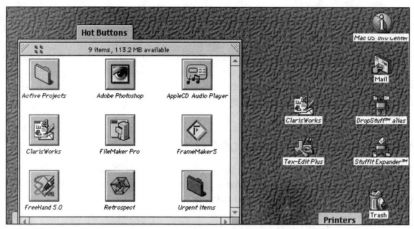

Figure 27-2: Keep frequently used items handy with aliases of them on the desktop or in pop-up windows.

STEP-BY-STEP

Permanently Removing *alias*

If you always remove the word *alias* from the end of new alias names, you may prefer never to have the word appended to file names at all. You can make a change with ResEdit so that Finder never appends *alias* to the names of new aliases. Follow these steps:

1. Make an alias of ResEdit and place it on the desktop.

2. Open the system folder and Option-drag Finder onto the desktop, which creates a duplicate the Finder. Drag this duplicate Finder onto the ResEdit icon to open it.*

   You see a window full of icons, each icon representing a different type of resource in the Finder.

3. Double-click the STR# resource type, opening a window that lists all the Finder's string-list resources by number.

4. Locate STR# resource number 8200 and double-click it to open it. (In Mac OS 7.6–7.6.1, open STR# resource number 20500.) The alias suffix is in string #1. This is the text that the Finder appends to the original file name to make up the alias name.

5. Change the string to one blank space rather than making it completely empty, so that the names of original files and their aliases will be different.

6. To finish, close all the ResEdit windows or simply quit ResEdit. Answer Yes when you are asked if you want to save your changes.

7. To see the results of your work, drag the original Finder into a folder outside the system folder, then drag the altered Finder into the System Folder and restart your computer.

*Always work on a copy of the original file when using ResEdit. You might think ResEdit keeps your changes only in the computer's memory until you save them to disk because the program asks whether you want to save changes before closing a file or quitting the program. But that alert is a cruel joke. As you make changes to a file, ResEdit actually updates the file on disk. If you get the alert and answer No, ResEdit reverses the changes and your file is safe. But if your computer crashes (does anyone have a computer that does not crash?), or ResEdit quits unexpectedly before you have the opportunity to reverse your ResEdit changes, you'll find the changes in place when you restart your computer and reopen the file with ResEdit. Be aware, and may the power of ResEdit be with you.

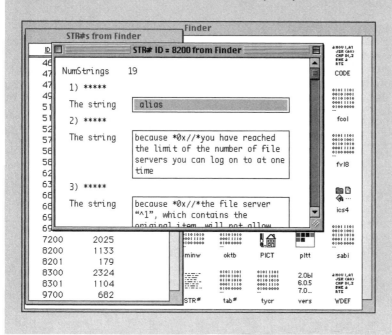

Express access to CD-ROMs

Cut through the drudgery of wading through folders on a CD-ROM by making aliases of items inside the CD-ROM folders. Because CD-ROMs are permanently locked, you must put the aliases on your hard disk (or a floppy disk). Opening an alias makes a beeline to the original item on the CD-ROM.

Cataloging items on floppy disks

You can use aliases to keep track of, and quickly open, items on floppy disks — even floppies that aren't inserted into your computer. Make aliases of the items on a floppy disk by selecting them and ⌘-Option-dragging them to your startup disk. (If you use the Make Alias command to make the aliases, you have to copy the aliases to the startup disk and then delete the aliases from the floppy disk.) When you need the item again, the Mac OS tells you the name of the disk to insert so that it can open the alias's original item. If you change your mind or can't find the needed disk, click the Cancel button. Figure 27-3 is an example of a disk insert message.

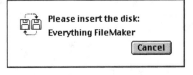

Figure 27-3: If you open an alias whose original item is on a disk that's not inserted, the Mac OS prompts you to insert the specific disk.

Making many aliases

You can make aliases for several items in the same window at the same time. First, select all the items. Then in Mac OS 8–8.5, you can ⌘-Option-drag the items within the same window, to a different window, or to the desktop. Alternatively, in any version of the Mac OS you can use the Make Alias command (⌘-M). An alias appears for every item that you selected. All the new aliases are selected automatically so that you can drag them to another place without having to manually select them as a group. If you accidentally deselect the items, you can easily group them together for reselecting by arranging or sorting the window by kind or date created.

Reverting to standard icons

You can revert to an item's standard icon after replacing the icon with custom graphics. Just select the item and use the Finder's Get Info command (⌘-I) to display the item's Info window. Select the icon in the Info window and a box appears around the icon to indicate that you have selected the icon. Choose Clear or Cut from the Edit menu or press the Delete key.

Fixing blank icons

Sometimes a file that you copy onto your disk ends up with a generic (blank) icon. You really don't want to rebuild your desktop files just to fix one icon (especially if you have a large disk). Instead, open the icon's Info window (⌘-I) and select the icon in the Info window. Now copy, paste, and cut the icon — in that order. If you are lucky, the correct icon shows its face.

Here's how it works: copying the icon makes it possible to paste; pasting the icon causes the Finder to internally mark the file as one that has a custom icon; and cutting the icon causes the Finder to unmark the file and restore its standard icon. You can't do the cutting step unless you have done the pasting step, and you can't do the pasting step unless you have done the copying step.

STEP-BY-STEP

Customizing Folder Icons

If you think you have too many boring, look-alike folders cluttering your desktop, you can enliven those folders by superimposing relevant application icons. Follow these steps:

1. Copy a folder icon from its Info window (which you display by choosing the Finder's Get Info command) and paste the icon into a color paint program.

2. Open the folder that contains the application whose icon you want to use, view the folder window by Small Icon and take a screen snapshot of the application icon. (To take the screen shot, press ⌘-Shift-4 and drag a selection rectangle around the icon.) Hold down the Control key while releasing the mouse button to copy the screen shot onto the Clipboard.

3. In the color paint program, paste the icon on top of the pasted folder icon.

4. Copy the composite icon from the paint program, paste it into the folder's Info window, and close the Info window.

When you select the custom icon in the paint program, you must take care to select a rectangular area no larger than 32 x 32 pixels (the maximum size of an icon). If you select a larger area, including lots of white space around your custom icon, the Finder shrinks the selection to 32 x 32 when you paste it into the folder's Info window, and your custom icon ends up shrunken. If you select an area smaller than 32 x 32, the Finder centers the selection in the folder's icon space, and the custom icon does not align horizontally with a plain folder icon (which is flush with the bottom of its icon space).

You can avoid this rigmarole by using the freeware utility Folder Icon Maker by Gregory Robbins. Just drag a great-looking application or document icon to Folder Icon Maker and presto — Folder Icon Maker creates a new folder with a small version of that icon superimposed on it.

The custom icons obscure any subsequent changes that you make to the folder's color (by changing its label) or to the folder's file-sharing status (with the Finder's Sharing command).

Pictureless icons

If your desktop gets so cluttered that you can hardly find the icon for an inserted floppy disk, you may wish that you could decrease the icon size to the bare minimum — nothing — leaving just the item name on your desktop. You can do this in Mac OS 7.6–8.1 by replacing icons with white space. This trick does not work in Mac OS 8.5.

First, in Mac OS 8–8.1, make sure the Icon Arrangement option of the View Options command (located in the Finder's View menu) for the desktop is set to None. In Mac OS 7.6–7.6.1, make sure the "Always snap to grid" option is turned off in the Views control panel.

Next, open an empty folder and take a picture of a small area of white space by pressing Control-⌘-Shift-4 and dragging a small selection in the folder window's white background. With your white space copied to the Clipboard, use the Finder's Get Info command (⌘-I) on each desktop item that you want to view by name, and paste the white space over the icon in each item's Info window. Pasting the white space leaves only the item's name visible. Four items without icons fit into the space previously occupied by two items with icons, as shown in Figure 27-4.

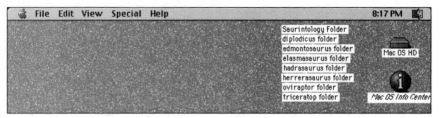

Figure 27-4: Items on the desktop take less space if you "white out" their icons.

Distinctive volumes

It's not unusual to have more than one hard disk icon on the desktop. This happens if you have more than one disk drive or you have partitioned a large hard drive into multiple volumes (see "Partitioning Hard Disks" in Chapter 6). While it's not hard to identify each disk volume by name, you find it easier to tell them apart if their icons look different. You can certainly make disk volumes distinctive by giving each a different custom icon. A subtler alternative that you may find every bit as effective is to make each volume icon a different color. To colorize a volume icon, select it and choose a colored label from the Labels submenu of the File menu (Mac OS 8–8.5) or from the Labels menu (Mac OS 7.6–7.6.1).

Bad disk icon

If you have problems with a custom disk icon — for instance, if your hard disk icon appears as a generic document icon — try the freeware utility Disk Rejuvenator from Aladdin Systems. This utility is also handy if you have a problem accessing your hard disk from standard Open dialog boxes. If you have problems with a custom folder icon, drag the folder's contents to a new folder and then drag the troublesome, now-empty folder to the Trash.

Desktop and Startup

This section covers tips for customizing your desktop, as well as the sights and sounds that you see and hear during and after startup.

Rebuilding the desktop

To rebuild the desktop of any disk whose icon normally appears on the desktop after startup, press ⌘-Option while starting your computer. For each disk in turn, the Finder asks whether you want the disk's desktop to be rebuilt. To rebuild the desktop of a floppy disk or another removable disk whose icon is not on the desktop, press ⌘-Option while inserting the disk. Figure 27-5 is an example of a rebuild confirmation dialog box.

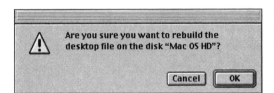

Are you sure you want to rebuild the desktop file on the disk "Mac OS HD"?

Cancel   OK

Figure 27-5: You must confirm rebuilding each disk's desktop individually.

Custom startup screen

Instead of the plain old "Welcome to Mac OS" startup screen, your computer can display a special picture. If your system folder contains a file named StartupScreen that contains a PICT resource with ID 0, the graphic image in that resource replaces the standard startup screen. You can use any of several programs to create such a startup screen for your computer, or you can create one using just ResEdit and the Scrapbook (see the sidebar "Creating Your Own Startup Screen"). Figure 27-6 is an example of a custom startup screen.

If you use a graphics program to create your custom startup screen, save the file as Startup Screen or StartupScreen as the file type (generally by choosing it from a pop-up menu in the Save As dialog box). In some graphics programs, you choose Resource File as the type of file to save and then specify a resource ID of 0 instead.

Startup movie

If you have QuickTime installed, you can have a movie play during startup by naming it Startup Movie and placing it in the System Folder. (To halt the startup movie, press ⌘-period(.) or any other key.)

Startup sounds

You can put a sound file in the Startup Items folder (inside the System Folder) and that file will play when you start your computer.

If your computer has a microphone, you can use the SimpleSound program or the Sound control panel to record a message for the next person who uses the computer, or just for fun. (To halt startup sounds, press ⌘-period(.).)

Figure 27-6: You can make a custom startup screen to replace the "Welcome to Mac OS" message.

Squelching the startup chime

Have you ever wanted to silence the computer's startup chime? On some Mac models, you can't quiet the startup chime by turning down the volume level in the Monitors & Sound control panel. If you want to eliminate the computer's startup chime, try one of these methods:

✦ Plug an earphone or headphones into the sound output port—you don't have to wear them.

✦ Plug in a $\frac{1}{8}$-inch flathead nylon screw that you have cut to $\frac{5}{8}$ inches in length and tied to a string for easy removal. The screw is less bulky and quieter than headphones, plus you can close the port cover if you use a PowerBook. *Be sure to use nylon and not metal so you don't create a short circuit!*

✦ On a desktop computer with speakers in the monitor, turn on the monitor a few seconds after starting the computer. (This happens automatically with the AppleVision 1710AV monitor because the monitor and its speakers don't turn on until the computer's ADB port comes to life, which happens after the startup chime.)

If your Mac does silence its startup chime when you turn down the sound volume all the way, you may wish to have the sound volume automatically turned up again after startup. You can accomplish this with a couple of very simple AppleScript applications, shown in Figure 27-7.

STEP-BY-STEP

Creating Your Own Startup Screen

If you don't have a graphics program that can save a startup screen but you do have ResEdit, you can use it and the Scrapbook to create your own startup screen file. Follow these steps:

1. Paste the image that you want to use as a startup screen into the Scrapbook.

2. Close the Scrapbook and use ResEdit to open a copy of the Scrapbook file (located in the System Folder).

   ResEdit displays a window containing icons that represent different types of resources in the Scrapbook file.

3. Open the Scrapbook file's PICT-resources icon and scroll through the images until you see the one that you want for your startup screen.

4. Copy the PICT resource that you want to use.

5. Create a new document in ResEdit and paste the PICT resource that you just copied. Save it with the name StartupScreen in the System Folder.

6. Open the PICT-resource icon in the new document, select the image that you just pasted, and choose Get Resource Info (⌘-I) from the Resource menu. In the Resource Info window that appears, change the ID number to 0.

7. Quit ResEdit and click the Yes button when you are asked whether you want to save the changes that you made.

8. Restart your computer to see the custom startup screen.

To create AppleScript applications that turn off the system sound during shutdown and turn it on during startup, follow these steps:

1. Open the Script Editor program (in the AppleScript folder inside the Apple Extras folder). In the script editing window that appears, type the following one-line AppleScript statement:

   ```
   set volume 0
   ```

2. Choose Save As from the File menu. In the Save As dialog box, open the Startup Items folder so that the script will be saved there. In addition, choose Application from the pop-up menu so that the script is saved as an application. Also turn on the Never Show Startup Screen option to prevent a dialog box from appearing every time the script application runs.

3. Change the AppleScript line to the following, replacing *x* with a number from 1 (lowest volume) to 7 (highest volume):

```
set volume x
```

4. Repeat step 2 to save this script as an application, except this time save it in the Startup Items folder.

5. Quit Script Editor.

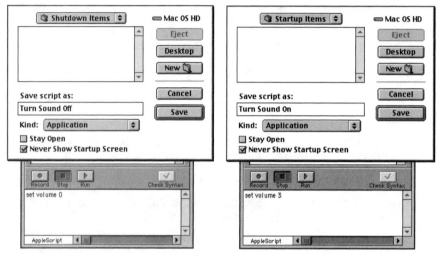

Figure 27-7: Two one-line AppleScript applications that turn system sound off (left) and on (right).

Bigger pointers

If your computer's pointer is just too small for you to comfortably keep track of in its travels around your desktop, try out Robert Abatecola's shareware Fat Cursors. Fat Cursors enlarges both the arrow pointer and the I-beam-shaped text pointer.

Several utilities just make it easier to locate a normal-sized pointer. Eyeballs installs a pair of eyes that watch your pointer from the menu bar. FindCursor, ZoomToCursor, and CursorBeacon each create a different type of visual commotion around the pointer when you press a specified key combination.

Startup booby trap

Don't hold down the Power-on key on the keyboard for more than a second or two when starting a Power Mac. Doing so sets the stage for the unexpected appearance of the mysterious programmer's window (a dialog box—containing only a greater-than symbol—that provides access to a limited set of program debugging tools known as the Mini Debugger). This baffling window appears sometime later, seemingly unbidden and definitely unwanted, when you press the ⌘ key. (You can make the programmer's window appear at will by holding down the ⌘ key and pressing the Power-on key on the keyboard.)

If the programmer's window appears on your screen, you can usually resume work without restarting by typing the letter G (short for Go) and pressing Return. If you type anything else and press Return, you may have to restart, losing all unsaved work.

If you hold down the Power-on key too long when starting up and later press Control-⌘, the computer restarts as if you switched the power off and on. In this case, you have inadvertently invoked the emergency restart sequence, which normally involves holding down Control-⌘ and pressing the Power-on key. *Warning: Don't use this technique as a shortcut for the Restart command.* Use it only in lieu of restarting with the power switch — for example, if your computer crashes.

Better file-sharing startup

Although you can have the Mac OS automatically connect to shared folders and disks at startup, doing so can really slow network performance (especially if everyone on the network does it). To reduce network traffic while keeping shared folders and disks conveniently accessible, use aliases to connect to them whenever you need them. To set up the aliases, use the Network Browser (Mac OS 8.5) or the Chooser (any Mac OS version) to connect to the shared folders and disks. Then select the shared folders and disks and make aliases. Put copies of the aliases on the desktop, in the Apple Menu Items folder, and anywhere else you want quick access to the shared items.

When you open the alias of a shared folder or disk, or drag something to the alias, your computer automatically asks you for a password and then connects to the shared folder or disk. Similarly, you can make aliases of items inside the shared folders and disks and use those aliases to simplify accessing the original items over the network.

Unfortunately, aliases of shared items do not always work correctly when the original items are on file servers that use the Windows NT Services for Macintosh.

Thawing a frozen program

Applications sometimes freeze and don't respond to ordinary controls such as Cancel buttons or pressing ⌘-period(.). When this happens use the Force Quit command: press ⌘-Option-Esc. This combination brings up a dialog box with a Force Quit button and a Cancel button. Clicking Cancel (not Force Quit) sometimes seems to act like a whiff of ammonia for a program that has passed out. It doesn't often work, but when it does it beats the alternatives. Be sure to save your work and restart the computer right away after reviving a frozen program.

Custom System Beeps

You can create your own custom system alert sounds on your computer from any audio CD. Follow these steps:

1. Using the AppleCD Audio Player, play the audio CD from which you want to make the alert sound and note the track and time where the passage you want to record starts. Pause the CD a few seconds before the start of the passage.

2. Open the Monitors & Sound control panel and click the Sound button. Set the volume control to a comfortable level. If your Monitors & Sound control panel has a Sound Monitoring Source option, set it to CD. If your Monitors & Sound control panel has a Sound Input option, set it to Internal CD. If your Monitors & Sound control panel has a Listen or Playthrough option, turn it on. Then switch to the Alert view by pressing the Alert button.

3. Switch to the Audio Player and click or press the Play button (or the spacebar). Immediately switch to the Monitors & Sound control panel and click the Add button, then the Record button (the timing can be tricky). Click the Stop button to finish your new alert sound — a second or two at most is plenty. The figure below shows this step in progress.

4. Name and save your new alert sound.

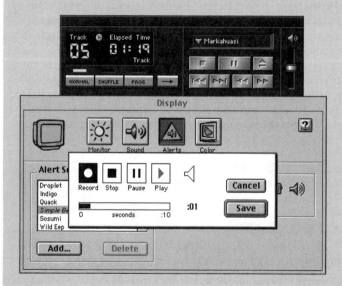

If you want more control over recording short segments from an audio CD, try Theo Vosse's freeware utility GrabAudio (described in Chapter 26).

First or last in a hurry

In most folder and disk windows, you can highlight the item that comes first alphabetically by pressing any number key or the spacebar. In most cases, you can highlight the item that comes last alphabetically by pressing the Option key along with any number key.

These tricks (which stem from the capability to select an item by typing the first part of its name) work fine unless you have many item names that come after a bullet (•), including names beginning with most accented capital letters, most symbols you type with the Option and Shift keys, and some symbols you type with the Option key alone.

If nothing is selected in the active Finder window (or on the desktop, if no window has racing stripes to indicate it is the active one), you can highlight the first or last item by pressing Tab or Shift-Tab. With an item highlighted, pressing Tab or Shift-Tab highlights the item that follows or precedes it alphabetically, and pressing an arrow key highlights the closest item on the desktop in the direction of the arrow.

Startup messages

Do you like to have reminders at startup, but don't want to use Stickies? Create a clipping file of your notes and place an alias of it in the Startup Items folder. Rename it to be alphabetically last, so it opens after other startup items. At startup, the Finder does not have to launch an application to display the note, which you can easily dismiss with ⌘-W. If you keep the clipping on your desktop, you can view it anytime you want within seconds.

To edit a clipping file directly (without dragging it to the Note Pad or some other application), get the freeware FinderNote by Jae Ho Chang, eMusicas Software (described in Chapter 26).

Futuristic Finder

Want to glimpse the future, when Web browsers may usurp the Finder's role? If you drag a folder into a browser window of Netscape Navigator, it lists the folder contents. In Microsoft Internet Explorer, type *file://localhost/* to see a list of disks on your desktop, and click a disk name to see its contents. Files and nested folders become clickable links, and if you click an HTML file (a Web page), a text file, a JPEG graphic file, or another file format that the browser can handle, it displays the file's contents. You can even save the listing in the browser window as a file. Figure 27-8 is an example of a futuristic Finder.

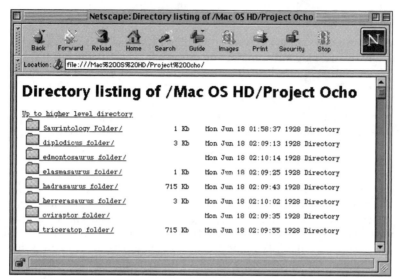

Figure 27-8: Use a Web browser to peruse the contents of your folders and disks.

You can also view files for which you have configured the browser to use a plug-in or a helper application. For instance, you can view a QuickTime movie by clicking its file name in the browser window if you have configured the browser application to use the QuickTime plug-in or the MoviePlayer application. It's a perfect way to catalog and browse clip art.

Folders and Windows

The tips in this section involve customizing and the manipulating the Finder windows and folders.

Locking folders

Everyone knows how to lock a file with the Finder's Get Info command, but how do you lock a folder? You can do it with one of the options normally used for setting access privileges of a shared folder. Just select the folder that you want to lock and choose Sharing from the Get Info submenu of the File menu (Mac OS 8.5) or from the File menu (Mac OS 7.6–8.1) to bring up the folder's file-sharing privileges window. In this window, check the box labeled "Can't move, rename, or delete this item." For this trick to work, file sharing must be turned on in the File Sharing or Sharing Setup control panel, whichever your computer has. (You don't have to actually share the folder or change any other sharing options.)

Special folder replacement

Should you happen to discard one of the special folders inside the System Folder, you can make a replacement by using the Finder's New Folder command (File menu). After creating a new folder, change its name to that of the special folder you want: Apple Menu Items, Control Panels, Extensions, Fonts, Preferences, Startup Items, and so forth. Close the System Folder, wait a few seconds and reopen it, and its icon gets the distinctive appearance of the special folder that you're creating.

Closing all but one window

Here's a quick way to close all the Finder windows except one in Mac OS 8.5. Drag the window you want kept open to the bottom of the screen to make it a pop-up window. Next, close all remaining open windows by Option-clicking the close box of any open window or by pressing ⌘-Option-W. Finally, drag the pop-up window back to the middle of the screen to make it a regular window once more.

Special folder mistakes

The Finder sometimes makes mistakes when it puts items in the System Folder's special folder for you. The Finder may put some items in the correct places and incorrectly leave others in the System Folder itself. For example, it may put font files and font suitcases in the Fonts folder but leave a folder containing fonts in the System Folder. To correct this problem, you must open the folder containing fonts and drag the fonts to the System Folder icon or to the Fonts folder.

Abridged system folder

Does finding the Apple Menu Items folder, Startup Items folder, or some other item in your System Folder take too long? Make aliases for the System Folder items that you access often — including an alias of the System Folder itself — and consolidate the aliases in a new folder. You can open and find an item in that folder faster than you can in the System Folder.

To make the new folder look like a System Folder, copy the icon from the System Folder's Info window and paste it into the new folder's Info window.

STEP-BY-STEP

Labeling System Clutter

Installer programs simplify the process of updating or installing software, but too many of these programs rudely scatter files all over the System Folder without so much as a by-your-ieave. Some installers even commit the unforgivable offense of overwriting your existing control panels and extensions with older versions. Although you may be able to limit this subterranean mischief by doing a custom installation, there's an easy method for keeping tabs on the changes. Follow these steps:

1. Before running an installer program, label every item that you want to keep track of in the System Folder. In Mac OS 8–8.5, use the Label command in the Finder's File menu, as shown in the figure below. In Mac OS 7.6–7.6.1, use the Label menu. After labeling the items, restart your computer.

   Labeling the contents of your System Folder after a clean installation of the Mac OS starts you on the right foot when it comes to resolving conflicts and crashes. Use the Preferences command (Mac OS 8–8.5) or the Labels control panel (Mac OS 7.6–7.6.1) to rename one of the labels as "Mac OS."

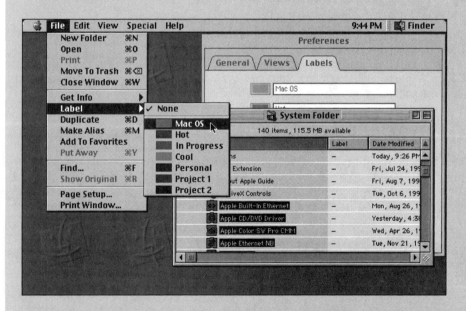

2. Back up your hard disk and run the installer. If the installer forces you to restart the computer but you don't want new extensions loaded until you see what they are, disable extensions (by holding down the Shift key during the restart).

3. To locate the new items, select the System Folder and choose Find from the Finder's File menu. This displays the Find File section of the Sherlock program in Mac OS 8.5 or the Find File program in Mac OS 7.6–8.1. Set the search criteria to find any item in

the Finder selection whose label is *none.* When the list of found items appears, you can select all, copy it, and paste the list into the Scrapbook or any text document for later reference. You can also select any number of found items quickly and change the label using the Open Enclosing Folder command (⌘-E).

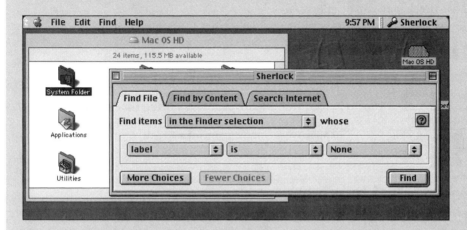

At best, labeling system files can help you reduce System Folder clutter and save RAM and hard disk space. At the very least, you know exactly which files the installer added. All else being equal, knowledge is always better than ignorance.

Replicating custom view settings

In Mac OS 8–8.1 (but not in Mac OS 8.5), the Finder's View menu affects only the active folder or disk window (or the desktop if no window is active). There are two ways to apply the View settings to any number of folder windows. One way doesn't require any additional software. To begin, create a new folder, open it, and use the View menu to set its view as you wish. Then duplicate the empty folder (⌘-D or Option-drag) on the same disk as an older folder whose view options you want to change, and drag the old folder's entire contents (⌘-A to select all) to the duplicate empty folder. Finally, copy the name from the old, now empty folder, trash the old folder, and paste the name on the replacement folder. Repeat with a new duplicate of the empty folder for each old folder that you want to have the same view settings. This procedure is still a lot of work, but less work than applying multiple View commands to each old folder.

A second approach is to use the Finder View Settings shareware by Alessandro Levi Montalcini. You can use it to override all folder-specific view settings in Mac OS 8–8.1 or to change the view settings for a batch of folders.

Removing items from the System Folder

Be sure to put items that you drag from the System Folder's special folders in the Trash, on the desktop, or in an ordinary folder. If you merely drag items from the Control Panels folder or Extensions folder to the main level of the System Folder, those items may still be effective.

Easy startup items

If you want an item to open at startup time, put an alias of it in the Startup Items folder. Don't put original items there because returning them to their original locations when you no longer want them opened at startup time can be a drag.

When you finish using an alias, you can drag it to the Trash, or in Mac OS 8–8.5, use the Finder's Move to Trash File command (⌘-Delete).

Seeing desktop items

If the windows of open programs obscure desktop icons, you can hide those windows by choosing Hide Others from the Application menu while the Finder is active. If the Finder windows cover desktop icons, you can close all the windows at the same time by pressing Option while clicking the close box of any the Finder window. With Mac OS 8–8.5, you can collapse all of the active application's windows by Option-clicking the active window's collapse box.

Shrunken tabs

Is the bottom of your screen becoming crowded with pop-up window tabs? Shrink the size of the tabs. Grab a tab you'd like to shrink and drag it up until its pop-up window becomes a regular window. Now position some remaining tabs about ½ to ¾ inches apart. Now drag the window back down to the bottom of your screen, between the two close-set tabs until you see it change back to a tab. The tab will keep its new smaller size even if you later drag it to a new position.

Drag to scroll

You can scroll a folder or disk window without using the scroll bars. In Mac OS 8.5, press the ⌘ key and start dragging inside a folder or disk window. The pointer changes to look like a gloved hand and the window contents scroll as you ⌘-drag.

Alternatively, in any Mac OS version you can simply place the mouse pointer in the window and drag toward the area that you want to view. When you drag the pointer up, down, left, or right past the window's active area scrolling begins. Dragging past a window corner scrolls diagonally. To scroll slowly, drag just to the window's edge (and continue holding down the mouse button). Increase scrolling speed by dragging beyond the window's edge.

Manipulating background windows

Sometimes you need to get at something in a background window that's covered by a window in front, but you don't want to bring the background window forward. For instance, you might want to drag some carefully selected icons from the front-most Finder window to a folder in a background window. If you can see any part of the background window, you can move it without bringing it to the front by ⌘-dragging the background title bar or window frame. If you're using Mac OS 7.6–7.6.1, you can only drag a window by its title bar (not by its frame).

Also, you can collapse a window in the background without bringing it to the front by ⌘-double-clicking it. (These tricks only work with background windows that belong to the active application.)

When windows open unbidden

Many CD-ROMs are set up to open windows automatically when you insert them. Some of these windows are full of custom icons and can take an inordinately long time to display. To keep windows from opening, simply hold down the Option key while inserting the CD. The same trick works for other types of removable disks.

Expanding multiple folders

You can use keyboard commands to see the contents of multiple folders in a window that's set to list view. Select the folders (press ⌘-A to select all) and press ⌘-right arrow(→) to expand the selected folders and see their contents. To also expand all folders contained in the selected folders, press ⌘-Option-right arrow(→). Pressing ⌘-left arrow(←) collapses all selected folders, and pressing ⌘-Option-left arrow(←) collapses all selected folders and all folders in them.

Finding empty folders

You can force empty folders to the bottom of a window. With Mac OS 8–8.5, just turn on the Calculate Folder Sizes options with the View Options command in the View menu, and then choose the "by Size" item from the Sort List or Arrange submenu of the View menu. With Mac OS 7.6–7.6.1, use the Views control panel and the Finder's View menu.

If you want to find all the empty folders on your disk, use the Sherlock program (Mac OS 8.5) or the Find File program (Mac OS 7.6–8.1). Set it to find items whose folder attribute is empty. This capability to search for folders that are or are not locked, shared, or empty is not very well known but can be extremely useful. After finding all shared folders, you can select some or all of the found folders and use the Sharing command in the Sherlock program or the Find File program to change the access privileges of all the selected folders at once. Figure 27-9 shows the Find File section of the Sherlock program set to find empty folders; the Find File program looks very similar.

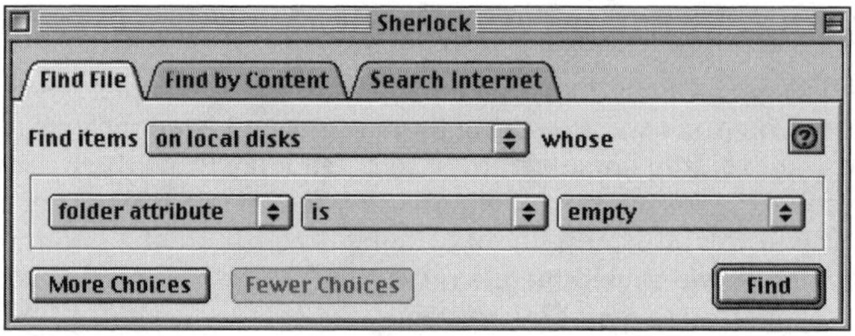

Figure 27-9: To find empty folders, set up a Find File search as shown here.

STEP BY STEP

Copy Fitting

When you copy batches of files from your hard disk to floppies or other removable disks, you must do some arithmetic beforehand so that the Finder won't tell you that there's not enough room on the disk. To have the Finder help you figure out how many files will fit on a floppy or a removable disk, follow these steps:

1. Create a new folder on the hard disk.

   The new folder must be in a window, not directly on the desktop.

2. Use the Finder's Get Info command (⌘-I) to bring up the folder's Info window.

3. Begin dragging files to be copied into the folder.

   As you drag, the Finder updates the folder's size in its Info window.

4. When the size approaches 1.4MB for a high-density floppy, 800K for a double-sided floppy, or 94MB for a Zip disk, stop dragging files into the folder; the disk will be nearly full.

If the Trash is empty, you can collect items in it instead of a specially created folder. This method has two advantages: You can quickly return all items to their original places by choosing the Put Away command from the File menu (⌘-Y), and you don't have to wait for the Finder to make copies of items that come from several disks. (The Finder doesn't copy items to the Trash, but it must copy items that you drag from one disk to a folder on another disk.) The Get Info command reports the size of the Trash only to the nearest K; however, it gives you the exact number of bytes in a folder.

If you have a large hard disk, you may notice that there is some space left over on the floppy disk after you copy the files there. This is because the smallest possible file takes less space on a floppy disk than on a hard disk unless the disk was initialized with the Mac OS Extended format in Mac OS 8.1–8.5. With the Mac OS standard format, the difference between a file's size on a floppy and a hard disk increases as the capacity of the hard disk increases. For example, on a 2GB hard disk each file uses a minimum of 32K and your average error per file copied will be 16K. This can add up pretty quickly. An alternative method that avoids this problem is to use the ShrinkWrap program (described in Chapter 26) to create an unlocked 1400K disk image, mount that on the desktop, and then copy stuff to it. When it's full, you can copy from it to a floppy. The extra copying to and from the disk image doesn't take very long because ShrinkWrap keeps the disk image contents on the hard disk (or in RAM, which is even faster).

The Trash

This section's tips are all about throwing stuff away and retrieving it from the Trash if you change your mind.

Stop all Trash warnings

The next time you empty the Trash you can skip the standard Trash warning (for example, "The Trash contains 104 items, which use 3.9MB of disk space. Are you sure you want to remove these items permanently?"). First select the Trash icon, and then choose the Get Info command (⌘-I). In the Trash Info dialog box that appears, turn off the "Warn before emptying" option — you'll never see the Trash warning again. Figure 27-10 shows the Trash Info dialog box with the warning option turned off.

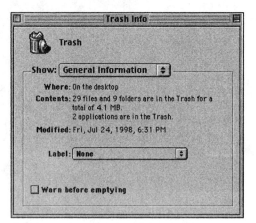

Figure 27-10: Use the Get Info command to disable the warning that appears when you empty the Trash.

Discarding locked items

When you use the Empty Trash command, the Finder normally doesn't discard locked items that you dragged to the Trash. Instead of unlocking each locked item with the Finder's Get Info command (⌘-I), you can simply press Option while choosing Empty Trash from the Special menu.

Retrieving trash

To put items that are currently in the Trash back where they came from, open the Trash, select the items, and choose Put Away (⌘-Y) from the Finder's File menu. The Finder returns each selected item to its previous folder, although not necessarily to the same place in the folder window.

Rescuing items

Sometimes, the Trash contains a folder named Rescued Items. This folder usually contains formerly invisible temporary files that were found when you started your computer. The Rescued Items folder may appear after a system crash, and you may be able to recreate your work up to the time of the system crash from the contents of the Rescued Items folder.

Apple Menu

Use the tips in this section to get more organized with the Apple menu.

Apple-menu organization

After you add more than a few items to the Apple menu, it becomes a mess. You can group different types of items by prefixing different numbers of blank spaces to their names — the more blank spaces, the higher on the Apple menu.

Prefixing a name with a hyphen or exclamation point makes the name appear below names that are prefixed with spaces and above names that have no prefixes. To make items appear at the bottom of the Apple menu, prefix them with a ◊ (Option-Shift-V) or • (Option-8). Figure 27-11 shows how these prefixes affect the order of items.

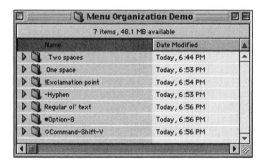

Figure 27-11: Use special keyboard characters and extra spaces to arrange items in a list to your liking.

If you have a hard time remembering what all the special symbol keyboard commands are, use the Key Caps utility located under the Apple menu, or try Günther Blaschek's excellent shareware program PopChar Pro, which automatically pops up a list of all letters, numbers, and symbols available in the current font when you move the pointer to a predesignated hot spot.

Fast Apple-menu changes

To add or remove Apple-menu items quickly, list the Apple Menu Items folder in the Apple menu. How? Make an alias of the Apple Menu Items folder and put the alias in that folder.

Too-full Apple menu

If your Apple menu contains so many items that you must scroll to see them all, consider organizing them in folders within the Apple Menu Items folder. The contents of each folder appear in hierarchical submenus if the Submenus option is turned on in the Apple Menu Options control panel. Figure 27-12 is an example of Apple-menu subfolders.

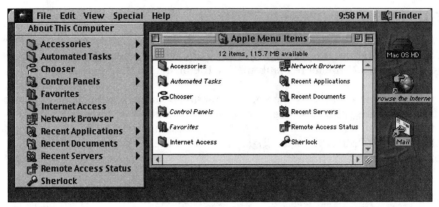

Figure 27-12: Keep your Apple menu short by putting items in folders inside the Apple Menu Items folder.

Universal Show Clipboard

Some application programs lack a Show Clipboard command; others that do have such a command use a private Clipboard whose contents may look different when pasted into another program. Put a Show Clipboard command in your Apple menu and then use the command to review the standard Clipboard contents from any application program.

First, make an alias of the Clipboard file, which is in the System Folder. Then place the alias in the Apple Menu Items folder and rename the alias Show Clipboard. Now choose Show Clipboard from the Apple menu; your computer switches to the Finder and opens the Clipboard.

Invisible file aliases

Do you crave the convenience of accessing items stored in the invisible Desktop Folder from the Apple Menu? Because the Desktop Folder is invisible, alias-creating utilities are of no help.

The trick is to access your computer via file sharing. When you access your computer from another machine via file sharing, the Desktop Folder becomes visible at the root level of your hard disk. Create an alias of the Desktop Folder (be sure to lock that Desktop Folder alias in its Info window to prevent it from becoming invisible) and transfer the alias to your computer. If you're using Mac OS 7.6–7.6.1, don't try to find the original item of a Desktop Folder alias by clicking the Find Original button in the alias's Info window unless you want to crash your system. Using the Show Original command in Mac OS 8–8.5 does not seem to cause a crash.

If your computer isn't on a network, borrow a computer and temporarily network it to your computer by connecting the two computer's printer ports with LocalTalk connectors or a serial printer cable. Alternatively, you can buy a disk utility such as File Buddy (described in Chapter 26) to make an alias of the invisible Desktop Folder.

STEP-BY-STEP

The non-ABCs Approach to Arranging Menu Items

Forcibly reordering items in the Apple menu by placing spaces or special symbols at the beginning of the items' names has side effects that you may not like. The spaces or symbols visibly alter the names and conspicuously shift the names to the right. To invisibly force the order you want, follow these steps:

1. Open the Note Pad or a new document in SimpleText or a word processor.

2. Press Return to create a blank line, select the blank line, and copy it to the Clipboard.

3. Switch to the Finder.

4. In the Apple Menu Items folder, select the name of the item that you want to appear at the top of the Apple menu.

5. Press the up-arrow (↑) key to move the insertion point to the beginning of the selected name and then paste.

6. The entire name goes blank, but don't fret—just press Return or click outside the name, and the name springs back into view.

   The renamed item jumps to the top of the window if you're viewing by list. To increase an item's alphabetic buoyancy, paste the blank line two or more times at the beginning of the item's name.

Some programs don't work properly with documents or folders whose names contain blank lines. In particular, you may be unable to print PageMaker or QuarkXPress documents in which you have placed a PostScript graphics file whose name begins with a blank line. If you have trouble after pasting a blank line into the name of a file or folder, remove the item from the Apple Menu Items folder, replace it with an alias, and then try this naming trick on the alias.

STEP-BY-STEP

Hierarchical Information Manager

You can turn your Apple menu into a contact database. By treating folder names as single-line entries in a database, you can easily create an elegant hierarchical database of often-used addresses, phone numbers, client contacts, and other information that you are tired of fumbling for on your crowded desktop or hard disk.

You can access the data instantly from the Apple menu and its submenus, and view the data by traversing the menu structure without actually choosing any menu item. (When you finish viewing the data, just drag the mouse pointer away from the menus and release the mouse.) For a persistent display, choose the menu item whose submenu contains the data that you want to see; the Finder opens the folder that contains the data.

Adding, deleting, and modifying data is a snap. Follow these steps:

1. Choose the menu item whose submenu you want to change and open the folder in which you need to make changes.

2. To add a line of data, use the Finder's New Folder command (⌘-N) and type the data as the new folder's name (up to 31 characters).

3. To change data, edit the corresponding folder names.

4. To remove a line of data, drag corresponding folders to the Trash.

5. To add a submenu, open a folder and add folders to it.

Because items appear alphabetically by name in the submenus, you may have to put extra spaces or other special characters at the beginning of folder names to arrange the names in the order you want. (You usually have to do this with a multiple-line address, for example.)

Another neat trick: Use aliases to duplicate data that you want to appear in several places in the database. After making an alias of the folder that you want to clone, simply drag the alias to the folder that represents the other location in the database where you want the information to appear. Cloned parts of your hierarchical database stay up-to-date because aliases don't contain any duplicate data that can get out of sync; the aliases simply point to the folders that contain the actual data.

No matter how large your database of folders becomes, the Finder always calculates its size on disk as zero! Yes, this is too good to be true. In fact, your data, consisting only of nested named folders, is kept in the startup disk's invisible directory file, which contains information about the hierarchical organization of fields and folders on that disk. The Finder reports only the sizes of aliases and other actual files that you may have in your hierarchical folders.

Keeping contact information in a hierarchical Apple menu has two advantages over using contact-database software such as Now Contact: You can always locate your contacts without opening (or keeping open) another program, and you can find any contact quickly without typing or even remembering a name. Managing hundreds of contacts is easier with contact-database software, though.

Apple menu options

If you use the Apple Menu Options control panel to list recently used documents, applications, and servers but don't necessarily want all three submenus active, set the number to zero in the Apple Menu Options control panel for those submenus that you don't want to activate. The items with a zero value disappear from the Apple menu.

Fonts

This section has tips for working with and modifying the System Folder's Fonts folder. When making changes to the Fonts folder, remember that any fonts that you add generally aren't available to open programs until you have quit the open programs and reopened them. Moreover, you must quit *all* open programs before removing fonts from the Fonts folder.

Duplicating fonts

Because you can't rename individual fixed-size or TrueType fonts with the Finder, you can't duplicate them in the same folder (you can't have two items with the same name in the same folder). However, you can rename or duplicate PostScript fonts and font suitcases.

To duplicate a fixed-size or TrueType font, press Option and drag the font to another folder or to the desktop. (Dragging to another disk automatically makes a copy of the font on the target disk.)

You can create a new, empty font suitcase file by duplicating an existing font suitcase file, opening the duplicate, and dragging its contents to the Trash. Figure 27-13 shows a duplicated font suitcase.

Deleting a damaged font

If you somehow manage to damage a font suitcase, you may not be able to delete it simply by opening the Fonts folder and dragging the suitcase to the Trash. Try dragging the Fonts folder from the System Folder to the desktop first. Then open the Fonts folder and drag the damaged suitcase to the Trash. Empty the Trash and put the Fonts folder back in your System Folder. If you can't drag the damaged suitcase to the Trash, try this: With your original Fonts folder still sitting on the desktop, create a new folder named Fonts inside the System Folder. Drag everything except the damaged suitcase from the old Fonts folder (on the desktop) to the new Fonts folder. Restart the computer and then drag the old Fonts folder (which still contains the damaged suitcase) to the Trash.

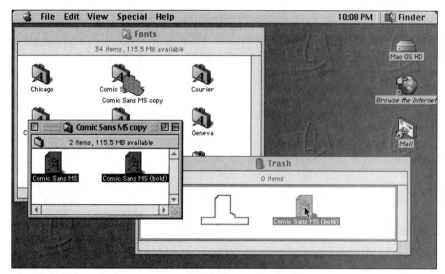

Figure 27-13: Make a new, empty font suitcase by duplicating an existing font suitcase and dragging its contents to the Trash.

STEP-BY-STEP

Personalized Sample Text

You don't have to read about "cozy lummoxes" and "smart squids" (or "razorback frogs and piqued gymnasts" if you use Mac OS 7.6–7.6.1) when you open a TrueType or fixed-size font file in the Finder. Use ResEdit to change the sample text as follows:

1. Open your System Folder, and press Option as you drag a copy of the Finder to the desktop.

2. Open this duplicate Finder with ResEdit.

3. Open the duplicate Finder's STR# resource icon, and then open the STR# resource whose ID is 5816. (With Mac OS 7.6–Mac OS 7.6.1, open STR# resource ID 14516.)

   A window appears that displays the sample text.

4. Edit the text to your liking.

5. Quit ResEdit, answering Yes when you are asked whether you want to save your changes.

6. Drag the original Finder from your System Folder to a folder outside the System Folder, and drag the modified Finder from the desktop to the System Folder.

7. Restart your computer and test the results of your modifications.

Summary

In this chapter, you learned some tips for the desktop, and how to organize the Mac OS virtual desktop for better efficiency. You also learned that you don't have to use the same, boring (even if they are 3-D) icons everybody else uses. Customizing icons, either by altering the default icon, using a custom icon, or removing the icon completely, is easy.

In this chapter, you picked up some tips on enlivening the startup process. You can change the look of your startup screen. You can also have your computer play a QuickTime movie, display a message, or a play a sound during startup.

This chapter also gave you several ideas for working with folders and windows. You can lock folders with the Sharing command. You can also scroll windows without using the scroll bars and move background windows without making them active. You can manage your pop-up window tabs if they get out of hand. You can set the view options for your folders. In addition, you can use the Sherlock program or Find File program to spot empty folders.

You also got some tips on working with the Trash. You can stop Trash warnings with the Get Info command and you can remove locked items by pressing the Option key. The Put Away command makes it easy to retrieve items from the Trash.

This chapter gave you some tips for organizing your Apple menu and some ideas for adding items to it. You can change the order of items by prefixing their names with blank space and other special characters. You can add a universal Show Clipboard command to the Apple menu and you can access the entire contents of your desktop from the Apple menu.

Finally, this chapter told you how to create new font suitcases and how to delete damaged font suitcases.

✦   ✦   ✦

Discover More Tips and Secrets

This second chapter of tips and tricks covers shortcuts and productivity boosters for your system in general: Open and Save dialog boxes, file sharing, Mac OS extensions and control panels, using the Mac OS with your applications, and memory and performance issues. Finally, the tips section ends with a few Mac OS "Easter eggs."

To use some of the tips in this chapter, you need a copy of ResEdit, Apple's no-cost resource editor. You can get ResEdit from Apple's Software Updates library (http://www.apple.com/swupdates/), online services such as America Online (keyword: filesearch), and Macintosh user groups. You can also get a copy of ResEdit from Macworld's Macdownload software library (http://macdownload.com). For more sources of shareware and freeware, see "Where to Get Utility Software" in Chapter 26.

Open, Save, and Navigation Services

The tips in this section will help you zoom through the dialog boxes that appear when you choose Open, Save, Save As, and other disk-related commands. All of these tips apply to the classic Open and Save type of dialog box. As noted in the descriptions of individual tips, some tips also apply to the Open and Save dialog boxes' heir-apparent, the Navigation Services dialog boxes introduced in Mac OS 8.5.

Find an alias's original item

You can go quickly to an alias's original item in an Open, Save, and Navigation Services dialog box by pressing Option while opening the alias (by double-clicking it, for example). Alias names appear in italics in these dialog boxes, just as they do in the Finder windows.

Folder switching

If you find that you frequently go back and forth between two folders, put an alias of each folder in the other. Whichever folder you are in, you can go to the other in one step by opening its alias. In Mac OS 8.5, bookmark your frequently visited folders using the Favorites pop-up in the Navigation Services dialog box.

Aliases for favorite folders

Putting aliases of your favorite folders on the desktop or inside disk windows enables you to open a favorite folder quickly from an Open, Save, or Navigation Services dialog box. Instead of working your way down through one branch of your folder structure and then working you way up another branch to the folder that you want, you zip to the desktop level or the disk level, and then open the alias of the folder that you want. This process is like jumping from one branch of a tree to the root level and then jumping to a spot on another branch without crawling up the trunk and along the other branch.

You can get to aliases of favorite folders on the desktop quickly by pressing ⌘-D. Get to aliases at the disk-window level by choosing the disk from the pop-up menu in an Open or Save dialog box, or the Shortcuts pop-up menu in a Navigation Services dialog box.

Sidestepping a double-click

As usual, you can open an item in an Open dialog box by double-clicking the item. If, before you release the mouse button, you realize that you double-clicked the wrong item, continue holding down the mouse button and drag the pointer to the item that you want to open. When you release the mouse button, the currently selected item opens.

This trick also works when you are opening a folder in a Save dialog box, but does not work in a Navigation Services dialog box (but see the next tip).

Canceling a double-click

To cancel a double-click in an Open, Save, or Navigation Services dialog box, hold down the mouse button on the second click and drag the pointer outside the dialog box before releasing the mouse button.

Shared folder access from the Save dialog box

Don't you hate it when you get into a Save dialog box only to find that you aren't connected to the shared folder that you want to save in? Just make an alias of the Recent Servers folder and put it on the desktop. Now you can quickly open the Recent Servers folder from any Save dialog box and then open and connect to any shared folder or disk in the Recent Servers folder. Beats a trip to the Chooser any day. (If you don't have an alias of the Recent Servers folder on the desktop, you can open the folder from the Apple Menu Items folder. Still beats a trip to the Chooser.) Figure 28-1 is an example of getting to a shared folder via an alias in the Save dialog box.

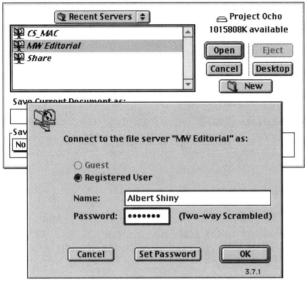

Figure 28-1: Save yourself a trip to the Chooser by placing an alias of the Recent Servers folder on the desktop.

File Sharing and Networking

This section describes tips for easier networking, plus ins and outs for file sharing under Mac OS 7.6–8.5.

Picking a secure password

Pick a password that is easy for you to remember but difficult for other people to guess. For better security, mix letters with numbers; try replacing the letters I and O with the numbers 1 and 0. Another trick is to use the initial letters of an easy-to-remember phrase. For example, "The White House is at 1600 Pennsylvania Avenue" becomes TWHia1600PA. Don't use birthdays, anniversaries, or family members' names.

Want to make sure you haven't chosen a too-obvious password? Ask a good friend, relative, or coworker to play spy: have them try to guess your password, writing down their guesses on a piece of paper. If your password is on the list, or is very similar to one on the list, choose a less-obvious password.

Sharing disks or outer folders

When you share a folder, the Mac OS won't let you share the outer folder or the disk that contains it. You have to drag the shared folder to another place or unshare it before you can share the outer folder or disk. To avoid this situation, share from the highest level of your disk and folder structure.

Improved file-sharing performance

For best performance of your computer, share as few of your folders as possible. The more items that others can access on your computer, the greater the demands on your computer's performance. Sharing too many folders can slow your system to a crawl. When you need to share numerous files or to share a folder simultaneously with several users, consider setting up a dedicated computer to act as a centralized file server for the shared information. (A great way to recycle older computers.)

Faster file sharing

If you've ever shared files from your computer, you know how bogged down your Mac can get, especially if the file sharing is done remotely. Combat slow system performance by creating a RAM disk and placing all the items that you wish to share on it. Then share the RAM disk by selecting the RAM disk and choosing Sharing from the Get Info submenu of the File menu (Mac OS 8.5) or from the File menu (Mac OS 7.6–8.1).

Drag to share

Here's a slick way to share your disks and folders. Forget the Finder's Sharing command. Instead, open the File Sharing control panel and click the Activity Monitor tab. Now simply drag a folder or disk that you want to share into the Shared Items area of the control panel. The item's sharing information appears in its Info window (Mac OS 8.5) or sharing window (Mac OS 8–8.1). Turn on the option "Share this item and its contents" and set the access privileges.

Trouble renaming hard disks

Are you stymied because you're unable to change the name of your computer's hard disk? Make sure file sharing is turned off in the File Sharing control panel or the Sharing Setup control panel, whichever you have. While file sharing is on you can't change the name or icon of an item that's available for network access.

Cut file-sharing red tape

Getting access to shared items involves wading through a fair amount of bureaucracy, whether you use the Chooser or Mac OS 8.5's Network Browser. Aliases cut through the red tape.

First, access a shared disk or folder one time, using the Chooser or the Network Browser. Next, select the shared item or any folder or file in it, then choose Make Alias from the File menu (⌘-M). Finally, copy the alias to your desktop or hard disk. An alias keeps track of its original item even if the original item is on another networked computer.

After you make an alias of a shared item, you can access it by opening the alias either from the Finder or from an Open command's dialog box. Dragging something to the alias of a shared disk or folder also accesses that shared item automatically. You still must enter a password unless you initially accessed the original item as a guest. If the shared item is not available (when, for example, the computer where the item resides is turned off), a message tells you so.

Aliases of shared items don't always work if the shared items are located on servers that use Windows NT Services for Macintosh.

Office on a disk

Because aliases can give you nearly automatic access to items on a networked computer via file sharing, take the previous tip a step further: put an alias of your hard disk on a floppy disk for quick access to your files from any computer on your network.

For this trick to work, your computer must have file sharing turned on. You can check the status of file sharing and turn it on if it is off by using the File Sharing control panel (Mac OS 8–8.5) or the Sharing Setup control panel (Mac OS 7.6–7.6.1). You can also use the Control Strip if it is installed on your computer.

With file sharing turned on, insert a floppy disk and make an alias on it for each of the other disks on your computer's desktop. Eject and lock the floppy.

As long as file sharing is active on your computer, you can use this floppy disk to access your hard disk from any other computer on your network. Simply insert the disk, open the alias for the disk that you want to use, and enter your password when asked. Correctly entering your password gives you access to all applications, folders, and documents on your disk from any remote Mac OS computer. You don't have to bother with opening the Chooser, selecting AppleShare, selecting your computer, and typing your name as the registered user.

An alias on your floppy disk may not work as expected if the alias's original item has the same name as a disk on the computer you're using. For example, if your hard disk is named Mac OS HD and the hard disk on the computer you're using to access it also has a hard disk by that name, opening the alias on your floppy may open the local hard disk instead of your hard disk over the network. You can work around this problem by temporarily renaming the hard disk on the computer you're using. Remember that if the computer you're using has file sharing turned on, you must turn it off before you can rename any of the computer's disks. If you make any of these changes to a borrowed computer, be sure to change them back when you finish.

What people have trashed

Items from your shared disk or folder that someone has dragged to the Trash—but not yet permanently removed—on another computer do not appear in your Trash. The Mac OS puts those items in folders whose names begin Trash Can #. You cannot see these folders with the Finder because they are in an invisible folder inside the shared folder or disk. To see the Trash Can # folders, use a utility program such as Norton Utilities for Macintosh from Symantec (408-253-9600, http://www.symantec.com) or File Buddy (described in Chapter 26).

Log-in shortcuts

When connecting to a shared folder or disk, you may have a choice of connecting as a guest or a registered user. In the dialog box that gives you this choice, you can press ⌘-R for Registered User or ⌘-G for Guest, eliminating an extra trip to the mouse. This shortcut is especially nice for keyboard-oriented folks.

Control Panels and Extensions

This section includes the what, where, and why of control panels and extensions, along with tips on how to get the most out of them.

Take a picture

You can take a picture of your desktop with a built-in feature of the Mac OS. Pressing ⌘-Shift-3 takes a picture of your whole screen; ⌘-Shift-4 lets you drag out a rectangular picture selection. Use Caps Lock and ⌘-Shift-4 to take a picture of a window in the active application by clicking the window. To place the picture on the Clipboard instead of in a SimpleText picture file on your startup disk, add the Control key to either of those key combinations.

In Mac OS 8–8.5, you can even capture the screen while a menu is open (but not a pop-up menu). Click the menu title to open the menu, and then press a key combination to capture all or part of the screen. To capture the screen while a pop-up menu is open or the mouse button is pressed, you need a screen-capture utility such as the shareware Screen Catcher from St. Clair Software (http://www.stclairsw.com), the shareware Snapz Pro from Ambrosia Software (http://www.ambrosiasw.com), or the shareware Flash-It by Nobu Toge.

Easy Access shortcuts

Instead of using the Easy Access control panel to turn Mouse Keys, Slow Keys, or Sticky Keys on and off, you can use the keyboard. (To get Easy Access, you must do a custom installation of the Mac OS, as described in Chapters 31 and 32.)

The Mouse Keys feature of Easy Access enables control of the pointer from the keyboard. To turn Mouse Keys on or off, press ⌘-Shift-Clear. Mouse Keys requires a numeric keypad to work.

The Slow Keys feature of Easy Access guards against accidental keystrokes by requiring that a key be held down for a second or two before the keystroke is entered. To turn Slow Keys on or off, hold down the Return key for about 10 seconds. After 5 seconds you'll hear a beep; 5 seconds after that you'll hear an ascending tone (on) or a descending tone (off).

The Sticky Keys feature of Easy Access lets you type keyboard combinations such as ⌘-S one key at a time. To turn Sticky Keys on or off, press the Shift key five times in a row without moving the pointer.

Big map

You can enlarge the world map in the Map control panel by pressing Option while opening the control panel. To magnify more, press Shift-Option while opening the map. Figure 28-2 shows the world map at various sizes.

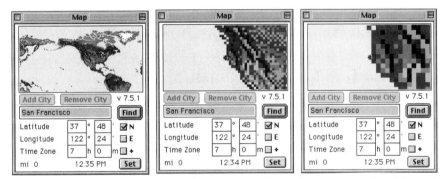

Figure 28-2: You can zoom in on the Map control panel to get more detail (sort of).

Time zone tracking

If you regularly contact people in multiple time zones, you can use the Map control panel to keep track of local times for those people. With the Map control panel open, type the name of the city and click the Find button. Then type the person's name over the city name and click the Add City button. Now you need only type a person's name in Map and click the Find button to find his or her time zone.

If you want Map to remember a person whose city isn't on the map, you can substitute a known city in the same time zone or add the unknown city. Whenever you add a new place or person to Map, verify the time zone and correct it, if necessary.

Hidden free beep

The Scrapbook includes an extra system alert sound that you can paste into the Alert Sounds section of the Sound control panel. If the Sound control panel is not in your Control Panels folder, you'll find it in the Apple Extras folder on your startup disk. You can't paste alert sounds into the Monitors & Sound control panel, which replaces the Sound control panel in the Control Panels folder with Mac OS 8–8.5.

If you threw away the extra system alert, you can get it again by installing a new copy of the Scrapbook file. For instructions on getting the standard Scrapbook File, refer to "Scrapbook Renewal" in the next section.

Virtual memory turn-off

Instead of opening the Memory control panel on those occasions when you need to turn virtual memory on or off, restart your computer while holding down the ⌘ key. Holding down the ⌘ key at startup automatically disables virtual memory; restarting without pressing ⌘ restores virtual memory to its previous settings. Holding down the Shift key during startup also disables virtual memory along with all extensions, whereas ⌘ does not disable all extensions. However, some third-party extensions or control panels may be disabled individually by a ⌘ key restart. If you have a startup file that's sensitive to the ⌘ key, check its documentation or Read Me files to see if you can change the key that acts as a disabler during startup.

Stuck in the past

If your Time and Date control panel insists that it's really 1956, you aren't stuck in a time warp — you just need to replace the lithium battery on the system board. When the computer is off, the battery keeps the clock ticking and powers the parameter RAM (PRAM), which stores settings for many control panels, including Mouse, Keyboard, and Startup Disk. You'll find Apple part numbers for batteries for all but the latest Macs, which shouldn't need batteries yet, in Apple's Technical Information Library article 11751, which is available on the Web (http://til.info. apple.com/techinfo.nsf/artnum/n11751).

Apple considers the clock battery replaceable on some desktop Macs and includes instructions in the owner's manuals for these models. You can remove the Mac's cover (as described in the computer's manual), eyeball the battery, and decide for yourself whether you want to try replacing it. You'll find pictures of the battery location in many models on The Macintosh Battery Web site (http://www.academ. com/info/macintosh/).

The specific procedure for replacing a clock battery varies because the clock battery location depends on the computer model. The following description gives an idea of the work involved.

Remember that while the cover is off the computer you could accidentally damage something inside that would be expensive to repair. Proceed with caution; if you're the least bit squeamish, let a technician do the work.

Before replacing the battery it's a good idea to use the free TechTool program (described in Chapter 26) to save the settings stored in the computer's parameter RAM (PRAM). The PRAM stores a number of control panel settings as well as secret settings (such as the number of hours the computer has been used); removing the battery may reset these settings to factory defaults. To replace a Mac's clock battery, remove the computer's cover and touch the metal power supply housing to drain off any static charge you may be carrying. Next, pry off the plastic cage that covers the battery. Carefully note the orientation of the old battery's positive and negative ends. Then pop out the old battery and snap in a new one with the same orientation as the old one. Replace the battery cage and the Mac cover, and restart the computer. If you saved PRAM settings with TechTool, use it now to restore the settings. Otherwise, check your control panel settings and change them as needed.

Clock tricks

Sometimes when you're on a deadline, the last thing you want to know is the date and time. To turn off the menu bar clock, Option-click it. Repeat the procedure to display the clock again. To switch the menu bar clock from the time to the date, simply click the clock — the date appears for 5 seconds and then switches back to the time.

PowerBook airport security

When you take a PowerBook through airport security and are asked to turn it on, the last thing you want to do is wait through a lengthy start-up. Waking a sleeping PowerBook is fast enough, but who wants to waste battery power while the PowerBook sleeps through check-in? Instead, use the Password Security control panel. The Password Security dialog box comes up quickly on startup and proves that you have a computer, not a bomb. Then press the Cancel button to shut down quickly so you can make your plane. Whatever you do, don't forget your password, because you can't bypass the Password Security dialog box by starting up with the Shift key pressed or by starting up from a CD or a floppy disk — the password control is handled at the disk-driver level. You'll have to take your PowerBook with proof of purchase to an authorized service center, where a technician can bypass the security dialog box.

If you have an older-model PowerBook, you can't use the Password Security control panel. In this case, either hold down the Shift key for a fast startup at the airport or download one of the many quick-start extensions available online. John Bullock's Scout's Honour, John Bascombe's Airport Quickstart, and Jon Wind's Zorba are all freeware extensions designed to provide quick startup and shutdown for airport security agents. And they work on any model PowerBook.

Applications and Accessories

In this section, you'll find tips for using Mac OS 7.6–8.5 features while working with your applications and accessory programs.

MoviePlayer controls

The standard controller for a QuickTime movie is full of hidden controls, including:

✦ Make the sound level louder than its normal maximum by holding down the Shift key while clicking the speaker icon and adjusting the sound level with the volume slider.

✦ Adjust the sound level by pressing the up arrow (↑) and down arrow (↓) keys.

✦ Turn the sound on or off by Option-clicking the speaker icon.

✦ Alternately start and pause playback by pressing either the Return key or the spacebar.

✦ Step forward or backward by pressing the right arrow (→) or left arrow (←).

✦ Play the movie forward by pressing ⌘-right arrow(→).

✦ Play the movie backward by ⌘-clicking the reverse-step button or pressing ⌘-left arrow(←).

✦ Control the playback direction and speed by Control-clicking either step button to reveal a jog shuttle.

✦ Jump to the beginning or end of the movie by Option-clicking a step button, as indicated by the direction of the step button.

When you open a movie with the MoviePlayer program, versions 2.5.1 or 3.0 Pro (but not 3.0 standard), these additional hidden controls become available:

✦ Select part of a movie by pressing the Shift key while dragging or clicking the play bar and then using the Cut, Copy, or Clear command in the Edit menu. After cutting or copying part of a movie, you can paste it anywhere in the same movie or another movie. To deselect your movie snippet, ⌘-click anywhere in the gray bar.

✦ Make the movie window an optimal size for playback by pressing the Option key while dragging or clicking the size box.

Audio CD AutoPlay

With QuickTime 2.5–3.0, which installs as part of Mac OS 7.6–8.5, you can have your computer automatically play an audio CD during startup (by placing an alias of Track 1 from any audio CD into the Startup Items folder) or any time that you insert an audio CD into the CD-ROM drive. Turn on the Enable Audio CD AutoPlay option in the AutoPlay section of the QuickTime Settings control panel. This feature starts playing the CD earlier during startup than the Startup Items method. If the CD starts playing automatically but you don't hear anything, you probably need to change the sound input settings in your Monitors & Sound control panel so that the sound source is the CD drive and the Listen option is turned on. Figure 28-3 shows the QuickTime Settings and Monitors & Sound control panels.

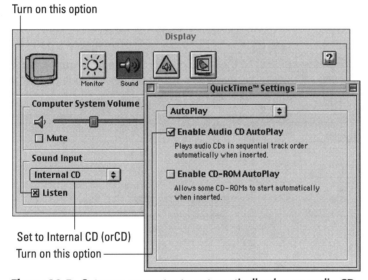

Figure 28-3: Set your computer to automatically play an audio CD inserted in the CD-ROM drive.

The other option in the AutoPlay section of the QuickTime Settings control panel, Enable CD-ROM AutoPlay, can cause problems. When this option is turned on, your computer can become infected with the AutoStart 9805 Worm (as described at the end of "Audio CDs" in Chapter 16).

Scripted calculator

You can copy the text of a calculation — for example, 69.65+26.98+14.99*.0725 — and paste it into the standard Calculator control panel. Be sure to use the asterisk symbol (*) for multiplication and the slash (/) symbol for division, and don't include any blank spaces in the text you copy.

STEP-BY-STEP

Audio-Only QuickTime Movies

It's easy to record a passage from an audio CD as a sound file—the QuickTime system extension makes it possible. (Keep in mind that many uses of sounds copied from a CD constitute a violation of copyright law unless you first obtain permission from the copyright holder.) You just need SimpleText and an audio CD. Then follow these steps to record the CD passage:

1. Insert the audio CD you want to use for your clip.

2. Open SimpleText and choose Open from SimpleText's File menu.

3. In the Open dialog box that appears, open the audio CD, select the track you want to record, and click the Convert button to bring up a Save dialog box.

4. In the Save dialog box, name the sound-only movie and select a folder location for it.

5. Still in the Save dialog box, click the Options button to bring up QuickTime's Audio CD Import Options dialog box. Adjust the slider controls to specify which part of the audio track to include, set the sound-quality options, and close the Audio CD Import Options dialog box. The following figure shows this dialog box.

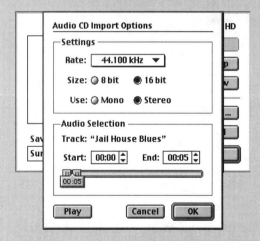

6. Back in the Save dialog box, click the Save button.

   QuickTime copies the audio data from the CD to the movie file. The following figure shows an example of an audio-only movie open in Simple Text and the movie file's icon in the Finder.

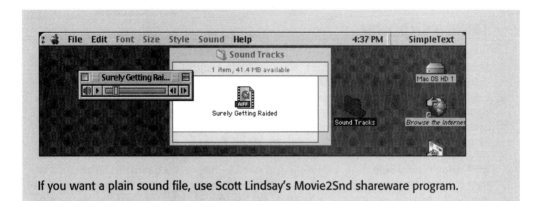

If you want a plain sound file, use Scott Lindsay's Movie2Snd shareware program.

Scrapbook renewal

If you tossed one of the items that was preinstalled in the Scrapbook, you can get it again by reinstalling the Scrapbook from the Mac OS installation CD or disks. Temporarily move your current Scrapbook File from your System Folder to the desktop. Next, do a custom installation of the Mac OS, selecting Scrapbook in the Apple Menu section of the Install Mac OS window (Mac OS 8.5) or the Install System Software window (Mac OS 7.6–8.1). (See Chapters 31 and 32 for detailed instructions on doing a custom installation.) This should install a new Scrapbook File.

Open the new Scrapbook File. Drag the missing item to the desktop to create a clipping file that contains it. Select the Scrapbook File that you previously dragged to the desktop, choose Put Away from the Finder's file menu, and click OK when the Finder asks whether it's OK to replace the Scrapbook File in the System Folder with the one that you're moving (putting away) from the desktop. Open the Scrapbook again, and drag the clipping file from the desktop to the Scrapbook window.

Note Pad notetaker

The next time you need to look through a plain text document — especially if you want to find specific text in it — try the Note Pad. Although the Note Pad has no Open command in its File menu, it can display the contents of a plain-text document, including SimpleText documents and text clipping files. To view a text file, you simply drag its icon to the open Note Pad. Even better reasons for using the Note Pad are that it opens instantly and ordinarily uses less than half the memory of SimpleText and other text editors such as BBEdit Lite and Tex-Edit Plus. Moreover, the Note Pad can search read-only SimpleText documents (the kind with a "newspaper" icon), which SimpleText itself can't do.

Take a clipping

Instead of saving text or pictures in files created in an application (such as SimpleText or a word processor), you can make a clipping file. Select part of a document that you want to make into a clipping file and try to drag it to the desktop or to the icon or window of a folder or disk. If the application you're dragging from supports drag-and-drop editing between applications, the Finder creates a clipping file containing what you dragged. If nothing happens, or if the selection changes when you try to drag to the desktop, the application you're dragging from doesn't work with drag-and-drop editing. In that case, you can make a clipping file by selecting, copying, and pasting into a document of an application that does work with drag-and-drop editing, and dragging to the desktop from there. Applications that work include SimpleText, Note Pad, Stickies, and the Scrapbook. Once you've created your clipping file, rename it so that you can tell at a glance what's in it. If you forget, just double-click the clipping file; the file opens without launching an application.

While a clipping file is open, you can copy its entire contents and paste the copied contents into a document. Another way to get the contents of a clipping file into a document is to drag the clipping file to the document window. The document window you drag to must belong to an application that supports drag-and-drop editing between applications.

SECRETS

Placing Graphics in SimpleText

How do people get graphics into a Read Me file or other SimpleText document, and how do they give it the special newspaper-style icon that designates a read-only SimpleText document? As you may know, the obvious methods — pasting graphics into the text and locking the file with the Finder's Get Info command — don't work. You need a secret keystroke and a resource editor such as Apple's ResEdit. Here is the procedure:

1. Open the SimpleText document that you want to enrich with graphics. Place the insertion point wherever you want to insert a graphic and press Option-spacebar followed by several blank lines to leave space for the graphic. (The number of lines isn't critical; you can adjust it later.)

2. Paste the graphics into the Scrapbook.

3. Use ResEdit to open a copy of the SimpleText document.

   If ResEdit tells you that opening the document will add a resource fork (where SimpleText stores graphics) and asks if you want to do that, answer OK. If ResEdit doesn't ask about adding a resource fork, then the document already has one.

4. One by one, in the order of their intended appearance, copy each graphic from the Scrapbook and paste it into the SimpleText document's ResEdit window.

   When you paste the first graphic, a PICT resources icon appears in the window.

5. Open the PICT resources to see the individual PICT graphics you pasted. Select each graphic and choose Get Resource Info from ResEdit's Resource menu (or press ⌘-I). In the Resource Info window that appears, change the ID number. Make the ID number 1000 for the graphic you want placed first, 1001 for the graphic to be placed second, and so on.

(continued)

(continued)

6. Close all the ResEdit windows, saving changes when asked.

7. Open the edited document file using SimpleText.

> Q: Can GOOs be played as Allies with the Kitab Al-Azif?
>
> A: Yes. However doing so is usually an exercise in futility since they have no values. The MSGS rules (pg. 8) offer the following clarification: "Allies that are reduced to a zero Card Value (via Spells or Events), or that have no listed value, are buried in your Story Deck immediately." Thus, unless you've managed to somehow give your GOO a value, it's going to be buried the second it hits the table.
>
>
>
> The Kitab Al-Azif, Knee Deep in Doom and Enchanted Weapons: This one takes a few different elements, but it's well worth the work (for Sheer Fun Value at the least). The premise is this: some of the best decks I've seen stack up all the requirements for several adventures, and then allow you to play multiple adventues in very short order. So, what you do is play out your first several adventures, the whole time using the Kitab to play Monsters as Allies, and handing them Enchanted Weapons as you are able. (Yes, your opponents will begin to sweat.) Play through your Adventures until you reach 15 points. Hopefully, you should have 20 points of Monsters laid out as Allies by then, all equipped with Enchanted Weapons. After playing that Adventure that brought you up to 15, immediately Pass. Pass. Commit all your Enchanted

You should see a graphic in each place you inserted an Option-space. The graphics are always centered in the document window. If a graphic overlaps text, simply add blank lines for additional space.

Sometimes graphics seem to vanish after you add or remove a line. To display the images, scroll the document or collapse and expand the window to refresh it.

8. To prevent other people from changing the document and to give it the newspaper-style icon, close it and use ResEdit's Get File/Folder Info command to change the document type to ttro.

Close a Stickies note without warning

When you click a Stickies note close box, a dialog box pops up asking you to confirm that you want the note deleted. To skip the warning, Control-click the note's close box.

Custom Connect To

The Connect To utility is preset to connect you to Apple's Web site on the Internet at http://www.apple.com. You can change the preset Internet address (URL) using Apple's Script Editor program (which is in the AppleScript folder inside the Apple Extras folder). You use the Script Editor to modify the AppleScript commands inside Connect To. That's right, Connect To is an AppleScript application even though it doesn't look like one because it has a custom icon. Before you can use Script Editor on Connect To, you must use ResEdit or another utility to change Connect To's internal file type. Follow these steps:

1. Make a copy of Connect To. Because the Script Editor application can't open the copy until you change its file type, open the copy of Connect To with ResEdit.

2. Choose the Get Info command from ResEdit's File menu, and in the Info window that appears, change the file type from APPD to APPL. Quit ResEdit, saving your changes.

   The APPD file type designates an application that the Finder automatically puts in the Apple Menu Items folder when you drag them to the System Folder icon. The APPL file type is for ordinary applications, including AppleScript applications.

3. Open the copy of Connect To with Script Editor. Look for the following command near the beginning of the script — set default URL to "http://www. apple.com" — and change the URL to the one that you want used by default. Save the changes and close Script Editor

4. You can copy the custom icon from the original Connect To and paste it onto the modified copy so that it, too, has the custom icon. You can also use ResEdit to change the type of the modified copy to APPD, although it will work perfectly well with the type APPL.

5. Replace the original Connect To with the modified copy and restart your computer.

Secret search criteria

By pressing one key you can search for files and folders by several secret criteria. You can find files and folders that are invisible, have custom icons, or have names and icons that can't be changed. To use these criteria, Option-click the leftmost pop-up menu in the Find File section of Mac OS 8.5's Sherlock program or the Find File program of Mac OS 7.6–8.1. This trick also enables you to search file contents for text you specify in Mac OS 7.6–8.1, where searching by content is not normally available as it is in Mac OS 8.5. Figure 28-4 shows these additional search criteria at the bottom of the pop-up menu in the Find File section of the Sherlock program; the Find File program looks very similar.

Batch copy or delete

Have you ever heard this jibe from a Windows user? "At least in Windows you can delete or copy a batch of files by typing a command such as Copy C:\draw*.eps D:." Ever since System 7.5, Mac OS users have had the same functionality through the Find File program or, in Mac OS 8.5, the Sherlock program. Use Sherlock or Find File to find a batch of files from multiple folders on one disk or on multiple disks. You can then select all or any part of the found items and drag the batch from the Items Found window to the Trash or to any disk or folder.

There is a catch to making this trick work in Mac OS 8–8.1. Due to an anomaly in Mac OS 8–8.1's the Finder, you must make an alias of the Trash and drag selected items from the Items Found window to the Trash alias. If you drag from the Items Found window directly to the Trash in Mac OS 8–8.1, nothing happens. This indirect method works in Mac OS 8.5 but is not required.

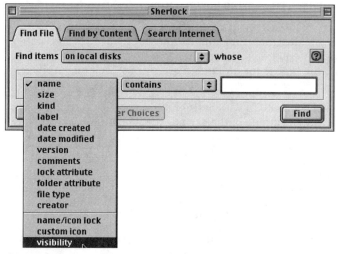

Figure 28-4: Reveal secret search criteria by Option-clicking the leftmost pop-up menu in a Find File search.

Autoclose Find File

You can quit the Find File program (in Mac OS 7.6–8.1) while opening a found item by holding down the Option key and double-clicking the item in Find File's Items Found window. This trick saves you the trouble of reactivating Find File in order to quit it. The Option-key shortcut also works with Find File's Get Info, Sharing, Open Enclosing Item, and Print commands. The Option-key shortcuts do not work in Find File's successor, Mac OS 8.5's Sherlock.

Hide windows while switching

To hide the active program's windows as you switch to a particular program, press Option while choosing the other program from the Application menu, or press Option while clicking another program's window. You hide windows and switch to the Finder by pressing Option while clicking the desktop or a the Finder icon.

If you have displayed the Application Switcher window in Mac OS 8.5 (by tearing off the Application menu), Option-clicking in it will hide the current application's windows.

Hide windows to boost performance

When you have several programs open, you can spend a great deal of time waiting while inactive programs redraw portions of their windows as dialog boxes come and go. This delay is particularly protracted when you're using virtual memory, because the window redrawing may require disk access. Eliminate the delay by choosing Hide Others from the Application menu. Hidden windows don't require updating.

About This Computer contextual menu

If you choose About This Computer from the Apple menu in Mac OS 8–8.5, you can do more than review a list of open programs and the memory they use. Control-click any listed program to pop up a contextual menu from which you can bring up Mac OS Help or switch to the program.

Fix unreadable floppies

Getting the dreaded message "This disk is unreadable by this Macintosh. Do you want to initialize the disk?" after inserting a once-good floppy disk? Possibly the floppy was formatted or written on a different computer. What to do if this is an old archive disk with essential data? A trick with the Disk First Aid utility works in most cases to read and repair floppies that have become unreadable. Disk First Aid is included with the Mac OS installation software.

When you get the "This disk is unreadable" message, immediately eject the disk and open Disk First Aid. With Disk First Aid as the active application, insert the problem floppy again. In Disk First Aid's window, select the floppy's icon and click the Verify button. When Disk First Aid finishes verification, it should tell you the disk needs repairs. Click the Repair button, and when Disk First Aid finishes, it will probably tell you that it successfully repaired the disk.

This trick works only if you insert the floppy while Disk First Aid is the active application and if you have it verify before you have it repair. If you skip the verify step, the repair step ends unsuccessfully.

Memory and Performance

The tips in this section help you make the most of your computer's memory and increase its performance.

Quitting startup programs

If you have several programs opening during startup, you may have to quit some of them later to free memory to open another program. Naturally, you want to quit the programs that are the least important to you. You get the maximum benefit from quitting those programs if they are the last items opened during startup. To make that happen, rename the items in your Startup Items folder so that the most important item comes first alphabetically, the next most important comes second, and so on. Better yet, you can avoid renaming original items by placing aliases in the Startup Items folder.

Reducing system memory size

You can reduce the Mac OS memory size (as reported by the About This Computer menu item in the Apple menu) to its minimum by pressing Shift while restarting your computer. Look for the message "Extensions Off" (Mac OS 8.5) or "Extensions Disabled" (Mac OS 7.6–8.1) during startup. This message confirms that you have suppressed loading of all items in the Extensions folder, the Control Panels folder, and the System Folder that would increase the Mac OS memory size. You have also bypassed opening items in the Startup Items folder, reduced the disk cache to its minimum size, forced virtual memory off, and prevented file sharing from starting.

None of these changes persists when you restart without pressing Shift. To make persistent changes, you must disable items with the Extensions Manager control panel (or drag items out of the special folders) and then change settings in the Memory and File Sharing (or Sharing Setup, in Mac OS 7.6–7.6.1) control panels.

You can also save memory by turning off file sharing if you're not using it. Reducing the disk cache size reduces the Mac OS memory size K for K — but slows system performance.

QUICK TIPS

An Extra Maintenance Disk

If you want to fix or optimize your only hard disk with a utility program that can't be run from the disk it's fixing (and the program won't fit on a floppy and you don't have a high-capacity removable disk such as a Zip disk), use a RAM disk as follows:

1. Use the Memory control panel to create a RAM disk just the size of the application you need to use. After you restart the computer, the RAM disk will use part of the computer's RAM as if it were a disk.

2. Restart, copy the utility program you need from the hard disk to the RAM disk, and open the program from the RAM disk.

3. If you can't work on your hard disk because it's the startup disk, restart from a Mac OS installation CD.

Fragmented memory

To check for fragmented memory, add up the memory sizes of all the open programs and the Mac OS as listed in the About This Computer window. Then subtract this sum from the total memory reported there. Also subtract 300K to 600K (depending on monitor resolution and number of colors) if your computer doesn't have dedicated video memory known as VRAM (video RAM). In this case, your computer uses its main memory, sometimes called DRAM (dynamic random access memory), for the screen image. Examples of Macs in that category include a Power Mac 6100, 7100, or 8100 with a monitor connected to the system board video port. If the number you come up with is substantially less than the largest unused block, your unused memory is probably fragmented into two or more blocks.

To consolidate fragmented memory, quit all open programs and then open them again. Restarting your computer also fixes fragmentation and may reduce the amount of memory used by the Mac OS as well.

You can avoid memory fragmentation by planning the order in which you open and quit programs (see "Quitting Startup Programs" earlier in this section). First, open the programs that you're least likely to quit first; and last, open the programs that you're most likely to quit last. When you need more memory to open another program, quit the most-recently opened program. If that doesn't free enough memory, quit the next most-recently opened program, and so on. This method frees a contiguous chunk of memory. Quitting programs helter-skelter leads to memory fragmentation.

Best partition sizes

If you work with many small files on a large hard disk that doesn't use Mac OS 8.1–8.5's Mac OS Extended format, you can save a significant amount of disk space by partitioning the disk into several smaller volumes. This is because the Mac OS file system allocates a minimum amount of disk space for each file, regardless of its actual contents. The minimum file size for a particular disk is set when it is initialized and is incrementally larger for larger disks (or volumes). For example, a short memo that takes up 16.5K on a 1GB hard disk would take only 4K on a 230MB volume, saving 12K per small file.

Most formatting programs set a minimum file size of 4K on volumes with capacities between 224MB and 255MB, 8K on volumes with capacities between 480MB and 511MB, 16K on volumes between 992MB and 1023MB, and so on.

If you work mostly with large files, large volumes are more efficient. The Mac OS Extended format, available in Mac OS 8.1–8.5, nearly eliminates the file size advantage of partitioning a hard disk into smaller volumes.

Shortcuts to sleep

A computer that's capable of sleep will go to sleep if you use these shortcuts rather than the Sleep command in the Finder's Special menu or the Control Strip:

✦ Press the Power key to bring up the Restart-Sleep-Shut Down alert box and click the Sleep button.

✦ On a PowerBook, Control-click the menu-bar battery icon. The battery icon is a feature of the menu-bar clock, which you set up with the Date & Time control panel. This method does not work with Mac OS 8–8.5.

✦ Press ⌘-Shift-0 (zero) if you're more of a keyboard person and are using a PowerBook.

✦ Press ⌘-Option-Power if you're a keyboard aficionado using a desktop Mac that's capable of sleep. Be sure you press this key combination precisely. Other key combinations very similar to this one will shut down or restart the computer unceremoniously and may result in data loss and disk corruption. Don't use this shortcut unless you have an excellent memory for key combinations and careful fingers.

Sleeping desktop computers

Some desktop Macs can't be put to sleep with the Energy Saver control panel. If you have one of these Macs, you can use the shareware control panel Sleeper from St. Clair Software to make some parts of your system sleep. Sleeper spins down hard disks and dims the display after periods of inactivity. You can use Sleeper's screen dimming in conjunction with another control panel that reduces power on an Energy Star monitor, such as Apple's Energy Saver control panel, and you can have Sleeper bring up a screen saver, such as After Dark, instead of dimming the display. Sleeper does not affect CD-ROM drives, tape drives, or the processor and other system-board circuitry, all of which remain fully active.

RAM disks

You can speed up surfing the Internet's World Wide Web by putting your Web browser program's disk cache on a relatively small RAM disk. With its cache on a RAM disk, the Web browser reloads pages it has saved to the cache more quickly, accesses the hard disk less frequently, and cleans up its cache almost instantaneously. To get set up, use the Memory control panel to create a RAM disk of 1MB to 5MB. After restarting to mount the RAM disk, set the Web browser to use the RAM disk for its cache. For example, in Microsoft Internet Explorer, the standard browser installed with Mac OS 8.1–8.5, you make this setting in the Advanced section of the Preferences dialog box. Note that the memory you allocate to a RAM disk is reported as part of the Mac OS by the Finder's About This Computer command.

To reclaim the memory used by a RAM disk, you must turn off the RAM disk feature and restart your computer. You can avoid this hassle by creating a RAM disk with the RamBunctious program (described in Chapter 26). It creates a RAM disk as an application (sounds weird, but it's true), and you get your memory back as soon as you quit or drag the RAM disk icon to the Trash. You can even automate mounting the RAM disk before opening the Web browser by using the ShrinkWrap shareware to create the RAM disk (see "Using AppleScript with Applications" in Chapter 23).

Download to RAM disk

When using an online service such as America Online or CompuServe, download files to a RAM disk rather than to your hard disk to save on download time. This can be especially useful when downloading the latest multidisk Mac OS update from Apple. Just make sure that you don't forget to save your RAM disk contents before shutdown.

Cables in a pinch

If you ever need to replace your ADB keyboard cable but can't find one at the local computer shop, head to a store that sells video gear and buy an S-video cable of the desired length instead. You can get a cable that's longer than the original, but Apple recommends that ADB cables be no longer than 5 meters. If your monitor cable needs an extension, you may be able to use an IBM PC Joystick Extender cable, which you should be able to pick up at a computer store for about $5. This cable works with most Mac OS monitors, but causes ghosting with some combinations of monitor and computer.

Eggs and Hacks

Apple's software engineers, true to their kind, have sprinkled Easter eggs — cute or funny animations or other surprising actions — in their work. To finish things off, here's a list of some of the treasures you can find hidden within the Mac OS.

About the Finder

In the Finder, pressing Option changes the first command in the Apple menu to About The Finder. Choose this command, and instead of the usual memory usage chart, you see a mountain range picture similar to the one that adorned the Finder 1.1 in 1984. (Some say this is a picture of the mountains around Silicon Valley.) With Mac OS 7.6–7.6.1, you see the original black-and-white picture. Mac OS 8–8.5 substitutes a 3-D color picture. Wait about 10 seconds, and credits start scrolling up the screen. Figure 28-5 shows the About The Finder window.

Figure 28-5: The credits are rolling for the Mac OS.

Sing it to me

If your computer has text-to-speech software installed, four of the supplied voices sing rather than speak text. The Bad News voice sings to the tune of a Chopin Prelude. The Good News voice sings to the tune of "Pomp and Circumstance." The Pipe Organ voice sings to the tune of the theme music for the "Alfred Hitchcock Presents" television show. The Cellos voice sings to the tune of Edvard Grieg's "In the Hall of the Mountain King" from *Peer Gynt.* To hear the tunes clearly, you need to have these voices sing (speak) a selection of text without punctuation marks. When these voices encounter punctuation, they start their tunes over.

Try this: In a new SimpleText document, type "la la la" several times in succession. Select what you have typed, copy it, click at the end of the document, and keep pasting it until you have a dozen lines of "la la la" in the document. Choose one of the singing voices from the Voices submenu of the Sound menu and use the Speak All command to hear the voice sing. Bonus: Some of the novelty voices, such as Boing, Bubbles, and Hysterical, also sound pretty weird when you have them speak this text.

STEP-BY-STEP

Finder Hacks

If you have itchy fingers and an idle copy of ResEdit, you can put a personal stamp on your Mac's Finder. This sidebar lists some interesting changes, or *hacks,* that you can make to the Finder. The basic procedure is the same for all the hacks listed below. As a rule, always use ResEdit on a copy of the original file instead of the original file itself. (For the reasons why, see the "Permanently Removing *alias*" sidebar in the "Icons" section of Chapter 27.)

✦ Change the suffix for an alias as follows:

1. Open STR# resource.

2. Open resource 8200 (Mac OS 8–8.5) or 20500 (Mac OS 7.6–7.6.1).

3. Change the alias suffix in string #1 to something else (up to 31 characters).

✦ Change the initial name of a new folder as follows:

1. Open STR# resource.

2. Open resource 4500 (Mac OS 8–8.5) or 11250 (Mac OS 7.6–7.6.1).

3. Alter string #3 to change *untitled folder* to something else (up to 31 characters).

✦ Change the sample text displayed when you open a TrueType or fixed-size font as follows:

1. Open STR# resource.

2. Double-click resource 5816 (Mac OS 8–8.5) or 14516 (Mac OS 7.6–7.6.1).

3. Edit the phrase in string #1.

✦ Change or modify keyboard shortcuts in the Finder (adding ⌘-T as the keyboard equivalent for Empty Trash, for instance):

1. In Mac OS 8.5, open fmn2 resource ID 522 (File), 523 (Edit), 524 (View), or 525 (Special). In Mac OS 8–8.1, open fmn2 resource ID 521 (File), 522 (Edit), 523 (View), or 524 (Special). In Mac OS 7.6–7.6.1, open resource 1252 (File), 1253 (Edit), 1254 (View), 1255 (Special), or 1256 (Label).

2. Select the third character before the command name, and change it to the letter to use with the ⌘ key as the keyboard equivalent for the command.

Note that there are actually two fmn2 resources for each menu in the Mac OS 8–8.5 Finder. The resource IDs listed above are used when the Simple Finder option is turned off in the the Finder's Preferences dialog box. Add 6 for the ID used when the Simple Finder option is on, but note that in this case, keyboard shortcuts are intentionally omitted from all the Finder commands.

Successfully performing any of these hacks gains you membership in the Loyal Order of the DogCow ("All hail Clarus — aya, aya, moof!"), which entitles you to wear an extralarge T-shirt and shorts to work and to litter your workspace with candy-bar wrappers and empty cola cans!

Tell me a joke

If you have Speech Recognition 1.4.1–1.53 installed and turned on, you can get your computer to tell you knock-knock jokes. You say, "Tell me a joke." The computer responds, "Knock, knock." You reply, "Who's there?" The computer answers with a name or some word, such as "orange." You repeat the word and then say "who?" Figure 28-6 shows a transcript of one of these jokes in the speech feedback window.

Figure 28-6: Get Speech Recognition to tell you a joke.

Summary

In this chapter of system-related tips and tricks, you found ways to navigate through Open, Save, and Navigation Services dialog boxes more efficiently. You can use the keyboard instead of the mouse. You can use folder aliases to jump from one folder directly to another. And you can side-step or cancel a misplaced double-click.

File sharing is very handy, especially when you know a few tricks. You can improve performance by sharing fewer folders and by putting shared files on a RAM disk. Cut file-sharing red tape with aliases. Carry around replicas of all your hard disks on a single floppy disk; they're fully functional as long as you're near your network.

There are a number of useful, hidden shortcuts for your control panels and system extensions. You can activate Easy Access features with the keyboard. Add a hidden alert sound to the Sound control panel. Temporarily turn off virtual memory when you start up your Mac. Hide the menu-bar clock, or toggle it from date to time. And if you're tired of waiting for your PowerBook to start up when you take it through airport security, use a utility to avoid the wait. This chapter also gave you some tips for getting the most from applications and accessories. You can operate the QuickTime movie controller from your keyboard. Set your computer to automatically play any audio CD that you insert in the CD-ROM drive, or make an audio-only QuickTime movie. Customize the preset Web page in the Connect To application. Magnify the Map control panel. Copy or delete a batch of items all at once (without typing a DOS-style command). Hide a program's windows while switching to another program. In addition, you can boost performance by hiding windows.

If your memory isn't what it should be, use the tips in this chapter to reduce system memory size and relieve fragmented memory. If you have a lot of memory, use part of it for a RAM disk. With a RAM disk, you can accelerate your Web browser's handling of its cache, speed up downloading of files, or even run a utility program to perform maintenance on your hard disk. Sleep won't help your computer's memory, but tips in this chapter tell you several ways to put your computer to sleep quickly.

In conclusion, this chapter revealed a couple of Easter eggs and disclosed a list of Finder hacks that work in Mac OS 7.6–8.5.

✦   ✦   ✦

Troubleshoot Problems

No computer, not even a Macintosh, is trouble-free. Inevitably, your computer will experience some mishap or other — a freeze, crash, startup problem, or strange behavior of some type. These problems can have a range of causes, from conflicts caused by various system extensions or old applications to misconfigured hardware devices, corrupted system software, or faulty hardware. It would be impossible to discuss all the problems that you might encounter, but there are general principles that can be applied to a variety of problems.

This chapter discusses the sorts of problems that all Macs are likely to experience at some time or other. In addition, you look at steps to reduce the likelihood of problems occurring and to minimize the consequences that result when problems do occur. You also learn about specific tools that can make troubleshooting more painless.

Although it's possible to solve some problems by trial and error, you can avoid much of the headache by taking steps to understand what is actually happening and applying techniques sensibly.

Preventive Measures

The best way to deal with a problem is to prevent it from happening in the first place. Of course, some problems will occur regardless of anything you do in advance. Nevertheless, a bit of prevention can go a long way.

Backups

A computer user who does not make backups is like a trapeze artist who practices without a net or a sky diver who fails to check his or her parachute before jumping. You may be lucky for a while, but it simply is not worth the risk to your life or your data, as the case may be. The question is not whether you will accidentally delete an important file or whether your hard disk or other storage device will fail; the only question is when it will happen. There are times when it pays to be a pessimist, and at no time is the payoff greater than when you are able to recover gracefully from what could otherwise be disaster for you and your data.

At one time, Mac users could back up all their files conveniently on diskettes. In this era of multigigabyte hard drives, that is no longer practical. For many Mac users, a backup device such as a tape drive or removable disk (a Zip, a Jaz, SyQuest, or magneto-optical drive) has become a necessity, along with appropriate backup software. A discussion of backup hardware and software is beyond the scope of our discussion, but reviews of these devices and software programs do appear periodically in publications such as *Macworld.* Useful backup programs include Retrospect and Retrospect Express from Dantz Development (510-253-3000, http://www.dantz.com/) and Personal Backup from ASD Software (909-624 2594, http://www.asdsoft.com/).

Whichever backup hardware and software you choose, it is important to perform backups regularly. A six-month-old backup may not be much help if disaster should strike. Don't forget to make backups of files that are on diskettes or other removable media but that are not on your hard disk.

Periodic maintenance

You can use many of the tools available for troubleshooting before problems become evident. In some cases, your Mac may already be experiencing problems that you are unaware of. By catching problems in the early stages, you can save yourself (and your Mac) a lot of grief.

Disk diagnostics

If the directory structure of a Mac disk—whether a hard disk, floppy disk, Zip, or other removable disk—becomes damaged, you may experience a variety of problems, including inability to access one or more of your files. In severe cases, the entire contents of a disk may become inaccessible.

Apple's Disk First Aid (which was introduced in Chapter 25 and is described in more detail in the "Troubleshooting Tools" section of this chapter) can detect and repair problems with the directory structure of a Mac disk. It's a good idea to run Disk First Aid periodically on your disks, even if you aren't experiencing any problems. Apple recommends running Disk First Aid monthly as a precautionary measure; if you use your Mac intensively on a regular basis, you may wish to run Disk First Aid more often than that.

Other utilities, notably commercial products such as Tech Tool Pro from Micromat Computer Systems (800-829-6227, http://www.micromat.com/) and Norton Utilities for Macintosh from Symantec (408-253-9600, http://www.symantec.com/) can perform a check similar to Disk First Aid's, sometimes fixing problems that Disk First Aid can't. Before running a commercial disk utility, make sure that it is fully compatible with your Mac model and the version of the Mac OS you are running.

Rebuilding the desktop

If the desktop database on your hard disk becomes damaged, you may see generic (blank) icons instead of the distinctive icons that tell you what kind of file you're looking at. Another symptom of desktop database trouble is being unable to open documents by double-clicking their icons or by dragging compatible documents to them, even if the icons are not generic. Also, problems with the desktop database can cause folder and disk icons to display slowly, although the type of view and the view options you have selected also have an effect on performance.

Apple recommends rebuilding the desktop monthly. You probably won't hurt anything by rebuilding frequently but it may be a waste of your time, because rebuilding can take several minutes per disk depending on the number of applications and files you have. You can try rebuilding once a month, and keep up with that schedule if you feel it improves the performance of the Finder. In any case, it is a good idea to rebuild the desktop at least once a month if you install software frequently.

You can rebuild the desktop by restarting your computer with the ⌘ and Option keys held down. At the end of the startup cycle, the Finder displays an alert asking you to confirm that you want to rebuild your disk. Figure 29-1 is an example of this alert.

CAUTION

Rebuilding Without Restarting — A Dubious Practice

It's possible to rebuild the desktop on your startup disk without restarting the computer, although there is some risk involved. What you do is close all folder and disk windows, close all control panels, put away any open dialog boxes, and then force the Finder to quit by pressing ⌘-Option-Esc. That brings up an alert box in which you click the Force Quit button if you're sure you want to go through with this. Then all the desktop icons, the folder and disk windows, and the Finder menus go away as the Finder quits. Now hold down the ⌘ and Option keys until the Finder displays its alert asking you to confirm rebuilding the desktop. The risk in forcing the Finder to quit is that you're not giving it a chance to clean up after itself; for example, by closing the desktop database in an orderly fashion. That's right, forcing the Finder to quit could induce problems with the desktop database! You face even more weirdness if you leave control panels or dialog boxes open when you force the Finder to quit, because the Finder won't be able to save any changes you've made to settings in those windows.

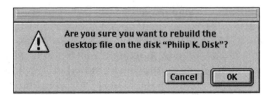

Figure 29-1: Rebuild the desktop by restarting your Mac while pressing ⌘-Option.

If more than one disk is connected to your computer when you rebuild the desktop, the Finder displays a separate alert box for each disk in turn. The same is true if you have partitioned your hard disk into multiple volumes (each with its own desktop icon).

You can rebuild the desktop database on floppy disks and other removable disks by pressing ⌘ and Option while inserting the disk. The Finder displays its confirmation alert before rebuilding.

If you are experiencing problems that appear to be the result of a corrupted desktop database and rebuilding the desktop does *not* solve the problem, use the Extensions Manager control panel (described in "Troubleshooting Tools" later in this chapter) to choose just the base extensions before restarting. In the case of severe corruption of the desktop, you may wish to use a utility such as the freeware utility TechTool or its commercial sibling TechTool Pro from Micromat to remove the desktop database completely, forcing a new one to be built from scratch. (If you remove the desktop database in this way, you will lose any comments that you entered in the Info window of files and folders in the Finder.)

Disk defragmentation

Just as the Mac's RAM can become fragmented (as described in Chapter 16), disk space can become fragmented as well. In addition, unlike applications that each must reside in a single contiguous block of RAM, files themselves (including applications) can become fragmented on a disk. A single file may be split into several pieces spread around in different locations physically on a disk. Fragmentation degrades disk performance because the disk drive must take extra time to move from one piece of a file to the next.

A fragmented file is analogous to a single track on an audio CD being split into multiple segments, so that the beginning of the track might be at the beginning of the CD, the middle at the end, and the end of the track some place in the middle. If audio CDs were mastered in that fashion (which, fortunately, they are not), you would likely notice a delay as the CD player's laser moves to play the next segment.

In a disk with no fragmentation, each file physically resides in a single contiguous block. As a disk begins to fill up and new files are created and deleted with increasing frequency, files and the free space start to become fragmented. Disk performance can suffer, often severely, if the fragmentation becomes heavy. In addition, a heavily fragmented disk is more likely to experience a variety of problems, including corrupted directory structures and damaged files.

Without any special software, you can eliminate fragmentation by copying the entire contents of a disk onto another disk, erasing the disk, and copying everything back. A better solution is to use a commercial disk defragmentation utility, such as SpeedDisk, a component of the Norton Utilities from Symantec (408-253-9600, http://www.symantec.com/), or DiskExpress Pro or PlusOptimizer from Alsoft (800-257-6381, http://www.alsoft.com/). Note that older disk optimization utilities are not compatible with the Mac OS Extended format (HFS Plus); you should check for compatibility before attempting to run a disk optimizer on a Mac OS Extended volume.

Before optimizing any disk, it is especially important to make a full backup, because virtually every byte on the disk may be erased and moved to a different location.

Protection from computer viruses

Although computer viruses are not nearly as prevalent on Macs as on Windows PCs, Mac viruses do exist, and many of the so-called "macro viruses" developed on PCs can infect Macs. Viruses can invade your computer through documents or applications that you have downloaded from the Internet, through electronic mail attachments, or through any type of removable disk (including floppy disks) you may use with your computer. Although some viruses may be relatively innocuous, doing little more than taking up space on disk and slowing down your computer a bit, others can be highly destructive, causing crashes and erasing files.

The only way to protect your Mac from computer viruses is to install an antivirus utility on your computer. Antivirus software can warn you if a virus attempts to infect your system, scan your disks for viruses that may be lurking (or may already have caused some damage), and eradicate almost any virus that it finds. The most popular free antivirus software program, John Norstad's Disinfectant, alas, is no longer being updated, but several commercial antivirus utilities are available. These include Dr. Solomon's Virex (781-273-7400, http://www.drsolomons.com/) and Norton AntiVirus for Macintosh from Symantec (408-253-9600, http://www.symantec.com/). Whichever antivirus software package you choose, it is essential to keep it up-to-date, as each time a new virus appears the antivirus packages must generally be updated to recognize it.

Keeping software up-to-date

Believe it or not, a good portion of the software on your computer may be infested with bugs. (*Bugs* in this case refers to programming errors or other flaws in software, not garden-variety insects.) Some of these bugs may be features not working as documented, and others may be more serious, causing crashes or data loss. Even the Mac OS is not immune to bugs.

BACKGROUNDER

Computer Viruses, Worms, and Trojan Horses

A computer *virus* is a piece of software designed to spread itself by illicitly attaching copies of itself to legitimate software. Although not all viruses perform malicious actions (such as erasing your hard disk), any virus can interfere with the normal functioning of your computer.

A macro virus is a virus written in the *macro language* of an application (a programming language that allows you to automate multiple-step operations within an application). By far, most macro viruses infect Microsoft Word (version 6.0 and later) and Excel (version 5.0 and later) documents. Like other viruses, macro viruses can be very destructive.

Viruses, alas, are not the only potentially destructive software that you may encounter. *Worms* are similar to viruses in that they replicate, but they do not attach themselves to files. A *Trojan horse* is an intentionally destructive program masquerading as something useful such as a utility, software updater, or game. Although worms and Trojan horses are not viruses, most commercial antivirus programs can detect and remove them.

Usually, once a software publisher becomes aware of a problem, it takes action to correct it right away, usually by providing free updaters, which update the software to a newer version, or by documenting workarounds. In some cases, a bug may be an incompatibility with some other software or hardware product. You can keep informed of bugs and bug fixes by registering your products, often by sending in a postcard that came packaged with the product, and by checking the publisher's Web site frequently. Late-breaking news regarding the Mac OS, including announcements of updates and compatibility information, can be found at Apple's Mac OS Web site (http://macos.apple.com/macos/latebreak/) and Apple's Software Updates library (http://www.apple.com/swupdates/).

One thing to remember is that older software may not be compatible with the most recent Mac OS from Apple, despite extensive compatibility testing by Apple and software publishers. For this reason, it is often a good idea to keep all your software current — applications, your Mac OS, and any third-party operating system extension you have installed.

Good (and bad) housekeeping practices

In the course of using your computer, some activities help minimize problems, while others are all but guaranteed to create them.

Shutting down

You can create problems through seemingly innocent actions such as shutting down your computer. The proper way to shut down your computer is to press the Power key and click the Shut Down button in the alert box that appears. As a shortcut, you can press ⌘-Shift-Option-Power. You can also shut down by choosing Shut Down from the Finder's Special menu.

CAUTION

When to Wait Before You Update

Every piece of software—including software updates—may have bugs. Unless you are experiencing a severe problem that an update is designed to correct, it often makes sense to wait at least a few days (or weeks) before installing a just-released update. Over the years, there have been many cases of a software publisher (including Apple) pulling an update from distribution because of serious bugs that were not foreseen by the programmers. In many cases, bugs in an update are documented in the accompanying Read Me file. Although Read Me files rarely make stimulating reading material, reading them before installing can save you much grief.

If you must run older software on your computer (for example, if a product you need is no longer being updated), it is especially important to exercise caution before updating the Mac OS. Although incompatibilities are often documented in the Mac OS Read Me files, some incompatibilities may not yet be discovered. These surprises are another reason why backups are so important.

If you shut down your computer by switching off the power, you may damage the disk directory. The Disk First Aid program (discussed in "Troubleshooting Tools" later in this chapter) can usually repair this type of damage. However, you're better off not causing the damage in the first place. Left uncorrected, disk directory damage leads to more directory damage and may eventually result in lost data.

Installing software

Before installing any software, there are a few precautions you should take. First, peruse the Read Me files and the installation instructions. You may discover that the program is not compatible with your particular Mac model or the Mac OS version you are using. Be suspicious of any software more than a year or so old.

Older software, especially utilities, system extensions, and games, can be a hazard. Before installing older software, check whether an update or a more recent version is available. Be particularly cautious of third-party extensions and control panels from companies other than Apple.

If you have enough disk space, it's usually best to install software using the easy, standard, typical, or default installation for the type of computer you have (desktop or portable). If you perform a custom installation, you can too easily omit a component that may be essential for the software to run. If the default installation will not install all the components you need or want, you can usually install those items separately by running the installer a second time.

Finally, before installing any software, it is a good idea to restart your computer. Depending on the software, you may want to disable some or all of your system extensions before beginning installation. You can do this by using the Extensions

Manager control panel to choose base extensions only or by restarting with the Shift key held down.

Experimenting

Although experimenting with your Mac is an excellent way to learn, it is important to take care in what you do. In particular, avoid removing items from the System Folder or files from the folders in which your applications reside unless you are certain the items are not needed. These files may be essential to the operation of your Mac or your applications, and they may not function unless they are in a specific location.

Cleaning up and reducing clutter

Just as furniture accumulates dust and desks accumulate papers, your Mac can accumulate a significant amount of clutter. The clutter can manifest itself in unneeded items on your desktop, duplicate files on your hard disk, old applications that you no longer run, and documents that you just don't need any more.

QUICK TIPS

Protecting Your Mac from Unauthorized Experimentation

If other people use your Mac, there are a couple of precautions you can take to reduce the damage they might cause. These steps won't be effective against people with malicious intent, more advanced users, or even particularly inquisitive children, but they may be helpful if you allow friends, relatives, or colleagues to use your computer occasionally.

✦ To reduce the risk of accidentally removing items from the System Folder and the Applications folder, you can use the General Controls control panel to turn on the options "Protect System Folder" and "Protect Applications folder." Turning on these options prevents items at the top level of the System Folder and Applications folder from being moved, removed, or renamed. Items in folders within the System Folder and Applications folder, however, can still be moved, removed, or renamed.

✦ To hide some of the more advanced features of the Finder from casual users in Mac OS 8–8.5, you can turn on the Simple Finder option in the Finder's Preferences dialog box, which you display by choosing Preferences from the Finder's Edit menu. After turning on the Simple Finder option, only the most basic commands appear in the Finder's menus, eliminating items such as Move to Trash, Make Alias, and Sharing.

Although these precautions can help thwart a casual user from messing up your machine, you will need to use a special utility to provide any real protection. Apple's At Ease can provide some protection, as can more robust security programs such as FolderBolt-Pro from Kent Marsh (800-962-0701, http://www.kentmarsh.com/), FileGuard from ASD Software (909-624 2594, http://www.asdsoft.com/), or Norton DiskLock from Symantec (408-253-9600, http://www.symantec.com/).

Although there's not necessarily any harm in being a packrat, unneeded clutter can slow you down, slow your computer, and increase the likelihood of running into problems. In particular, having different versions of the same application can result in unpredictable behavior, and older applications may not be fully compatible with your other, more recent software. In addition, clutter can make it hard to find the files or applications you need. Having a large number of files in a single folder can reduce performance, and keeping your system clean will lessen the likelihood of running out of disk space.

Periodically, you might want to take some time to clear up the clutter taking over your hard disk, deleting old applications, aliases you no longer use, and files whose purpose ceased to be relevant. A utility such as Apple System Profiler or Spring Cleaning from Aladdin Systems (408-761-6200, http://www.aladdinsys.com/) can help simplify the cleanup process.

Troubleshooting Tools

The proper tools are just as important to a Mac user as they are to a carpenter or mechanic. Of course, the tools are generally software, not hammers and screwdrivers. The Mac OS comes with a number of utilities that can make troubleshooting much less of chore, and there are third-party utilities that pick up where Apple's utilities leave off or fall short. Many Mac problems cannot be solved without using these tools.

Apple System Profiler

The Apple System Profiler (described in Chapter 25), normally the first item under the Apple menu, makes it easy to get detailed information about your Mac's hardware and software configuration.

This utility aids in troubleshooting in several ways. If you call Apple's or another company's technical support number, the technician will likely ask you specific questions about your Mac's configuration. Chances are, the answers to those questions are in one of Apple System Profiler's reports. In addition, having a printed report from Apple System Profiler handy while you are reading Read Me files or news of software updates can alert you to potential incompatibilities.

Moreover, the information that this utility provides can help you troubleshoot problems more easily. You can use the device and network information to troubleshoot certain hardware configuration problems. You can create reports about extensions and control panels that separate items that are part of the Mac OS from items from other sources. These reports, used in conjunction with the Extensions Manager (described later in this section), can aid in resolving extension conflicts. The System Folder Information report can tell you whether you have multiple System Folders on your startup disk (generally not a good practice). The Application Information report makes it easy to see which versions of applications you have installed and whether you have multiple copies of your applications. Figure 29-2 shows the version of Apple System Profiler that comes with Mac OS 8.5.

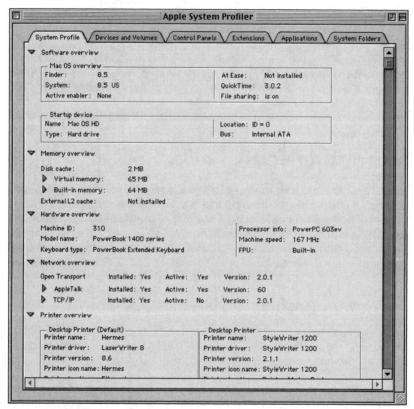

Figure 29-2: The Apple System Profiler provides a wealth of information about your Mac's configuration.

If you have never run Apple System Profiler before, it is a good idea to create and print a detailed report of your Mac's configuration. If at some point you begin to experience problems, you can print another report and see what has changed. Figure 29-3 is an example of the report created by the Apple System Profiler that comes with Mac OS 8.5.

Disk First Aid

Disk First Aid (introduced in Chapter 25) is Apple's tool for detecting and correcting problems with the directory structure on a Mac hard disk. Disk First Aid is found on a Mac OS installation CD-ROM and on a Disk Tools disk. With Mac OS 7.6–8.5, you also have a copy of Disk First Aid in the Utilities folder on your startup disk.

Only the most recent versions of Disk First Aid can repair damage to the startup disk. With the older versions of Disk First Aid, you must start your computer from a CD-ROM, Disk Tools disk, or another disk to repair damage to your usual startup disk. (These versions can still test the startup disk and report problems.) Also, file sharing must be turned off for Disk First Aid to check for or repair damage.

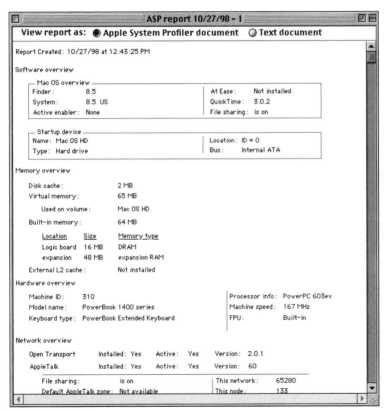

Figure 29-3: Use Apple System Profiler to generate detailed reports such as this one.

To use Disk First Aid, simply open it and select the disks you wish to check. Each disk has an icon in the Disk First Aid window. You can select multiple disks by Shift-clicking each one or by holding down the Shift key while dragging across them. Then click Verify to check the selected disks or click Repair to check and correct any problems found on the selected disks. It is a good idea to Verify or Repair at least twice, since Disk First Aid may be able to find or correct different problems on different passes. Figure 29-4 is an example of the Disk First Aid window.

If Disk First Aid finds problems that it cannot fix, you may need to use another utility to correct the problem or, as a last result resort, back up and reinitialize your hard disk.

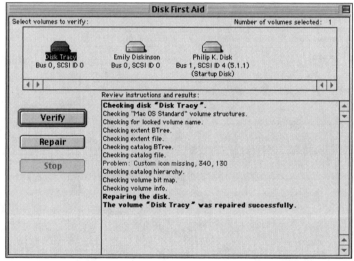

Figure 29-4: Disk First Aid can correct problems with the directory structure on a Mac disk.

Drive Setup

The Drive Setup utility allows you to test, initialize, and partition Apple hard disk drives and some other kinds of storage media (such as some removable cartridge disks and magneto-optical disks). Drive Setup performs the same functions (and more) as Apple HD SC Setup and Internal HD Format, supplied with earlier versions of the Mac OS. Apple HD SC Setup is still required for Mac OS 7.6 or 7.6.1 on some older Mac models; it is completely superseded by Drive Setup in Mac OS 8–8.5. (For details, see "Preparing for Installation" in Chapter 30.) You can usually find Drive Setup on a Mac OS startup CD-ROM, on a Disk Tools disk, and in the Utilities folder on your startup disk.

If you have a non-Apple hard disk, you need to use the disk utility program that came with your hard disk or that you purchased separately, such as Hard Disk Toolkit from FWB Software (650-482-4800, http://www.fwb.com/) or LaCie Storage Utilities from LaCie (503-844-4500, http://www.lacie.com/).

This section discusses the capabilities that Drive Setup provides and how to use them.

Updating the driver

The driver on a hard disk (or removable disk) is the software that tells the Mac how to access the information on the disk. Updating the driver can sometimes correct certain disk-related problems. In addition, if your hard disk does not have the latest version of the driver (for example, if your disk was formatted with an older version of Drive Setup), you may wish to update your driver. Newer drivers may provide better performance and improved reliability.

To update the driver, select the disk you wish to update in the main Drive Setup window and choose Update Driver from the Functions menu. If you update the driver on your startup disk, the new driver will not be available until you restart your computer. Figure 29-5 is an example of Drive Setup's main window with one disk selected and ready to have its driver updated.

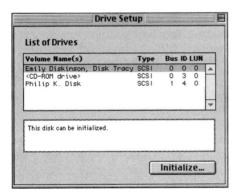

Figure 29-5: Drive Setup allows you to initialize, test, and update the drivers on Apple hard disk drives and some removable media.

Testing a disk

Drive Setup can perform a comprehensive test of a disk by copying and saving a block of data from the disk, writing and verifying a test pattern onto the disk, restoring the original data, and checking that there is no discrepancy. This test is different from the one that Disk First Aid performs. Disk First Aid just checks the validity of the disk directory structure for consistency with the files written on the disk; Drive Setup actually tests every sector of the disk surface to ensure that it can be both read and written in a consistent and predictable manner. Drive Setup can mark any unreliable blocks that it finds so that no data is stored there. Drive Setup displays a message describing any problems that it finds.

To perform the comprehensive read/write test on your startup disk, you will need to start up from another disk, such as a Mac OS startup CD-ROM or Disk Tools floppy disk. Otherwise, Drive Setup will perform a less comprehensive read-only test. Also, if your computer is capable of sleep, be sure it is set to never sleep using the Energy Saver control panel or PowerBook control panel, whichever your computer has. To test a disk with Drive Setup, select the disk you wish to test in the main Drive Setup window and choose Test Disk from the Functions menu. The comprehensive disk test can take several hours to complete on a large hard disk, although you can stop the test at any time without the risk of damaging anything.

Initializing a disk

Initializing a disk prepares it for storing Mac files. It also erases all the files and folders on the disk. Before initializing a disk that has any files or folders on it, you must first make backup copies of the ones you want to keep.

When Drive Setup initializes a disk, it erases the disk by creating a new disk directory just like the Finder's Erase Disk command. Erasing does not actually clear out what was stored in old files, but it allows the Mac OS to reuse the disk for new files by writing over the old content (just as you can record over a used videotape or audiotape). In addition, you can set an option to have Drive Setup format the disk surface during initialization. Formatting a disk records new timing marks on the disk surface and checks for bad spots on the disk. You can also set an option to have Drive Setup write zeros over the entire surface of a disk while initializing it, completely and irretrievably replacing all data. You may be able to recover files after erasing a disk, but you can seldom recover file contents after formatting. You can never recover file contents after zeroing-out the disk surface.

Normally, Drive Setup does not format a disk or write zeros across it during initialization. You set these options by choosing Initialization Options from the Functions menu. This displays a dialog box in which you can select either or both of two options: "Low level format" and "Zero all data." Selecting either of these options will significantly increase the time it takes to initialize a disk. If you select either of these options, you should make sure your computer with not go into sleep mode. Use the Energy Saver control panel or the PowerBook control panel to adjust sleep settings (see "Sleep, Startup, and Shutdown Settings" in Chapter 11).

To initialize a disk, select it in the main Drive Setup window and click the Initialize button. Drive Setup displays the Initialize dialog box, in which you confirm that you want to proceed with initialization even though this will erase all data on the disk. Figure 29-6 is an example of Drive Setup's Initialize dialog box.

The Initialize dialog box contains a Custom Setup button, which you can click to divide the disk into several volumes or choose the type of disk format. Clicking this button displays the Custom Setup dialog box shown in Figure 29-7.

Figure 29-6: Initializing a disk erases all files and folders on it.

If you divide the disk into multiple volumes, each volume will have a separate disk icon on the desktop after initialization. You work with each volume as a separate disk. There are a few advantages to partitioning a large disk. First, you may be able to store and access information more quickly with a smaller partition. Second, if you are using a Mac OS Standard partition (as opposed to a Mac OS Extended partition), you will effectively increase your overall storage capacity, because smaller files will take up less space. Finally, if you wish to install multiple operating systems on this disk in addition to the Mac OS, you will need to create partitions for the other operating systems. Note that partitioning an already initialized disk will erase any data that may be present. (For more information, see "Partitioning Hard Disks" in Chapter 6.)

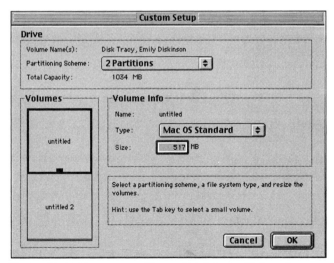

Figure 29-7: You can partition a disk into multiple volumes and choose the type of disk format using Drive Setup.

If you click the Custom Setup button in Mac OS 8.1–8.5, you can choose the type of disk format for each disk volume. You can have a volume initialized using the Mac OS Standard format (also known as HFS) or the Mac OS Extended format (also known as HFS Plus). The Mac OS Extended format has a number of advantages over Mac OS Standard format, but there are also some potentially serious drawbacks. (For more information on the Mac OS Extended format, see "Working with Disks" in Chapter 5.)

Mounting and write-protecting disks

If a disk attached to your system does not appear on the desktop, you can use Drive Setup to mount it. Simply select the disk you wish to mount in the main Drive Setup window and choose Mount Volumes from the Functions menu. You can use this command to mount a disk that you have removed by dragging its icon to the Trash.

Disks generally mount automatically on the desktop during startup, but you can change this behavior if the disk is one that Drive Setup supports. You can also write-protect (lock) a disk so that data can be read from it, but not written to it. After selecting the disk in the main Drive Setup window, choose Customize Volumes from the Functions menu. This displays a dialog box in which you can select "Automount on startup" to make sure that the disk mounts automatically on startup. (For internal hard disks, this option is normally selected.) In the Customize Volumes dialog box, you can also select "Write protected" to lock the disk. Figure 29-8 is an example of this dialog box.

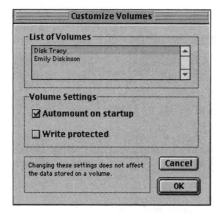

Figure 29-8: Set a disk to mount automatically on startup or write-protect a disk using Drive Setup.

Extensions Manager

Many Mac problems can be traced to extensions — those operating system additions whose icons you see marching across the bottom of the screen when your Mac starts up. Third-party (non-Apple) extensions and older extensions tend to be the most problematic. The Extensions Manager control panel (described in "Managing Startup Items" in Chapter 10) greatly simplifies troubleshooting extension problems.

CAUTION

Don't Let the Mac OS Extended Format Jeopardize Your Data!

Before converting a disk to the Mac OS Extended format, make certain that all your disk utility software is compatible. Ask each software publisher whether their utility will work with the Mac OS Extended format. Then search your disks for incompatible versions of disk utilities and isolate them in a special folder or remove them. Inadvertently using an incompatible utility may damage a disk that uses the Mac OS Extended format. For example, Norton Disk Doctor versions 3.5.1 and earlier can render Mac OS Extended disks unusable. Norton Disk Doctor 3.5.2 safely recognizes Mac OS Extended disks and ignores them. The latest version of Disk First Aid, included in Mac OS 8.5, can repair some of the damage caused by disk utilities that are incompatible with the Mac OS Extended format, but it is best not to take any chances.

Furthermore, you must use Mac OS 8.1–8.5 to see the contents of a disk in Mac OS Extended format. If you open a Mac OS Extended disk with Mac OS 7.6–8, all you see is a document that explains why you can't see the disk's contents.

The Extensions Manager actually controls all kinds of startup items, including extensions, some control panels, shared program libraries, communications tools, and more. For brevity, all startup items are commonly referred to as *extensions*.

Configuring for troubleshooting

To use Extensions Manager effectively for troubleshooting, it's usually a good idea to start by making a copy of the set of extensions that you are currently using. To do this, click the Duplicate Set button and pick a name for the copy. You will then be able to make changes to the duplicate set and compare it with your original configuration. You can also save the set as a text file (by choosing Save Set as Text from the File menu) and print it out. If you want a report that lists only Apple extensions or only non-Apple extensions, use the Apple System Profiler instead of Extensions Manager.

It is often best to view the list of extensions by package, so that you can easily enable or disable groups of related items all at once. To set this grouping, choose As Packages from the View menu. In addition, you can more easily see which items are disabled if you sort the list of extensions by the On/Off column in the Extensions Manager. To sort this way, click the On/Off column heading. Then you can make the disabled items appear at the top of the list by clicking the triangular sort direction indicator at the right end of the column headings. Figure 29-9 is an example of the Extensions Manager set to view by package and sorted by On/Off status with the disabled items listed first.

If you're not sure whether you need a particular extension, click its icon in the Extensions Manager. Then look at the bottom of the Extensions Manager window to see information about the item. If you don't see the item information section of the window, click the disclosure triangle labeled Show Item Information.

It is a good idea to disable any extensions that you are quite sure you don't need, because many extensions take up memory and may conflict with other extensions, the Mac OS, or particular applications. (If you are unsure whether you need a particular extension made by Apple, it's best to leave it enabled.) If you do decide to disable any extensions, you should make a note of which ones you disable. Then restart your Mac and test your system by trying a variety of your usual daily activities to make sure you haven't inadvertently disabled features you need.

Troubleshooting extensions systematically

Taking a systematic approach is the most efficient way to troubleshoot extension problems. First, disable all extensions by restarting your Mac with the Shift key held down. (Alternatively, you can choose All Off from the Edit menu in Extensions Manager and then restart your computer; holding down the Shift key has the advantage of not changing the settings in Extensions Manager.) If the problem persists after disabling all extensions, then the problem you have been experiencing is not the result of an extension conflict. Because some extensions are necessary for the normal operation of your Mac or its applications, your Mac will behave differently when you restart with all extensions disabled; some features will not be available, including the capability to access a CD-ROM drive or a network.

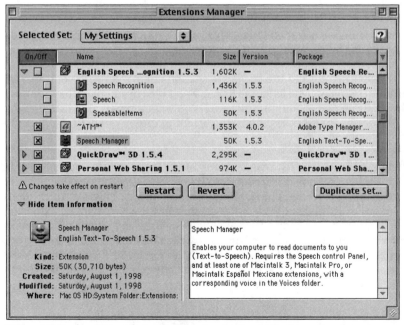

Figure 29-9: Use Extensions Manager to enable or disable extensions. For convenience, view by package and sort by On/Off status.

The next step is to choose the Mac OS base set from the pop-up menu at the top of the Extensions Manager and restart again. If you are able to duplicate the problem, then one or more of the items enabled in the base extension set may be damaged or not compatible with your computer. In either case, you will likely need to reinstall the Mac OS.

Not all the base extensions are essential for the normal operations of all Macs. For example, you don't need the network-related extensions if you are not on a network, and you might not need the text-to-speech extensions if you don't want your Mac to talk to you.

If you don't run into any problems with just the base extensions enabled, the next step is to choose the Mac OS All set and see whether the problem occurs again. Even if the problem does not occur, you might want to go through the additional items in the Mac OS All set and disable those items that you are sure you don't need. Again, if you make changes, you should note them, restart your Mac, and test your system.

QUICK TIPS

Get Info about an Extension

For some extensions, you get little useful information at the bottom of the Extensions Manager window. In these cases, you may wish to choose Get Info from the Extensions Manager's File menu. This displays the selected item's Info window (in the Finder), where you will probably find the publisher's name and the copyright date. The publisher's name may give you a clue as to the extension's purpose.

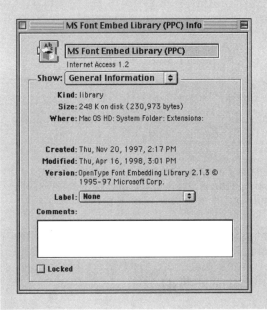

QUICK TIPS

Changing the Order in Which Extensions Load

In some cases, you may be able to resolve an extension problem by changing the order in which the Mac OS loads extensions when your Mac starts up. The Mac OS extensions load in this order: first, items in the Extensions folder load alphabetically; then items in the Control Panels folder load alphabetically; and finally, any startup items in the System Folder itself load alphabetically.

To change the order in which extensions load, change their names. For example, if you place a space character in front of the name of an extension, that extension will load before extensions that start with a letter of the alphabet. In addition, a tilde (type Shift-` for ~) or a degree symbol (type Option-Shift-8 for °) at the beginning of an extension's name causes the extension to load after extensions whose names start with a letter. To force a control panel to load before all other control panels regardless of their names, move it to the Extensions folder. Then for convenience, put an alias of this control panel in the Control Panels folder.

The next step is to start enabling extensions made by companies other than Apple. It is best to do this individually or by package, restarting and testing after each change. Troubleshooting extension problems can be time consuming, but sometimes there is no other way to solve a particular problem.

Other utilities

Although you can correct many types of Mac problems using only the software that Apple provides, there is still a need for utility programs from other companies. These utilities have some capabilities that Apple's software lacks and can aid in troubleshooting problems when Apple's utilities fall short.

No Mac user should be without these types of utilities:

✦ **Backup software.** Having good backup software and using it regularly allows you to recover from serious crashes and other problems without having to worry about losing your data.

✦ **Antivirus software.** Although viruses are the cause of only a small proportion of Mac problems, viruses can be extremely destructive and cause serious problems. No matter how careful you are, the only way to protect yourself from viruses is with a good antivirus program.

✦ **Diagnostic utilities.** Commercial utility packages such as the Norton Utilities and TechTool Pro duplicate some of the functionality of Apple's utilities, but also can do a lot more. These programs can sometimes correct disk problems that Disk First Aid misses and often offer additional features, such as the capability to optimize a disk.

Before installing utility software, it is important to make sure that it will be compatible with your Mac model, Mac OS version, and disk format (Mac OS Standard or Extended).

Recovering from Freezes and Crashes

The steps you take right after a problem occurs can determine how quickly a problem can be resolved. Some actions can make the problem worse or even create new problems. This section describes the steps to take, in order, if your Mac or an application should freeze or crash.

Document the problem

In many cases, simply restarting your computer can solve the problem. However, if you do not document exactly what happened and ignore the problem, chances are excellent that the problem will occur again, possibly with more serious consequences.

Right after the problem occurs, you should make a note of the following:

✦ What you did immediately prior to the problem.

✦ What other applications were running at the same time.

✦ Whether you had recently installed any other software.

✦ What exactly happened, including the precise wording of any error messages.

This information can often allow you to figure out the cause of the problem fairly quickly or at least narrow down the causes.

Wait

If your Mac appears to be frozen, wait at least a minute or so before taking action, particularly if the pointer has become the wristwatch icon. Even if the pointer has not changed to a different icon, it is still possible that your Mac is performing some time-consuming operation. If the problem occurs during startup, it is best to wait at least several minutes, because at startup the Mac OS performs some diagnostics and may be repairing itself.

Use the keyboard to recover

If nothing happens when you click the mouse or the mouse pointer is frozen, try using the keyboard to recover.

Canceling an interminable operation

Sometimes an application takes so long to complete an operation that you wonder if it is stuck and will never finish. In fact, you may occasionally encounter a programming error that does make an application get stuck. One of these key combinations may unstick the application and give you full control of your system:

✦ ⌘-period(.) cancels the operation in progress.

✦ ⌘-S saves the current open document.

✦ ⌘-Q quits the application running in the foreground.

If you are able to recover from a frozen mouse using these key combinations, it is a good idea to restart your Mac.

Forcing an application to quit

If ordinary keyboard shortcuts do not allow you to save your work and quit an application gracefully, the next step is to attempt to force the application to quit. After forcing an application to quit, you can save your work in other open applications and restart your computer.

To force an application to quit, press ⌘-Option-Esc. If this key combination is successful, an alert box appears that gives you the option to "Force Quit" the application or cancel. This alert box warns that all changes that you have made to documents since you last saved them will be lost. If you're using Mac OS 8–8.5, this alert box also advises you to restart the computer after the forced quit. Figure 29-10 shows the Force Quit dialog box in Mac OS 8.5.

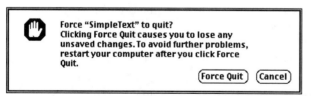

Figure 29-10: Force an application to quit by pressing ⌘-Option-Esc when more graceful methods fail.

If an application gets in so much trouble that you must force it to quit, it may have corrupted other open applications or even the Mac OS. This corruption may not surface immediately, but some time later you may encounter another freeze or crash with more devastating results. Guard against additional problems by restarting your computer after forcing an application to quit. Yes, restarting is an ordeal. Do it anyway.

In some cases, after clicking the "Force Quit" button, nothing happens or your Mac becomes completely frozen. In this case, you will have to force your Mac to restart, as described next.

Restart your computer

The proper way to restart your computer is, of course, to press the Power key or choose Restart from the Special menu in the Finder. If you press the Power key, an alert box appears, asking whether you want to cancel, shut down, restart, or sleep (if your computer is capable of sleep). You can bypass this alert box and restart by pressing ⌘-Option-Power or shut down by pressing ⌘-Option-Shift-Power. If there are any open applications when you use these restart methods, the Mac OS tells them to quit in an orderly fashion. You get a chance to save any unsaved changes before the computer restarts.

Sometimes the orderly methods for restarting don't work and you have to force your Mac to restart. You can usually force a restart by pressing ⌘-Control-Power to restart your computer. When you force a restart, any work you have not saved is lost.

If ⌘-Control-Power does not work, then switch off the power to your Mac. If your Mac does not have a power switch, then unplug the computer from the wall. If you need to shut down your Mac, wait at least 30 seconds before turning it on again. If you switch off the power to your Mac, any changes that you have not saved are lost.

Some older Mac models have a reset button on the computer itself (not on the keyboard). This reset button is marked with a triangle. Pressing this button restarts the machine. If you press the reset button, any changes that you have not saved are lost.

Run Disk First Aid

After forcing your Mac to restart, it is a good idea to run Disk First Aid or a similar utility. If you use Mac OS 8.5, you may not have to do anything. After a crash, Mac OS 8.5 automatically performs the same check that Disk First Aid performs unless you have turned off the option "Warn me if computer was shut down improperly" in the General Controls control panel. When Mac OS 8.5 performs its automatic disk check and repair, you see an alert box advising you that an improper shutdown occurred. This alert box also contains a gauge that measures the progress of the automatic disk check and repair.

System Error Messages

Unlike a crash or a freeze that prevents your Mac from functioning without any warning or explanation, the Mac OS is capable of recognizing some types of serious error conditions and reporting them to you. These errors can be problems specific to a single application or to the Mac OS.

System errors can often be traced to an incompatibility, such as between an application and the Mac OS, the Mac OS and an extension you added, or an application and an extension. Other system errors can be traced to a single application, damaged system software, or the settings of a particular control panel.

Applications that quit unexpectedly

If an application encounters a serious problem, it may quit unexpectedly without crashing or freezing the entire system. The Mac OS displays an alert box that tells you a particular application has quit unexpectedly due to an error. The alert box may identify the type of error with an error code number. Figure 29-11 is an example of this alert box.

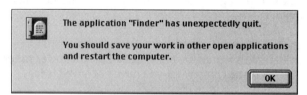

Figure 29-11: The Mac OS alerts you when an application quits unexpectedly without crashing the entire system.

When an application quits unexpectedly, make a note of the error code (if there is one included in the alert); save your work in open applications and quit them; and restart your computer. Then see whether you can duplicate the problem. For help troubleshooting applications, see "Application Problems" later in this chapter.

General system errors

Sometimes a serious error occurs that prevents you from using any open application (including the Finder). In this case, the Mac OS displays a system error alert. System errors are also known as *bombs* because the alert box that reports one has a bomb icon in it. Figure 29-12 shows one of these alert boxes.

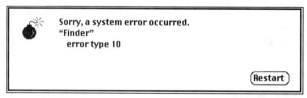

Figure 29-12: A system error alert tells you that a serious error prevents the use of any application.

If a system error occurs, you must restart your computer. You may be able to do this by clicking the Restart button in the system error alert box. Often this button does not work, and you have to force the computer to restart as described in the previous section. Be sure to use Disk First Aid to check and repair the hard disk after a system error.

System error messages and codes

System error messages and error code numbers are frequently vague or so technical as to make sense only to Mac programmers. Nevertheless, by looking up the error message or code number reported in an alert box, you may discover clues leading to a solution to the problem. A list of system error messages and codes is available on the Internet in Apple's Tech Info Library (http://til.info.apple.com/techinfo.nsf/artnum/N1749). Regardless of whether the error message makes sense to you, it is important to write it down, because it may help a technical support person narrow down the cause of the problem.

Startup Problems

Some Mac problems can prevent your Mac from starting. Instead of a smiling Mac icon that normally appears at the beginning of the startup process, you may see a flashing disk icon or a flashing System Folder icon with a question mark in its center. Alternatively, you may see a sad Mac icon. It's also possible that your computer may freeze during the startup process. Startup problems can result from an extension conflict, improperly connected hardware devices, or corrupted, missing, or damaged system software.

It is normal for a Mac to start much more slowly after a crash. However, if a sad Mac icon or the flashing question mark icon appears on startup, it is likely that the Mac OS has become corrupted or there is a hardware problem.

If you are experiencing startup problems, the first thing to do is to make sure that all your hardware devices are connected properly. In particular, make sure that you have turned on all your SCSI devices (such as external disk drives and scanners) before you turn on your Mac. It is also important to make sure that the SCSI chain is terminated properly. (If one or more devices on the SCSI chain is turned off, there is a good chance the SCSI chain is *not* terminated properly.) You also should make sure that each SCSI device has a unique SCSI ID number. Apple System Profiler can help resolve SCSI conflicts. (For more information about SCSI issues, choose Help or Mac OS Guide from the Help or Guide menu in the Finder, and search for the term SCSI.)

Assuming that you find no hardware configuration problems, try restarting with the Shift key held down to disable extensions. (You will need to use the ⌘-Control-Power key combination to restart if your Mac has frozen during startup.) If you are able to restart successfully, you can assume that the problem is the result of an extension conflict. (See the discussion of Extensions Manager in the earlier section "Troubleshooting Tools.") If the problem turns out not to be an extension conflict, you might want to try resetting the PRAM (parameter RAM), as described in "Systematic Troubleshooting Steps" later in this chapter.

If you are still unable to start successfully, try starting from another disk such as a Mac OS CD-ROM or Disk Tools floppy disk. On many Mac models, you can force the machine to start up from a CD-ROM by holding down the C key when restarting. You can only start your computer from a CD-ROM that contains a System Folder for a Mac OS version that's compatible with your computer. If necessary, you can force the computer to eject the CD-ROM currently in the drive by holding down the CD-ROM eject button when you restart the computer; you will then have the opportunity insert a startup CD-ROM. If your Mac doesn't start from the CD-ROM while you are holding down the C key and you're sure the CD-ROM has a System Folder, try restarting your computer while holding down the ⌘, Option, Shift, and Delete keys. This key combination causes the Mac to ignore the internal hard disk when looking for a startup disk. If this trick works, you can then use Drive Setup or another utility to mount the hard disk, and you can run a diagnostic program such as Disk First Aid. In any case, once you have successfully started from another disk, you can run diagnostics or reinstall the Mac OS, if needed.

You can troubleshoot many types of problems that interfere with the normal startup of a Mac by following the procedures described in the "Systematic Troubleshooting Steps" section later in this chapter.

Application Problems

Applications may crash or fail to open for a number of different reasons. There may not be enough free memory, the application's memory partition may be too small, there may be a conflict between the application and the Mac OS or an extension, the preference file (or files) may be corrupted, or the application itself may be damaged.

Memory problems

An application that doesn't have enough memory may crash. When this happens, you typically see an alert box naming an application that unexpectedly quit because of an error of type 1, 2, or 3. In some cases, the alert message may not name a specific application; instead it says that application "unknown" has unexpectedly quit. (If you keep track of which applications you are running, you should be able to determine what the unknown application was.) Figure 29-13 is an example of this alert box.

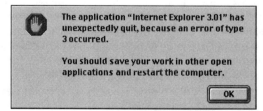

> The application "Internet Explorer 3.01" has unexpectedly quit, because an error of type 3 occurred.
>
> You should save your work in other open applications and restart the computer.
>
> [OK]

Figure 29-13: An error of type 1, 2, or 3 may be the result of insufficient application memory.

If your applications crash in this unceremonious manner, check your computer's memory usage by choosing About This Computer from the Apple menu as described in Chapter 16. If the largest available block of memory is small or memory has become sufficiently fragmented, there may not be enough available memory to give the next application you open its preferred amount. You may still be able to open the application, but it will get less than its preferred amount of memory. The application may get as little as the minimum amount of memory set for it in its Info window.

You can check and adjust an application's memory requirements in its Info window. First, select the application in the Finder. Then, in Mac OS 8.5, choose Memory from the Get Info submenu. This submenu is in the Finder's File menu and in the application's contextual menu. In Mac OS 7.6–8.1, choose Get Info from the Finder's the File menu.

An application's Info window lists three memory sizes: Suggested, Minimum, and Preferred. Very often applications are less reliable when they get less than the Suggested size. If an application seems to crash when its current memory size (as reported in the About This Computer window) is less than its Suggested size (as reported in its Info window), try changing its Minimum size so that it is at least as much as its Suggested size. Some applications are more reliable when they have more memory than the Suggested size. Try setting the Preferred size higher than the Suggested size. You must quit an open application before you can change its Minimum or Preferred memory sizes.

If your computer never seems to have enough memory available to give applications their preferred memory sizes, you need to increase the total amount of memory available. You can increase (or turn on) virtual memory in the Memory control panel, install more memory, or use memory-optimizing software. Turning on virtual memory actually reduces the memory requirements of most applications on a PowerPC Mac and a few applications on other Macs. All these techniques are detailed in "Increasing Total Memory" in Chapter 16.

Corrupted preferences

Applications store settings and status information in preference files and folders located in the Preferences folder within the System Folder. If a preference file becomes damaged, an application may crash, exhibit unusual behavior, or refuse to run at all.

If you experience problems with a specific application, locate the preference file or folder for the application in the Preferences folder and drag it to another folder or the desktop. The next time you open the application, it creates a new preference file (or folder) automatically. Although you will probably lose all your personal preference settings for the application, you may find that the application behaves properly with its new preferences file. If removing a preferences file does not resolve the problem, you can restore your personal preference settings by dragging the old preferences file back to the Preferences folder.

Some applications place several items in the Preferences folder, sometimes in a single folder. It is possible that the application will not run at all once you have removed a particular item from the Preferences folder. In this case, it may take some experimentation to determine which files can safely be removed.

When to reinstall

If you have ruled out insufficient memory and corrupted preference files as the cause of a problem with a specific application, it may be that the application file or a file associated with it has become damaged or corrupted.

Sometimes an application will not run or be incapable of carrying out certain operations if it cannot find particular files. This situation can arise if an application was installed using a custom installation that omitted necessary files. An application may also be unable to find files it needs if you change System Folders after installing it. You change System Folders when you start up from a different disk and when you do a clean installation of the Mac OS.

You can usually restore missing application files by installing the application again from the original disks or CD-ROM. Be sure to use the easy installation or standard installation, not the custom installation unless you know specifically which files are missing. You may also be able to restore missing files from a backup, but figuring out which files are required can be difficult.

Patches and updaters

A solution to a problem you are experiencing with an application may be available as a patch or updater from the publisher. See the discussion on keeping your software up-to-date in the section "Preventive Measures" earlier in this chapter.

Technical support and other resources

Generally, no one knows an application better than the people who created it. Many software publishers have Web pages with detailed discussions of problems and solutions. In addition, some publishers provide excellent support by telephone. Taking advantage of the support resources provided by the publisher can often lead to a quick and relatively painless solution.

In addition, there are numerous other resources that you can make use of, such as user groups, Internet discussion groups, and Web sites. These sources are detailed in the section "Troubleshooting Resources" at the end of this chapter.

Systematic Troubleshooting Steps

Many Mac problems can be solved through the series of systematic troubleshooting steps presented in this section. Not all of these steps are relevant for all problems; tailor the steps you take to the specific problem. However, it's best not to skip a step unless you are sure it will have no bearing on the problem. (Most of these steps are described in more detail elsewhere in this chapter.)

Back up

At the first sign of trouble, make sure you have recent copies of your important files. The problems you are experiencing could damage files, or the problems could lead to other problems that damage your files. If at all possible, retain old backup files that you made before your trouble began. Avoid deleting or replacing old backup files while you're having trouble. Your trouble may have already damaged some files, and backup copies of damaged files will also be damaged. Old but healthy backup files are better than new but damaged backup files. See the discussion of backups in the section "Preventive Measures" earlier in this chapter.

Document the problem

Take detailed notes about the problem, about what you were doing immediately before the problem occurred, and about any software that you may have installed recently. (Be sure to keep the notes on paper rather than on your computer because a crash can make the notes inaccessible.)

Run diagnostics

After any sort of crash, it is a good idea to run a diagnostic utility such as Disk First Aid. If Disk First Aid tells you that it cannot fix a problem, try a commercial diagnostic program such as the Norton Utilities or TechTool Pro. Running a commercial diagnostic program in addition to Disk First Aid is a good idea in any case, because these utilities can catch and fix problems that Disk First Aid might miss. (See the discussion of Disk First aid and other utilities in the section "Troubleshooting Tools" earlier in this chapter.)

Before running a diagnostic utility, it is best to restart your computer from another disk. Many diagnostic utilities cannot fix some types of problems if they are run from the startup disk that you wish to check. (All but the most recent versions of Disk First Aid cannot correct problems on the startup disk.)

In addition, if you are experiencing a system-wide problem and the problem goes away when you start from another disk, there is very likely a problem with the Mac OS or some item in the System Folder of your normal startup disk. The remainder of this section discusses several possible causes and cures for Mac OS problems.

Check for viruses

Although the vast majority of Mac problems are not the result of viruses, it is still important to rule out viruses as a cause. Any current commercial antivirus utility does a good job of finding and eliminating viruses that have infected your disks. See the description of viruses and related phenomena in the section "Preventive Measures" earlier in this chapter.

Resolve extension problems

Extension conflicts are among the most common problems that Mac users experience. See the discussion of Extensions Manager in the section "Troubleshooting Tools" earlier in this chapter.

Rebuild the desktop

When the desktop database becomes badly corrupted, a variety of different problems can result. Rebuilding the desktop can correct a number of otherwise mysterious Mac ailments. See the discussion of desktop rebuilding in the section "Preventive Measures" earlier in this chapter.

Zap the PRAM

The Mac stores certain systemwide preferences in an area of nonvolatile memory called *PRAM* (parameter RAM). On Macs with PCI expansion slots, additional system settings are stored in another area of persistent memory called *NVRAM* (nonvolatile RAM). Restoring the PRAM and NVRAM to the factory presets can solve a number of different problems. When the PRAM or NVRAM becomes corrupted, your Mac may not be able to start at all.

The settings for a number of control panels, including Memory, Monitors, Sound, Monitors & Sound, Keyboard, Mouse, Trackpad, AppleTalk, Date & Time, and Map reside in PRAM or NVRAM. Before resetting the PRAM and NVRAM, you should take note of the settings of those control panels.

To reset (or "zap") the PRAM, restart your Mac and immediately press ⌘-Option-P-R. You will most likely need to use both hands to do this (unless you have very large hands). Keep those keys held down until you hear the startup chime twice in succession.

On a PowerBook 5300, 190, or 1400, you must shut down the computer to reset its PRAM. Then turn on the PowerBook and immediately press ⌘-Option-P-R. A single chime will be heard, the screen will go dark, and the green sleep light will go on and stay on. Press the Reset button (on the back of the PowerBook) once or twice and the PowerBook will start after a brief pause. If the Reset button doesn't work, press the Power key on the keyboard.

To reset the NVRAM on a Mac with PCI slots, you must first shut down your computer. You can't reset the NVRAM when you restart, only after a full shutdown. Press the Power key to turn on the computer and immediately press ⌘-Option-P-R. You must press these keys before you see the gray screen on your monitor. After the gray screen appears, you can continue pressing ⌘-Option-P-R to reset the PRAM.

After resetting the PRAM or NVRAM, you may need to go back and make some changes to your control panels. In particular, you may need to adjust your video and sound settings; your network, printer, and modem connections; and your memory settings.

Perform a clean installation of the Mac OS

A clean installation of the Mac OS, as described in Chapters 30 to 32, creates a brand-new System Folder. Although a clean installation is one of the most laborious troubleshooting options available, in some cases it may be the only solution.

The real work of performing a clean installation is not in running the installer program. The hard part of a clean installation is in getting the new System Folder to behave like the old one, but without the problems. The new System Folder will not contain any extensions, control panels, fonts, preference files, or application support folders that you added over time to the old System Folder.

After performing a clean installation, do not immediately move items from your old System Folder to your new one if at all possible. Instead, install extensions, control panels, fonts, and application support folders from the original installation disks. In any case, proceed with caution when adding items to the new System Folder because it is entirely possible that in doing so you may reinstate the problem. (However, you significantly reduce the likelihood of that happening if you perform all the steps mentioned in this section.) Add items a few at a time and test your system for a while before adding more.

Back up and initialize your startup disk

Initializing your hard disk is the most drastic step you can take to resolve a thorny problem. If you take this step, you start on a clean state — an empty hard disk. You initialize most Apple hard disks and some other brands as well with Drive Setup. If you use Mac OS 7.6–7.6.1 and have an older Mac, you use Apple HDSC Setup instead. If you have a hard disk not supplied by Apple, use the disk utility program that came with the hard disk or that was purchased separately. (See the discussion of initializing a disk with Drive Setup in "Troubleshooting Tools" earlier in this chapter.)

Before taking this step, you should first exhaust all other options. But if diagnostic programs such as Disk First or Norton Utilities detect problems that they cannot fix, initializing may be the only option.

Before initializing your hard disk, it is essential that have a complete backup of your hard disk. Initializing completely erases your hard disk. It is a good idea to have at least two complete backups just in case one turns out to be damaged.

When you restore data to a freshly initialized disk, it is best to install the Mac OS and your applications from the original disks rather than rely on the copies from the backup. When possible, restore only your data files from the backup. It is a good idea to restore items gradually, rather than all at once.

What to do when nothing works

If none of the steps described previously leads to a solution to the problems you are experiencing, it is entirely possible that you have a hardware problem. Before taking your Mac into the shop, you might want to take advantage of the other troubleshooting resources described at the end of this chapter.

Performance Problems

Some Mac problems manifest themselves in slow performance rather than in crashes or system errors. The causes of performance problems are often the same as the causes of other problems, and the general troubleshooting techniques presented in this chapter can often solve performance problems as well.

If your Mac has been performing more slowly than usual, here are a few possible causes and solutions.

Memory problems

Check the settings in the Memory control panel. If virtual memory is turned on (as it normally is), you may run into performance problems. The higher you set the amount of virtual memory, the more likely you are to encounter performance problems. You will probably first notice sluggishness when you switch between different applications. To avoid severe slowdowns, do not set the total amount of memory to more than about two times the actual built-in memory. In addition, applications run more slowly if there is not enough free RAM for them to occupy their "preferred" memory partition size.

It is also possible that your disk cache size is too small. If you click the Use Defaults button in the Memory control panel, the Mac OS sets a recommended disk cache size based on the amount of built-in memory in your computer.

For more information on virtual memory and the disk cache, see Chapter 16.

Disk fragmentation

When the files on a disk become fragmented, disk performance can suffer considerably. See the discussion of disk optimization in "Preventive Measures" earlier in this chapter.

Viruses

Some viruses may have no noticeable effect on your computer other than to slow it down. A virus-checking program can detect and eliminate most of the viruses that have infected your computer. See the description of viruses and related phenomena in "Preventive Measures" earlier in this chapter.

Video performance

If you have a video card that offers graphics acceleration, be sure to install any software that came with it.

In addition, you can improve the video performance considerably on some Mac models by reducing the number of colors displayed on the screen using the Monitors & Sound control panel or the Control Strip. For most applications, 256 colors are adequate, although thousands of colors are better for graphics-intensive activities, including surfing the Web. Also, some QuickTime movies are optimized for playback with thousands of colors. Millions of colors look great, but are required primarily for graphics professionals and people who edit high-resolution photographic images.

Troubleshooting Resources

Resolving Mac problems can be much simpler and much more pleasant if you take advantage of the available resources.

Macintosh Help and other onscreen documentation

Believe it or not, your Mac may already know the answer to a pesky problem that has been plaguing you — all you have to do to find the answer is ask. You can search for and browse detailed information about how to use your Mac, including troubleshooting information, right on your computer screen. You can get this onscreen help in the Finder by choosing Mac OS Help from the Help menu (Mac OS 8.5), Help from the Help menu (Mac OS 8–8.1), or Mac OS Guide from the Guide menu (Mac OS 7.6–7.6.1). In addition, choosing Show Balloons from these menus displays useful information in cartoon-style balloons when you point at things on the screen. (For more information, see Chapter 8.)

QUICK TIPS

Speed Up Your Mac

By changing the settings in a few control panel panels, you can make your Mac faster (or at least seem faster):

✦ In the General Controls control panel, you can reduce the number of times a menu item "blinks" (flashes on and off) when you select it. By default, it will blink three times; turning menu blinking off (or reducing the number of blinks) can make your Mac's response time noticeably faster. In General Controls, you can also increase the speed at which the insertion point blinks, which can make your Mac seem faster.

✦ In the Mouse or Trackpad control panels, you can increase the pointer-tracking speed. This is particularly useful if you have a large screen. You can also adjust the double-click speed.

✦ In the Keyboard control panel, you can increase the speed at which a key being held down begins to repeat. You can also increase the rate at which it repeats.

Mouse and keyboard settings are discussed in detail in Chapter 11.

Some of the information in Mac OS 8.5's onscreen help is not available through the Help menu in Mac OS 8–8.1. Instead, this information is available in a separate program whose icon is normally on the desktop, the Mac OS Info Center. This program displays a variety of information, including troubleshooting pointers and links to Apple's Web pages, in your regular Web browser.

Finally, numerous Read Me files are installed with the Mac OS and the applications you install. These onscreen documents often provide helpful troubleshooting information. Look for them in the main level of the startup disk, in the Mac OS Read Me Files folder on the startup disk, and in the folders of individual application programs.

Documentation, manuals, and books

Many computer users treat manuals as a last resort. Although manuals can indeed be useful when all else fails, it's better to consult them when you first get started with a product, not when problems start arising. In addition, there are several books devoted exclusively to Mac troubleshooting, including Ted Landau's comprehensive *Sad Macs, Bombs, and Other Disasters and What to Do About Them* (3rd edition, 1997, Peachpit Press; ISBN: 0201688107).

Internet resources

If you have access to the Internet, a wealth of excellent troubleshooting resources is available to you. These are a few places to start:

✦ **Apple Tech Info Library** (http://til.info.apple.com/). The Tech Info Library is Apple's technical support database. You can use it to search for information on literally thousands of Mac problems. In Mac OS 8.5, you can easily access the Tech Info Library using the Sherlock program, as described in "Searching the Internet" in Chapter 17.

✦ Apple's **Basic Troubleshooting** site (http://www.info.apple.com/ basictroubleshooting). This site provides basic information on Mac troubleshooting, including tips and solutions to common problems.

✦ **MacFixIt** (http://www.macfixit.com/). An excellent independent source of information on troubleshooting Mac problems, MacFixIt often documents software incompatibilities before Apple does.

✦ **Macintosh Crash/Freeze Tips** (http://www.zplace.com/crashtips/). This site has detailed information on resolving many specific problems that can cause your Mac to crash.

✦ **Macintosh Guide: Troubleshooting** (http://www.cis.yale.edu/macguide/ Trouble/Trouble.html). This page provides a detailed troubleshooting flowchart and links to other Mac troubleshooting sites.

✦ **Usenet newsgroups**. Usenet newsgroups are online discussion forums (or bulletin boards) where participants can post questions and read responses from other participants. Useful newsgroups for troubleshooting Mac problems include comp.sys.mac.system, comp.sys.mac.apps, comp.sys.mac.comm, and comp.sys.mac.hardware.misc. (See Chapter 17 for more information about newsgroups.)

User groups

One of the best ways to take advantage of the skills and experience of knowledgeable Mac users is to join a user group. To find a user group near you, see Apple's User Groups page at http://www.apple.com/usergroups/ or call Apple at 800-538-9696.

If there is no Mac user group located near you, consider joining one of the larger Mac user groups, such as the Berkeley Macintosh Users Group (BMUG) (510-549-2684, http://www.bmug.org/) or the Arizona Macintosh Users Group (AMUG) (602-553-8966, http://www.amug.org/). You will still be able to take advantage of membership benefits such as newsletters, various discounts, and access to extensive libraries of freeware and shareware, even if you cannot attend local meetings.

Technical support from Apple and other companies

In addition to having extensive technical support resources on the Web (see Apple's Technical Support Online page at http://www.info.apple.com/ techsupportonline), Apple also offers technical support by telephone. For the first 90 days after purchasing a Mac, you can get free "up-and-running" support by calling 800-500-7078. Apple also provides free general information and answers to frequently asked questions through an automated service at 800-SOS-APPL. In addition, Apple offers technical support for a fee at 888-APL-VALU.

If you are having a problem with a hardware or software product from a company other than Apple, the best way to resolve the problem is to take advantage of that company's technical support services. Many companies offer technical support through their Web sites and technical support hotlines.

Summary

In this chapter, you looked at a variety of Mac problems and possible solutions. You started by looking at preventive measures, including making backups, protecting yourself from computer viruses, and performing periodic maintenance such as running disk diagnostics, rebuilding the desktop database, and optimizing your disks. These preventive measures can help reduce the occurrence and severity of problems.

Next, you saw how to use specific utilities, including Apple System Profiler, Disk First Aid, Drive Setup, and Extensions Manager to make troubleshooting easier. You learned what to do when faced with freezes and crashes, system errors, startup problems, and application problems. You also learned how to take a systematic approach to solving a variety of problems. Then you looked at a few suggestions for dealing with performance problems.

Finally, you took a brief peak at the resources available in books, on the Internet, and by telephone for troubleshooting Mac problems.

✦   ✦   ✦

Installing
the Mac OS

◆　◆　◆　◆

Get Ready to Install

Installing a newer Mac OS version on your computer is not something you can do casually. This chapter describes what you need to do to prepare for installation. First, you need to assess the equipment requirements and compare the features of newer Mac OS versions to determine which version is best for your computer. Second, you need to obtain the installation software. Third, you need to prepare for installation by making a backup copy of your disk, checking its condition, and more. Fourth, you need to decide whether to install a brand-new copy of the Mac OS or upgrade your existing System folder with the new Mac OS. In case you need to have two versions of the Mac OS installed on the same disk, this chapter concludes by telling you how to switch from one to the other.

You will find the actual installation instructions for Mac OS 8–8.5 in Chapter 31 and the installation instructions for Mac OS 7.6–7.6.1 in Chapter 32.

Comparing Mac OS Versions

If you use an old version of the Mac OS, you may be wondering whether your Mac can be upgraded to a newer Mac OS version and which version is best for you. To help you answer these questions, this section lists the equipment requirements for the Mac OS versions covered in this book. This section also summarizes the features of Mac OS versions as far back as System 7.5. (Prior to Mac OS 7.6, the versions were named "System" instead of "Mac OS.") You can use this information to determine which versions your Mac can use now, how much more memory and disk space you might need to add to use a more recent Mac OS version, and whether the features of a newer version are worth the effort and expense of upgrading.

QUICK TIPS

Check Your Computer's Vital Statistics

You can easily find out how much memory or disk space your computer has or which version of the Mac OS it uses. If the Apple System Profiler program is listed in your Apple menu, choose it. Check the System Overview section or the System Profile section of this program for the system version and the amount of built-in memory on your computer. Then check the Volumes section or the Devices and Volumes section to learn the amount of disk space available.

If the Apple System Profiler isn't available on your computer, you can use other methods to get your computer's vital statistics. To learn the Mac OS version and the amount of memory that are installed on your Mac, make the Finder the active application (choose it from the Application menu at the right end of the menu bar) and choose About This Computer or About This Macintosh from the Apple menu. The About This Computer window or the About This Macintosh window reports the Mac OS version number in the upper-right corner. If this window displays an amount labeled Built-in Memory, that's how much memory is installed in your computer. If you don't see an amount labeled Built-in Memory, then the amount labeled Total Memory tells how much memory your computer has installed. (In System 7–7.5.5, the Built-in Memory amount isn't reported if it's the same as Total Memory, which happens when virtual memory is turned off in the Memory control panel.)

To check the amount of hard disk space available, open the icon of the hard disk where you want to install the Mac OS. The available space is reported at the top of the disk's window.

If the amount of memory or hard disk space is reported in K (kilobytes), you can convert to MB (megabytes) by dividing the number of K by 1,024 (for example, 2,048K ÷ 1,024 = 2MB).

Equipment requirements

The more recent the Mac OS version, the greater its equipment requirements. The newer versions require more powerful processors, more built-in memory, and more hard disk space. The disk space requirements vary quite a bit, depending on several factors. One factor is the selection of Mac OS modules you install. Another factor in Mac OS 8.1–8.5 only is the format of the hard disk; less space is required on a disk that uses Mac OS Extended format than a disk that uses Mac OS Standard format. If the disk uses the Mac OS Standard format, then the disk capacity also affects the amount of space used by the Mac OS. Smaller disks use less disk space.

Table 30-1 compares the processor, memory, and disk requirements for Mac OS 7.6–7.6.1, Mac OS 8–8.1, and Mac OS 8.5.

Table 30-1 **Mac OS Equipment Requirements**			
	Mac OS 8.5	**Mac OS 8–8.1**	**Mac OS 7.6–7.6.1**
Processor (factory installed)	PowerPC	PowerPC or 68040[1]	PowerPC, 68040, or 68030[1, 2]
Built-in memory	16MB minimum (with virtual memory set to 24MB) 24MB highly recommended	12MB minimum (with virtual memory set to 20MB) 20MB highly recommended	8MB minimum 16MB recommended
Disk space	95MB–210MB	50MB–140MB	40MB–120MB

[1] The QuickDraw 3D option included with Mac OS 7.6–8.5 requires a PowerPC processor.

[2] Mac OS 7.6–7.6.1 doesn't work on a Mac SE/30, IIx, or IIcx even though these models were factory-equipped with 68030 processors.

Feature summary

Table 30-2 lists the major features and capabilities added to or removed from the Mac OS beginning with System 7.5.

Table 30-2 **Mac OS Features at a Glance**					
Feature	**8.5**	**8–8.1**	**7.6–7.6.1**	**7.5.3–7.5.5**	**7.5–7.5.1**
Appearance themes	●	○	○	○	○
Multiple system fonts	●	○	○	○	○
Sound tracks	●	○	○	○	○
Text smoothing	●	○	○	○	○
Icon badges	●	○	○	○	○
Application Switcher window	●	○	○	○	○
Help Viewer	●	○	○	○	○
Icons in window title bars	●	○	○	○	○
Standard view options	●	○	○	○	○

● Included with this version of the Mac OS.   ○ Not included with this version of the Mac OS.

(continued)

Table 30-2 *(continued)*

Feature	8.5	8–8.1	7.6–7.6.1	7.5.3–7.5.5	7.5–7.5.1
Smart scroll bars	●	○	○	○	○
Resize list view columns	●	○	○	○	○
QuickTime 3 Pro	●	○	○	○	○
Favorites folder	●	○	○	○	○
Navigation Services	●	○	○	○	○
Find by Content (Sherlock)	●	○	○	○	○
Search Internet (Sherlock)	●	○	○	○	○
File Exchange control panel	●	○	○	○	○
Folder actions	●	○	○	○	○
Faster AppleScript	●	○	○	○	○
Faster network copies	●	○	○	○	○
Network Browser	●	○	○	○	○
Internet control panel	●	○	○	○	○
Internet location files	●	○	○	○	○
Network time servers	●	○	○	○	○
Multilingual Web browsing	●	○	○	○	○
Euro currency symbol	●	○	○	○	○
Mac OS Extended format	●	●[1]	○	○	○
Platinum appearance	●	●	○	○	○
Charcoal system font	●	●	○	○	○
Desktop pictures	●	●	○	○	○
Window collapse box	●	●	○	○	○
Draggable window frame	●	●	○	○	○
Button views	●	●	○	○	○
Pop-up windows	●	●	○	○	○
Improved View menu	●	●	○	○	○
View options for each folder	●	●	○	○	○
Simple Finder	●	●	○	○	○
Spring-loaded folders	●	●	○	○	○

1 Mac OS Extended format is available in Mac OS 8.1 but not Mac OS 8.

● Included with this version of the Mac OS.   ○ Not included with this version of the Mac OS.

Feature	8.5	8–8.1	7.6–7.6.1	7.5.3–7.5.5	7.5–7.5.1
Contextual menus	●	●	○	○	○
Sticky menus	●	●	○	○	○
Move To Trash command	●	●	○	○	○
Show Original (of alias)	●	●	○	○	○
Improved Sharing window	●	●	○	○	○
Simultaneous Finder operations	●	●	○	○	○
Apple Location Manager	●	●	○	○	○
Internet Setup Assistant	●	●	○	○	○
Internet applications	●	●	○	○	○
Personal Web Sharing	●	●	○	○	○
Mac OS Runtime for Java	●	●	○	○	○
Multiprocessor support	●	●	●	○	○
ColorSync	●	●	●	○	○
OpenDoc	●	●	●	○	○
Cyberdog	○	● [2]	●	○	○
QuickDraw 3D	●	●	●	○	○
Apple Remote Access	●	●	●	○	○
MacLinkPlus	○	●	●	○	○
Power key turns off	●	●	●	●	○
Smarter file sharing for removable disks	●	●	●	●	○
Desktop printing	●	●	●	●	○
Translucent icon drag	●	●	●	●	○
Text-to-speech	●	●	●	●	●
AppleScript and scriptable Finder	●	●	●	●	●
Apple Guide	●	●	●	●	●
QuickDraw GX printing	○	○	○	●	●
QuickDraw GX typography	●	●	●	●	●

[2] Cyberdog is included with Mac OS 8 but not Mac OS 8.1.

● Included with this version of the Mac OS.   ○ Not included with this version of the Mac OS.

(continued)

Table 30-2 *(continued)*					
Feature	**8.5**	**8–8.1**	**7.6–7.6.1**	**7.5.3–7.5.5**	**7.5–7.5.1**
PowerTalk	○	○	○	●	●
Open Transport networking	●	●	●	●	○
Find File program	●	●	●	●	●
Easy Open	●	●	●	●	●
Big desktop patterns	●	●	●	●	●
Special Documents folder	●	●	●	●	●
Hide desktop in background	●	●	●	●	●
Apple-menu submenus	●	●	●	●	●
Launcher	●	●	●	●	●
Drag-and-drop editing	●	●	●	●	●
Classic networking	○	○	○	●	●
Control Strip	●	●	●	●	●
Stickies	●	●	●	●	●
Menu bar clock	●	●	●	●	●
Collapsible windows	●	●	●	●	●
Improved Scrapbook	●	●	●	●	●
Improved Note Pad	●	●	●	●	●

● Included with this version of the Mac OS.   ○ Not included with this version of the Mac OS.

Obtaining Installation Software

Installation software—the installer program, installer script, and pieces of software to be installed—comes on several forms of media. You may install from a set of floppy disks, in which case the installer program asks by name for each disk it needs and ejects the disk it no longer needs. As an alternative to floppy disks, you can put the installation software on a hard disk or removable hard disk as described in the sidebar "Net Install." But you're most likely to install from a CD-ROM.

Installation CD-ROMs

When more than a few floppy disks are involved in the installation process, Apple generally makes a CD-ROM that contains the installation software. The installation CD-ROM usually includes extra software that won't fit on an equivalent set of floppy disks. Some versions of the Mac OS are available *only* on CD-ROM.

STEP-BY-STEP

Net Install

Installing software from a set of floppy disks is considerably slower than installing from a hard disk or CD-ROM, and you have to pay attention so that you know when the installer program needs the next floppy disk. Moreover, installing from floppies is a huge inconvenience if you have to install the same software repeatedly (for example, on a number of networked computers). Rather than installing from floppy disks, you can use them to create an installation folder on a hard disk and install from there. Here's the simplest method:

1. Create a new folder on the hard disk that you want to use for installation. If you need to install the same software on several networked computers, create the new folder on a network file server or a shared hard disk.

2. Copy each floppy disk to the new folder. To copy a floppy, insert it and drag its icon to the new folder's icon.

3. For convenience, make an alias of the installer program in the first installation folder and put the alias in the same folder as the set of installation folders.

You end up with a set of installation folders having the same names as the installation floppy disks. It's important to keep all of the installation folders in the same folder on the hard disk and not to change their names. The installer program won't work if you relocate or rename any folders.

To install from the set of installation folders, you simply start the installer program in the first installation folder by double-clicking its icon or an alias of it. If you have trouble installing from a set of installation folders — for example, the installer program asks you to insert a floppy disk when it should use the next installation folder — try putting a copy of the installer program and the installer script file into the same folder as the set of installation folders, and then start the installation with that copy of the installer program. (To copy the installer program and the script file, open the first installation folder and press the Option key while dragging the installer program and the script file to the folder that contains the set of installation folders.)

An alternative method of putting installation software on a hard disk involves creating a disk image file for each floppy disk. This method requires more effort, but it works in cases when the simpler method described above fails. You create the disk image files with a utility program such as Apple's free Disk Copy or Aladdin's ShrinkWrap shareware. For more information on disk image files, see the sidebar "Disk Image Files."

Major releases of the Mac OS, such as Mac OS 8.5, are sold in stores and through catalogs. Apple usually makes upgrades to the latest major release available at lower cost to Mac OS owners through the Apple Order Center (800-293-6617; 716-447-7305 fax). The Apple Order Center also distributes minor releases of the Mac OS and some updates to individual Mac OS pieces for a shipping fee.

BACKGROUNDER

Disk Image Files

Software you obtain from the Internet, America Online, CompuServe, or other online sources may come in the form of disk image files. You can use these files to create a set of installation floppy disks. Two such utilities are Apple's free Disk Copy and Aladdin Systems' ShrinkWrap program (for availability, see "ShrinkWrap" in Chapter 26). With ShrinkWrap or Disk Copy 6.1 or later, you don't have to make floppy disks to install from the disk image files. ShrinkWrap 3.0 and Disk Copy 6.1 and later can mount any number of disk image files directly onto your desktop. It's as if you had inserted a whole bunch of floppy disks simultaneously. Because you can mount all of the "disks" needed for installation, you don't have to sit in front of your computer to swap floppies. Once you start the installation process, it proceeds without further attention from you. Disk Copy comes with Mac OS 8–8.5.

You may use an installation CD-ROM in your computer directly, or you may access it over a network. Using installation software over a network is much the same as using it from a CD-ROM in your computer's CD-ROM drive.

Online installation software

Apple maintains a software library on America Online, CompuServe, and the Internet, and you can copy software from those sources to your hard disk. New versions of individual Mac OS pieces show up in Apple's online software library before they're available on CD-ROM or floppy disk. The library also contains older versions of many Mac OS pieces, including System 7.0.1 complete (other Mac OS versions are not available from the library). Here's how to access Apple's software:

✦ On the Internet, point your Web browser to http://www.apple.com/support/ and follow the links to the software library or a featured item.

✦ On America Online, use the keyword **applecomputer** to go directly to the Apple Computer window. All software is located in the software area of that window.

✦ On CompuServe, use the Go word **APLSUP** to take you to the Apple Computer Support forum, where you can find Apple USA SW Updates, or use the Go word **APLWW** to access the Apple Worldwide Software Updates Forum.

Note that major upgrades to the operating system, such as Mac OS 7.6, Mac OS 8, and Mac OS 8.5 are not available for free downloading online. These must be purchased from a software retailer. However, incremental updates (such as the updater to change Mac OS 7.6 into 7.6.1 or 8 to 8.1) are available for free downloading.

Preparing for Installation

Before installing new Mac OS software—whether that means upgrading to the latest version of the Mac OS, installing a new Mac OS technology, or installing Mac OS 8.5 to replace System 7.5 (or something even older)—you need to determine whether the new software will work with the software you already have. Ideally, you would make a list of every piece of software that's not part of the Mac OS and then check with the software publishers or distributors to make sure the versions you have are compatible with what you're about to install. If you have the time and patience to do that, great; if not, at least do the following to minimize the risk of incompatibilities:

✦ Make a backup of your hard disk and of any RAM disk you have.

✦ Verify the directories of all your hard disk volumes.

✦ Update hard disk driver software.

✦ Turn off any security, virus protection, and screen-saver software.

✦ Turn on standard extensions.

✦ Read the text files on the installation disk—in Mac OS 8.5, they are "Installing Mac OS 8.5" and "About Mac OS 8.5"—for known incompatibilities and disable, remove, or upgrade any incompatible software that you have.

✦ Optionally, label all items in your System Folder with the Labels submenu of Finder's File menu (Mac OS 8–8.5) or the Labels menu (Mac OS 7.6–7.6.1 and System 7–7.5.5). After installation, the new items will be the unlabeled ones.

✦ If you are installing on a PowerBook, make sure it's plugged in.

✦ If you're installing on a computer that can go to sleep, make sure it won't go to sleep during installation.

The remainder of this section discusses these tasks in more detail.

Backing up disks

If you use more than one hard disk, or if your hard disk is partitioned into multiple volumes, make backups of all of them. Making backups is like buying car insurance—it's a terrific imposition and you hope it's a total waste of effort. Do it anyway.

If you have a RAM disk, copy its contents to another disk before upgrading or installing any Mac OS version. Alternatively, you can save the RAM disk as a disk image file using Apple's free Disk Copy program or Aladdin Systems' ShrinkWrap shareware. The RAM disk may be turned off and its contents lost during the installation process.

Backing up today's large hard disks onto floppy disks is impractical. You need some type of high-capacity backup storage device, either another hard disk of equal or greater capacity, a tape drive, an Iomega Zip drive, an Imation SuperDisk, or a hard disk with removable cartridges. If you have a second hard disk, you can back up your main hard disk by simply dragging its icon to the backup disk's icon. That method isn't very efficient if you want to keep your backup up-to-date on a regular basis, but it's adequate for preinstallation purposes.

You could back up onto removable disks by dragging folder icons, but it's simpler to use a special backup utility such as Retrospect Express or DiskFit from Dantz Development (925-253-3000, http://www.dantz.com). These utilities automate the process of backing up a large hard disk onto several smaller removable disks. Retrospect Express and DiskFit also make it easy to keep your backup files current. Each time you back up, they copy only the files and folders that have changed since the last backup. That minimizes the amount of time and number of removable disks you need for backup.

If you have a tape drive, you must use backup software such as Dantz's Retrospect. You can't back up folders to a tape by dragging icons in the Finder.

Verifying disk directories

It's important to check the condition of a disk before installing the Mac OS on it. The installation software automatically checks the disk as part of a normal installation of Mac OS 7.6–8.5.

You can check disks any time with Apple's Disk First Aid utility, which comes with the Mac OS. Disk First Aid checks the condition of a disk's directory, which keeps track of where files are stored on the disk, and can often repair any problem it finds. The Mac OS maintains each disk directory automatically, updating it every time you save changes to a file or create a new file. The directory can become damaged when the computer freezes or crashes, when an application quits unexpectedly, and so on. The damage may be so slight that you don't notice a problem, but over time the damage can grow and become irreparable. Disk First Aid is easy to use — you simply select one or more disks in its window and click the Verify or Repair button. Figure 30-1 is an example of the Disk First Aid window.

Disk First Aid versions 8.1 and earlier have a limitation that you can avoid by starting your computer from a Disk Tools floppy disk or a Mac OS CD-ROM and opening the copy of Disk First Aid from there. A version of Disk First Aid earlier than 8.2 can't repair problems it finds on the current startup disk or on the disk that contains the running Disk First Aid program. This limitation doesn't get in your way if you start from a Mac OS installation CD-ROM and run Disk First Aid from it. If you don't have a Mac OS installation CD-ROM, you can start up from the Disk Tools floppy disk that comes with a set of installation floppy disks for a major release of the Mac OS.

CAUTION

Norton Utilities and Mac OS Extended Format

Do not use Norton Utilities version 3.5.1 or earlier with a hard disk that has been initialized (erased) in the Mac OS Extended format. This format, which is also known as HFS Plus, is optional with Mac OS 8.1–8.5. You can damage a Mac OS Extended hard disk with Norton Utilities 3.5.1 and earlier. If you suspect you have damaged a Mac OS Extended disk by using Norton Utilities 3.5.1 or earlier on it, avoid making further changes to it and contact Symantec Technical Support immediately (541-465-8440). Symantec has a repair procedure that can be done over the phone and is free of charge to registered owners of Norton Utilities.

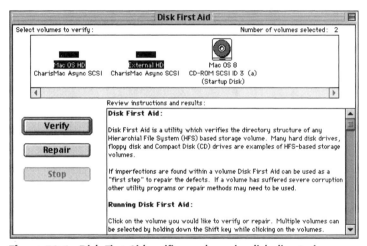

Figure 30-1: Disk First Aid verifies and repairs disk directories.

Some disk problems are beyond Disk First Aid's restorative powers. If Disk First Aid says it can't fix a problem, put the problematic disk through the repair process several more times anyway. The problem may be one that Disk First Aid can fix bit by bit. If after several repair attempts Disk First Aid doesn't tell you that the disk appears to be okay, you need to bring in a high-priced disk mechanic — TechTool Pro from Micromat Computer Systems (800-829-6227, http://www.micromat.com/) or Norton Utilities from Symantec (408-253-9600, http://www.symantec.com). TechTool Pro and Norton Utilities can detect and fix significantly more problems than Disk First Aid. If they can't repair the disk, they may be able to recover individual files that the Finder can no longer access. After recovering lost files and copying them to another disk together with other files that haven't been backed up, you can resurrect the disk by reformatting it.

Updating hard disk driver software

The driver software that resides on every hard disk and removable hard disk cartridge must be compatible with the Mac OS version in use or problems can result. For example, old driver software made by Transoft causes a problem with the Mac OS. The old Transoft driver considers the startup disk to be ejectable, which causes the Mac OS to display a message asking you to insert the startup disk when you shut down the computer, even though the startup disk was never ejected. To check whether your startup disk has a Transoft driver, select the disk's desktop icon and choose Get Info from the Finder's File menu. If the Info window's "Where" information contains "NS-SCSI" or "NS-ACAM" then the disk contains a Transoft driver. Transoft drivers were distributed with various brands of hard disks, notably APS Technologies, as well as with Transoft's SCSI Director formatting utility. The problem does not affect APS hard disks with Power Tools software versions 3.0 and later, nor does it affect Transoft SCSI Director version 3.0.9 and later.

Updating disk driver software takes just a minute and generally doesn't affect disk contents in any way. (To update the driver on an old hard disk formatted with Apple's HD SC Setup version 2.0, you must reformat the hard disk, erasing the disk contents in the process.)

If you're installing Mac OS 8–8.5 on an Apple hard disk, the installer program updates the driver for you—there's no need to run a separate program. If you're not installing on an Apple hard disk, you need to use the most recent version of the formatting utility program last used on the disk.

Apple hard disk utilities

You update the driver software of an Apple-brand hard disk with one of these formatting utility programs from Apple: Drive Setup or Apple HD SC Setup. The one to use depends on the make and model of your computer and the Mac OS version you're installing:

✦ **Drive Setup.** Use this utility to update the hard disk driver before installing Mac OS 7.6–7.6.1 on any Apple Power Macintosh or any Apple Macintosh computer that has an IDE (not SCSI) internal hard disk, except a PowerBook 150. Apple Macintosh computers with IDE hard disks include the PowerBook 190, 1400, 2300, and 5300; the Performa and LC 580 series; the Performa, LC, and Quadra 630 series; and the Performa 5200, 5300, 5400, 6200, and 6300 series. You do not need to (and in fact cannot) update the driver of a PowerBook 150's internal hard disk, because the driver is in the PowerBook 150's ROM.

You can also use Drive Setup to update the hard disk driver on any computer before installing Mac OS 8–8.5. However, you don't need to do this because the installer program for Mac OS 8–8.5 updates the driver for you.

✦ **Apple HD SC Setup.** Use this utility to update the hard disk driver before installing Mac OS 7.6–7.6.1 on a Quadra (except 630 series), Centris, LC (except 580 and 630 series), Mac II, Classic, SE, or PowerBook with a SCSI internal hard disk. This utility does not work with any IDE hard disks.

The Apple HD SC Setup program is obsolete after installing Mac OS 8–8.5. To test, format, partition, mount, or update the driver software of a disk with Mac OS 8–8.5, use the Drive Setup program in the Utilities folder on the startup disk.

CAUTION

Mac OS 8 Driver Compatibility

The hard disk driver software installed with Mac OS 8–8.5 is not compatible with computers that have 68000 processors. If a hard disk that uses Apple driver software is connected when you install Mac OS 8–8.5, you won't be able to use that hard disk subsequently with a Mac Plus, SE, original Classic, Portable, or PowerBook 100 computer.

CAUTION

Turn Off At Ease Security before Updating Driver

If your computer has Apple's At Ease software installed, you should turn off its disk security feature before updating your hard disk's driver with Drive Setup 1.3.1 or later. Otherwise you may be greeted by a flashing question mark when you next start up the computer. To turn off At Ease disk security, follow these steps:

1. Start the At Ease Administration program.

2. Choose System Settings from the Security menu.

3. Make sure the option "Prevent users from bypassing security by starting up from a floppy disk" is not selected.

If you neglect to follow this procedure before updating the hard disk driver, you can work around the problem by following these steps:

1. Restart from the Mac OS installation CD-ROM. (With the flashing question mark displayed, insert the CD-ROM and hold down the C key until you see the Welcome message.)

2. Use the Apple HD SC Setup program or the Drive Setup program from the CD-ROM to update the driver again. The hard disk icon should appear on the desktop.

3. Do one of the following:

   • If you used Drive Setup, restart the computer and turn off At Ease's disk security option (follow the three steps above). Restart again and use Drive Setup 1.3.1 or later to update the driver one more time. Then restart and turn on At Ease's disk security.

   • If you used Apple HD SC, restart the computer and back up important files. Then initialize (erase) the hard disk with Drive Setup 1.3.1 or later. Finally, restore files from backup and turn on At Ease's disk security.

Other hard disk utilities

You generally need a disk-formatting utility program other than Drive Setup or Apple HD SC Setup to update the driver software on a brand of hard disk other than Apple. Likewise, you need a different formatting utility to update the driver on an Apple hard disk whose driver someone once updated using a non-Apple formatting utility.

If you have an internal or external hard disk from a company other than Apple, contact the company for the latest version of its hard disk formatting utility. If that version is more recent than the one you have, use the more recent version to update your non-Apple hard disk's driver.

You can also switch to a different brand of driver software, such as Hard Disk Toolkit from FWB Software (415-463-3500, http://www.fwb.com). However, once you switch from an Apple driver to another brand, you generally can't switch back. Before switching to another brand of driver software, consider that Apple always updates its hard disk driver software to be compatible with the latest Mac OS. Other companies sometimes take longer than Apple to update their hard disk drivers for the latest Mac OS. The startup disk is particularly susceptible to incompatibilities between disk driver software and the Mac OS, so don't switch the startup disk from an Apple driver to another brand without good reason.

Configuring extensions

Some system extensions and control panels can interfere with installing or upgrading Mac OS 8–8.5. To avoid problems caused by antivirus, security, screen-saver, or energy-saver software, be sure to do the following before you begin the installation process:

✦ Disable At Ease or other security software that locks or restricts access to files, folders, or disks.

✦ Disable software that protects against viruses.

✦ Turn off screen-saver software.

✦ Deactivate all but the standard set of extensions and control panels for your version of the Mac OS, plus any other extensions and control panels required for installation, as follows:

- If you are upgrading from System 7–7.1.4, turn off all extensions by holding down the Shift key while restarting your computer.

- If you're upgrading from or reinstalling Mac OS 7.6–8.5 or System 7.5–7.5.5, open the Extensions Manager control panel and from its pop-up menu choose the extensions set that activates all the standard extensions for your Mac OS version. This extension set's name begins with your Mac OS version and may include the word *only* or *all,* as follows: System 7.5 Only, Mac OS 7.6 all, Mac OS 8 all, Mac OS 8.1 all, or Mac OS 8.5 All. Figure 30-2 shows this setting in Mac OS 8.1.

- If you have special equipment that requires extensions or control panels to start up, turn them back on in the Extensions Manager.

✦ Make sure the computer is not set to go to sleep or shut down automatically.

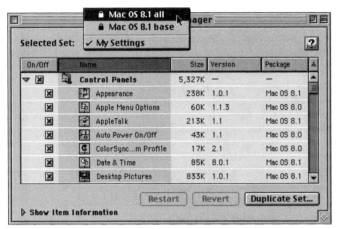

Figure 30-2: Activate only the standard extensions and control panels (plus any that are required for special equipment).

Tracking installer program actions

When you update the Mac OS or reinstall it, the installer program does more than add entirely new items. It also removes existing items from the startup disk (for which the installation software includes replacements), and then copies the replacements into the correct places on the startup disk. But the installer program gives you no record of what it has done. You can use the Labels submenu of the Finder's File menu (Mac OS 8–8.5) or the Labels menu (Mac OS 7.6–7.6.1 and System 7–7.5.5) to keep tabs on the changes by following these steps:

1. Print a report of the System Folder contents before using the installation software. To do that, open the System Folder, use the View menu to view the window contents as a list, choose Select All from the Edit menu, and press ⌘-Option-right arrow(→) to expand all folders within the System Folder. Then choose Print Window from the File menu to print the hierarchical list of System Folder contents.

   Alternatively, you can make a document containing an alphabetical list of everything in the System Folder. This is easy to do with the Finder's Find command. Start by opening the startup disk icon and selecting the System Folder icon. Next choose Find from the Finder's File menu, and set the search criteria to find items in the current Finder selection whose name is not "????" (or any other name you know doesn't exist). When the list of found items appears, you can select all, copy the items, and paste them into the Scrapbook, the Note Pad, or any text document for later reference. Figure 30-3 shows an alphabetical list of System Folder items that has been pasted into the Note Pad.

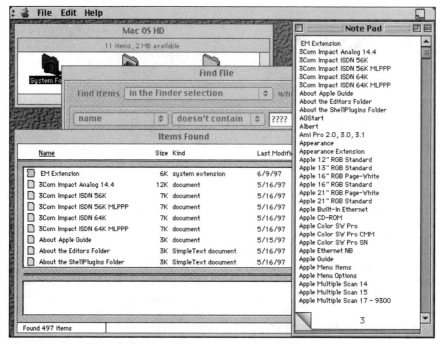

Figure 30-3: Use Find File (System 7.5–7.5.5 and Mac OS 7.6–8.1) or the Sherlock program (Mac OS 8.5) to make a list of all System folder items in the Note Pad.

2. Label every item that you want to keep track of in the System Folder. The simplest method is this: After expanding all folders as described in step 1, choose Select All from the Edit menu and choose one of the labels from the Label submenu of the File menu (Mac OS 8–8.5) or the Label menu (Mac OS 7.6–7.6.1 and System 7–7.5.5).

Alternatively, you can use multiple labels to categorize items. For example, you could label all items that are part of the Mac OS with one label and all items you have added with a different label. Use the Finder's Preferences command (Mac OS 8–8.5) or the Labels control panel (Mac OS 7.6–7.6.1 and System 7–7.5.5) if you want to change label names or colors (see "Labeling Items" in Chapter 6).

3. Install the Mac OS as described in Chapters 31 or 32. The installation process removes some of the items you labeled and adds other items, which are all unlabeled.

4. To see which items are new or replacements look in the System Folder for unlabeled items. You can search for unlabeled items in the System Folder using the Find File section of the Sherlock program (Mac OS 8.5) or the Find File program (Mac OS 7.6–7.6.1 and System 7.5–7.5.5). Start by selecting the

System Folder icon or folders inside it if you want to look for new items only in them. Next, set the Find File criteria to search for items in the Finder selection whose label is None (or is not the label you applied in step 2).

To determine which items are completely new and which have been deleted, print another report or make another alphabetical list of the System Folder contents following the procedures described in step 1. Compare the newer and older reports or the newer and older alphabetical lists. Brand-new items appear in the newer list but not in the older list. Deleted items appear in the older list but not in the newer list.

The one thing this procedure does not tell you is which unlabeled replacement items are newer versions of the items they replaced and which replacements are the same versions as the items that they replaced. However, there's a rough correlation between an item's version and its modification date. So you can get a rough idea of which items are new versions by using the Sherlock program or the Find File program to find the unlabeled items and then viewing the found items by date. Items at the top of the list are more likely to be new versions than are items at the bottom of the list.

Installing on a PowerBook

Although you can install or upgrade the Mac OS on a PowerBook under battery power, it's better to have the PowerBook plugged in, especially if you're installing from a set of floppy disks. If you are called away during installation, the PowerBook could go to sleep if it's operating on batteries.

You cannot install or upgrade the Mac OS correctly on a PowerBook's hard disk when it is in SCSI disk mode. A PowerBook is in SCSI disk mode when it is connected with a SCSI adapter cable to another computer and that computer is using the PowerBook as an external hard disk. In this scenario, you would be running the installer program on the other computer, not on the PowerBook, and the installer program would not install the pieces of the Mac OS specifically designed for PowerBooks.

To install or update the Mac OS correctly on a PowerBook, you must run the installer program on the PowerBook. You can use a set of floppy disks, a CD-ROM (in a drive connected to the PowerBook or in a shared drive you access over a network), and so on.

Performing a Clean Installation

Ordinarily, Apple's installation software upgrades the Mac OS that already exists on a computer, merging the new with the old. You get some entirely new items and some replacements for existing items that haven't changed, but preference files and files that contain your data are not replaced. For example, installing Mac OS 8.5 replaces the Scrapbook program but not items you have added to the Scrapbook file. Upgrading the existing Mac OS is the right thing to do unless your system has become unreliable and you can't seem to resolve its problems.

You can usually eliminate nagging system problems by installing a pristine copy of the Mac OS. This is known as a *clean installation,* and it's a favorite tonic of telephone technical support personnel because it's so effective. The trouble is, a clean installation of the Mac OS forces you to laboriously reinstall all of the control panels, extensions, fonts, Apple menu items, Startup items, and anything else that you have added to your System Folder since you started using your computer. You also have to reconfigure your control panels and reset options in most of your application programs because all of their settings are kept in preference files in the System Folder. And that's not all. You also need to reinstall application programs that keep auxiliary files and folders in the System Folder, such as most Claris and Adobe applications. Sure, you could copy files from the old System Folder to the new one, but that defeats the purpose of a clean installation, which is to stop using old, possibly damaged files. Performing a clean installation of the Mac OS is like moving to a new apartment because your old one smells bad. It might be easier to figure out what's causing the stink and fix it. (For troubleshooting guidance, see Chapter 29.)

Before going to the trouble of a clean installation, you should try replacing the Mac OS files in the System folder without touching the other files you have added there. To do this, you must be able to start your computer from the Mac OS installation CD (as described in "Startup Problems" in Chapter 29). Then you can drag the System file, Finder file, and System Resources file (Mac OS 8.5 only) out of the System Folder on your normal startup disk. Finally, do a standard installation — not a clean installation — of the Mac OS, as described in Chapter 31 or 32.

There are times when a clean slate is the simplest cure, or at any rate a useful diagnostic tool, because a computer clearly doesn't have a hardware malfunction if it works reliably with a cleanly installed System Folder. Apple's installation software makes it easy to do a clean installation of Mac OS 7.6–8.5. You'll find specific instructions for Mac OS 8–8.5 in Chapter 31, and for Mac OS 7.6–7.6.1 in Chapter 32.

After doing a clean installation, you may find that your printer's icon is missing from the left side of the Chooser. This means that the printer driver software for your printer is not included with the Mac OS. In this case, you must reinstall the software that came with your printer. Better yet, check with the printer's manufacturer to see if updated software is available. Note that older Apple StyleWriter and Color StyleWriter printers can use the latest StyleWriter and Color StyleWriter drivers installed with the Mac OS (see "Comparing Printer Driver Software" in Chapter 14).

Using Multiple Systems

You can switch between two versions of the Mac OS if necessary, even if you have only one hard disk. To install a second System Folder on a disk, perform a clean installation as described in the previous section. As part of a clean installation, your old System Folder is renamed Previous System Folder. Go ahead and change its name and the name the new System Folder if you can think of something more descriptive, such as System Folder 8.5 and System Folder 8.1. The System Folder can have any name and still function properly.

Apple ordinarily advises against installing two System Folders on the same disk, claiming you can't be sure which System Folder will be used during startup and become the active (or blessed) System Folder. Although multiple System Folders can lead to confusion, they don't have to lead to disaster. You can designate which System Folder will be the blessed one during the next startup or restart by using the System Picker utility (described in Chapter 26). Mac OS 8–8.5 requires System Picker 1.5 or later.

If you can't get System Picker, you can switch to a System Folder by deblessing all the others. To debless a System Folder, open it and drag the System file into the Startup Items folder. If you want to switch System Folders, first debless the current System Folder (the one with a small Mac OS badge). Then bless another System Folder by opening it, opening its Startup Items folder, and dragging the System file from the Startup Items folder to the System Folder. Close the System Folder window and make sure the System Folder icon now has a badge, indicating it's currently blessed.

Summary

After reading this chapter, you know which features and capabilities were added to, and in a few cases removed from, successive Mac OS versions. From reading this chapter you also know what kind of processor, how much RAM, and how much hard disk space the various Mac OS versions require.

In this chapter, you read that major releases of the Mac OS are sold on CD-ROMs and floppy disks. You can get software updates from the Apple Software Updates library on the Internet, America Online, and CompuServe.

This chapter recommended that before installing a new version of the Mac OS, you back up your disks, verify disk directories, update hard disk driver software, and turn off all but the standard Apple extensions and control panels plus any that are required for any special equipment on your computer. This chapter also explained how you can track installation activity with the Labels menu. In addition, this chapter made suggestions for trouble-free installation on PowerBooks.

Also covered in the chapter were the pros and cons of a clean installation. Although a clean installation prevents the carrying over of damaged files from the previous Mac OS, a normal installation is usually quite effective and not nearly as much work.

This chapter concluded by telling you how to switch systems when more than one is installed on your hard disk.

✦　　✦　　✦

Install Mac OS 8–8.5

Since the earliest days of the Macintosh, installing system software has been easy. Mac OS 8–8.5 makes it even simpler with its improved superinstaller, Mac OS Install. This program coordinates the installation of the basic system software as well as a host of supplemental modules such as Internet Access, QuickDraw 3D, Text-to-Speech, and more.

You set up the installation by selecting a destination disk and by optionally selecting a clean installation. Then you can do any of these types of installations:

+ **Standard installation** includes the basic system software modules and the most common supplemental modules. For Mac OS 8 and 8.1, you can select which supplemental modules you want included. All installed modules are automatically tailored for the type of Mac that's running Mac OS Install. (To select modules for Mac OS 8.5, you must do a custom installation.)

+ **Custom installation** includes only the modules you select, and gives you the opportunity to selectively install portions of each module.

+ **Universal installation** includes everything needed to start any kind of Mac, not just the kind that's running Mac OS Install.

+ **Minimal installation** takes as little disk space as possible, either for the kind of Mac that's running Mac OS Install or all kinds.

Before starting installation, you must make sure your computer can use the Mac OS version you want to install.

Compatibility

Unfortunately, Mac OS versions 8–8.5 aren't for everybody. Some Macs can't use these versions at all. On other Macs, you can install Mac OS 8–8.5 only after fixing problems. This section details these restrictions. (For a comparison of equipment requirements for Mac OS 7.6–8.5, see "Comparing Mac OS Versions" in Chapter 30.)

Processor requirements

Mac OS 8.5 requires a computer with a PowerPC processor. You can generally tell by a Mac's model name whether it can use Mac OS 8.5 or not. Any model with G3 in its name can use Mac OS 8.5, and so can the iMac. In addition, older models whose names contain four digits — for example, PowerBook Duo 2300, Power Mac 6100, and Performa 5200 — can use Mac OS 8.5. If a model's name has only three digits, it must use Mac OS 8.1 or earlier.

A Mac that has been upgraded with the logic board of a four-digit model can also use Mac OS 8.5. For example, a PowerBook Duo 230 that has been upgraded with a 2300 logic board can use Mac OS 8.5. A Mac that has a PowerPC upgrade card added to its logic board can't use Mac OS 8.5. For instance, a PowerBook 540c or a Quadra 650 with a PowerPC upgrade card must use Mac OS 8.1 or earlier.

Mac OS 8 and 8.1 don't require a PowerPC processor. They also work on Macs that were factory-equipped with 68040 processors. Nevertheless, Apple recommends using a PowerPC computer with Mac OS 8–8.1. In fact, many of Mac OS 8– 8.1's best features, such as the native Finder, benefit PowerPC computers the most.

A Mac with a 68030, 68020, or 68000 processor can't use Mac OS 8–8.5, even if the Mac has an accelerator card with a 68040 or PowerPC processor. These systems must use Mac OS 7.6.1 or earlier. (All Macs with 6800 or 68020 processors, and some with 68030 processors, must use System 7.5.5 or earlier. For details, see Chapter 32.)

iMac computers

iMac computers can use Mac OS 8.5, and some iMac computers can also use a special version of Mac OS 8.1. This special version of Mac OS 8.1 includes an extra file, Mac OS ROM, in the System Folder. iMacs that can use this special version of Mac OS 8.1 come with installation software for it on a CD-ROM. The regular version of Mac OS 8.1 does not work with iMac computers.

Mac 5200, 5300, 6200, and 6300 computers

Some Performa and Power Macintosh computers in the 5200, 5300, 6200, and 6300 series can't use Mac OS 8–8.5 until a hardware problem is fixed. The problem does not affect the 5260, 6320, or 6360 models. You can test for the problem by using the 5xxx/6xxx Tester utility in the Utilities folder on the Mac OS CD-ROM. In addition, the installation software for Mac OS 8–8.5 checks for the problem and alerts you if repairs are needed. The repairs are covered under an Apple warranty extension program that's in effect until 2003.

Accelerated 6100, 7100, 8100, and 9150 computers

The Mac OS Install program may not recognize a Power Mac or Performa 6100, 7100, 8100, or 9150 computer whose clock speed has been boosted with an accelerator. If this happens to you, remove the accelerator while installing Mac OS 8–8.5. If that's not feasible, and you're installing Mac OS 8, you can install each software module individually by running its Installer program. For a description of the basic procedure, see "Installing Mac OS Enhancements" in Chapter 32. You'll find the individual Installer programs in folders inside the Software Installers folder on the Mac OS 8 CD-ROM. You can't install Mac OS 8.1–8.5 by installing software modules individually.

Installation on removable disks

If you wish to install Mac OS 8.5 on an Iomega Zip or Jaz disk, you must reconfigure the virtual memory settings or install Iomega driver version 6.0.2 or later. The Iomega driver included with Mac OS 8.5 does not allow using the Zip or Jaz disk as a virtual memory disk. To reconfigure the virtual memory settings, restart with the ⌘ key held down, open the Memory control panel, turn on the Virtual Memory option, select a disk other than a Zip or Jaz disk, and restart. You can use a Zip or Jaz disk for Virtual Memory if you install version 6.0.2 or later of the Iomega driver. It's available from the Iomega Web site (http://www.iomega.com).

400K floppy disks

Mac OS 8–8.5 can't use 400K floppy disks. If you have information on 400K floppies, copy it to another disk before installing Mac OS 8–8.5.

Program memory requirements

Some programs need more memory with Mac OS 8–8.5 than with Mac OS 7.6.1 and earlier. If a program refuses to open with Mac OS 8–8.5, try increasing its minimum memory size by 200K or 300K in its Info window. You can display this window by selecting the program's icon and choosing Get Info from the Finder's File menu (for more information, see "Adjusting Application Memory Use" in Chapter 18).

Monitor resolution

Your monitor resolution may change after you do a clean installation of Mac OS 8.5. You can adjust your monitor resolution using the Monitors & Sound control panel or the Control Strip (see "Monitor Adjustments" in Chapter 11).

Standard Installation of Mac OS 8.5

A standard installation of Mac OS 8.5 includes the basic system software and several supplemental system software modules. If you want to pick and choose the modules to be installed, you must do a custom installation. For an explanation of the custom installation procedure, including a list of the system software modules, see "Custom Installation of Mac OS 8.5" later in this chapter.

The Mac OS Install program leads you through the four steps necessary to install Mac OS 8.5. In the first three steps, you select a destination disk, read a document about installing Mac OS 8.5, and agree to a software license. In the fourth step, you set a couple of options before you start installation. When you finish these four steps, the Mac OS Install program checks the condition of your hard disk's directory, updates your hard disk driver software (if you have an Apple hard disk), and then installs the basic system software and some common supplemental system software modules.

Starting the Mac OS Install program

To start the Mac OS Install program, insert the Mac OS 8.5 CD-ROM disc, find the Mac OS Install program, and double-click its icon. After a few seconds, the Install Mac OS 8.5 window appears, displaying some introductory information. Click the Continue button in this window to begin installation. Figure 31-1 shows the introductory information in the Install Mac OS 8.5 window.

Figure 31-1: Read the introductory information in the Install Mac OS 8.5 window.

Selecting a destination

The first step to installing the Mac OS is to choose a disk for it. A pop-up menu lists the available disks. When you choose a disk from the pop-up menu, the Mac OS

Install program reports the disk's system software version and the amount of free space available. This step also gives you the option of selecting a clean installation. (For general advice on doing a clean installation, see "Performing a Clean Installation" in Chapter 30.) Figure 31-2 shows this first step in the Install Mac OS 8.5 window.

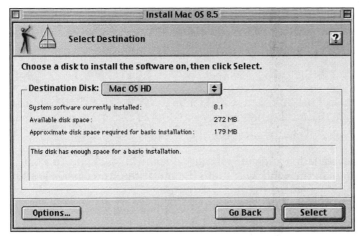

Figure 31-2: Choose a hard disk and optionally select a clean installation.

A standard installation of Mac OS 8.5 requires 170MB to 210MB of free space. The exact amount depends on your computer model. If you want to make more space available on the hard disk you've chosen, you can switch to the Finder, delete some files from that disk, and then switch back to the Mac OS Install program. (Use the Application menu at the right end of the menu bar to switch to and from the Finder.)

If you want to do a clean installation, click the Options button at the bottom of the Install Mac OS 8.5 window. In the dialog box that appears, turn on the option Perform Clean Installation and click OK.

After choosing a destination disk and deciding whether to perform a clean installation, click the Select button at the bottom of the Install Mac OS 8.5 window to go to the second step. You can also go back to the introduction by clicking the Go Back button.

If you chose a destination disk that already has Mac OS 8.5 installed, the Mac OS Install program displays an alert box explaining the situation and giving you three choices: Reinstall, Add/Remove, or Cancel. If you want to choose a different destination disk, click Cancel. If you want to replace the system software with a clean copy, click Reinstall. If you want to add or remove portions of the system software, click Add/Remove. If you click Add/Remove, the Mac OS Install program skips the second and third installation steps and switches from a standard installation to a custom installation. In this case, you should continue reading at "Custom Installation for Mac OS 8.5."

Reading installation information

In the second installation step, the Install Mac OS 8.5 window displays a document containing last-minute installation information for Mac OS 8.5. It's tempting to skip this document, but the information provided actually is important, and you should at least skim it for the mention of your computer model, printers you use, and software you use. You can print the document by clicking the Print button at the bottom of the window. You can also save the document on disk, but there's no need to because it's already available on the installation CD-ROM.

The CD-ROM contains other text documents with additional information about Mac OS 8.5. You would be wise to read these documents as well. You don't have to quit the Mac OS Install program to read these documents. You can switch to the Finder (by choosing it from the Application menu) and double-click the documents whose names begin with "About" in the CD-ROM window.

After reading the installation and compatibility document, click the Continue button at the bottom of the window to go to the third step. You can also return to the previous step by clicking the Go Back button.

Agreeing to the software license

In the third installation step, the Install Mac OS 8.5 window displays a license agreement. The license agreement is filled with lawyerspeak, but you should look through it so you know what you're agreeing to. For example, one provision states that you may only install the software on one computer at a time. You can print the license agreement or save a copy on disk by clicking the Print or Save button at the bottom of the window.

Click the Continue button when you're ready to go to the last step. A small dialog box appears, asking if you agree or disagree with the terms of the license. You cannot continue with the installation unless you click the Agree button!

Selecting options

In the last installation step, you set some options, as detailed in the following paragraphs, before starting installation. In addition, you can initiate a custom installation instead of a standard installation (see "Custom Installation of Mac OS 8.5" later in this chapter). Figure 31-3 shows the last step of the Mac OS Install program for Mac OS 8.5.

The hard disk driver update option

The Mac OS Install program normally updates the driver software on Apple hard disks. If you don't want this to happen, click the Options button at the bottom of the Install Mac OS 8.5 window and in the dialog box that appears turn off the Update Apple Hard Disk Drivers option. (For more information on updating hard disk drivers, see "Preparing for Installation" in Chapter 30.)

The installation report option

The Mac OS Install program normally creates a report that details which files were installed and where. You can suppress this report by clicking the Options button at the bottom of the Install Mac OS window and turning off the Create option in the dialog box that appears.

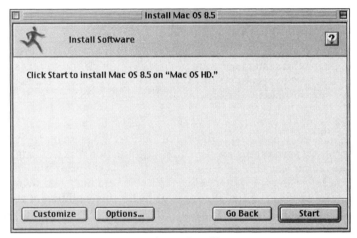

Figure 31-3: Set options and start installing Mac OS 8.5.

Installation starts

To begin the installation, click the Start button in the Install Mac OS window. The Mac OS Install program checks the destination disk's directory to ensure that files can be written to the disk properly. Next, the Mac OS Install program updates the drivers of Apple hard disks unless you have turned off the Update Apple Hard Disk Drivers option, as described previously. These procedures in no way affect the contents of your disk.

After checking the disk directory and updating Apple hard disk drivers, the Mac OS Install program begins installing system software modules. A standard installation proceeds automatically unless you are installing from floppy disks or a problem occurs. If you are installing from a CD-ROM, a standard installation doesn't require more of your attention until it finishes. If you are installing from floppy disks and the Mac OS Install program needs a different disk, the program ejects the disk that it is using and asks you to insert the disk it needs.

You can always cancel an installation that's underway by clicking the Cancel button. If you cancel an installation in progress, the Mac OS Install program displays an alert asking how you want to proceed. You can stop installation, skip installation of the module currently being installed, or try installing again.

When you restart the computer after a successful installation, Mac OS Setup program opens automatically and asks you for information to configure the computer. (For details, see "Mac OS Setup Assistant" at the end of this chapter.) In addition, after the first restart, the Finder may automatically rebuild the desktop database of all disks (see "Checking the Desktop Database" in Chapter 10).

Standard Installation of Mac OS 8 or 8.1

A standard installation of Mac OS 8 or 8.1 includes the basic system software and your choice of supplemental system software modules. Although you can pick and choose the supplemental modules to be installed, you must do a custom installation to install portions of modules (see "Custom Installation of Mac OS 8 or 8.1" later in this chapter).

The Mac OS Install program leads you through the four steps necessary to install Mac OS 8 or 8.1. The first three steps are selecting a destination disk, reading a document about installing Mac OS 8 or 8.1, and agreeing to a software license. In the fourth step, you select the software modules that you want installed. When you finish these four steps, the Mac OS Install program checks the condition of your hard disk's directory, updates your hard disk driver software (if you have an Apple hard disk), and then automatically runs a subordinate Installer program for each system software module you selected. This section describes the installation process.

Starting the Mac OS Install program

To start the Mac OS Install program, insert the Mac OS CD-ROM disc or the Mac OS Install Me First floppy disk, find the Mac OS Install program, and double-click its icon. After a few seconds, a window appears, displaying some introductory information. This window is titled Install Mac OS 8 or Mac OS 8.1 Install. Click the Continue button in this window to begin installation. Figure 31-4 shows the introductory information in the Mac OS 8.1 Install window.

Selecting a destination

The first step to installing the Mac OS is to choose a disk for it. A pop-up menu lists the available disks. When you choose a disk from the pop-up menu, the Mac OS Install program reports the disk's system software version and the amount of free space available. This step also gives the option of selecting a clean installation. (For advice on doing a clean installation, see "Performing a Clean Installation" in Chapter 30.) Figure 31-5 shows this first step in the Mac OS 8.1 Install window.

Figure 31-4: Read the introductory information in the Mac OS Install program's window.

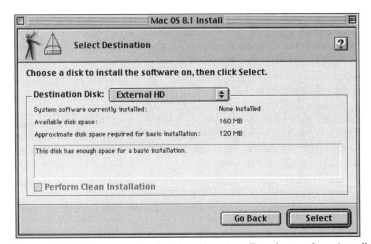

Figure 31-5: Choose a hard disk and optionally select a clean installation.

A standard installation of Mac OS 8 requires about 95MB of free space, and Mac OS 8.1 requires about 120MB. In each case, the exact amount depends on your computer model. If you elect to install more or fewer software modules than are included in a standard installation, you will need more or less free disk space. Unfortunately, the Mac OS Install program does not help you figure out how much more or less disk space you will need for a nonstandard installation. If you want to make more space available on the hard disk you've chosen, you can switch to the Finder, delete some files from that disk, and then switch back to the Mac OS Install program. (Use the Application menu at the right end of the menu bar to switch to and from the Finder.)

After choosing a destination disk and deciding whether to perform a clean installation, click the Select button at the bottom of the Mac OS Install program's window to go to the second step. You can also go back to the introduction by clicking the Go Back button.

If you choose a destination disk that already has the same version of the Mac OS as you're about to install, the Mac OS Install program displays an alert box explaining the situation and giving you three choices: Reinstall, Add/Remove, or Cancel. If you want to choose a different destination disk, click Cancel. If you want to add or remove portions of the system software, click Reinstall. If you click Add/Remove, the Mac OS Install program skips the second and third installation steps and switches from a standard installation to a custom installation. In this case, you should continue reading at "Custom Installation of Mac OS 8 or 8.1."

Reading installation information

In the second installation step, the Mac OS Install program's window displays a document containing last-minute installation information for Mac OS 8 or 8.1. It's tempting to skip this document, but the information provided actually is important, and you should at least skim it for the mention of your computer model, printers you use, and software you use. You can print the document by clicking the Print button at the bottom of the window. You can also save the document on disk, but there's no need to because it's already available on the installation CD-ROM or floppy disk.

The CD-ROM or floppy disk contains other text documents with additional information about the Mac OS version you're about to install. You would be wise to read these documents as well. You don't have to quit the Mac OS Install program to read these documents. You can switch to the Finder (by choosing it from the Application menu) and double-click the documents whose names begin with "About" in the CD-ROM or floppy disk window.

After reading the installation and compatibility document, click the Continue button at the bottom of the window to go to the third step. You can also go back to the previous step by clicking the Go Back button.

Agreeing to the software license

In the third installation step, the Mac OS Install program's window displays a license agreement. The license agreement is filled with lawyerspeak, but you should look through it so you know what you're agreeing to. For example, one provision states that you may only install the software on one computer at a time. You can print the license agreement or save a copy on disk by clicking the Print or Save buttons at the bottom of the window.

Click the Continue button when you're ready to go to the last step. A small dialog box appears, asking if you agree or disagree with the terms of the license. You cannot continue with the installation unless you click the Agree button!

Selecting modules and options

In the fourth step of a standard installation for Mac OS 8 and 8.1, the Install Mac OS window displays a checklist of software modules from which you select the ones you want to install. You also have the option of turning off the updating of Apple hard disk driver software. You click a button to start installation. Under the control of the Mac OS Install program, each selected module is installed by a separate Installer program. During a standard installation, the individual Installer programs do not require any response from you unless you are installing from floppy disks or a problem occurs. Figure 31-6 shows the last step of the Mac OS Install program configured for a standard installation of Mac OS 8.1.

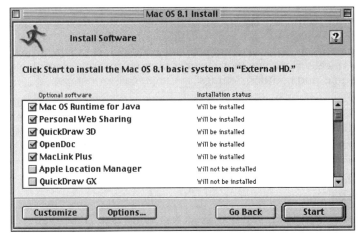

Figure 31-6: Select modules for a standard installation of Mac OS 8 or 8.1.

Setting the hard disk driver update option

The Mac OS Install program normally updates the driver software on Apple hard disks. If you don't want this to happen, click the Options button at the bottom of the Mac OS Install program's window and in the dialog box that appears turn off the Update Apple Hard Disk Drivers option. (For more information on updating hard disk drivers, see "Preparing for Installation" in Chapter 30.)

Selecting modules

There are ten optional modules in the checklist for a standard installation of Mac OS 8 or 8.1. Some may be selected initially, but you can easily change the selection by clicking the modules' checkboxes. To display information about a module, click its information button at the right side of the checklist. These optional modules are available in the standard Mac OS 8 or 8.1 installation:

✦ **Mac OS Runtime for Java** lets you run Java applets and applications on your computer (see the description of Apple Applet Runner in "Accessory Program Encyclopedia" in Chapter 25 for more details).

✦ **Personal Web Sharing** lets your computer host a Web site (see "Sharing Your Own Web Site" in Chapter 17 for more details).

✦ **QuickDraw 3D** makes viewing and manipulating three-dimensional models and objects just as easy as watching QuickTime movies (see "Viewing QuickDraw 3D Objects " in Chapter 16 for more details).

✦ **OpenDoc** provides the underlying foundation for creating compound documents using diverse plug-in software components instead of conventional applications (see "OpenDoc Compound Documents" in Chapter 24 for details).

✦ **MacLink Plus** can translate between Windows and Mac OS files (see "Translating Documents" in Chapter 7 for details).

✦ **Apple Location Manager** assists in switching groups of control panel settings all at once, typically when you move your computer from one place to another (see "Date, Time, and Location Settings" in Chapter 11 for details).

✦ **Cyberdog,** which is not included with Mac OS 8.1, is Apple's groundbreaking software (based on OpenDoc) for incorporating live Web pages and other Internet content into documents together with ordinary text, pictures, movies, sound (see "Sending and Receiving E-mail" and "Browsing the World Wide Web" in Chapter 17 for details).

✦ **QuickDraw GX** provides extensive typography enhancements (see "QuickDraw GX Typography" in Chapter 13 for details).

✦ **Text-To-Speech** lets your computer speak text aloud (see "Text-to-Speech" in Chapter 22 for details).

✦ **Apple Remote Access Client** lets your computer connect to a remote AppleTalk network by modem (see "Making a Remote Network Connection in Mac OS 7.6–8.1" in Chapter 19 for details).

Starting installation

To begin the installation, click the Start button. The Mac OS Install program checks the destination disk's directory to ensure that files can be written to the disk properly. Next, the Mac OS Install program updates the drivers of Apple hard disks unless you have turned off the Update Apple Hard Disk Drivers options, as described above. These procedures in no way affect the contents of your disk.

After checking the disk directory and updating Apple hard disk drivers, the Mac OS Install program gives control to a succession of subordinate Installer programs, one for each Mac OS 8 module to be installed. Each Installer program briefly displays the message "Preparing to install" and then displays the folders (or disks) it needs and begins installation. When you install from the Mac OS 8.1 CD-ROM, Mac OS Install runs the Installers for Mac OS 8 first. Then it runs the Installer for Mac OS 8.1 Update, LaserWriter 8.5.1, and Open Transport 1.3. The individual Installer programs do not display welcome messages or offer installation options.

When you restart the computer after a successful installation, Mac OS Setup program opens automatically and asks you for information to configure the computer. (For details, see "Mac OS Setup Assistant" at the end of this chapter.) In addition, after the first restart, the Finder may automatically rebuild the desktop database of all inserted disks (see "Checking the Desktop Database" in Chapter 10).

Custom Installation of Mac OS 8.5

A custom installation of Mac OS 8.5 provides the opportunity to select individual system software modules and to select individual components of modules. For example, you must do a custom installation to install the Easy Access and CloseView control panels, which are part of the Mac OS 8.5 module. A custom installation also provides the opportunity to remove all or part of a module.

To do a custom installation of Mac OS 8.5, follow the first three steps of the four-step procedure that you use for a standard installation as described in "Standard Installation of Mac OS 8.5" earlier in this chapter. In the fourth step, click the Customize button in the Install Mac OS 8.5 window. Clicking the Customize button reveals a checklist of available system software modules. Each module can be included or excluded individually. You can also include or exclude portions of some modules. Figure 31-7 shows the last step of the Mac OS Install program configured for a custom installation.

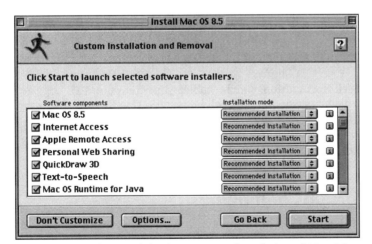

Figure 31-7: Select modules for a custom installation of Mac OS 8.5.

Selecting modules

There are 11 modules in the checklist for a custom installation of Mac OS 8.5. The first eight modules are initially selected because they are part of a standard installation. You can easily change the selection by clicking a module's checkbox.

To display information about a module, click its information button at the right side of the checklist. You can choose from these modules:

✦ **Mac OS 8.5**, which includes the core system software (described in detail throughout Chapters 4–15, 18–21, and 23–25).

✦ **Internet Access**, which includes Microsoft Internet Explorer or Netscape Navigator, Microsoft Outlook Express, Internet Setup Assistant, Connect To, Internet control panel, StuffIt Expander, and Installer for DropStuff with Expander Enhancer (all described in detail in Chapter 17).

✦ **Apple Remote Access**, which lets your computer connect to the Internet, a remote TCP/IP network, or a remote AppleTalk network by modem (see "Making a Remote Network Connection Mac OS 8.5" in Chapter 19 for details).

✦ **Personal Web Sharing**, which lets your computer host a Web site (see "Sharing Your Own Web Site" in Chapter 17 for more details).

✦ **QuickDraw 3D**, which makes viewing and manipulating 3D models and objects just as easy as watching QuickTime movies (see "Viewing QuickDraw 3D Objects" in Chapter 16 for more details).

✦ **Text-To-Speech**, which lets your computer speak text aloud (see "Text-To-Speech" in Chapter 22 for details).

✦ **Mac OS Runtime for Java**, which lets you run Java applets and applications on your computer (see the description of Apple Applet Runner in "Accessory Program Encyclopedia" in Chapter 25 for more details).

✦ **ColorSync**, which manages color to improve consistency from scanner to monitor to printed page (see "Monitor Adjustments" in Chapter 11 for details).

✦ **QuickDraw GX**, which provides extensive typography enhancements (see "QuickDraw GX Typography" in Chapter 13 for details).

✦ **English Speech Recognition**, which enables your computer to recognize North American English speech (see "Speech Recognition" in Chapter 22 for details).

✦ **World Wide Web Access**, which lets you view multilingual text using the WorldScript system software and multilingual application software (see "Languages Preferences" in Chapter 11 for details).

Selecting portions of modules

You can selectively install portions of a module by choosing Customized Installation from the pop-up menu next to the module's name. This brings up a dialog box that contains a checklist of components and, in some cases, groups of components that you can install. To expand a component group, click the disclosure triangle next to it. You can get information about a component by clicking its information button at the right side of the checklist. Select the components that you want to install by clicking the appropriate checkboxes. You can select all or none of the components by choosing from the pop-up menu at the top of the dialog box. Figure 31-8 shows the checklist of components for the Mac OS 8.5 module.

Custom Installation of Mac OS 8 or 8.1

A custom installation of Mac OS 8 or 8.1 gives you the opportunity to select individual system software modules and to select individual components of modules. For example, you must do a custom installation to install the Easy Access and CloseView control panels, which are part of the Mac OS 8 module. A custom installation also gives you the opportunity to remove all or part of a module. Do a custom installation only if you are sure that you know which individual items must be present for a module to work properly.

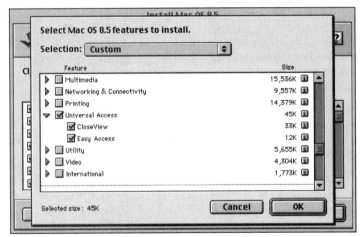

Figure 31-8: Select components to be installed from one Mac OS 8.5 module.

To do a custom installation of Mac OS 8 or 8.1, follow the first three steps of the four-step procedure that you use for a standard installation as described in "Standard Installation of Mac OS 8 or 8.1" earlier in this chapter. In the fourth step, click the Customize button in the Mac OS Install program's window. Clicking the Customize button expands the checklist of available software modules by adding four that are not listed in a standard installation. Each module can be included or excluded individually. You can also include or exclude portions of some modules. Figure 31-9 shows the last step of the Mac OS Install program configured for a custom installation.

Selecting modules

There are 14 modules in the checklist for a custom installation of Mac OS 8 or 8.1. The last ten modules are the same as for a standard installation and are described in "Standard Installation of Mac OS 8 or 8.1" earlier in this chapter. These four modules appear at the top of the checklist only for a custom installation:

✦ **Mac OS 8**, which includes the core system software (described in detail throughout Chapters 4–15, 18–21, and 23–25).

✦ **Mac OS Info Center**, which provides an overview of system software features, some troubleshooting pointers, and a list of places to start exploring the Internet; you view all this with a Web browser after installation.

✦ **Internet Access**, which includes Netscape Navigator (Mac OS 8) or Microsoft Internet Explorer (Mac OS 8.1), Claris Emailer Lite, Internet Dialer, Internet Setup Assistant, Connect To, Internet Config, StuffIt Expander, and Installer for DropStuff with Expander Enhancer (all described in detail in Chapter 17).

✦ **Open Transport PPP**, which lets you connect your computer by modem to remote TCP/IP networks such as the Internet (for details, see "Making a Dial-Up TCP/IP Connection" in Chapter 19).

You select which of the 14 modules will be installed by clicking their checkboxes. You can display information about a module by clicking its information button at the right side of the checklist.

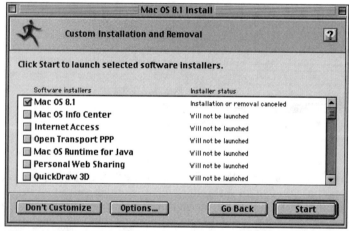

Figure 31-9: Select modules for a custom installation of Mac OS 8 or 8.1.

Selecting portions of modules

In a custom installation, you must interact with a subordinate Installer program for each module that you select. This interaction provides the opportunity to select specific components to be installed or removed. The Mac OS Installer program gives control to the Installer program for each selected module in turn. Some of the Installer programs display an initial welcome message that you must dismiss in order to see the Installer's main window, which describes what will be installed. Figure 31-10 shows the Installer for the main Mac OS 8 module.

To install a complete module, choose Easy Install from the pop-up menu in the Installer's main window and click the Install button in that window. (If the Installer has no pop-up menu, simply click the Install button.)

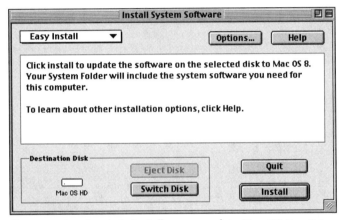

Figure 31-10: Ready to install one complete Mac OS 8 or 8.1 module.

To selectively install portions of the module, choose Custom Install from the pop-up menu in the Installer window. The Installer lists the components and, in some cases, groups of components that you can install. To expand a component group, click the disclosure triangle next to it. You can get information about a component by clicking its information button at the right side of the Installer window. Select the components that you want to install by clicking the appropriate checkboxes, and then clicking the Install button. Figure 31-11 shows the Custom Install section of the Installer for the main Mac OS 8 module.

To selectively remove portions of the module, choose Custom Remove from the pop-up menu in the Installer window. Select the components or groups of components that you want removed, and click the Remove button.

Figure 31-11: Select components to be installed from one Mac OS 8 or 8.1 module.

Universal Installation of Mac OS 8–8.5

When you perform a standard installation, the Mac OS Install program installs the correct files and resources for the computer model you're using. This is very handy as it keeps your System Folder from becoming bloated with unnecessary files. However, it makes life difficult if you're installing Mac OS 8–8.5 on a different computer than it will be used on. For instance, if you install Mac OS 8.1 on a PowerPC computer's Jaz or SyJet removable disk and then move the removable disk to a Quadra, which has a 68040 processor, the Quadra won't be able to start from the disk.

To get around this problem, you need to perform a universal installation. This places all of the files for all Mac models onto the selected hard disk. The resultant System Folder is much larger, but it will be able to start any kind of computer that can use the Mac OS version you install. If you're creating an emergency startup Zip disk for use with Norton Utilities, for instance, you'll probably want to do a universal installation so that it can be used on any computer.

To create a universal installation of Mac OS 8–8.5, you must do a custom installation as described previously in "Custom Installation of Mac OS 8.5" and "Custom Installation of Mac OS 8 or 8.1." In the last step of the Mac OS Install program, be sure to select the Mac OS 8.5, Mac OS 8.1, or Mac OS 8 module. You don't have to select the other modules (Internet Access, Text-To-Speech, and so on) if you know you're not going to need them with this disk. Then bring up the checklist of components for the Mac OS module, and select the "Universal System for any supported computer" component. When you're ready to proceed with installation, click the Start button (Mac OS 8.5) or the Install button (Mac OS 8–8.1). You should be able to use the resulting disk to start any computer that can use the Mac OS version you installed.

Minimal Installation of Mac OS 8–8.5

Unlike Mac OS 7.6–7.6.1, there is no option for a minimal floppy installation of Mac OS 8–8.5. You can't install Mac OS 8–8.5 onto a floppy disk. The only way to get Mac OS 8–8.5 on a floppy disk is to copy the 1MB System Folder from a Disk Tools floppy disk to another floppy disk. The resulting system software looks and works more like Mac OS 7.6 than 8–8.5, but it does start a computer that requires Mac OS 8–8.5. (You can make Disk Tools floppy disks from the image files in the Disk Tools folder on the Mac OS CD-ROM.)

Mac OS 8–8.5 on a Zip disk

It is possible to squeeze a standard installation of Mac OS 8 on a 94MB Zip disk or an 88MB SyQuest cartridge. Mac OS 8 seems to fit on these disks even though Apple says you need 95MB of hard disk space.

To fit Mac OS 8.1 on a Zip disk, you must exclude some of the system software modules that are normally included in a standard installation. Be sure to include the Mac OS 8.1 module.

To fit Mac OS 8.5 on a Zip disk, you must do a custom installation. In the last step of the Mac OS Install program, select only the Mac OS 8.5 module. Then choose Customize Installation from the pop-up menu for the Mac OS 8.5 module to bring up the checklist of components, and select the component "System software for this computer." You can also select other components as long as the selected size reported in the bottom left corner of the dialog box does not exceed about 96,000K.

Minimal System Folder

The smallest System Folder you can install with the Mac OS Install program takes about 11.5MB (Mac OS 8), 18.1MB (Mac OS 8.1), or 13.7MB (Mac OS 8.5). To get a minimal System Folder, you must do a custom installation as described previously in "Custom Installation of Mac OS 8.5" and "Custom Installation of Mac OS 8 or 8.1." In the last step of the Mac OS Install program, select only the Mac OS module. Then bring up the checklist of components for the Mac OS 8.5, Mac OS 8.1, or Mac OS 8 module, and select only the Core System Software component from the checklist of installable components. The resulting svelte System Folder starts fast and uses substantially fewer megabytes of RAM than a standard System Folder because it includes only a few control panels and extensions.

Mac OS Setup Assistant

The first time you start up the computer after installing Mac OS 8–8.5, the Mac OS Setup Assistant program opens automatically. It asks you for some basic information about yourself and how you will use your computer. It requests the information in several sections, which it displays one at a time. After entering information in one section, you go to the next section by clicking the right-arrow button (→). You can also go back to the previous section by clicking the left-arrow (←) button. You enter information in these sections:

✦ **Regional preferences**, which sets the keyboard layout and the formats for time, date, text, and numbers based on the region or language you select.

✦ **Name and organization**, which identify you when your computer is connected to a local network. In addition, some application programs pick up this information automatically to save you typing.

✦ **Time and date**, which set your computer's clock and calendar. They establish the creation date and modification date for each of your files, set the date on e-mail you send, and so forth.

✦ **Geographic location**, which is used to adjust for time-zone differences.

✦ **Finder preferences**, which lets you set the Simple Finder option in Mac OS 8.5 (see "Simple Finder" in Chapter 5).

✦ **Computer name and password**, which identifies your computer when it is connected to a local area network and which prevents other network users from accessing your computer as its owner.

✦ **Shared folder**, which lets you create and name a folder whose contents can be accessed by everyone connected to your local network.

✦ **Printer connection**, which specifies whether your printer and computer have a direct connection or a network connection. If your printer has a network connection and is turned off, the Setup Assistant will not notice it and you will have to use the Chooser to select it later (see "Choosing the Default Printer" in Chapter 14).

✦ **Printer type**, which appears if you specified a direct printer connection. It also specifies which driver software and port the printer uses.

✦ **Printing connection**, which appears if you specified a network printer connection. It lets you specify your favorite network printer. If your favorite printer isn't listed or no printers are listed, don't worry. You can use the Chooser later to designate your favorite printer (see "Choosing the Default Printer" in Chapter 14).

When you finish entering the printer type or printer connection, the Mac OS Setup Assistant displays a Conclusion section. This section contains three buttons: Show Details, Cancel, and Go Ahead. If you want to recap the information you entered, click Show Details. If you want to quit the Mac OS Setup Assistant without having it save any of your information, click Cancel. If you want the Mac OS Setup Assistant to create settings based on the information you entered, click Go Ahead.

If you click Go Ahead, the Mac OS Setup Assistant configures your system with the information you entered. When it finishes, it gives you two choices: Quit or Continue. If you want to begin working immediately, click Quit. If you want to set up an Internet connection now, click Continue. Clicking the Continue button opens the Internet Setup Assistant program, which is described in detail in "Setting up an Internet Connection" in Chapter 17.

Summary

This chapter explained how to install Mac OS 8, 8.1, and 8.5. It told you which computer models are compatible with each version and what to do if yours isn't. You learned how to perform a standard installation and how to customize that installation to suit your needs. This chapter also described how to do a universal installation on an external disk so that the external disk can start any computer capable of using the Mac OS version you installed. In addition, this chapter told you how to create a startup disk with a minimal Mac OS 8–8.5 System Folder. Finally, this chapter described how to use the Mac OS Setup Assistant when you restart after installing Mac OS 8–8.5.

✦　　✦　　✦

Install Mac OS 7.6.1 and Mac OS Enhancements

Although the latest Mac OS is great, your computer may require something older than Mac OS 8.5 or even Mac OS 8. Mac OS 7.6.1 is the latest version that you can use on a Mac that was originally equipped with a 68020 or 68030 processor. The first section of this chapter discusses Mac OS 7.6–7.6.1 compatibility topics in detail.

If your computer now has Mac OS 7.6, you can upgrade it to version 7.6.1 from a set of floppy disks or a folder of installation software. If your computer has System 7.0–7.5.5, you can install Mac OS 7.6 or 7.6.1 from a CD-ROM or a set of floppy disks. If you have a CD-ROM or floppy disks that install Mac OS 7.6, you can subsequently upgrade to Mac OS 7.6.1. The second section of this chapter tells you how to install Mac OS 7.6.1 or Mac OS 7.6 from a CD-ROM or a set of installation floppy disks. The third section of this chapter explains how to upgrade Mac OS 7.6 to 7.6.1.

Whether your computer uses the latest Mac OS or an earlier version, you can periodically enhance it by installing an upgraded module such as the latest QuickTime. The last section of this chapter tells you how to install these individual modules.

Compatibility

Although many Mac models can use Mac OS 7.6–7.6.1, not all can. In addition, some of the individual Mac OS 7.6–7.6.1 modules are not compatible with either every Mac model or with all Mac software. Also, newer versions of several modules are available for separate installation. The following paragraphs detail these conditions.

Core requirements

The Mac OS 7.6 and 7.6.1 core software requires a Mac that was originally equipped with a 68030, 68040, or PowerPC processor and that has a 32-bit clean ROM. The following models can't use Mac OS 7.6: Plus, SE, SE/30, II, IIx, IIcx, Portable, PowerBook 100, original Classic, and original LC. System 7.5.5 is the latest version that those models can use. Those models cannot be made eligible for Mac OS 7.6 by installing the MODE32 software to enable 32-bit addressing or by installing hardware accelerators. (Models older than a Mac Plus can't use System 7.0 or later.)

A number of Mac OS models can use Mac OS 7.6.1 but not Mac OS 7.6. These models are the Power Mac 4400, 5500, 6500, 7300, 8600/200, 9600/200, 9600/200 MP, and 9600/233. To install Mac OS 7.6.1 on these models, you must install from a full set of 7.6.1 installation software, which is available from the Mac OS Up-to-Date program (800-335-9258, http://www.apple.com/macos/up-to-date/). On these models, you can't install Mac OS 7.6 and then upgrade it to Mac OS 7.6.1.

Newer Mac models that originally shipped with Mac OS 8–8.5 cannot use Mac OS 7.6–7.6.1 at all. These models include the iMac, all Power Mac G3 models, and all PowerBook G3 models. Each of these must use a Mac OS version the same as or newer than the version it came with.

QuickDraw 3D

QuickDraw 3D requires a PowerPC processor. You can't install it on a computer with a 68030 or 68040 processor. A newer version of QuickDraw 3D is included with QuickTime 3.0, which is available from Apple's QuickTime Web site (http://www.apple.com/quicktime/).

OpenDoc, Cyberdog, and LaserWriter 8.4

OpenDoc, Cyberdog, and the LaserWriter 8.4 printer driver require a common piece of software on computers without PowerPC processors. The software, called the CFM 68K Runtime Enabler 4.0, is included with Mac OS 7.6.1 but not with Mac OS 7.6. Without the 68K Runtime Enabler 4.0, you cannot use OpenDoc, OpenDoc Essentials, Cyberdog, or LaserWriter 8.4 on a computer with a 68030 or 68040 processor.

A few application programs also require the CFM 68K Runtime Enabler 4.0, including Apple Telecom 3.0, Apple Games Sprockets, and the Apple Media Tool. The 68K Runtime Enabler 4.0 is included with the Mac OS 7.6.1 Update and is available separately from Apple's Software Updates library (http://www.info.apple.com/swupdates/). You don't need the 68K Runtime Enabler 4.0 on a computer with a PowerPC processor.

Cyberdog 2.0 is available from Apple's Cyberdog Web site (http://www.cyberdog.apple.com). Newer versions of the LaserWriter printer driver are available from Apple's Software Updates library (http://www.info.apple.com/swupdates/).

Mac 5200, 5300, 6200, and 6300 series

Some Performa and Power Macintosh computers in the 5200, 5300, 6200, and 6300 series can't use Mac OS 7.6 or 7.6.1 until a hardware problem is fixed. The problem does not affect the 5260, 6320, or 6360 models. You can test for the problem by using the 5xxx/6xxx Tester utility in the Utilities folder on the CD-ROM. In addition, the Mac OS 7.6 and 7.6.1 installation software checks for the problem and alerts you if repairs are needed. The repairs are covered under an Apple warranty extension program that's in effect until 2003.

Open Transport

If you have installed Open Transport 1.1.2 or newer, it will be replaced with an older version when you install Mac OS 7.6 or 7.6.1. After installing Mac OS 7.6 or 7.6.1, you must reinstall your newer version of Open Transport. A newer version of Open Transport is available separately from Apple's Software Updates library (http://www.info.apple.com/swupdates/).

AppleShare Workstation software

If your computer has AppleShare Workstation software installed, you must make sure it is version 3.6.3 or later before installing Mac OS 7.6 or 7.6.1 over a network. Apple Workstation 3.6.3 is included in the Utilities folder of the Mac OS 7.6 or 7.6.1 CD-ROM. To install it, drag its icon to the System Folder icon of the startup disk.

QuickDraw GX drivers

If you have a printer that doesn't use LaserWriter 8 or another Apple printer driver software and you want to install QuickDraw GX, you need to get a QuickDraw GX driver for your printer. Once QuickDraw GX is installed, you will not be able to print without a GX driver. Mac OS 7.6 and 7.6.1 includes GX printer drivers for Apple printers. Contact the maker of your printer for assistance.

Adobe Acrobat

If your computer has Adobe Acrobat installed and you use the Mac OS 7.6 or 7.6.1 installation software to install or remove QuickDraw GX, Acrobat will display a message about missing fonts each time that the computer starts. Reinstall Acrobat to stop the message — simply disabling QuickDraw GX with the Extensions Manager control panel does not stop the message.

Apple Remote Access

If you install Apple Remote Access Client software after installing Open Transport PPP, a message tells you that a more recent version of Open Transport PPP is already installed. Respond that you want to use the newer version of Open Transport PPP.

System 6

You can't install Mac OS 7.6 or 7.6.1 directly over System 6. You must either install System 7.0 or later, or do a clean installation of Mac OS 7.6 or 7.6.1.

Installing Mac OS 7.6 or 7.6.1

This section tells you how to use a CD-ROM or set of floppy disks that contain complete installation software for Mac OS 7.6 or Mac OS 7.6.1. First, this section describes what you can install as part of Mac OS 7.6 or 7.6.1. Next, this section gives you step-by-step instructions for setting up the installation. Following the setup instructions, you'll find separate instructions for doing a standard installation, a custom installation, or a universal installation of Mac OS 7.6 or 7.6.1. For instructions on upgrading from Mac OS 7.6 to 7.6.1, see the next section, "Upgrading to Mac OS 7.6.1."

Selecting Mac OS 7.6 or 7.6.1 modules

The installation software for Mac OS 7.6 and 7.6.1 lets you install any of ten separate software modules. The modules you can install include the following:

✦ Mac OS 7.6 or 7.6.1 core software

✦ OpenDoc 1.1.2

✦ OpenDoc Essentials Kit 1.0.1

✦ QuickDraw 3D 1.0.6 (with Mac OS 7.6) or 1.5.1 (with Mac OS 7.6.1)

✦ MacLinkPlus 8.1

✦ Apple Remote Access Client 2.1

✦ Cyberdog 1.2.1

✦ Open Transport PPP 1.0

✦ English Text-To-Speech 1.5

✦ QuickDraw GX 1.1.5

Setting up for Mac OS 7.6 or 7.6.1 installation

The complete installation software for Mac OS 7.6 and 7.6.1 includes a simplified installation program called Install Mac OS. You can use this program to install some or all Mac OS modules, and you have the option of performing a clean installation (see "Performing a Clean Installation" in Chapter 30). The Install Mac OS program will help you update the disk driver software on most of your Apple-brand hard disks. In addition, you can have it check the condition of the hard disk on which the Mac OS modules will be installed (see "Preparing for Installation" in Chapter 30).

The Install Mac OS program begins by leading you through some of the preparatory tasks that ensure a successful installation of Mac OS 7.6 or 7.6.1. To prepare for installing some or all Mac OS modules, be sure to read Chapter 30, and then follow these steps:

1. Insert the CD-ROM disc or the Install Me First floppy disk for Mac OS 7.6 or 7.6.1, and find the Install Mac OS program.

2. Start the Install Mac OS program by double-clicking its icon.

   After a few seconds, the Install Mac OS window appears, as shown in Figure 32-1.

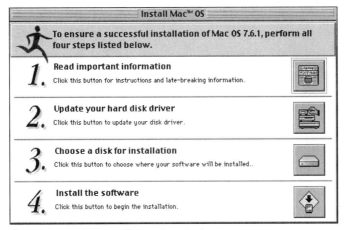

Figure 32-1: The Install Mac OS window.

3. Click the button for task 1 in the Install Mac OS window. The SimpleText program displays a document containing last-minute installation information for Mac OS 7.6. After reading, attending to, and optionally printing that document, close its window and switch to the main Install Mac OS window.

   You can skip step 3 if you read the document "Installing Mac OS 7.6" located on the installation CD-ROM or floppy disk before starting Mac OS Install.

4. Click the button for task 2 in the Install Mac OS window. An alert provides the opportunity to skip this task if none of your hard disks have Apple drivers. If you click the Continue button, the Drive Setup or HD SC Setup program opens, whichever is appropriate for your computer. Select each Apple hard disk and click the Update Driver button or the Update button to update its driver software, then quit the Drive Setup or HD SC Setup program and switch to the main Install Mac OS window.

   To update the driver software of hard disks that have non-Apple driver software, see "Preparing for Installation" in Chapter 30. You can skip this step if you have already updated the driver software on your hard disks.

5. Click the button for task 3 in the Install Mac OS window. A dialog box appears in which you choose the disk on which you want to install the Mac OS modules. Choose the disk by name and click the Select button.

   If you skip this task, then in task 4 the Install Mac OS program will display a dialog box that asks you to specify the disk on which to install the Mac OS.

6. Click the button for task 4 in the Install Mac OS window when you are ready to select the Mac OS modules that you want installed.

7. Do one of the following:

   • Use the procedure in "Standard Installation of Mac OS 7.6 or 7.6.1" if you want to install the basic Mac OS modules plus some or all of the additional modules, each in its entirety.

   • Use the procedure in "Custom Installation of Mac OS 7.6 or 7.6.1" if you want to install any of the Mac OS modules partially or completely.

   • Use the procedure in "Universal Installation of Mac OS 7.6 or 7.6.1" if you want to install a Mac OS that can start any computer capable of running Mac OS 7.6 or 7.6.1.

Standard installation of Mac OS 7.6 or 7.6.1

A standard installation of Mac OS 7.6 or 7.6.1 always includes the Mac OS core module. A standard installation also includes the OpenDoc and OpenDoc Essentials modules, if they will work on your computer. Other modules you can optionally install are QuickDraw 3D, MacLinkPlus, Apple Remote Access Client, Cyberdog, Open Transport PPP, English Text-To-Speech, and QuickDraw GX. Use the Install Mac OS program to select the optional modules you want to install. Then under the control of the Install Mac OS program, each selected module is installed by a separate Installer program. The individual Installer programs do not require any response from you unless you are installing from floppy disks or a problem occurs.

The following steps explain how to do a standard installation of Mac OS 7.6 or 7.6.1 and, optionally, how to a clean installation:

1. Start the Install Mac OS program and go through its four numbered tasks as previously described in steps 1 through 6 in "Setting Up for Mac OS 7.6 or 7.6.1 Installation."

   After you complete all of the numbered tasks, a dialog box appears in which you can select the Mac OS modules you want installed, as shown in Figure 32-2.

2. Select the Mac OS modules that you want installed by clicking the appropriate checkboxes.

   The Install Mac OS program may select some modules by default, depending on the type of computer you're installing on. The three basic modules — Mac OS, OpenDoc, and OpenDoc Essentials — are not shown because they are always included in a standard Mac OS 7.6 and 7.6.1 installation. (OpenDoc and OpenDoc Essentials are included only if they will work on your computer.)

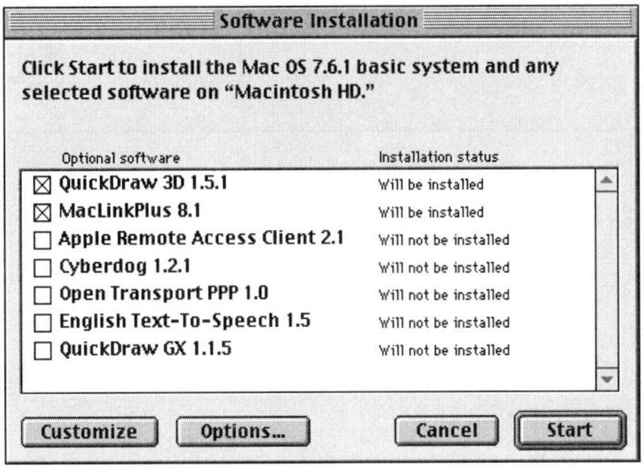

Figure 32-2: The standard Software Installation dialog box in the Install Mac OS program.

3. To perform a clean installation, click the Options button in the standard Software Installation dialog box. A dialog box appears in which you select the option "Create new System Folder (clean installation)" and then click OK.

4. Verify that the disk named at the top of the standard Software Installation dialog box is where you want the software installed (click the Cancel button and go back to step 1 if it isn't). Then click the Start button in the standard Software Installation dialog box to begin installation.

The Install Mac OS program checks the condition of the disk on which it's going to install the software and tries to fix any problems it finds. While checking, it displays a progress gauge. If you want to stop the installation at this point, click the Stop button and go back to step 2.

5. The Install Mac OS program gives control to a succession of subordinate Installer programs, one for each Mac OS module to be installed. The first Installer program displays an Apple license agreement for you to read and optionally print. If you agree to its terms, click the Agree button and installation begins.

Each Installer program briefly displays the message "Preparing to install." If you are installing onto the startup disk and other programs are open (such as SimpleText), the Installer displays an alert message advising you that it can't continue while other applications are open. You can click a Cancel button to cancel installation or click a Continue button to have the Installer quit the other open applications. (The Installer also turns off file sharing if it is on.) As each application quits, it may come to the front and ask whether you want to save any changes that you haven't yet saved. After quitting the other open applications, the Installer displays the folders (or disks) it will need and begins installation, as shown in Figure 32-3.

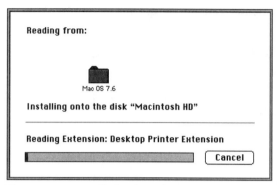

Figure 32-3: Installation is under way.

A standard installation proceeds automatically unless you are installing from floppy disks or a problem occurs. The individual Installer programs do not display welcome messages or offer installation options. If you are installing from a CD-ROM, a standard installation doesn't require more of your attention until it finishes. If you are installing from floppy disks and the Installer needs a different disk, the Installer ejects the disk that it is using and asks you to insert the disk it needs.

You can always cancel an installation that's under way by clicking the Cancel button. If you cancel an installation in progress, the Install Mac OS program displays an alert asking how you want to proceed. To stop installation, click the alert's Stop button and go back to step 2. To skip installation of the module currently being installed, click the alert's Skip button. To try installing the current module again, click the alert's Try Again button.

6. When the last Installer finishes, the Install Mac OS program asks whether you want to continue to install additional Mac OS modules. If your answer is yes, click the Continue button to repeat steps 2 through 5 to install the modules. Otherwise quit the Install Mac OS program and restart the computer to use the new system software.

As the startup disk and any other hard disks appear on the desktop during the first restart after installation (or later, in the case of removable hard disk cartridges), the Finder may automatically rebuild the desktop database files (see "Checking the Desktop Database" in Chapter 10).

Custom installation of Mac OS 7.6 or 7.6.1

A custom installation of Mac OS 7.6 or 7.6.1 gives you the choice of installing any of the following modules: Mac OS, OpenDoc, OpenDoc Essentials, QuickDraw 3D, MacLinkPlus, Apple Remote Access Client, Cyberdog, Open Transport PPP, English Text-To-Speech, and QuickDraw GX. In addition to installing complete modules, you can selectively install portions of each module. For example, the following are some of the components you can selectively install from the Mac OS module:

✦ Printer driver software for a kind of printer you haven't used before

✦ Control Strip, which provides quick access to various control-panel settings

✦ Easy Access, which lets you move the pointer with the numeric keypad, type a key combination one stroke at a time, and so on

✦ Close View, which can magnify the entire display image

Do a custom installation only if you are sure that you know which individual items must be present for a module to work properly. If you're not sure, do a standard installation as previously described in "Standard Installation of Mac OS 7.6 or 7.6.1."

In a custom installation, you use the Install Mac OS program to select the modules you want installed, and the Install Mac OS program has individual Installer programs install the modules you select. You must interact with each Installer program to specify whether you want it to install all or part of its module.

The following steps tell you how to custom install Mac OS 7.6 or 7.6.1, and, optionally, how to do a clean installation:

1. Start the Install Mac OS program and go through its four numbered tasks as previously explained in steps 1 through 6 in "Setting Up for Mac OS 7.6 or 7.6.1 Installation."

   After you complete all of the numbered tasks, the standard Software Installation dialog box appears, in which you can select modules to be installed and indicate that you want to do a custom installation (review Figure 32-2).

2. Click the Customize button in the standard Software Installation dialog box to change to the Custom Software Installation dialog box, as shown in Figure 32-4.

3. Select the modules of Mac OS 7.6 or 7.6.1 that you want installed by clicking the appropriate checkboxes.

   Only the selected modules will be installed. You will have an opportunity later to selectively install portions of each module as it is installed.

4. Click the Options button in the Custom Software Installation dialog box if you want to do a clean installation or disable checking of the destination disk's condition.

   A dialog box appears in which you can turn on or off the options "Create new System Folder (clean installation)" and "Check Destination Disk." If the disk checking option is absent then you are doing a standard installation, which always includes the disk check.

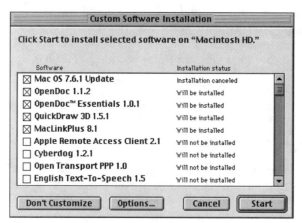

Figure 32-4: The Custom Software Installation dialog box in the Install Mac OS program.

5. Verify that the disk named at the top of the Custom Software Installation dialog box is where you want the software installed (click the Cancel button and go back to step 1 if it isn't). Then click the Start button in the Custom Software Installation dialog box to begin installation.

   Unless you disabled the Check Destination Disk option in step 4, the Install Mac OS program checks the condition of the disk on which it's going to install the software and tries to fix any problems it finds. While checking, it displays a progress gauge so you can monitor its progress. If you want to stop the installation at this point, click the Stop button and go back to step 3.

6. The Install Mac OS program gives control to a succession of Installer programs, one for each Mac OS module you selected in step 3.

   Before displaying its main window, each Installer except the one for the OpenDoc Essentials module first displays a welcome message. After you dismiss that, some Installers display an Apple license agreement for you to read and optionally print. You must agree to its terms to continue installation. The Installer displays its main window, which describes what will be installed (see Figure 32-5).

7. Do one of the following:

   • To install a complete module, choose Easy Install from the pop-up menu in the Installer's main window and click the Install button in that window. (For the OpenDoc Essentials module, simply click the Install button, because its Installer has no pop-up menu.)

   • To selectively install portions of the module, choose Custom Install from the pop-up menu in the Installer window. The Installer lists components, and in some cases groups of components that you can install. To expand a component group, click the disclosure triangle next to it. You can get information about a component by clicking its information button at the right side of the Installer window. Select the components that you want to install by clicking the appropriate checkboxes, and then click the Install button (see Figure 32-6).

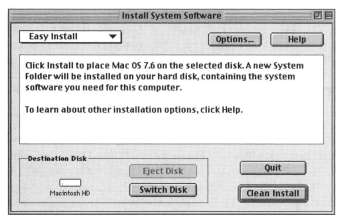

Figure 32-5: Ready to install one complete Mac OS module.

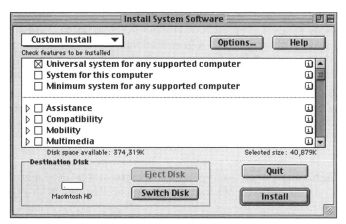

Figure 32-6: Select the components to be installed from one Mac OS module.

After you click the Install button, the Installer briefly displays the message "Preparing to install." If you are installing onto the startup disk and other programs are open (such as SimpleText), the Installer displays an alert message advising that it can't continue while other applications are open. You can click a Cancel button to cancel installation or click a Continue button to have the Installer quit the other open applications. (The Installer also turns off file sharing if it is on.) As each application quits, it may come to the front and ask whether you want to save any changes that you haven't yet saved.

After quitting the other open applications, the Installer displays the folders (or disks) that will be needed and commences installation. If you are installing from floppy disks and the Installer needs a different disk, the Installer ejects the disk that it is using and asks you to insert the disk it needs.

You can always cancel an installation that's under way by clicking the Cancel button and quitting the Installer program. If you cancel an installation in progress, the Install Mac OS program displays an alert asking how you want to proceed. To stop installation, click the alert's Stop button and go back to step 3. To skip installation of the module currently being installed, click the alert's Skip button. To try installing the current module again, click the alert's Try Again button.

8. When the last Installer finishes, the Install Mac OS program asks whether you want to install additional Mac OS modules. Click the Continue button if you want to repeat steps 3 through 7 to install additional modules, otherwise quit the Install Mac OS program and restart the computer to use the new system software.

Universal installation of Mac OS 7.6 or 7.6.1

Normally the Install Mac OS program installs only the Mac OS software for the type of computer it's running on. For example, Install Mac OS installs mobility software only on PowerBook models. If you want to install the Mac OS software needed to start any type of Mac OS computer — a universal Mac OS — you must do a distinct type of custom installation. Perform steps 1 through 8 as previously outlined in "Custom Installation of Mac OS 7.6 or 7.6.1," with the following exceptions:

✦ In step 3, be sure to select the Mac OS module.

✦ In step 7, as each Installer program takes its turn, specify these conditions:

- Mac OS 7.6 Installer — choose Custom Install from the Installer's pop-up menu and select either "Universal system for any supported computer" or "Minimum system for any supported computer." You may also select other listed components that you want installed by clicking their checkboxes.

- OpenDoc — choose Easy Install from the Installer's pop-up menu.

- OpenDoc Essentials — nothing to specify.

- QuickDraw 3D — choose Easy Install.

- MacLinkPlus — choose Easy Install.

- Remote Access Client Install — choose Easy Install.

- Cyberdog Installer — choose Easy Install.

- Open Transport PPP — choose Custom Install and select all components if the universal Mac OS is to be used with PowerPC processors and 68030 or 68040 processors. Easy Install is OK if it is to be used with only one type of processor.

- English TTS Installer — choose Easy Install.

- QuickDraw GX Installer — choose Custom Install and, preferably, select all components; at minimum, select the "Base QuickDraw GX Software for any Macintosh" component.

Upgrading to Mac OS 7.6.1

Mac OS 7.6.1 can be installed as an upgrade to Mac OS 7.6. There are two versions of the upgrade installation software. The Mac OS 7.6.1 Update works with all computers that can use Mac OS 7.6 except PowerBook 3400s. The Mac OS 7.6.1 Update for PowerBook 3400 upgrades a PowerBook 3400 from Mac OS 7.6 to 7.6.1. Both of these upgrades are available from Apple's Software Updates library (http://www.apple.com/swupdates/).

Neither of the upgrades works with a computer that can't use Mac OS 7.6 but that can use 7.6.1, including a Power Mac 4400, 5500, 6500, 7300, 7600, 8600, and 9600. To upgrade any of these computers, you must use the Mac OS 7.6.1 CD that is distributed only through the Mac OS Up-To-Date program (800-335-9258, http://www.apple.com/macos/up-to-date/).

Perform the following steps to upgrade to Mac OS 7.6.1 using the Mac OS 7.6.1 Update installation software or the Mac OS 7.6.1 Update for PowerBook 3400 installation software:

1. If your Mac has System 7.5.5 or earlier, install Mac OS 7.6 by following the instructions in "Installing Mac OS 7.6 or 7.6.1" earlier in this chapter.

2. Insert the first Mac OS 7.6.1 floppy disk or open the Mac OS 7.6.1 Update folder and start the Installer program by double-clicking its icon.

3. The Installer program displays an Apple license agreement for you to read and optionally print. Click the Agree button to continue.

   The Installer's main window appears. This window identifies the disk on which the software will be installed and describes what will be installed, as shown in Figure 32-7.

4. Make sure the destination-disk name is the one on which you want to install the software. If you have more than one hard disk, you can switch disks by clicking the Switch Disk button.

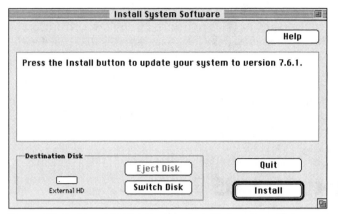

Figure 32-7: Mac OS 7.6.1 Update Installer's main window.

5. Click the Install button in the main Installer window to begin installation.

The Installer briefly displays the message "Preparing to install." If you are installing onto the startup disk and other programs are open (such as SimpleText), the Installer displays an alert message advising you that it can't continue while other applications are open. You can click a Cancel button to cancel installation or click a Continue button to have the Installer quit the other open applications. (The Installer also turns off file sharing if it is on.) As each application quits, it may come to the front and ask whether you want to save any changes that you haven't yet saved. After quitting the other open applications, the Installer displays the folders (or disks) it will need and commences installation, as shown in Figure 32-8.

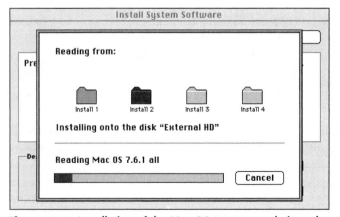

Figure 32-8: Installation of the Mac OS 7.6.1 upgrade is underway.

If you are installing from floppy disks and the Installer needs a different disk, the Installer ejects the disk it used and asks you to insert the next disk it needs. You can always cancel an installation by clicking the Cancel button.

When the Installer finishes upgrading to Mac OS 7.6.1, it tells you to restart the computer to use the new system software.

After upgrading to Mac OS 7.6.1, you can still install individual components of Mac OS 7.6 such as desktop printing or the Control Strip. You can use the Mac OS 7.6 CD-ROM or floppy disks as described in "Custom Installation of Mac OS 7.6 or 7.6.1."

Installing Mac OS enhancements

Apple periodically releases new or upgraded system software modules that you can add to your existing installation of the Mac OS. Examples from the past include QuickTime, Open Transport, LaserWriter, QuickDraw GX, and PlainTalk. Apple typically makes upgraded modules available through various areas on its Web site, including these:

✦ Software Updates library (http://www.apple.com/swupdates/)

✦ QuickTime (http://www.apple.com/quicktime/)

✦ Speech (http://www.apple.com/speech/)

✦ ColorSync (http://www.apple.com/colorsync/)

✦ AppleScript (http://www. applescript.apple.com)

You install most add-on system software with an Installer program, and these steps usually apply:

1. Locate the Installer program for the add-on software, and start the Installer by double-clicking its icon.

2. If the Installer displays a welcome message, dismiss it to proceed with the installation.

3. If the Installer displays a license agreement, you must agree to its terms to continue installation.

4. When the Installer's main window appears, confirm that the destination disk is correct. If you have more than one hard disk, you can switch disks by clicking the Switch Disk button (see Figure 32-9).

5. Do one of the following:

   • To install the complete add-on software module, choose Easy Install from the pop-up menu in the Installer's main window and click the Install button in that window. If there is no pop-up menu in the Installer window, simply click the Install button.

• To selectively install portions of the add-on software module, choose Custom Install from the pop-up menu in the Installer window. The Installer lists components, and in some cases groups of components, that you can install. To expand a component group, click the disclosure triangle next to it. You can get information about a component by clicking its information button at the right side of the Installer window. Select the components that you want to install by clicking their check boxes, and then click the Install button (see Figure 32-10).

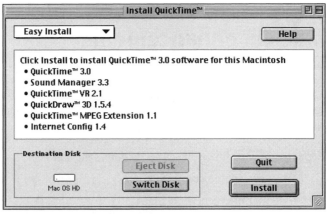

Figure 32-9: An Installer's main window.

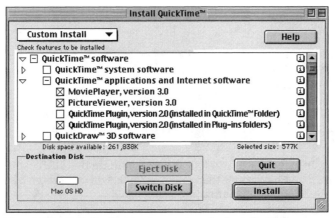

Figure 32-10: Selecting components to be installed from an add-on software module.

The Installer briefly displays the message "Preparing to install" and then commences installation. If you are installing from floppy disks and the Installer needs a different disk, the Installer ejects the disk that it used and asks you to insert the next disk it needs. You can always cancel an installation by clicking the Cancel button.

When the Installer finishes, it may ask if you want to quit or continue doing installations. Quit unless you want to repeat steps 4 and 5 to install the module on other disks. Alternatively, the Installer may tell you to restart the computer to use the new system software.

Summary

This chapter told you how to install Mac OS 7.6 or 7.6.1 on a computer that's using System 7.5.5 or earlier. You can install Mac OS 7.6 or 7.6.1 in its entirety, or you can selectively install portions of any module. This chapter also told you how to upgrade from Mac OS 7.6 to Mac OS 7.6.1. In addition, you learned how to enhance the Mac OS by periodically installing individual software modules such as the latest version of QuickTime.

✦   ✦   ✦

QuickDraw GX Printing

I f you choose to install QuickDraw GX with Mac OS 7.6–7.6.1, you get both an advanced typography (described in Chapter 13) and an enhanced printing system. Why are you reading about an enhanced printing system in an appendix? Despite GX printing's benefits, it is not a popular program. Apple decided to remove the printing enhancements from QuickDraw GX beginning with Mac OS 8 and standardize on non-GX printing.

The main features of QuickDraw GX printing in Mac OS 7.6–7.6.1 are:

+ **Desktop printer icons** give you drag-and-drop printing and improved management of background printing, including the capability to redirect a print job from one printer to another. This feature is similar to the desktop printing described in Chapter 14.

+ **Simplified Page Setup and Print commands** offer simple options, or at the click of a button they offer expanded options in participating applications — options such as choosing a printer at print time and combining multiple page sizes and margins in a single document. In addition, you can drag the Page Setup and Print dialog boxes around the screen.

+ **Printer extensions** add special effects such as watermarks and multiple pages per sheet of paper to every participating application.

+ **Portable Digital Documents** allow you to view and print fully formatted documents without the applications that created them and without the fonts used to create them.

+ **Printer sharing** enables you to share printers that themselves don't connect to a network and (optionally) to secure any shared printer with a password. This feature is similar to the printer sharing described in Chapter 14.

As with non-GX printing, you set up and control printing the same basic way, regardless of the application you are using or the type of printer you have. All applications use the same printer driver software to prepare the page image for and to communicate with a particular type of printer. For each printer you use, you select a driver and set up a desktop icon with the Chooser.

To print documents, you use standard Page Setup and Print commands that are enhanced in applications designed to take full advantage of QuickDraw GX printing. In applications that are merely compatible with GX printing, you use Page Setup and Print commands that are similar to the commands without GX printing (described in Chapter 15).

All GX printing occurs in the background, so you don't have to wait for documents to finish printing before continuing with other work. If several documents are waiting to be printed on a particular printer, you can use its desktop icon to manage the queue of waiting print requests.

This appendix describes the software that you need and the methods that you use with QuickDraw GX-enhanced printing. If your Mac uses Mac OS 7.6–7.6.1 and has QuickDraw GX installed, this appendix is for you. If your Mac does not have QuickDraw GX installed or it uses Mac OS 8–8.5, refer to Chapters 14 and 15.

Checking for GX Printing

Your Mac may have the QuickDraw GX printing enhancements if it uses Mac OS 7.6–7.6.1. QuickDraw GX is included with the complete installation packages for Mac OS 7.6–7.6.1, but is not part of the standard installation.

If you're not sure whether your Mac has QuickDraw GX with enhanced printing, you can tell for sure by opening the Chooser and looking for printer icons whose name end with GX. Looking in the Extensions folder (inside the System Folder) for printer driver files whose name end with GX is not a foolproof method because those files can be present even if the rest of QuickDraw GX is absent. Likewise, checking for the QuickDraw GX extension file is inconclusive because QuickDraw GX 1.1.6 does not include printing enhancements. Also, the presence of desktop printer icons does not guarantee that you have GX-enhanced printing because desktop printing software is available without QuickDraw GX.

Comparing GX Printer Driver Software

QuickDraw GX with printing enhancements needs its own printer driver software for each type of printer you use. A GX printer driver prepares an image of each page to be printed in a format that the printer can interpret, and then sends the

page descriptions to the printer. The printer drivers used by non-GX printing
do not work with GX-enhanced printing. Installing QuickDraw GX with printing
enhancements adds these printer drivers to the Extensions folder, as shown in
Figure A-1:

✦ **LaserWriter GX** for printing on PostScript printers, such as Apple's LaserWriter
   Plus, II, IINT, IINTX, IIf, and IIg; Personal LaserWriter IINT, IINTR, and 320;
   LaserWriter Select 360; and LaserWriter Pro 600, 630, and 810. LaserWriter GX
   takes the place of LaserWriter, LaserWriter 8, and PSPrinter, but it can coexist
   on a network with those non-GX printer drivers. LaserWriter GX does not use
   PPD files.

✦ **Color StyleWriter 2400 GX** for printing on a Color StyleWriter 2200 or 2400.

✦ **Color StyleWriter Pro GX** for printing on a Color StyleWriter Pro.

✦ **StyleWriter GX** for printing on a StyleWriter 1200, StyleWriter II, or original
   StyleWriter.

✦ **PDD Maker GX** for creating portable digital documents as described in "Using
   Portable Digital Documents (PDDs)" later in this appendix.

✦ **LaserWriter 300 GX** for printing on a LaserWriter Select 300 or Personal
   LaserWriter LS.

✦ **ImageWriter GX** for printing on an ImageWriter or ImageWriter II.

✦ **ImageWriter LQ GX** for printing on an ImageWriter LQ.

✦ **LaserWriter IISC GX** for printing on a LaserWriter IISC.

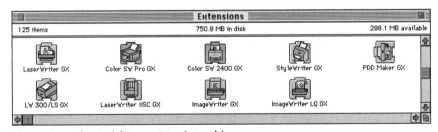

Figure A-1: The QuickDraw GX printer drivers.

Non-GX printer drivers remain in the Extensions folder after the installation of
QuickDraw GX, but you can't use any of those drivers for GX-enhanced printing.
You may be able to print with a non-GX printer driver by using Apple's GX Helper
software (as described in "Bypassing GX Printing" later in this appendix). For the
best results with GX-enhanced printing, you should get GX drivers from the makers
of devices such as fax/modems, non-Apple printers, and portable document makers.

Extending GX Printing Capabilities

You can add to the basic functions of a printer driver by installing printing-extension software in the Extensions folder. Some printing extensions give you access to a particular printer's features, such as its resolution and the size and capacity of its paper trays. Other printing extensions modify the appearance of a document during the printing process. For example, a printing extension could provide the option of watermarking every page with a light-gray text message (such as *Draft*) or a faint picture (such as a company logo); the ordinary contents of each page would print over this watermark.

Apple includes a GX printing extension with some versions of QuickDraw GX for printing multiple minipages per sheet of paper. Additional printing extensions are available from other companies, such as Peirce Print Tools from Peirce Software (408/244-6554, http://www.peircesw.com). Peirce Print Tools adds nine new printing capabilities to every application (even if the application hasn't been updated to use GX print dialog box) including double-sided printing, multiple pages per side, and watermarks.

Using GX Desktop Printer Icons

With QuickDraw GX 1.1.5 and earlier installed, you do not use the Chooser to choose an output device for printing; instead, you use the Chooser to create desktop printer icons for each printer, fax/modem, or other output device that you use. After creating the desktop printer icons, you use the Finder, not the Chooser, to choose and set up a printer. Background printing is always on for all devices; you cannot turn it off with the Chooser.

Creating desktop printer icons

Installing QuickDraw GX 1.1.5 or earlier creates a desktop printer icon for the printer that was selected in the Chooser before installation. If you use more than one printer, or if you had not selected a printer in the Chooser before installing QuickDraw GX, you use the Chooser to create desktop printer icons. Each printer must have its own icon. If you use three LaserWriters, for example, you need three LaserWriter GX desktop icons. You cannot print to a printer until you create a desktop icon for it.

Selecting a type of printer

To create a desktop printer icon for any device, open the Chooser. Each printer or other output device for which there is a GX printer driver in the Extensions folder appears as an icon in the Chooser. On the left side of the Chooser window, select the icon of the driver that you want to use. If you see a list of network zones in the lower-left corner of the Chooser window, select the zone of the printer for which you want to make a desktop icon. (If you don't see a list of zones, your network has no zones.) Figure A-2 shows an example of the Chooser ready for selecting a GX printer driver.

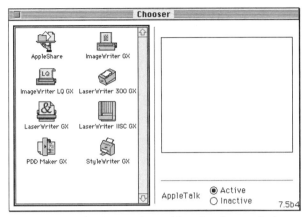

Figure A-2: Selecting a printer driver for the GX desktop printer icon.

Selecting a networked printer

After selecting a printer driver, you can select a specific printer (or a specific printer connection) on the right side of the Chooser window. If there is a Connect Via pop-up menu at the top of the Chooser window, use it to choose the type of connection for the type of printer or other output device that you're setting up. Choose AppleTalk for a device that is connected to a LocalTalk or EtherTalk network; choose Servers for a shared device (described in "Sharing Printers under QuickDraw GX" later in this appendix); choose Serial for a device that is connected without a network adapter box to the Mac's modem or printer port; or choose SCSI for a device that is connected to the Mac's SCSI port. The pop-up menu lists only relevant choices for the selected driver; it does not list all choices for all drivers. The pop-up menu does not appear for drivers that have no connection options.

If you choose AppleTalk as the Connect Via option for the selected printer, a list of the names of all printers of that type that currently are available on your network displays. Select the specific printer that you want by clicking its name. You can also select a listed printer by typing the first part of its name. (To select by typing, a heavy border must surround the list of printer names; if a heavy border doesn't surround the list, press Tab until it does.) Figure A-3 shows an example list of printers that use the LaserWriter GX driver.

If your network has zones, the names of printers in the currently selected zone are displayed. You can select a different zone in the lower-left part of the Chooser. The Chooser does not display a list of zones unless your network has more than one zone.

Selecting a directly connected printer

If you choose Serial as the Chooser's Connect Via option for the selected GX printer driver, the Chooser lists the ports to which the printer can be connected. You select a port by clicking it in the Chooser. Figure A-4 shows an example list of ports for a directly connected printer.

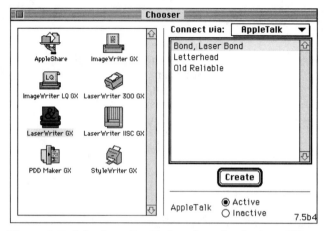

Figure A-3: Selecting a PostScript printer for the LaserWriter GX driver when the Chooser's Connect Via option is AppleTalk.

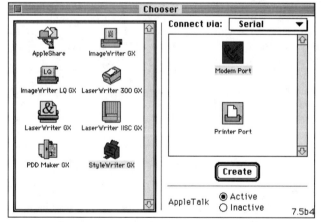

Figure A-4: Selecting a port for a directly connected printer when the Chooser's Connect Via option is Serial.

Creating the printer icon

After selecting a specific printer or other device, click the Create button to create a desktop icon for that printer or device. This icon refers only to the printer or device that was selected when you clicked the Create button. If you need a desktop icon for another printer or device of the same type, you must select it and click Create again.

Choosing the default printer

After creating desktop printer icons for all the printers you use, you must designate which one you want to use by default. First, select the printer's desktop icon; a Printing menu appears next to the Finder's Special menu. Choose Set Default Printer from that menu. The Finder indicates the default printer by drawing a heavy black border around its desktop icon. The Printing menu is only available in the Finder. Figure A-5 shows a couple of desktop printer icons and the Printing menu.

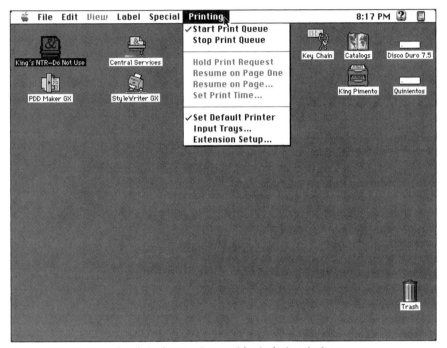

Figure A-5: Setting the default GX printer with Finder's Printing menu.

Changing printer setup

The Finder's Printing menu contains commands not only for designating the default printer, but also for changing the setup of any printer that has a desktop icon. The Input Trays command specifies the type of paper present in the paper trays of the printer whose desktop icon is selected. Your options vary according to the number of and types of trays installed in the currently selected printer. The paper tray settings are used by the Print command of applications that have adopted GX printing (see "Using the GX Print Command" later in this appendix). Figure A-6 is an example of the dialog box in which you specify the type of paper that is in a printer's paper tray.

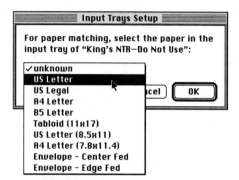

Figure A-6: Specifying the type of paper in a printer's input tray or trays.

The Extension Setup command specifies which of the available GX printing extensions (installed in the Extensions folder) to use with the printer whose desktop icon is selected. The active extensions are applied in the order listed, from top to bottom. You can change the order of printing extensions by dragging them up or down the list in the Extension Setup dialog box. Figure A-7 is an example of the dialog box in which you set up GX printing extensions.

Figure A-7: Specifying which GX printing extensions are active for a printer and the order in which they apply.

The other commands in the Finder's Printing menu are covered in "Managing GX Printing" later in this appendix.

Using the GX Page Setup Command

Before printing a document, you need to format the document pages. You must specify the type of paper, page orientation, reduction or enlargement factor, and other formatting options. The exact options available depend on the type of printer you are using and on whether the application in which you choose the Page Setup command (usually from the File menu) has adopted GX printing. The following section describes the GX Page Setup command in applications that have adopted GX printing; the section after describes the GX Page Setup command in applications that have not adopted GX printing.

In addition to the options described in these sections, you may encounter options added by printing extensions or by individual application programs. For information on these options, see the documentation for the software that is responsible for them.

GX Page Setup in participating applications

Applications that take full advantage of GX printing offer the same general Page Setup options for every type of output device. These applications display a simple Page Setup dialog box that you can drag to a different location by its title bar. Figure A-8 is an example of the simple GX Page Setup dialog box displayed by applications that have adopted GX printing.

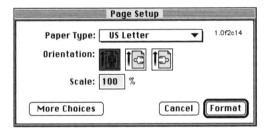

Figure A-8: Setting basic LaserWriter GX page attributes in applications that have adopted GX printing.

In the simple GX Page Setup dialog box, the Paper Type pop-up menu lists the paper sizes that are available on the selected printer. (For example, tabloid size — 11 x 17 inches — is available on LaserWriters but not on StyleWriters.) You also can choose one of three page orientations and enter a reduction or enlargement percentage.

Clicking the More Choices button in the simple Page Setup dialog box expands the dialog box. The expanded Page Setup dialog box includes all the basic options of the simple dialog box and, permits you to choose a printer from a pop-up menu. The Format For pop-up menu lists every type of printer for which the Extensions folder contains a GX printer driver; the menu also lists the name of every printer with a desktop icon. Choosing a printer from this pop-up menu does not change the default printer; use the Finder's Set Default Printer command for that purpose. Figure A-9 is an example of the expanded GX Page Setup dialog box displayed by applications that have adopted GX printing.

The icons on the left side of the expanded GX Page Setup dialog box represent panels of options. Many printers, including all StyleWriters and ImageWriters, have only the General panel of options.

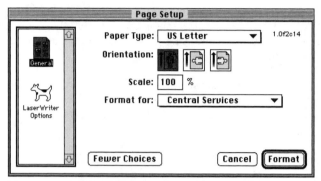

Figure A-9: Setting all LaserWriter GX page attributes in applications that have adopted GX printing.

The LaserWriter GX dialog box has a LaserWriter Options panel for setting a few PostScript options. LaserWriter GX has fewer PostScript options than the non-GX LaserWriter Page Setup dialog boxes described in Chapter 15. LaserWriter GX sets the missing options automatically for best results. Figure A-10 shows the LaserWriter Options panel of the LaserWriter GX Page Setup dialog box displayed by applications that have adopted GX printing.

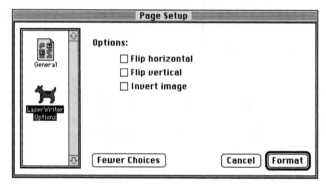

Figure A-10: Setting LaserWriter GX PostScript options in applications that have adopted GX printing.

GX Page Setup in nonparticipating applications

When QuickDraw GX printing is active, you still can use the Page Setup command in applications that have not been updated to take full advantage of GX printing. These Page Setup options are similar to the options offered when GX is inactive (for details, refer to Chapter 15). Notably you cannot choose a printer in the Page Setup dialog box of an application that has not been updated for GX printing. Before using the Page Setup command in such an application, you must choose the printer by selecting its desktop icon and using the Finder's Set Default Printer command (as described in "Choosing the Default Printer" earlier in this appendix). Figures A-11 and A-12 are examples of the Page Setup options offered for a couple of printers in applications that have not adopted GX printing.

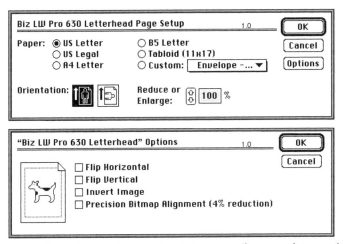

Figure A-11: Setting LaserWriter GX page attributes and PostScript options in applications that have not adopted GX printing.

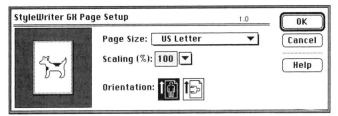

Figure A-12: Setting StyleWriter GX page attributes in applications that have not adopted GX printing.

Using the GX Print Command

After setting page formatting options with the Page Setup command, you can print a document by choosing the Print command (located in the File menu of most applications). In the Print dialog box, you can specify the range of pages, the number of copies, and a paper source. You may have additional options, depending on the type of printer and on whether the application in which you choose the Print command has adopted GX printing. The following section describes the GX Print command in applications that have adopted GX printing; the section after describes the GX Print command in applications that have not adopted GX printing.

In addition to the options described in these sections, you may encounter options that have been added by printing extensions or by individual application programs. For information on these options, see the documentation for the software that is responsible for them.

GX Print in participating applications

Applications that take full advantage of GX printing offer the same general Print options for every type of output device. These applications display the simple Print dialog box that you can drag to a different location by its title bar. Figure A-13 shows an example of the simple GX Print dialog box displayed by applications that have adopted GX printing.

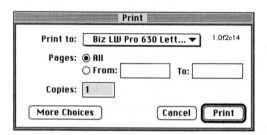

Figure A-13: The simple GX Print dialog box that is displayed by applications that have adopted GX printing.

In the simple GX Print dialog box, you can choose the printer you want to use from the Print To pop-up menu. The initial choice for a new document is the default printer (as designated by the Finder's Set Default Printer command), but you can choose any printer that has a desktop icon. You can also specify a range of pages and the number of copies to print.

Clicking the More Choices button in the simple Print dialog box expands the dialog box. The expanded Print dialog box includes all the general options of the simple dialog box. You can also specify a paper source — automatic or manual paper feed — and whether multiple copies will be collated as they are printed. Figure A-14 is an example of the expanded GX Print dialog box that is displayed by applications that have adopted GX printing.

Some printers provide additional Print options. With PostScript printers, for example, you can choose to have the page images saved as a PostScript file by choosing PostScript from the Destination pop-up menu. With a StyleWriter, you can choose one of three print qualities from the Quality pop-up menu.

You can access still more Print options by clicking one of the icons on the left side of the expanded Print dialog box. All printers have the General panel of options; most printers have the Print Time and Paper Match options as well. Still more panels of options may be provided by GX printing extensions in the Extensions folder (inside the System Folder).

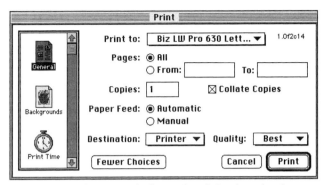

Figure A-14: The expanded GX Print dialog box that is displayed by applications that have adopted GX printing.

The Print Time options determine when your document will be printed. You can elect to have the computer notify you when printing starts, when printing ends, or at both times. Figure A-15 shows the Print Time options of the GX print dialog box that is displayed by applications that have adopted GX printing.

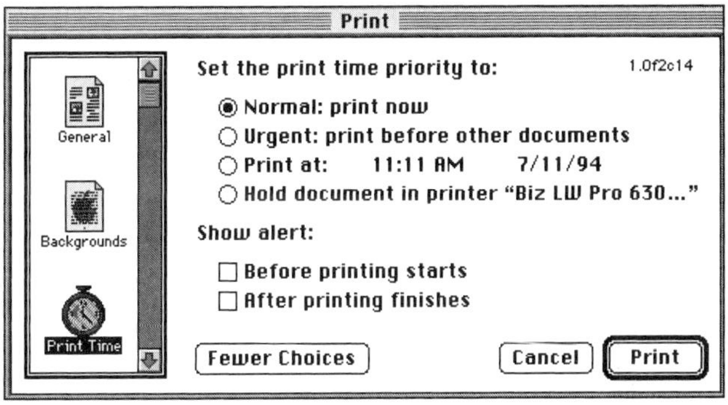

Figure A-15: The GX Print Time options.

The Paper Match options set the type of automatically fed paper and its source. One option is to have the printer driver deduce the type of paper and its source based on the information you specified with the Finder's Input Trays command (described in "Setting Up a Printer" earlier in this appendix). Alternatively, you can select a different type of paper (which you have put or intend to put temporarily in the paper tray). If you select a particular tray or paper, you can specify how you want the printer driver to handle pages that are too large. You can have the excess portion cropped at the left and bottom margins; you can have pieces of the page printed full-size on multiple sheets of paper that you later tape together; or you can have the page scaled to fit the paper. Figure A-16 shows the Paper Match options of the GX print dialog box that is displayed by applications that have adopted GX printing.

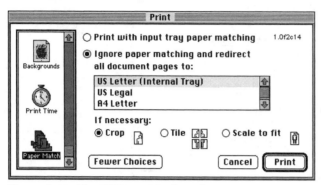

Figure A-16: The GX Paper Match options.

GX Print in nonparticipating applications

In an application that has not been updated to take full advantage of QuickDraw GX, choosing the Print command displays a dialog box similar to the one that appears when QuickDraw GX is inactive (for details, refer to Chapter 15). Notably, you cannot choose a printer in the Print dialog box of an application that has not been updated for GX printing. Before using the Print command in such an application, you must be sure to choose the printer by selecting its desktop icon and using the Finder's Set Default Printer command (as described in "Choosing the Default Printer" earlier in this appendix). Figures A-17 and A-18 show the Print options for a couple of printers in applications that have not adopted GX printing.

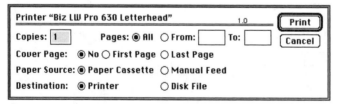

Figure A-17: Setting LaserWriter GX Print options in applications that have not adopted GX printing.

Managing GX Printing

When you click the Print button in a GX Print dialog box, the GX printer driver and any GX printing extensions create page descriptions for the pages to be printed, saving the page descriptions in a file for later printing. Normally, these files print in the background automatically while you continue working. You can view and manage the queue of waiting print files for each printer individually by using the desktop printer icons and the Finder's Printing menu.

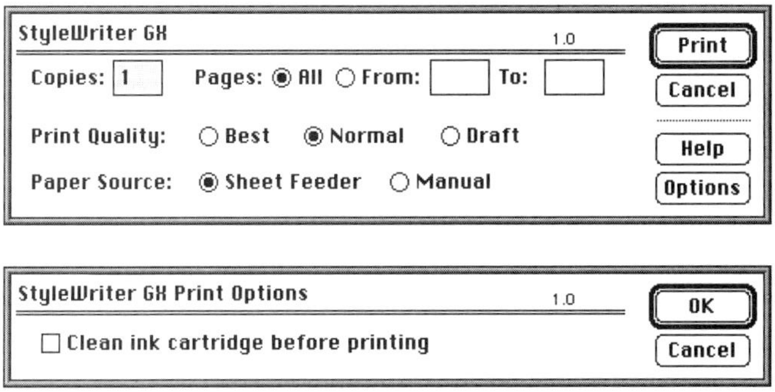

Figure A-18: Setting StyleWriter GX Print options in applications that have not adopted GX printing.

The Finder controls background printing for QuickDraw GX. As long as the Finder is open (even in the background) printing proceeds normally. If the Finder is not open, nothing prints. The Finder normally is not open when At Ease (version 2 and earlier) is present. It's best not to use At Ease 2 and earlier versions with QuickDraw GX.

Viewing a print queue

At any time, you can see the queue of files waiting to be printed on a particular printer by opening that printer's desktop icon in the Finder. Opening a desktop printer icon brings up its window. A desktop printer's window identifies the file that it is printing, reports the status of that print job, and lists the files that are waiting to be printed. You can sort the list of waiting print files by name, number of pages, number of copies, or print time. Choose a sort order from the View menu or click the column heading in the desktop printer's window. Figure A-19 shows a GX printer's window.

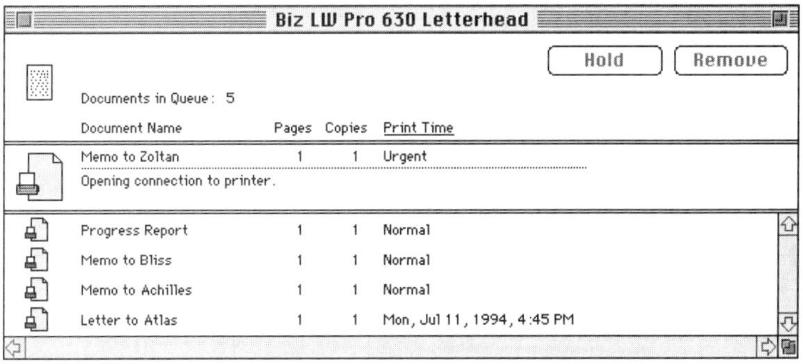

Figure A-19: Viewing queued print files in a GX desktop printer.

You can preview any print file onscreen by simply double-clicking the file's icon. The SimpleText application opens the file and displays one page. Use the Next Page and Previous Page commands in SimpleText's Edit menu to see other pages.

Redirecting a print file from one printer to another is quite easy. Simply drag the printer file from its current location to the desktop icon or window of another printer.

Changing the print order

Files in a desktop printer's window print in the listed order when the list is sorted by print time. Urgent files are listed first, followed by normal files and files with specific print times. You can change the order of urgent files and the order of normal files by dragging them up and down in the window. You cannot drag an urgent file below the first normal file, and you cannot drag a normal file above the lowest urgent file. You can, however, change a normal file to an urgent file (and vice versa) by selecting the file and choosing Set Print Time from the Finder's Printing menu. You also can use the Set Print Time command to schedule a file to print at a specific time and date.

You can postpone printing a file indefinitely. Select the file in the desktop printer's window and click the Hold button or choose Hold Print Request from the Finder's Printing menu.

To resume printing a file that is on hold, select it and then click the Resume button in the desktop printer's window. Clicking this button displays the Resume Print Request window in which you can specify the page at which you want printing to resume. (Instead of clicking the Resume button, you can choose Resume on Page One or Resume on Page from the Printing menu.)

Starting and stopping printing

To stop all printing on a particular printer, select its desktop icon and choose Stop Print Queue from the Printing menu. A small stop sign appears on the printer's desktop icon.

To start printing again, select the printer's desktop icon and choose Start Print Queue from the Printing menu.

Sharing GX Printers

Since the first Apple LaserWriter it has been possible to share printers that connect directly to a network. QuickDraw GX extends printer sharing in two ways: it enables sharing most printers that connect directly to computers (as opposed to networks) and it can limit access to a networked printer. In both cases, the printer must have a desktop icon (which means that it must have a GX printer driver in the Extensions folder). For details on creating a desktop printer icon, refer to "Using GX Desktop Printer Icons" earlier in this appendix.

To share a directly connected printer or to restrict access to a networked printer, select the printer's desktop icon and choose Sharing from the Finder's File menu. A printer-sharing window appears, as shown in Figure A-20.

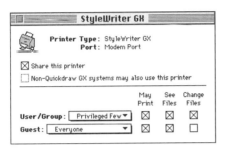

Figure A-20: Setting up sharing of a directly connected printer.

In the printer-sharing window, turn on the "Share this printer" option. If you want people who do not have QuickDraw GX to be able to share this printer, turn on the "Non-QuickDraw GX systems may also use this printer" option. (This option is not available for all types of printers.) From the User/Group pop-up menu, choose a registered user or group to which you want to give special access. Use the Guests pop-up menu to specify whether you want to allow all network users, or only users in your zone, to access the shared printer as guests. Unlike registered users and members of groups, guests do not have to enter a password to access a shared printer. (For information on creating registered users and groups, see "Identifying Who can Access Your Shared Items" in Chapter 21.)

Turn on and off the various access privileges for guests and for the designated user or group. The May Print privilege allows printing on the printer. The See Files privilege allows the display of all the waiting print files for the shared printer. The Change Files privilege allows changing of the sequence of print files and the removal of print files.

There is a catch to sharing a printer that is directly connected to your computer: your hard disk must store all the print files waiting to be printed by everyone who's using your printer, and your computer must print those files in the background. If you continue working while your computer handles all that background printing, you may notice a performance slowdown.

Using Portable Digital Documents

QuickDraw GX's print files actually are portable digital documents (PDDs). PDDs are document files that anyone who has QuickDraw GX can view and print without the applications and fonts that were used to create them. One of Apple's GX printer drivers, PDD Maker GX, facilitates creating PDDs from any application. PDDs can be sent to other QuickDraw GX users for viewing and printing with SimpleText. A PDD retains all its text formatting and graphics.

Creating a PDD is as easy as printing. To create a PDD with an application that has not been updated to use QuickDraw GX printing, select the PDD Maker GX's desktop icon and choose Set Default Printer from the Finder's Printing menu. You also can choose PDD Maker Setup from the Printing menu to select a folder in which to save PDDs by default. (You can always select a folder other than the default folder at the time you actually create a PDD.) Then you can switch to the application in which you want to create a PDD and use the Page Setup and Print commands as though you were printing to a printer.

When you create a PDD, the Print dialog box has a Save button instead of the usual Print button. Clicking the Save button brings up an ordinary Save dialog box, in which you select a folder and type a name for the PDD file. This Save dialog box also has a pop-up menu from which you choose the fonts that you want to include in the PDD. Your choices are to include all fonts used in the document, all fonts except the standard 13 fonts found on most PostScript printers, or no fonts. Fonts included in a PDD work only with that PDD and they cannot be extracted and installed in anyone's system. Figure A-21 shows the dialog box for saving a PDD file.

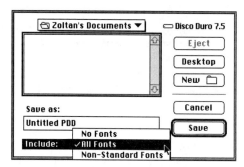

Figure A-21: Saving a portable digital document (PDD).

Bypassing GX Printing

Printing with QuickDraw GX requires a GX printer driver, but you may be able to bypass QuickDraw GX to use a printer, fax modem, or other output device that has no GX printer driver. Installing Apple's QuickDraw GX Helper system extension, which requires a custom installation with some versions of QuickDraw GX, enables you to turn off GX printing for applications individually. Installing QuickDraw GX Helper in the Extensions folder adds the command Turn Desktop Printing Off to the Apple menu in applications that allow bypassing of GX printing.

When you choose Turn Desktop Printing Off from the Apple menu, QuickDraw GX Helper tries to find a non-GX printer driver that is equivalent to the current default desktop printer. For example, if the currently selected desktop printer uses the LaserWriter GX driver, then QuickDraw GX Helper tries to find the original LaserWriter driver (version 7.2 or earlier). If the original LaserWriter driver is not in your Extensions folder, then QuickDraw GX Helper tries to find the LaserWriter 8 driver. (Thus, if you want QuickDraw GX Helper to use the LaserWriter 8 driver, make sure the original LaserWriter driver is not in your Extensions folder.)

If QuickDraw GX Helper successfully substitutes a non-GX printer driver for the current default desktop printer, you can use the Page Setup and Print commands as though QuickDraw GX were not installed (as described in Chapter 15). To choose a different non-GX printer driver, select an equivalent desktop printer and then choose Set Default Printer from the Finder's Printing menu.

When GX printing is turned off in one application, you can still use GX printing in other applications.

Step-by-Step

Non-GX Printer Drivers without GX Equivalents

If you want to use a non-GX printer driver for which no equivalent desktop printer exists, you may have to use a bit of chicanery. You will need a copy of Chooser version 7.0 or 7.1, which comes with System 7.0.1 or System 7.1, respectively. When you have one of these Choosers, follow these steps:

1. In the Finder, select a LaserWriter desktop printer and choose Set Default Printer from the Finder's Printing menu.

   If you don't have a LaserWriter desktop printer, use the Chooser to create one.

2. Switch to the application in which you want to use the non-GX printer driver and choose Turn Desktop Printing Off from the Apple menu.

   A message appears, advising you that QuickDraw GX Helper has selected the (non-GX) LaserWriter driver as a substitute for the current default printer.

3. Click OK to dismiss the message.

4. Open Chooser version 7.0 or 7.1 and select the non-GX printer driver's icon on the left side of the Chooser window.

   You must use either Chooser version 7.0 or 7.1; versions 7.3 and later do not work.

5. On the right side of the Chooser window, select the port (for non-network devices) or the specific device (for network devices).

6. Click OK to dismiss the Chooser.

7. Use the Page Setup and Print commands to output documents with the selected non-GX printer driver.

If you use the Finder's Set Default Printer command again, you must repeat steps 4 through 6 to reselect the non-GX printer driver.

Summary

In this appendix, you learned that on a computer with QuickDraw GX version 1.1.5 and earlier, you use the Chooser to create desktop printer icons and the Finder's Printing command to select a printer.

You use an application's Page Setup command to format the printed page, and use the application's Print command to print pages. The Page Setup and Print commands are different in applications that have adopted GX printing than in applications that have not.

You also learned in this appendix how to manage background printing with GX desktop printer icons. The print files inside GX printer icons are portable digital documents (PDDs) that anyone can see and print with SimpleText.

Although GX printing requires GX printer drivers, by installing QuickDraw GX Helper you can bypass GX printing in individual applications.

✦   ✦   ✦

Glossary

68K applications   Programs written for Macs with 68000, 68020, 68030, and 68040 processors. These programs also work on Macs with PowerPC processors, but more slowly than programs written expressly for PowerPC processors.

active program   The program whose menus are currently displayed in the menu bar.

adorn   The process of changing the formatting of a *subscriber*.

alert box   A window in which the Mac OS or an application program notifies you of a hazardous situation, a limitation in your proposed course of action, or an error condition.

alias   A stand-in or agent for a real program, document, folder, or disk. The alias does not duplicate the item it represents; instead, the alias points to the item it represents.

allocation block size   The smallest amount of space that can be allocated to a file on a volume. Larger volumes have a larger allocation block size.

antialias   The process of smoothing text by blending its jagged edges with the color of the background. Text-smoothing is an option of Mac OS 8.5's Appearance control panel and of the ATM control panel.

Apple events   The Mac OS language for *interapplication communication (IAC)*. Applications can send Apple events messages to one another. When an application receives an Apple event, it takes an action according to the content of the Apple event. This action can be anything from executing a particular command to taking some data, working with it, and then returning a result to the program that sent the Apple event.

Apple Guide   A help system that provides step-by-step interactive instructions for completing certain tasks.

AppleScript   An English-like programming language that you can use to send *Apple events* to programs. With AppleScript you can write your own programs, called *scripts,* to perform complex tasks easily. For example, you can use an AppleScript to move data between many applications.

AppleTalk   The networking protocol built into all Mac OS computers and most LaserWriter printers for passing messages and information to each other. The content that is passed back and forth could be *Apple events,* page images to be printed, e-mail, file contents, or any other kind of information. The content and the protocol can be transmitted through *LocalTalk* cabling, *Ethernet* cabling, or other media.

applets   Small Java programs that are commonly embedded in Web pages to make them more interesting or useful.

application program   Software that enables a computer to perform set of related tasks for a specific purpose, such as word processing, working with spreadsheets or graphics, or Web browsing. See *program* and *software.*

authentication   The process of identifying a user's ID and password in order to make a network connection.

autoscrolling   The process of scrolling through a window or a list without using the scroll bars by placing the pointer in the window or the list, pressing the mouse button, and dragging toward the area you want to view.

background program   A program that runs during the intervals, typically less than $1/8$ of a second long, when the active program isn't using the computer. It usually works while the active program waits for you to do something.

balloon help   A help system that makes a cartoonlike balloon appear when you drag the mouse slowly over a standard object in the Mac OS interface. The balloon may tell you what the object is, what it does, or what happens when you click it.

binary file   A file of formatted text, pictures, sound, movies, other data, or program code.

BinHex   A method of encoding a *binary file* into a plain text file so it can be sent over a network. A BinHexed file must be decoded back into a binary file before it can be used on the receiving computer.

bit   A single binary digit.

bitmap font   Same as *fixed-size font.*

blessed   A term used for the active System Folder.

bookmark   A way to store *Web page* locations (*URLs*) that you want to remember and go to frequently.

bug   A programming error or other flaw in software. A minor bug may affect what you see or how a program works in a noncritical way. A serious bug may cause crashes or data loss.

built-in memory   Apple's term for *RAM.*

case-sensitive   Describes a password in which capitalization matters. For instance, capital *A* is not the same as lower case *a*.

character   A written representation of a letter, digit, or symbol; a basic element of a written language.

Clarus   See *DogCow*.

click-and-a-half   A gesture used to make a disk or folder spring open that is performed by beginning to double-click the disk or folder but not releasing the mouse button after the second click.

clean installation   This type of installation deactivates your old System Folder and installs a new one with new copies of Mac OS software. You must then reconfigure control panels, reinstall application programs, and reset preferences in them.

client   A program that requests and receives information or services from a server.

clipping file   A file created by the Finder to hold material that has been dragged from a document to the desktop or a folder window.

codec   Compressor-decompressor software or hardware. (See *compressor*.)

color picker   The dialog box in which you specify a custom color either by clicking a color wheel or by entering color values.

compile   To put a *script* in an internal format that *AppleScript* can run. Before compiling a script, AppleScript checks it for things that AppleScript doesn't understand. For example, if you forget a parenthesis where AppleScript expects to find one, it lets you know.

compression algorithm   A method for compressing and decompressing data. Each compression algorithm generally works best with one type of data, such as sound, photographs, video or motion pictures, and computer-generated animation. Three characteristics of a compression algorithm determine how effectively it compresses: compression ratio, image fidelity, and speed.

compression ratio   Indicates the amount of compression and is calculated by dividing the size of the original image by the size of the compressed image. Larger compression ratios mean greater compression and generally mean poorer image quality.

compressor   Something that compresses data so that it takes less space to store, and decompresses compressed data back to its original form for playing or changing. A compressor may consist of software, hardware, or both. Sometimes also called *codec,* a shortened form of "compressor-decompressor."

conditional   A programming command that evaluates a condition (stated as part of the conditional) to determine whether another command or set of commands should be performed. (Also referred to as a *conditional statement.*)

container   An OpenDoc part that can contain other parts.

contextual menu   A menu that lists commands relevant to an item that you Control-click.

control panel   A small program that you use to set the way some part of the system looks and behaves.

custom installation   You can selectively install portions of the Mac OS modules. Do this only if you are sure that you know which individual items must be present for the software to work properly.

cyberbutton   A button you can add to an OpenDoc document and link to a location on the Internet. Clicking the button takes you to the Internet location.

dead keys   The keys that generate accented characters when typed in combination with the Option key and in proper sequence. For example, typing Option-E followed by O generates ó. The Key Caps desk accessory outlines the dead keys when you press the Option key.

default button   The button in a dialog box or alert box that has a heavy border. It represents the action you'll most often want to take. If the most common action is dangerous, a button representing a safer action may be the default button.

default browser   The Web browser application that launches when you open the Browse the Internet program, use the Connect To program, open an Internet *location file,* or otherwise don't specify a particular browser application.

desk accessory   A type of program that doesn't have documents and can't receive Apple events.

desktop database   Invisible files used by the Finder to keep track of the location, icon, and Info window comments for every file, folder, and disk. The Mac OS keeps it hidden because you don't use it directly.

dialog box   A window that displays options you can set.

digital signature   Functions as a handwritten signature, identifying the person who vouches for the accuracy and authenticity of the signed document.

DIMMs   Dual in-line memory modules.

disk cache   Improves system performance by storing recently used information from disk in a dedicated part of memory. Accessing information in memory is much faster than accessing information on disk.

DogCow   Also known as Clarus, it is the official mascot of Mac hackers and is pictured in many Page Setup Options dialog boxes.

domain name   The part of a *URL* that identifies the owner of an Internet location. A domain name has the form companyname.com, organizationname.net, schoolname.edu, militaryunitname.mil, governmentagencyname.gov, and so forth.

double-click speed   The rate at which you have to click so that the Mac OS perceives two clicks in a row as a single click.

download   The process of receiving software or other computer files from another computer, over a network, generally through a modem and telephone line.

dpi (dots-per-inch)   A measure of how fine or coarse the dots are that make up a printed image. More dots-per-inch means smaller dots, and smaller dots mean finer (less coarse) printing.

drag   To move the mouse while holding down the mouse button.

drag-and-drop editing   To copy selected text, graphics, and other material by dragging it to another place in the same window, a different window, or the desktop. This capability works only with applications that are designed to take advantage of it (such as SimpleText, Stickies, Note Pad, the Scrapbook, and the Finder).

drag-and-drop open   To drag a document to a compatible application in the Finder thereby highlighting the application, and then releasing the mouse button, causing the application to open the document.

drop box   A shared folder in which network users may place items, but only the folder's owner can see them.

easy installation   Installs all of the software components that are recommended for your computer model.

edition   A file that contains a live copy of the material in a *publisher*. When the publisher changes, the edition is updated. *Subscribers* contain copies of editions.

enclosing folder   The folder that contains another folder.

encryption   The process of making messages or files unrecognizable, for example to someone who taps into your network without authorization.

Ethernet   A high-speed standard for connecting computers and other devices in a network. Ethernet ports are built into many newer Mac OS computer and LaserWriter printer models. Its connectors and cabling cost more than *LocalTalk* equivalents.

EtherTalk   A type of network that uses *AppleTalk* software and communications protocols over *Ethernet* cabling.

extension   A software module that is loaded during startup and adds features or capabilities to the Mac OS. See also *file name extension*.

fair use   Defines the criteria that must be considered before using another person's copyrighted work (printed or recorded materials).

file ID number   The number that the Mac OS uses internally to identify the original item to which an alias is attached even if you have renamed or moved that original item.

file mapping   The technique used by the Mac OS of treating a program file as part of *virtual memory* so that fragments of a program are only loaded into memory as needed.

filename extension   The last part of a filename that follows a period and indicates the kind of file on the Internet and a DOS or Windows computer. (Also referred to as a filename suffix.)

file server   A computer running a program that makes files centrally available for other computers on a network.

file sharing   Allows you to share files, folders, and disks with people whose computers are connected to yours in a network.

file spec (specification)   Part of an AppleScript command that tells the Mac OS exactly where to find a file or folder.

firewall   A special program or programs on a local area network whose purpose is to prevent Internet users from getting into the local network and to stop local network users from sending sensitive information out.

fixed-size font   Contains exact pictures of every letter, digit, and symbol for one size of a font. Fixed-size fonts often are called *bitmap fonts* because each picture precisely maps the dots, or *bits,* to be displayed or printed for one character.

font   A set of *characters* that have a common and consistent design.

font family   A collection of differently styled variations (such as bold, italic, and plain) of a single *font.* Many *fixed-size, TrueType,* and *PostScript* fonts come in the four basic styles: plain, bold, italic, and bold italic. Some PostScript font families include 20 or more styled versions.

Fonts folder   Located in the System Folder, this folder includes all *fixed-size, PostScript,* and *TrueType* fonts.

font suitcase   A folderlike container specifically for *fixed-size* and *TrueType* fonts. You can create a new font-suitcase file by duplicating an existing font-suitcase file, opening the duplicate, and dragging its contents to the Trash.

fps (frames-per-second)   Measures how smoothly a motion picture plays. More frames-per-second means smoother playback.

fragmented memory   See *memory fragmentation.*

frame   One still image that is part of a series of still images, which, when shown in sequence, produce the illusion of movement.

frame rate   The number of frames displayed in one second. The TV frame rate is 30 fps in the United States and other countries that use the NTSC broadcasting standard; 25 fps in countries that use the PAL or SEACAM standard. The standard movie frame rate is 24 fps. (See also *fps*.)

freeware   Free software distributed through user groups and online information services. Most freeware is copyrighted by the person who created it; few freeware programs are in the public domain.

FTP (File Transfer Protocol)   The data communications *protocol* used by the Internet and other TCP/IP networks to transfer files between computers.

FTP site   A collection of files on an FTP server available for downloading.

full motion   Video displayed at frame rates of 24 to 30 fps. The human eye perceives fairly smooth motion at frame rates of 12 to 18 fps. (See also *fps* and *frame rate*.)

gamma correction   A method the computer's video circuitry uses to balance color on a monitor. Color balancing is necessary because the intensity of color on a monitor does not correspond uniformly to the intensity of the video signal that generates the picture on the monitor.

glyph   A distinct visual representation of one character (such as a lowercase *z*), multiple characters treated as one (such as the ligature æ), or a nonprinting character (such as a space).

grid fitting   The process of modifying characters at small point sizes so they fit the grid of dots on the relatively coarse display screen. The font designer provides a set of instructions (also known as *hints*) for a *TrueType* or *PostScript* font that tells the Mac OS how to modify character outlines to fit the grid.

groups   Collections of individual registered users. You can grant specific access privileges for a shared item to a group instead of to a single user.

guest   A network user who is not identified by a registered name and password.

hack   A programming effort that accomplishes something ingenious or unconventional.

hacker   A person who likes to tinker with computers, and especially with computer software code. Some hackers create new software, but many hackers use programs such as ResEdit to make unauthorized changes to existing software.

handler   A named set of *script* commands that you can execute by naming the handler elsewhere in the same script. Instead of repeating a set of commands several times in different parts of a script, you can make the set of commands a handler and invoke the handler each place you would have repeated the set of commands.

helper application   A program that handles a particular kind of data encountered on the Internet.

home page   The page that a Web browser displays when you first open it.

hot spots   Places in a QuickTime VR panorama that you can click to go to another scene in the panorama or to a QuickTime VR object.

hyperlink   Underlined text on a *Web page* that, when you click it, takes you to another page on the same or a different Web site.

icon   A small picture that represents an entity such as a program, document, folder, or disk.

initialization   A process that creates a blank disk directory, whose effect is the same as erasing the disk. Initialization actually wipes out the means of accessing the existing files on the disk without actually touching the content of files.

insertion point   A blinking vertical bar that indicates where text will be inserted if you start typing.

installation   Places a new or updated version of software on your disk.

interapplication communication (IAC)   The technology that enables programs to send each other messages requesting action and receiving the results of requested actions. In the Mac OS, IAC is called *Apple events* and is the basis of *AppleScript*.

Internet   A worldwide network that provides e-mail, Web pages, news, file storage and retrieval, and other services and information.

Internet Service Provider (ISP)   A company that gives you access to the Internet via your modem.

kerning   Adjusting the space between pairs of letters so the spacing within the word looks consistent.

label   A means of categorizing files, folders, and disks. Each label has its own color and text, which you can change with the Labels control panel.

LAN   See *local area network*.

language script system   Software that enables the Mac OS to use an additional natural language such as Japanese. Multiple languages can use one language script system (for example, the Roman script is used for English, French, Italian, Spanish, and German).

launch   The opening of a program that you want to use.

ligature   A glyph composed of two merged characters. For example, *f* and *l* can be merged to form *fl*.

link   See *hyperlink*.

live object   An *OpenDoc* plug-in that has been through a certification process to ensure that it works and plays well with others.

local area network (LAN)   A system of computers that are interconnected for sharing information and services and are located in proximity such as in an office, home, school, or campus.

localization   The development of software whose dialog-box messages, screens, menus, and other screen elements use the language spoken in the region in which the software is sold.

LocalTalk   A relatively low-speed standard for connecting computers, printers, and other devices to create an *AppleTalk* network. LocalTalk uses the built-in printer ports of Mac OS computers and the LocalTalk ports of many LaserWriter printers.

location file   A file that, when opened, takes you to a location on the Internet or a local area network.

lossless   A type of compression algorithm that regenerates exactly the same data as the uncompressed original.

memory fragmentation   The condition wherein available memory has become divided into multiple disjointed blocks, with each block separated by an open program. The Mac OS cannot automatically consolidate fragmented memory nor open a program in multiple blocks. You can fix memory fragmentation by quitting all open programs.

memory-management unit (MMU)   A part of the 68030, 68040, or PowerPC processor chip, the MMU is required for virtual memory.

memory partition   The piece of memory that a program has for its exclusive use while it is open.

memory size   The amount of memory allocated to a program when you open it. You can change a program's minimum and preferred memory sizes with the Get Info command.

modem   A device that connects a computer to telephone lines. It converts digital information from the computer into sounds for transmission over phone lines and converts sounds from phone lines to digital information for the computer. (The term *modem* is a shortened form of *modulator-demodulator*.)

modem script   Software consisting of the modem commands necessary to start and stop a remote access connection for a particular type of modem.

movie   Any time-related data, such as video, sound, animation, and graphs that change over time; and Apple's format for organizing, storing, and exchanging time-related data.

mount   To make a disk's contents available to the computer. In the case of hard disks, this happens every time you start up the computer. You can also use the Drive Setup utility program or a similar disk utility to mount disks.

multimedia   A presentation combining text or graphics with video, animation, or sound, and presented on a computer.

multitasking   The capability to have multiple programs open simultaneously.

navigate   Opening of disks and folders until you have opened the one that contains the item you need; and to go from one *Web page* to another.

network   A collection of interconnected, individually controlled computers, printers, and other devices together with the hardware, software, and protocols used to connect them. A network lets connected devices exchange messages and information.

network administrator   Someone who sets up and maintains a centralized file server and other network services. The network administrator does not control access to folders and files on the server's disks; that is the responsibility of each person who puts items on the disks.

network interface card (NIC)   An internal adapter card that provides a network port.

network location   A type of file that opens a particular file server in the Mac OS 8.5 Network Browser.

networking protocol   A set of rules for exchanging data over a *network*.

newsgroup   A subject on the Internet's *Usenet*. It is a collection of people and messages pertaining to that particular subject.

notebook   A part of Cyberdog where you keep track of your favorite Internet locations. You can add notebooks to any OpenDoc document.

object   A kind of information, such as words, paragraphs, and characters, that an application knows how to work with. An application's *AppleScript* dictionary lists the kind of objects it can work with under script control.

online information service   A source that provides shareware and freeware directly to your computer through telephone lines and modems. Examples include America Online (800-827-6364), CompuServe (800-800-2222), and various Internet sites. Except for the Internet, online information services charge access fees and retrieval fees.

OpenDoc   An extension of the Mac OS that makes it easy to work on many types of data in a single document without switching applications.

OpenDoc editor   Software that lets you view and perhaps edit a particular kind of data (such as graphics, audio, or video) in an OpenDoc document.

operating system   Software that controls the basic activities of a computer system. Also known as *system software*.

original item   A file, folder, or disk to which an *alias* points, and which opens when you open its alias.

orphaned alias   An *alias* that has lost its link with its original item (and, therefore, the Mac OS cannot find it).

outline font   A font whose *glyphs* are outlined by curves and straight lines that can be smoothly enlarged or reduced to any size and then filled with dots.

owner   A registered user or group that can assign access privileges to a shared folder; and the person who can access all disks and folders (even those not explicitly shared with the Sharing command). This latter owner's name and password are set in the File Sharing or Sharing Setup control panel.

package   A logical grouping of files that are related, such as all of the items that make up fax software, or all of the parts of QuickTime.

palette   A window that contains controls or tools or displays auxiliary information for the application program that you're currently using.

part   An *OpenDoc* plug-in component that lets you work on a particular kind of content, which could be text, graphics, sound, movies, spreadsheets, charts, databases, Web pages, e-mail, or something else.

partition   To divide a hard drive into several smaller volumes, each of which the computer treats as a separate disk. Also, another name for any of the volumes created by dividing a hard drive.

password   A combination of letters, digits, and symbols that must be typed accurately to gain access to information or services on the Internet or a *local area network*.

peer-to-peer file sharing   The process of sharing folders, disks, and their contents with other people's computers — not a central file server — on a network.

PhoneNet   An inexpensive LocalTalk cabling system for connecting computers, printers, and other devices to an *AppleTalk* network.

pixel   Short for picture element, a pixel is the smallest dot that the computer and monitor can display.

pixel depth   The number of memory bits used to store each pixel of a displayed image. The number of colors available depends on the number of bits. For example, 256 colors require 8 bits per pixel, and 32,768 colors require 16 bits per pixel.

point of presence (POP)   An entry point to the Internet. Also, a telephone number that gains access to the Internet through an Internet service provider.

pop-up menu   A menu that is not in the menu bar, but that is marked with an arrowhead and pops open when you click it.

PostScript font   An outline font that conforms to the specifications of the PostScript programming language. PostScript fonts can be smoothly scaled to any size, rotated, and made to follow a curved path. Originally designed for printing on LaserWriters and other PostScript output devices, the ATM software makes PostScript fonts work equally well onscreen and with non-PostScript printers. (Compare *TrueType*.)

PostScript printers   Printers that interpret PostScript commands to create printable images.

PPD (PostScript Printer Description)   A file that contains the optional features of a PostScript printer such as its resolution and paper tray configuration.

PRAM (parameter RAM)   A small amount of battery-powered memory that stores system settings such as time, date, mouse tracking speed, speaker volume, and choice of startup disk.

Preferences folder   Holds files that contain the settings you make in control panels and with the Preferences commands of application programs.

primary script   The *language script system* used by system dialog boxes and menus. If you are working on a computer that is set up for English, Roman is your primary script; your secondary script can be any other installed language script, such as Japanese.

printer driver   Software that prepares pages for, and communicates with, a particular type of printer. This software resides in the Extensions folder inside the System Folder.

print job   A file of page descriptions being sent to a particular type of printer. Also called a *print request* or *spool file*.

print request   See *print job*.

print server   A computer or a program on a computer that manages one or more shared printers on a network.

program   A set of coded instructions that direct a computer in performing a specific task.

program linking   The process of sharing programs by sending and receiving *Apple events* across a network. You must turn on program linking in the File Sharing or Sharing Setup control panel, and you can use the Finder's Sharing command to enable or prevent linking to individual programs.

protocol   See *networking protocol*.

publisher   A section of a document, a copy of which has been saved as an *edition* for other documents to subscribe to.

RAM   Random-access memory, which is physical memory built into the computer in the form of electronic chips or small circuit boards called DIMMs or SIMMs.

RAM disk   Memory that is set aside to be used as if it were a very fast hard disk.

registered user   Network users who must enter their names and any passwords that you've assigned them before they can connect to your computer to share files or programs.

repeat loop   An arrangement of *AppleScript* commands that begins with a Repeat command and ends with an End Repeat command. AppleScript executes the commands between the Repeat and End Repeat commands for the number of times specified in the Repeat command.

resolution   The perceived smoothness of a displayed or printed image. Printed resolution is measured in dots-per-inch (*dpi*). A high-resolution printed image has more dots-per-inch than a low-resolution printed image.

resolve an alias   What the Mac OS does to find the original item that is represented by an *alias*.

resources   Information such as text, menus, icons, pictures, or patterns used by the Mac OS, an application, or other software.

ROM   Read-only memory.

root level   The main level of a disk, which you see when you open the disk icon.

root part   The part (or the part whose stationery) you use to create a new *OpenDoc* document.

script   A collection of *AppleScript* commands that perform a specific task. Also, short for *language script system,* which is software that defines a method of writing (vertical or horizontal, left-to-right, or right-to-left). A script also provides rules for text sorting, word breaking, and the formatting of dates, times, and numbers.

script applications   AppleScript scripts saved as applications.

scripting additions   Files that add commands to the *AppleScript* language, much as plug-in filters add menu commands to Photoshop or the contents of the Word Commands folder add various features to Microsoft Word. Scripting additions reside in a folder called Scripting Additions, which is in the System Folder.

script recording   A process in which *AppleScript* watches as you work with an application and automatically writes a corresponding *script.*

selection rectangle   A dotted-line box that you drag around items to select them all.

server   A program that provides information or services to clients on demand.

shareware   Low-cost software distributed through user groups and online information services. Shareware depends on the honor and honesty of people who use it. You're expected to pay the author a small fee if you plan to use the software.

Shift-click   Holding down the Shift key while clicking the mouse to select multiple items or a range of items.

SIMMs   Single in-line memory modules.

software   One or more programs, which consist of coded instructions that direct a computer in performing a task.

sound track   A set of related sounds that may accompany various actions you perform with menus, windows, controls, and icons in Mac OS 8.5. Also, an audible part of a movie.

spool file   See *print job*.

spooling   A printer-driver operation in which the driver saves page descriptions in a file (called a *spool file*) for later printing.

standard installation   This type of installation installs basic modules such as the Mac OS and QuickTime plus any additional modules you select. Each module is installed in its entirety.

startup disk   A disk with the Finder and System files in its System Folder, and which allows the computer to begin operation.

Startup Items folder   Items placed here are opened automatically when your Mac is started.

stationery pad   A template document that contains preset format and contents.

subdirectories   The equivalent in other operating systems to folders in the Mac OS.

submenu   A secondary menu that pops out from the side of another menu. A submenu appears when you place the pointer on a menu item that has an arrowhead at the right side of the menu.

subscriber   A copy of an *edition* that has been placed in a document and that can be updated automatically when the edition is updated by its *publisher*.

suite   In AppleScript, a group of related commands and other items.

swash   The fancy tail on an alternate, decorative form of a character, or the character with its fancy tail. To use swashes, you need QuickDraw GX, a GX font that includes swashes, and an application that lets you set the text style to show swashes.

system enabler   A plug-in software component that modifies the Mac OS to work with a particular computer model.

system extension   See *extension*.

System file   Contains sounds, keyboard layouts, and language script systems as well as the basic Mac OS software.

System Folder   Stores the essential software (including the Finder, the System file, control panels, and extensions) that gives the Mac OS its unique appearance and behavior.

system software   Software that controls the basic activities of a computer system. Also known as the operating system.

theme   A group of all the settings in the Appearance control panel in Mac OS 8.5.

thread   A string of messages about the same subject.

track   One channel of a QuickTime movie, containing video, sound, closed-captioned text, MIDI data, time codes, or other time-related data.

tracking   The overall spacing between letters in an entire document or text selection. Text with loose tracking has extra space between the characters in words. Text with tight tracking has characters squeezed close together.

tracking speed   The rate at which the pointer moves as you drag the mouse.

transceiver   A connector box that converts a general AAUI Ethernet port, which is built into many Mac models, to the specific kind of port needed for a particular type of Ethernet cable in a network.

translator   A program that translates your documents from one file format to another file format, such as a PICT graphic to a GIF graphic.

Trojan horse   Intentionally destructive software that masquerades as something useful such as a utility program or game.

TrueType   The outline font technology built into the Mac OS. TrueType fonts can be smoothly scaled to any size onscreen or to any type of printer.

Type 1 font   A PostScript font that includes instructions for grid fitting so the font can be scaled to small sizes and low printer resolutions with good results.

universal installation   Yields a version of the Mac OS that can be used by any compatible Mac model.

UNIX   A complex and powerful operating system whose TCP/IP networking protocol is the basis of the Internet.

unmount   To remove a disk's icon from the desktop and make the disk's contents unavailable without deleting the items in that disk permanently.

unshielded twisted-pair (UTP)   The type of cable used in a 10Base-T Ethernet network.

upload   The process of sending files from your computer to another computer.

URL (Universal Resource Locator)   An Internet address. This can be the address of a *Web page,* a file on an *FTP* site, or anything else that you can access on the Internet.

Usenet   A worldwide Internet bulletin board system where people can post messages and join discussions about subjects that interest them.

user group   An organization that provides information to people who use computers. Many user groups, such as BMUG (510-549-2684), have extensive libraries of *shareware* and *freeware,* which they distribute on floppy disk for a nominal fee. For the names and phone numbers of user groups near you, call Apple's referral line (800-538-9696).

variable   A container for information in a *script*. You can place data in a variable and then use it elsewhere in the script.

virtual memory   Additional memory made available by the Mac OS treating part of a hard disk as if it were built-in memory

virus   Software designed to spread itself by illicitly attaching copies of itself to legitimate software. Some viruses perform malicious actions, such as erasing your hard drive, and even seemingly innocuous viruses can interfere with the normal functioning of your computer.

volume   A disk or a part of a disk that the computer treats as a separate storage device. Each volume has a disk icon on the desktop.

Web browser   A program that displays *Web pages* from the Internet.

Web page   A basic unit that the World Wide Web uses to display information (including text, pictures, animation, audio, and video clips). A Web page can also contain *hyperlinks* to the same page or to other Web pages (on the same or a different Web server).

Web server   A computer or a program running on a computer that provides information to a Web browser program.

worm   Software that replicates like a virus but without attaching itself to other software. It may be benign or malicious.

write protect   The process of locking a disk so that it cannot be erased, have its name changed, have files copied onto it or duplicated from it, or have files or folders it contains moved to the desktop or trash.

Index

Continued

Continued

Continued

Continued

Continued

Continued

my2cents.idgbooks.com

Register This Book — And Win!

Visit **http://my2cents.idgbooks.com** to register this book and we'll automatically enter you in our fantastic monthly prize giveaway. It's also your opportunity to give us feedback: let us know what you thought of this book and how you would like to see other topics covered.

Discover IDG Books Online!

The IDG Books Online Web site is your online resource for tackling technology — at home and at the office. Frequently updated, the IDG Books Online Web site features exclusive software, insider information, online books, and live events!

10 Productive & Career-Enhancing Things You Can Do at www.idgbooks.com

- Nab source code for your own programming projects.

- Download software.

- Read Web exclusives: special articles and book excerpts by IDG Books Worldwide authors.

- Take advantage of resources to help you advance your career as a Novell or Microsoft professional.

- Buy IDG Books Worldwide titles or find a convenient bookstore that carries them.

- Register your book and win a prize.

- Chat live online with authors.

- Sign up for regular e-mail updates about our latest books.

- Suggest a book you'd like to read or write.

- Give us your 2¢ about our books and about our Web site.

You say you're not on the Web yet? It's easy to get started with IDG Books' *Discover the Internet,* available at local retailers everywhere.